EUROPEAN

MW00774349

The rediscovery of Roman law and the emergence of classical canon law around AD 1100 marked the beginnings of the civil law tradition in Europe. Between the twelfth and eighteenth centuries, a highly sophisticated legal science of a truly European dimension was developed. Since then the different European states have developed their own national legal systems, but with the exception of England and Ireland they are all heirs to this tradition of the *ius commune*.

This historical introduction to the civil law tradition, from its original Roman roots to the present day, considers the political and cultural context of Europe's legal history. Political, diplomatic and constitutional developments are discussed, and the impacts of major cultural movements, such as scholasticism, humanism, the Enlightenment and Romanticism, on law and jurisprudence are highlighted. This contextual approach makes for a fascinating story, accessible to any reader regardless of legal or historical background.

RANDALL LESAFFER is professor of legal history and dean of the Law School at Tilburg University, the Netherlands. He also teaches cultural history at the Law School of the Catholic University of Leuven.

EUROPEAN LEGAL HISTORY

A cultural and political perspective

RANDALL LESAFFER

Translated by
JAN ARRIENS

CAMBRIDGE
UNIVERSITY PRESS

CAMBRIDGE UNIVERSITY PRESS
Cambridge, New York, Melbourne, Madrid, Cape Town, Singapore, São Paulo,
Delhi, Dubai, Tokyo, Mexico City

Cambridge University Press
The Edinburgh Building, Cambridge CB2 8RU, UK

Published in the United States of America by Cambridge University Press, New York

www.cambridge.org
Information on this title: www.cambridge.org/9780521877985

This English translation © Randall Lesaffer 2009

First published 2009
3rd printing 2010

Printed in the United Kingdom at the University Press, Cambridge

A catalogue record for this publication is available from the British Library

Library of Congress Cataloguing in Publication data
Lesaffer, Randall.
[Inleiding tot de Europese rechtsgeschiedenis. English.]
European legal history : a cultural and political perspective / Randall Lesaffer, Jan Arriens.
p.   cm.
Includes index.
ISBN 978-0-521-87798-5 (hardback)   1. Law – Europe – History.
I. Arriens, Jan.   II. Title.
KJ147.L473 2009
349.4–dc22
2009010957

ISBN 978-0-521-87798-5 hardback

To Sabien

CONTENTS

PREFACE

Over the past few decades, the process of European integration and the debate on a common private law in Europe have made their impact felt on the study of legal history at European universities. Whereas post-Roman legal history had traditionally been studied in terms of national history, now the European perspective dominates the field.

In the past twenty years, several surveys of the history of the civil law tradition have been published. This book adds to their number. In it, the historical development of civilian jurisprudence takes centre-stage. The common law tradition is dealt with in the briefest of ways, the sole purpose of its inclusion being to indicate when and where the English law has taken its own direction. The focus here is on the Mediterranean region for Antiquity and on western Europe for the centuries since. As a result of the origins of this book, the Low Countries receive some additional attention. I have decided to retain these pieces from the original Dutch version of the book because they serve to illustrate more general trends. Moreover, I am sure nobody will be harmed by learning something of the history of these lands. Scandinavia and eastern Europe are not covered.

What sets this book apart from other introductions and surveys is that it puts legal history in a broader context. A great deal of space is devoted to political and cultural history, as much in fact as to the legal developments properly speaking. It is hoped that this will make European legal history more accessible for those readers both in Europe and beyond who lack a sufficient background in general European history, and give legal developments more sense and meaning, by relating them to their context. On the other hand, this might also allow historians and other interested readers to relate legal history to a context they know better.

This book is based on the classes in legal history that I have taught at Tilburg University for almost ten years now. It unmistakably bears the traces of the fact that I have also been teaching cultural history at the Law School of the Catholic University of Leuven since 1998. The influence of my teacher and good friend Dirk van den Auweele is evident throughout.

The members of the Legal History Section at Tilburg University have all contributed to the book. Erik-Jan Broers, Klaas Dijkhoff, Raymond Kubben, Tessa Leesen, Thomas Lina, Olga Tellegen-Couperus, Karlijn van Blom, Jan-Hendrik Valgaeren and Beatrix van Erp-Jacobs have enriched the book with their suggestions and comments. David Ibbetson took great trouble in reading and commenting on the final manuscript and made many valuable suggestions. I should also like to thank all those who have helped shape my views on law, legal history and cultural history over the years. In particular, I wish to acknowledge Maurice Adams, Philip Allott, Clifford Ando, Dominique Bauer, Raoul Bauer, James Crawford, Reginald De Schryver, Peter Haggenmacher, Dirk Heirbaut, Mark Janis, Benedict Kingsbury, Georges Martyn, Jos Monballyu, Stephen Neff, Paul Nève, Michel Oosterbosch, Andreas Osiander, Amanda Perreau-Saussine, Ignacio Rodriguez, Fred Stevens, Raoul van Caenegem, Laurent Waelkens, Bart Wauters, Alain Wijffels and Willem Witteveen.

This book first appeared in 2004 in Dutch as *Inleiding tot de Europese rechtsgeschiedenis* with Leuven University Press. Jan Arriens, to whom I am most indebted, translated the text which I then revised and updated. From the first time I came forward with the idea of producing an English version of the book, Finola O'Sullivan at Cambridge University Press gave it her full, enthusiastic support. Richard Woodham, Carol Fellingham Webb and Chantal Hamill at the Press put in a great deal of hard work and devotion in the final laps of the publication process. My parents and in-laws, Amber, An, Andreas, Jana, Fauve, Joost, Maurane, Rebecca, Wim and Sabien, as well as all my other 'birthday-party friends', I thank for keeping work on this book and other projects from becoming an even larger part of my life.

Brugge

1

Introduction

Quand on parle de l'amour du passé, il faut faire attention,
c'est de l'amour de la vie qu'il s'agit; la vie est beaucoup
plus au passé qu'au présent. Le présent est un moment toujours
court, et cela même lorsque sa plénitude le fait paraître éternel.
Quand on aime la vie, on aime le passé parce que c'est le présent
tel qu'il a survécu dans la mémoire humaine.
Ce qui ne veut pas dire que le passé soit un âge d'or:
tout comme le présent il est à la fois atroce, superbe,
ou brutal, ou seulement quelconque.

Marguerite Yourcenar, *Les yeux ouverts.*

1   *Towards a new* ius commune?

1   The end of the Cold War and the integration of Europe

The end of the Cold War triggered an acceleration in the process of European integration. For France and Britain, the unification of Germany (1990) was only palatable if its power would be safely embedded within Europe. These countries feared they would be overshadowed by a strong and unified Germany and wanted to tie it down in the European structures. In 1992, the Maastricht Treaty transformed the European Community into the European Union (EU). Apart from the traditional economic and monetary integration, steps were taken towards greater co-operation in the field of foreign policy, defence and justice. In the 1990s, a timeframe was established for the introduction of a single currency, which became a fact on 1 January 2002. Moreover, the collapse of the communist bloc paved the way for the expansion of the EU to the east. In 2004, ten new member states acceded to the EU, most of them former Eastern bloc countries; in 2007, Bulgaria and Romania joined. The rejection of the European constitution by French and Dutch voters in 2005 put an – at least temporary – end to this period of accelerated integration and left the European Union facing an uncertain future. Nevertheless, Europe is today more a fact of life than it was before.

In the climate of renewed Euro-optimism in the 1990s and the early years of the twenty-first century, the idea of a unified European law made headway. This applies primarily to private law and much less to public law. Whereas numerous advocates of ongoing European unification have traditionally dreamed of a federal Europe and ultimately almost turned the idea of a European constitution into reality, hardly anyone would dream of standard national constitutions or administrative systems. For many, that would amount to the nightmare of a centralised European super state having come true. Although co-operation between the member states of the EU was enhanced in certain areas of crime control, the harmonisation, let alone unification, of criminal law does not appear realistic. Criminal law and prosecution have traditionally been among the prime concerns of any government. Justice and internal security belong to the essence of national sovereignty. The difficulties surrounding the implementation of the Schengen Agreement and, after 11 September 2001, the introduction of a European arrest warrant, show just how jealously the European member states guard their autonomy in this area.

There is a bigger constituency for a common private law of Europe. Over recent decades, relations between citizens and businesses in the European Union have become unmistakably more numerous and more intense. Whereas previously only larger companies were active in international markets, a substantial proportion of the customers and suppliers and, in some cases, even the employees of small and medium-sized businesses are now foreign. Ever more businesses have establishments in different European countries. The European authorities are encouraging this process of internationalisation by the liberalisation of such sectors as the postal service, energy, telecommunications, insurance and banking. Modern means of communication have added an international dimension to retailing. The mobility of private individuals, be they employees, students, migrants or tourists, is increasing in leaps and bounds.

In legal terms, all these relationships pertain to private law. Although the mass of European legislation and regulations is growing and the European courts are becoming more important, the countries of the Union each have their own municipal systems of private law. In recent years, the idea has gained ground to try and change this. During the 1990s, leading academics from many European law faculties pushed for a European *ius commune*, that is, a common private law for Europe. For many, the ultimate goal of this process is a European civil code to replace the existing, municipal civil codes.

2 The civil law tradition

Proponents and opponents alike agree that the unification of European private law and the drafting of a common civil code is no easy matter. The biggest problem in this regard is the dividing line between the civil law tradition prevailing in continental Europe and the common law tradition prevailing in England and Ireland.

In the civil law countries, private law – as other parts of the law – has largely been codified by the national legislature. Although the civil codes of distinct countries differ from one another as regards concepts, rules, structure and methodology, there are sufficient similarities for us to speak of a truly continental civil law tradition. There are several historical explanations for this.

First, the historical context in which the various municipal codes were drafted is largely the same. The codification movement was inspired and promoted by the natural law and Enlightenment thinkers of the seventeenth and eighteenth centuries. With the exception of the United Kingdom, codification took place in virtually all the countries of western and central Europe in the eighteenth and nineteenth centuries. In that sense, it was a truly European movement.

Second, the majority of European and also non-European civil codes spring from two 'models': the French *Code civil* of 1804 and the German *Bürgerliches Gesetzbuch* of 1896/1900.

Third and most importantly, the codification of the eighteenth and nineteenth centuries did not mark a radical break with pre-codification law. In contrast to what certain authors of the great civil codes and the generations of lawyers immediately afterwards asserted, the civil codes were in large measure inspired by the 'old' law. The codification did not mark an absolute caesura in the development of the civil law. Old legal practices and doctrines retained much of their relevance. Although codification took place within national states and, certainly as far as the German codification was concerned, in an atmosphere of nationalism, the new civil codes preserved much of the civil law tradition.

3 The civil and common law traditions

The civil law tradition has its origins in the late eleventh century, in the rediscovery of ancient Roman law in Italy. This marked the beginning of a European legal science based on the study of the compilation of Roman law promulgated by the Byzantine Emperor Justinian (529–65), the *Corpus Iuris Civilis*, and of canon law texts. This scholarly démarche was genuinely European in nature. It also gained a foothold in England. Until codification, the study of law was to a large extent co-terminous with the study of Roman and canon law. This amalgam of 'learned law' – Roman and canon – is also known as the *ius commune*. Even after the 'nationalisation' of private law began to take shape from the sixteenth century onwards, this historical *ius commune* continued to provide a common core on which national legal systems were able to draw. By giving the name *ius commune* to their ideal, contemporary advocates of a European private law system have sought to link up with historical tradition.

Even though this European tradition of *ius commune* crossed the English Channel, the dividing line between the civil and common law traditions goes back in part to the difference in impact of the *ius commune*. The early formation, from the twelfth century onwards, of a national system of law – the common law – meant that the influence of Roman law in England was more restricted then on the continent. At a formal level, the gap between England and the mainland was only widened by the codification movement: on the English side of the Channel, codification was rejected and a system of private law based on custom and case law and far less on legislation continued to hold sway.

As a result it comes as no surprise that the debate about the desirability and feasibility of a European civil code is often conducted in terms of whether or not the gap between the continental and English legal systems can be bridged. Advocates like to point out that there are no insurmountable differences inherent in the overall body of substantive law from both traditions, while opponents assert that the English will never accept a civil code.

4   The rise of European legal history

This book focuses on the historical development of the civil law tradition from the late eleventh century onwards. Since this tradition started with the rediscovery and renewed study of ancient Roman law, its historical evolution must of necessity also be covered. In Part I we examine the history, significance and most important features of ancient Roman law up to its codification under Emperor Justinian (the seventh century BC to the sixth century AD). Part II and the epilogue deal with the history of the European legal tradition from the fall of the Western Roman Empire to the present. Common law is dealt with only in passing, with the sole purpose of indicating how the differences between the two traditions came about.

Efforts to introduce a European system of private law have stimulated interest in the legal history of Europe in pre-codification times. The advocates of the new *ius commune* – legal historians and lawyers – search the past for arguments to support their case. The historical *ius commune* provides a point of reference. Where previously handbooks and introductions on the history of law were traditionally written from the viewpoint of national history, surveys of European legal history are now clearly in vogue.[1]

This book adheres to this trend. This does not in any way mean that we are interested only in the facts and developments that underpinned the historical unity and coherence of the civil law tradition. The rediscovery of Roman law and the expansion of canon law led to the flourishing of a European legal science that exerted a major influence on legal practice. But, however real and substantial these unifying factors were, the numerous local, regional and later national legal systems were equally real and substantial. Throughout the history of the civil law tradition, unity and diversity keep one another in check. It is through the dynamics produced by these opposing forces that the civil law tradition has evolved.

2   A cultural-historical approach

5   External and internal legal history

Legal history may be approached either internally or externally. Internal legal history is the study of particular legal rules or concepts in or across certain periods. External legal history regards a legal system as a whole and looks at it from the outside. In this book, we confine ourselves to the external history of the civil law tradition. In the first place, the book focuses on the creation and enforcement of law. It embraces the study of legal sources and legal institutions. It is difficult to disentangle these from their political and constitutional context. Therefore, the external history of law cannot be entirely divorced from political history and the internal history of public law.

6   The civil law tradition and its cultural context

The perspective is somewhat broader again. The historical development of law is examined against the background of cultural history. Law in general and legal science in particular are determined by their intellectual and cultural context. Studying legal and cultural history together allows

---

[1] Manlio Bellomo, *The Common Legal Past of Europe, 1000–1800*, Washington 1995; O.F. Robinson, T.D. Fergus and W.M. Gordon, *European Legal History*, London 1994; Peter Stein, *Roman Law in European History*, Cambridge 1999.

us to understand the interaction between law, society and culture more effectively. In this way, the law emerges as an instrument for modelling society according to the dictates of a particular worldview and ideology. It also becomes clear how, in Europe's intellectual and cultural history, legal science has sometimes acted as a trailblazer and precursor for other disciplines.

'Cultural history' is understood in terms of its original meaning. Cultural history arose as an academic activity in the nineteenth century, but its intellectual roots go back further, to the Enlightenment of the eighteenth century. Following in the footsteps of the natural scientists, the historians of the Enlightenment sought to lay bare the 'laws' that ruled the chain of causes and effects that was history to them. Their optimism about their own times and their admiration for a few other civilisations and epochs – the Athens of Perikles (495–429 BC), the Rome of Cicero (106–43 BC), the Italian Renaissance (AD 1450–1530), the France of Louis XIV (1643–1715) – meant that above all they wanted to understand the dynamics of an extolled civilisation in its entirety. They were in search of the spirit of an age, the essence of a civilisation, a leading idea or concept that permeated and determined all. In this way, one could discover what historical law or laws made a civilisation great. The concrete facts and details came a distant second. Or, as the great French Enlightenment philosopher François-Marie Arouet, better known as Voltaire (1694–1778), put it in the introduction to his *Le siècle de Louis XIV*:

> It is not just an account of the life of Louis XIV that we are seeking to write; our subject is greater than that. We shall be seeking to paint for posterity not the actions of a single man but the spirit of the people in the most enlightened century there has ever been.[2]

The first major works of cultural history by professional, academic historians date from the nineteenth and early twentieth century. Jakob Burckhardt (1818–97) made his reputation with *Die Kultur der Renaissance in Italien* (*The Civilisation of the Renaissance in Italy*, 1860), in which he interpreted the Italian Renaissance in terms of the rise of the individual. The Dutch historian Johan Huizinga (1872–1945) obtained lasting renown with his *Herfsttij der Middeleeuwen* (*The Waning of the Middle Ages*, 1919).

---

[2] 'Ce n'est pas seulement la vie de Louis XIV qu'on prétend écrire; on se propose un plus grand objet. On veut essayer de peindre à la postérité, non les actions d'un seul homme, mais l'esprit des hommes dans le siècle le plus éclairé qui fut jamais.' Voltaire, *Le siècle de Louis XIV*, Paris 1994, 1.

The first, mainly German, cultural historians were indebted to the philosophy of history of Georg Wilhelm Friedrich Hegel (1770–1831). According to Hegel, history was not the accidental outcome of a myriad chance events and individual decisions, but was propelled forward by an all-pervasive *Geist* (spirit). The history of a nation was nothing other than the maturation process of the nation's *Volksgeist*. Each age was determined by a *Zeitgeist*.

Cultural historians seek to lay bare the spirit of an epoch. They try to discover a pattern in the multiplicity of events and developments and look for an all-explanatory determinant. As Huizinga wrote, 'the object of cultural history is culture'.[3] At first sight, this statement of the obvious provides little comfort to those wishing to define cultural history, but it is nevertheless significant. As vague and all-embracing as the term 'culture' is, the term 'cultural history' is equally vague and all-embracing. Cultural history differs fundamentally from every other branch of historiography. Political history, economic history, the history of art, legal history and intellectual history: all these are concerned with one aspect of human activity. Cultural history is not: it covers all the aspects of human life and in that sense encompasses all other subdisciplines. Even so, cultural history does not coincide with general history. It is not the sum of all historical subdisciplines. It is a search for the essence, the spirit of an age and a culture that helps to explain this age and culture for all areas of human life. Cultural history is always general in nature and, to use a contemporary buzzword, multidisciplinary.[4] It does not content itself with analysis; it also synthesises and integrates.

The difference between cultural history and every other branch of the historical tree is a bit like the different ways in which one can look at an impressionist painting, such as the *Japanese Bridge* (*Bassin aux nymphéas*, 1899) by Claude Monet (1840–1926). The paint has been pressed on to the canvas in thick, multicoloured blobs. The forms have not been separated by lines; the colours merge into one another. Stand up close to the painting and all you see is blotches. If you want to see a pond with water lilies you need to take a step backwards and take in the whole. In this book, the law and its history are not regarded as independent variables but are placed in their cultural setting. We stand up to the painting and inspect

---

[3] Johan Huizinga, *De taak der cultuurgeschiedenis*, Groningen 1995, 82.
[4] 'Cultural history differs from political and economic history in the sense that it only deserves its name in so far as its remains concerned with deeper considerations and the general. The state and enterprise exist as a whole but also in their details. Culture exists only as a whole.' Huizinga, *De taak der cultuurgeschiedenis*, 83.

the blotches of law; but we often also stand back and look at the place of those blotches within the whole.

Yet, this book is not a true 'cultural history' of the civil law tradition. That would demand a far greater integration of law within its cultural context than is aspired to. But to some extent, legal history is related, if not integrated, to the main cultural and intellectual evolutions with which the law interacted.

This approach implies a mild criticism of one of the major pitfalls of university education and research in our time: the exaggerated drive for specialisation resulting in the fragmentation of knowledge into ever smaller and more autonomous areas. Recent decades have seen a phenomenal increase in the knowledge available. Academics have responded by entrenching themselves in a minuscule part of their field. They know more and more about less and less. The safety of detail is preferred to the risks of synthesis. Overspecialisation hinders communication between specialists from different fields and reduces scholars' added value for society. In relation to the study of law, exaggerated specialisation not only threatens the coherence of the law itself but widens the gap between law and society. Overspecialisation is a daily assault on the collective consciousness and the collective memory of the intellectual elites. It does its bit towards the fragmentation of culture and society.

3   Periodisation in history

7   Petrarch and the traditional periodisation of history

Historical periodisation is never neutral. Periodisation means that certain historical events or trends are put in the spotlight while others are relegated to the background. Everything that underlines the internal unity of an epoch is brought to the fore; everything that suggests otherwise is dusted under the carpet. An event marking the caesura between two epochs is given undue exposure and puts other events in the shade.

In modern European historiography, traditionally four major epochs are distinguished: Antiquity (up to AD 476), the Middle Ages (476–1453), the Early Modern Age (1453–1789) and the Modern Age (1789 to present). Often, the post-1945 years are considered a distinct epoch and are referred to under the term 'contemporary history'. In this book the Modern Age concludes with the First World War.

What might appear to be a fourfold or fivefold division of history in fact rests on the foundations of a threefold division going back as far as the early Renaissance or even the proto-humanist Petrarch (Francesco Petrarca, 1304–74). As the terminology indicates, the Early Modern Age and the

Modern Age are closely connected. They are the eras of the emergence of modernity and, as such, stand in a dialectic relationship with 'Antiquity'. Together they form the 'Modern Age' in a broad sense. The differences between the two periods, and the importance of the French Revolution of 1789 that divides them, is particularly stressed in France and the Low Countries. In other countries, such as Britain, the gap is less deep.

In essence, this traditional periodisation is a by-product of the self-image and worldview of Renaissance and modern Europe and the judgements they implied about Antiquity, the Middle Ages and the Modern Age. It is little more than what is known in the Anglo-American world as the 'Whig interpretation of history' on a European scale.

Already in the fourteenth century, Petrarch observed that, in his own age, the West was undergoing a cultural revival for the first time since the fall of the Western Roman Empire. In the works of the great poet Dante Alighieri (1265–1321) and the painter Giotto di Bondone (1266–1337), he glimpsed a new dawn for literature and the fine arts. It was Petrarch who first used the terms *antica* (old) and *nuova* (new) in this context. The intervening period between classical – Graeco-Roman – Antiquity and his own New Age was in his eyes a barbaric era to be labelled *medium aevum*, that is, the Middle Ages.

By the early eighteenth century, the threefold classification between Antiquity, the Middle Ages and the Modern Age had become established. During the nineteenth century, the opinion gained ground that the beginnings of modernity could be traced to the Italy of the late fifteenth and early sixteenth centuries. The rediscovery of classical Antiquity by the scholars and artists of that time set in motion a cultural movement dubbed the 'Renaissance' by historians Jakob Burckhardt (1818–97) and Jules Michelet (1798–1874). Petrarch was considered an early forerunner of the Renaissance and humanism. His thinking is sometimes referred to as the false dawn of humanism. With the name Renaissance (or rebirth), Burckhardt and Michelet wanted to indicate its key characteristic: the study of classical Antiquity as a model. The Italian Renaissance marked at one and the same time the rebirth of classical culture in the West and the birth of modern, Western civilisation. The Middle Ages – a period of a thousand years – were by and large portrayed in a negative light.

8   The Renaissance of the Twelfth Century

In 1927, the American historian Charles Homer Haskins (1870–1937) published his magnum opus: *The Renaissance of the Twelfth Century*.

According to Haskins, the crucial caesura in Western history was not the Renaissance of the fifteenth and sixteenth centuries but that of the twelfth century.

In his book, Haskins contended that the period between 1070 and 1225 was marked by a general revival of economic, political, legal, religious, intellectual and artistic life in western Europe. This revival too was a 'renaissance' in the sense that it rested on a distinctive rediscovery of Antiquity. Haskins – whose basic tenets were later adopted by many other historians – argued that modern Western culture could be traced back to the Renaissance of the Twelfth Century.

What is to a certain extent true for general history certainly applies to legal history. The beginning of European legal science – the backbone of the civil law tradition – coincides with the beginning of the Renaissance of the Twelfth Century. Moreover, the rediscovery of Roman law and the emergence of classical canon law from 1070 onwards provided an important foundation for this Renaissance of the Middle Ages.

9   An alternative periodisation

This book uses an alternative periodisation of history rather than the traditional one. The three-way breakdown into Antiquity, the Middle Ages and the Modern Age has been preserved, but the boundaries have been shifted. The major caesura marking the beginning of European or Western civilisation has been brought forward by some four to five centuries. Since it is now generally accepted that the revival of Europe stems from as far back as the late tenth (Germany and England) and eleventh centuries (France), the year 1000 has been taken as the starting point for the emerging of European civilisation. Strictly speaking, it would be more correct to talk of years, or rather decades, of transition – that is, stretches of no man's land between the ages – rather than to use specific years.

In this way, we arrive at a new three-way classification. First, there is the age of the ancient civilisations around the Mediterranean. We could speak of the age of Mediterranean civilisations. Of these civilisations, this book discusses only the Roman one. On account of the codification by the Eastern Roman Emperor Justinian, this age stretched into the sixth century. This is then followed by a period referred to here as the Early Middle Ages (sixth to tenth century). The period of European civilisation starts around the year 1000. Alternatively, we might refer to the Early Middle Ages as the 'Short Middle Ages' in the sense of a shortened period of transition between the Mediterranean and European civilisations.

The periodisation of history

The traditional periodisation		The periodisation in this book	
Antiquity	until AD 476	Age of the Mediterranean civilisations	until AD 565
Middle Ages	476–1453	Early Middle Ages	500-1000
Early Middle Ages	476–1070	Age of the European civilisations	1000–1914
High and Later Middle Ages	1070–1453	Late Middle Ages	1000–1453
Early Modern Age	1453–1789	Early Modern Age	1453–1648
Modern Age	1789–1945	Modern Age	1648–1914
Contemporary Era	1945 to present	Post-Modern Age	1914 to present

The period of European civilisation has been further subdivided into three ages: the age of scholasticism from 1000 to 1453 (the Late Middle Ages), the age of humanism from 1453 to 1648 (the Early Modern Age) and the age of rationalism from 1648 to 1914 (the Modern Age). This three-way classification is based on a cultural-historical logic. Each age is understood in terms of its central ideology, its views on God, man, nature and truth which dominated the intellectual and cultural life of that age – including legal thinking. This does not in any way imply that there were no counter-currents to these core beliefs. These counter-currents did, however, evolve in dialogue with the mainstream and could to a certain extent be explained by the latter. A prime example is provided by Romanticism as a reaction to the rationalism of the Enlightenment.

10 The end of modernity

The triumph of reason during the eighteenth and nineteenth centuries was at the same time the triumph of modern, European civilisation. These centuries were characterised by an unparalleled advance of science and technology. Thanks to their technological supremacy, the European powers conquered and colonised the greater part of the world. After 1914, the European model was increasingly contested from both within and without. The drama of the First World War (1914–18) dealt a heavy blow to Europe's power and self-perception. The twentieth century is in more than one sense an age of transition or, as Eric Hobsbawn put it, an *Age of Extremes.*[5] Whereas the European model – more accurately referred to from the twentieth century onwards as the Western model – brought prosperity, knowledge and freedom for an ever-increasing share of the world's population, there were also growing doubts. A sense of crisis and uncertainty first took hold among the artistic and intellectual elites and later among the middle classes.[6] Two world wars, genocides, numerous disasters of human origin and the continuing deprivation of large parts of the world all served to undermine the optimism of modernism. Postmodernism as a term came in vogue to denote the discontent with the basic tenets of modern culture – it is a term largely devoid of meaning, but nevertheless historically accurate. The post-1914 period is, accordingly, excluded from the part of the book covering the era of European civilisation. It forms the subject of a separate part – one that is incomplete, and in fact no more than a brief epilogue. This epilogue is pervaded by the sense one has that the twentieth century is a period of transition. The new paradigm to which that transition will lead is not yet clear. In the meantime, the twentieth century has been labelled the age of voluntarism.

Like any history, let alone any broad outline of a large tract of it, this history of the civil law tradition cannot lay any claims to completeness or objectivity. It is just one more interpretation of a history that is ultimately too variegated to be encapsulated within a single narrative. Like any history it probably has more to say about the author and the latter's own context than about the past. Ultimately, telling the 'story' of the past is another method of studying the present. As the Belgian historian Henri Pirenne (1862–1935) put it, 'Je m'intéresse à l'homme parce que je suis historien.'[7]

Further reading

1. On the debate about a common European private law: B. de Witte and C. Forder, eds., *The Common Law of Europe and the Future of Legal Education*, Deventer 1992; M. Gebauer, *Grundfragen der Europäisierung des Privatrechts*, Heidelberg 1998; A. Hartkamp, E. E. Hondius, A. Verbeke and R. Zimmermann,

---

[5] Eric Hobsbawm, *Age of Extremes: the Short Twentieth Century, 1914–1991*, London 1994.
[6] 'My conclusion is that the current wave of scepticism and despair, which looks ahead to nothing but destruction and decay, and dismisses as absurd any belief in progress or any prospect of a further advance by the human race, is a form of élitism – the product of élite social groups whose security and whose privileges have been most conspicuously eroded by the crisis, and of élite countries whose once undisputed domination over the rest of the world has been shattered.' E. H. Carr, *What is History?*, London 2001, li–lii.
[7] 'I am interested in man because I am a historian.'

Towards a European Civil Code, 3rd edn, The Hague 2004; P. Legrand, 'European Legal Systems are Not Converging', *International and Comparative Law Quarterly*, 45 (1996) 52–81; O. Remien, 'Illusion und Realität eines europäischen Privatrechts', *Juristenzeitung*, 47 (1992) 277–84; J. Smits, *The Making of a European Private Law: Towards a* Ius Commune Europaeum *as a Mixed Legal System*, Oxford 2002; R. Zimmermann, 'Civil Code and Civil Law: the "Europeanization" of Private Law within the European Community and the Re-emergence of a European Civil Science', *Columbia Journal of European Law*, 1 (1994/1995) 63–105.

2. Recent interpretations of European legal history from the perspective of the historical antecendents to a common private law of Europe: M. Bellomo, *The Common Legal Past of Europe, 1000–1800*, Washington 1995; R. C. Van Caenegem, *European Law in the Past and the Future: Unity and Diversity over Two Millennia*, Cambridge 2002; R. Zimmermann, *Roman Law, Contemporary Law, European Law: the Civilian Tradition Today*, Oxford 2001.

3. General surveys of European legal history: H. Coing, ed., *Handbuch der Quellen und Literatur der neueren europäischen Privatrechtsgeschichte*, 7 vols., Munich 1973–88; J. Gilissen, *Introduction historique au droit. Esquisse d'une histoire universelle du droit. Les sources du droit depuis le XIIIe siècle. Eléments d'histoire du droit privé*, Brussels 1979; H. Hattenhauer, *Europäische Rechtsgeschichte*, 4th edn, Heidelberg 2004; J. M. Kelly, *A Short History of Western Legal Theory*, Oxford 1992; P. Koschaker, *Europa und das Römische Recht*, Munich and Berlin 1947; J. H. Merryman, *The Civil Law Tradition*, 2nd edn, Stanford 1985; O. F. Robinson, T. D. Fergus and W. M. Gordon, *An Introduction to European Legal History: Sources and Institutions*, 3rd edn, London 2000; P. Stein, *Roman Law in European History*, Cambridge 1999; R. C. Van Caenegem, *An Historical Introduction to Private Law*, Cambridge 1992; Van Caenegem, *Judges, Legislators and Professors: Chapters in European Legal History*, 2nd edn, Cambridge 1993; Van Caenegem, *An Historical Introduction to Western Constitutional Law*, Cambridge 1995; T. G. Watkin, *An Historical Introduction to Modern Civil Law*, Aldershot 1999; A. Watson, *The Making of the Civil Law*, Cambridge, Mass. 1981; J. M. Zane, *The Story of Law*, 2nd edn, Indianapolis 1998.

4. On the role of Roman law in the formation of modern legal systems: W. W. Buckland and A. MacNair, *Roman Law and Common Law*, Cambridge 1965; J. P. Dawson, *The Oracles of the Law*, Ann Arbor 1968; H. F. Jolowicz, *Roman Foundations of Modern Law*, Oxford 1957; P. Stein and J. Sand, *Legal Values in Western Society*, Edinburgh 1974; R. Zimmermann, *The Law of Obligations: Roman Foundations of the Civilian Tradition*, Oxford 1996.

5. On cultural history as a historical discipline: P. Burke, 'Cultural History: Past, Present and Future', *Theoretische Geschiedenis*, 13 (1986) 187–96; Burke, *Varieties of Cultural History*, New York 1997; R. Chartier, *Cultural History*

between Practices and Representations, Cambridge 1988; E.H. Gombrich, *In Search of Cultural History*, Oxford 1969; J. Huizinga, *De taak der cultuurgeschiedenis*, Groningen 1995.

6. On historiography: M. Bloch, *The Historian's Craft*, Manchester 1992; H. Butterfield, *The Whig Interpretation of History*, London 1931; Butterfield, *Man and his Past*, Cambridge 1955; E.H. Carr, *What is History? (With a New Introduction by Richard J. Evans)*, London 2001; R.C. Collingwood, *The Idea of History*, New York 1956; R.J. Evans, *In Defence of History*, London 1997; J.L. Gaddis, *The Landscape of History: How Historians Map the Past*, Oxford 2002.

7. On the Renaissance of the Twelfth Century: Marcia L. Colish, *Medieval Foundations of the Western Intellectual Tradition, 400–1400*, New Haven and London 1997; Charles H. Haskins, *The Renaissance of the Twelfth Century*, Cambridge, Mass. and London 1927; Francis Oakley, *The Medieval Experience*, Toronto 1988; R.N. Swanson, *The Twelfth-Century Renaissance*, Manchester and New York 1999.

8. For a recent survey of European cultural history: N. Davies, *Europe: a History*, Oxford 1996; P. Rietbergen, *Europe: a Cultural History*, 2nd edn, London 2006.

PART I

Ancient Roman law

2

Suum cuique tribuere
(Ancient Rome, *c.*1000 BC–AD 565)

A   Politics and the state

1   *Aeneas and the origins of Rome*

Arma virumque cano, Troiae qui primus ab oris
Italiam fato profugus Laviniaque venit,
Litora, multum ille et terris iactatus et alto
Vi superum, saevae memorem Iunonis ob iram,
Multa quoque et bello passus, dum conderet urbem,
Inferretque deos Latio, genus unde Latinum,
Albanisque patres atque altae moenia Romae.[1]

11   The beginnings of Rome: legend and history

The men who poured the myths about the origins of Rome into their classical mould were the historian Livy (59 BC–AD 17) and the poet Virgil (70 BC–19 BC).[2] The genealogy of the legendary founders of the city, the twins Romulus and Remus, went back to the Trojan hero Aeneas. The Roman myths tied in with the greatest epic of Greek civilisation, Homer's *Iliad*. According to this epic, the Greeks, after a war lasting ten years, destroyed the city of Troy on the Hellespont, the narrow strait separating Europe from Asia. Of the Trojan heroes only Aeneas managed to escape. After lengthy wanderings, he landed on the coast of Latium. There, he founded the town of Lavinium, from which the later kings of

---

[1] Virgil, *Aeneid* I, vv. 1–7. 'Of arms I sing and the man who first from the coasts of Troy, exiled by fate, came to Italy and Lavinian shores; much buffetted on sea and land by violence from above, through cruel Juno's unforgiving wrath, and much enduring in war also, till he should build a city and bring his gods to Latium; whence came the Latin race, the lords of Alba, and the walls of lofty Rome.' Translation by H. Rushton Fairclough, *Virgil: Eclogues, Georgics, Aeneid I–VI* (Loeb Classical Library 63), Cambridge, Mass. and London 1916. Also see Livy, *Ab urbe condita* 1.1–6.

[2] At the end of the third century BC, the early Roman historians Quintus Fabius Pictor and Lucius Cincius Alimentus had already laid down the great outlines of Rome's originating myths.

Alba Longa came. Romulus and Remus were the grandsons of one of the kings of that town.

The fact that the Romans traced their roots back to a hero from Greek literature is telling. Nor is the choice of an enemy of the Greeks as the forefather of Rome accidental. Rome was influenced by Greek culture. The poet Horace (65–8 BC) had already written 'Graecia capta ferum victorem cepit.'[3] Greek literature, philosophy, rhetoric and art were admired, adopted and imitated by the Romans. That influence precedes the Roman conquest of Greece in the second century BC; through the Greek colonies in southern Italy, Rome had already come into contact with the Hellenic civilisation at a much earlier point of its history – probably as early as the seventh and sixth centuries BC.

In this light, it comes as no surprise that the Romans looked to the Greeks in constructing their foundational myth. Even so, it is striking that it should have been Aeneas – the loser in the most famous Greek epic – who was adopted as a forefather, rather than a Greek hero like Odysseus or Herakles. The choice symbolises the way in which the Late Republican Roman elite dealt with the Greek civilisation. The Roman conquerors admired the art, culture and science of the vanquished Greeks and consciously adopted elements from them. It was, however, no slavish admiration: as conquerors of the Greek world the Romans regarded themselves as the new masters of Greek culture. For them, the Hellenisation of Rome was not the assumption of a foreign culture but the confiscation of the spoils of war.

The Romans did not just adopt; they adapted the Greek heritage to their own liking. Greek culture enriched Roman identity, but it did not completely transform it. It was subjugated to it and, to some extent, absorbed by it. The choice of Aeneas, an enemy of the Greeks, as forefather of the Romans needs to be viewed in this light. Through the conquest of Greece, the descendants of Aeneas avenged Troy.

12   Greek culture and Roman law

In no other field – except maybe that of warfare – did the Romans contribute so much as in that of law. In the centuries following the conquest of Greece around 150 BC, Roman culture reached a state of high development. The first century BC and the first and second centuries

---

[3] 'The conquered Greece in turn conquered the savage victor.' Horace, *Epistolae* 2.1.157–63; translation by H. Rushton Fairclough, *Satires, Epistles, Ars Poetica* (Loeb Classical Library 194), Cambridge, Mass. and London 1926.

AD represented the heyday of Roman literature, philosophy, science and architecture. In these fields, the Romans borrowed heavily from the Greeks and barely managed to improve on or rival the Greek accomplishments. Similarly, the rise of Roman law in this period may in part be traced back to Hellenisation, although the Greek influence was more limited and less lasting in this than in other areas. It was the pragmatic genius of the Romans and not the systematic thought of the Greeks that led Roman law to such heights.

Roman law was without doubt the most sophisticated and highly developed legal system from Antiquity. It was also the most influential on later history. It was the rediscovery and study of Roman law in the late eleventh century that triggered the development of European legal science and the civil law tradition. The ancient Roman law which was handed down to later times was a product of more than a thousand years of legal development. That history forms the subject of this chapter.

2   The beginnings of Rome and the Regal Period
(Seventh century to 509 BC)

13   The foundation of Rome

According to Roman tradition, the foundation of Rome by Romulus and Remus took place in 753 BC. After the murder of his brother, Romulus became the first king of the city. There were six further kings. The last three were not Romans but Etruscans. In 509 BC, King Tarquinius Superbus (Tarquin the Proud) was driven out and Rome became a republic.

The reality is more prosaic than these legends as told by Livy and other Roman historians. The Romans came from two Indo-European tribes, the Latins and the Sabines, who had settled in Latium, the region around Rome, in the second millennium BC. The hills on which Rome was later to be built, or at least some of them, were already populated by Latin and Sabine tribes by the start of the first millennium BC.

Whether Rome as a town was rationally planned and thus 'founded', or gradually grew from these settlements is still a matter of contention. Whichever is the case, its development from a cluster of small settlements on the hills of Rome to a walled town with stone-built public buildings was accomplished by the last quarter of the seventh century BC. Around that time, Rome also reached a kind of political unification and organisation resembling that of a city-state. Ironically enough, the foundation of the town may not have been a purely 'Roman' matter. Apart from the

Latins and the Sabines, the Etruscans played a prominent if not the leading role in the early growth of the town.

The Etruscans were of different ethnic origins and spoke a different language from the Latins and the Sabines. By the late seventh century, under Phoenician and Greek influence, they had attained a high standard of civilisation, urbanisation and political organisation. Their area of control was located north of Rome in what is now Tuscany, to which they gave their name. The Etruscans did not form a unified state but constituted a loose federation of city-states. They had important trade contacts with the Greek colonies in southern Italy and Sicily and with the Carthaginian establishments on that island. The hilly area occupied by the Latins and Sabines was of strategic value to them as it dominated several fords in the River Tiber, which otherwise blocked the north–south route west of the Appenine mountains. This explains their presence and influence in the Roman area. Some historians consider that the construction of a town amidst the Latins and Sabines, the future Romans, was prompted by the desire to control the north–south trade route that ran through the Latin and Sabine territory. They regard the foundation of Rome as the unilateral action of a more developed people in the territories of some backward tribes. More recent archaeological finds, however, indicate that the Latins and Sabines had already achieved a high degree of development themselves. This induced some historians to conclude that the foundation or growth of the town of Rome was a Latin–Sabine achievement, in which Etruscans may have partaken but not played the leading role. The Greek influence that stimulated urbanisation in Tuscany may well have had an impact directly on the Latins and Sabines.

Roman historians accepted that the last three of their seven kings were Etruscans. This, apart from other evidence, indicates that the 'Romans', through or upon the foundation of the town, fell under Etruscan dominance. Under the traditionally held belief that Rome was an Etruscan foundation, these three 'last' Etruscan kings may have been the only kings who ever ruled the Roman city-state, while the previous 'Roman' kings – if they existed – may have been little more than tribal leaders of the Latins and Sabines living in the smaller settlements. More recent archaeological evidence and the interpretation of the literary sources based on this suggest that some kings at least preceded the three Etruscans kings after Rome became a city-state sometime in the late seventh century BC. Some even doubt that there were any Etruscan kings at all. But at least, in any interpretation of Rome's early political history, it remains highly plausible that the last two Roman rulers were usurpers, most probably foreigners, and most likely Etruscans. They broke through the traditional power constraints that came from the co-operation between the king and the Latin–Sabine aristocracy and amassed an almost unlimited *imperium* of political, legal and military power. They resembled Greek tyrants more than traditional kings. Thus the revolution of 509 BC that ended the monarchy and established the Republic was triggered.

14   Patricians and plebeians

Originally, the Latin and Sabine population consisted of a number of large *gentes* (clans), the members of which were all said to descend from a single, often legendary ancestor. The large *gentes* such as that of Gaius Iulius Caesar (100–44 BC), the *gens Iulia*, traced their lineage back to major heroes and even gods. Caesar claimed that he descended from Aeneas and, through him, from the goddess of love, Venus. At the head of each *gens* stood a clan leader, the *pater familias*. For the rest, however, there was a high degree of equality within the *gentes*. Within the *gens*, all property was collective.

During the course of the ninth century BC, class distinctions emerged when the leaders of the clans, the *patres familias*, put an end to the system of collective property and laid personal claim to the lion's share of the clan's property. In this way, a group of clan leaders and their close kin – their family – set themselves apart from the majority of the population. When the kings increased their power as a result of a number of conquests, at first they tried to remain on friendly terms with the leaders of the *gentes* by giving them some of the captured lands. On the other hand, they incorporated the population of those conquered areas into the state by granting them citizenship, thereby creating a counterweight to the indigenous elite. Many immigrants from the Etruscan areas also obtained citizenship during that period. Gradually, a distinction arose between the patricians – the leaders of the old *gentes* – and the plebeians, ordinary people, consisting of the vast majority of the original inhabitants of the Roman territory, the population of the territories that had been annexed and numerous immigrants.

3   *The Early Republic (509–264 BC)*

15   The rise of the plebeian order

The coup of 509 BC against the last Etruscan ruler Tarquinius Superbus was led by the patricians, who no longer wanted a king and decided to divide the king's old *imperium* among various magistrates to be elected each year. To begin with, these were only patricians. The Republic was a fact. The early centuries of the Republic were marked by the class struggle between the patricians and plebeians, on the one hand, and by ongoing wars on the other. Towards 264 BC, the latter resulted in the subjugation of the whole of Italy south of the River Po.

With the expulsion of Tarquin, the plebeians lost their political patron and found themselves exposed to the caprice of the patricians. During the first few centuries of the Republic, the patricians controlled and monopolised the most important institutions of state: the Senate and the magistrature. Right from the early years of the Republic, the patricians and plebeians came into sharp conflict with one another. Gradually, the latter attained more political rights. In 471 BC, they obtained the right to set up their own popular assembly without the patricians (*concilium plebis*) and to make laws (*plebiscita*) applying only to themselves. In 451 BC, the *ius civile* – the law of and for the Roman citizenry – was written down in the Twelve Tables. In the Regal Period as under the Early Republic, the law consisted primarily of the rules of the *mos maiorum*, the customs of the ancestors, the recording of which now served to constrain the arbitrariness of the priesthood. At that time the priests were still all members of the patriciate. They were responsible for the interpretation of the *mos maiorum*. Now that the law was written down and everyone who could read was able to consult it, the priesthood lost part of its power over the law. In the course of the fifth century BC, a new institution was introduced: that of the plebeian tribunes. Whereas all other magistratures were the preserve of the patricians, the tribunes came from the *plebs*. They were the representatives and defenders of the plebs. They were inviolable and had the power to veto any decision by any public body (the right of intercession). They could even block decisions by other tribunes. Gradually, the ordinary magistratures became accessible to the plebeians. In 367 BC, the *leges Liciniae Sextiae* even granted the plebeians access to the highest political magistrature – the consulate. From 342 BC onwards, one of each year's two consuls had to be plebeian. By the third quarter of the third century BC, often both consuls stemmed from the plebeian order. Since the former magistrates and, from the second century onwards, also the plebeian tribunes were appointed to the Senate, more and more plebeians entered this powerful body. The *lex Hortensia* of 287 BC determined that the *plebiscita* or popular laws of the *concilium plebis* were binding on the entire Roman population, including the patricians. In this way, they obtained an equivalent status to the laws issued by other popular assemblies of which the patricians did form part (the *comitia*). During the second and first centuries BC, the *concilium plebis* was to become an instrument in the hands of the plebeian tribunes to push through legislation against the will of the Senate and the ruling class.

16 An oligarchic republic

The inclusion of plebeians in the magistrature and the Senate saw the disappearance of the political importance of the old patrician *gentes* as a separate class. The system did, however, remain oligarchic. Apart from a few – nineteen to be precise – patrician clans, a number of plebeian families now appeared at the top of Roman politics. Between 233 and 133 BC, nearly 80 per cent of all consuls came from twenty-six families, some of them patrician and others plebeian. From the second century BC onwards, it becomes more relevant politically to draw a distinction between senatorials and plebeians than between patricians and plebeians. The senatorial order consisted of several hundred families of patrician or plebeian origin that governed the city politically. The senatorial order controlled the Senate, the magistrature and the pontifical colleges. The electoral system gave them a grip over the popular assemblies. The power of the senatorial order was further enhanced by the system of the *clientela*, under which a Roman citizen or a foreigner would place himself under the protection of a powerful Roman. In exchange for this protection, the client promised political support to his patron.

In principle, people became senators after having served a term as quaestor or tribune. In most cases, the members were elected from families who already numbered senators among their ancestors. Nevertheless, in each generation, 'new men' (*homines novi*) made their way into the ranks of the magistrature and the senatorial order. Although the Senate was a fairly closed group, by allowing some new men into its ranks the senatorial order managed to co-opt the more dynamic and ambitious elements from among the *plebs* and thus continually replenish its own forces.

17 The conquest of Italy

After the fall of the monarchy, the young Republic was almost constantly at war with its neighbours. In 493 BC, Rome made an alliance, the Cassian Treaty (*foedus Cassianum*), with the Latin towns around Rome. It was a permanent alliance against all external enemies of the Romans and the Latins. According to tradition, Rome was not simply just another member of the Latin League; it was the equal partner of all the other members together. At any event, Rome was dominant within the League. In 396 BC, the Romans extended their territory north of the Tiber by the conquest of the Etruscan city of Vei.

Around 390 BC, the Romans suffered a defeat against a tribe of Celts, the Senones, who came from the region between the Alps and the River Po. Rome itself was sacked. For the next half a century, Rome had to reassert itself in central Italy and fight many of the towns and peoples it had formerly subdued. Between 340 and 280 BC, Rome succeeded in overcoming its main opponents in Italy, the Etruscans to the north and the Samnites to the south. Between 281 and 272 BC, Rome fought a drawn-out war with the major Greek city in southern Italy, Tarente. Rome's victory over the city and its foreign ally, King Pyrrhus of Epirus (318–272 BC), gave it control over *Magna Graeca*, the south of the peninsula. The main reason why Rome's former enemies suffered its domination was that Rome had proved to be the sole power capable of protecting Italy against the Celtic invasions. After the Second Punic War (218–201 BC) and the victory over Hannibal, whose invasion of Italy had received great support from the Celts, Rome extended its sphere of influence north of the Po and subdued the Cisalpine Celts in their own territories.

The Romans did not turn Italy into a centrally administered polity for some centuries. All through Italy, colonies of Roman citizens or Latin allies were founded. The subjected cities and peoples closest to Rome often received full Roman citizenship, citizenship without the right to vote (*sine suffragio*) or Latin rights – that is, similar rights as the Latin allies had received under the Cassian Treaty. Although exceptionally some were enfranchised, the conquered tribes and cities further away normally had to accept an alliance treaty with Rome, becoming *socii populi Romani*. The defeated tribe or city lost part of its own territory and gave up control over foreign policy. In time of war, the Italian allies were required to provide troops. They did, however, just as the cities which had been enfranchised, retain a large measure of autonomy in domestic affairs. Often, the leaders of the non-enfranchised peoples received, immediately or with time, some form of citizenship.

After the Social War (91–88 BC), citizenship was awarded to the entire population south of the Po, as a result of which Roman law was applied throughout the peninsula. Even then, however, no centralised administration was established. The Roman government remained first and foremost that of the city of Rome. Although gradually an increasing number of citizens from other cities in Italy won a seat in the Senate, they did so not as representatives of those tribes or cities but, just like any other Roman citizens, in their own name. Anyone aspiring to a political career could not escape moving to Rome and becoming truly Roman.

4 The conquest of the Mediterranean (264–27 BC)

18 The great civilisations of Antiquity

During the last three millennia BC, the Mediterranean and Middle East produced a number of major civilisations and empires: the Sumerian, Egyptian, Babylonian, Hittite, Assyrian, Persian, Phoenician and Greek. During the last millennium BC, first the Persians and then the Macedonian King Alexander the Great (336–323 BC) managed to conquer most of the heartlands of the old civilisations. From the ninth century BC, the Phoenicians and the Greeks also set their sights on the western part of the Mediterranean. The Phoenicians founded Carthage on the coast of what is now Tunisia, from where they colonised Sicily, Sardinia, the Balearics and the Spanish coastal areas. The Greeks founded colonies in Italy, Sicily, southern France and Spain.

Between the third century BC and the start of the Christian era, the Romans conquered the entire Mediterranean region and a large part of the Middle East. In doing so they united the lands where all the great civilisations of Antiquity had flourished. Furthermore, they penetrated deeply into the northern regions of Europe and brought large parts of the continent into contact with Mediterranean civilisation.

19 Rome's conquest of the Mediterranean

Many historians have sought the explanation for Rome's spectacular expansion within and without Italy in its aggressive, bellicose and militaristic nature. Whereas it cannot be denied that the Roman Republic was certainly all that, in this it was not exceptional. Most of its Italian and Mediterranean competitors shared these characteristics. In the anarchical world of the Mediterranean, these characteristics were necessary for survival.[4] What made Rome exceptional, and explained its achievement, was that it proved better at war. For this, two explanations can be advanced. First, there was Rome's exceptional capacity to assimilate the peoples it subdued and harness them to its own interest. Thanks to this, Rome could draw on a vast pool of men and resources and could outlast

[4] Arthur M. Eckstein has convincingly argued this in *Mediterranean Anarchy, Interstate War, and the Rise of Rome*, Berkeley 2006.

its enemies in the many protracted wars it had to fight. Second, through the long experience of its many wars, Rome achieved superiority in terms of organisation, logistics and discipline over most of its enemies. If the Romans had such a successful learning curve, it was probably partly owing to the fact that it was such a long one.

Rome's ascendancy over Italy brought it on to a collision course with other great powers of the Mediterranean. In the war against Tarente, Rome had already had the chance to cut its teeth against the Greek armies of Pyrrhus of Epirus. In 264 BC, the First Punic War between Rome and Carthage broke out. At stake was control over the island of Sicily. The war ended in 249 BC in Roman victory and the conquest of the island by Rome. In the aftermath of the war, the Romans annexed Sardinia and Corsica and subjugated the Celtic tribes living in northern Italy between the Po and the Alps. During the Second Punic War (218–201 BC), Rome was almost brought to its knees by the Carthaginian general Hannibal (249–183 BC). In 218 BC, Hannibal led an army from Spain across the Pyrenees and the Alps into Italy, taking the Romans by surprise. For sixteen years, he roamed through the peninsula, leaving a trail of destruction behind. On three separate occasions, he destroyed a Roman army in the field. He was not, however, able to capture the city of Rome, and ultimately Rome won what became a war of attrition. The young general Publius Cornelius Scipio Africanus Major (235–183 BC) first captured the Carthaginian territories in Spain and then invaded Africa, thus forcing Hannibal to leave Italy. At Zama (202 BC), he defeated the legendary general.

With its victory over Carthage, Rome established its hegemony around the western Mediterranean. The city now turned its attention to Carthage's allies in Greece and the East. By 146 BC, Macedonia and Greece had been subdued. The Hellenic kingdoms established in Asia Minor, Syria and Palestine by the successors of Alexander the Great were overrun by Gnaeus Pompeius Magnus (Pompey) (106–48 BC) in the 60s BC. Octavian, later Emperor Augustus (27 BC–AD 14), added the last large, independent kingdom in the Mediterranean, Egypt, to the Roman Empire in 30 BC. Octavian's adoptive father, Caesar, had conquered Gaul up to the Rhine during the 50s BC. From that point onwards, present-day Belgium and the south of the Netherlands also formed part of the empire. In the reign of Augustus, the remainder of the Netherlands and Germany up to the River Elbe were temporarily occupied (until AD 9). Augustus also annexed all the regions south of the Danube. Under Claudius (AD 41–54), England was added to the Roman Empire.

5 Political organisation under the Late Republic (264–27 BC)

20 An oligarchic republic

During the Regal Period, Rome had three important political institutions: the king, the Senate and the popular assemblies. By the end of that period, the king enjoyed a virtually unlimited *imperium*. He was the supreme commander of the army, high priest, chief justice and legislator. After their successful coup of 509 BC, the patricians decided to carve up the military and administrative *imperium* of the king and divide it among various magistrates. The king's religious power was taken over by priests, among whom the leading figure was the *pontifex maximus*, the chairman of the powerful college of *pontifices*, literally bridge-builders. The Senate and popular assemblies continued to exist.

The Greek philosopher Aristotle (384–321 BC) distinguished three forms of government, and this distinction was adopted by Roman scholars, remaining a classical topos of political doctrine until the Modern Age. First comes monarchy, the form of government whereby one person holds power. Second, there is aristocracy, the rule by a small group of the very best from among the citizens. Third, there is democracy, in which the supreme power resides with the people. In the Renaissance, reference began to be made to the Roman state as the Roman *respublica*. But for the Romans, the term simply meant 'the public affairs'. According to the Roman orator Marcus Tullius Cicero (106–43 BC), the Roman Republic was a hybrid form in which the consuls – the most senior magistrates – constituted the monarchical element, the Senate the aristocratic element and the popular assemblies the democratic element.

> Since this is true, the kingship, in my opinion, is by far the best of the three primary forms, but a moderate and balanced form of government which is a combination of the three good simple forms is preferable even to the kingship. For there should be a supreme and royal element in the state, some power also ought to be granted to the leading citizens, and certain matters should be left to the judgment and desires of the masses.[5]

In reality, the Senate dominated the daily affairs of state. The Roman Republic was an aristocracy or oligarchy, under which the members of a small elite – the leading figures from the senatorial order – constantly vied for power among themselves.

[5] Cicero, *De republica* 1, 69; translation by Clinton Walker Keyes, *Cicero: De republica, De legibus* (Loeb Classical Library 213), Cambridge, Mass. and London 1928.

21   The popular assemblies

The popular assemblies, the *comitia*, were gatherings of all Roman male, adult citizens. They were convened by the magistrates. The highest magistrates – the consuls, praetors and censors – were elected in the most important of the three types of *comitia*, the *comitia centuriata*. Here, the consuls' legislative proposals were put to the vote. The *centuriata* were divided into 193 centuries – originally army units – each of which had one vote. The centuries were divided into five property classes and one unpropertied class. The first and wealthiest class, which had few members and included the senatorial order as well as the equestrians, controlled 98 of the 193 centuries: 80 for the senatorial order and 18 for the equestrians. The poorest class, the *infraclassem* – that is, those without property, including the urban proletariat – had only five centuries. This system guaranteed a minority of the voters the majority of the votes. After the *centuriata* in terms of importance came the *comitia tributa*. This body elected the lower magistrates and could also make laws. The *tributa* consisted of thirty-five tribes, of which thirty-one represented the rural areas around Rome. The rural *tribus* were sparsely populated; generally speaking, only the more affluent landowners took the trouble to go to Rome in order to vote. The majority of the urban *plebs* were concentrated in just four urban tribes. The third *comitia*, the *curiata*, lost its political importance under the Republic and ultimately retained just a few formal duties, such as homologating certain adoptions.

The layered voting in the *comitia* neutralised the power of the masses. The poorest classes held little weight in the elections. It was partly for this reason that the *concilium plebis*, an assembly in which only plebeians were allowed to participate, arose. This assembly was also subdivided into thirty-five *tribus*.

In the earlier days of the Republic, only the *comitia*, more particularly the *comitia centuriata* and the *comitia tributa*, could legislate and make statute law (*lex*, pl: *leges*). Until 339 BC, all the statutes had to be confirmed by the Senate. In that year, the order was reversed. Henceforth, the magistrates were required to submit their proposals to the Senate for approval before they went to the popular assemblies. Since the will of the Senate and that of the *comitia* generally coincided, the role of the *comitia* in the drafting of laws became steadily smaller. Under the leadership of a number of historic plebeian tribunes, the *concilium plebis* obtained a greater role. After the *lex Hortensia* of 287 BC, the *concilium plebis*, just like the *comitia*, held the power to legislate for all classes. The statutes promulgated by the *concilium plebis* were known as *plebiscita* (plebiscites). Whereas the *comitia* had to be convened by a magistrate, the *concilium plebis* could be convened only by the plebeian tribunes. They also submitted the legislative proposals to the *concilium*. In principle, these proposals were first submitted to the Senate. Strictly speaking, that was not mandatory, but it became a standard practice during the second century BC. During the final centuries of the Republic, the *concilium* and the plebeian tribunes were the true engines behind the legislative process. Radical proposals with significant political, administrative or social impact were often tabled by the plebeian tribunes and voted on in the *concilium plebis*. During the late second and first centuries BC, this led on a number of occasions to sharp clashes between the Senate and radical tribunes.

Since the popular assemblies – the *comitia* and *concilium plebis* – did not allow open debate but moved to an immediate vote, the magistrates would often convene a *contio* in advance of the actual popular assembly. This was a gathering of the people independent of the structure of one of the popular assemblies. It provided a forum to debate the magistrates' proposals; it was here that great political speeches, such as some by Cicero, were delivered.

22   The Senate

The Senate's roots lay with the meeting of the *patres* (heads, literally fathers) of the old *gentes* during the Regal Period. The Senate was a place of dialogue among the clan leaders themselves and between these and the king. After the expulsion of the king, the Senate, as the only permanent political body, played a leading role in the day-to-day business of the Republic. Although the *senatusconsulta* (Senate decisions) were formally speaking merely advisory opinions for the magistrates and the popular assemblies, in reality the Senate dominated the decision-making process. The Senate also arrogated foreign policy and the treasury to itself.

The Senate owed its position to its composition. It was the forum where the leading men in the Republic met and discussed the business of state. It consisted of all former magistrates. From the second century BC, plebeian tribunes also joined the Senate more or less automatically after they resigned their office. Membership was for life. The Senate worked in fact with a system of co-optation. Anyone from the right family who was put forward by their kin for election to the political offices – the magistratures – could have legitimate hopes of being elected and would thus become a senator. Before the dictatorship of Lucius Cornelius Sulla (138–78 BC, dictator 81–79 BC), the Senate had approximately three hundred members. Since many of these executed duties in the provinces or the army or were simply no longer active, there were seldom more than two hundred present. Under the dictatorship of Sulla, the Senate was expanded to some six hundred members.

23   The magistrates

The magistrates were the annually elected officials of the Roman Republic. The former royal *imperium* was divided up among them. In the early stages of the Republic, there were just two or more magistrates of equal rank, each with an equal *imperium*. The *imperium* included both military and administrative power. From the end of the second century BC at the latest, this also included the *iurisdictio* – namely, power and control over the dispensation of justice. As time went by, more offices were added and a hierarchy of higher and lower magistrates came into being. In 367 BC, the various magistracies were established and codified by the *leges Liciniae Sextiae*. In 180 BC, the *lex Villia Annalis* established concrete rules about the *cursus honorum*, the sequence of offices one had to hold in order to reach the highest office of consul, and about the minimum age requirements for each office. The statute also stipulated a two-year interval between the holding of two consecutive offices in the *cursus honorum*. In 81 BC, the dictator Sulla refined the rules and brought the numbers of magistrates into line with the needs of the rapidly growing empire. The rules were designed to prevent one man from arrogating too much power. First, there was the rule that magistrates held office for one year and could in principle only be re-elected after a minimum interval. Second, there was the principle of collegiality: no magistracy was exercised by just one individual. Each office was always held by a number of persons, each of whom had the same power. Magistrates holding the same office could act independently from one another, but each magistrate could veto his colleagues' decisions (*prohibitio* in advance of the decision, *intercessio* after the decision was taken). The *lex Villia Annalis* of 180 BC also allowed magistrates to veto the decisions of all lower magistrates. These veto powers provided a means of checking and reining in each officeholder. Third, while in office, magistrates were immune from prosecution by the courts. But, with the exception of the censors, they could be held to account for their actions as magistrate upon relinquishing office. The prosecution of former magistrates was the order of the day; it was one element in the struggle for power between rival clans and factions. It was a sword of Damocles hanging over the head of any magistrate who made too many and too powerful enemies while in office.

The lowest magistracy was the quaestor. Sulla laid down that nobody could become a quaestor before the age of thirty; before, one had to have served for ten years in the army. He also increased the number of quaestors from eight to twenty. The quaestors were assistants of the consuls and praetors, their duties extending to the supervision of financial affairs.

The second office was not a compulsory step in the *cursus honorum*. It was that of the aedile (*aedilis*), who was responsible for public buildings and temples, markets and commerce, water and grain supplies and the organisation of festivals and games. They also acted as judges in commercial disputes, especially those concerning the purchase and sale of slaves and cattle. The fact that the aediles needed to draw on their own financial resources for the performance of their duties placed this office beyond the reach of many. It was, however, an excellent method for gaining the voters' favour in the struggle for the two highest offices: those of praetor and of consul.

The office of praetor was first established in 367 BC. To begin with, the praetor was a junior colleague of the consuls, with fewer powers and less authority. It was probably not until the third or even second century BC that the praetors were given responsibility for the dispensation of justice in Rome. Sulla set the number of praetors at eight. A minimum age requirement was introduced by the *lex Villia Annalis*; in Sulla's law of 81 BC this was thirty-nine years. The person elected with the most votes became urban praetor (*praetor urbanus*) and was responsible for the administration of civil law in the city of Rome. The peregrine praetor (*praetor peregrinus*) was concerned with the dispensation of justice for disputes in which foreigners were involved. Others were responsible for special courts while others again were given a province, that is an area outside Italy under Roman control or where Rome waged a war, to act there as Rome's representative and as military commander.

The highest office of all was that of consul. Every year, two consuls were elected. These were the political and military leaders of the Republic. Traditionally one, or if necessary both, acted as supreme commander in the many wars waged by the Roman Republic inside and outside Italy. The consuls alternately presided over the Senate and prepared the activities of the Senate and the *comitia*. The minimum age for a consul was forty-two (but lower for a patrician). According to a statute of 151 BC (*lex de consulatu non iterando*), one had to wait ten years in order to be allowed to stand for the consulate a second time. During the second and first centuries BC, numerous exceptions were made to these rules for all sorts of reasons.

The office of censor was one of the most coveted and prestigious and was, in practice, reserved for former consuls. Two censors were elected every five years for a period of eighteen months. The censors took a *census* – the list of names of the Senate, the equestrian class and the various categories of the popular assemblies – awarded public works and upheld traditional morality, the *mos maiorum*. Their term of office was concluded with a major ceremony, the *lustrum*.

24   The princes of the Senate

The successful completion of the *cursus honorum* with the promotion to the consulate gave the Roman politician a place at the top. Anyone who became consul elevated his family and all his descendants to the nobility, irrespective of whether he came from a patrician or a plebeian family. These *nobiles* or nobles formed a small band at the top of the senatorial order. The vast majority of consuls came from the same thirty noble families. The nobility consequently remained a small group. If it was difficult for a non-noble to be elected as consul, for a *homo novus* or new man – someone who was the first of his family to enter the Senate – it was all but impossible. The few who managed to do so, such as Marcus Porcius Cato the Censor (235–149 BC), Gaius Marius (158–83 BC) or the orator Cicero, took no little pride in this feat.

The Senate was subject to a strict hierarchy. In practice, only a limited number of senators would take the floor during the debates. The presiding consul would introduce the issues and invite others to speak according to the strict hierarchy. The presiding consul was followed by the consuls-elect for the next year – if these had already been elected – and the *consulares*, or ex-consuls. *Consulares* were generally called to speak in order of seniority. They dominated the Senate and assured continuity in Roman policy. One of the older *consulares* would be designated by the censors as *princeps senatus*. His name appeared at the top of the list of senators and he was the first of the *consulares* allowed to speak. After the *consulares* came the praetors-elect, the ex-praetors and the incumbent praetors. In this way the list of the magistracies was ticked off. The real backbenchers – the *pedarii*, that is, those who had never got further than quaestor – were rarely if ever called to speak.

The *consulares* – the great political and military leaders – were at the helm of the ship of state. The cornerstone of the power and influence of a former consul was his *auctoritas* (personal authority) and his *dignitas* (personal dignity). There were many dimensions to a politician's *auctoritas* and *dignitas*: the family to which he belonged, a *cursus honorum* culminating in one or more consulates or the office of censor, the political and military achievements during a period of office as magistrate or provincial governor, the celebration of a military triumph, generosity in organising festivals and ceremonies and funding public works, membership of one or more pontifical colleges, the number and type of clients and friends with whom he associated, the family ties he managed to establish with other *gentes*, and his success as a speaker in the Senate, the popular assemblies or the courts.

Under the Republic, the Senate grew into the most powerful organ of state. It was the assembly of all the great political and military leaders. It was the sole body that was at once permanent and small enough to be effective. The Republic was, accordingly, government by the Senate. For many centuries, the principles of annuality and collegiality of the magistracies prevented the concentration of power in the hands of a single person or dynasty. Day-to-day Roman politics was a matter for several dozen or at most several hundred members of the nobility, senators and their families. It was dominated by the ongoing struggle for power among the members of this oligarchy. The Senate was the most important battlefield in this permanent war. Only in the confrontation with the other two classes would the ranks within the Senate close, and then not always.

25   The priesthood and the dictatorship

Reference should also be made to another institution that had great political relevance, the pontifical colleges. The most important of these colleges were those of the *pontifices*, under the direction of the *pontifex maximus* (high priest), and of the *augures*, the official diviners of the will of the gods. Initially, the colleges filled their ranks by means of co-optation; later the priests were elected by the people. The office was held for life. For a long time, membership of the colleges was restricted to the patricians. By the time of the Late Republic, this had changed, but the same families who provided most of the magistrates also monopolised the large pontifical colleges. The priests did not form a separate class. Generally speaking, leading politicians were elected to the colleges. Initially, the administration of justice was in the hands of the *pontifices*; later they were displaced by the praetors and aediles. The priests did, however, retain authority over the religious courts. Since the priests played a major role in public festivities and ceremonies, membership of one of the more prestigious colleges led to public notoriety. In addition, many public meetings were preceded by the reading out of an augury, creating room for all sorts of manipulation by the *augures*. On more than one occasion, a meeting was postponed or a decision enforced for religious reasons.

In times of emergency, the Senate could suspend the normal operation of the institutions of state. A dictator with an unlimited *imperium* would then be appointed for a limited period of time. Once the state of emergency had been lifted the dictator would stand down again. During the turbulent first century BC, dictators for life were appointed on two occasions: Sulla and Caesar.

6   *The challenges of empire*

26   The transformation of society and the economy

The spectacular expansion of the Roman Empire after Hannibal had been defeated radically transformed Roman society and the Roman state. To begin with, Rome was a community of farmers and warriors. The republican institutions were designed for the administration of a city-state. The conquest of Italy had wrought changes, but Rome nevertheless remained a fairly small city with an agricultural mentality. It had little impact on the system of political administration since Rome granted the subjugated tribes self-government. But by the end of the second century BC, the Roman elite found itself at the head of an empire comparable with that of Alexander the Great.

The conquest of an empire and the expense and responsibilities this brought produced new social tensions. The Roman farmers in Italy suffered from the almost continuous warfare. The destruction wrought by Hannibal had plunged many families into misery. Even worse were Rome's numerous wars outside Italy. The Roman army was a citizens' army: all male citizens, with the exception of members of the unpropertied class, were required to serve in the army. Until the third century BC, military campaigns were generally confined to spring and summer and were conducted close to home. They did not lead to any long-term dislocation of agricultural activity. The wars in Spain, Africa and Greece of the second century BC changed all this. The soldiers remained under arms for the full duration of the campaign. The maximum period of service was twenty years. When soldiers returned home upon completion of their service, they often had great difficulty in readjusting themselves to peaceful lives as farmers and family men, always assuming their farms and families were still there for them to go back to. This and other factors led to the demise of family farming and small landholding throughout Italy. The lands previously owned by small landholders ended up in the hands of a few wealthy families. These also appropriated the lands taken by Rome from conquered tribes and cities in Italy. Thus, country estates or *latifundia* that thrived on cheap labour, hired hands and slaves emerged. Small farmers were driven from the market. Later, Italian farmers also had to compete with cheap grain imported from Sicily, Africa – nowadays Tunisia – and Egypt.

Slavery also played an increasing role in trade, mining and industry. As a result of the numerous conquests, the Roman slave markets in the third and second centuries BC were flooded with cheap labour. Although this was to benefit many Roman families, providing them with plenty of domestic servants, the wealthier families profited the most. Thanks to these slaves, they were able to set up larger trading and industrial enterprises, so that ordinary Roman citizens became economically marginalised. With the pauperisation of an element of the Roman population, Rome found itself confronted, from the late second century BC onwards, by the problem of a growing urban proletariat. Their ranks were further swelled by large numbers of freed slaves who were granted citizenship upon their release. Numerous foreigners from conquered areas also made their way to the city. Social tensions in Rome increased in leaps and bounds. Some senators responded to this by portraying themselves as defenders of the common people. They demanded reforms such as the reallocation of land, the distribution of grain at reduced rates, the extension of citizenship rights in Italy and restrictions on the power of the Senate.

27   The equestrian order

But the rise of the empire also brought fortune to many non-senatorial families. During the second century BC, a new order began to emerge among the plebs: the *equites* (knights or equestrians). This group was drawn from that element of the citizenry who were wealthy enough to perform their military service on horseback. Gradually, this group of more affluent citizens evolved into a separate middle class. The equestrians gradually came to control trade, industry and banking in and outside Rome. Senators were subject to strict limitations with regard to commercial, maritime and industrial activities. By tradition, they were required to invest their wealth in land and farming. Although many senators circumvented this by means of legal arrangements with slaves, freedmen and family members, the regulations left room for the equestrian order. The spectacular expansion of the empire around the Mediterranean basin in the second and first centuries BC provided an economic stimulus for the equestrians. Through their tax farming businesses and as bankers, ship-owners and entrepreneurs, the equestrians controlled the huge flows of money between Italy and the rest of the empire.

The majority of the equestrian order kept out of politics, which remained the domain of the senatorial order. Those equestrians who did venture into politics and have success became senators themselves and promoted their families to the senatorial order. As a result of this co-optation of new elements from the dynamic strata of the population, the senatorial order was continually replenished and the political elite remained in touch with the economic elite. Nevertheless, the two groups each had their own interests.

During the second and especially the first centuries BC, the two orders came into conflict over financial, economic and legal issues. One such source of conflict was the control over the special criminal courts, the *quaestiones perpetuae*. Certain offences, often with a political dimension to them, were tried before these jury courts. They were a powerful weapon in the political struggle among senators themselves and in the struggle of the other orders against the senatorial elite. One of the disputes between the equestrian order and the senatorial order was whether the jury should consist of equestrians or of senators, or of members of both orders. Another point of dispute related to tax farming. Every few years the Roman Senate issued tax contracts. Equestrians could buy the right, by advancing the tax to the treasury, to collect taxes in those provinces subject to taxation, in particular the province of Asia – in what is now western Turkey. This resulted in numerous abuses, on the part of both the provincial governors drawn from the senatorial order and of the *publicani* (tax collectors), and led to sharp clashes between the two elites.

28   The proconsuls

The expansion of Roman conquests outside Italy tested the political, administrative and military organisation of the Republic to and beyond its limits. As indicated above, the republican institutions were geared not to an empire but to a medium-sized city-state. The Republican constitution was aimed at maintaining the equilibrium within the leading elite in Rome. It was not intended for the efficient administration of an empire. The defence of and control over the empire was left to the magistrates/military commanders assigned to the provinces. In the course of the second and first centuries BC, some of these amassed such power that they became uncontrollable, independent power brokers within the Republic. Ultimately, this led to the demise of the Republic and the establishment of an autocratic regime.

As mentioned, the Roman army was initially a citizens' army, with citizens required to bear arms for the duration of a campaign. On account of the continual and protracted wars of the second century BC and the pauperisation of part of the population, the supply of recruits had become exhausted by the end of that century. The proletariat – the propertyless *infraclassem* – was after all excluded from compulsory military service. *Proletariat* Under the threat of a Germanic invasion of Italy, the Roman general Gaius Marius managed to implement an important reform at the end of the second century BC. He admitted the proletariat to the army and provided the soldiers with long-term appointments in return for pay. In a short space of time, the army was transformed from a conscript army into a professional one, thereby weakening the link between Roman society and the military. Loyalty to the state was supplanted by loyalty to one's own commander.

During the Republic, the army was commanded by the consuls and the praetors. That meant that they could be in command for no more than one year. Since, in the earlier days of the Republic, the campaigns seldom went on for any longer than that, this did not present many problems. If a war did drag on, the newly elected magistrate would simply take over the command or the commander-in-chief's *imperium* would be temporarily extended.

From the second century BC onwards, the wars were generally conducted from or in a particular *provincia*, that is an area outside Italy *provincia* within or at the fringes of the Roman 'Empire'. During the Late Republic, the term *provincia* could refer to any region that came – or, according to Rome, should come – within the sphere of influence of the Roman Empire and to which a magistrate or promagistrate was sent. The Romans denoted a region they had subjugated as being *sub imperio Romano*. *sub* Literally, this means 'under the power of Rome', but it is often mislead- *imperio* ingly translated as 'within the Roman Empire'. In truth, often submission *Romano* to Rome implied only that the people living there recognised their defeat by Rome and accepted its lead, its hegemony, in foreign and military affairs. But in most cases, Rome left the subject people a great amount of autonomy in their internal affairs. Belonging to the 'Roman Empire' did not necessarily mean the existence of an effective Roman administration, or that the inhabitants even had tax or legal obligations vis-à-vis Rome. In some cases, such as in Sicily or the Roman province of Asia, there was far-reaching Roman involvement and it would be fair to speak of a genuine provincial governor. In more peripheral provinces, the Roman magistrate was, apart from being the army commander, in truth more of an ambassador than a governor. This non-governance of the larger part of its 'empire' by Rome did not change until after the end of the Republic.

The political representation of Rome in a province and the military command over the operations of war in those parts were bound up together. Whereas previously, the provinces had been assigned to magistrates for a period of one year, the custom arose of extending the *imperium* of the magistrates in question or even of assigning the provinces and commands immediately to former consuls and praetors for several years. These would then act as proconsul or propraetor – literally, deputy consul or praetor – for a period of three, five or even more years. The major generals of the first century BC, such as Sulla, Pompey and Caesar, conducted their conquests as proconsuls in one or more provinces.

In this way, certain individuals managed to acquire great renown, power and wealth. Pompey and Caesar built up fortunes at the expense of subjected peoples. This enabled them to buy the support and votes of numerous friends and clients in the Roman Senate and the popular assemblies. They and other generals evolved into independent power brokers within the Republic. During their lengthy spells as proconsuls, they were able to assure themselves of the personal loyalty of their troops. During the last few decades of the Republic, the resources of the conquered areas were concentrated in the hands of a few *generalissimi*; the Senate lost its grip over the 'empire' outside the city and outside Italy.

7   The Age of Revolution at the end of the Republic (133–27 BC)

29   Optimates and populares

In modern historiography, the hundred years after the revolt by Tiberius Sempronius Gracchus in 133 BC is often designated as the Age of Revolution. During this period, Rome was plagued by political unrest and outright civil war. In 133 BC, the plebeian tribune Tiberius Sempronius Gracchus clashed with the majority of the Senate when he resorted to unconstitutional measures in order to enforce his proposals for land reform. His violent death marked a turning point in the political history of Rome. Tiberius Gracchus and his younger brother Gaius (d. 122 BC), who ten years later trod in his brother's footsteps, won a place in collective memory as the forerunners of the *populares*.

The first century BC saw a division in the Senate between the conservative majority of the *optimates*, and the radical minority, the *populares*. The *optimates* were the defenders of the hegemony of the Senate and of the constitutional and social status quo. Ranged against them were the

populares, the advocates of reform who sought support from the equestrian order and the plebs. It would, however, be wrong to conceive of
the *populares* as a party of and for the people. They were not ordinary
members of the public; the *populares* were senators and many, such as
Caesar, Lucius Sergius Catilina (108–63 BC) or Publius Clodius Pulcher
(c.92–52 BC), came from the oldest noble families in Rome. The *populares*
set themselves apart from their opponents in that they sought support
from the people and eagerly made use of the possibilities afforded by the
tribunate and the *concilium plebis* in order to further their personal ambitions or political programmes. In doing so, they challenged the monopoly
of the Senate over government. In order to assure themselves of popular
favour, the *populares* generally identified themselves with a populist programme of land reform, grain distribution and the extension of citizenship, and portrayed themselves as the successors of the Gracchi or the
great, populist general Gaius Marius. Equally, however, they sought support from the wealthy equestrian order and from Roman citizens in Italy
and the provinces. The *populares* were populists who, for reasons of personal ambition, turned against the system whereby power was dispersed
among the elite and consequently sought a power base outside the elite,
among the people; their populism was generally a means and not an end.
The struggle between the *populares* and *optimates* may have reflected the
social tensions in Roman society, but was above all the umpteenth episode
in the struggle between the most powerful members and clans within the
senatorial order itself.

30   The fall of the Republic

It was not so much the social unrest that led to the fall of the Republic as
the failure of the republican institutions to keep the great generals under
control. The Senate in Rome proved incapable of reining in the ambitions of those who had conquered the empire. The revolt by the Gracchi
was followed by several decades in which various leaders sought to push
through new land reforms. During the 90s BC, the demands by the Italian
allies for citizenship became the biggest issue of contention. The stub-
born rejection of these demands by the majority of the Senate and the
plebs led to the outbreak of war between Rome and its Italian allies (the
Social War, 91–88 BC), during which tension between the *optimates* and
populares reached a boiling point. Ultimately, this gave rise to the clash
between the two greatest generals of the time: Marius and Sulla. After
having been stripped of the proconsulate and his command in Greece and
Asia through the agency of Marius, Sulla took a step without precedent

in Roman history: he marched his own troops on Rome and took the city (88 BC). After a lengthy war in the East, Sulla was to repeat this a second time. Upon this occasion, Sulla was appointed by the Senate as dictator for life (81 BC). He made use of this unlimited power to reform the republican institutions before withdrawing from the scene (79 BC).

Sulla's *coup d'état* led to other, similar interventions. In the next generation, three powerful men emerged who each managed to acquire great fame, power and wealth: Marcus Licinius Crassus (115–53 BC), Pompey, who liked to be called Magnus (the Great), and Gaius Iulius Caesar. During the 60s BC, Crassus and Pompey vied for the top spot in Rome. Both, in doing so, sought popular favour. In 60 BC, Caesar, an ally of Crassus, forged an alliance between Pompey, Crassus and himself that was to go down in history as the first triumvirate. This was not a *coup d'état* but a coalition in which the three agreed to support each other's candidates and proposals in elections and votes. The triumvirate laid the basis for Caesar's ascent to the top. Caesar was elected consul for 59 BC and was later assigned the provinces from which he was to conquer Gaul in the next decade.

After the death of Crassus in 53 BC, Caesar and Pompey gradually became estranged. Caesar had managed to project himself as the main *popularis*, as a result of which Pompey drifted towards the *optimates*. The irreconcilable attitude adopted by the leaders of that group towards Caesar triggered a new civil war, leading to the death of Pompey (48 BC) and the dictatorship of Caesar. After Caesar's murder in 44 BC, a third major civil war broke out, which was to span thirteen years. Many luminaries of Roman politics, including the orator Cicero, were to meet their end during this war. In 42 BC, Caesar's political heirs won the upper hand over his murderers (Battle of Philippi). The three most important leaders formed the second triumvirate. On this occasion, however, this was a genuine *coup d'état*. The three granted themselves a virtually unlimited *imperium* as *triumviri rei publicae constituendae* (three men for the restoration of the Republic) and divided the empire up among themselves. Mark Antony (Marcus Antonius, 82–30 BC), Caesar's loyal lieutenant, received all the provinces in the East. Marcus Aemilius Lepidus (90–12 BC) was assigned various provinces in the West but was deposed by the third *triumvir* in 36 BC. The third was Caesar's adopted son, Gaius Iulius Caesar Octavianus (63 BC–AD 14), who, as a nineteen-year-old youth, astonished friend and foe alike by taking up position alongside the powerful Antony. In 31 BC, the struggle between Octavian and Antony and the latter's lover, the Egyptian Queen Cleopatra (59–30 BC), entered its final stage. Antony and Cleopatra's fleet was defeated at Actium off the Greek coast and the two lovers committed suicide. After the annexation of Egypt, Octavian returned to Rome as sole ruler in 27 BC.

Octavian

8   Augustus (27 BC–AD 14)

31   Augustus

Upon his return to Rome in 27 BC, Octavian faced the challenge of restoring the peace and prosperity of Rome, Italy and the empire after decades of political unrest and civil war. The internal power struggle had severely disrupted the ranks of the senatorial and equestrian orders. Italy's economy was in disarray. The exodus from the countryside to the city had assumed major proportions and the ranks of the urban proletariat in Rome were greatly swollen. Countless Roman families had lost their farms and Rome had lost its hold over the provinces.

The death of Mark Antony left Octavian as the sole survivor of the *triumviri* of 43 BC. Upon his return to Rome, however, he returned his power to the Senate and the people of Rome. Octavian wanted to restore the Republic – or at least that's what he said. In return, the Senate bestowed upon him the honorary name Augustus, or Venerable. In addition he was given a number of powers by the Senate that confirmed his position as the strong man of the state. The year 27 BC is traditionally regarded as the definitive end of the Republic and the start of the Imperial Age.

Octavian = Augustus

Although Augustus was out to consolidate his power, the alternation of power between himself and the Senate was not just a show for public consumption. This claim that he intended to restore the Republic was more than propaganda. Augustus did not enjoy total supremacy. The events of 27 BC were not a farce enacted by an all-powerful Octavian and a powerless Senate. Octavian may have eliminated all his immediate opponents but was aware that he would be unable to stay in power while simultaneously restoring order without the consent of the major families and the political elite. The form of government that was worked out was a compromise between the former *triumvir* and the majority of the Senate. Augustus did not aspire to be crowned king. Since the expulsion of the last king, the concept of kingship in Rome was taboo. The rumours that Caesar wanted the throne had played a role in his demise. In addition, Augustus made a serious effort while in office to restore republican

Imperial age (end of the republic)

values, way of life and social relations and tried to extend a new dignity to
the Senate. At the same time, both Augustus and a majority of the Senate
were clear that a return to the situation of the 50s BC was neither feasible
nor desirable. It was feared that the wounds from the past would lead to
renewed civil war if Augustus were to retire. The events of 27 BC were the
result of laborious negotiations between Augustus and the Senate. The
ascendancy of the former *triumvir* was confirmed, while the honour of
the Senate was to some extent restored.

During the forty years in which he was in power, Augustus managed
to maintain peace and stability in the empire. He made use of artists and
men of letters as propagandists to promote his authority and policies.
The works of the historian Livy and the poet Virgil were designed to add
lustre to the traditional values and life-style of the Republic. Augustus's
policies were aimed at the restoration of agriculture, industry and commerce, the reassertion of Rome's grip over the empire, an enhanced level
of administrative efficiency inside and outside Italy, and the revival of
republican morality at public and family level. Augustus expanded the
ranks of the Senate and the equestrian orders with new elements so as to
re-establish the pool of political and military leaders. Increasing numbers
of non-Italians made their way into the Senate. In this regard, Augustus
was continuing a policy that had been launched under Caesar. Finally,
he rounded off the borders of the empire – in Europe up to the Rhine
and Danube, and in North Africa to the Sahara. He also reorganised the
provinces. A certain degree of Roman administration was slowly introduced around the empire. All the provinces were given a genuine provincial governor, either a promagistrate or an imperial official. The cities
and tribes continued, however, to retain a high measure of autonomy in
domestic affairs and numerous semi-independent client states continued
to exist within the borders of the empire.

The longer Augustus remained in power, the more pressing the matter of his succession became. Since Rome was formally a republic and
Augustus was not a monarch, it was not axiomatic that there should be a
new 'Augustus' after his death. The success and the length of Augustus's
administration, however, rendered a complete restoration of the Republic
improbable. Ultimately, Augustus adopted Tiberius, his wife's son from
her first marriage and one of the most successful generals and administrators in his own right under Augustus, and conferred far-reaching
powers on him. After the death of Augustus, Tiberius (AD 14–38) took
over his stepfather's position. The new form of government, which went
down in history as the Principate, was thereby confirmed.

9   The Roman Empire under the Principate (AD 14–284)

32   Further expansion

The Principate saw the biggest expansion of the Roman Empire. Emperor Claudius (AD 41–54) added Britannia (England) to the empire. Trajan (98–117) captured Dacia (Romania) and temporarily also the areas between the Euphrates and Tigris, largely present-day Iraq. His nephew and successor Hadrian (117–38) put an end to the policy of conquest and opted instead for a defensive strategy. Hadrian annexed most of the client-states of semi-independent rulers and city-states located within the empire's sphere of influence and fortified the borders with forts and walls where there were no natural lines of defence. Hadrian's Wall in northern England bears witness to this new strategy to the present day. The new strategy spread the benefits of Roman rule – mainly security – over large parts of Europe, further and further away from the Mediterranean. It also made the costs of imperial defence rise.

The first two centuries of the Principate were a period of relative peace, the *pax Romana*. Most of the wars took place on the borders of the empire. There were, however, a number of military coups in the second half of the first century and at the end of the second century. Although there were some clashes between provincial governors and their armies, the empire was not seriously affected and the consequences of the struggle for power remained largely limited.

33   Romanisation

The second century was the high point of the empire. The core areas of the empire were at peace. The reigns of the intelligent, intellectual and culturally minded emperors Hadrian (117–38), Antoninus Pius (138–61) and the philosopher Marcus Aurelius (161–80) still stand out in collective memory among the finest periods in European history.[6] The prosperity brought by peace did not, however, benefit the urban population of Rome itself. The problem of the urban proletariat did not go away; on the contrary, its ranks were if anything strengthened by foreigners, freedmen, Roman farmers and craftsmen who had been driven out of business.

Under the Principate, Rome was transformed from a group of regions administered by the conquering city-state into something more like a

---

[6] The Franco-Belgian author Marguérite Yourcenar evoked and idealised the period in her masterly novel *Mémoires d'Hadrien*, Paris 1951 (translation by Grace Frick as *Memoirs of Hadrian*, London 1955).

genuine empire. It was through military conquest that Rome had amassed most of its empire. But the foundation stone of the empire's endurance was the successful association of the local elites – especially the landowning classes – from the conquered territories with Rome and what it stood for. Rome, through its armies, its laws and its local representatives, guaranteed these elites their security, their privileges and their riches. In their stead, these elites provided the empire with loyal, local administrators who could be trusted to guard Roman interests with which they identified, while keeping a great deal of leeway in the internal administration of their towns and tribes. They proved their allegiance to Rome by subscribing to the cult of the emperor and by assimilating parts of Roman-Greek culture. Increasing numbers of provincials succeeded in attaining Roman citizenship until the *constitutio Antoniniana* granted this right in 212 to all free-born inhabitants of the empire. This helped, at least partially, to harmonise the administrative and fiscal systems of the subjugated areas; more importantly, it made Roman law the law of the entire empire. In this process of integration, the Roman elite of senators and equestrians also lost its Roman and even its Italian character. More and more members of the provincial elites pursued careers in the army, the imperial civil service or the Senate. From the second century onwards, most of the emperors no longer came from Italy itself. The families of Trajan, Hadrian and their direct successors came from Spain. The general Septimius Severus (193–211), whose dynasty governed Rome for nearly half a century, came from Libya. The new members of the elite did, however, often receive their education in Rome and launched their careers there. This began to change in the third century, when the throne fell increasingly into the hands of professional soldiers. Many of the great emperors in the post-AD 250 period saw Rome for the first time after ascending to the throne; some emperors never went there at all.

10   *The emperorship under the Principate (AD 14–284)*

34   *Princeps inter pares*

The Principate of Augustus and his successors was not a genuine monarchy. Formally, the Republic continued to exist and the old institutions all remained in place. The emperorship only gradually became institutionalised. The later designation of the emperor as Caesar Augustus indicated this. At the outset, these were not titles, but names. The first four successors of Augustus, all belonging to the dynasty of the *Iulii Caesares* by adoption or blood ties, bore the names Caesar Augustus as *cognomines*. But later as well, emperors who no longer had any family links with Caesar continued to dignify themselves with these names, and the names gradually turned into titles. Similarly the term *palace* bears witness to the gradual transformation of the emperorship from a de facto situation into a constitutional office. *Palatium* refers to the Palatine Hill where Augustus, like most of the wealthy Romans in the Late Republic, lived. His residence developed into the seat of imperial government. These evolutions symbolise the gradual transformation of Rome from a republic with a highly monarchical element under Augustus into a genu- ine imperial monarchy at the end of the third century, with the accession of Diocletian (284–305). His reign marks the end of the Principate and the beginning of the Dominate.

Although formally speaking not a monarch, Augustus was the pivotal figure in the state. How did this come about? In the first place, Augustus was able to draw on incomparable *dignitas* and *auctoritas*. The appeal to personal prestige and authority as the basis for power in the state was in accordance with republican tradition. The conferment and systematic use of Augustus as a name were part and parcel of that strategy. Augustus liked to portray himself as *princeps inter pares* (first among equals), which is why we refer to the Principate. Augustus assumed the position of the republican *princeps senatus*, that is, the principal senator. Since he him- self permanently held the censorial power and it was one of the privileges of the censors to designate the *princeps senatus*, he was automatically assured of that position.

In addition, Augustus based his power on the permanent accumula- tion of various republican positions and magistracies, which gave him exceptional power. Needless to say this ran counter to the traditional republican constitution. In the first place, Augustus was assigned the pro- consular *imperium* over various provinces. These were mainly the per- ipheral provinces that had recently been added to the empire. It was also in these regions that most of the legions were stationed. Augustus was furthermore given a special *imperium*, making him the supreme com- mander of the army. He held the consulate from 31 to 23 BC, which gave him extensive power in Rome and Italy.

In 23 BC, a serious crisis between Augustus and the Senate erupted, with the *princeps* threatening retirement. Augustus emerged stronger from the crisis. He gave up the consulate – which he henceforward would only assume a few more times – but was awarded the *tribunicia potestas*. This gave him a right of veto, while he himself was rendered immune to the veto exercised by the real plebeian tribunes. The *tribunicia potestas* guaranteed his permanent inviolability – the *tribunicia sacrosanctitas*, a privilege already bestowed upon him and his wife Livia in 36 BC – and gave him the power to convene the Senate and the *concilium plebis* and to submit legislative proposals to those bodies. He also had himself assigned an *imperium proconsulare maius*. This meant that he obtained supreme administrative powers in all the provinces, putting him above the actual provincial governors. This special *imperium* was bestowed for five years, but was then renewed time and again with little trouble. In 19 BC, a life-long *imperium consulare* was added. This gave Augustus the power and immunity of a consul without having that status, thus granting him *imperium* in Rome and Italy and so allowing him to preside over the Senate and the popular assemblies and command troops in Italy. The *imperium consulare* also encompassed the powers of the censor, namely compiling the list of the Senate and control over public morals, or the *regimen morum*. After the death of Marcus Aemilius Lepidus, the former *triumvir* and high priest, Augustus had himself elected as high priest.

35   Succession

The unconstitutionality of the emperor's position at the outset of the Principate rendered his succession problematical. Since there was no formal position, there could be no formal rules of succession. The emperor would seek to arrange his succession while still alive by designating someone as heir and successor. That person – generally a blood relative or in-law – would be adopted and be conferred part of the imperial power before the death of the incumbent emperor. If nobody was in place or if the successor was unable to accede, a struggle for power would ensue and the prize would go to the strongest. On the odd occasion, the Senate would manage to put forward a candidate. In most cases, however, it was the imperial guard, the praetorian guard, or one of the major field armies that resolved the issue. As early as the first century, various generals would march on Rome at the head of their troops in order to claim the throne. On one occasion the throne was even sold by the praetorian guard to the highest bidder. The 'lucky' winner was able to hold on to the supreme office only briefly before he, too, was murdered. However, these chronic political crises at the top did not severely disrupt the empire or fatally weaken it.

11   *The erosion of the republican institutions*

36   The emperor and the Senate

Augustus left all the republican institutions in place, even making efforts to restore the Senate to some of its former glory. Ultimately, however, the concentration of power in the hands of the emperor could in the end only erode the republican system of governance, the first principle of which was the distribution and limitation of power. Gradually, the republican political and legal institutions were eroded. Power was transferred to the emperor and his court. Over a period of three centuries, this de facto situation became increasingly formalised, until eventually, after 284, the illusion could no longer be sustained and the designation of Rome as a *respublica* had become no more than a hollow epithet.

That matters would turn out this way was by no means clear cut under Augustus or even under his initial successors. Many senators, including some from Augustus's own circle and family, dreamed of a restoration of the Republic. At no point was Augustus certain of the continuation of his regime and its persistence beyond his death. In contrast to what historians have traditionally asserted, the Senate was not a powerless instrument under the early Principate. It did, of course, lose some of its most important powers to the emperor, such as control over foreign policy and a large part of the treasury. The Senate also often acted as the emperor's obedient voting machine. On many occasions, however, the powerful clans within the Senate managed to close ranks and offer resistance. The fact that a number of emperors sowed death and decay among the ranks of the Senate may be said to betoken the continuing relevance of the senators rather than their inconsequentiality. Various emperors were in turn murdered at the behest of the Senate. Whatever the formal and actual power of the Senate, it remained the assembly of representatives of the powerful, wealthy and influential clans and families. Apart from various old republican families, ever more new clans from Italy and the provinces were added. For the emperor, the Senate represented a pool of potential allies, opponents and outright competitors. Certainly up to the year 200, Roman politics remained a struggle for power between the most powerful senators, headed by the emperor.

37   The decline of the republican institutions

Augustus's attempt to restore the standing of the Senate was prompted not by idealism but by well-understood self-interest. Augustus brought the Senate up to strength with representatives drawn from all over the empire, at the same time ensuring himself a solid majority. In this way, he increased the supply of potential magistrates and provincial governors. Under Augustus and Tiberius the most important powers of the popular assemblies shifted to the Senate, including the powers to legislate and to elect magistrates. Formally the *comitia tributa* and the *concilium plebis* retained a role during the first century, but they turned into compliant voting machines that rubber-stamped the emperor's proposals as approved by the Senate. Furthermore, the popular assemblies were no longer representative of the Roman citizenry. In practice, only the inhabitants of the city of Rome attended. Citizens from Italy and the provinces, which formed the backbone of the empire, were rarely if ever present.

Formally speaking, the Senate had only advisory powers in the legislative process. Since the popular assemblies became a formality and even dropped out of the legislative process entirely after the first century, that limitation lost all relevance. The jurists of the Principate held that the decisions taken by the Senate had force of law. In practice, most of the legislative proposals came from the emperor. Tiberius formally transferred the election of the magistrates from the popular assemblies to the Senate. The candidates nominated by the emperor were generally elected without further ado. This does not mean that such nominations were not preceded by negotiations with and among the major clans. The Senate retained control over the *aerarium* or public treasury. Already under Augustus, however, the emperor had a separate exchequer, the *fiscus*, into which other sources of revenue were paid and over which the emperor alone had control. In the third century, the two treasuries were merged into the imperial *fiscus*.

The various magistracies continued to exist. Only the office of censor disappeared entirely after the first century. The consulate remained a coveted position. The biggest honour was to be consul in a year in which the emperor chose to act as a colleague by being elected consul himself. Caesar and Augustus introduced the practice of appointing what could be a number of consuls each year, succeeding one another in rapid succession. In doing so they sought to drive up the available supply of provincial governors and to bind more families to themselves. Since the most important powers of the consul in the military and political fields were exercised by the emperor, the main significance of the office of consul was that it led to a position as provincial governor and army commander in the capacity of proconsul. The office of the praetor also continued to exist. The praetors retained control over the traditional courts, but their sphere of influence was curtailed with the advent of the new imperial courts. In addition, the emperors appointed special praetors with extraordinary powers. In 23 BC, Augustus appointed two *praetores aerarii* who were given day-to-day management of the ordinary exchequer, thereby depriving the quaestors of their prime task. The position of quaestor remained important as an entry ticket to the Senate. The position of plebeian tribune survived as an honorific office without much substance.

12 The emergence of the imperial civil service

38 The rise of the imperial bureaucracy

In the days of the Republic, Rome did not have a civil service. The day-to-day administration was handled by the magistrates and promagistrates, who did not dispose of an army of civil servants. The consuls had twelve *lictores* who acted as bodyguards, messengers and sometimes secretaries. In practice, the magistrates made use of the services of private staff: slaves, freedmen and paid servants.

Similarly, Augustus made use of members of his own household in exercising his military, administrative and legal responsibilities. His house on the Palatinate gradually obtained the allure and standing of an official imperial residence. His personal staff and servants (*minister*) dealt with the affairs of state. In most cases, these staff were freed slaves, often of Greek origin. Gradually their duties became more official in nature and they turned into genuine civil servants. From the second century onwards, it was no longer considered acceptable for them to be freedmen, and civil servants were instead recruited from among the equestrian order – many members of which, nevertheless, had freedmen among their ancestors. Senators – potential opponents and competitors of the emperor – were excluded from these new positions.

Emperor Hadrian organised his civil service into various bureaus or departments. The most important of these were the *rationibus* (finance), *a memoria* (appointments and personnel), *a libellis* (imperial correspondence with citizens) and *ab epistulis* (imperial correspondence with civil servants and senators). On top of this there were the *fisci Caesaris* or the various imperial treasuries.

Already during the earlier stages of the Principate, the emperors had, to curb the power of traditional magistrates, inaugurated some new offices, which they entrusted to members of the equestrian order. The most important position was that of *praefectus praetorio,* or commander of the imperial bodyguard. In the second century, an important administrative and legal dimension was added to this position and the commander of the guard grew into a kind of prime minister, second only to the emperor. From that point on the praetorian prefect was also assigned a purely military colleague. The office of praetorian prefect was held by a number of the greatest jurists in Roman history, such as Papinian, Ulpian and Paul. Apart from the praetorian prefect, there was also the *praefectus urbi*, a senator responsible for the administration of the *urbs*, meaning the city of Rome itself.

39   The concentration of power

The emergence and extension of the imperial civil service reflected the growth of imperial power and the transformation of the Republic into a genuine monarchy. The civil servants were instrumental in curtailing the actual power of the magistrates and the Senate, usurping their competence. Being freed slaves or equestrians, with few exceptions their ranks did not include any senators. They were the emperor's personal protégés, elevated by him from slavery or the middle classes. They were appointed, paid and dismissed by the emperor and depended on him for their power and careers. The magistrates were senators, elected by their colleagues. However much the election might be stage-managed by the emperor, it nevertheless gave the magistrates some autonomy vis-à-vis their ruler. Furthermore, the magistrates generally belonged to families whose fortune and standing did not derive entirely from the emperor.

To a greater extent than the old senatorial order, the civil servants provided a guarantee for an efficient, centralised system of administration. Since their office and power sprang from one and the same source, they acted in a somewhat more co-ordinated fashion than the republican magistrates had or did. The civil service was hierarchically structured according to the principle of the delegation of power from top to bottom. Conversely, a citizen could take his grievances and complaints up the rungs of the administrative ladder until eventually reaching the emperor.

The emperor surrounded himself by a council or *consilium*. Apart from leading senators, this consisted in particular of civil servants and people drawn from the emperor's immediate circle. From the time of Hadrian onwards, experts – especially jurists – were also represented on the council.

Not just the civil service, but also the army saw a growth in its power. Apart from the generals drawn from the senatorial order, there arose a class of career generals and officers drawn from all strata of society and all parts of the empire and even further afield. The existence of a professional army was not new. What was new was that the highest military positions were entrusted to non-senators, that is, non-politicians. This led to alienation between the army and the traditional Roman elite.

13   *The crisis of the third century (235–84)*

40   Army reform

During the half-century after the death of the last emperor of the dynasty of Septimius Severus in 235, the empire found itself in a deep political crisis. Between 235 and 284 no fewer than fifty emperors and counter-emperors succeeded one another.

The main cause of this crisis was not internal, but external. For the first time in centuries, Rome saw itself confronted with a competing great power, the Persian Empire under the Sasanian dynasty. Between 240 and 272, the Sasanians defeated the Romans three times, capturing or killing no fewer than three emperors. At the same time, the Roman frontiers to the north at the Rhine and Danube came under increasing pressure from Germanic and other tribes living outside the empire. It took the Romans the better part of two generations to adjust to the new strategic situation and overcome the new threats. In the meantime, the defeats and the reforms which followed disrupted the stability of government, without, however, mortally weakening the empire.

The grand strategy of the Roman Empire, introduced by Emperor Hadrian, proved inadequate to address the new threats, or rather, proved to be inadequately implemented. The early emperors had stuck to the old republican grand strategy. The Roman Empire consisted of a number of core provinces around the Mediterranean such as Greece, Spain, southern Gaul, Asia Minor, Egypt and Africa, which were more Romanised or civilised than the peripheral territories. Around them lay a number of border provinces. Within and without the provinces, and most particularly these latter provinces, Rome tolerated numerous client-states and other small states that were subject to Rome only in terms of foreign policy. These states acted as buffer zones against external attacks on the empire. The Roman army was stationed not at the outer frontiers but deeper in the border provinces, closer to the Mediterranean. No troops needed to be wasted on garrisons along the enormously long border lines of the empire. If an invading army cut through the buffer zone, the corps located at some distance from the borders would have the time to prepare and launch a counterattack. This strategic deployment allowed for a relatively small army – under Augustus around 400,000 men – to defend the empire, thus keeping the costs down. A precondition for the success of this strategy was the offensive orientation of the Roman Empire. Rome conducted a constant, active diplomacy of intervention and involvement among neighbouring peoples. The borders were permeable. Minor incursions by the enemy did not necessarily elicit a response by the Roman army, but could be dealt with by the client-states; on the other hand, a divide-and-conquer policy and the permanent threat of intervention by the legions ensured that the neighbouring peoples remained reasonably peaceable. Rome also exercised a policy of permanent terror against its neighbours. Sooner or later any harm inflicted on the empire would be avenged. When Trajan launched a campaign against the Parthians in the early second century AD, he let it be known that he was coming to avenge the defeat of Crassus in 53 BC.

Hadrian chose to seal off the borders hermetically. In doing so, he abandoned the dream of Augustus and his immediate successors of extending the empire to 'the Ocean encircling the world'. Hadrian incorporated the large client-states into the provinces and strengthened the borders, along which the troops were thinly spread. The Persian and other attacks of the third century proved that the Roman army was too small to seal off the empire's borders effectively against other great powers. Once the borders were pierced and the border troops defeated, it took too long to mobilise a sufficiently large field army to counterattack and prevent deep incursions in the direction of or into the heartlands of the empire. Also, while Hadrian's reform had transferred the centre of gravity of the army from close to the centre in Italy to the borders of the empire, the political centre of gravity had not followed. The wars of the third century made this situation untenable. The time it took the imperial government to adjust to the new strategic challenge from without was also the time of the internal challenges to its stability and of the many military coups.

To restore the military balance, Rome had to transform its military. First, the size of the Roman army was drastically increased, to half the size again of its former complement. Second, the army's strength was concentrated in three disputed border areas: the Rhineland, the Danube north of the Balkans, and the eastern provinces facing the Persian Empire. Third, the bureaucracy and the political power behind keeping the army financed and functioning had to move closer to the front lines of the empire. After 235, few emperors ruled from Italy. They brought their government closer to where the main military action was. In the short term, this was the single most important cause of the many coups of the third century. The closer association of the emperor with one or two armies left the other armies neglected in terms of money and privileges. These 'orphaned' armies time and again promoted their own commanders to the emperorship. This political instability was more or less brought under control by Emperor Diocletian (284–305) and his successors, who divided the empire between two or even four imperial colleagues, and split the bureaucracy up accordingly. Thus, they adjusted the political reality to the dictates of military necessity. This could not prevent further coups from happening in the fourth and early fifth centuries, but it made them less disruptive to the system. Even if the emperors fought with one another, or when there was only one emperor, there were now at least several imperial bureaucracies, each serving its own field army.

41 Tax reform

In order to strengthen the army and overcome the new external threats, central government had to raise more taxes. This was achieved not so much by raising the total amount of taxes paid, but by confiscating a larger part of the tax income of local authorities and diverting it to the imperial *fiscus*. In this way, tax increase did little to cripple the economy, which remained strong all through the third and fourth centuries in most parts of the empire. In the short run, the tax increases of the third century would not weaken the empire nor spell in any way its future demise. But in the long run, they changed the parameters for co-operation between imperial government and local elites and influenced the conditions of the latter's loyalty. This would contribute to the collapse of the Western Roman Empire in the second half of the fifth century.

By the third century, the economic and political elites of the conquered peoples and cities of the Roman Empire had adjusted well to Roman rule. Local elites had become Romanised. They provided their children with a classical Roman education. They spoke the language of the empire, Latin in the West and Greek in the East. Everywhere, towns were built and modelled after the Roman example, featuring public fora and halls, temples, public baths and theatres. Landowners had adopted the forms and organisation of Italian country life by building large agricultural estates, *villae*. In exchange for their loyalty to the Roman state and a cut of local tax income, Rome provided law and order, the primary function of which was the protection of the interests of the propertied class, especially the landowners. Also, Rome secured them against external invasions. Although Roman law applied everywhere and local governmental institutions had been partially harmonised, local autonomy remained important. Increasingly, members of the Romanised elites made their careers in the imperial civil service and army, often attaining the top tiers. The elites of the different provinces of the empire felt they were adopted into the Roman Empire and its self-declared superior civilisation and not oppressed by it.

The reforms of the third century, more particularly the growing share of local wealth taken by the imperial government, would change the cost/benefit equation of being part of the Roman Empire. In the short run, the loss of local tax incomes made an administrative career in local government less attractive and stimulated the members of provincial elites to join the imperial civil service. After retirement, they often took office in their home towns. This in fact strengthened the cohesion of the empire. But in the long run, the increase in the costs of imperial security and law and order also meant that the loyalty of provincial and local landowners and power brokers rested now more than ever on the effectiveness with which central government delivered its part of the bargain.

14   Diocletian and the establishment of the Dominate (284–395)

42   The Dominate

In 284, general Diocletian assumed power. The new emperor came from the Balkans. He was an energetic and competent administrator, but had little affinity with Rome or with its traditions. He was the emperor who completed the great reforms of the third century and vested the government on new foundations. With his accession and the consolidation of his power, the period of crisis was brought to a successful ending.

Diocletian transformed the regime into a genuine monarchy, presenting himself as a potentate in the tradition of the old empires of the pre-Hellenic and Hellenic East. The emperor became more than ever the embodiment of the state. His veneration as a divinity – which had been rather common in the East since the days of Augustus – became even more central to the system. From now on, the emperor was referred to as *dominus*, rather than as *princeps inter pares*. The change of terminology was significant: *dominus* is the term used for a master by his slaves. The emperor was no longer the first Roman citizen or senator but was master of the empire and its inhabitants. This new reality was reflected in a court ceremonial that had its roots in the veneration of the Persian Great Kings. Nothing was further from the republican tradition than the *adoratio* (or, in Greek, *prokynesis*), which required people to prostrate themselves at the emperor's feet.

Diocletian imposed a rigid military, administrative and fiscal system. He realised that the new military realities necessitated more than one ruler and appointed a fellow emperor or second *Augustus*. Diocletian divided the empire into an eastern and a western half. He himself opted for the eastern part, the new centre of gravity of the empire from where the wars with Rome's main rivals had to be fought. Both *Augusti* designated a colleague of lower rank or *Caesar* to command the other great field armies and to succeed the *Augusti*. In 305, Diocletian and his colleague abdicated in favour of their two *Caesares*, who in turn designated new *Caesares*. During the next generation, matters went awry and a struggle for power erupted that finally was resolved in 326 in favour of Constantine the Great (313–37).

43 The rise of Christianity

Emperor Constantine is celebrated in history as the first emperor to recognise Christianity. During the course of the third century, this new religion had won a substantial following throughout the empire. The sporadic persecutions of the early imperial age became somewhat more systematic, but did not produce much effect. Constantine decided to change tack and to recognise Christianity.

Constantine also built a new, second capital in the East: on the site of the former Byzantium arose Constantinople, present-day Istanbul. Constantine referred to this city as the new Rome. In the western part of the empire, old Rome steadily lost importance. For decades, the city had no longer acted as the imperial residence, although it did continue to house the Senate. Under Constantine and a number of his successors, the empire was once again united under a single emperor. However, in 395, upon the death of Theodosius the Great (379–95), the split into Eastern and Western empires became definitive. It was Theodosius who, after 390, recognised Christianity as the sole religion, prohibiting all other religions.

15 *The state under the Dominate (284–565)*

44 The emperor as *dominus*

During the third century, the imperial regime was effectively transformed into a military and bureaucratic monarchy. Most of the emperors were generals who had come to power through the agency of their own troops. Their administration was buttressed by an expanding, powerful bureaucracy. The regime's lack of political legitimisation made the veneration or sacralisation of the emperor all the more important. The deification of the emperor or, under Christianity, his elevation to the status of God's deputy on earth, rendered imperial power autonomous from any earthly power. It was no longer dependent on approval by the Senate and the people of Rome. 'Governing under the authority of God our Empire which was delivered to us by the Heavenly Majesty,' stated Emperor Justinian when he gave instruction for the codification of Roman law.[7]

---

[7] *Constitutio Deo auctore*, translation by Alan Watson, *The Digest of Justinian*, Philadelphia 1998.

The system of government under the Dominate cut across the Roman republican traditions, which had still commanded, at least outward, respect under the Principate. Under the Republic, the most powerful individuals and bodies, including the magistrates and the Senate, owed their position, at least in theory, to the popular assemblies. The magistrates were granted an *imperium* for one year, together with personal inviolability. Upon relinquishing office, they became private citizens again, just like anyone else. The Senate was the assembly of the *optimi*, or the best among the citizenry. The state, or *respublica*, was the business of all. Ultimately the state was nothing other than the Senate and the people of Rome.

Diocletian identified the emperor with the state, the *respublica*. Although the Senate and the various magistracies remained in existence, and even though reference continued from time to time to be made to the republican traditions that were intimately bound up with the emperorship, the mask had fallen. The identification of the emperor as *Dominus et Deus* (Master and God) made it clear that the emperor was a genuine monarch, a king or *basileus* – the title given by the Greeks to the Persian and Hellenic kings. The new emperorship was consistent with the Eastern, monarchical traditions of the great empires such as Assyria, Egypt and Persia or that of Alexander the Great and his Hellenic successors. The emperor was no longer the most powerful of the citizens. As ruler he was of a different order than the citizens, who were all equally subject to him. Like the Pharaohs in ancient Egypt or the Persian kings, the emperor was identified with the gods. His power stemmed not from the people, but from the gods. The appeal to the divine origin of power – an ancient tradition in the East – entailed a reversal of the legitimisation of government power from an ascending to a descending theory of power.

45   Ascending and descending theory of power

The question concerning the source of power of a particular government or ruler is one of the key issues of political theory. Since Antiquity, governmental authority has often been legitimated on the basis of the delegation of power: power has been delegated to the government from an original source. Broadly speaking, two groups of theories can be distinguished.

On the one hand, there is the descending theory of power. Power comes 'from above'; it is delegated to the ruler by a hierarchically higher power. In the case of the supreme ruler of the state or people, the source of their power will generally be God or the gods. The most important practical consequence of such a legitimisation is that the ruler is independent of those he governs. Not being appointed by them, he is not required to render account to them.

On the opposite side, there is the ascending theory of power. In this case, power comes 'from below', that is, from persons or bodies that are subordinate to the ruler. Historically, such theories have been developed in order to curb the power of the ruler. Often, but not always, under this theory, subjects retain the right to depose their ruler.[8]

46   Emperor and church

In Rome, religion and state ideology had always been closely intertwined. The demise and final rejection of the traditional Roman religion went hand in hand with the loss of republican tradition. Constantine the Great and a number of his successors discovered the possibilities offered by monotheistic Christianity for the legitimation of their absolute power: the one emperor as God's vicar on earth. Christianity became the religion for the new, political ideology. Both had Eastern and Hellenic roots. The emperors sought to engage the church in the administration of the empire. Constantine and his successors gave the church a place in their bureaucratic apparatus, for example by requiring the civil service to implement the judicial decisions over private disputes made at episcopal audiences (*episcopalis audientia*). Conversely, they involved themselves with internal, ecclesiastical matters, including theological disputes. Since religious belief had become a central pillar of imperial power and the church had become an institution of state, the unity of religious belief and the church had become a matter of state. Any divergent interpretations were declared heretical and suppressed. Even so, all sorts of diverse ideas and interpretations of Christianity were to persist both inside and outside the church for a long period of time.[9]

47   The reform of the imperial bureaucracy

The senatorial order lost its position as a distinct political class. Membership of the Senate was turned into a badge of honour for meritorious civil servants. Conversely, senators gained access to the civil service. With the Senate being usurped by the civil service, it was eliminated

---

[8] Walter Ullmann, *Principles of Government and Politics in the Middle Ages*, London 1966.
[9] The novel *Julian* (New York 1962) by the American author Gore Vidal provides a stirring picture of the political struggle surrounding Christianity in the fourth century. It tells the story of Emperor Julian the Apostate (361–3), who turned against Christianity and tried to restore traditional religion.

as an autonomous power and as a counter-balance against the might of
the emperor and his professional civil service.

The Senate lost the last of its major political and legal competencies.
In practice, it was demoted into a kind of municipal council for the city
of Rome. The magistratures were reduced to honorific positions. The
presidency of the Senate was conferred on the highest civil servant in the
city, the *praefectus urbi* or city prefect. Constantine, moreover, installed
a second Senate in Constantinople. The imperial council was known
henceforth as the *consistorium*. It now existed almost entirely of senior
officials and generals. The central administration was also reformed by
Constantine. Four bureaus headed by senior civil servants were set up in
the new capital, all equal in rank with the city prefect. The *quaestor sacri
palatii* was responsible for the dispensation of justice, as a kind of minister
of justice. The *magister officiorum* presided over the imperial secretariat
but was also head of the imperial police. The *comes sacrarum largitionum*
and the *comes rerum privatarum* each had responsibility for parts of the
state treasury.

Diocletian and Constantine also reorganised the provincial structure
of the empire. Diocletian assigned each of the four co-emperors a *praefectus praetorio* who acted as a kind of prime minister in his part of the
empire. After Constantine had emerged as victor from the civil war of the
310s–320s, the system of two *Augusti* and two *Caesares* was abolished, but
the four prefectures remained. Each was headed by a *praefectus praetorio*
with both civil and military powers. Together with the emperor, the praetorian prefect was the highest judge of appeal. He exercised control over
the dioceses and the provinces. Each prefecture consisted of a number of
dioceses, which in turn consisted of various provinces. In certain areas
of the empire, there were still provinces that came directly under the
emperor. In charge of a diocese was a *vicarius*, while a province was run
by a *praeses*. These too were now imperial civil servants and not promagistrates. The *vicarii* and *praesides* had administrative and legal responsibilities and acted as the highest judges in their territories.

16   The fall of the Western Roman Empire

48   Decline and fall

Since Edward Gibbon (1737–94) published his monumental *Decline and
Fall of the Roman Empire* at the end of the eighteenth century, there has
been an ongoing debate among historians about the fall of the Western
Roman Empire. Until recently, the 'fall' was understood in terms of a

long process of internal decay, which had, according to Gibbon, already begun at the end of the second century and which seriously weakened the Roman Empire in the fourth and fifth centuries, allowing the Germanic tribes from northern and eastern Europe to destroy and overrun the West between 376 and 476.

Gibbon theory

Historians adhering to Gibbon's theory have always had a hard time explaining why the Western Roman Empire collapsed and the Eastern Roman Empire survived. For a long time, it was held that the Eastern Empire was more urbanised, making it more defensible, and that its economy suffered less than that of the western half from the imperial tax regime.

Recent scholarship has greatly amended these views. Most historians today reject the classical thesis of three centuries of irreversible decline. As was expounded above, the Roman Empire indeed underwent a grave crisis during the third century, but this was overcome by the end of that century. Recent archaeological finds have shown that the economy remained vibrant in almost all parts of the empire until at least the late fourth century and that the new taxation policy did little to cripple it.

49   Huns and Germans

Many historians today defend the view that the Western Roman Empire collapsed because of external pressure. The Germanic tribes that after its fall divided the territories of the Western Roman Empire among themselves also caused its downfall in the first place. That they could do so is to be explained in terms rather of their military strength and some luck, than of the empire's weakness and its propensity to fall.

Since before Christian times, northern, central and eastern Europe had been subject to large migratory flows of Germanic and other tribes. Around 100 BC, Marius destroyed a Germanic force at the gates of Italy. Caesar legitimated his conquest of Gaul by claiming he had to save it from being overrun by Germanic barbarians. Propaganda or not, thanks to Caesar's conquest, Rome was able to keep the Germanic tribes at bay from the Mediterranean for another four hundred or so years.

Germanic tribes

From the time of Caesar to the late fourth century, trade, diplomacy and chronic warfare had drawn the Germanic tribes living to the north of the Rhine and Danube within the Roman orbit. As a consequence, the Germanic peoples of north-western and central Europe had become more 'civilised' and less 'barbarian'. Many tribes had turned to agriculture and had grown more prosperous and numerous. Land ownership had made these tribes less egalitarian and had led to the emergence of a broad but distinct aristocracy of propertied free men. Also, from the third and fourth centuries onwards, federations of tribes under a sole leader or king, which had before been quite sporadic and unstable, became more frequent and more stable. All in all, the Germanic tribes the Roman Empire faced at the end of the fourth century were much stronger than their ancestors that Caesar had faced.

Prior to the invasions of the late fourth century, Germanic tribes had already been living within the empire. It was a common Roman policy to resettle defeated enemies from outside the empire within a province. Since the first century BC, the Roman army had also taken in foreign auxiliaries. By the third and fourth centuries, Germanic auxiliaries had assumed a significant role in the imperial defence. In particular, numerous Germanic leaders had made a career as officers in the Roman army, at times attaining the top tiers. Slowly, the Germans were becoming part of the empire and of the imperial power structure. In itself, this was nothing new and did in no way spell the eventual doom of the empire. The assimilation of foreign tribes and peoples into the empire – be they peoples whose territories had been conquered by the Romans or peoples who had been settled within the borders of the empire – and the rise of their elites to the very top of the Roman bureaucratic and military structure had been the essence of empire for several centuries. Meanwhile, many Germanic tribes, some allies of the Romans, many not, remained outside its borders.

From the third quarter of the fourth century, the migration of the Huns – a Mongolian people – from Asia to the west caused a new wave of migrations in the direction of the Mediterranean. The age of the great migrations was under way. In 376, a coalition of Gothic tribes pierced the Roman defences at the Danube and forced its way into the empire. After several years of warfare, during which the Goths scored some major victories (for example, the Battle of Hadrianople, 378), they made their peace with the Eastern Roman emperor and were settled within the empire. It was their aim not to destroy or slice away a piece of the empire, but to be accepted within its fold and gain a stake within the Roman Empire, as so many other tribes and peoples had done before them. In 406, several Germanic tribes – the Burgundians, the Vandals and the Suevi – crossed the Rhine and made their way through Gaul and Spain. In 409, the Romans withdrew their army from Britannia, leaving the local, Romanised population to defend itself against Saxon invaders. Meanwhile, the Goths, newly unified under their King Alaric (395–411), marched on Italy in the hope of obtaining a more advantageous treaty from the Western Roman

Emperor Honorius (393–423), who withdrew to Ravenna. When this failed, Alaric had the city of Rome sacked (410) in an ultimate attempt to force the emperor's hand. After the death of Alaric, his brother and successor Athaulf (411–15) led the Goths to south-western Gaul where they settled. In the decades to come, these Goths – whose King Athaulf had married the emperor's sister Galla Placidia (c.390–450) – allied themselves with the Roman emperor and helped him reconquer Spain from the Suevi and the Vandals. Although the second wave of invasions of the first decade of the fifth century had cost the Western Roman Empire effective control over part of its territory – Britannia, western Gaul and north-western Spain – its cultural and economic heartlands were safe. The Germanic tribes effectively ruling parts of the empire did this more often than not as confederates and in the name of the empire.

In the 430s and 440s, however, disaster struck. The Vandals crossed to Africa. In 439, they captured Carthage and overran the province of Africa, the West's granary and one of its most important provinces in terms of tax income. The joint counterattack of the two emperors failed. New attempts could not take place because, at around the same time, the new Hunnic king, Attila (440–53), attacked the empire.

Halfway through the fourth century, the Huns had appeared on the borders of Europe, north of the Black Sea. It was their westward migration which triggered the first Gothic invasion of 376. During the years around 400, the Huns must have moved further westwards, to the Great Hungarian Plain, thus presumably causing the 406 attack of the Germans on the Rhine. Since then, they had often rendered their services as allies or mercenaries to Rome. Now, under Attila, they turned upon the empire, looking for new plunder and riches. During the 440s, Attila crossed the Danube several times and rampaged through the Balkans, at one time reaching Constantinople. After 450, he turned to Gaul (451), where he was defeated on the Catalaunian Fields by a coalition of Romans and Germans, and Italy (452). After his death in 453, his empire – a lose federation of tribes dominated by the Huns – quickly disintegrated. Ironically, it was this more than anything that caused the Western Roman Empire's final demise.

The Hunnic attack of the 440s had prevented the Romans from recovering Africa. Thus the most strategic possession of the Western emperors was lost to them. From that time onwards, the Germanic tribes who had settled in Gaul and Spain gradually lost interest in an allegiance to Rome – or, rather, Ravenna – as the Roman emperor had few means left to conquer or buy them. Attila's invasions, though ultimately failures, thus did mortally wound the Western Empire. But it was the fall of the Huns that finally undid the Western Empire. For better or worse, the Huns had played a central role in the balance of power between Romans and Germans since the early fifth century, at times as allies against the Germanic invaders, at others acting as catalysts to unite the Germans with the Romans. Now that they disappeared from the scene and the emperor had little left to offer the Germans, the Western Empire was doomed. During the 460s and 470s, the Germanic kings increasingly started to behave as autonomous rulers in the parts of the empire where they had settled. The local, Romanised elites adjusted and shifted their allegiance from the Roman emperor to the Germanic kings, who guaranteed them at least part of their property and secured them against new attacks. This transition was all the more natural, as the Germanic kings often assumed the insignia and titles of Roman officials, acting in the name of the Roman emperor – initially of the West, or after his deposition in 476, of the East. In 476, Odovacar (c.435–93), a Germanic leader who had led a coalition of former Germanic and other allies and vassals of the Huns into Italy and taken service in the imperial army, deposed the last Western emperor, Romulus Augustulus (475–6). The insignificance of the last Roman emperor was illustrated by the fact that Odovacar did not even deem it necessary to kill him, but just pensioned him off.

Odovacar was not the first military commander to depose a Western Roman emperor, but he would be the last. No new emperor came forward in the West, nor was one proposed by the emperor in the East as had been done before. Thus did Odovacar's action signify the end of the Western Roman Empire as a working, political structure. Though Odovacar himself probably did not understand the historic implications of his coup, he accompanied it with a symbolic deed to match them. The Germanic commander, who assumed the Roman title of *patricius* claiming to have received it from the Eastern emperor, sent the insignia of the imperial office to Constantinople, and there they remained.

50   The endurance of the empire

Although the Western Roman Empire no longer existed, it lived on in people's minds. The Latin, western part of Europe continued to consider itself as part of the empire. The fact that there was no longer an emperor or any effective imperial authority did not destroy the notion of empire. The Germanic kings governed their new territories first as rulers of their tribes. Their power was legitimated in personal rather than territorial terms: they bore the title of king of the Franks, Goths or Saxons, rather than king of

Franconia, Gothenland or Saxony. However, when it came to the administration of the indigenous population of the Roman territories that they
had conquered, they portrayed themselves as provincial governors and
officials of an absent emperor or of the Eastern Roman emperor. When
western Europe was once again Christianised and the church became
subject to the authority of the Bishop of Rome, the pope, in the course
of the seventh and eighth centuries, the notion of unity received a fresh
impulse. The concept of empire was so closely interwoven with Rome that
even the fall of the emperors was unable to sever that link.

The Eastern Roman Empire survived the migrations of the fifth century.
This was largely because the Roman supremacy at sea had for the most
part kept the core economic areas of the eastern part of the empire – the
Middle East, Asia Minor and Egypt – beyond the reach of the invaders. In
the end, the Eastern Roman emperors managed to defeat the invaders. In
the early sixth century, Emperor Justinian the Great (527–65) recaptured
Italy, North Africa and southern Spain. After his death, these territories
were once again lost. This marked the definitive end of Roman authority
in the West. The brief re-conquest of Italy under Justinian was, however,
to have major consequences for legal history. The Eastern Roman Empire
held on for nearly another millennium as a Christian, Greek-speaking
empire with Constantinople as its capital. As a result of the conquests
by Islam in the seventh century, Egypt and the Middle East were lost.
After the year 1000, the empire rapidly crumbled away, until eventually
Constantinople was conquered by the Ottoman Turks in 1453.

B   Culture and the law

1   The laws of gods and men

The law is like a bow. It is designed to be bent almost indefinitely, but
never to be broken.

51   Law in archaic Greece

In recent years, the celebrated British comic writer Tom Holt has tackled
a number of historical novels set in Antiquity. In *Alexander at the World's
End*,[10] he recounts the adventures of Euxenus, cynical philosopher,
tutor and evil genius of Alexander the Great. Through the eyes of this
fictional counterpart to Alexander's real-life mentor, Aristotle, the
world of the conqueror of the Persian Empire comes to life. But

[10] London 1999.

Euxenus's worldviews are often closer to those of a twentieth-century cynic than those of a contemporary of Alexander. Nevertheless, his metaphor of law could have come from the lips of an Athenian sophist of the fifth or fourth century BC. For Euxenus, the law is an instrument, a weapon for men to bend the world to their will. Whereas such a conception of law might have been conceivable for a sophist, it would have been inconceivable for the Greeks of before the Athenian Golden Century, the fifth century BC.

During the archaic period (until the eighth century BC), the Greeks did not perceive of law as an autonomous body of rules, distinct from religion or morality. In his great epic, the *Iliad*, Homer refers to *themis*.[11] *Themis* (plural *themistes*) indicates a judgment. It is breathed into the ear of the judge by the goddess *Themis*, or another deity. The law manifests itself only in the act of rendering judgment over a concrete dispute. It does not exist as an autonomous system of rules, as objective law. *Themistes* are the particular manifestation in a specific dispute of a general, imperative order.

By this order was understood everything which was natural and had been given to man. No distinction was drawn between a natural and a legal order or even between a divine and a human order. In the *Iliad* and in Homer's other epic, the *Odyssey*, gods and men are subject to the same rules about what ought and ought not to be. These are not made or determined by man, but have been given to him. As such, they transcend human will and thus are immutable. 'Law' is not an instrument in the hands of men to mould the world to their liking.

Already Homer had used yet another term to indicate law: *dikè*. Although it is difficult to draw a sharp distinction between the two concepts, it is generally accepted that *dikè* had more of a human dimension. The introduction of this second concept shows how people were gradually becoming aware of the existence of man-made law, of human law. Homer himself did not, however, go as far as to recognise that man himself could create law. For Homer, *dikè*, just like *themis*, signified dispute or judgment. Nevertheless, we find here a greater measure of human autonomy when it comes to judgment. *Dikè* is derived by human beings from *themis*, and is not directly infused by the gods.

Homer also used the term *nomos*. With this, the Greeks referred to custom: what people were used to do and consequently accepted as normal or the norm. Archaic Greek law, like that of most primitive societies

[11] The text of the *Iliad* as we know it dates from the eighth century BC, but the epic refers to events from the twelfth century BC.

including Roman society, consisted primarily of customary law. That which answered to the usages and practices of society and had been regarded by society since time immemorial as natural and just was considered to be law. Of necessity, the law accorded with the ideas and values common among the people; it was essentially democratic. Since the law went back to earlier generations and times, it was perceived as immutable and eternal. Whereas in reality it had been formed by the customs of generations, people thought that law had been given to them by the gods or by even more ancient forces. As long as people were not aware of any change in the law, there was no need to address the question of whether man could make law. The dominance of tradition and custom blended seamlessly with the understanding of history. Hesiod, an Athenian writer of the eighth century BC, divided history into four ages: the gold, silver, bronze and iron age. Each period was gloomier than the last. The Greeks looked back nostalgically to the most remote ages, when gods and heroes still walked the earth. The forefathers were regarded as superior beings who still knew and faithfully observed divine commandments.

52   Statute law

The close relation between law and religion started to weaken in the course of the eighth to sixth centuries BC. Many Greek city-states were marked by social and political conflicts between the aristocracy and the majority of the people. In response to the suppression of their rights and the arbitrariness of the ruling classes, the people demanded that the law be written down. It was the age of the great legislators such as Lycurgus in Sparta (eighth century BC) and Draco and Solon in Athens (seventh and sixth centuries BC). By setting down the law on stone or bronze tablets and displaying these in the *agora* or market square, the law was brought within the grasp of a far greater part of the people. It was, furthermore, recorded once and for all. Inadmissible violations of or changes in the law by the ruling class could be unmasked more readily.

All this reveals that people had grown aware of human abilities to make and change law. All in all, however, this was still not considered to be acceptable. On the contrary, most statute laws did little other than confirm and record existing law. Legislators such as Lycurgus and Solon evolved into legendary figures invested with almost divine authority. Changing the law by introducing new statutes was forbidden or otherwise made exceptionally difficult. In many city-states, it was stipulated that anyone proposing a change in the law would be executed or banished, or at least that anyone proposing a change that was not adopted would face such a punishment. Old customs outside the recorded statutes were ascribed to the gods and to mythical heroes.

2   Fas *and* ius *in archaic Roman law*

53   *Fas* and *ius*

As was the case for archaic Greece, the archaic Roman law of the Regal Period and the Early Republic was closely intertwined with religion. The oldest core of Roman law consisted of the traditional morals and customs that had been handed down from generation to generation and reached back to the remotest ancestors (*mos maiorum*). These rules gave expression to the natural order and related to both gods and men. The order laid down by the *mos maiorum* was willed by the gods.

Even our earliest sources indicate that the Romans distinguished between *fas* and *ius*. *Fas* governed the relationship between gods and men. Anything running counter to those rules was *nefas* (taboo) and disrupted the harmony between the Romans and their gods. A deed that was *nefas*, even if committed by a single individual, would call the wrath of the gods on the entire Roman people. Sickness, war and natural disaster would afflict the city and its inhabitants. The curbing and punishment of *nefas* therefore concerned the entire Roman people.

The rules of *ius* governed the relations between the Roman citizens themselves. Anyone breaking those rules committed *iniuria* (an injury or a wrong). Initially, *ius* only governed the relations between members of different *gentes*. Disputes between members of the same *gens* were an internal affair of the *gens* and were resolved within the *gens*, without any outside or public interference. When, later on, the *gentes* broke up into smaller *familiae*, the application of *ius* was greatly extended.

Ius was designed to guarantee peace among the Roman citizens. The judicial resolution of disputes was designed to stop people from taking justice into their own hands and to prevent disputes from escalating into blood feuds. *Ius* did not lay any claim to completeness; there did not exist legal rules for every dispute. Only those disputes that were regulated by *ius* could be brought before the courts. Other disputes had to be resolved by the parties themselves, either by negotiation or, if necessary, by the application of the time-honoured *ius talionis*, the law of retaliation of an eye for an eye and a tooth for a tooth. The fact that *ius* was a substitute for self-help appears from various rules in archaic Roman law. If somebody wounded a fellow citizen, the latter would have a right to punitive damages (*poena*). In case of serious mutilation, it was possible

for the victim to renounce *poena* and to take revenge by t
perpetrator himself.[12] Under archaic law, public authority
limited and passive role in the judiciary process. The cot
of ordinary citizens, assessed who was in the right and v
wrong and handed down judgment. Both the prosecution
mentation of the judgment were left to the discretion of the injured party.
Ius protected the private interests of the citizens. It was up to them to
ensure that the matter came to trial and that the judgment was enforced.
Society's sole concern was to prevent the violent escalation of the conflict
and to maintain order in society.

During the Early Republic, the distinction between *fas* and *ius* did not
signify that *ius* was a completely secular body of law. During the Regal
Period, the kings were responsible for the application of both kinds of law.
Under the Early Republic, jurisdiction in matters of both *fas* and *ius* fell
to the college of *pontifices* or priests. Furthermore, *ius* retained its ritual
character. Under *fas*, a trial was designed to appease the wrathful gods.
A trial was in essence a ritual ceremony and the punishment of a deed of
nefas constituted a propitiatory sacrifice for the gods. But a similar ritual
nature was reflected in the procedure before the common courts, which
applied *ius*. Also, the Romans held to the immutability of *ius*.

3 Ius civile *and the Law of the Twelve Tables*

54 *Ius civile*

The Romans referred to their *ius* as *ius Quiritium* or *ius civile*. This was
the law of and for the Roman citizens (*civis* = citizen): *of* the Roman citizens because it originated from them and *for* the Roman citizens because
it applied to them only. *Ius civile* did not apply to disputes between Roman
citizens and foreigners. As was the case for most primitive law systems,
Roman law was applied personally, and not territorially. The ethnic background of the parties, not the place here an event occurred, determined
whether Roman law was applicable or not.

The *mos maiorum* formed the core of the *ius civile*. This was an amalgam of rules and institutes of law that were handed down from generation
to generation. According to the second- and third-century Roman jurists,

---

[12] 'If he has maimed a part (of a body), unless he settles with him, there is to be talion ...
If he has broken a bone of a free man, 300, of a slave, 150 (asses) are to be the pen-
alty.' From the Law of the Twelve Tables, 8.2 and 8.3, translation M. H. Crawford and
J. C. Claud, *Roman Statutes*, vol. II, London 1996.

before the Republic was founded, there were also statute laws promulgated by the king (*leges regiae*). It is, however, more probable that these laws were of a more recent date but were later on ascribed to the kings. This would be in accordance with the Greek custom of ascribing laws to legendary lawmakers.

55   The Law of the Twelve Tables

The Law of the Twelve Tables marks a turning point in the early history of Roman law. Halfway through the fifth century BC, at the height of the conflict between the patricians and the plebeians, the latter demanded that the law be recorded. The priests, who at the time were all patricians, had a monopoly over the interpretation of the law and, thus, were able to amend the law to their own liking. Recording the law would put an end to such vagaries and prevent the priests from changing the law. *Ius civile* may have been distinct from divine law, but its authority was still vested in the customs and mores of remote ancestors. As such, it was considered to be, or that it ought to be, immutable. The duty of the king and, under the Republic, of the priests, was not to adapt or change the law, but to guarantee its application. The Law of the Twelve Tables came out of a conservative reaction, the purpose of which was to stop the development of the law by the priests and to preserve traditional law.

In 451 BC, a ten-person commission, the *decemviri legibus scribundis*, was appointed. During the *decemviri*'s term in office, all other magistracies were suspended. The story goes that a delegation was sent to Athens in order to study the laws of Solon. This is highly unlikely. What might be true is that the Romans visited a number of the Greek cities in southern Italy. At any event, ten tables of law were promulgated in 450 BC; two more were added the next year.

A substantial part of *ius civile*, both customary and statute law, was written down. Nevertheless, the assertion by the historian Livy that the Law of the Twelve Tables was 'the source of all public and private law' goes too far.[13] The Twelve Tables contained primarily rules of private law, criminal law and procedural law and only a few rules of constitutional law and sacral law. By and large, the Twelve Tables recorded existing *ius civile*, although various amendments will have been made. From 449 BC onwards, the Law of the Twelve Tables formed the core of *ius civile*. The rules of the *mos maiorum* that had not been included in the Tables remained valid regardless.

---

[13] Livy 3.34.6.

56 Statute law

In the centuries after 449 BC, the popular assemblies, *comitia* and *concilium plebis*, would from time to time adopt statute laws which amended or added to the Law of the Twelve Tables. Of these, the *lex Aquilia*, a plebiscite on tort law from 287 BC, is the best-known instance from the Republican period. Generally speaking, however, legislation under the Republic played only a marginal role when it came to private law. In the field of public law, the assemblies were more active.

The resolutions of the Senate — *senatusconsulta* — had advisory value only. In practice, they were generally observed by the magistrates and/or followed up by the popular assemblies. One does, however, need to wait until the Principate before they could genuinely be regarded as statute laws.

[handwritten marginalia: lex Aquilia]

[handwritten marginalia: senate only, sivian optimion (adunce)]

4 Legis actio *and the role of the priest*

57 The two stages of the *legis actio* procedure

Under archaic Roman law, civil procedure was based on the *legis actio*. It was a two-stage procedure: the stage *in iure* (in law) and that *apud iudicem* (before the judge). The term *in iure* referred to *iurisdictio* – the power to regulate and oversee the administration of justice. To begin with, *iurisdictio*, most probably, belonged to *pontifices* or priests. At the latest, half way through the second century BC, *iurisdictio* became part of the *imperium* of the magistrates.

First, the plaintiff and the defendant appeared before the priest (*in iure*). The latter would establish whether the dispute fell under the provisions of the *ius civile*, allowing for a trial to be held. If so, the priest referred the case to the judge or judges (*apud iudicem*). If not, the case could, on principle, not be brought before the judge. In the second phase, evidence was tabled and the case was pleaded and adjudged.

This two-stage division went back far in time. Many modern scholars have claimed that in the Regal Period, the king, who was also the high priest, determined the kind of evidence the litigants could use to prove their case. Often this involved an appeal to the gods, either by taking an oath under which one invoked the wrath of the gods if one failed to speak the truth or by various methods of divination, such as augury – the study of the flight of birds – or reading signs in the death throes or entrails of a sacrificial animal by the *haruspex*. The king-priest indicated the type of rite appropriate for the dispute in question. Only then could the evidence be adduced and a judgment be reached.

58   *In iure*

During the time of the Republic, the distinction between the two stages of the *legis actio* procedure was sustained. But their concrete significance evolved. In the first stage, it was established whether the dispute came under the *ius civile*, meaning under the application of one of the existing *legis actiones* (action on the basis of the law, somewhat similar to a writ). A *legis actio* was a procedural ritual. The parties were required to undertake certain ritual acts and to pronounce solemn formulas. By so doing, they brought a factual dispute within the field of the law and transformed it into a legal dispute. Each *legis actio* could be used to enforce various rights protected by the *ius civile*. By using a certain *legis actio*, one indicated the kind of right one wished to defend or claim before the court. In this way the claim was made in terms of the law. It was then possible for the judge to pronounce on the dispute in the second stage.

[margin handwritten note: procedural aspects]

The *ius civile* provided for only a limited number of such *legis actiones*. In the second century AD, Gaius would distinguish five *legis actiones*, three to obtain a judgment and two to enforce the sentence. Four of these were already present in the Law of the Twelve Tables; only a single one was added after 449 BC.

The oldest form was the *legis actio sacramento*, the action by means of a ritual wager. This could be used *in rem* or *in personam*. The *legis actio sacramento in rem* was applied in order to vindicate a thing, while the *legis actio sacramento in personam* concerned a claim with respect to another person.

The *legis actio sacramento in rem* provides a good example of the ritual nature of the procedure. Both parties appeared before the priest, later the magistrate. The plaintiff formulated his *vindicatio* (claim) whereby he grasped the thing concerned or touched it with a staff and uttered some ritual words; the defendant did exactly the same. The priest then commanded them to let go of the thing. At the end, the plaintiff challenged the defendant to take an oath (*sacramentum*) under which he was required to provide a monetary stake which he would lose if he were found against. The defendant did the same. The loser of the *apud iudicem* proceedings forfeited the stake in this ritual wager to the state treasury, while the winner obtained the right to demand the value of the thing from the loser. The latter could escape this payment by handing over the thing. This complex enforcement mechanism indicated the private character of the whole procedure. The government did not provide any guarantee that the object of dispute would be ceded by the loser. Instead it armed the parties with indirect means of coercion they were required to employ themselves.

Procedure by *sacramentum* was of general application ... If the action was *in rem*, movables, inanimate and animate, provided they could be carried or led into court, were claimed in court in the following manner. The claimant, holding a rod and laying hold of the actual thing – let us say a slave – said: 'I affirm that this man is mine by Quiritary rights according to his proper title. As I have declared, so look you, I have laid my staff on him', and at that moment he laid his rod on the man. His opponent spoke and did the selfsame things. Both parties having thus laid claim, the praetor said: 'Unhand the man, both of you'. They did so. The first claimant then put the following question to the other: 'I ask, will you declare on what title you have laid claim?' and he answered: 'By laying on my staff I have exercised my right'. Thereupon the first claimant said: 'Seeing that you have laid claim unrightfully, I challenge you by a *sacramentum* of 500 *asses*'. And his opponent likewise said: 'And I you'.[14]

Appeal to the judge was possible only in those situations in which the *ius civile* provided for one of the *legis actiones* to be applied. The five *actiones* were each used for various kinds of dispute. A distinction needed therefore to be drawn between the five forms of litigation and the many disputes for which a legal remedy could be provided by application of these five forms. Thus the *legis actio sacramento in rem* could be applied to claim ownership over a slave or some cattle – the legal remedy would then be known as *rei vindicatio* – but also in order to resolve a dispute concerning *patria potestas*, paternal authority. The task of the priest in the *in iure* stage consisted of establishing whether there was a *legis actio* applicable to the dispute in question and whether to allow (or disallow) the commencement of proceedings.

The first stage of the *legis actio* procedure was highly formalistic. The *legis actiones* were religious in origin. Even under the Republic, they kept much of their ritualistic character. The plaintiff and the defendant were required to take well-defined actions and to pronounce particular words so that the *legis actio* selected could be applied. As Gaius wrote, pronouncing the wrong words could invalidate the whole action. The Law of the Twelve Tables stated that one could take legal action if someone had cut down one's trees. Gaius related the story of a man whose vines were cut down. Upon pronouncing the applicable words, he substituted 'vines' for 'trees'. His case was thereby invalidated.

The actions of the practice of older times were called *legis actiones*, either because they were the creation of statutes (of course, in those days the

---

[14] Gaius, *Institutiones* 4.13 and 16; translation by Francis de Zulueta, *The Institutes of Gaius, Part I: Text with Critical Notes and Translation*, Oxford 1946.

praetorian edicts, whereby a large number of actions have been introduced, were not yet in use), or because they were framed in the very words of statutes and were consequently treated as no less immutable than statutes. Hence it was held that a man who, when suing for the cutting down of his vines, had used the word 'vines', had lost his claim, because he ought to have said 'trees', seeing that the Law of the Twelve Tables, on which his action for the cutting down of his vines lay, spoke of cutting down trees in general.[15]

Apparently, the priests did apply the proceedings for trees to vines. However, this extensive interpretation of the law did not make it acceptable for the words themselves to be amended.

59   *Apud iudicem*

During the second stage, *apud iudicem*, the case was pleaded and evidence was produced. The judge or judges ruled which of the two parties had told the truth and rendered judgment. They were not professional judges but rather jurors, citizens appointed by the priest and the parties in order to rule on the dispute in question. For some cases, the jury could number as many as a hundred or more.

The *apud iudicem* stage was much less formalistic than the first stage. The judges were there primarily to establish who spoke the truth. If the jury found for the plaintiff, it attributed the claim as it had been defined during the *in iure* stage. If the ruling went for the defendant, the claim was rejected and the defendant absolved.

Both parties were given the opportunity to argue their case before the court or to have it argued by an advocate. Each had to produce evidence for the claims and allegations he made. Documentary evidence was rare. Witness statements and oral pleadings decided most cases. The judges were at liberty to seek the assistance of an advisory council or *consilium* of experts, constituted for the occasion. The judges were not always familiar with the law. Nevertheless, some judges, especially senators and equestrians, would regularly serve upon a jury and thus gain experience in law.

There was no provision for appeal. At the end of the first stage, both parties signified their agreement with the proceedings, including the choice of the judge(s). This meant that they undertook to respect the sentence. The winner in the proceedings was himself responsible for its enforcement. To this end, there were again two *legis actiones*. Sometimes, with consent of the priest, it was possible to detain the convicted person in order to enforce compliance with the verdict.

---

[15] Gaius, *Institutiones* 4.11.

60 Roman law as a set of remedies

Modern lawyers are familiar with the distinction between substantive and procedural law. In the Early Republic, there was no such distinction. The *ius civile* was a system of procedural rules that provided a legal remedy for a large but ultimately limited number of disputes. If there was no legal remedy, there was no title or right. The existence of a substantive legal rule was the consequence of the existence of a legal remedy. In present-day law, substantive law takes primacy. For each subjective right derived from substantive law, a remedy is available to take the case to court: *ubi ius, ibi remedium*.[16]

An example will illustrate the difference. Most continental civil law systems recognise a general principle of liability for wrongful action. Article 1382 of the French Civil Code of 1804 states that 'anyone who, through his act, causes damage to another by his fault shall be obliged to compensate the damage'.[17] In the new Dutch Civil Code this runs: 'anyone committing an unlawful deed towards another that may be ascribed to him is obliged to compensate the other party for the damage suffered in consequence' (Article 6:162, 1). Furthermore, any dispute concerning liability can be referred to the court.

Roman law did not contain any such general rule of liability for wrongful action. The Law of the Twelve Tables did, however, provide a number of legal remedies for specific cases in which damage had been done:

> In cases where a four-footed animal is alleged to have committed *pauperies*, a right of action is derived from the *Twelve Tables*, which statute provides that that which had caused the offence (that is, the animal which caused harm) should be handed over or that pecuniary damages should be offered for the amount of the harm done.[18]

Similarly, the *Lex Aquilia* offered specific remedies for specific instances of, in particular, damaging somebody's property:

> The first chapter of the *lex Aquilia* provides as follows: 'If anyone kills unlawfully a slave or female slave belonging to someone else or a four-footed beast of the class of cattle, let him be condemned to pay the owner the highest value that the property had attained in the preceding year.'[19]

---

[16] Literally, wherever there is a right, there is a remedy.
[17] Translation by Walter van Gerven, Jeremy Lever and Pierre Larouche, eds., *Tort Law* (*Ius Commune* Casebooks for the Common Law of Europe), Oxford and Portland, Oreg. 2000, 57.
[18] D. 9.1.1 (Digest); translation by Alan Watson, *The Digest of Justinian*, 2nd edn, vol. I, Philadelphia 1998.
[19] D. 9.2.2.

> In its third chapter the *lex Aquilia* says: 'In the case of all other things
> apart from slaves or cattle that have been killed, if anyone does damage
> to another by wrongfully burning, breaking, or spoiling his property, let
> him be condemned to pay to the owner whatever the damage shall prove
> to be worth in the next thirty days.'[20]

Other legal remedies could be applied for other types of damage, but
there were also all sorts of situations in which the law did not provide any
remedies.

61   The priests and the interpretation of the *ius civile*

In principle, only those disputes could be taken to court for which the
ius civile provided a legal remedy. After the promulgation of the Law of
the Twelve Tables, new *legis actiones* and new remedies could only be
introduced by the popular assemblies. The view that the *ius civile* should
remain unchanged still dominated. Laws creating new remedies, such as
the *Lex Aquilia*, were rare. For some time, the priests could, however, prevent the legal system from becoming too rigid and losing touch with the
needs of the evolving Roman society. Since they controlled the first stage
of legal proceedings, they enjoyed a virtual monopoly over the interpretation of the *ius civile*. In addition, they were often consulted for legal
advice on all sorts of legal actions. As the Roman Republic expanded
and the city grew during the fourth and third centuries BC, increasingly
diverse and complex legal disputes were submitted to the courts. In order
to find answers in the *ius civile* to these new questions, the priests had to
interpret the various *legis actiones* in a most extensive way. As we have
seen, it was accepted that people litigated about vines although the law
only mentioned trees. But the creative work of the priests went further
than these analogous reasonings. Gradually, through the improper use
of the *legis actiones*, they developed new legal concepts and techniques.
A much-quoted example concerns the development of *in iure cessio* as a
way of transfer of property from the *legis actio sacramento in rem*. The
priests used this action originally meant for ownership claims for the
purposes of an ordinary transfer of property when ownership was not
disputed. For *in iure cessio*, the old and new owners would appear before
the priest. The new owner would demand the property according to the
rites of the *legis actio sacramento in rem*. If the priest then asked the 'coun-
terparty' for a response, the latter would do nothing and remain silent.
The case would then be awarded to the 'plaintiff'. It may justly be claimed

[20] D. 9.2.27.5.

that the priests provided the first impetus for the development of legal science in Rome. This jurisprudential activity was, from the very first, interwoven with legal practice.

5   Public law and private law

62   *Ius* and *fas*, public and private law

To some extent, the division between *fas* and *ius* lies at the root of the modern distinction between private and public law. The enforcement of *fas* was *res publica*, a public affair, and concerned the whole Roman people. If somebody committed *nefas*, the harmony between the Roman people and their gods was disturbed. Offences against *fas* were initially prosecuted by priests on behalf of the *respublica*. By punishing the offender, the Romans hoped to reconcile the gods with the Roman people. Some legal historians find here an explanation for the origins of the death penalty: the offender was sacrificed to the gods. In any case, the death penalty often applied to *nefas* and was performed in a very ritual way. Offences against *fas* were religious in nature, such as the use of incantations, or directly affected the *respublica*, such as treason. They were insults against the gods, the embodiment of the Republic.[21]

From the distinction between *fas* and *ius* comes the distinction between *crimina publica* (crimes) and *delicta privata* (delicts). From the outset, ordinary crimes such as theft and defamation fell under the second category. They came before the ordinary court where all other civil law disputes were dealt with and fell within the sphere of private law. The victim himself had to prosecute, as only private interests had been harmed. It was up to him to assess whether or not he desired redress. If that was not the case and he decided against prosecution, no one would do so in his place.

Anyone found guilty of a *crimen publicum* became *sacer*, dedicated to the gods, and forfeited his life. It is unclear whether this status was assigned upon conviction or whether a person had already forfeited his life by committing the crime itself. In principle, the *comitia centuriata* were authorised to hear offences subject to the death penalty. Anyone

---

[21] This deification of the state is reflected in the myth that Romulus ascended to the gods and joined Jupiter, the supreme god, after his death. Under the Early Republic, the *fetiales* or priests of Jupiter Optimus Maximus would act in cases of declarations of war and peace treaties. This symbolised the fact that the war and the treaty were matters for Rome itself. Jupiter Optimus Maximus, whose temple stood on the Capitol, was the personification of the state.

condemned to death by a magistrate could appeal to the people (*provocatio ad populum*). As the proceedings and the punishment lost their religious nature, the category of *crimina publica* was extended to crimes of a less religious nature than those traditionally coming under *fas*. Towards the end of the Republic, it became possible for *crimina publica* to be prosecuted not only by magistrates but by any citizen. In the second century BC, the *quaestiones perpetuae* emerged. These courts were competent to hear a particular offence, such as corruption by provincial administrators, electoral corruption or public violence. They were jury courts in which senators and equestrians sat. They played a major role in the struggle for power within the senatorial order.

In this way, criminal law evolved away from traditional *fas*. It lost its religious character but retained its public law dimension. Although most offences were prosecuted by private individuals, the *ratio* of criminal law was still to exact punishment upon the offenders rather than to indemnify their victims. Another part of *fas* evolved into *ius sacrum* or religious law. This regulated religious practices as well as the organisation of the priesthood, but also continued to cover certain legal actions such as a particular form of adoption.

The Romans themselves did not yet draw a distinction between private and public law as two separate branches of the law with their own logic and fundamental rules. They did, however, introduce the terminology and distinguished two spheres of law. Around AD 200 the greatest of Roman jurists, Ulpian, defined these spheres as follows:

> There are two branches of legal study: public and private law. Public law is that which respects the establishment of the Roman commonwealth, private that which respects individuals' interests, some matters being of public and others of private interest. Public law covers religious affairs, the priesthood, and offices of state. Private law is tripartite, being derived from principles of *ius naturale, ius gentium,* or *ius civile*.[22]

6   *The influence of Greek philosophy and rhetoric 1*

63   Philosophy and rhetoric

Under the Late Republic, Roman law underwent a fundamental change, losing much of its religious character. From the end of the second century BC, an autonomous legal science started to develop. Also, a particular body of law, *ius gentium*, applicable to cases involving foreigners, emerged.

---

[22] D. 1.1.2.

All these changes, to some extent, reflect Rome's political, economic and cultural rise under the Late Republic. Particularly in the cultural domain, Rome borrowed from Greece. The conquest of Macedonia and Greece in the first half of the second century BC strengthened the cultural bonds between Greece and Rome. Greek orators and philosophers came to Rome, often to teach there. It became fashionable for young Roman aristocrats to complete their education with a tour of Greece, where one would take instruction from Greek philosophers and orators. Caesar and Cicero did so. As a writer, orator and philosopher, Cicero played a significant role in disseminating Greek knowledge and ideas among the Roman elite.

The Greeks never developed an autonomous legal science. Greek philosophy and rhetoric, rather than Greek law, were instrumental in the formation of Roman jurisprudence. Various Greek philosophers and rhetoricians formulated propositions and opinions which were of direct relevance for the law.

The history of Greek and hence all Western philosophy began in the sixth century BC, in the Ionic-Greek cities on the west coast of present-day Turkey. The so-called natural philosophers, such as Heraclitus and Thales of Milete, searched for a single, original principle that determined the whole of nature and history. A number of these Ionic natural philosophers moved to Athens.

The fifth century BC was the Golden Age of Athens. The Athenian *polis* or city-state was a democracy in which every citizen had certain rights of political participation. The important political decisions were taken in the popular assembly, generally after lengthy debate. Rhetoric was a powerful and necessary tool for anyone aspiring to a political career. The Athenian sophists of the fifth century BC were the first teachers in the art of rhetoric and disputation. According to the sophists, a rhetorician had to possess the ability to persuade his public of any conceivable proposition. What was important was not knowledge and truth but the power of persuasion. Contemporary and later opponents often upbraided them for their opportunism.

The Athenian Golden Age was the age of the great philosopher Socrates (469–399 BC), whose life and thought were recorded by his most famous disciple, Plato (427–347 BC). Socrates can, to some extent, be considered a sophist as he elevated dialogue and debate into an art form. In contrast to the sophists, however, he regarded debate as an instrument not of persuasion but of truth. For Socrates, knowledge of the truth led to moral behaviour. Understanding of virtue led to virtuous conduct. Socrates and

Plato laid the foundations of Greek moral philosophy. They took a stand against the amoral principles of the sophist rhetoricians, accusing them of practising the art of deception. In later centuries, the battle between Socrates and Plato and the sophists was continued by the proponents of the philosophical and rhetorical traditions. The philosophers argued that they strove for truth, while the rhetoricians had only mastered the art of persuading their listeners that what they said was also the truth. Since rhetoric was vital for a successful political career, both in Greece and later in Rome, the teachers of rhetoric enjoyed the most success. It should, however, be said that many of them also had a philosophical interest. In any case, both philosophy and rhetoric contributed towards the development of dialectic logic and the theory of argumentation.

During the course of the second century BC, Rome fell under the spell of Greek thought. Famously, in 155 BC, an Athenian embassy consisting of three philosopher-orators paid a visit to the city. Among the Athenians was Carneades, a representative of the New Academy. Entirely in the sophist tradition, he defended the view that a trained orator should be able to persuade his hearers of any stance whatever. In order to support his thesis, he offered to defend a proposition in the forum and then to refute it the next day. He evidently had success among the Roman population, at least to the extent that the great Roman statesman and orator Marcus Porcius Cato the Censor, who portrayed himself as the defender of Roman tradition, asked the Senate to complete the negotiations with the Athenians swiftly, so that they would not have to remain in Rome for too long. This story demonstrates that the Romans inherited from the Greeks the tension between the rhetorical and philosophical traditions.

7   *The sophists and the mutability of the law*

64   Human law

Even if they failed to develop a genuine legal science, the sophists still had a major influence on legal thought in classical Greece. They challenged the link between human and divine law. The sophists noted that the customs of the various tribes and city-states differed greatly from one another. Why should not each city-state have its own specific laws? Custom and law, both of which they referred to as *nomos*, were ultimately based on nothing more than convention, on usages that commanded widespread support. The basis of the law was consequently consent among the citizens. The law was not divine in its origin. The idea was born that the law was manmade and consequently subject to human will. What man had made, he could unmake.

65   Human law and morality

But the sophists also proposed more far-reaching conclusions. As the law was not divine in its origin, it did not necessarily sustain the order of things as it was willed by the gods – or, in modern times, morality. Recognition that the law was manmade led the sophists to question its morality. What guaranteed that manmade law was in accordance with the will of the gods, with a higher morality? It is the eternal question of the relation between law and justice.

To the mutable *nomos*, the sophists opposed the immutable and eternal *fysis* (nature). It was in these terms that the contrast between human law and natural law – the law contained in human nature itself – was later to be constructed. Natural law was given to humankind at the beginning of time. It is immutable and beyond human will. *Nomos* by contrast is based on consent and need not be in accord with the 'laws' of nature. Human law is morally neutral. Law is what people say the law is, irrespective of its substance. It is not sanctioned by any higher norm. The sophist Antiphon (fifth century BC) took an even more radical step. He stated that people were by nature concerned with their own interests and inclined to dominate other people. This immutable 'law of nature' gave each human being the freedom to trample on human law when it was in his interest.

Many sophists, as well as Socrates and Plato, opposed the radical implications drawn from Antiphon. In his dialogue *Crito*, Plato described the final hours of Socrates after he had been condemned to death. Crito advised Socrates to escape; everything was arranged. Socrates refused. Even if he had been unjustly treated under the law, he considered that he had to abide by the law. The laws were based on convention, but that convention was binding, even if it worked to one's disadvantage. The interest of the *polis* came first. To do otherwise would be to risk the destruction of the state and society. Socrates let the laws speak to him:

> But we say that whoever of you stays here, seeing how we administer justice and how we govern the state in other respects, has thereby entered into an agreement with us to do what we command; and we say that he who does not obey does threefold wrong, because he disobeys us who are his parents, because he disobeys us who nurtured him, and because after agreeing to obey us he neither obeys us nor convinces us that we are wrong, though we give him the opportunity and do not roughly order

him to do what we command, but when we allow him a choice of two
things, either to convince us of error or to do our bidding, he does neither
of these things.[23]

The sophists had taken an irreversible step by recognising the existence of
a law subject to human volition. The law was grounded in the consent of
the members of the *polis*. There was nothing to prevent those members or
the *polis* itself abolishing, amending or supplementing that law by means
of new agreements. For the first time, the law was perceived as a flexible
instrument in the hands of men.

66   Antigone

The question as to whether human law needed to be in accord with the
higher, eternal standards of divine and natural law was not answered by
the Greeks. The Greek philosophers did not take their interpretation of
divine, natural and human law far. The most familiar and clearest text
from classical Greek literature in which the distinction between the various kinds of law is brought out is not a legal text but a fragment from
Antigone by the great Athenian dramatist Sophocles (496–406 BC).
Antigone was the daughter of King Oedipus of Thebes. The new king, her
uncle Creon, decreed on pain of death that one of Antigone's brothers
should not be buried. Among the Greeks, it was a sacred duty on the part
of the relatives of the deceased to look after his mortal remains. If not, the
soul of the departed person would never enter the underworld. Antigone
therefore faced a dilemma: should she follow the law of the gods or that of
the king? She chose the former and was caught. When brought before her
uncle, she challenged him as follows:

> Yes, for it was not Zeus who made this proclamation,
> Nor was it Justice who lives with the Gods below
> That establishes such laws among men,
> Nor did I think your proclamations
> Strong enough to have power to overrule,
> Mortal as they were,
> The unwritten and unfailing ordinances of the gods.
> For these have life, not simply today and yesterday,
> But for ever, and no one knows how long ago they were revealed.[24]

---

[23] Plato, *Crito*; translation by Harold North Fowler, *Plato: Euthyphro, Apology, Crito,
Phaedo, Phaedrus* (Loeb Classical Library 36), Cambridge, Mass. and London 1914.

[24] Sophocles, *Antigonè* vv. 450–8, translation by Hugh Lloyd-Jones, *Sophocles: Antigone,
The Women of Trachis, Philoctetes, Oedipus at Colonus* (Loeb Classical Library 21),
Cambridge, Mass. and London 1994.

67 Cicero, the Stoa and the law of nature

It is difficult to discern to what extent Greek influence was responsible for the important changes Roman law underwent in the Late Republic. What is certain is that Greek scholars and orators increasingly settled in Rome from the second century BC onwards and helped disseminate Greek ideas. In his philosophical and political works, Cicero developed a theory of natural and of human law. According to him, some rules of conduct were inherent in human nature. Ultimately these stemmed from God. These precepts were reasonable, in the sense that human beings were able to discover and discern them through their reason. For Cicero this natural law was the supreme law (*ius*).

> Law is the highest reason, implanted in Nature, which commands what ought to be done and forbids the opposite. This reason, when firmly fixed and fully developed in the human mind, is Law. And so they believe that Law is intelligence, whose natural function is to command right conduct and forbid wrongdoing ... Now if this is correct, as I think it to be in general, then the origin of Justice is to be found in Law, for Law is a natural force; it is the mind and reason of the intelligent man, the standard by which Justice and Injustice are measured ... But in determining what Justice is, let us begin with that supreme Law which had its origin ages before any written law existed or any state had been established.[25]

Natural law was the measure of objective justice that applied to all people. This universalism betrayed the influence of the Stoa on Cicero. The Stoa was a philosophical tradition that had emerged in the Greek world in the fourth and third centuries BC. The Stoics believed in the existence of a single, natural society of all men. Cicero labelled this in Latin *societas humana*, or human society. He also raised the question of the relationship between the supreme law, the law of nature, and human law. He unequivocally rejected the utilitarianism of the sophists. Legal rules that were not in accord with nature and the supreme law led to injustice.

> But the most foolish notion of all is that belief that everything is just which is found in the customs or laws of nations. Would that be true, even if these laws had been enacted by tyrants? ... For Justice is one; it binds all human society, and is based on one Law, which is right reason applied to command and prohibition. Whoever knows not this Law, whether it has been recorded anywhere in writing or not, is without Justice.
>
> But if Justice is conformity to written laws and national customs, and if, as the same persons claim, everything is to be tested by the standard

---

[25] Cicero, *De legibus* 1.18–19, translation by Clinton Walker Keyes, *Cicero: De republica, De legibus* (Loeb Classical Library 213), Cambridge, Mass. and London 1928.

of utility, then anyone who thinks it will be profitable to him will, if he is able, disregard and violate the laws. It follows that Justice does not exist at all, if it does not exist in Nature, and if that form of it which is based on utility can be overthrown by utility itself. And if Nature is not to be considered the foundation of Justice, that will mean the destruction [of the virtues on which human society depends]. For where then will there be a place for generosity, or love of country, or loyalty, or the inclination to be of service to others or to show gratitude for favours received? For these virtues originate in our natural inclination to love our fellow-men, and this is the foundation of Justice … But if the principles of Justice were founded on the decrees of peoples, the edicts of princes, or the decisions of judges, then Justice would sanction robbery and adultery and forgery of wills, in case these acts were approved by the votes or decrees of the populace.[26]

Even so Cicero did not go as far as demanding that the human laws be in accordance with natural law in order to be binding and enforceable. The fact that legal rules were unjust did not necessarily mean that they could be left aside. In fact, neither Cicero nor the jurists of the imperial age made any pronouncements on the subject. The Christian scholars of the Middle Ages were the first to state that human law should be in accordance with divine and natural law for it to be binding.

68   The jurists of the imperial age and natural law

The jurists of the imperial age similarly used the concept of natural law, but paid little attention to its metaphysical dimension. Natural law was a vague concept. It embraced the rules and institutes that were perceived as natural and reasonable and that were to be found among all peoples. It was not considered to be promulgated by the gods – divine law – but was to be found in nature, inherently present in people and things themselves. It was a set of rights and obligations that arose from the fact of being born and being human and not from any human decision. This inherent law included the right to self-defence, the duty to care for one's own children and the right to inherit property from relatives. Roman legal scholars associated the law of nature with the *ius gentium*, the law the Romans applied to aliens. Both systems had a universal application; they applied to all peoples.

The jurists of the imperial age no more established a strict hierarchy between natural law and human law than Cicero had done. The validity of human law did not depend on compatibility with natural law. Ulpian, for

---

[26] Cicero, *De legibus* 1.42–3.

example, noted that the desire to be free was inherent to all human beings but that slavery had been introduced by the *ius gentium*.[27]

8 Per formulam *procedure and* ius praetorium

69   The expansion of Rome and the challenge to the *ius civile*

During the final centuries of its existence, the Roman Republic changed radically. In the space of a few generations Rome evolved from a medium-sized city-state into the greatest empire in the Mediterranean. The expansion, the massive inflow into the city of foreigners and slaves, the granting of citizenship to tens of thousands of new citizens from Italy and the provinces, the upsurge of trade, mining and industry, and the accumulation of enormous wealth by a few hundred families meant that the courts were flooded with new kinds of disputes and cases. Increasingly, cases were brought forward for which the *ius civile* offered no answer. At the time of the Law of the Twelve Tables, when the *ius civile* was codified, Rome was still a small city-state. The archaic law had been tailored to the needs of a small city and agricultural community. Now, the gap between the law and social reality was widening. As Rome expanded, so the law needed to expand.

Renewal and change did not come through legislation. After the Law of the Twelve Tables, a few statute laws were passed that supplemented or amended the *ius civile*, but these remained exceptional. The use of statute law as an instrument for legal change, particularly in the field of private law, ran counter to tradition. Wholly consistent with the logic of a system of law that was largely procedural, change came from the administration of justice itself, by the emergence of a new kind of legal procedure.

70   *Iurisdictio* of the praetor

It was, however, no longer the *pontifices* who controlled the courts. From 300 BC onwards, their control over the courts and their monopoly of legal interpretation were increasingly challenged. The fact that certain priests began issuing their opinions publicly meant that knowledge about the law was disseminated outside the pontifical colleges. In 367 BC, the *praetura* was set up. At first, the praetor was a *collega minor* or assistant of the consuls. In due course, *iurisdictio* was added to the praetor's *imperium*. This *iurisdictio* concerned not the pronouncement of judgments but control over the proper administration of justice and the courts. In the course

----

[27]   D. 1.1.4.

of the next century, the new magistracy was expanded further. By the second half of the second century BC at the very latest, the praetor had displaced the priests as the presiding officer of the courts.[28] Henceforth, the urban praetor presided *in iure*. This was the praetor who had obtained the most votes in the elections. The replacement of the priests by the praetor was part and parcel of a more general process of secularisation of the law. One must, however, guard against overestimating the social impact of that change: the praetors were drawn from the same pre-eminent senatorial families as the priests. The change did, however, mean that the administration of justice was now controlled by magistrates who were elected for one year only and no longer by priests elected for life. Although a good many praetors had built up a thorough legal knowledge as experienced politicians, administrators and/or advocates, there were inevitably some who had little if any legal knowledge or experience. This provides part of the explanation for the emergence of the jurists in the late second and the first centuries BC. Apart from the praetor, the aediles also gained judicial powers in certain areas.

71   Extensive interpretation by the praetor

It was the magistrates, especially the *praetor urbanus*, who were responsible for the development of Roman law under the Late Republic. As noted previously, ever more disputes came before the courts for which the *ius civile* afforded no solution. Few new rules were introduced into the *ius civile* by legislation; strictly speaking, the *ius civile* largely remained as it was. The procedural logic of the old law was not abandoned. Just like the priests before them, the praetors attempted to broaden the application of the *ius civile* with its limited arsenal of *legis actiones* by means of an extensive interpretation of the existing law. In doing so, they departed increasingly from the original content of the rules of the *ius civile*. When a dispute arose to which no *legis actio* applied, the praetors often allowed the case to go through anyway. They would then grant an *actio utilis* or an *actio in factum*. In the case of an *actio utilis*, permission to have the case tried by the judges was granted for a case that was similar to one that

---

[28] In the literature it is fairly generally accepted that the judicial powers came into the hands of the magistrates at a much earlier point, indeed already in the Early Republic before the appointment of the *praetura*. The priests did, however, continue to play a dominant role in the interpretation of the law as advisers to these magistrates. Olga Tellegen considers, however, that the replacement of the priests by the magistrate is of much later date. This view is endorsed here. See Olga Tellegen-Couperus, *A Short History of Roman Law*, London and New York 1993, 22; Tellegen-Couperus, 'Pontiff, Praetor, and *Iurisdictio* in the Roman Republic', *Legal History Review*, 74 (2006) 31–44.

was described by the *ius civile*. So the right to commence proceedings was granted to an alien on the basis of an action that could normally only be brought by a citizen. The praetor created an *actio utilis* by means of an analogous interpretation of the dispute in question and the dispute coming under the existing *legis actio*:

> Be X judge. If it appears that a golden cup had been stolen from Lucius Titus by Dio the son of Hermaeus or by his aid and counsel, on which account, if he were a Roman citizen, he would be bound to compound for the wrong as a thief, [he must condemn him; if it does not appear, then he must absolve him].[29]

An *actio in factum* was a legal remedy granted *ad hoc* by the praetor in a specific case on the basis of the actual facts. It was here that the praetor moved furthest away from the *ius civile* and where he played his most innovative role.

72   Legal change and the fiction of immutability

Formally speaking, the *ius civile* was still considered to be immutable. The praetor did not alter the existing law as such, but improved or supplemented it; as a magistrate the praetor was unable to change the law, but was responsible for its correct and effective application. The later jurist Aemilius Papinianus (d. 212) wrote on this subject: 'Praetorian law is that which in the public interest the praetors have introduced in aid or supplementation or correction of the *ius civile*.'[30]

The notion was retained, even though it was a fiction, that the praetor was not formulating or introducing any new legal rules. He acted as if he were only disclosing applications for the old, immutable law that had been dormant within it but had only been disclosed now within the context of this new case. In reality, however, he did grant new remedies, the *actiones utiles et in factum*, or so-called praetorian actions, and in doing so, he created new enforceable rights and obligations. The activity of the praetors was substantial and innovative. In fact, all sorts of new legal concepts, such as possessory interdicts and the concept of good faith in contract law, have their origin in praetorian law.

73   Praetorian law

In this way, there gradually emerged a second body of law beside the existing *ius civile*. This is normally referred to as *ius honorarium* (law of the

---

[29] Gaius, *Institutiones* 4.37.   [30] D. 1.1.7.1.

magistrates) or, more narrowly, *ius praetorium* (praetorian law).[31] Like the *ius civile*, praetorian law was not a logical and internally coherent system but an organically evolved body of case law, of legal remedies. The new law was as casuistic and procedural in nature as the old law, but was more extensive and less exclusive. During the Late Republic, the praetors granted remedies for countless new cases. In this way, they adapted Roman law to the new needs of society. They developed it into a sophisticated and finely meshed body of law which provided a myriad different solutions for an ever increasing number and variety of cases.

Under their *imperium*, the praetors disposed of the *ius edicendi*, the power to promulgate edicts. These were general regulations by means of which the magistrates made clear how they would exercise their *imperium*. From the second century BC onwards, the *praetor urbanus* would annually promulgate an edict upon taking office by which he announced which legal remedies he would be applying that year. To begin with, the praetor was not bound by his edict. He was at liberty to allow legal remedies that had not been provided for in it. Although the praetor was free to determine the content of his edict, it was customary for a new praetor largely to adopt that of his predecessor(s), albeit with some omissions, improvements and additions. In this way, the edict expanded from year to year. In 67 BC, it was decided by plebiscite that the praetor would henceforth abide by his own edict. This was an attempt to keep arbitrariness on the part of the praetors within bounds. Towards the beginning of the Principate, the edict was as good as fixed, with little if any further evolution.

74   Procedure *per formulam*

The massive introduction of new remedies by the praetors radically changed the nature of the Roman civil trial. Apart from the *legis actio* procedure, there emerged a new procedure, the procedure *per formulam*. During the course of the second century BC, the *lex Aebutia* stipulated that the procedure *per formulam* could be used in a number of instances in which the older procedure would previously have had to be used. Augustus promulgated two laws under which the procedure *per formulam* obtained the same validity in virtually all cases for which a *legis actio* would previously have been required. Although not abolished, the *legis actio* procedure subsequently fell into disuse.

---

[31] The two terms tend to be used interchangeably. In fact, *ius honorarium* is broader as it extends to the law of magistrates other than the praetors, such as the aediles.

The fundamental difference between the *legis actio* procedure and that of the *formula* pertained to the use of *legis actiones* or *formulae* respectively. The division into two stages with their respective functions was retained. During the *in iure* stage, the two parties appeared before the praetor and submitted their case. In mutual consultation with the parties, the praetor then drew up the *formula* describing the dispute and setting out the various legal remedies and exceptions. The judge or judges were also designated in it. Both parties were required to concur with the *formula*. By means of such concurrence (*litis contestatio*, joinder of issue), the plaintiff and defendant declared that they would abide by the verdict of the actual judge (*iudex*).

To begin with, the praetors drew up a new *formula* for each individual case in respect of which they granted a praetorian action. While that remained the case, the praetors did little to formulate new rules of law. Their actions had significance *inter partes* (among the parties) only and not *erga omnes* (towards all). Halfway through the second century BC, however, the praetors began to draw up standardised *formulae* that outlined a dispute in general terms with fixed and variable elements. The *formulae* became standard provisions, each of which could be applied to a number of similar cases. This higher degree of abstraction owed much to the influence of the Greek philosophers and rhetoricians. It resulted in the articulation of somewhat more general legal rules, so that Roman law became more flexible in its application. It did not, however, amount to a separation of substantive law and procedural rules.

In contrast to the *legis actio* procedure, the procedure *per formulam* lacked any ritual or religious basis. The *formulae* were stripped of any ritualistic dimension, instead straightforwardly and clearly articulating the nature of the case and the applicable rule. The shift in emphasis from form to content meant that the *formulae* could be more easily transformed and adapted to deal with new cases. They were more open and flexible than the *legis actiones*. An example of the importance of the procedure *per formulam* for the formation of law is the introduction of the concept of *bona fides* (good faith) in contract law. Under the *ius civile*, contractual obligations essentially arose only from the observance of certain forms. The praetors accepted that at the basis of the obligation stood the *fides* or faith placed in the given word. The praetor therefore allowed proceedings to be instituted in respect of four types of contract – sale, hire, partnership and mandate – even if the formal requirements of the *ius civile* had not been observed or if foreigners were involved in the agreement. According to the praetor, good faith required the observance of the agreement, irrespective as to whether or not the formal requirements of the *ius civile* had been observed.

The *formula* consisted of various elements. In the first place there was the appointment of the judge, second, the presentation of the facts (*demonstratio*), third, the statement of claim (*intentio*) and fourth, the authority for the judge to condemn or absolve (*condemnatio*).

> Be X judge. If it appears that Aulus Agerius deposited the silver table with Numerius Negidius and that by the fraud of Numerius Negidius it has not been returned to Aulus Agerius (*intentio*), do thou, judge, condemn Numerius Negidius to Aulus Agerius in as much money as the thing shall be worth. If it does not appear, absolve (*condemnatio*).[32]

The judge in the second stage (*apud iudicem*) could only establish whether or not the conditions of the *formula* had been fulfilled. All the legal arguments for and against the conviction were already contained in the *intentio*. Apart from arguments in favour of the plaintiff the praetor could include exceptions in favour of the defendant (*exceptiones*). An example:

> X must be the judge. If it appears that the defendant ought to pay to the plaintiff 1,000 sesterces (*intentio*) and if it has not been agreed between the plaintiff and the defendant that the money should not be sued for (*exceptio*), he must condemn him; if this does not appear, then he must absolve him (*condemnatio*).[33]

All this does not mean that the judges in the second stage did not play any role in the formation of new law. The fact that the praetor allowed matters to proceed to the second stage with a new *formula* did not necessarily imply that the judge did nothing but blindly apply the *formula*. It will have happened on more than one occasion that the legal remedy failed because the *formula* did not properly outline the case in question. The *sententiae* (judgments) handed down by the judges certainly contributed to the evolution of praetorian law as they taught the praetors which *formulae* were successful and which were in need of amendment. The judges also frequently gave new interpretations to the *formulae*, which then served as a precedent for later proceedings.

9   *The* ius gentium

75   Roman *ius gentium*

During the last centuries of the Republic, the number of non-citizens living in Rome and in Italy greatly increased. More and more, the courts

---

[32] Gaius, *Institutiones* 4.47.   [33] Tellegen-Couperus, *Short History*, 55.

found themselves dealing with disputes in which at least one non-citizen was involved. In such cases, the courts did not apply the *ius civile*. As early as 242 BC, a second praetor, the peregrine praetor, was appointed. This praetor held *iurisdictio* over all cases involving non-citizens.

The peregrine praetors developed the Roman *ius gentium*, the law of nations. This body of law had little to do with what later came to be understood under the term law of nations, namely the law governing relations between states – nowadays public international law. Roman *ius gentium* was not international law, as it was of Roman origin. Neither was it public law. It was a kind of universal private law. It was applied to all cases brought before the Roman court in which one or more foreigners were involved. It was applied to all foreigners, irrespective of their origins. Since it was developed by the peregrine praetors, it was *ius honorarium*, and even, *ius praetorium*. Like the urban praetor, the peregrine praetor drew up an edict, later known as the provincial edict, in which he summed up the *formulae* he would be admitting in the coming year. As with the ordinary edict, this edict became ever more sizeable through successive changes and supplements made by the various praetors.

Right from the start, the *ius gentium* was totally separate from the *ius civile*. As a result, it escaped the formal constraints of that law. The procedure *per formulam* first emerged through the endeavours of the *praetor peregrinus*. This praetor enjoyed a large measure of freedom and was more at liberty than the urban praetor to focus on the substance of the dispute. In this way, the *ius gentium* could evolve into a system of fairly general rules in which considerations of reasonableness and fairness were dominant. It reflected the general attitudes towards law and justice prevailing among both Romans and other peoples.

It will come as no surprise that the jurists from the imperial age associated *ius naturale* and *ius gentium* with one another. The Roman law of nations seemed a more concrete embodiment of the basic rules of law that were enshrined in human nature itself and were common to all humankind. During the second century AD, the jurist Gaius referred to natural reason as the source of the law of nations:

> Every people that is governed by statutes and customs observes partly its own special law and partly the common law of all mankind. The law which a people established for itself is special (*proprium*) to it, and is called *ius civile* (civil law) as being the special law of that *civitas* (state), while the law that natural reason established among all mankind is followed by all peoples alike, and is called *ius gentium* (law of nations, or law of the world) as being the law observed by all mankind.[34]

[34] Gaius, *Institutiones* 1.1.

Ulpian distinguished natural law and the law of nations from one another in that the former applied to all living creatures and the latter only to human beings. His assertion was adopted by Emperor Justinian together with Gaius's definition in his *Institutiones*. This indicates that the law of nations was generally regarded as a more detailed elaboration of natural law, based as it was on natural reason, the main attribute distinguishing man from beast.[35]

10   *The emergence of legal science in the second and first centuries BC*

76   The emergence of an autonomous legal science

In contrast to ancient Greece and all other ancient civilisations in the Mediterranean, in Rome an autonomous, secular legal science, practised by a distinct group of legal specialists or jurists, emerged. Its beginnings may be traced to the second and first centuries BC. Under the Late Republic, the priests lost their monopoly over the knowledge and interpretation of the law. Apart from the priests, other members of the senatorial order gained legal expertise. The more elaborate and complex Roman law became, the more litigants, judges and praetors called on these 'specialists' for counsel. It was from this advisory practice that legal science or jurisprudence emerged. The legal science was primarily concerned with private law. The *ius sacrum* or religious law was also the object of expert study. Public law was the least commented upon and studied.

After the first few generations, the activities of the Roman jurists became distinct from those of the advocates. By tradition, any Roman citizen who had to defend himself before the court or the popular assemblies had the right to be assisted by an *advocatus* (literally, one called to assist). For a young Roman from the senatorial order with political ambitions, pleading before the court was an excellent way to gain notoriety and popularity. The advocate-orators were primarily members of the senatorial order or ambitious young men from the equestrian order. One of the obligations of a *patronus* was to assist his clients before the court or at least to arrange for someone else to assist them. It was, furthermore, forbidden to accept payment for services as an advocate, although it was customary to accept gifts. The wealthy clients of Cicero – the greatest orator and advocate of his time – knew that a villa on the Neapolitan coast would constitute a suitable expression of their gratitude for winning an important case ...

---

[35] D. 1.11.4. and *Inst.* 2 pr. and 2.1.

Advocates were primarily orators (*oratores*). They were schooled in rhetoric and not necessarily in the law. Cicero in fact complained that some *oratores* who appeared before the court did not know enough about the law: 'And yet, it was not eloquence, or the art of speaking, or copiousness that was wanting in those counsel, but knowledge of the *ius civile*.'[36] Cicero, himself both an orator and a scholar, did not consider himself a jurist. He did, however, consider that a good orator should have at least a minimal knowledge of his subject. In that sense, he regarded a minimum of legal expertise an indispensable tool for any serious advocate.

> Accordingly, that a man, ignorant of these and similar laws of his own community, should roam with a large following from court to court, haughtily and with head upraised, eager and assured in mien and countenance, directing his gaze hither and thither, and holding out and tendering protection to clients, aid to friends, and the illumination of his talent and advice to well-nigh every citizen, is not all this to be considered something extremely scandalous?
>
> And since I have spoken of the effrontery of men, let us go on to chastise their slackness, and laziness. For even if this legal study were a matter of great difficulty, yet its great utility should urge men to undergo the toil of learning. But, by Heaven, I should not say this with Scaevola listening, were he not himself in the habit of affirming that he thinks no art easier of attainment.[37]

In other places, Cicero also did not spare his criticism of the lack of style and eloquence among jurists: 'But as it is you admit that a man may be learned in the law without possessing this eloquence which we are investigating and that many such have appeared.'[38]

Like advocates, jurists were drawn from among the ranks of senators and magistrates. On the basis of their experience as advocate, judge, magistrate, senator and/or priest and their special interest in the law, a number of senators became true legal experts. They were systematically consulted by praetors and other magistrates, judges, advocate-orators and litigants on points of law. The first great jurists of the second and the early first centuries BC were at the same time great orator-advocates. In the second half of the first century BC, these two activities became separated. Nevertheless, the study of rhetoric remained an important element in the training of a jurist during the imperial age. The jurists were, however, no longer regularly practising as advocates at the same time.

---

[36] Cicero, *De oratore* 1.167, translation by E. W. Sutton and H. Rackham, *Cicero: De oratore books I–II* (Loeb Classical Library 348), Cambridge, Mass. and London 1942.
[37] Cicero, *De oratore* 1.184–5.   [38] Cicero, *De oratore* 1.236.

77   The activities of the jurist

According to Cicero the activity of a jurist was threefold:

> If again the question were, who is rightly described as learned in the law,
> I should say it is the man who is an expert in the statutes, and in the cus-
> tomary law observed by individuals as members of the community, and
> who is qualified to advise (*ad respondendum*), direct the course of a law-
> suit (*ad agendum*), and safeguard a client (*ad cavendum*), and in this class
> I should refer to Sextus Aelius, Manius Manilius and Publius Mucius.[39]

Respondere or responding refers to rendering advisory opinions on points
of law in the context of a specific case. It was the most important activity
of the Roman jurists. As we have already seen, the jurists were consulted
not just by the litigants themselves but also by the advocate-orators,
judges and in some cases even the praetors. With the odd happy exception, judges and praetors were not themselves jurists, although this did
not necessarily mean that they were totally unfamiliar with the law. As
former quaestors, popular tribunes or aediles and as senators, the praetors certainly had administrative and/or legal experience. Many judges
were also drawn from the senatorial and equestrian orders. By tradition,
it was customary for a magistrate to enlist the assistance of a council of
advisers, or *consilium*, for the exercise of his office. Jurists generally gave
their counsel orally and in public, in the forum. They did so free of charge.
The great jurists surrounded themselves with a few disciples. During the
early centuries, training as a jurist consisted of little other than following,
listening and, most probably, clerking for an accomplished jurist. In many
cases, the advisory opinion was copied down by the jurist's disciples.

The second activity of the jurists was *agere*, that is, acting. Initially, this
also included pleading before the court, including in the second stage of
the trial. Towards the end of the Republic, this became far less frequent.
Agere was then confined to the *in iure* stage of a legal action. The jurist assisted the litigants and the praetor in the selection of the *actio* and
in drawing up the *formula*. The *apud iudicem* stage was the arena of the
orator-advocate. This stage, which was primarily concerned with the facts
and with persuading the judges of the truth of the matter, turned on oral
argument. It was here, and particularly before the criminal courts such
as the *quaestiones perpetuae*, that the art of oratory reached its apogee in
Rome. Finally, there was *cavere*. This involved drawing up written documents such as documentary evidence, contracts and wills. A number of
jurists developed and published standard models for this purpose.

---

[39] Cicero, *De oratore* 1.212.

78   The jurists of the Late Republic

From all this, it is evident that the Roman jurists were closely involved
with legal practice: they were in the true sense of the word *jurisperiti*,
experienced in the law. They were as much practitioners of law as they
were scholars. They made a major contribution to the further formation
and sophistication of Roman law, and especially of the *ius praetorium*.
Roman jurisprudence was characterised by a major concern for the fairness and reasonableness of the administration of law. The jurists helped
Roman law to transcend its traditional formalism.

Among the great names of early Roman jurisprudence in the late
Republic – the so-called *veteres* or elders – reference must be made
to Sextus Aelius Paetus (consul in 198 BC, censor in 194 BC), Marcus
Porcius Cato the Censor (234–149 BC, consul in 195 BC, censor in 184
BC), Manius Manilius (consul in 148 BC), Publius Mucius Scaevola
(d. 113 BC, consul in 133 BC), the latter's son Quintus Mucius Scaevola
Pontifex Maximus (*c.*140–82 BC, consul in 95 BC), Gaius Aquilius Gallus
(d. before 44 BC, praetor in 66 BC) and Servius Sulpicius Rufus (d. 43 BC,
consul in 51 BC). The most important form of legal literature from that
time was collections of *formulae*, that is, models for legal practice, and
responsa. These writings did not do much for the scientific systematisation of Roman law. They only reported the legal opinions given and the
remedies used in specific cases. But from the start, the jurists contributed
much to the further sophistication and growth of Roman case law in the
context of the procedure *per formulam*.

Even so, early Roman jurisprudence also saw some more systematic
works in which the law was discussed as a whole and in a logical, consistent
order. One example is provided by the eighteen books of Mucius Scaevola
Pontifex Maximus concerning the *ius civile*. While the classification of the
law by Scaevola may have been rudimentary, we need to bear in mind that
someone had to be the first to bring some order into the unordered mass
of historically grown legal remedies. Someone had to be the first to draw
a distinction between persons, property and actions and to establish how
those categories differed from one another. It is uncertain whether even
this threefold classification was in fact recognised by Scaevola.

11   *The influence of Greek philosophy and rhetoric 2*

79   Greek logic and Roman jurisprudence

As opposed to the Romans, the ancient Greeks never developed an
autonomous legal science. Already Cicero was conscious of Roman

superiority in the field of law:

> You will win from legal studies this further joy and delight, that you will most readily understand how far our ancestors surpassed in practical wisdom the men of other nations, if you will compare our own laws with those of Lycurgus, Draco and Solon, among the foreigners. For it is incredible how disordered, and well-nigh absurd, is all municipal law other than our own; on which subject it is my habit to say a great deal in everyday talk, when upholding the wisdom of our own folk against that of all others, the Greeks in particular.[40]

Nevertheless, the first Roman jurists certainly took part of their inspiration from the Greek rhetorical and philosophical traditions. Since the fifth century BC, a debate had been waged between the Greek 'rhetoricians' and 'philosophers' about the place of truth in the rhetorician's discourse. This ongoing battle was reinvigorated in the second century BC. The New or Sceptical Academy, which emerged in Athens during the second century BC and of which Carneades was a member, supported the classical proposition of the sophists: what mattered was not truth but persuasion. But this did not prevent the defenders of the New Academy holding that it was important for a rhetorician to be knowledgeable, at least about his subject if not in more general terms. In addition, the New Academy provided a new stimulus for the study of dialectical logic. Dialectical logic was the common ground on which both rhetoricians and philosophers stood. Of everything the Greeks contributed to Roman scholarship, dialectical logic was of the greatest significance in the emergence of Roman jurisprudence. It reached the Roman elites thanks to their interest in rhetoric. The fact that the oldest jurists were also trained rhetoricians and that the separation into two activities came only later was of major importance for the early development of Roman jurisprudence.

80   Plato

The writings of Plato and Aristotle left a deep mark on numerous Hellenistic rhetoricians and philosophers. Later, the scholastic theologians and philosophers of the Middle Ages highlighted the differences between Plato and Aristotle and underplayed their similarities. The two Greek philosophers came to be seen as the founding fathers of two opposing philosophical traditions: Plato of the rationalist and Aristotle of the empirical. Thereby, it was all too easily overlooked that the ideas of the two great philosophers overlapped to a large extent and that Aristotle,

---

[40] Cicero, *De oratore* 1.197.

who was one of Plato's students, built on the work of his master, particularly as regards dialectical logic. The central ideas of Plato's philosophy –
particularly as it was understood in the Middle Ages – can be found in his
allegory of the cave:

> Picture men dwelling in a sort of subterranean cavern with a long
> entrance open to the light on its entire width. Conceive them as having
> their legs and necks fettered from childhood, so that they remain in the
> same spot, able to look forward only, and prevented by the fetters from
> turning their heads. Picture further the light from a fire burning higher
> up and at a distance behind them, and between the fire and prisoners and
> above them a road along which a low wall has been built, as the exhibitors
> of puppet-shows have partitions before the men themselves, above which
> they show the puppets...
>
> See also, then, men carrying past the wall implements of all kinds that
> rise above the wall, and human images and shapes of animals as well,
> wrought in stone and wood and every material, some of these bearers pre-
> sumably speaking and others silent...
>
> When one was freed from his fetters and compelled to stand up sud-
> denly and turn his head around and walk and to lift up his eyes to the
> light, and in doing all this felt pain and, because of the dazzle and the
> glitter of the light, was unable to discern the object whose shadows he
> formerly saw, what do you suppose would be his answer if someone told
> him that what he had seen before was all a cheat and an illusion, but that
> now, being nearer to reality and turned toward more real things, he saw
> more truly?[41]

For Plato, everything on earth is no more than a shadow, an imperfect
reflection, of what is outside the physical world in the World of Ideas. The
Ideas include general concepts such as goodness and beauty as well as more
concrete ideas such as man, animal or tree. The Ideas are independent
of their material and concrete manifestations. They are general, internal
and immutable concepts which dwell outside the physical world, but are
reflected into it. According to Plato, true knowledge comes from understanding these Ideas. This can best be achieved by a kind of migration of
the soul – metempsychosis – from the physical world to the ideal world. In
Plato's view, the human soul is not of the physical order. It is purely spiritual in nature and is bound up with, but does not form part of, the body
and the physical order. The soul carries with it the memory of another life,
the life in the World of Ideas from which it has tumbled. The soul carries
true understanding with it but is not aware of it. Metempsychosis means

---

[41] Plato, *The Republic* 7.514–15, translation by Paul Shorey, *Plato in Twelve Volumes: The
Republic*, vol. II (Loeb Classical Library 276), Cambridge Mass. and London 1935.

that the soul regains insight into the World of Ideas. Migration is a sudden anamnesis, a sudden remembrance. Similarly, Plato's teacher Socrates taught his pupils that all knowledge was inborn, but was lost at birth and needed to be remembered.[42] True knowledge – of the World of Ideas – is ingrained in man. The study of physical phenomena, of nature, can never yield true understanding. The key to that kind of understanding is to be found not within the confinement of the physical world, but outside of it; not in the physical but in the metaphysical world, with the human spirit forming a gateway between the two worlds. Once one gains insight into the Ideas, it is possible by a process of deduction to arrive at knowledge of the more concrete and earthly manifestations of those Ideas. Rather than, for example, studying all deeds of goodness, one needs properly to understand the Idea of Goodness. That insight enables one to recognise all acts of goodness and distinguish them from other acts. For Plato, not experience but abstract reasoning leads to the understanding of the Ideas, and of the First Idea. Once this is achieved, rational deduction suffices to move from the First Idea to knowing all.

81 Aristotle

Aristotle does not reject the existence of the Ideas as such. For Aristotle, the distinction between the physical and the ideal is not so sharp. His theory of 'hylemorphism' is the cornerstone of his system. Each phenomenon has two dimensions: *hylè* (substance or matter) and *morphè* (form). In the case of a marble statue, the marble is the matter from which it is made, and the image is the form. Even if the well-defined statue disappears, the matter may be lost but the form or image continues to exist as an idea. Each phenomenon has matter and form. But apart from its existing, actual form, each piece of matter also has other, potential forms. A piece of wood may be a tree, a plank or a bench. The matter can be transformed so that it corresponds to one or other potential, ideal form. The forms are to Aristotle what the ideas are to Plato – actually, Aristotle himself referred to *morphè* as *eidos*, idea. They are timeless, general concepts that exist independently of matter and physical reality. Although Aristotle does not have any clear metaphysical framework such as Plato's World of Ideas, he recognises the existence of a higher, abstract reality beyond physical matter. The most perfect form is pure form, which does not require matter. It is pure spirit; it is God.

---

[42] See Plato's dialogue *Meno*. This text was also known to the great Church Fathers.

According to Aristotle, physical phenomena stand not aloof from the higher sphere of form. Each object and each living being carries within it the desire for the perfect form and seeks the actualisation of an ever higher and purer form. It carries within it the potentiality for change and improvement. Where Plato regarded the physical world as a false reflection of higher reality, for Aristotle it was an as yet incomplete realisation of the higher ideas. It is the place where the ideas are transfixed into matter and where each phenomenon seeks to achieve a higher form. Physical reality is continually evolving towards higher forms and, ultimately, God. There is no strict dualism between the physical and the ideal world, but an evolutionary link between the physical and metaphysical realities. Logically, Aristotle attaches greater value to the physical world than Plato did.

For this reason, Aristotle, in contrast to his master, regards the study of physical phenomena as useful and necessary in the quest for true knowledge. By observing physical phenomena, human beings can discern which attributes are common to various things and which distinguish them from one another. It is, for example, possible to discern the essence of the concept of 'tree' in the form of various trees by establishing what is common to all species of tree and what makes them different from bushes or flowers. In various acts of goodness, one needs to discern the general attributes of 'goodness' that make it possible to grasp their 'form'. Translated to a less metaphysical and more practical level, this means that the recognition of common features enables one to formulate general theses until one eventually arrives at the most general and fundamental theses that apply in all circumstances and in all disciplines. The knowledge of what is general is arrived at by induction, by the injection of general rules and categories into the empirical study of the concrete.

82   Science and systematisation

For significant elements of his epistemology, Aristotle was indebted to his teacher, Plato. Aristotle holds that, once the most general rules and categories have been defined, one can discover ever more concrete and more detailed theses by way of deduction. Ultimately, one arrives at the concrete, unique phenomena. With this, Aristotle introduced the ideal of systematisation of the Western scientific tradition. Science consists of ordering all phenomena according to a system of categories which, in turn, consist of subcategories, etc., until one arrives at specific phenomena. A distinction is drawn between *genera* (classes) and *species* (specific phenomena). All classes and phenomena should be named and defined. Science is categorisation and definition.

A scientific discipline is complete when all particular phenomena have been defined and classified into categories and subcategories. Aristotle applies observation and induction as well as abstract and deductive reasoning. According to Aristotelian logic, each concept is defined by (1) summarising all the attributes it shares with other members of the same class or subclass, and (2) describing all the attributes that turn it into a separate subclass or a unique phenomenon. In this way a discipline – whether we are talking about astronomy, zoology, logic itself, politics or law – is transformed into a pyramid of classes, subclasses and concepts within which each piece of data is classified. In his *Topika*, Aristotle applies his epistemology to the process of finding arguments by categorisation and definition. According to Cicero, Aristotle goes a step further than the Stoic thinkers. Cicero accuses them of being solely concerned with assessing existing arguments and of defining their place within the system of all true knowledge. The *Topika* of Aristotle enables the logician to test the validity of his arguments by re-placing them in the wider context of all knowledge.

> Every systematic treatment of argumentation has two branches, one concerned with invention of arguments and the other with the judgment of their validity; Aristotle was the founder of both in my opinion. The Stoics have only worked in the latter of the two fields. That is to say, they have followed diligently the ways of judgment by means of the science which they call dialectic, but they have totally neglected the art which is called topics, an art which is both more useful and certainly prior in the order of nature.[43]

83   Cicero's *topica*

The ideas of Plato and Aristotle were adopted and elaborated by the leading philosophical and rhetorical schools of the Hellenistic period (late fourth to second century BC). During that period, their ideas became applicable to distinct, increasingly autonomous disciplines, such as rhetoric. From the second century BC onwards, the Roman elite became more familiar with Greek thought. Gradually, the Romans entered into the debates on rhetoric and philosophy, and started to write on them.

The works of Cicero acted as a conduit for the dissemination of Greek thought among the Roman elite and provide us with an excellent source for establishing whether and how Greek ideas penetrated in Rome. As a rhetorician and scholar, Cicero drew on both the Greek rhetorical and the

[43] Cicero, *Topica* 6, translation based on H. M. Hubbell, *Cicero: De inventione, De optimo genere, Topica* (Loeb Classical Library 386), Cambridge, Mass. and London 1949.

Platonic-Aristotelian philosophical traditions to construct his theory ˌ logic. Thus he refers on a number of occasions in his works on rhetoric to the theory of dialectics. The prime task for the orator is *inventio*, the search for the right arguments to plead the case. To this end, the orator must make use of the *topica*.

In his *De oratore* or *On the art of oratory*, Cicero defines what according to him – and to Greek tradition – constitutes science. If one wishes to make the law the object of scientific study, the same approach needs to be taken as to other scientific disciplines:

> I see that in my desire to be brief, I have spoken a little obscurely, but I will try to express myself, if I can, in clearer terms. Nearly all elements, now forming the content of arts, were once without order or correlation: in music, for example, rhythms, sounds and measures; in geometry, lines, figures, dimensions and magnitudes; in astronomy, the revolution of the sky, the rising, setting and movement of heavenly bodies; in literature, the study of poets, the learning of histories, the explanation of words and proper intonation in speaking them; and lastly in this very theory of oratory, invention, style, arrangement, memory and delivery, once seemed to all men things unknown and widely separated from one another. And so a certain art was called in from outside, derived from another definite sphere, which philosophers arrogate wholly to themselves, in order that it might give coherence to things so far disconnected and sundered, and bind them in some sort of scheme. Let the goal then of the *ius civile* be defined as the preservation, in the concerns and disputes of citizens, of an impartiality founded on statute and custom. We must next designate the general classes of cases, restricting these to a small fixed number. Now a general class is that which embraces two or more species, resembling one another in some common property while differing in some peculiarity. And species are subdivisions, ranged under those general classes from which they spring; while all names, whether of general classes or of species, must be so defined as to show the significance of each. A definition of course I may describe as a concise and accurate statement of the attributes belonging to the thing we would define.
>
> I would therefore append illustrations to what I have said, were I not mindful of the quality of the hearers of this discourse: as it is, I will briefly summarize my plan. For if I am permitted to do what I have long been projecting, or if someone else anticipates me, preoccupied as I am, or does the work when I am dead, first dividing the entire *ius civile* into its general classes, which are very few, and next distributing what I may call the subdivisions of those classes, and after that making plain by definition the proper significance of each, then you will have a complete art of the *ius civile*, magnificent and copious but neither inaccessible nor mysterious.[44]

---

[44] Cicero, *De oratore* 1.187–90.

, the scientific study of law means the subdivision of the
law into *genera* and *species* and drawing up definitions for
According to Cicero, Servius Sulpicius Rufus's achievement
realising this ambition for the systematisation of the law.
icero was clearly exaggerating in flattering his friend, the pas-
ructive. It shows that according to Cicero, the scientific study
of the law is an application of Greek dialectic logic.

> Scaevola, and many others too, had great practical experience of the *ius
> civile*; [Servius Sulpicius Rufus] alone made of it an art. This he could never
> have attained through knowledge of the law alone had he not acquired in
> addition that art which teaches the analysis of a whole into its component
> parts, sets forth and defines the latent and implicit, interests and makes
> clear the obscure; which first recognizes the ambiguous and then distin-
> guishes; which applies in short a rule or measure for adjudging truth and
> falsehood, for determining what conclusions follow from what premises,
> and what do not. This art, the mistress of all arts, he brought to bear on all
> that had been put together by others without system, whether in the form
> of legal opinions or in actual trials.[45]

84   Roman jurisprudence between systematisation and casuistry

Cicero was, however, overly optimistic. Pouring the mass of Roman law
into the mould of a scientific system turned out to be an enormous challenge that was to occupy European jurists for the better part of two thousand years. Science presupposed the construction of a system of classes,
subclasses and concepts under which a place was assigned to all possible
concrete and unique phenomena. In law, this meant that the scholar
should predict and provide a solution for each possible case that could be
legally distinguished from another. This was, of necessity, a utopia, if only
because of the fact that society was constantly evolving. Furthermore,
the early Roman jurists were grappling with the casuistic and procedural nature of Roman law. The systematisation of the law into classes and
subclasses implied that there were general solutions for general problems
and that there were therefore more general legal concepts and legal rules.
Roman law was, however, a system of legal remedies that had evolved historically in the context of specific legal disputes.

A number of legal scholars from the first century BC and first
and second centuries AD, nevertheless, took some steps towards the

---

[45] Cicero, *Brutus* 152, translation after G.L. Hendrickson, *Cicero: Brutus* (Loeb Classical
Library 342), Cambridge, Mass. and London 1939.

systematisation of Roman law. The subdivision into public and private law became the *summa divisio* of law. In the *Institutiones* of Gaius, written around 160 by an otherwise little-known jurist from the provinces, we find a subdivision of civil law that is at the basis of our modern subdivisions. The *Institutiones* were a concise, systematic overview of the law and acted as an introductory textbook. Gaius followed a classification of civil law that may already have been regarded as classical at that time and that had evolved in the first centuries BC and AD. In the first place, Gaius distinguishes the law of persons, second, the law of property and third, the law of procedure. 'The whole of the law observed by us relates either to persons or to things or to actions.'[46] The law of property covered the law of things, the law of succession and the law of obligations.

The subdivision of the law of obligations into contracts and torts was also already known,[47] but the further subdivision of the branches of civil law remained primitive and incomplete. The jurists of the time saw greater merit in proposing, delineating and defining legal and other concepts such as obligation (*obligatio*), contract (*contractus*) and injury (*iniuria*), together with the introduction and elaboration of more general concepts such as good faith or fairness.

The concern with systematisation was particularly evident among the earlier generations of jurists. Later, during the heyday of Roman jurisprudence, it receded into the background. Then, more than ever, the focus was on casuistry. The jurists classified the mass of concrete legal remedies into larger and smaller categories and developed general concepts and rules helping them to understand, define and substantiate the law somewhat more effectively. But overall, their first concern was to find for each case a solution that could be fitted into the complex of existing law while at the same time being equitable. In that sense, they became caught up with describing and interpreting an ever more vast and sophisticated arsenal of legal remedies and rules.

12   *Classical Roman law*

85   Classical Roman law

The three hundred years between 50 BC and AD 250 – broadly speaking the Principate – marked the age of classical Roman law. The generation of jurists from the reigns of the Emperor Septimius Severus and his dynasty (early third century) marked the absolute high point thereof. The bulk

---

[46] Gaius, *Institutiones* 1.8.   [47] Gaius, *Institutiones* 3.88.

of the *Digest*, the great anthology of Roman jurisprudence compiled in the time of Emperor Justinian, stemmed from this generation. As the law of the Principate is referred to as classical Roman law, that of the Late Republic can be referred to as pre-classical Roman law, and that of the Dominate as post-classical Roman law.

Periodisation of the history of ancient Roman law

Regal Period and Early Republic	archaic Roman law
Late Republic	pre-classical Roman law
Principate	classical Roman law
Dominate	post-classical Roman law

At the start of the Principate, the praetor's edict had by and large reached its definitive form. Only a few further *formulae* were added. The development of new rules under the *ius honorarium* slowly came to an end. Around AD 130, Emperor Hadrian instructed the jurist Publius Salvius Julianus (d. 170/180) to record and fix the praetorian edict. It may be that Julian did not confine himself to the edict of the urban praetor but also examined those of the peregrine praetor and the aediles. At any event, Hadrian ordained that Julian's edict should apply for all time. It is referred to as the *edictum perpetuum* or perpetual edict. The decision by Hadrian was less radical than it might appear at first sight. The evolution of the praetorian edict had as good as come to a halt a century before and the praetors had long lost much of their role in the formation of new law.

Under the Principate, the role of the praetors in the renewal and modification of the law was taken over by the great jurists. To a greater extent than before, they concentrated on providing their expert opinions – *responsa* – in specific cases. In contrast to earlier practice, these opinions were now issued in writing and under seal. The leading jurists published their opinions in collections of *responsa*.

86   The emperor and Roman jurisprudence

It was the jurists of the classical age who brought Roman law to its highest peaks. They introduced new models for legal practice and, through an extensive interpretation of the existing legal remedies, allowed a broader and more refined application of the law. Under the early Principate, the emperors awarded certain jurists the *ius publice respondendi ex auctoritate principis*, literally the right to respond under the authority of the *princeps*. Whether this privilege had already been assigned by Augustus or whether it was introduced by his successor Tiberius (AD 14–38) is subject to debate. It has also been alleged that the assignment of the *ius respondendi* meant that only those jurists who enjoyed this privilege were permitted to issue opinions. This appears unlikely. In fact, the opinions of the jurists holding the *ius respondendi*, formally speaking, held no more authority than those of other legal scholars. After all, the emperorship was not yet an official position so that the *ius respondendi* could not be official in nature. In practice, however, the opinions were generally followed by praetors and judges.

In awarding this privilege, the emperors may have aspired not so much at influencing jurisprudence as at reclaiming it for themselves. By granting the privilege to the most authoritative experts, the emperors found favour with these individuals and managed to associate themselves with their opinions. The later jurists Gaius and Papinian maintained that the scholars' opinions were binding if they concurred. According to some Romanists, Emperor Hadrian put an end to the custom of granting the *ius respondendi*. They claimed that Hadrian began issuing legal opinions himself by means of *rescripta*. Whether or not this is true is unclear. What is clear is that later emperors, including the Septimii Severi, often issued opinions. The *rescripta* were imperial letters in answer to a question submitted to the emperor by a citizen. The jurists who drew up these *rescripta* for the emperor now became civil servants in the emperor's pay.

Like their predecessors, the jurists of the early Principate were generally drawn from the ranks of the Senate. From the second century onwards, many jurists worked for the imperial civil service. Of these, many came from the equestrian order. At the high point of Roman law, around AD 200, a certain competition arose between the jurists from the imperial offices who drew up *rescripta* for the emperor and independent, senatorial jurists who, as in the past, issued *responsa* on their own initiative. The downfall and loss of autonomy of the Senate led to the loss of a tradition of jurisprudence that was independent of the emperor. After 250, Roman jurisprudence was past its peak.

The absolute torchbearers of Roman jurisprudence lived and worked around AD 200. They all made major careers in the service of Emperor Septimius Severus and his immediate successors. The fact that two of them, Papinian and Ulpian, were liquidated by their political enemies is a clear indication of their political importance. Their legal significance is evident from the scale and lasting fame of their output. Aemilius Papinianus was a contemporary of Emperor Septimius Severus, of whom he was also a confidant. From 205 to 211, Papinian was *praefectus praetorio*, a kind of prime minister. Before then, he carried responsibility, as secretary *a libellis*, for the imperial correspondence. Julius Paulus and Domitius Ulpianus (d. 223/4) also worked for the Severi. Both achieved the rank of *praefectus praetorio*. The last of the great classical jurists to whom reference should be made is Herennius Modestinus, who was *praefectus vigilum* or commander of the city cohorts of Rome. His death around 250 marks the end of the classical age of Roman law.

87 Literary production

Foremost among the scholarly literary production of the Principate were the *responsa* collections of individual jurists. The expert opinions contained in the *responsa* were classified according to one of two customary systems. One was to follow the classification that had been designed for the *ius civile*: law of succession, law of persons, law of obligations and property law. Alternatively, the rather more complex sequence of the praetorian edict would be followed. This second classification covered the rules of both the *ius civile* and the *ius honorarium*. After that, legal questions relating to statute law, senatorial decisions and the imperial constitutions were covered, once again in a fixed order. Among the *responsa* collections, the *Digesta* or *Pandectae* occupied a special place. These were anthologies from the advisory opinions of a single author. The *Digesta* of Julian constitutes one of the best-known examples.

Apart from these collections and anthologies of *responsa*, reference should be made to the great commentaries. In these, the author commented on a particular legal source: the edict, a statute law or a Senate decision. He respected the sequence of the text and did not opt in favour of a more systematic or logical sequence. Great jurists such as Sextus Pomponius (second century AD), Ulpian and Papinian wrote elaborate commentaries on the edict of the praetors. Gaius authored a commentary on the provincial edict, that is, the model edict applied by the provincial governors in their jurisdictions. Similarly, the works on the *ius civile* by two older legal scholars, especially the *Iuris civilis libri XVIII* by Quintus Mucius Scaevola Pontifex Maximus and the *Iuris civilis libri III* by Massurius Sabinus (first century AD), were the subject of commentaries. Pomponius, Paul and Ulpian all wrote a commentary *ad Sabinum*.

Reference has already been made to short textbooks, namely *Institutiones* or *Institutes*. This was the leading genre in which systemisation was given precedence over casuistry. Of these introductions, only the second-century AD *Institutiones* of Gaius survives. Although Gaius was a comparatively unimportant jurist in his own age, his short work gained considerable success during the Dominate. When jurisprudence had passed its peak, Gaius's concise and intelligible work found particular favour. The development of the genre makes it clear that legal instruction was also evolving. This training was no longer restricted to clerking for a particular jurist. During the course of the second century, a genuine law school arose in Rome, while in the third century a similar school emerged in Beirut. Later schools were added in Carthage, Alexandria, Caesarea, Athens and Constantinople (425). The training lasted approximately five years. To begin with, the *Institutiones* of Gaius would be studied, followed by the *responsa* collections. The course was completed by a study of imperial legislation.

Differentiae (differentiations), *Definitiones* (definitions) and *Regulae* (rules) were short collections of legal rules and concepts. Monographs, in which one particular legal subject was handled exhaustively, were rare.

Compared with that of the Principate, the literary output of the Dominate is modest. Most important and abundant were adaptations from collections of *responsa* and *rescripta* by the classical jurists. These were intended for both teaching and practice. In itself, this literature exemplifies the decline of Roman jurisprudence: the work of the great predecessors was studied and re-edited. Equally indicative of this decline were the so-called *epitomae* and the *compilationes*. Once again, these were based on the works of jurists from the classical age. An *epitome* was an anthology of fragments from the works of one or more jurists. The most famous are the *Sententiae* of Paul and the *Epitome* of Ulpian. A *compilatio* (compilation) also contained elements of imperial legislation. These were handy books designed to make the most important legal rules and opinions accessible. The *Fragmenta Vaticana*, a fragment from such a compilation discovered in 1821, contained excerpts from both scholarship and imperial legislation. Classical law had become too rich, too complex and too sizeable for the legal practitioners and scholars of the Dominate.

13   The cognitio extraordinaria

88   Imperial courts and procedure

Under the Principate, a new civil procedure emerged: the *cognitio extraordinaria*. In truth, the term refers to a series of procedures which share some common features. The *cognitio extraordinaria* was a one-stage trial. The judge, who heard the case as well as rendered judgment, was an imperial official.

The new procedure first emerged in the provinces. The *iurisdictio* for disputes between Roman citizens in conquered territories belonged to the representative of Rome, the Roman magistrate or pro-magistrate present there acting as governor, or his deputies. In principle, their role was the same as that of the praetor in Rome. But because it was often hard to find enough Roman citizens to act as jurors, the provincial governors and their deputies quite quickly took it upon themselves to render judgment. In criminal cases, this was customary even from the beginning. Because of this, the distinction between the two stages of the trial faded and disappeared. The governor or his deputy selected the applicable *formula*, heard the case and rendered judgment.

When Emperor Augustus won the *imperium* over numerous provinces, he delegated his powers of jurisdiction to officials acting on his behalf. From then onwards, single-stage proceedings became more general, also in civil cases. Later, the new arrangement spread from the imperial provinces to the senatorial provinces, to Italy and, finally, in the third century, to Rome. There it was used side by side with the old procedure *per formulam* until this was abolished in 342. The imperial judges applied the same law and the same actions and *formulae* as the praetors.

The *cognitio extraordinaria* was applicable to both criminal and civil cases. Under the new procedure, the judge had a much more active role than the praetor and the judges had played under the old procedure. The judge could if necessary summon the defendant himself; judgment by default was possible. In contrast to the lay jurors from the second stage of the old procedure *per formulam*, the judges, as officials representing the emperor, were vested with public authority. The concurrence of the parties with the proceedings lost its relevance. In practice, litigation had for some time no longer presupposed the voluntary submission of the dispute by both parties to the court, but now the final traces of those distant origins disappeared. Criminal prosecution increasingly became a concern of the state, taken into hand by state officials. The judge also gained the authority to order investigatory actions. The criminal trial became inquisitorial instead of accusatorial. On the other hand, the right of each Roman citizen to prosecute crimes was curbed; only the victims of a crime could bring a case to court. With the *cognitio extraordinaria* also came the right to higher appeal. The fact that the judge was a civil servant meant that it was always possible to appeal to his hierarchical superior and, ultimately, to the highest of them all, the emperor himself.

14   Imperial legislation and the first codifications

89   Imperial legislation

Under the Principate, the popular assemblies, including the *concilium plebis*, lost their control over the legislative process. Although formally they retained legislative power, they had in fact become rubber stamps for the emperor's proposals. Gradually, they were convened less frequently. Although strictly speaking, the Senate decisions were merely advisory opinions, already in the final decades of the Republic, it increasingly happened that Senate decisions were not submitted to the popular assemblies but were applied immediately. In the first century AD, this practice became more widespread. During the second century, legislative activity was largely confined to the Senate. The jurists of the second and third centuries accepted that the *senatusconsulta* had force of law. Thus Papinian included Senate decisions alongside statute laws, plebiscites, imperial decisions and opinions of the jurists among the sources of the *ius civile*.[48] In reality, most Senate decisions were introduced by the emperor. The emperor's proposal, which the emperor read out (or had read out) in his *oratio*, was generally adopted as it stood. Many jurists quoted the text of the imperial *oratio* in their works as though this were the Senate's decision itself. In this way, the legislative power shifted from the Senate to the emperor. The evolution was completed in the third century.

In the earlier days of the Principate, the emperors did not have any legislative power as such. Like any magistrate, however, they could promulgate *edicta* (edicts) and *mandata* (mandates). Edicts contained general rules, while mandates were a kind of circular with concrete instructions for subordinate officials. The emperor was frequently asked for a legal opinion. The imperial civil service would reply in the form of a *rescriptum* (rescript) which, strictly speaking, was addressed only to the inquirer but in practice was generally applied. Similarly, the judgments or *decreta* (decrees) handed down by the emperor or his authorised representatives were in practice *erga omnes* precedents and enjoyed force of law. As the emperorship became more firmly established, these four forms of imperial decisions came to be regarded as genuine statute laws. During the third century, they became the sole form of statute law, making the emperor's monopoly over the legislation a fact. The four types of imperial legislation were given the collective name *constitutiones* (constitutions).

---

[48]   D. 1.1.7. See also Pomponius D. 1.2.2.12 and Gaius, *Institutiones* 1.2.

The imperial age saw an increase in legislative activity. Although, during the Principate, statute law was mainly concerned with matters of criminal, religious and public law, important inroads into private law, particularly in the fields of family and property law, were made. Once the great font of the jurists' creativity had dried up halfway through the third century, imperial legislation became the primary source of law. The *edicta*, now also known as *leges generales* (general laws), drove the other three types of imperial legislation into the background during that period.

During the Dominate, imperial legislation was by far the most important source of law. The decline of customary law, case law and jurisprudence as legal sources was related to the transformation of Rome from an aristocratic republic into a military and bureaucratic dictatorship. Legislation became the most suitable instrument for the central government to intervene directly in society and impose a uniform system of law on the entire empire.

90   Early codifications and the Law of Citations

The increase in the mass of imperial legislation made it necessary to publish these laws in major collections or compilations. As early as the third century, some jurists included important *rescripta* in their *responsa* collections. The decline of independent *responsa* in favour of the imperial *rescripta* created the need for a new form of compilations. The earliest examples of compilations of imperial constitutions were the *Codex Gregorianus* (291) and the *Codex Hermogenianus* (295), both named after their compilers.[49] The *Codex Gregorianus* was a collection of constitutions, starting from the reign of Hadrian. The constitutions followed the same traditional thematic ordering as the digests. The *codex Hermogenianus* contained mostly constitutions from the years 293 and 294 and was classified chronologically. Like the old *responsa* collections, these *codices* were the product of private initiatives; they were not compiled on instruction by the emperor. It is, however, more than likely that the authors were imperial civil servants.

During the fourth century, the call to enhance the clarity and accessibility of the law became ever louder. The number of *responsa* and *rescripta* was huge. Many were mutually contradictory and there was often doubt as to what should and should not be regarded as authoritative. The judges, administrators and citizens in Italy and the provinces needed a more

---

[49] They are called *codex* rather than *liber* since these were no longer scrolls but bound books as we still have to the present day.

straightforward and clear-cut system of law that provided greater certainty and a clearer frame of reference. The transformation of the Roman Empire from a loose structure to a more integrated empire administered by a central bureaucracy called for more legal unity. The emperors of the Dominate took initiatives themselves to compile the law and to establish what they considered to be authoritative sources of law. They also wanted to bring the huge legacy of classical jurists within their orbit.

Emperor Constantine was the first to promulgate legislation granting formal authority to certain works by classical jurists while imposing a prohibition on the use of other works (321). A hundred years later, in 426, the Eastern Roman emperor Theodosius II (408–50) and Western Roman emperor Valentinianus III (425–55) jointly promulgated the Law of Citations. This statute stipulated that only the works of Papinian, Ulpian, Paul, Modestinus and Gaius could be quoted in the context of a legal dispute and that only they had force of law. In the event of disagreement among those who had written something concerning a certain point of law, the majority opinion would prevail. In the case of a tie, Papinian's opinion would be decisive. If he did not have a relevant opinion on the subject, the judge would be at liberty to choose from the various propositions. By means of these rules, the emperors sought to inject order into the mass of scholarly opinions. At the same time they confiscated the body of private jurisprudence and made it their own.

The same emperors also issued instruction in 429 for the compilation of a code which, in addition to the two existing *codices*, would also contain the *leges generales* since Constantine, as well as the most important texts of the classical scholars. This ambitious plan was abandoned in 435 and it was decided to confine matters to the collection of the imperial constitutions since the time of Constantine. The book was completed in 438 and is known as the *Codex Theodosianus*. The *Codex* was divided into sixteen chapters, in turn subdivided into thematic titles. The laws were chronologically arranged within each title. The code primarily contained rules of public law.

15   The codification of Emperor Justinian

91   Justinian's first Code

The Eastern Roman emperor Justinian (527–65) sought further codification of Roman law. As early as 528, he appointed a commission to draw up a new collection of imperial constitutions. The strongman on the ten-member commission was Tribonian, from 530 onwards *secretarius sacri palatii.* The commission was ordered to make a complete collection of imperial legislation that would not merely supplement but replace the existing codes.

The work was completed by the following year. The speed with which the commission worked was, among other things, a result of the fact that collections had been made for teaching purposes in the law schools of Constantinople and Beirut. The new code was more than just a collection. The term compilation – from *compilare*: to plunder – is appropriate. The commission had been given the power to select from the existing laws, to resolve discrepancies and even to change laws. The code was divided into twelve books and further subdivided into titles according to the system of the Perpetual Edict. The *Codex Justinianus*, also known as *Codex vetus* or Old Code, was promulgated in 529 and was to be replaced as early as 534. The text has been lost.

92   *Digesta* and *Institutes*

Justinian did not limit himself to the codification of imperial legislation. He also had the literature of the classical jurists codified. In 530, he instructed Tribonian to draw up an anthology from the entire legacy of the Roman jurists. Tribonian was allowed to appoint a commission himself. This was granted extensive powers. It was not just to make selections but was also to resolve discrepancies and to amend texts:

> We therefore command you to read and work upon the books dealing with Roman law, written by those learned men of old to whom the most revered emperors gave authority to compose and interpret the laws, so that the whole substance may be extracted from them, all repetition and discrepancy being as far as possible removed, and out of them one single work may be compiled, which will suffice in place of them all. Others too have written books dealing with the law whose writings have not been received or used by any later authors, but we do not regard these works as being worthy of intruding upon our ordinance.[50]

It was particularly fortunate that the emperor ordered that the name of the jurists and the work from which it had been drawn be placed above each excerpt; most of the texts of the great Roman legal scholars were preserved only in the Justinian collection. The work, the *Digesta*, was divided into fifty books and further subdivided into titles. The order of the *Codex*, which went back to the praetor's edict, was maintained. This sequence was partly logical but was also, to a significant extent, the result of historical

---

[50]   *Constitutio Deo auctore* 4.

tradition. The *Digesta* made little headway towards the further systematisation of the Roman legal heritage.

The *Digesta* – also known as *Pandectae* – were promulgated as early
as 533. The book had force of law. The selected passages from the works
of generations of legal scholars were consequently invested with statutory authority. Justinian, moreover, forbade other scholarly opinions
not contained in his *Digesta* from being cited in court. According to the
promulgation act, the collection comprised some 150,000 lines, while the
commission had read three million lines in 2,000 scrolls. In total, excerpts
from the works of thirty-nine jurists have been preserved, of which texts
written by Ulpian account for about 40 per cent.

Justinian's purpose was to inject order into the large and unwieldy
mass of Roman jurisprudence. But he went further: he forbade anyone
from adding commentaries on or interpretations of the *Digesta* in the
future. In doing so, he tried to freeze jurisprudence in a similar to way to
that in which Hadrian had frozen the evolution of praetorian law by laying down the edict. The interpretation of the law was a prerogative of the
emperor himself:

> We command that our complete work, which is to be composed by you with
> God's approval, is to bear the name of the *Digest* or *Pandekts*. No skilled
> lawyers are to presume in the future to supply any commentaries thereon
> and confuse with their own verbosity the brevity of the aforesaid work ...[51]
>
> ... that no one, of those who are skilled in the law at the present day
> or shall be hereafter, may dare to append any commentary to these laws,
> save only insofar as he may wish to translate them into the Greek lan-
> guage in the same order and sequence as those in which the Roman words
> are written (*kata poda*, as the Greeks call it); and if perhaps he prefers
> to make notes on difficulties in certain passages, he may also compose
> what are called *paratitla*. But we do not permit them to put forward other
> interpretations – or rather, perversions – of the laws, for fear lest their
> verbosity may cause such confusion in our legislation as to bring some
> discredit upon it. This happened also in the case of the commentators on
> the Perpetual Edict, who, although the compass of that work was moder-
> ate, extended it this way and that to diverse conclusions and drew it out to
> an inordinate length, in such a way as to bring almost the whole Roman
> legal system into confusion. If we have not put up with them, how far
> can vain disputes be allowed in the future? If any should presume to do
> such a thing, they themselves are to be made subject to a charge of fraud,
> and moreover their books are to be destroyed. But if, as we said before,
> anything should appear doubtful, this is to be referred by judges to the

[51] *Constitutio Deo auctore* 12.

very summit of the empire and made clear by the imperial authority, to which alone it is granted both to create laws and to interpret them.[52]

Hereby, Emperor Justinian affirmed himself as the sole legislator, the sole source of law in his empire.

Apart from the codification of statute law and jurisprudence, Justinian took yet another step. In 533, following the example of the old *Institutiones*, Justinian had an introductory textbook on Roman law drawn up for teaching purposes. The *Institutes* of Justinian owed a great debt to those of Gaius. The three-way classification into persons, things and legal actions and the division into four books were also retained, although the four books were now systematically subdivided into paragraphs.

93   Justinian's second *Codex* and the *Novellae*

After the promulgation of the *Digest* and the *Institutes*, Justinian had the *Codex* revised. Since 530, many new laws had been issued, particularly in connection with the codification of the *Digest* and the *Institutes*. The new *Codex* was ready as early as 534. A great many laws disappeared from the new code, while there were all sorts of supplements and amendments. Like the old code, the new one consisted of twelve books. Book 1 concerned religion and the church as well as some major constitutional and procedural matters, books 2 to 8 private law, books 9 to 12 public law. The further subdivision into titles followed that of the *Codex vetus*. The collection contained no fewer than 4,600 laws, of which the oldest dated to the time of Hadrian. Four hundred of these dated from the reign of Justinian himself, which says something about the proliferation of legislation.

Justinian was unable to undertake further codification of the legislation that he himself promulgated after 535. A considerable number of his constitutions concerned family law and succession law. There were various private collections, the so-called *Novellae Constitutiones* or new laws. The most important of these official collections were the *Authenticum*, which comprised 134 constitutions, and the *Collectio Graeca* containing 168 constitutions of Justinian and his immediate successors. The latter has been used, since the sixteenth century, as the foundation for what became known as the fourth part of Justinian's codification, the *Novellae*.

94   The *Corpus Iuris Civilis*

Justinian's legislative efforts may be regarded as a genuine codification. His ambition consisted of collecting and sifting the entire amalgam of

---

[52] *Constitutio tanta* 21.

legislation, case law and jurisprudence and replacing it with one great collection. Anything that did not appear in his new collection was abolished. The Justinian collection was the only source of law. It laid claims to exclusivity and completeness. What Justinian did not aspire to was a far-reaching renewal of the law. Substantively, the work was confined to the collection, selection and at most harmonisation and improvement of existing law. Justinian's codification explicitly built on a millennium of legal tradition. It was a reorganisation of Roman law, not a radical reform.

In terms of later legal development, the Justinian collection acted as a conduit for transmitting the achievements of one thousand years of legal development to later generations. The rediscovery of the Justinian *Digest* in the eleventh century sparked off the advent of legal science in western Europe. In the sixteenth century, the Justinian codification was given the name *Corpus Iuris Civilis*. The *Corpus* consisted of, in the following order, the *Institutiones, Digesta, Codex* and *Novellae*.

16 Suum cuique tribuere

95 Casuistry

Few of the works of the great jurists of the classical age have been preserved in their original form. Thanks to the *Digest*, however, we have thousands of excerpts from the *responsa* collections, commentaries and other writings of the classical jurists. The *responsa* stand out for their conciseness. In a few words, the jurist would outline the case and put forward a legal solution by indicating the legal remedy which he considered to be applicable. The argumentation as to why the application of a particular legal remedy had been decided upon generally remained sketchy in the extreme and was often not spelt out at all. The principle, rule or reasoning on which the opinion rested was only implied but not expressed; it can be reconstructed only through a close analysis of the circumstances of the case and wordings of the opinion. This shows that it was not the force of argument but the name and reputation of the jurist that were decisive for the authority assigned to an opinion.

Above all, however, this approach is illustrative of the particular nature of Roman law and jurisprudence. The great classical jurists were not system-builders. Their prime concern was not to forge the mass of legal rules into a logical and consistent system of general principles, doctrines and specific rules under which the solution to each particular case would be dictated by its position within the whole. Roman jurisprudence involved an ever more refined distinction of specific cases, with ever more detailed and fine-tuned legal remedies and rules. The aim of jurisprudence was the same as that of legal practice: *suum cuique tribuere*, that is, giving each his due.[53]

Inevitably, the casuistic character of Roman law and jurisprudence, in combination with the scholarly tradition of the *topica* to which the jurists were necessarily indebted, did not prevent the articulation of general principles, rules and concepts. This was done by means of induction. The articulation and definition of the *genera* – the groupings and classes – were the consequence of a growing awareness of their existence that followed from and did not precede the drawing up of new legal remedies. If a Roman jurist had to counsel on a new case, he would seek to find, adapt or draw up a legal remedy for that case. During this process, it would sometimes happen that a new principle, a new rule or a new causality linking the case to the legal remedy was 'discovered'. In this regard, the principle, rule or causality was – at least at the conscious level – the product and not the cause of the solution to the case.

96   Lex Aquilia

Title 9.2 of the *Digest* on tort law provides a number of *responsa* that illustrate this well. In Chapter 1 of the *Lex Aquilia* it was laid down that anyone who killed another person's slave or a four-footed animal belonging to the cattle family was required to reimburse the owner for the highest value of the slave or the animal over the past year. In his commentary on the edict, Ulpian quotes the following case:

> Thus, if someone does damage through being pushed by somebody else, Proculus writes that neither is liable under the *lex*; the one who pushed is not liable because he did not kill, nor is the one who was pushed because he did not do the damage unlawfully. According to this view, an *actio in factum* will be given against the one who pushed.[54]

The question underlying the case was whether pushing one person on to another and thus killing a third person fell within the meaning of the word *occidere* (to kill) from the *Lex Aquilia*. If that was not the case, the praetor could permit an *actio in factum*. The distinction between direct and indirect causation is not explicitly drawn here, but to the modern

---

[53] 'Iuris praecepta haec sunt: honeste vivere, alterum non laedere, suum cuique tribuere': D. 1.1.10 ('The basic principles of right are: to live honourably, not to harm any other person, to render to each his own').

[54] D. 9.2.7.3.

lawyer, as it did to some Roman lawyers, it would logically constitute the underlying question.

The distinction between fault or negligence (*culpa*) and malice (*dolus*) is reflected in a number of cases. The following example – once again a fragment from Ulpian's commentary on the edict – is often quoted:

> Ulpian, *Edict, book 18*. Julian also put this case: A shoemaker, he says, struck with a last at the neck of a boy (a freeborn youngster) who was learning under him, because he had done badly what he had been teaching him with the result that the boy's eye was knocked out. On such facts, says Julian, the action for insult does not lie because he struck him not with intent to insult, but in order to correct and teach him; he wonders whether there is an action for breach of the contract for his services as a teacher, since a teacher only has the right to administer reasonable chastisement, but I have no doubt that action can be brought against him under the *Lex Aquilia*.[55]

From other examples, we know that the 'unlawful killing or damage' – a requirement for the application of the *Lex Aquilia* – presumed fault (*culpa*).

> Paul, *Sabinus, book 10*. If a pruner threw down a branch from a tree and killed a slave passing underneath (the same applies to a man working on a scaffold), he is liable only if it falls down in a public place and he failed to shout a warning so that the accident could be avoided. But Mucius [Scaevola] says that even if the accident occurred in a private place, an action can be brought if his conduct is blameworthy; and he thinks there is fault when what could have been foreseen by a diligent man was not foreseen or when a warning was shouted too late for the danger to be avoided …[56]

From the case of the shoemaker it is evident that *culpa* needs to be conceptually distinguished from *dolus*. Whereas *dolus* means that a person wishes to inflict harm through his actions, *culpa* only means that the condemned deed can be assigned to the perpetrator, for example because the latter acted carelessly, but without the intention to do damage. *Culpa* refers to the imputability of the action; *dolus* to the object of causing damage or death.

97   The *Digest* and European jurisprudence

For a contemporary jurist the juridical rules, concepts and reasonings underlying the *responsa* will be rather easy to discern. But in the case of

---

[55] D. 9.2.5.3.   [56] D. 9.2.31.

these and other examples, it needs to be borne in mind that the Roman jurists drew such distinctions for the first time and that they did so because they were confronted by a case compelling them to do so. It is in the ongoing 'discovery' and use of new legal rules, distinctions and institutes that the Roman legal genius lies. In this regard, the jurist was concerned not with elaborating and formulating a doctrine of causality or of fault but only with the practical applications. Theory was only developed in so far as required for the specific case.

Thus, in the *Digest*, the Romans left behind a treasure hoard of concrete cases and sophisticated legal solutions that shrouded the underlying general principles, rules and concepts. Later jurists would find them there, but it was still up to them to formulate a consistent doctrine of law. From the rediscovery of the *Digest* in the late eleventh century onwards, European jurists would examine the enormous anthology of Roman jurisprudence for hundreds of years in what seems a perpetual intellectual treasure hunt. From the multiplicity of material left behind by the Romans, European jurists managed to construct a consistent system of private law. This process of just less than a thousand years forms the scarlet thread running through European legal history from the eleventh century onwards.

Further reading

1. On early and Republican Roman history: M. Crawford, *The Roman Republic*, 2nd edn, London 1992; G. Forsythe, *A Critical History of Early Rome: From Prehistory to the First Punic War*, Berkeley, Los Angeles and London 2005; M. Grant, *The History of Rome*, London 2002; R. E. Mitchell, *Patricians and Plebeians: The Origin of the Roman State*, Ithaca 1990; T. Mommsen, *Römische Geschichte*, 3 vols., Leipzig 1854–6 (available as *The History of Rome*, London and New York 1996); H. H. Scullard, *A History of the Roman World, 753 to 146 BC*, 6th edn, London 2002.

2. On Greek civilisation, rhetoric and philosophy and their impact on Rome: C. Freeman, *The Greek Achievement: the Foundation of the Western World*, New York and London 1999; E. S. Gruen, *The Hellenistic World and the Coming of Rome*, Berkeley 1984; Gruen, *Studies in Greek Culture and Roman Politics*, Leyden 1990; Gruen, *Culture and National Identity in Republican Rome*, Ithaca 1992; W. C. K. Guthrie, *History of Greek Philosophy*, 6 vols., Cambridge 1962–83; A. A. Long, *Hellenistic Philosophy: Stoics, Epicureans, Sceptics*, London 1974; C. Rowe and M. Schofield, eds., *The Cambridge History of Greek and Roman Political Thought*, Cambridge 2000.

3. On the Age of Revolution (first century BC): P. A. Brunt, *The Fall of the Roman Republic and Related Essays*, Oxford 1988; A. Everitt, *Cicero: a Turbulent Life*,

London 2001; A. Goldsworthy, *Caesar: the Life of a Colossus*, London 2006; E. S. Gruen, *The Last Generation of the Roman Republic*, Berkeley 1974; T. Holland, *Rubicon: the Triumph and Tragedy of the Roman Republic*, London 2003; A. Keaveney, *Sulla: the Last Republican*, 2nd edn, London and New York 2005; A. Lintott, *Judicial Reform and Land Reform in the Roman Republic*, Cambridge 1993; T. N. Mitchell, *Cicero: the Ascending Years*, New Haven and London 1979; Mitchell, *Cicero: the Senior Statesman*, New Haven and London 1991; Josiah Osgood, *Caesar's Legacy: Civil War and the Emergence of the Roman Empire*, Cambridge 2006; H. H. Scullard, *From the Gracchi to Nero: a History of Rome from 133 BC to AD 68*, 4th edn, London 1980; R. Seager, *Pompey the Great: a Political Biography*, 2nd edn, Oxford and Malden 2002; D. Shotter, *The Fall of the Roman Republic*, London and New York 1994; R. Syme, *The Roman Revolution*, Oxford 1939.

4. On Augustus and his government: A. Everitt, *The First Emperor: Caesar Augustus and the Triumph of Rome*, London 2006; P. Southern, *Augustus*, London and New York 1998.

5. On imperial history: A. R. Birley, *Septimius Severus: the African Emperor*, London 1971; Birley, *Hadrian: the Restless Emperor*, London 1997; J. Carcopino, *Daily Life in Ancient Rome: the People and the City at the Height of the Empire*, London 1991; M. Goodman, *Rome and Jerusalem: the Clash of Ancient Civilizations*, London 2007; M. Grant, *The Roman Emperors: a Biographical Guide to the Rulers of Imperial Rome, 31 BC–476 AD*, New York 1985; C. Wells, *The Roman Empire*, 2nd edn, London 1992.

6. On Roman expansion and imperial strategy: E. Badian, *Roman Imperialism in the Late Republic*, 2nd edn, Ithaca 1968; A. M. Eckstein, *Mediterranean Anarchy, Interstate War and the Rise of Rome*, Berkeley, Los Angeles and London 2006; W. V. Harris, *War and Imperialism in Republican Rome, 327–70 BC*, 2nd edn, Oxford 2000; R. Kallet-Marx, *Hegemony or Empire: the Development of the Roman* Imperium *in the East from 148 to 62 BC*, Berkeley, Los Angeles and Oxford 1995; E. N. Luttwak, *The Grand Strategy of the Roman Empire: From the First Century AD to the Third*, Baltimore and London 1976; S. P. Mattern, *Rome and the Enemy: Imperial Strategy in the Principate*, Berkeley, Los Angeles and London 1999.

7. On the late empire and the fall of the Western Roman Empire: P. Brown, *The World of Late Antiquity: From Marcus Aurelius to Muhammad*, London 1971; T. S. Burns, *Rome and the Barbarians, 100 BC–AD 400*, Baltimore and London 2003; A. Cameron, *The Later Roman Empire*, London 1993; S. Corcoran, *The Empire of the Tetrarchs*, Oxford 1996; J. A. S. Evans, *The Age of Justinian: the Circumstances of Imperial Power*, London and New York 1996; P. Garnsey and C. Humfress, *The Evolution of the Late Antique World*, Cambridge 2001; E. Gibbon, *Decline and Fall of the Roman Empire* (1776–8), Everyman's Library edn, 6 vols., London 1910; W. Goffart, *Barbarians and Romans, AD 418–584: the*

Techniques of Accommodation, Princeton 1980; P. Heather, *The Fall of the Roman Empire: New History of Rome and the Barbarians*, London 2005; A. H. M. Jones, *The Later Roman Empire: a Social, Economic and Administrative Survey*, 3 vols., Oxford 1964; N. Lenski, *Failure of Empire: Valens and the Roman State in the Fourth Century AD*, Berkeley 2002; P. Mitchell, *A History of the Later Roman Empire, AD 284–641: the Transformation of the Ancient World*, London and Malden 2006; J. Moorhead, *Justinian*, London 1994; Moorhead, *The Roman Empire Divided, 400–700*, Harlow 2001; W. Pohl, ed., *Kingdoms of the Empire: the Integration of Barbarians in Late Antiquity*, Leyden, New York and Cologne 1997; B. Ward-Perkins, *The Fall of Rome and the End of Civilization*, Oxford 2005; S. Williams, *Diocletian and the Roman Recovery*, London 1985; S. Williams and G. Friell, *The Rome that Did Not Fall: the Survival of the East in the Fifth Century*, London and New York 1999.

8. On the rise of Christianity: P. Brown, *Authority and the Sacred: Aspects of the Christianisation of the Roman World*, 2nd edn, Cambridge 2002; Brown, *The Rise of Western Christendom: Triumph and Diversity, AD 200–1000*, 2nd edn, Oxford 2003; H. Chadwick, *The Church in Ancient Society: From Galilee to Gregory the Great*, Oxford 2001; C. Freeman, *The Closing of the Western Mind: the Rise of Faith and the Fall of Reason*, London 2002; R. Lane Fox, *Pagans and Christians in the Mediterranean World from the Second Century AD to the Conversion of Constantine*, London 1986.

9. On the history of Roman law: J. Harries, *Law and Empire in Late Antiquity*, Cambridge 1999; H. F. Jolowicz and B. Nicholas, *Historical Introduction to the Study of Roman Law*, 3rd edn, Cambridge 1972; M. Kaser, *Römische Rechtsgeschichte*, 2nd edn, Göttingen 1976; W. Kunkel, *Römische Rechtsgeschichte*, 14th edn, Cologne 2005 (available in an older version as *An Introduction to Roman Legal and Constitutional History*, Oxford 1966); G. Mousourakis, *The Historical and Institutional Context of Roman Law*, Aldershot 2003; O. F. Robinson, *The Sources of Roman Law: Problems and Methods for Ancient Historians*, London 1992; A. Schiller, *Roman Law: Mechanisms of Development*, The Hague and New York 1978; O. E. Tellegen-Couperus, *A Short History of Roman Law*, London and New York 1993; F. Wieacker, *Römische Rechtsgeschichte. Quellenkunde, Rechtsbildung, Jurisprudenz und Rechtsliteratur*, 2 vols., Munich 1988–2006; H. J. Wolff, *Roman Law: an Historical Introduction*, Oklahoma 1951.

10. On archaic Roman law: A. Watson, *Rome of the XII Tables: Persons and Property*, Princeton 1972; Watson, *The State, Law and Religion: Pagan Rome*, Athens, Ga. and London 1992.

11. On the Roman state and constitution: T. C. Brennan, *The Praetorship in the Roman Republic*, 2 vols., Oxford 2000; J. A. Crook, *Consilium principis: Imperial Councils and Counsellors from Augustus to Diocletian*, Cambridge 1955; F. de Martino, *Storia della costituzione romana*, 7 vols., Naples 1962–75;

J. Gonzalez, 'The *Lex Irnitana*: a New Copy of the Flavian Municipal Law', *Journal of Roman Studies*, 76 (1986) 147–243; J. H. Liebeschuetz, *Barbarians and Bishops: Army, Church and State in the Age of Arcadius and Chrysostom*, Oxford 1990; A. Lintott, *Imperium Romanum: Politics and Administration*, London 1993; Lintott, *The Constitution of the Roman Republic*, Oxford 1999; F. Millar, *The Emperor in the Roman World (31 BC–AD 337)*, London and Ithaca 1977; T. Mommsen, *Römisches Staatsrecht*, 3 vols., 3rd edn, Leipzig 1887–8; R. J. A. Talbert, *The Senate of Imperial Rome*, Princeton 1984.

12. On Roman statute law: D. Daube, *Forms of Roman Legislation*, Oxford, 1956; T. Honoré, *Emperors and Lawyers*, London 1981; Honoré, *Law in the Crisis of the Empire, 379–455 AD*, Oxford 1998; John F. Matthews, *Laying Down the Law: a Study of the Theodosian Code*, New Haven and London 2000; D. Pugsley, *Justinian's Digest and the Compilers*, vol. I, Exeter 1995.

13. On the judiciary and legal procedure: J. A. Crook, *Legal Advocacy in the Roman World*, London 1995; A. H. J. Greenidge, *The Legal Procedure of Cicero's Time*, Oxford 1966; M. Kaser and K. Hackl, *Das römische Zivilprozessrecht*, 2nd edn, Munich 1996; J. M. Kelly, *Roman Litigation*, Oxford 1966; Kelly, *Studies in the Civil Judicature of the Roman Republic*, Oxford 1976; O. Lenel, *Das Edictum perpetuum*, 3rd edn, Leipzig 1927; E. Metzger, *A New Outline of the Roman Civil Trial*, Oxford 1997; J. Powell, ed., *Cicero the Advocate*, Oxford 2004.

14. On Greek influence on Roman law: D. Daube, *Roman Law: Linguistic, Social and Philosophical Aspects*, Edinburgh 1969; M. Ducos, *Les Romains et la loi. Recherches sur les rapports de la philosophie grecque et de la tradition romaine à la fin da la République*, Paris 1984; G. A. Kennedy, *The Art of Rhetoric in the Roman World, 300 BC–300 AD*, Princeton 1972; J. W. Jones, *The Law and Legal Theory of the Greeks: an Introduction*, Oxford 1956; P. Stein, *Regula Iuris: From Juristic Rules to Legal Maxims*, Edinburgh 1966.

15. On Roman jurisprudence: R. A. Bauman, *Lawyers in Roman Republican Politics: a Study of Roman Jurists in their Political Setting, 316–82 BC*, Munich 1983; Bauman, *Lawyers and Politics in the Early Roman Empire*, Munich 1989; B. W. Frier, *The Rise of the Roman Jurists: Studies in Cicero's Pro Caecina*, Princeton 1985; T. Honoré, *Gaius*, Oxford 1962; Honoré, *Tribonian*, London 1978; Honoré, *Ulpian: Pioneer of Human Rights*, 2nd edn, Oxford 2002; O. Lenel, *Palingenesia iuris civilis*, Leipzig 1889; F. Schulz, *History of Roman Legal Science*, Oxford 1946; A. Watson, *Law Making in the Later Roman Republic*, Oxford 1974.

16. On Roman private law: A. Borkowski and P. du Plessis, *Textbook on Roman Law*, 3rd edn, Oxford 2005; W. W. Buckland and Peter Stein, *A Textbook of Roman Law from Augustus to Justinian*, 3rd edn, Cambridge 1963; D. Johnston, *Roman Law in Context*, Cambridge 1999; M. Kaser, *Das römische Privatrecht*, 2 vols., 2nd edn, Munich 1971–5; R. W. Lee, *The Elements of Roman Law with*

a Translation of the Institutes of Justinian, 4th edn, London 1956; E. Metzger, ed., *A Companion to Justinian's Institutes*, London 1998; B. Nicholas, *An Introduction to Roman Law*, Oxford 1962; D. Pugsley, *The Roman Law of Property and Obligations: an Historical Introduction to Some of the Main Institutions*, Cape Town 1972; F. Schulz, *Classical Roman Law*, Oxford 1951; J. A. C. Thomas, *Textbook on Roman Law*, Amsterdam 1976; A. Watson, *The Spirit of Roman Law*, Athens, Ga. 1995. Also see A. Berger, *Encyclopedic Dictionary of Roman Law*, Philadelphia 1953.

17. The main sources of Roman law in English translation are to be found in: M. H. Crawford, ed., *Roman Statutes*, 2 vols., London 1996; A. C. Johnson, P. R. Coleman-Norton and F. C. Bourne, eds., *Ancient Roman Statutes*, Austin 1961; *The Institutes of Gaius*, translation by W. M. Gordon and O. F. Robinson, London 1988; text, translation and commentary by F. de Zulueta, 2 vols., Oxford 1946–53; *The Theodosian Code and Novels*, translation by C. Pharr, Princeton and London 1952; *The Institutes of Justinian*, text, translation and commentary by J. A. C. Thomas, Amsterdam 1975; *Justinian's Institutes*, text and translation by P. Birks and ed. G. McLeod, London 1987; *The Digest of Justinian*, translation by A. Watson, 2 vols., 2nd edn, Philadelphia 1998. For the Latin text of the whole Justinian codification, the *Corpus iuris civilis*: *Institutiones, Digesta*, eds. T. Mommsen and P. Krueger, 16th edn, Berlin 1954; *Codex*, ed. P. Krueger, 11th edn, Berlin 1954; *Novellae*, eds. R. Schoell and W. Kroll, 6th edn, Berlin 1954.

PART II

The civil law tradition

3

Correctio
(the Early Middle Ages, *c.*500–1000)

A   Politics and the state

1   The end of Antiquity and the formation of Europe

Decedente atque immo potius pereunte ab urbibus Gallicanis liberalium cultura litterarum … nec repperire possit quisquam peritus dialectica in arte grammaticus, qui haec aut stilo prosaico aut metrico depingeret versu … Vae diebus nostris, quia periit studium litterarum a nobis, nec reperitur rethor in populis, qui gesta praesentia promulgare possit in paginis.[1]

98   The Dark Middle Ages

With these words, Bishop Gregory of Tours (538/9–94) opened his chronicle about the Frankish kings of the Merovingian dynasty and their rule over Gaul. The idea of decay conveyed by his words lingered on in the collective memory of the West. The centuries between the fall of the Western Roman Empire and the eleventh century are often captured in terms of political, economic and cultural decline. The collapse of Roman authority in the West brought an end to Graeco-Roman civilisation. Culturally speaking, the Germanic conquerors of the Roman Empire lagged behind the Romans. They proved incapable of maintaining Roman civilisation or of replacing it with anything worthy of the name. Europe entered an age of decline and disruption: the Dark Middle Ages. This view of the era after the fall of the Roman Empire fits into the overall negative view of the Middle Ages held by the humanists, which survived well into the twentieth century. Even the re-evaluation of the Late Middle

---

[1] 'In the towns of Gaul the writing of literature has declined to the point where it has virtually disappeared altogether … nor can one find one man schooled in dialectics or grammar who could depict these things in prose or verse … What kind of period is this, in which the study of literature had perished and no one is to be found who is capable of writing down what is happening these days.' Gregory of Tours, *Historia Francorum*, preface, translation after Lewis Thorpe, *History of the Franks*, London 1974.

Ages by Haskins in 1927 with the publication of his *Renaissance of the Twelfth Century* led to little if any adjustment in the way the Dark or Early Middle Ages were perceived.

Nevertheless, already in the nineteenth century, some historians indicated a few significant periods of cultural revival in the five hundred years between the downfall of the Roman Empire and the year 1000. Like the great 'Renaissance' of the fifteenth century, these were labelled 'renaissances', thus giving the term a more general meaning than it initially had. It now referred to any cultural revival that drew on classical Graeco-Roman culture. The most important of such 'renaissances' in the Early Middle Ages was the Carolingian Renaissance in the Frankish Empire around 800. Other renaissances include the Ostrogothic in Italy around 500, the Anglo-Saxon in Britain in the early seventh century, the Visigothic in Spain in the same period and the Ottonian in Germany in the late tenth century.

99   The transformation of the Mediterranean and the formation of the West

But even this revision fails to do justice to the period 500–1000. It cannot be denied that the collapse of the Roman Empire set off a period of decay. We may also justly label the period between 500 and 1000 as a period of transition between the Graeco-Roman and the western European civilisation, which only truly emerged after the year 1000. But in this transition, the Early Middle Ages were more than a passive conduit; they were crucial for the formation of western European civilisation as they were marked by the confrontation and interaction of the Graeco-Roman, Judaeo-Christian, Germanic and Celtic cultures. It is out of the amalgamation of those cultures that a new civilisation arose. The various 'renaissances' from the sixth to the tenth century need to be considered in this light. More than just movements that drew on the heritage of Antiquity, these were pivotal for the formation of a western European culture in which Graeco-Roman, Judaeo-Christian, Germanic and Celtic elements were forged together.

The Early Middle Ages were crucial for yet another reason. The fall of the Western Roman Empire and the ultimate expulsion of the Eastern Roman emperors from the western part of the Mediterranean put an end to the political and, in due course, the cultural unity of the Mediterranean world. The rise of Islam and the conquest by the Arabs of a large part of the countries to the east and south of the Mediterranean, including the Iberian peninsula (711), led to the disintegration of the old Mediterranean civilisation into three distinct civilisations: the Arab-Islamic in the south, the Greco-Christian in the east and the Latin Christian in the west. Western Europe was cut off from the wealthier and more developed eastern and southern parts of the Mediterranean. It was thrown back on to its own resources. Halfway through the eighth century, the disintegration of the Mediterranean world was a fact. It was precisely out of this turmoil that the West was born.

2 The Germanic conquest of the West

100 The Germanic kingdoms

By the end of the fifth century, a handful of 'Germanic' kingdoms had filled in the power vacuum left by the fall of the Western Roman Empire.[2] The Visigoths settled in southern Gaul and from there conquered the larger part of Spain. The Vandals founded a kingdom in southern Spain and overran the former Roman province of Africa, present-day Tunisia. The Burgundians established themselves in the Rhône Valley, while Belgium and northern France fell to the Franks, who had already been settled there in the fourth century. The greater part of what is now the Netherlands, north of the Rhine, came into the hands of the Frisians. On the British islands, the Celtic population was overrun by the invading Anglo-Saxons; many migrated to the west (Wales, Cornwall and Ireland), the south (Brittany) and the north (Scotland). In Italy, Odovacar's rule was terminated by the Ostrogoth Theodoric the Great (475–526), who invaded the peninsula at the behest of the Eastern Roman emperor. The mighty Ostrogothic kingdom was destroyed by Belisarius (505–65), a general under Emperor Justinian. Finally, in 568, the Langobards or Lombards invaded northern Italy and put an end to the Byzantine domination of Italy, with the exception of a few enclaves in the south and along the Adriatic coast.

101 Conquest and integration

Although the invasions and the conquests of the fourth to sixth centuries brought a great deal of destruction and chaos, the Germanic invaders did

---

[2] The term 'Germanic' is used to denote the conquerors of the Western Roman Empire. In truth, the invading peoples were often loose 'federations' of tribes of various, not always Germanic, origins. Moreover, the Germanic tribes themselves resulted from centuries of assimilation between originally Scandinavian Germans and other groups – such as Celts, Sarmatians and Skythians.

not aim at destroying Roman civilisation and driving out the people living in their newly won territories. To begin with, they had never aimed at overthrowing the Roman Empire, but rather at winning a place in it, and eventually, when it collapsed, taking it over.

The Germanic conquerors of the Western Roman Empire, in general, stood at a lower level of civilisation than the Romans. But they were certainly no mindless, primitive barbarians who had nothing in common with their new subjects. First, the Germanic tribes had originally come from Scandinavia. Between the fifth and third centuries BC, they had migrated south into Europe and had settled in the territories north of the Rhine and Donau that had long been Celtic. Germanic culture mixed with Celtic culture to the extent that it is hard to indicate what was specifically Germanic. Thus, the Germanic invaders and the existing populations of the Western Roman provinces that had been Celtic – Gaul, Britain and Spain – had much common ground to stand on. Both partook in the same traditional 'Germano-Celtic' culture that had been dominant in much of Europe north and west of Italy before the Roman conquest and had, particularly in the northern parts of the Roman Empire, been only partially erased by Romanisation.

Second, there were the long-established contacts with the Roman Empire itself. The first contacts between the Germans and the Romans date as far back as the second century BC. Roman conquests up to the Rhine and Danube in the days of Caesar and Augustus had brought many Germanic tribes within the Roman political, cultural and economic orbit. By the third and fourth centuries AD, major Germanic tribes had won a foothold in the Roman Empire and many Germanic aristocrats made careers within it. Long before the demise of the Western Empire, their Romanisation had begun. After their victory over the Roman Empire, the Germanic invaders further adopted elements of Roman culture.

Upon their conquest, the Germans did not systematically displace the existing population, confiscate their property or upset the political, administrative, economic and ecclesiastical structures. During the first period after the collapse of imperial power in the West, many features of Roman civilisation remained more or less intact. But inevitably, with time, the effects of the disappearance of central Roman authority were felt. The Romanised indigenous elites, who for centuries had lived in close alliance with the Romans, now shifted their allegiance to their new Germanic masters. They started culturally to adapt to and assimilate with the Germanic elite. In many respects, this was a return to their own roots.

With time, Roman culture and administration faded. The lack of a central government, administration and fiscal system and the disappearence of the inducements to 'be Roman' that went with these contributed to the gradual decay of Roman culture.

The last centuries of the Roman Empire and the first centuries of the Early Middle Ages were thus marked by a slow but gradual process of mutual adaptation. While during the first century or so after the fall of the Western Empire, the Germanic invaders and the indigenous but Romanised elites remained clearly distinguishable, from the sixth century onwards the process of integration really took off. The new culture was partly Roman, and partly Germano-Celtic. It was from this drawn-out process of transformation that the West was born.

102 Roman influences on the Germanic conquerors

Chief among the Roman influences on their Germanic vanquishers were the role of the written word, Christianity and the domainial system. The Germano-Celtic culture was based on an oral tradition, whereas the written word played a central role in Roman education, administration and law. The gradual decline of the Roman schooling system would, on the one hand, diminish the role of the written word throughout western Europe during the Early Middle Ages. On the other hand, the Germanic elites came to grant a greater role to writing than they had before.

Between the fourth and seventh centuries, most of the Germanic invaders converted to Christianity. Initially, many of them opted not for the Catholic faith of the Roman Empire and the Bishop of Rome but for one of the many 'heresies': Arianism. It may be that in doing so they were seeking to assert their special status vis-à-vis the Romanised population and their independence vis-à-vis the emperor in the East. In the course of the sixth and seventh centuries, the Germanic kings one by one converted to Catholicism.

In addition, the economic positions of power of the indigenous elites were respected by the Germanic invaders in most parts of Europe. During the final stages of the empire, these elites had largely withdrawn from the cities and consolidated their power by building large, rural *villae* (estates or domains). Dozens of families lived on and around the lands owned by the *dominus* (lord) of the domain in question. In most cases these people became legally dependent on the lord in one way or another. The Germanic conquerors, who were mostly farmers, preserved and adopted the domainial system. In the modern historiography on the Middle Ages, the terms manor and manorial system are also used.

103   Tribal kings and Roman administrators

The initial separation between Germanic and indigenous elites was reflected in the political structure of the newly established kingdoms. On the one hand, the Germanic kings ruled their own people as tribal or popular leaders. In the Germanic tradition, there was no abstract notion of the state as an autonomous body politic with a fixed territory. The title held by the king, which referred to the people he governed and not to the territory – *rex Francorum, rex Visigothorum* – reflected its personal character. The migrations had, of course, strengthened the personal dimension of leadership.

On the other hand, the Germanic kings wanted to consolidate their rule over the indigenous, Romanised population. This they did by leaving the existing Roman structures in place and/or adopting them for better or for worse. Many Germanic kings had a Roman magistracy conferred on them by the Roman emperor in Constantinople or appropriated a Roman official title in addition to their Germanic title. This they did in order to strengthen their position of power vis-à-vis their Germanic competitors and to increase their legitimacy in the view of the people living in their new territories. The latter was all the more important since the original population was more numerous than the Germanic invaders, except perhaps in the very northernmost part of what had been the Roman Empire. The effects of the distinction between Germanic and indigenous people were also felt in the field of law.

3   *The Frankish Empire under the Merovingians and the Carolingians*

104   The Merovingians

Among the Germanic kingdoms ultimately one emerged as the strongest: the Frankish. The Franks were a relatively small group of Germanic tribes which from the third century onwards lived north and east of the Rhine. Already in the fourth century, some Frankish groups were allowed into the Roman Empire. By the early fifth century, Frankish groups had established themselves in the area between the Rhine and the Seine. At the end of the fifth century, one of the many Frankish tribal kings, Clodowech or Clovis I (482–511) of the house of Merovech, subjugated all other Frankish rulers and tribes. In order to ensure the support of the Gallo-Roman elites in Gaul and of 'their' Catholic Church, he had himself baptised as a Catholic in Reims in 496. In doing so, he laid the foundation for the long-lasting alliance between the church of Rome and the Frankish kings.

Apart from being a shrewd politician, Clovis was also an excellent general. Under his control the Frankish Empire expanded over the larger part of Gaul, present-day France. Clovis defeated the last Roman commander in Gaul, Syagrius (d. 487), subjugated the Alamans in the Rhineland and drove the Visigoths across the Pyrenees to Spain. His successors annexed the Burgundian kingdom on the Rhône as well as Thuringia and Bavaria in present-day Germany. By means of their conquests, Clovis and his sons consolidated their domestic position. The Germanic king was first and foremost an army commander who depended on his success as a general. He could rely on the loyalty and obedience of his warriors, but had to reward them for their loyalty and courage. Apart from territorial gains, the king needed booty for this purpose. Expansion and conquest were necessary for the establishment and consolidation of strong royal authority.

Clovis divided his empire among his sons into separate *regna* (kingdoms). Numerous domestic disputes and civil wars among his descendants weakened the dynasty. The history of the late Merovingians of the sixth and seventh centuries reads as a catalogue of murder, betrayal and bloody revenge among the various branches and members of the family. Although the entire Frankish Empire did on several occasions briefly fall under the control of a single king, as under Dagobert I (629–39), none of the Merovingians could rival Clovis. The internal divisions made new conquests outside the empire's borders impossible from around 530 onwards. This meant that the kings no longer had sufficient new lands and plunder to ensure the loyalty of their powerful subjects and were forced to give away their own lands. By 700, the dynasty had become impoverished and had undermined its own power base. The fact that the Franks were able to maintain their position in Gaul and the Rhineland was due not so much to their own strength as to the weakness of their Germanic opponents in Spain and Italy, who also had to worry about keeping the Byzantines at bay.

105   The Carolingians

From the seventh century onwards, a new, powerful clan came to the fore in the Frankish Empire: the Carolingians. The Carolingians held the office of mayor of the palace under the kings of Austrasia, the eastern part of the Frankish Empire. The mayor of the palace was the head of the royal household. Since the king's personal household assisted him in the administration of his realm, the mayor also stood at the head of the military and political apparatus. Pippin of Herstal (c.650–714) was the first of the Carolingians who managed to become mayor of the palace for all the Frankish kings at once. His son Charles Martel (688–741) and grandson Pippin (Pepin) III the Short (714–68) followed in his footsteps. In addition, the Carolingians could draw on their enormous landholdings. They were one of the foremost families to benefit in the seventh century from the weakness of the Merovingian kings by swindling them out of numerous estates.

During the first half of the eighth century, matters reached boiling point. The invasion of Spain in 711 by Islamic Arabs and Berbers and the rapid conquest of the Iberian peninsula brought the Frankish Empire into the front line of the Islamic onslaught on Europe. The Merovingian kings or southern dukes could not stop them, although Duke Odo of Aquitaine (d. c.735) initially inflicted a heavy defeat on the Arabs (Battle of Toulouse, 721). The mayor, Charles Martel, defeated the Arabs at the Battle of Poitiers – actually fought at Moussais-la-Bataille – in 732. He, like Odo before him, owed this success to the use of heavy cavalry in addition to the traditional foot soldiers. The battle was, however, not so decisive in stopping the Islamic attack on Gaul as traditional historiography has made out. Charles Martel and his son had to fight another thirty years to eject the Islamic forces from Gaul. In this, they were greatly helped by the revolt of the Berbers in the Maghreb and Spain against their Arab overlords and the internal troubles in the Arab Empire which led to the effective secession of al-Andalus, Islamic Spain, from the Caliphate (756). The victory at Poitiers and the successful fight against the Islamic invaders afterwards did a great deal in strengthening the Carolingians' position in the Frankish Empire. After 732, Charles Martel and his son Pippin the Short definitively took over power in all but name.

In 750, Pippin the Short decided to bring the legal situation in line with reality. According to tradition, Pippin asked Pope Zacharias (741–52) whether it was acceptable for the Frankish kings no longer to hold effective power. The pope replied that it was preferable for whoever held power also to be king.

> Burchard, the bishop of Würzburg, and the chaplain Fulrad were sent to Pope Zacharias to ask him whether it was good that at that time there were kings in Francia who had no royal power. Pope Zacharias informed Pepin that it was better for him who [really] had the royal power to be called king than the one who remained without [effective] royal power. By means of his apostolic authority, so that order might not be cast into confusion, he decreed that Pepin should be made king.[3]

[3] Paul Edward Dutton, ed., *Carolingian Civilization: a Reader*, Peterborough 1993.

This sufficed for Pippin. In 751, he had the last Merovingian king deposed and placed in a monastery. An assembly of Frankish magnates confirmed Pippin as king and Archbishop Boniface anointed him in Soissons. Three years later the new pope, Stephen II (752–7), came to Francia in order to anoint Pippin and his two sons, Carloman and Charles, later Charlemagne.

The kingship of Pippin and his sons rested on two pillars: acclamation by the Frankish aristocracy and the support of the pope and the church. This put an end to the centuries-old alliance between the dynasty of Clovis and the church. Instead, there was now co-operation between the Carolingians and the successors of Peter. For the popes, this was stark necessity. As Bishop of Rome the pope regarded himself not just as head of the church in the West but also as governor of the city of Rome and the lands around it, that is, the true successor of the emperor. On this basis, the pope ruled over middle Italy like a secular prince. From the early seventh century onwards, the Lombard kings in northern Italy threatened the pope's position. The pope needed a new ally to provide him with military assistance against his foes. After ascending to the throne, Pippin entered Italy, consolidating the pope's power in middle Italy (755).

For their part, Pippin and his sons needed the support of the pope and the church in order to consolidate their newly won position. Although powerless, the Merovingians, as the successors of the legendary Clovis, still enjoyed a certain prestige and inviolability. By allowing himself to be anointed by the bishops and the pope, Pippin sought to demonstrate that his kingship had been sanctioned by God. The anointment was a reference to the Old Testament, in which the earliest kings of Israel – Saul, David and Solomon – were anointed by prophets on behalf of God. The approval by the church gave Pippin's kingship a sacral quality that was more evident and more current than that of the Merovingian kingship. Furthermore, the clergy – bishops, priests and monks – exercised a virtual monopoly over education, writing and scholarship, so that the church's support was indispensable for the organisation and administration of the empire.

106   Charlemagne and the aegis of the Frankish Empire

The advent and assumption of power by the Carolingians marked the beginning of a new expansion of the Frankish Empire. The new rulers needed conquests and spoils in order to assure themselves of the support of the greedy aristocracy and the church. Pippin of Herstal and Charles Martel fought the Frisians for control of the Dutch territories north of the Rhine. The most important expansion of the kingdom took place under Charlemagne (768–814). He completed the conquest of the Low Countries. He also subjugated Saxony in what is now northern Germany and extended his kingdom to the east, from the Baltic to present-day Austria. The Celtic tribes in Brittany were driven to the western part of their peninsula. At the request of the pope, Charlemagne invaded Italy several times. In 774, he decided to put an end to the Lombard threat once and for all, defeating their armies and having himself proclaimed king of the Lombards. Charlemagne confirmed the dominion of the pope over Rome and surrounding areas. The Papal State would last for more than one thousand years (until 1870). Later, Charlemagne conducted a number of less successful expeditions against the Arabs in Spain.

Thanks to these conquests, the empire of Charlemagne, King of the Franks, Lombards, Saxons, Thuringians and Bavarians – to name just a few of the Germanic tribes over which he held sway – extended over the larger part of the Latin West. With the exception of Britain and southern Italy, he governed all the territories that had once formed part of the Western Roman Empire and were still Christian. Charlemagne considered that he could lay claim to the title of emperor and during his visit to Rome at Christmas 800, he was crowned as emperor by the pope. Under the dominion of Emperor Charlemagne the Latin West – or at least the larger part of it – was politically unified for the first time since the fall of the Roman Empire – and for the last time until Napoleon. This brief period of unity (774–843) was crucial for the formation of the West as a cultural area. It was also a time of cultural revival – the Carolingian Renaissance.

After his death in 814, Charlemagne was succeeded by Louis II the Pious (814–40), whom he had himself crowned the year before as co-emperor. Louis, undoubtedly the most intelligent and learned of the Carolingian kings, had no interest in further expansion. Instead he concentrated on the organisation of government and the reform of the church. The last ten years of his rule were overshadowed by quarrels and open warfare between Louis, who wanted to leave his empire entirely to his oldest son, and his younger sons. In this struggle Louis came out on the losing side. It was the beginning of the end of the Carolingian dynasty.

4   The Treaty of Verdun and the crisis of the West

107   The decline of the Frankish empire

After the death of their father in 840, the three sons of Louis the Pious continued to fight one another for the inheritance. In 843, they reached an agreement at Verdun. The oldest, Lothar I (840–55), became emperor and received the so called Middle Kingdom. This extended from the Netherlands across the Rhineland and the Rhône Valley to Italy. Lothar's name lived on in those of the duchies of Lower Lorraine (primarily Belgium) and Upper Lorraine (the area to the south on both banks of the Rhine). Charles the Bald (840–77) became king of West Francia, the future kingdom of France. Louis the German (840–76) received East Francia, the future kingdom of Germany. Following the death of their eldest brother Lothar, Charles and Louis divided up the northern part of Lothar's kingdom under the Treaty of Meersen in 870. Charles the Bald annexed the lands west of the River Scheldt. The larger part of the County of Flanders, which was then being formed, was therefore French. The remainder of the Low Countries came under the kings of Germany. The kingdom of Arles or Burgundy (the Rhône Valley) and the *regnum Italiae* (Italy north of Rome) became separate *regna* and were claimed by various branches of the Carolingians.

The late ninth and early tenth centuries were a period of deep crisis in western Europe. Like the Merovingians after Clovis, the Carolingians after Charlemagne and Louis the Pious rapidly went into decline. Although the dynasty still produced a number of strong rulers, none managed to measure up to their forefathers. The ongoing internal and dynastic struggle weakened the position of the kings and strengthened that of local magnates. The Carolingian treasury was exhausted. As they no longer benefited from the support of the king, everywhere in the empire bishops and abbots were obliged to ally themselves with local power magnates. The papacy also went through a dark period. Without the help of their Carolingian allies, the popes fell victim to the ambitions of local aristocratic families in and around Rome.

108 The Dark Age

Most of all, it was the invasions of Europe that caused the demise of royal authority. At the end of the ninth century, the Low Countries, France and the British Isles fell prey to raids and conquests by the Vikings, or Norsemen, from Denmark, Norway and Sweden. The Mediterranean areas suffered from attacks by Islamic raiders from Spain and North Africa. The Arabs established themselves in Sicily and southern Italy. Raids in southern France were the order of the day. A third threat came from the east: that of the Magyars or Hungarians. Following the Huns and the Avars (sixth and seventh centuries), this was the third people from the central Asian steppes to overrun eastern and central Europe.

In 955, the German King Otto I the Great (936–73), from the new Saxon dynasty, managed to defeat the Magyars decisively at Lechfeld. The Magyars retreated into what is now Hungary and in the course of a few centuries became fully incorporated into the Latin West. Later, in the fifteenth and early sixteenth centuries, Hungary was to become a bulwark of the Christian West against the Turkish invasions in Europe.

Particularly in West Francia, the invasions severely weakened royal authority and sounded the death-knell for the Carolingian dynasty. The kings failed to discharge their primary responsibility – the defence of the realm against foreign enemies. The royal army was not designed for this task. The invasions were generally brief and small raids rather than large-scale campaigns of conquest. The royal army consisted of batches of nobles and their followers who had been called upon by the king at the start of a campaign season to go to a particular part of the kingdom. If a particular area in the north faced marauding expeditions by the Vikings, it could take months before a royal army could be called up and arrive on the spot. By that time the enemy would have departed.

The failure of royal authority resulted in the far-reaching fragmentation of political, military and legal authority in the West. Local administrators, large landowners and even abbots and bishops took over the royal responsibilities of defence and administration. Needless to say they at the same time usurped royal powers and privileges, such as the right to mint, collect taxes and dispense justice. It was the age of the feudal system. Although the kingdoms nominally continued to exist, western Europe was in practice divided into literally hundreds of medium-sized and small entities – ranging from large duchies such as Normandy and Saxony to villages of a few hundred people – governed by local lords who acted as petty kings.

This political and legal fragmentation was coupled with an economic break-up. The domainial system had survived the Frankish era. Large domains, or manors, where several dozen peasant families would work the land under the authority of a local lord, dominated the rural landscape. With the invasions and the collapse of central political authority, these manors were thrown back upon their own devices to subsist and survive. International trade and even regional trade between domains largely withered. More than ever, the manors became autarkic economic entities that had to meet all their own requirements such as food, clothing, housing and tools. The virtual collapse of commercial activity meant the end for many towns. Europe fragmented into countless tiny farming communities living in isolation.

In so far as the Dark Middle Ages truly existed, these were the decades before and after 900. Compared with the Arab caliphates in Spain, Egypt and the Middle East and with the Byzantine Empire in Constantinople, western Europe at that time was an underdeveloped region.

109   The Ottonian dynasty

The first signs of the turning of the tide came during the second half of the tenth century. Here and there, local rulers managed to organise themselves more effectively against invaders. Fortifications and strongholds were built along the coasts on both sides of the North Sea to hold off the Norsemen. The Vikings managed to establish themselves in northern France (the Duchy of Normandy), England (the *Danelaw* around York) and even southern Italy (the Kingdom of Sicily), founding kingdoms and dynasties. Gradually, like the Hungarians, they were absorbed into the culture and political life of the Latin West. The Vikings brought fresh blood and new energy to bear. As warriors, adventurous seafarers, traders and administrators they were to make a major contribution to the revival of the West in the eleventh and twelfth centuries.

Both in Germany and in France, the Carolingians finally departed the stage in the tenth century. In Germany, power fell into the hands of the tribal dukes (of the Saxons, the Franks, the Bavarians and the Swabians). In 919, the Saxon Duke Henry I the Fowler (919–36) was elected German king. Henry broke with the old Frankish tradition of dividing up his kingdom among his sons – which was not common to most other Germanic peoples – appointing his son Otto as his sole successor. This son, Otto I the Great (936–73), managed to restore central royal authority in Germany, drove the Magyars out to the east and protected his realm, like Charlemagne, with a belt of margraviates – large and strong border provinces – such as the Eastern March, later Austria. Otto conquered the kingdoms of Arles and Italy. As king of Germany and Italy he considered himself to be in a position to reclaim the imperial title. In 962, he was crowned emperor by the pope in Rome. Thus, he became the founder of what was later called the Holy Roman Empire – a reference to its Christian nature and to its Roman origin. In fact, the new empire encompassed only the old Eastern Frankish kingdom and the larger part of the Middle Frankish kingdom, but this was sufficient for Otto to claim primacy over all other kings. Until 1806, the title of emperor (*Caesar* or *Caesar Augustus*) remained associated in the West with the combined kingship of Germany (the Romano-German king, *rex Romanorum*) and Italy (*regnum Italiae*). In 987, the last Carolingian king in France disappeared. Hugo Capet (987–96), Duke of Paris, secured the throne for himself and his Capetian successors.

5   *The Frankish kingship under the Merovingians*

110   The Roman concept of 'state'

The Germanic political system differed greatly from that of the late Roman Empire. The Romans had not held a fully accomplished abstract notion of the state, a notion of the state as autonomous legal personality, which transcended the people and/or the ruler. Historically, the body politic had been identified with the people, hence the expressions *Senatus Populusque Romanus* (Senate and People of Rome), *res publica* to refer to the Roman 'state' or its business, or *civitas* (the community of citizens). Still, the Romans distinguished between a sphere of public and of private law, thus limiting the effects of that identification. Under the Principate and Dominate, gradually, the emperor came to embody the empire as he assumed more and more of the *imperium*, or public authority. As *dominus*, he alone stood at the head of the machinery of the empire and was its personification. But the emperorship, with its standing bureaucracy and army, also transcended the physical person who bore it. It was eternal. The deification of the emperors in pagan times actually reflected this rather than the opposite. It was a new form of the sacralisation of the *res publica* that went back far in Roman history. Later, once Christianity had become the official religion, the emperor was seen as God's vicar on earth.

111   *Sippe*, tribe and people

The Germanic invaders did not have any abstract notion of the state. The *sippe*, a kin group or clan, lay at the foundation of the Germanic social and political organisation. A *sippe* was a large group of kin who shared a common ancestor. Including their slaves and servants, such a group could number several dozen or even hundreds of people. It may be compared to the original Roman *gens*. At the head of the kin group stood the *pater familias* or elder. He would take all the decisions concerning the kin group, manage the property and resolve disputes in consultation with the free-born members of the group. A number of kin groups formed a tribe. Matters or disputes transcending the individual kin groups were discussed in the meeting of the elders or of all free-born men of the tribe, the tribal assembly. It could also happen that the young men from various kin groups would serve the head of one large kin group as warriors and establish themselves around him. These heads were known as *principes* and formed the heart of the nobility (*nobiles*).

In the event of war, the members of the tribe elected a duke (*dux*) to lead military operations. This was a temporary position. No later than the time of the great migrations, it became, however, more permanent. The Romans often designated these tribal leaders as *rex* (plural *reges*, king), a title the Germanic leaders quickly assumed. This was a time of continuing migration and war, in which tribes grouped together into greater entities or peoples, such as the Visigoths, the Ostrogoths, the Burgundians and the Franks. Peoples generally consisted of tribes that were ethnically related, but this was not necessarily the case. At times of migration all sorts of kin groups and tribes would latch on to passing groups.[4] The tribal or popular assembly would elect a supreme leader or supreme king. Clovis's direct forefathers were only some among many Frankish tribal leaders; it was Clovis who managed to get all the Frankish tribes to recognise his authority and to be proclaimed king of the Franks.

112   Merovingian kingship

Under the impact of the migrations and the conquest of the Western Roman Empire, Germanic tribal leadership evolved into kingship. Roman conceptions and traditions as well as religious motives played a role.

Originally, tribal leadership depended on election and acclamation by the tribal or the popular assembly. Before the time of the migrations, the assembly had been the meeting of all free men of the tribe or people. It was, to some extent, the mustering of the army at the beginning of the campaigning season, somewhere between March and May (Marchfield or Mayfield). Here, laws were adopted, disputes were resolved and important decisions on agriculture, taxes and warfare were taken. During the migrations and the invasions of the Roman Empire, the assemblies profoundly changed in composition. Partly because of practical reasons – the tribes and peoples became more numerous and were constantly on the move – but also because of Roman influence, the assembly evolved into a meeting of the aristocracy, the so-called *nobiles* (nobles). Assemblies could be organised at any level – popular or tribal, general, regional or local.

By the end of the fifth century, Frankish kingship had become hereditary. For a long time, tribal leadership had, in most cases, been monopolised by one leading family. The assembly did not really have a free choice

---

[4] Etymologically the Dutch 'volk', German 'Volk' and Old English 'folc' are related to 'follow'.

but normally acclaimed the family member of the former leader who came out strongest. By the late fifth century, succession from father to son had become normal among the Merovingians. To accomplish this, the Merovingian kings would have their sons and successors acclaimed king during their own lifetime. With time, the election of the king became a mere acclamation of the candidate or candidates who had been designated, either by the previous king or by the rules of hereditary succession. As opposed to most other Germanic peoples, among the Franks it was customary to divide up the realm among the sons of the former king.

Germanic and Frankish kings were not supreme rulers like the late Roman emperors of the Dominate, who were accountable to God alone. The kingship was patriarchal and, to some extent, consensual: the king's power over his people was similar to that of the elder over his kin group. The king had the *mundium*, the responsibility and authority to take care of his people, to protect it and to do justice by each member of it. To this end, he held the *bannum*, that is, the right to command, punish and restrain. *Mundium* and *bannum* were indissolubly linked. The king's authority was dependent upon the discharge of his duty.

The Frankish kings ruled with the help and consent of the assemblies – general, regional or local. These assemblies had evolved into gatherings of magnates, prelates as well as the king's own ministers. While decisions were taken at the top by the king and his most trusted ministers, the assembly served to communicate the decision and ensure the consent of the realm's most powerful. The king and the assembly were locked in a permanent struggle for power. *Bannum* was a kind of law of the strongest: the stronger the king, the greater his freedom to act independently and impose his decisions on the assemblies; the weaker the king, the more the consent of the assembies had to be bargained for.

Germanic leadership and, at the outset, kingship were personal in nature. Having been acclaimed by the assembly, the king was in the first place king of his people or tribe and not of a particular territory. This also remained the case under the Merovingians, and to some extent, even the Carolingians. They were the leaders of various peoples at once. The Germans had a concept of 'people', but no concept of a territorial state. The personal relation between the king and his people was reflected in the concept of *fides* (loyalty) and the custom for all free men to take an oath of fealty to the king. During the Carolingian period, the companions of the king or *antrustiones* made their oath directly to him; the other free members swore loyalty to the *antrustiones* and were thus indirectly bound to him. In this way, the age-old pyramid structure of Germanic society of kin groups, tribes and people was reflected in the pyramid of free persons, nobility and the king.

At first, *regnum* (realm or kingdom) referred not so much to a particular territory as to a particular people. After the conversion to Christianity of the Germanic kings and peoples, it came to refer to the 'people of God' under the latter's *imperator* (emperor) or *rex* (king). The king was responsible not so much for the administration of a certain territory as for the care of his people. He was the military leader and the protector of church and faith. After the advent of the feudal system he also became the supreme liege or suzerain above all other lieges and vassals. As leader of the people he was responsible for military defence and for the maintenance of the peace among his people. He ensured that the customs (that is, the law) and his decisions were enforced.

The Merovingian kingship was hereditary, patriarchal, consensual and personal. Partly because of Roman influence, this last feature began to change under Clovis's successors. After the time of the great migrations, gradually, a bond was forged between the king and his territory. Ultimately, it was to take a further five or six centuries before this led to changing the royal title from *rex Francorum* to *rex Franciae*. But it was no longer felt acceptable for the Frankish Empire to be arbitrarily divided up among the sons of the king. The different Germanic territories the Merovingians and Carolingians had conquered and ruled, such as Austrasia, Neustria or Aquitania, lay at the basis of the different *regna* of which the Frankish Empire consisted. These *regna* could be divided up among the sons of the king but were not further subdivided. Whereas the Germanic kings who conquered the Roman Empire initially adopted Roman titles of office such as *patricius* or *comes* in order to legitimate their authority vis-à-vis the original, Romanised population, they subsequently ceased to do so. Nevertheless, Pippin the Short was to accept the title *patricius* one more time from the pope, particularly with a view to strengthening his position in Italy. One of the reasons why Charlemagne accepted the emperorship was to legitimate himself in the eyes of the 'Romans', the people from middle Italy. The personal application of the law was also suppressed in favour of a territorial application, on which more later.

6   The role of the church in the Frankish Empire

113   From pantheism to Christianity

From the Early Middle Ages to the turn of the twentieth century, the relation between church and state was a matter of severe contention in western

Europe. In Antiquity, there was little if any tension between religion and politics. Virtually all primitive civilisations adhered to one or another form of pantheism. The divine was immanently present in nature or, put differently, nature itself was divine. There was no opposition of the natural and the supernatural, nor a strict separation of the human and the divine. Polytheism was virtually universal, with the numerous forces of nature and life being represented by a multitude of divinities.

The Jews were one of the few peoples in Antiquity to break with this pattern. The early Christians, who sprang from Jewish culture, did the same. With their belief in a single god, the Jews broke not just with polytheism but also with pantheism. The God of the Old Testament was an aloof and mysterious God who, while involved with the world and humankind, also dwelled outside the world. Under the influence of Neoplatonism, the great Church Fathers underscored the dualism of the natural and the supernatural, the human and the divine.

The medievalist Francis Oakley claimed that all this had major implications for the concept of kingship and the relation between church and state.[5] In Antiquity, the deification of the king went along with pantheism. The king was regarded as a son of the gods or even as a god, the Egyptian pharaohs offering the best-known example thereof. In most ancient civilisations, the king was also supreme priest. There was no separation of church and state, religion and politics. In many cultures, such as the Roman one, priests did not form a distinct professional caste. The Roman priests were drawn from the political elite. One of the main functions of Roman religion was the sacralisation of public authority. In ancient times and under the Republic, Rome itself was sacralised and identified with some of the gods. Although eastern influences certainly had their share, the deification of the emperor in later times stood, to some extent, in that ancient tradition.

Jewish kings of the Old Testament such as Saul, David and Solomon did not share in such deification; they were not gods but were the one God's appointees on earth. They were not directly appointed by God, but held their authority through the mediating powers of prophets, who were authorised by God. Although there was not yet any question of a separate 'church' or clerical order, a dualism arose between the political and religious orders: kings and prophets were more than once ranged against one another. The kings ruled on earth but the prophets knew the will of God, which they then imparted to humans.

---

[5] Francis Oakley, *The Medieval Experience*, Toronto 1988, 108–15.

The same duality between the political and the religious permeates the New Testament. Statements by Jesus such as 'pay Caesar what belongs to Caesar, and God what belongs to God' and 'My kingdom does not belong to this world' had a marked effect on early Christian thinking.[6] Before the recognition of Christianity by Constantine the Great in the early fourth century, the Roman state and the Christian Church were often at loggerheads. The new religion saw no reason whatever to associate itself with the imperial government.

114   Church and state under the late empire

This was to change radically after the recognition of Christianity by Constantine and particularly with the elevation of Christianity to the empire's official religion. The church could no longer hold on to the strict separation of church and state. Under the late Roman Empire and in the Byzantine Empire, it found itself caught up in the ancient, traditional pattern of co-operation between political and religious authority. Constantine and his Christian successors, such as Theodosius and, in particular, Justinian, regarded themselves not just as God's appointees but as his vicars on earth and, thus, supreme heads of the church. The Christian Church and faith paid the price for their political recognition in the form of concessions to the old, pantheist traditions of the Graeco-Roman world.

At the First Council of Constantinople in 381, the bishops of Rome, Constantinople, Antioch, Jerusalem and Alexandria were appointed as the five patriarchs or heads of a part of the church. Nevertheless, although the pope, as Bishop of Rome and successor of the Apostle Peter, exercised primacy over the four other patriarchs, it was the emperor who governed the church. The late Roman and Byzantine emperors established a theocracy. The church was incorporated into the bureaucratic machinery of the empire. In each province, a bishop was appointed; in each diocese, an archbishop. The emperors assigned judicial and administrative duties and powers transcending the purely spiritual to these church officials. The state enhanced its control over the church but, at the same time, had increasing need of the church.

115   Gregory the Great and the Western Church

The collapse of imperial authority in the West and the conquest by the non-Christian Germanic tribes freed the Western Church from secular

---

[6] Mark 12:17 and John 18:36 (see also Matthew 22:21).

control. Justinian and his successors sought to retain control over Rome and the church in the former Western Roman Empire, but ultimately failed. Gradually, the Eastern and Western churches drifted apart. Although it was to take until 1054 before the break between the two churches – the Greek Orthodox Church in Constantinople and the Latin Catholic Church in Rome – was to be fully consummated, by the early seventh century the supreme authority of the Eastern emperor was little more than a pretence.

To free themselves from Byzantine control, the church and the popes needed the support of their Frankish allies. That support was also indispensable for the victory of Catholicism in the West. Although during and after the invasions of the Roman Empire, the Germanic tribes rapidly converted to Christianity, mostly they adopted Arianism, which Constantinople and Rome considered a heresy. Clovis was the first of the great Germanic kings to opt for the 'true' church. Most of the other Germanic monarchs followed in the course of the sixth and seventh centuries. The support of the Frankish kings helped the Roman Church to defeat its competitors in the West, to suppress Germanic paganism and to establish its own autonomy vis-à-vis the emperor in Constantinople.

The alliance between the popes and Frankish kings was also vital for the standing of the pope within the church. As the sole patriarch of the West, the bishop of Rome, the pope, was the foremost bishop in the West. Until the year 600, this primacy did not signify much. This only started to change with Pope Gregory I the Great (590–604), whose papacy was pivotal for the formation of the Western Church and hence of the Latin West itself. Gregory managed to wrest England from the Celtic-Irish Church, whose missionaries had won the island over to Christianity in the course of the previous century, and bring it under control of the Roman Church.[7] In the process, the last remaining serious competitor to the supreme authority of the pope over the church in the West was eliminated or, more accurately, driven out to the western fringes of Europe, the Celtic territories of Ireland, Wales, Scotland and Brittany. In addition, Gregory strengthened the papacy's grip over the Western dioceses. He built an ecclesiastical hierarchy of priests, bishops, archbishops and pope which gave every clergyman his place and was to assure the submission of all to the pope. The supreme authority of the papacy remained largely theoretical as the popes did not possess the legal and administrative instruments to exert effective control. Gregory's vision of papal

---

[7] Melvyn Bragg has written a fascinating novel on this conflict: *Credo*, London 1996.

supremacy, however, was there to stay. He and his successors enhanced
the role, scope and mass of ecclesiastical, or canon, law. In doing so, they
sought to reform the church's organisation and make it more efficient.
Gregory also sought to strengthen the unity of liturgy and theology. The
Roman (Julian) calendar was to be used all over Europe and supersede
all other – including the Irish – calendars. Finally, he greatly encouraged
the adoption wherever possible by abbeys of the rule of Saint Benedict of
Nursia (c.480–550). In addition to the episcopal hierarchy, the monasteries were supposed to form a second network that would disseminate to the
remotest extremities of the West the one true faith of the one true church
with its one liturgy and one law.

116   The two swords

The alliance between the popes and the Frankish kings not only provided
benefits for Rome but also threatened the autonomy of the church. Like
the Roman emperors before them, the Frankish kings engaged the clergy
and ecclesiastical hierarchy in the administration of their empire. In the
tension between the Judaeo-Christian and Graeco-Roman tradition, the
West once again shifted towards the Graeco-Roman end of the spectrum.
The clergy monopolised schooling, writing and the knowledge and use of
the language in which everything was written: Latin. In consequence, the
clergy's co-operation was indispensable for the administration of a large
empire such as the Merovingian and Carolingian. The kings attempted
to control the clergy by seeking to gain a say over their appointment. On
the other hand, the bishoprics and abbeys, just like the nobility, benefited from the numerous privileges and gifts – especially of land – that
they prised from the king. Under the Carolingians, the tithe, a tax of
10 per cent of all earnings payable to the church, was introduced in much
of Europe.

The alliance between the Frankish kings and the pope rested on a
precarious balance of power. Both had an interest in empowering the
other but felt threatened at the same time. The king supported the unification of church and faith since this was in the interest of the unity of
his kingdom. The pope supported the unity of the kingdom since this
advanced the unity of the church. Both, however, were aware of the danger of falling under the other's supremacy. As long as the Franks under
the Merovingians ruled only a limited part of the West, the Frankish
kings, unlike the Roman emperors, were unable to lay any claim on the
leadership of the church as a whole. While the kings were able to bring
the bishoprics and abbeys in their own territory under their control, the

papacy could safeguard much of its autonomy. The popes tolerated and supported the co-operation between the Frankish kings and the Frankish church as long as they themselves were recognised as the spiritual head of the whole church.

The duality between king and pope, between the secular and the spiritual, was given expression in what later became known as the theory of the 'two swords'. The doctrine stems from a statement by Pope Gelasius I (492–6) in 494 claiming that there were two *dignitates* (dignities) on earth: papal and regal. The former pertained to eternal life, the latter to temporal life. Neither Gelasius nor his immediate successors, however, recognised the full import of this doctrine. There were two powers to be distinguished, but this did not mean that they were therefore totally separated. Gelasius and his successors did not reject the view that the king as a secular leader had a say in the 'temporal' matters of the church, or that the king had spiritual authority. Not until later, during the Investiture Controversy (from approximately 1070), did the popes claim the full separation of church and state. It was at this time that the metaphor of the two swords or keys also arose. Christ had left two swords or keys on earth: that of spiritual and that of secular power.

117   Church and state under the Carolingians

The conquest of the larger part of the West by Charlemagne disrupted the balance of power. The alliance between Pippin the Short and the pope was forged because the latter needed military help against his Lombard foes in Italy. For their part, the Carolingians desired papal sanctioning for their usurpation of the Frankish crown. The anointment of Pippin the Short and his sons by the pope and bishops symbolised that the Carolingian kings had obtained their power from God. They therefore drew on a descending theory of power that was at variance with the Germanic tradition. In truth, the Carolingians based their kingship on both the Germanic tradition – acclamation and consent from the aristocracy – and the Judaeo-Christian tradition of divine sanction by anointment.

Under Pippin, Charlemagne and Louis the Pious, the new alliance between the Frankish kings and the popes allowed the former to strengthen their grip on the church. The Carolingians used their interventions in Italy on behalf of the pope to project themselves as protectors of the church. The coronation of Charlemagne at Christmas 800 by the pope was a double-edged sword for the latter. On the one hand, it was the pope who had taken the initiative with the goal of strengthening the autonomy of the Western Church vis-à-vis the Eastern Roman emperors.

Now that there was once again an emperor in the West, the emperor in Constantinople no longer had any reason to interfere with the church in Rome. On the other hand, Charlemagne and, to a much greater extent again, his son Louis the Pious and later again the Ottonian emperors, would use the imperial office to style themselves as the secular protectors or guardians of the church.

From Clovis onwards, the Frankish kings had been anointed by clergymen. The anointment not only conferred God's and the church's blessing on the king but bestowed episcopal powers on to him. The anointed of the Lord was *rex et sacerdos*, king and priest. The clerical dimension to the kingship legitimated the king's interference with church and faith. In fact, this notion of *rex et sacerdos* reflected the views of the great Church Father Saint Augustine (354–430) on the relation between the church and the Roman Empire. According to Augustine, political authority was only legitimate in so far as it created and safeguarded the peaceful conditions necessary to allow the faithful to live as good Christians. Under the Frankish interpretation of kingship, the king was responsible for law and peace in society. The king was to ensure that the church and the goods of the church were left untouched. In that sense, the king was the secular – that is, political, legal and military – guardian of the church. Some kings, however, including the great Carolingians and later the Ottonians, went a step further and claimed that – particularly if the pope and the ecclesiastical hierarchy remained at fault – they could involve themselves with ecclesiastical matters in order to promote the faith.

Since the recognition of Christianity by the Roman emperors in the fourth century, secular and spiritual authorities had always been both allies and competitors. This dynamic tension came from the blurring together of classical theocratic tendencies with the Jewish and early Christian tradition of separation of religion and politics. For most of the period, the two powers held one another in balance. But under the greatest rulers of the age such as Charlemagne, Louis the Pious or Otto the Great, the balance between church and state was broken to the benefit of the latter. Meanwhile, the tension smouldered and continued to grow, until its eruption in the late eleventh century.

7   Renovatio imperii, translatio imperii

118   *Renovatio imperii*

On Christmas Day 800, Charlemagne attended mass at Saint Peter's in Rome. During the ceremony, Pope Leo III (795–816) unexpectedly crowned him as emperor. According to Charlemagne's biographer Einhard (*c.*770–840), Charlemagne later revealed that if he had foreknown this, he would not have entered Saint Peter's that night.[8] This remark was not prompted by false modesty. What disturbed Charlemagne was not that he had become emperor but that the pope had invested him with this office. This is illustrated by the fact that it was Charlemagne himself who made his son Louis the Pious co-emperor and crowned him with his own hand in Aachen in 813. The pope was invited to witness the proceedings from the sidelines.

Leo III and Charlemagne held divergent views on Charlemagne's emperorship. The pope regarded his deed as a genuine *renovatio imperii* (renewal of the empire), in the sense of the *imperium Romanum* (the Roman Empire). With the coronation of Charlemagne, the pope wanted to make it clear to the Eastern Roman emperor that there was once again an emperor in the West who was of equal standing to the emperor in Constantinople. As we have seen, this was a move in the struggle for greater autonomy for the Western Church with regard to Constantinople. Charlemagne was, moreover, a more effective protector against the inhabitants of the city of Rome and the Papal State than the distant emperor in Constantinople. It was precisely because the pope needed the Carolingians in Italy that he wanted to legitimate their presence in the peninsula. What could serve this purpose better than bestowing the Roman emperorship upon them?

119   *Translatio imperii*

Although Charlemagne did aspire to the imperial dignity, the office held a different significance for him. As the conqueror of the Saxons and the Lombards, Charlemagne ruled over various peoples. His emperorship was a confirmation of the fact that he was king of many peoples, a king of kings. This placed the Frankish Empire in the tradition of great empires from the past such as the Babylonian, Persian, Macedonian or Roman empires, the 'emperors' of which had ruled over many peoples and kings.

For Charlemagne, the coronation was a *renovatio imperii* to the extent that it involved the recognition of his 'universal' authority over the Christian part of the former Western Roman Empire. It was in that sense that he sought recognition by his colleague in the East, which he did not

---

[8] Einhard, *Vita Karoli*, ed. O. Holder-Egger, Monumenta Germaniae Historica: Scriptores Rerum Germanicarum in Usum Scholarum, Hanover 1911.

obtain until 812. In the light of his alliance with the papacy and his own conquest of Italy, Charlemagne certainly had no difficulty acting as secular protector of the church – a role that the late Roman emperors had also assumed.

Apart from these two largely Roman elements, however, the emperorship had yet another meaning for Charlemagne. His empire was in the first place Frankish, as reflected in the ninth century in the doctrine of *translatio imperii* (transfer of the empire). This idea was based on a reference to the dream of Nebuchadnezzar as recorded in the Book of the Prophet Daniel in the Old Testament. The Prophet was able to relate and explain the dream to the king:

> As you watched, there appeared to your majesty a great image. Huge and dazzling, it stood before you, fearsome to behold. The head of the image was of fine gold, its chest and arms of silver, its belly and thighs of bronze, its legs of iron, its feet part iron and part clay. While you watched, you saw a stone hewn from a mountain by no human hand, it struck the image on its feet of iron and clay and shattered them. Then the iron, the clay, the bronze, the silver, and the gold were all shattered into fragments, and as if they were chaff from a summer threshing-floor the wind swept them away until no trace of them remained. But the stone which struck the image grew and became a huge mountain and filled the whole earth.
>
> That was the dream: now we shall relate to your majesty its interpretation. Your majesty, the king of kings, to whom the God of heaven has given the kingdom with its power, its might and its honour, in whose hands he has placed mankind wherever they live, the wild animals, and the birds of the air, granting you sovereignty over them all: you yourself are that head of gold. After you there will arise another kingdom, inferior to yours, then a third kingdom, of bronze, which will have sovereignty over the whole world. There will be a fourth kingdom, strong as iron: just as iron shatters and breaks all things, it will shatter and crush all the others. As in your vision, the feet and toes were part potter's clay and part iron, so it will be a divided kingdom, and just as you saw iron mixed with clay from the ground, so it will have in it something of the strength of iron. The toes being part iron and part clay means that the kingdom will be partly strong and partly brittle ... In the times of those kings the God of heaven will establish a kingdom which will never be destroyed nor will it ever pass to another people; it will shatter all these kingdoms and make an end of them, while it will itself endure for ever.[9]

This passage was already known in the West at the time of the Roman Republic. According to the Greek historian Polybios (*c*.200–120 BC), who lived and worked as a prisoner of war in Rome, Rome was the fourth and

---

[9] Daniel 2:31–42, 44.

final kingdom. A different interpretation was now assigned to the dream. History was a linear story that would end not with the fourth but with an eternal fifth empire. While the Roman Empire could continue to be regarded as the fourth empire after the Assyrian, Persian and Macedonian empires, the Franks laid claim to being the fifth kingdom, which would endure until the end of times. In the process, the universal claims of the Romans were transferred to the Franks. The imperial coronation of Charlemagne symbolised a genuine *translatio imperii* from one people to another. This transfer was shored up by the care Charlemagne devoted to his palace in Aachen, which was built to rival Rome as the centre of the West. Nor was reference made to the *Roman* Empire.

The notion of a 'Frankish' Empire held by Charlemagne and his successor was not at variance with the Christian nature of the empire. Here, the emperor and pope were in full agreement. The doctrine of *translatio imperii* meant that God's divine plan to salvage humanity would come to fruition under and with the kingdom of the Franks. The Franks were a new chosen people, the new Israel.

120   The coronation of Charlemagne and the Investiture Controversy

For Charlemagne, his imperial title was one instrument to enhance his authority over his vast, multi-ethnic empire. Charlemagne sought to obtain greater control over his empire, enlisting the service of both the clergy and the nobility. The so-called Carolingian Renaissance boils down to Charlemagne's and his son Louis's efforts to promote, reform and harmonise education, monastic life, liturgy and church organisation throughout the empire. The unity of the church, of its religious and intellectual life, was a foundation stone of a unified empire. The Christian faith and Latin – the language of all written texts and of government – transcended the differences between the various peoples and tribes of the 'Latin West' which made up the Frankish Empire. For Charlemagne and Louis, the imperial title provided a ready means of legitimating their interference with the church. As universal rulers of the West, they were, in line with their Roman predecessors, also the protectors and where necessary – filling the gap left by the pope – *correctors* (correctors or reformers) of the church. In that sense, the coronation of Charlemagne by Pope Leo III was, from the early ninth century onwards, to work out increasingly to the disadvantage of the pope. Particularly under Louis the Pious, it became an argument for limiting papal autonomy and strengthening imperial authority over the church.

The coronation of 800 was a significant event, not only for contemporaries but also and more particularly for subsequent generations. Well beyond the Middle Ages, Charlemagne lived on in the collective memory of the West as the greatest emperor ever and served as an example for later rulers. Many monarchs based their claims to power on their alleged descent from Charlemagne. For the better part of a millennium, emperors would consider Charlemagne's empire as the source of their own imperial authority. The interpretation of what Charlemagne's emperorship entailed, consequently, became a source of dispute for the supporters and opponents of later emperors. The coronation of Charlemagne by Pope Leo III sowed the seeds for a major dispute between emperor and church but, for the time being, the conflict smouldered beneath the surface. Only in the eleventh century would it erupt. During the Investiture Controversy (1070–1250), reference would often be made to the events of Christmas 800 by the advocates of both papal and imperial supremacy. The coronation of Charlemagne by the pope was understood in entirely different terms. The popes from the time of the Investiture Controversy invoked Charlemagne's coronation by Leo III in order to demonstrate the supremacy of spiritual over secular power. The coronation of the emperor, like the anointment of the Frankish king, was interpreted as evidence that the pope and the church appointed the emperor or king and consequently also had the power to depose him. Leo III himself had no such intention. He was too dependent on Charlemagne to exploit the potentialities opened up by his deed; not until three centuries later would his successors dare to do so. Leo III placed the imperial crown on the head of the conqueror of the Lombards, but then he prostrated himself at the feet of the emperor. By applying the *prokynesis* from the Byzantine court ceremonial in this way, he wanted once more to underline that for him Charlemagne was equal to the emperor in the East. Whatever the case may have been, the position of Leo III was much too weak for him to exert any supremacy over the new emperor. For their part, Charlemagne and his immediate successors considered that the emperorship had been directly conferred upon them by God and not by any papal or ecclesiastical mediation. As in the case of the anointment, the coronation of the emperor was simply a liturgical act. It was the symbolic implementation of the divine will. God, and not the pope or the church, had appointed the emperor.

121   Territorial organisation

Charlemagne did not found his power solely on his imperial title or on the divine sanctioning of his kingship; he also emphasised the personal, consensual and patriarchal – and hence also Germanic – elements of his kingship. On several occasions during his long reign, he ordered all free men in his empire to take a personal oath of fealty (*fides*) to him. He did so for the final time in 802, after his coronation as emperor. Charlemagne's vision of his leadership over the Latin West was based on a conjunction of Roman, Christian and Germanic elements.

Like their predecessors, the Carolingians made major efforts to secure the loyalty of the leading men of the empire, namely the higher clergy and the nobility. They did so by giving war booty and land to the most important warriors and the local magnates. This was fully in line with the tradition of the Germanic kings, who rewarded their warriors for their courage and services. Charlemagne, however, did so not simply by giving away royal lands and estates but by transferring them under a feudal contract.

The Frankish Empire was divided into several hundred *pagi* (counties), each of which was headed by a count. These were royal officials who were appointed, and if need be dismissed, by the king and who were responsible within their particular county for the administration, dispensation of justice, collection of taxes and military defence in the name of and subject to the authority of the king. In most cases, the counts were local nobles, large landowners or warriors. Charlemagne strengthened his grip over these local rulers in various ways. He regularly sent *missi dominici* (the king's envoys) throughout the empire in order to assist and check up on the counts. Although he expanded his palace in Aachen into a genuine centre of administration and education, Charlemagne travelled tirelessly throughout his territories. Quite early on, he appointed his sons as viceroys of the different *regna* that constituted his empire. These measures were highly important; ultimately the personal loyalty of the secular and spiritual aristocracy towards their king and its assent to his rule provided the first and most direct foundation of the king's power. In the case of a strong, powerful and authoritarian ruler such as Charlemagne, this worked to the advantage of the king. Charlemagne was the last Frankish king able to exploit this to the full.

8   *The feudal system*

122   The emergence of the feudal contract

Charlemagne's general use of the feudal contract was, however, his main historic legacy. The feudal system needs to be distinguished from the seigniorial system. Both systems evolved in the Early Middle Ages, the former in the eighth, the latter in the ninth and tenth centuries; both had their roots in Germanic tradition. Otherwise, the two systems differed greatly from one another.

The feudal system was, first and foremost, of military and administrative significance. It was based on an ancient Germanic tradition whereby an important man – a king, tribal leader or large landowner – surrounded himself with numerous warriors who swore him faithful service, or fealty. In exchange for their military service, the lord promised his warriors protection and upkeep. In *Beowulf*, an epic stemming from seventh-century Northumbria, the king was often referred to as the ring-giver – that is, the giver of gold rings and jewels. The relation between the lord and his warriors was based on a contract, known as *commendatio*, with mutual rights and obligations. During the turmoil of the great migrations and the invasions of the Western Roman Empire, the system was used to strengthen relations between rulers and their main subjects.

The feudal contract as such only emerged under the Carolingians. It built on the *commendatio* contract by combining it with another contract known to the Franks: the *beneficium* or *precarium* contract. Unlike the personal *commendatio* contract, this was a real contract. It dated from the time of the invasions and the Merovingians. In those turbulent times, many free men relinquished their landed property – *allodia* or allodial lands – to a local magnate in return for the latter's protection. The title to the property would then be transferred to the magnate but the usufruct – or at least an amalgam of rights and obligations that somewhat resembled Roman *usufructus* or usufruct – reverted to the former owner, a system known as tenure. The tenure could be free or not. In the former case, the tenure holder or tenant simply remained a free man; in the second case, he became a serf and was required, apart from having to pay a tribute, to labour on the lord's own lands at certain times and perform other menial tasks for his lord. In the case of a free tenure, the transfer of title to the land was referred to as *beneficium*, a practice applying particularly to secular tenure-givers such as kings or nobles, or as *precarium*, in the case of ecclesiastical tenure-givers such as bishops and monasteries.

The feudal contract combined *commendatio* and *beneficium*. The lord, referred to as the liege lord or liege, discharged his obligation to provide maintenance for his man, referred to as vassal, by giving him a *beneficium* in loan, that is, the man retained the usufruct of the *beneficium* as long as he lived. Later on, feudal contracts were restricted to free men.

123   Charlemagne and the feudal system

The Carolingians, and especially Charlemagne, applied the feudal contract systematically. Charlemagne wished to bind the leading members of the nobility, landowners, administrators and warriors of his empire more closely to himself. In order to prevent him from having to give away ownership of his royal lands as his Merovingian predecessors had done, he generalised the feudal contract under which he only had to depart from the possession of his lands for the lifetime of his vassals. Charlemagne made such compacts with his foremost subjects. Next to the traditional oath of fealty to the king, they now were also bound to their oath of homage given in the context of their feudal contract. In exchange for a *beneficium*, they undertook to provide their liege, the king, with aid and counsel (*auxilium et consilium*). 'Counsel' referred to their duty to advise the king in administering the realm, 'aid' to military service. The feudal relation between the king and his vassals, the main magnates of the realm, was personal and private.

By applying the system generally and entering into feudal contracts with the leading men of the empire, Charlemagne made the feudal system into a military and administrative instrument. The great military commanders of the empire would now be required to assist the king not just on the basis of the latter's royal *bannum* but also on account of a personal, contractual obligation. The combination of material advantage and the warrior's word of honour to his liege acted as a powerful incentive. Charlemagne went a step further by inducing each of his vassals to enter into feudal contracts of their own with local lords and warriors in their dominions, giving out parts of their *beneficia* to these men. The latter in turn entered into similar arrangements with even smaller landowners and lords. Through these several layers of subinfeudation, a pyramid of different layers of vassals up to the direct vassals of the king – also known as tenants-in-chief – and ultimately the supreme liege or suzerain came into being. Since the feudal contract was personal in nature, it did not provide the king with any direct claims on the vassals of his vassals. As it was later said, 'my vassal's vassal is not my vassal'. The vassal was unable to command the vassals of his vassals but could stipulate in the feudal contract with his vassal that the latter was required to assist him with a certain number of warriors, that is, sub-vassals. By generalising the system in this way, Charlemagne wished to ensure that all the warriors in his empire would receive a sufficiently large piece of land as a *beneficium* to enable them to pay for the necessary horses, weapons and equipment and to train as knights on horseback. As king of the Franks, Charlemagne could require all free men to take up arms for the defence of the realm, but the feudal system was required in order to provide an economic basis for a sufficiently large, well-trained cavalry.

To begin with, the *beneficium* normally consisted of a piece of land. The vassal was given a number of farms – including a number of serfs and/or free tenure-holders working for him – large enough for him to equip himself as knight and become proficient in warfare or to provide for the maintenance of a number of knights-vassals. By the eleventh century, the term 'fief' became common to denote the land held as *beneficium*.

Gradually, Charlemagne began giving other goods out as a *beneficium* as well, such as money or public offices such as those of palsgrave, steward or count. By the ninth century, this had become common practice. By being granted their public offices as *beneficia*, officials now held their office on a double basis. On the one hand, they held it on the basis of what we would call a public law investiture by the king, while on the other they held it as vassals of the king under a essentially private compact. In the case of offices with a territorial basis – such as that of count – the *beneficium* would often come with large landholdings within that county, thus setting up the count as both a royal official and an important landowner – if he had not been that in the first place. The *beneficium* or fief would thus encompass both landholding and office. In this way, the relationship between the king and his leading officials was extended, and gradually shifted, from the domain of public law to that of private law. The personal relation of dependence between the king and his vassals displaced the traditional relation between the king and his officials and broke through the distinctions between private and public law.

124   Feudality and the collapse of royal authority

As long as the suzerain was a strong ruler such as Charlemagne or Louis the Pious, the feudal system worked to the latter's advantage. Through the combination of *commendatio* and *beneficium*, the feudal contract had, from the outset, a personal and a real dimension. In its personal aspect, the focus of the feudal contract lay with the obligations of a vassal to his lord, while in its real aspect, its focus lay with the material benefits for the vassal. Charlemagne and Louis the Pious managed to exploit the feudal system largely to their own benefit. They placed the emphasis on the new, additional pledge of homage on the part of their vassals and kept their rights within bounds. During this period, the feudal system supported central authority.

All this changed radically in the ninth and tenth centuries. The success of the feudal system as a centralising instrument depended entirely on the strength of the suzerain, who was to hold the feudal pyramid together. As soon as the power of the king-suzerain weakened, his tenants-in-chief started to act more autonomously and amassed more power. After 840, the emphasis shifted increasingly from the personal to the real aspect of the feudal contract. The pledge of fealty on the part of the vassal towards his liege faded into the background. The feudal contract now became primarily a basis for the holding of office and land. This is demonstrated by various ways in which the feudal system evolved.

First, fiefs became hereditary. Formerly a *beneficium* was granted only for the duration of the life of both parties; it was a contract *intuitu personae*. Under Charlemagne, the practice already arose that if a vassal died the fief would be bestowed upon the latter's heir. The suzerain did, however, always retain the right to grant the *beneficium* to another person, for example if he did not regard the heir as suitable as a warrior or count. In the course of the ninth and tenth centuries, hereditary succession became a right. The heir of the deceased vassal was required to pay a levy, but was entitled to the fief. In this way, the situation arose that there were vassals – such as under-age children – who were incapable of discharging their military and other obligations as vassal. Later women were also allowed to inherit fiefs. This is a clear indication that the original, military function of feudalism was receding into the background.

Second, it was increasingly common for vassals to enter into feudal compacts with various liege lords at the same time. This plurality of feudal contracts was totally at variance with the personal element on which feudalism was originally based. The question now arose as to what a vassal should do if both his lieges laid claim to his services in order to fight one another. After the year 1000, situations arose in which kings became one another's suzerains or under which a suzerain would become the vassal of his own tenant-in-chief. All these elements demonstrate that land ownership and not military service had become the *ratio existendi* of the feudal system and that it was the vassal who benefited the most from this process. Around 1230, the jurist Accursius was to argue that ownership was divided between liege and vassal not in terms of ownership and usufruct but in terms of *dominium directum* and *dominium utile*. According to Accursius, the latter, which was assigned to the vassal, accounted for nine-tenths of all rights. The system was furthermore to remain the basis for a very large part of all land tenancy in western Europe until its abolition during the French

Revolution (1789), at which point the vassals became at a stroke the full owners of their former feudal fiefs.

As a result of these processes, feudalism in the ninth and tenth centuries contributed towards the collapse of royal authority and the decentralisation of power. The last kings of the Carolingian dynasty were barely capable of enforcing their authority upon their leading subjects/vassals. The latter neglected their duties under their feudal contracts, making use instead of their rights as counts and landowners to build up their power in and around their fiefs.

The relationship between the ruler and leading nobles under the feudal system now began to work against the ruler. Whereas Charlemagne had sought to double his relationship with his court officials, warriors and counts by the general extension of the feudal system, this relationship was now more exclusively viewed in terms of the feudal contract. The 'public law' or, more accurately, royal basis for appointment as court official or count was no longer doubled but displaced by the feudal *beneficium*. The vassal's neglect of his personal obligations towards his liege went along with the general neglect of his obligations as court official or count towards his king.

During the late ninth and the tenth century, royal and imperial – that is, public – power all but disappeared. Charlemagne's and his son's achievements in strengthening royal and imperial authority and building a central power structure did not outlive them long. What remained was a myriad of personal relations between the king, his tenants-in-chief and the latter's vassals. Under this new reality, each free man's position was rather determined by his direct or indirect feudal relation to the suzerain, the king, than by his natural subservience to the ruler of the Frankish people or the Frankish Empire. This usurpation of public authority by a system of private law contributed dramatically towards the political and legal fragmentation of the West in the ninth and tenth centuries.

9 The seigniorial system

125 Tenure and serfdom

Whereas the original function of the feudal system was military and administrative, the seigniorial system had an economic basis. In the decades before the fall of the Western Roman Empire, the Roman elite had increasingly withdrawn from the towns and established themselves in the country. Large rural estates, domains or manors were established, where large numbers of slaves (*servi*) tilled the ground in the service of their lord (*dominus*). The German conquerors of the West left this system intact and adopted it.

Under the influence of Christianity, the slaves obtained more rights and became serfs. At the same time a movement took place by which free farmers, from among both the original Romanised population and the Germans, relinquished their lands and freedom in favour of a local lord. In return they were given the land in tenure. The minority of these people remained free (*ingenui*) and were given free tenure, but many fell into bondage or serfdom. As serfs, they were tributary to their lord. In exchange for an annual, fixed tribute, which could be either a sum of money or a stake in the harvest, they could farm their land on their own account.

There were two kinds of serfs on the domains or manors. On the one hand there were the villains (*servi*). These were held in bondage for only as long as they held on to their tenure. Their bondage implied that they were, for instance, required to work the lord's own lands, the *demesne*, for a certain number of days. Apart from the land tribute, they also paid a poll tax, that is, a small tax to reflect their serfdom. If they gave up the tenure, they became free again and could leave the manor. By contrast, the other serfs (*mancipia*), who were generally descendants of earlier slaves, were bound not just to the land but also to the lord. They did, however, have certain rights and, in contrast to the case under ancient Roman law, were not regarded as *res* (goods). On the other hand, they were not permitted to leave the manor without the lord's consent and were subject to far more obligations.

126   Usurpation of royal authority

The late ninth and early tenth century saw the collapse of central authority. Local power magnates filled in the vacuum and usurped the king's political, legal and military authority within their territories. From this resulted the seigniorial system.

The term seigniory refers to a certain territory, large or small, the inhabitants of which came directly under the power of the lord. His power was similar to that of the king, or his regional official, the count. He exercised his power in his own name and not in that of the king or count, while at the same time – at least in theory – remaining subject to their authority. The seigniorial system refers to the fact that, during the crisis of royal authority, in virtually all parts of Europe, local and regional power magnates usurped royal authority in their territories, however large or small these might be. Since the king and sometimes also the counts were not themselves capable of defending their people and providing good governance, these local lords did so themselves. In some cases, the rulers expressly granted the local lords certain privileges (*libertates*). Apart from judicial and tax immunities, these could include the delegation of certain royal prerogatives and powers. In many cases, however, the lords simply usurped royal powers. Assumption of royal authority occurred at the level of the manors – in which case we can truly speak of seigniories – as well as at the level of counties or larger units such as margraviates or dukedoms – in which case we rather speak of principalities. Often, usurpation was layered between these levels. A duke, margrave or count would take over the most important royal powers, such as command of the army, high justice – for capital offences and important civil cases – and the mint, while the manorial lords assumed the daily administration of their manors as well as low justice. Low justice included, apart from petty crimes, the jurisdiction over serfs which had formerly belonged to the *vicarii* and *centenarii*, the royal representatives at the level of the sub-county level. The lords, who had previously only enjoyed authority over their free and unfree tenants as landowners, now became petty kings within their own domain.

Like the feudal system, the seigniorial system was both a cause and a consequence of the collapse of royal authority and the political fragmentation of Europe in the ninth and tenth centuries. Both systems shared another connection. In many cases, the original power base of the local magnates who usurped royal authority and thus became seigniorial lords or princes was their feudal fiefs. Only in a limited number of cases was the lord's power based on allodial land ownership (allodial seigniories), rather than feudal possession (feudal seigniories).

10   The Imperial Church under the Ottonians

127   The crisis of the church

Like the Carolingian monarchy, the papacy went through a deep crisis during the ninth and tenth centuries. Through their interference with the church, Charlemagne and Louis the Pious had jeopardised papal authority over the church and made the pope and the ecclesiastical hierarchy dependent on their support. After the collapse of royal authority in large parts of the West, the popes proved unable to restore their authority over the church. By the end of the tenth century, they had even lost their political control over their own diocese, Rome. The throne of Peter had become a pawn in the struggle between the clans in what had become the small provincial town of Rome. As such, its occupancy was not much more than that of Colosseum near the Forum, nothing but the symbol of a family's, often very temporary, ascendancy in the city of Rome.

Once the pope and kings had lost control over the church as a whole, abbeys and bishoprics all over western Europe fell within the grasp of local lords and princes. The higher clergy – bishops, abbots and monks of the great abbeys – were often the younger – or illegitimate – sons or siblings of local secular rulers. In this way, the regional power brokers gained financial and administrative control over the church institutions within their territories, laying claim to their revenues and interfering in their daily administration. Clerical discipline collapsed. Simony, the sale of ecclesiastical offices, and nicolaism, the marriage of priests, were common. The standard of education of many ordinary parish priests, and even higher clergymen, left much to be desired.

128   The Ottonians and the church

In the course of the tenth century, a new dynasty assumed power in Germany: the Ottonians. Like the Merovingians and Carolingians before them, the new dynasty, which also arrogated the imperial title in 962, forged an alliance with the church. To a greater extent than their Frankish predecessors, the Ottonians mobilised the church to administer their empire. Emperor Otto the Great and his successors systematically enfeoffed bishops and abbots, making them counts in those parts of the empire in which they held their ecclesiastical office. In this way, the Ottonians transferred secular authority over towns such as Cologne, Liége or Utrecht and the countryside around them to their local bishops. As vassals of the emperor, the bishops and abbots became secular rulers over large territories. This system had two advantages. First, the fact that bishops and abbots could, in principle, not marry meant that there were also no legitimate sons who could inherit their fief. Consequently, the fief reverted to the emperor upon the death of the count-prelate. Second, many prelates had enjoyed an education, were literate and had a command of Latin, which made them on average more suitable for administration than secular power magnates often were.

As the high clergy played a crucial role in the Ottonian machinery of power, it was vital for the emperors to have a say in the choice of who was to become bishop or abbot. During the crisis of the papacy, the Ottonians were successful in attaining control over the appointment – the investiture – of the high clergy. But once the papacy started to recover halfway through the eleventh century, confrontation between the emperor and the pope became all but inevitable. This became the Investiture Controversy.

B   Culture and the law

1   Germanic law

Ben diverso era il monaco scrivano immaginato dal nostro santo fonda-tore, capace di copiare senza capire.[10]

129   Customary law

The law of the Germanic peoples was in many ways far different from Roman law as it had developed over time. First of all, it should be clear that there was no such thing as a common law of the Germans. Each tribe, each people had its own law. But these various legal systems shared important common features. The term 'Germanic law', by consequence, does not refer to a single law system, but to a family of legal systems.

As with most primitive law, including Celtic law and archaic Roman law, Germanic law was predominantly customary law (*ewa*). A customary rule has two constitutive elements: a material (*corpus*) and a psychological (*animus*) one. The material element is the existence of usage or prac-tice (*usus*): a certain solution is repeatedly applied to a number of simi-lar cases. The psychological element consists of the consent among the people that the practice applies because the law dictates it (*opinio iuris*). With the Germans, this meant consent by the attendants of the assembly where the case was tried. As in most primitive legal systems, this consent rested on the belief that the practice was ancient. The authority of the law was founded in tradition, on the idea that the law was immutable.

Germanic law was unwritten. It was transferred from generation to generation through oral tradition. It existed in a culture where, gener-ally speaking, the written word played only a marginal role. Centuries of exposure to Greek and Roman civilisation had certainly familiarised the Germans with writing, but it never occupied the same place in their legal culture as it did with the Romans.

The orality of the law increased uncertainty about what the law said. It also allowed for the law to evolve constantly with the changing needs

---

[10]   Umberto Eco, *Il nome della rosa*, Milan 1980, 187. 'Quite different was the scribe-monk imagined by our sainted founder, capable of copying without understanding,' translation by William Weaver, *The Name of the Rose*, London 1983.

and mores, and to do so imperceptibly. This is the great paradox of all primitive customary law. While its authority is based on the belief that it is ancient and immutable, oral tradition allows for it constantly to evolve and adapt. Among the Germans as in other primitive cultures, if changes were noticed, these were explained away in terms of a restoration (*correctio*) of an old law that had been lost, or of a return to the proper understanding of a law that had been corrupted.

130   *Leges barbarorum*

The role of the king and the assembly was to ensure the correct application of the law, not to change it. By consequence, statute law held only a marginal place. After the invasions and the conquest of the Western Roman Empire, this started to change somewhat. Here, Roman influence told as Germanic kings took inspiration from the emperors and began to promulgate statute law, though far less than their Roman role models. In general, legislation was confined to the recording of existing law, the restoring of corrupted law and, more rarely, the supplementing and improving of it. In a minority of cases, statutes introduced new law.

Statute laws were promulgated by the king in front of the assembly. At the outset, in most of the Germanic kingdoms, the king was not to be considered a sovereign legislator, an autonomous source of law. He could legislate only with the consent of the assembly. The promulgation in the assembly expressed this. The king proposed the law and the assembly acclaimed it. Whether this reflected a true participation of the assembly in the decision-making process or not depended on the balance of power between the king and his leading subjects. For the most powerful kings such as Charlemagne, promulgation often meant little more than announcing new statutes to the magnates of his empire.

During the first centuries after the fall of the Western Roman Empire, in several of the Germanic kingdoms rather extensive recordings of the Germanic law were made and promulgated by the kings: the so-called *leges nationum Germanicarum* or *leges barbarorum*. As law was, generally speaking, applied personally and not territorially, in most cases these *leges* applied only to the Germanic subjects of the king. These recordings included both customary law and statute law. They were, for the most part, written in Latin. Their primary function was to set down the law and enhance legal certainty, not to change the law, although these recordings often included or were supplemented by recent royal decisions. In a few of the kingdoms, like that of the Lombards, these recordings were a reaction against Roman influence. In recording their law, the Germanic kings wanted to confirm the law and identity of their own peoples in relation to the Roman population they had conquered, even if, ironically, the very act of recording the law was an element of Romanisation. Examples of *leges barbarorum* include the *Lex Visigothorum* of 654 (also known as *Forum Iudicum* or *Fuero Juzgo*), the *Lex Burgundionum* (also known as *Lex Gundobada*), possibly from around 501, the *Lex Ripuaria* and the *Lex Salica*, initially recorded in the years 507–11, the *Pactus Alamannorum* from between 584 and 629 and its successor, the *Lex Alamannorum* from between 712 and 725, the *Lex Baiwariorum* of 743–4, the many 'dooms' promulgated by the various Anglo-Saxon kings in England from the early seventh century onwards, as well as the *Edicta* from the Lombard kings from between 643 and 755, the most famous of these being the *Edicta* of Rothari (643) and of Liutprand (713–35).

the law of the Visigoths [handwritten marginal note]

131 The Salic Law

The *Lex Salica* or Salic Law was a record of the law of the Salian Franks, from whom the Merovingians stemmed. It dated from the reign of Clovis and was probably made between 507 and 511. The law was later to be supplemented and re-promulgated by various kings. The latest version, the *Lex Salica emendata (Carolina)*, dates from the time of Charlemagne (798). The Salic Law provides a reasonably good impression of the content and nature of Germanic customary law.

The Salic Law comprised several dozen titles: the first version (*Pactus Legis Salicae*) sixty-five, the fourth a hundred and the fifth and final version of 798, seventy. In particular, it covered rules in relation to litigation and private law, in particular tort law.

For most offences, the Franks lacked any notion of public criminal law. Only a handful of crimes against the tribe or religion were subject to genuine punishments, generally the death penalty. As in the case of archaic Roman law, executions were often a kind of propitiatory sacrifice to appease the gods offended by the crime. With regard to the vast majority of 'offences', the governing authorities did not intervene with regard to prosecution or punishment. The offence was regarded not as an infringement against public order or, even less, the authority of the – non-existent – state, but as an injury against a private person. In that sense, proceedings did not differ from ordinary civil proceedings: it was a dispute between two or more private individuals, between perpetrator and victim. Prosecution was a matter for the victim and his kin; the goal was retribution.

The Salic Law was above all a catalogue of injuries and *compositiones* (singular: *compositio*, composition). The composition was a fixed and pre-determined indemnification that an offender was required to pay in order to buy off the justified revenge of the victim or his family. The more serious the offence was considered to be, the higher the amount.

> He who steals a suckling pig from the first or middle enclosure and it is proved against him, shall be liable to pay one hundred twenty denarii, i.e., three solidi.
>
> He who steals from the field a young pig that can live without its mother and it is proved against him, shall be liable to pay forty denarii, i.e., one solidus.
>
> He who kills a free Frank or other barbarian who lives by Salic law, and it is proved against him, shall be liable to pay eight thousand denarii, i.e., two hundred solidi.
>
> He who kills a count [shall be liable to pay] six hundred solidi.[11]

The basis of this system of compositions was the traditional *ius talionis*. In order to escape from the circle of revenge and counter-revenge, the law laid down a system of indemnification. If the proposed sum were paid by the offender and accepted by the victim, the latter would give up his right of revenge and the dispute would be at an end. Where that was not the case one reverted to the right of revenge. In this sense, the indemnification was not so much a monetary compensation for the damage, but more like punitive damages.

The *compositio* consisted of two elements: the *faidus* and the *fredus*. The *faidus* was the actual sum the offender had to give the victim to pay off the blood feud. The *fredus* – reflected in the etymologically related German word *Friede* – was a fine payable to the king or count by way of compensation for his role in settling the dispute. The king or count acted as guardian of law and order in society. He pronounced the final judgment handed down by the court – originally the assembly – and confirmed it with his *bannum*, that is the right to command observance and punish non-observance. The sentence then became binding; anyone violating it was guilty of breaking the king's or count's peace. The fine meant that an element of 'punishment' imposed by public authority had crept in and that there was a dimension of public law. Over the centuries the balance between *faidus* and *fredus* was to change in favour of the latter.

---

[11]   Translation by Katherine Fischer Drew, *The Laws of the Salian Franks*, Philadelphia 1991.

132   *Leges Romanorum*

Roman law was not swept away all of a sudden by the collapse of imper ial authority in the West. During the first centuries after the fall of the empire, it continued to be applied in much of western Europe. The Germanic kings allowed their Romanised subjects to continue to live under the Roman law and had their courts and ministers apply it to dis putes among them. In some cases, Roman law was even extended to the Germanic part of the population, as was the case with the Visigoths.

Roman law was, however, overly complex and extensive. It is highly doubtful whether it was ever applied in all its richness and complexity outside Rome and the other great cities of the Mediterranean. Already under the Dominate, significant efforts had been made to make Roman law more accessible and manageable. Justinian's codification had come too late to have any impact in much of the West, with the exception of parts of Italy. But the *Codex Theodosianus* was widely known through out the former Western Empire and had even been adopted by the Visigoths. After the imperial bureaucracy and judiciary had disappeared and their functions were taken over – or not – by the Germanic kings and their ministers, the need to simplify the law became even greater. Some Germanic kings – especially in southern Europe – applied Roman law rather well, but in general, kings, judges and litigants fell back on a limited number of summaries. Gradually, there emerged a simplified, so-called 'vulgar' Roman law based on a few surviving laws and texts from the time of the Dominate. In this, the evolution after the fall of the Western Empire only continued a process of simplification and vulgar isation that had already begun in the second half of the third century.

Shortly after their conquest, various Germanic kings decided to have the Roman law recorded, in simplified form: the so-called *leges Romanorum*. These Germanic codifications were anthologies of imperial legislation drawn from existing codes, such as the *Codex Theodosianus* which had found wide application in the West, and of writings by classical jurists such as Gaius, Papinian or Paul, taken from compilations and summar ies from the Dominate. They were made for the benefit of the 'Roman' subjects of the new Germanic kings, but in some cases were also extended to the Germanic population. Important examples of *leges Romanorum* include the *Lex Romana Visigothorum* promulgated by King Alaric II of the Visigoths in 506 (also known as the *Breviarium Alarici*), and the *Lex Romana Burgundionum* from the kingdom of the Burgundians on the Rhône. These efforts were not sustained, however. With time, as the Germanic tradition of orality settled in, recorded law was pushed further into the background. Roman substantive rules mainly survived – certainly at the local level – as a kind of 'Roman' customary law.

133   Personal and territorial application

In most of the Germanic kingdoms that replaced the Western Roman Empire, at the outset the law was applied personally. The Germanic conquerors lived by their own law, while the indigenous Romanised people continued to live under Roman law. But the various legal systems did not exist in isolation from one another. Over time, they started to interact, mutually influence one another, grow towards one another and even merge. The gradual intermingling of the various population groups certainly aided this. By the seventh or eighth century, in most of western Europe an open and eclectic legal system applied, which consisted primarily of customary law – some of it recorded, most not – and some statute law, the contents of which came from both Germanic and Roman law.

The relative importance of vulgar Roman law and Germanic law differed from the north to the south of Europe. In the more Romanised areas such as Italy, Spain and southern France, the 'Roman' population dominated and the impact of Roman law was greater. The customary law that thrived there was a kind of vulgar Roman law and references continued to be made to some Roman legal texts. In the north, where the Germanic population was bigger or the indigenous population had been less touched by Romanisation, Germanic – and Celtic – customary law became and remained dominant. The dividing line ran through the middle of France, to the south of Paris.

Several kings, in particular the Carolingians, had contributed to this process of mixture through their ambition to overcome the personal application of the law. They aspired to one law that would be territorially applied to all their subjects, regardless of their ethnic or cultural background. Charlemagne promulgated the *Lex Salica emendata* for all inhabitants of the empire: Franks, Germans and others. During the ninth and tenth centuries, the formation of countless small seigniories made it easy for the local lords to subject everyone to the same law within their relatively small territories. In that sense, the feudal and seigniorial systems and the fragmentation of public authority they brought contributed to the 'territorialisation' of the law.

2   *Courts and procedure in the Frankish Empire*

134   The *mallus*

Traditionally, the Germans brought and resolved their disputes before the assembly. According to the Roman historian Tacitus (Publius

Cornelius Tacitus, *c*.AD 55–120), the tribal leaders would generally seek to persuade the parties to resolve the dispute amicably and to have a particular outcome accepted rather than imposing a judgment. One could rather speak of arbitration.

By the Frankish era, this had changed. Still, the role of the 'judge' – the king, the count or their representatives – remained limited. He chaired the meeting, but did not decide upon the verdict. He was a judge 'in the old style'. The king held jurisdiction in the sense that he was responsible for the proper working of the courts and the observance of the law, but the authority to render judgment belonged to the people. The assembly was assisted in finding a verdict by a group of *sapientes* (wise men). These were generally older men chosen for their experience in dispute resolution, the knowledge of local law, and their familiarity with the region and the people involved. They listened to the parties and suggested the law which they considered to apply. They 'found' a judgment in the facts of the case and the customs applicable. The judge would then submit that solution to the people for approval or rejection. The judge would ultimately pronounce the verdict, approved by the assembly, and ensure its observance.

During the time of the invasions, the political and judicial organisation of the Germanic peoples was based on kin groups, tribes and peoples. Once the migrations were over and the various groups had settled, a territorial organisation arose. The smallest unit was now the *villa*, a small agricultural community encompassing the members of one or more old Germanic kin groups as well as the indigenous population. Various *villae* together formed a *centenarius* (hundred), which in turn formed part of a *pagus* (shire or county). Charlemagne's empire comprised some 300 *pagi*. At the borders of their empire, the Carolingians created margraviates or marches. These were areas that were bigger in size than the ordinary counties in order to provide the margrave with the necessary resources to defend the empire against external attacks. Dukedoms, in turn, were larger territories again, comprising various counties and often corresponding to the lands of a single German people such as the Saxons or Swabians. During the crisis of the ninth and tenth centuries, these 'mini-kingdoms' gained in importance, especially in the eastern part of the former Carolingian Empire, the later kingdom of Germany.

Since the time of the Merovingians, a 'ting' or assembly was held in each *pagus*, often referred to as a *mallus*, since the gathering was generally held on a hill. The *centenarii* had a similar assembly under the leadership of the *centenarius* (hundredman). Apart from disputes that were the preserve of the king or, increasingly, the ecclesiastical courts, all disputes between free members were in principle heard by the *mallus*. In earlier days, before there were permanent kings, a tribal assembly would be presided over by a judge, who was generally appointed for the occasion. Later this function was taken over by the king or, at the level of the *mallus*, by the count. As the king's deputy, the count was responsible for the proper administration of justice and the observance of the law, but his role as chairman of the *mallus* remained that of a judge of the old style. His task consisted of ensuring that the procedures were held in an orderly fashion. The royal power was reflected in the fact that the count urged a judgment from the members of the *mallus*. He would also subsequently read out the judgment reached by the *mallus*. This meant that the judgment was reinforced by the royal *bannum*. The judgment itself was reached by the assembled people. As in pre-Frankish times, it remained the task of the *sapientes* to propose a judgment or 'wisdom' on the basis of the applicable law. In the *mallus* these *sapientes* were also known as *rachinburgii* (those finding judgment). These were occasional jurors elected from the assembly. The number generally ranged between seven and thirteen.

Charlemagne sought to increase his control over the administration of justice at the county level. To this end, he took two important measures. First, he regularly sent *missi dominici* to the various counties and *malli* in order to check that the law was being correctly observed and to assist the counts. Second, he replaced the *rachinburgii* by *scabini* (aldermen); it was for this reason that courts were referred to later in the Middle Ages as the aldermen's bench or court. The position of aldermen was permanent. Although they were not professional judges but simply local notables presumed to be knowledgeable about local customary law, the change gave rise to a greater consistency in the interpretation and application of the law. On the other hand, the actual participation by the people in the judicial process diminished. The proposal made by the aldermen was generally followed.

135   Procedure

Before the *mallus*, procedures were accusatory. The trial was a legal action between two private individuals, the plaintiff and the defendant. The king or count did not prosecute unless royal property or rights were involved. It was up to the parties to table their arguments and evidence and in many cases even to indicate the customary laws they were basing their claims on.

The legal proceedings were almost entirely oral. Relatively little use was made of written documents. As far as witnesses were concerned, the number one could turn out in one's favour was generally more important than the substance of what they said. If neither of the parties was capable of persuading the court, an appeal to God was made. This was done by means of a trial by ordeal, or alternatively the parties would resort to a trial by battle in which they literally fought the matter out, either personally or through champions. The count would then declare the winner to be in the right.

Since the law was largely unwritten it was frequently subject to debate. The *rachinburgii* and aldermen played an instrumental role in determining the applicable law. But the parties themselves were also required to introduce the legal rules they were invoking and, if so requested, to prove their existence. To this end, different instruments of proof were developed and institutionalised in the Late Middle Ages.

136   The Palatinate Court

The eighth and early ninth century were marked by the increase of royal power both in the Frankish Empire and in England. Charlemagne and Louis the Pious, in particular, managed to enhance their power at the expense of traditional popular justice. This was reflected not just in the growing control of the king over the *mallus* but also in the increasing significance of the royal court. More and more cases were submitted directly to the king, thereby bypassing the *malli*.

Since time immemorial, it had been customary for nobles and free men to submit disputes to the king for mediation or arbitration. After the invasions, however, the role of the king grew. Apart from the jurisdiction he held as a judge of the old style, the king increasingly acted as a judge properly speaking, as a judge of 'the new style'. Like their counterparts among other Germanic peoples, the Frankish kings promulgated few laws and legal rules of universal application among all their subjects. By contrast, they frequently awarded privileges to particular subjects. In most cases, these privileges were grants of land, promises of royal protection, immunities from jurisdiction and from all different kinds of obligations. The king guaranteed that he would enforce those rights upon third parties. Observance of these rights came under the protection of his *mundium* and the authority of his *bannum* and were known as the 'peace' of the king or the land. As *rex et sacerdos*, the king extended his protection to all groups of vulnerable people, such as orphans and widows. Complaints in connection with these rights could be submitted directly to the king or his representative. In this way, the role and the significance of the royal court expanded. Increasingly, the king did not restrict himself to acting as mediator or arbitrator, but acted coercively. The king too sought the advice of a number of *sapientes*. In reality, these were the most important nobles, prelates and dignitaries attached to the royal court. They provided advice on the judgment, but it was the king – or his deputy – who ultimately determined the judgment. The king was the actual judge.

Under the Carolingians, a true royal court emerged: the Palatinate Court. Since the king was often not present in person, he was represented by the *comes palatii* (Count Palatine). The Palatine Court heard disputes concerning royal privileges and grants, especially of royal domains and lands (jurisdiction *ratione materiae*) or disputes in which certain individuals were involved, such as court officials or people under the protection of the ruler (jurisdiction *ratione personae*). There was no appellate procedure in Frankish law, so the Palatine Court did not act as a court of appeal. It did, however, exercise control over the county courts. Litigants could turn to the king if they found they had been treated unjustly in the *mallus*. Thus, complaints concerning the denial of justice (that is, refusal to hand down judgment) or false judgment (a judgment based on a mistaken interpretation of the law) could be referred to the king or to the Palatine Court. In principle, the king would then refer the matter to an ordinary court for a new verdict. Gradually, it became customary for the king himself or the Palatine Court to hand down a new verdict.

3   Iudicium parium

137   Plurality of legal systems and legal circles

As with the Roman population, the Germanic population was divided into separate orders. The Germans distinguished between *nobiles* (nobles), *ingenui* (free men) and *servi* (serfs). With time, the latter group split into villeins and slaves. The rising significance of cavalry (chivalry) in warfare and the feudal system ultimately led to a situation in which the nobility had a monopoly over the conduct of war, a process that was not completed until after 1000. Furthermore, the clergy came to form a third order of free men.

Out of the melting-pot of Germanic, Roman and eccleciastical tradition, Bishop Adalbero of Laon (d. 988) articulated the doctrine of the three orders: *oratores*, *pugnatores* and *laboratores*, or those who prayed, those who fought and those who toiled. Class distinction was ordained by God and could not be tampered with. Adalbero's classification of the three orders was to survive until the end of the eighteenth century as a leading social and juridical principle in western Europe.

These orders were more than social classes. Each order had its own legal status, living under its own laws, applied by its own courts. This is the system of *iudicium parium* (judgment by peers). By the year 1000, this system, combined with the territorial fragmentation caused by the feudal and seigniorial systems, gave rise to an extremely complex situation. There were canon law and canon courts for the clergy. Feudal cases were brought before feudal courts and were judged according to the feudal law. Within the seigniories, there were the aldermen's courts and seigniorial courts for free men and for serfs. The burghers – invariably free – of the many towns and boroughs that started to flourish after the year 1000 had their own municipal law and their own aldermen's courts. Finally, there were also the traditional, 'ordinary' royal and county courts that were in principle open to free men only. In many cases, these had been usurped by local lords or had stopped working.

In the same way as the political map, the juridical map of western Europe around the year 1000 provides a picture of far-reaching fragmentation. The Latin West had disintegrated into numerous political and juridical entities of varying size, each with its own territorial jurisdiction. This territorial fragmentation of jurisdictions and plurality of legal systems was doubled by the *iudicium parium* system, under which each class had its own law and institutions. The result was that there were literally thousands of customary law systems, applied in equally as many jurisdictions or legal circles by equally as many courts.

4 *The Augustinian ideology*

138 The intellectual contribution of the Early Middle Ages

In his masterpiece *The Name of the Rose*, the Italian semiotician and novelist Umberto Eco (b. 1929) has his main character, the young fourteenth-century Benedictine monk Adso of Melk, muse in the scriptorium of the abbey he is visiting about the monks from the earlier days of his order. They were capable of copying the great works of the ancients and the Church Fathers without needing to understand them: 'capace di copiare senza capire'.

These few words reflect the traditional assesment of early medieval intellectual history. In this understanding, the period's sole contribution to the cultural and intellectual development of the West was in copying and preserving the textual inheritance from Antiquity and the Church Fathers. The same was true for those periods of cultural revival such as the Carolingian Renaissance. The intelligentsia of the Early Middle Ages acted as passive conduits between the Roman era on the one hand and the Late Middle Ages and the Renaissance on the other.

It is indeed thanks to the copying activity of the Early Middle Ages that such a large part of the literature from Antiquity and early Christianity has been preserved. This picture is, however, somewhat lop-sided. Early medieval scholars did more than preserve and pass on the works of earlier times, also trying to understand and interpret the ideas contained in them and make them accessible to their contemporaries. These scholars adapted these ideas to their own needs. In this way, a synthesis was forged from the Graeco-Roman, Judaeo-Christian, and to a lesser extent, Celtic and Germanic intellectual and cultural traditions.

139   Saint Augustine

The Church Father Saint Augustine (354–430), Bishop of Hippo in North Africa, played a seminal role in creating an intellectual synthesis of Graeco-Roman and Judaeo-Christian traditions. Augustine managed to reconcile Christian theology, rooted as it was in Jewish tradition, with the Graeco-Roman philosophical and ethical tradition. The Roman Church was later to develop an all-embracing view on God, nature and humanity from the works of Augustine and a number of other Church Fathers and Christian scholars that was to shape the church and the Latin West into the eleventh century. It was Pope Gregory the Great who elevated Augustine's thought, mixed with that of Saint Benedict of Nursia, into the official doctrine of the church and hence of the West. Given the significance of Augustine's thought therein, it is legitimate to refer to this Gregorian doctrine as the Augustinian ideology, even if not all of Augustine's ideas were adopted or properly understood. As in the case of many great thinkers, it was Augustine's fate that his ideas took on a life of their own after he died. The main elements in Augustine's thinking are outlined below, in so far as they are relevant for the Augustinian ideology of the Early Middle Ages.

Augustine heavily drew on Neoplatonism, which was the dominant philosophical school under the late Roman Empire. Neoplatonism recycled much of Plato's thought, but also had some merit of its own. Its leading representative, the pagan Plotinus (204–70), adopted Plato's idealism and the dualism between the physical world and the World of Ideas. Plotinus advanced the idea that everything stemmed from and reverted to an originating Idea, 'the One', in the centre of his system. In addition, he distinguished the One as having three dimensions: the Supreme, the Spirit (*nous*) and the World Soul. Plotinus hereby unwittingly spanned the gap between Plato's concept of the One and the Christian concept of Holy Trinity.

Augustine's most important works were his *Confessiones* (Confessions), in which he related his conversion to Christianity, and his *De civitate Dei* or *The City of God*, written as an apology in response to the accusation that the departure from the old Roman gods had brought about the end of the Roman Empire and the destruction of the city of Rome in 410. Although Augustine's thinking does not form a coherent system, a number of essential ideas may be discerned that went to the heart of Christian thought in the Middle Ages.

140   *Ordinatio ad Unum*

The doctrine of original sin was a foundation stone of Augustine's theology. The book Genesis in the Old Testament relates how Adam and Eve were expelled from the Garden of Eden because they had eaten from the tree of knowledge, having been tempted by the devil. This had disrupted the original harmony between God and man. Man, from birth, was burdened by the original sin of Adam and Eve. Augustine's doctrine of original sin explained the central place baptism was to have in medieval theology. Through baptism, man's sinful nature is washed away; the baptised is reborn under a new 'nature': that of member of the church, the people of God. The church incarnates the continuing presence on earth of Jesus Christ who, through his life and death, had offered redemption from original sin and given people a new chance to save their souls. Salvation is conditional upon the acceptance of Christ's sacrifice, through faith in Christ and, of necessity, membership of his church. The dogma of original sin leads to the rejection of human nature as sinful: people are born into sin and face eternal damnation. Only through accepting Christ's sacrifice and adherence to the church can one's soul be saved in the afterlife. The autonomy of man as a natural being is rejected.

A second key notion in Augustinian thinking is the doctrine of participation. This goes back to Plotinus. Under this doctrine, the finality of each being springs from the fact that it forms part of a greater whole. The essence of each being lies outside itself. This results in a hierarchical worldview in which each being strives towards a higher reality and ultimately to the eternally unchangeable One, or God: the *ordinatio ad Unum*.

These views stem from Plato's idealism as recounted in the allegory of the cave. Truth is to be found not on earth or in nature, but beyond. Augustine combines this with Judaeo-Christian theology. God is the beginning and end of all creation. The natural or temporal world carries no purpose in itself. Eternal salvation is man's true purpose. Therefore, life on earth must be lived in preparation for eternal life and man must devote himself as much as possible to doing God's will. These ideas provide the basis for what was to become the central thesis of the Augustinian ideology of the Early Middle Ages: the rejection of the physical and temporal world and total orientation to the metaphysical world, to God and the afterlife. In the Augustinian view, life on earth is no more than a preparation for eternal life. Outside that context, human life has no value or purpose. The *ordinatio ad Unum* (orientation towards the One) permeates all aspects of human life. The medievalist Walter Ullmann (1910–83) speaks of a unipolar world vision. The subjection of the natural to the divine is, according to Ullmann, also universal – in terms of time and place – as well as total. With this, he means that it extends to all areas of human and social life.[12]

Augustine's basic ideas permeated the entire Western ideology and were decisive for the positions the church took in various areas.

141   Ecclesiology and canon law

In the first place, the unity of thought was reflected in ecclesiology, that is, the doctrines about the nature and role of the church. Since salvation can only be obtained through faithful membership of the church, the church is placed at the very centre of human existence. The church – the embodiment of Christ's continuing presence on earth – is the mediator between man and God. The ecclesiastical hierarchy or clergy has a monopoly over the administration of the sacraments such as baptism, the eucharist and later confession. The sacraments, particularly eucharist, symbolise Christ's sacrifice for mankind and man's acceptance of it, on which salvation is conditional. Ultimately, the final decision at the Last Judgment will depend on God's mercy. On this point, there is a difference between Augustine's writings and the Augustinian theology as elaborated by Gregory the Great and others. Augustine emphasises that human beings can only be saved by the mercy of or a decision by God and that human beings are unable to do anything about this in their lives. The fate of each soul has already been decided at the beginning of time; this is the doctrine of predestination. The church mitigated this by suggesting that people could nevertheless help determine their fate through faith and by doing God's will. Human will then becomes free and decisive, although God, who is outside all time, knows the outcome of the final reckoning in advance.

---

[12] See for his views on the Augustinian worldview: Walter Ullmann, *Medieval Foundations of Renaissance Humanism*, London 1977, 14–28.

Whatever the case may be, the propositions put forward by Augustine, like those of other Church Fathers, contributed towards the transformation of the church from a community of the faithful into a hierarchical, legal institution. The church faced the task of duplicating the natural order with an all-embracing ecclesiastical one. In the same way as Plato's soul, the church does not form part of the physical world. By means of baptism and inclusion into the church, human beings are divested of their nature and move to a different sphere. That sphere is beyond nature and, thus, artificial; it spans the gap between man and his salvation by God. The church is not part of the natural world and is not subject to the laws of nature. Instead it answers to a God-given, immutable order. Since that order is unnatural it has to be rendered explicit. This is the role of canon law: the creation of an artificial order and hierarchy setting the church apart from the natural order of the physical world.

The sacraments symbolise the mediating function of the church between man and God. Receiving the sacraments becomes the key element in the profession of faith. Personal, inner belief outside the church loses significance. Towards the year 1000, religion is turned into liturgy: the continual repetition of the same ritual, sacramental acts whereby the church reiterates Christ's sacrifice and man's acceptance of it and thus fulfils its mediating role. Canon law regulates this liturgy.

Since God and the divine order of things do not form part of the natural order, faith and the understanding of truth are not inherent in human nature. What Christians need to believe is determined in the dogmas of the church, in theology. Truth can only be acquired through studying theology or through mystical contact with God, a process clearly similar to Plato's metempsychosis. Therefore, not everybody can attain the same understanding of God and the divine will. By consequence, the people of God fall apart into two groups: laity and clergy. The latter form a separate hierarchy of priests and bishops, monks and abbots who stand outside and apart from the secular order. Their status too is regulated by canon law. The sacraments may be received only from the hands of the clergy, who hold a monopoly over the mediation between man and God.

142 Church and state

Second, Augustine's view of the state reflects the dominant role of religion and church in four ways. *Primo*, the state is no more natural than the church. The fall of man broke the natural relation between God and man. Man is, consequently, no longer able to live in nature but is subjected to a political organisation. This is regarded as a necessary evil. *Secundo,* the Church Father has an instrumental vision of the state. The only purpose of the state – in Augustine's time still the Roman Empire – lies in that it, in bringing order and securing peace, allows people to live as good Christians and to prepare for the afterlife. In that sense, Augustine defends the unity of the empire: as there is a single church, so there should be a single empire. Augustine considers the collapse of the empire as punishment for the sinfulness and faithlessness of man. *Tertio,* however much one may seek to do so, the *civitas terrena* (the state on earth) will never correspond with the heavenly ideal, the *civitas Dei.* Perfect peace and order on earth are unattainable but are nevertheless worth striving for. Augustine does, however, have little faith in change and progress and emphasises that it is better to maintain the existing order. The unattainability of 'heaven on earth' means that change does not measure up against the risk of disrupting the existing order. Augustine's political order is static. The static nature of political power was later reflected in the doctrine of the three orders, under which each person was assigned his or her fixed place. *Quarto,* the Augustinian ideology provides ammunition for a descending theory of power. Since the state has its place in the divine plan, secular authority ultimately comes from God. The emperor is God's appointee, not the people's.

143   History

Third, there is Augustine's interpretation of history. History is nothing but the fulfilment of God's preordained plan with mankind. There are six eras of a thousand years each. Each of these eras refers to one of the six days of creation. After all, to God a thousand years is but one day.[13] The birth or passion of Christ announces the final era – hence the expectation that the year 1000 or 1033 would usher in the end of time. This final era is the time of the church. Under this interpretation of history, the fall of the Western Roman Empire does not form an important caesura. To the contrary, the beginnings of the Roman Empire – the reign of Augustus – coincide with the coming of Christ. This helps to explain why the empire lived on in people's minds and why until well into the Middle Ages people regarded themselves not so much as the heirs but as part of the Roman tradition.

144   Intellectual tradition

Fourth, for Augustine and his followers, education and scholarship are only valuable inasmuch as they are instrumental towards understanding

---

[13] 'For in your sight a thousand years are as the passing of one day.' Psalms 90:4.

the divine. The study of language, the classical texts, philosophy, logic, rhetoric and nature are no more than keys towards a better understanding of God's word. Augustine's views had a double impact on early medieval scholarship and education. On the one hand, they legitimise the recovery by Christianity of Graeco-Roman scholarship. Herein lies the greatest and most lasting contribution of Augustine to the intellectual history of the West. Augustine, himself a teacher of rhetoric at Rome and Milan before his conversion to Christianity, emphatically defends the idea that Christians should learn and study the classical languages, literature and science in preparation for studying the Bible. Thereby, he facilitated the preservation of much of the literary inheritance of Antiquity, including the writings of pagan authors. In preserving their texts, the church is following the proposition that God in his wisdom has revealed some of his divine plan to a few pagan souls – *animae naturaliter Christianae* (souls by nature Christian).

On the other hand, all scholarship is, at least in theory, subordinated to the one true science, theology, and to the church. Put differently, theology is the sole and all-embracing science. In this way, the dividing lines between the various disciplines become blurred as each discipline ultimately obeys the same laws and is subject to the same truth, namely that of theology and the Bible. Theology came to encompass all kinds of disciplines during the Early Middle Ages. The insights on philosophy, ethics, physics, politics and law from early medieval scholarship are, to a large extent, contained in theological writings.

More generally, Augustine assigns no more than a minor place to reason in the quest for truth. Only through faith can one arrive at truth. Reason serves to persuade man to rely on his faith and the authority of the church. In reading and interpreting the Bible, one must allow oneself to be guided by the dogmas of the church, that is, by the ecclesiastical authorities. Around the year 600, Gregory the Great articulated his deep suspicion against free thought. Gregory equated intellectual freedom with pride, the worst of the seven mortal sins. Even so, the church of Gregory and his successors was instrumental in the survival of much of Graeco-Roman scholarship.

5   Education and scholarship during the Early Middle Ages

145   The survival of classical texts

By defending the intellectual heritage of Graeco-Roman Antiquity, Augustine and other Church Fathers ensured that it remained largely preserved. Within the church, the classical texts of great pagan authors were kept and copied and in some cases even taught and studied.

The process of simplification and vulgarisation that marked law and jurisprudence in late Roman times and after now marked education and scholarship in general. In the same way that anthologies were made from the works of the classical jurists for educational purposes and to answer practitioners' needs, the same happened with works of philology, logic, rhetoric, philosophy and natural sciences. It was the Roman summaries, anthologies, commentaries and Latin translations of ancient texts compiled and made from the second century onwards that were used by Christian scholars from the Early Middle Ages, not the original texts. Similarly, the first great Christian scholars such as Boethius (480–525/6), Cassiodorus (*c*.480–575) and Isidore of Seville (*c*.560–636) made Latin translations and summaries of works of classical philosophers, rhetoricians, natural scientists and literators, accompanied by commentaries. This gave rise to a limited canon of classical texts that was recovered by the medieval church and scholarship. In the field of philosophy, Plato and Neoplatonism were dominant. Of Aristotle only the books on logic containing his ideas on the classification of science into classes – referred to in the Middle Ages as *categoriae* – were known. Among the literary giants of Antiquity, Virgil was the most authoritative author, while Cicero was also considered important for his philological, rhetorical and philosophical work.

146   Church and education

From the sixth century onwards, monasticism spread all over western Europe. Having originated in the east of the former Roman Empire, monasticism took two forms: that of the solitary hermit – the word monk stems from *monos*, meaning *only, alone* in Greek – and that of monks or nuns living in a closed community. In the West, the second model gained the upper hand. The supreme figure in the development of monastic life, towering high above all other founders of orders and monasteries, is Saint Benedict. The Rule of Saint Benedict laid the foundations for the organisation of monasteries and abbeys in the Latin West for many centuries. Pope Gregory the Great, who was a great admirer of Benedict, wanted all monasteries to be organised along Benedictine lines and sought to make the Rule a universal one. Benedict's Rule established a balance for the monks between two activities: *ora et labora* (prayer and work). The monks were required to devote a large part of the day to liturgy, performing the sacraments, praying and praising God. Gregory assigned a major role to music, Gregorian chant. In addition, the monks were required to work in order to provide for their livelihood. As time went by, such work was also taken to include the copying of books in the scriptoria, and study. Partly as a result, it became possible for the Benedictine abbeys to have scriptoria in which not just the Bible and works of the Church Fathers, but also the works of classical authors were copied, summarised and in some cases commented upon. The monasteries established large libraries in which all this was preserved.

It was in the monasteries and, to a lesser extent, in the schools of the diocesan cathedrals and the royal palaces, that education was provided. Most of the pupils and students would ultimately become monks or priests. Some of these would, later in their lives, play a role in royal government. Particularly in the Carolingian age, students also included sons from noble families who were not being prepared for the church. The educational programme was organised along Roman lines. The ultimate purpose of education was the study of the Bible and the ability to perform the liturgy correctly.

147   Artes liberales

During the Carolinian Renaissance, Alcuinus (*c.*730–804), head of Charlemagne's Palatial School in Aachen, drew up the educational programme according to the classification of the seven *artes liberales* or liberal arts. That classification stemmed from a work by the fifth-century writer Martianus Capella, *The Marriage of Mercury and Philology*, an allegory in which the god Mercury, the quick-witted messenger of the gods who was practised in the art of love, goes in search of a wife. Ultimately, he finds her in Philology, the study of language. As a marriage gift Mercury gives his wife seven servants, the seven liberal arts. The work continues with a discussion of those seven *artes* or disciplines.

The extent to which the seven *artes liberales* also formed the canon of classical education in the Roman schools is subject to debate.[14] For us, it is only important that the Christian authors of the Middle Ages considered that they were following the Roman programme of education by providing instruction in the seven liberal arts. The seven *artes* were subdivided into two groups: the *trivium*, or the three disciplines generally corresponding with what we now refer to as the humanities, and the *quadrivium*, or the four disciplines corresponding more closely with exact sciences.

---

[14] Marcus Terentius Varro (116–27 BC) referred to nine liberal arts, also adding medicine and architecture. These latter lost their status among the *artes liberales* and became considered professional or traditional disciplines.

The *trivium* consisted of grammar, dialectics or logic, and rhetoric. Grammar was philology in a general sense. It concerned studying and learning to use Latin, in reading and writing. Grammar also included the reading and understanding of texts from the canon of the classical authors, such as Virgil, and Latin translations of Greek, pagan and Christian authors. Martianus Capella accordingly referred to them as *litteratura*. 'My duty in the early stages was to read and write correctly; but now there is the added duty of understanding and criticizing knowledgeably ... I have four parts: letters, literature, the man of letters, and literary style.'[15] Grammar also included the study of philosophy and logic. Some of the more original thinkers of the Early Middle Ages, such as Alcuinus, focused on the theory of categories (*categoriae*). According to this theory, all knowledge could be reduced to a system of general concepts (*genus*, plural *genera*) and specific manifestations (*species*). The basic texts for the study of logic were provided by the *Isagoge*, a commentary by the Neoplatonist Porphyrius (234–*c*.304), and Boethius's commentary thereon – and not the Greek original of Aristotle. In this way, the scholars of the Early Middle Ages triggered the development of a new logic that was to blossom from the eleventh century onwards: medieval dialectics. The emphasis was not so much on the construction of a comprehensive system of knowledge concerning a particular discipline; instead it was on the philosophical and theological consequences of the claims to truth of general categories and concrete phenomena. Rhetoric was considered the least important of the three disciplines of the *trivium* and steadily lost ground. The *quadrivium* too was overshadowed by grammar and logic. The four branches of the *quadrivium* were *arithmetica* (arithmetic), *geometria* (geometry), *astronomia* (cosmology) and *musica* (music), which was taught from a mathematical perspective. These four disciplines shrank to a few fragments of elementary arithmetic, a few topics useful to theology such as computation (biblical chronology) and some basic knowledge about geography and cosmology.

148 Carolingian Renaissance

The Augustinian ideology, the monastic libraries and the liberal arts form the three intellectual foundations on which the Latin West based its edifice of civilisation and scholarship during the Early Middle Ages. This culminated in the Carolingian Renaissance. This intellectual and cultural

---

[15] Martianus Capella, *De nuptiis Philologiae et Mercurii* 3.230–231, translation by William Harris Stahl, Richard Johnson and E. L. Burge, vol. II, New York 1977.

Renaissance served a political purpose. Charlemagne and Louis the Pious promoted the political and legal unity of their empire. The church was mobilised to actively promote administrative harmonisation, as well as cultural and intellectual unification.

Charlemagne took a great interest in education. As we have seen this was primarily, but not exclusively, concerned with the training of bishops, priests and monks. Charlemagne ordered that each bishop should set up a school. All through the empire, the same curriculum would be taught. Charlemagne also introduced this programme in his Palatial School at Aachen.

Carolingian education and scholarship aimed not so much at expanding existing knowledge as at understanding the eternal, immutable and perfect truth that is with God. Human knowledge is not perceived in terms of an expandable mass; God has preordained what man is capable of understanding. Christianity is a religion of revelation; God has revealed himself to humankind. For the medieval Christians, all knowledge has been revealed to humankind by God in the Bible and the other texts of the early Christian and classical canon. The truth is immutable and contained in these texts. The understanding of these texts may evolve and improve, but the texts themselves do not. Furthermore, the influence of Plato's idealism strengthens the static nature of scholarship. The object is not knowledge of physical phenomena but the most direct insight possible into the supreme truth.

The Carolingian sponsors of intellectual life had little faith in the ability of the scholars of their age to add anything to the understanding by the first Church Fathers of the Bible and the classical text canon. Most of all, they were fearful that their endeavours would corrupt the understanding of their great predecessors. Scholarship was hardly seen in terms of accumulation and growth of knowledge, but rather as the ongoing preservation, repetition and tradition of the same truth contained in the classical text canon. The immutability of knowledge strengthened and ensured the unity of thought. The theological approach to scholarship interacted with the political aims of the Carolingians. The empire needed a universal, total and immutable politico-ecclesiastical ideology or theology.

149   Carolingian education

During the Carolingian Renaissance, education and scholarship were, logically enough, concerned primarily with grammar and the improvement – *correctio* – of Latin. A thorough and correct knowledge of Latin was fundamental to an educational programme which served to prepare students for theology and liturgy.

> And let schools be established in which boys may learn to read. Correct carefully the Psalms, the songs in writing, the songs, the calendar, the grammar, in each monastery or bishopric, and the catholic books; because often some desire to pray to God properly, but they pray badly because of faulty books. And do not permit your boys to corrupt them in reading or writing. If there is need of writing the Gospel, Psalter and Missal, let men of mature age do the writing with all diligence.[16]

This fragment from one of the most important statutes of Charlemagne on education immediately betrays the purpose behind the entire Carolingian educational reform. Charlemagne and his associates were aware that inadequate knowledge and the corruption of Latin were responsible for the numerous errors made by the monks and other writers and scholars when copying and commenting upon the Bible and the Christian and classical authors. The result was that the truth given by God to human-kind through the Bible, the Church Fathers and the enlightened pagan authors had become obscured. Monks and priests therefore needed to be trained so that the old Christian and pagan texts could be correctly copied, free from corruption. Commenting upon and discussing the texts were of much less concern during the Carolingian Renaissance, although the movement did produce a number of important thinkers, including Alcuinus himself. Some of the intelligentsia also held that the time would come when a better understanding of the texts would be pos-sible. Until such time, the ancient texts had to be preserved unharmed. In the meantime, the monks were able to 'copiare senza capire'. In doing so the intelligentsia of the Early Middle Ages acted as a conduit between Antiquity and the Late Middle Ages and humanism. The irony is that it was precisely in this attitude that their original contribution to the devel-opment of the West lay: the Augustinian sacralisation of the classical canon contained the seeds of the intellectual revival after the year 1000. Furthermore, the ideal of immutability did not prevent the thinkers of the Carolingian Renaissance from further articulating and delineating the Augustinian ideology.

150   Liturgy

The static and even repetitive nature of education and scholarship emerged even more clearly in another area of cultural life: liturgy. Apart

---

[16] *Admonitio generalis* (789), translation by Dutton, *Carolingian Civilization*.

from education, the Carolingians were closely involved with monastic life. Louis the Pious undertook a reform of the monasteries, an initiative that was a precursor to the great reform of Cluny in the tenth and eleventh centuries. His aim was to harmonise religious life within the walls of the many monasteries and abbeys throughout the Frankish Empire. Formally, this was achieved by imposing the Rule of Benedict. In practice, the spirit of this Rule was distorted. In many abbeys, monks ceased to perform manual labour themselves. Only the work in the scriptoria and libraries could still be regarded as *laborare*. More than ever, the emphasis lay on liturgy. The monks filled their days with as many as seven services. In these, the Gregorian chant took centre-stage. Along with grammar, music accordingly assumed a central place in their education. The Gregorian liturgy and chant formed as it were the final step in the Carolingian educational programme. Furthermore, the monastic system symbolised the ideal of the unified, Carolingian society along the lines of Augustinian ideology. A network of monasteries, which all celebrated the same liturgy, emerged throughout the West. This was the consecration of a faith and a church based not on individual faith but on collective, institutionalised liturgy. Human salvation was assured not by devout living but by the institutionalised repetition of rites by a specially trained elite. The members of this elite were often the younger sons of noble families who could thus assure the spiritual welfare of their older warrior-brothers. The ideals of unity and immutability of empire and church meant that the top and the base increasingly drifted apart. In the same way that the monarch elevated himself above his people as God's representative on earth, so the church excluded the laity, its own people.

6   *The Carolingian Renaissance and the law*

151   *Capitularia*

Augustinian ideology also had an impact on legal thought. The static worldview fitted well with the primitive, Germanic conception of immutable law. The Carolingian Renaissance did not bring about any fundamental shift in this regard, even though Charlemagne and his successors were more active legislators than most of their predecessors. As legislators, they were concerned less with changing the law than with improving, harmonising and unifying it. However much this might lead to adjustments and reforms, it did not necessarily detract from the idea that royal intervention was aimed at the preservation, restoration and improvement of traditional law which had been corrupted over time.

Carolingian statute laws are referred to in historiography as *caputilaria* (literally, chapters). These were promulgated orally by the king in the presence of the leading nobles. In principle, the consent of 'the people' remained mandatory, but under a powerful monarch such as Charlemagne this was often little more than a formality. The written text had only instrumental and no constitutive value; it served only as evidence.

Much of Carolingian statute law fell under the ancient tradition of recording and supplementing 'popular' law. Except in the case of a major recording such as the *Lex Salica emendata* in which the entire Salic Law was recorded, this primarily took the form of the *capitularia legibus addenda* (that is, *capitularia* that had to be added to the statutes). These mostly pertained to private and criminal law. In addition, there were the *capitularia per se scribenda*. These were self-standing statutes which often introduced new rules. Although the distinction cannot be strictly applied, it is nevertheless fair to say that these were mainly used for interventions in the field of public administration, the judiciary, the church and the army. The reforms of the church, the monastic system and schooling were also implemented through *capitularia* – the so-called *capitularia ecclesiastica* in contrast to the *capitularia mundana*.

The upsurge in legislation proved to be brief. The fact that these statute laws dealt primarily with matters of government and church meant that their influence on the further development of law in Europe, with the possible exception of canon law, was not particularly great. The legislative activities of the Frankish kings went into decline after the year 900.

The restoration of the unity of the West under Charlemagne and Louis the Pious was short lived but nevertheless left behind deep traces on the political and constitutional history of Europe. In the first place, Charlemagne's empire breathed new life into the concept of empire and the idea of the unity of the West. In the second place, and more particularly, the Carolingian emperors, in their efforts to strengthen the unity of their empire, articulated a vision of culture, politics and kingship in which Roman, Christian and Germanic elements were interwoven. Even though their attempt failed, the age of Charlemagne was viewed with nostalgia in the centuries to follow. The Carolingian synthesis cast a long shadow before it.

7   *The decline of jurisprudence*

152   The decline of jurisprudence

Thanks to the short-lived re-conquest of Italy under Justinian in 554, a few copies of his great codification, including the *Digest*, reached the peninsula. The Byzantine dominion was, however, too brief and the text too extensive and complex for widespread distribution in the West. After the Byzantines had been driven out of northern and middle Italy, the Justinian codification fell into oblivion. Just a few scarce copies of the *Institutes* remained in circulation in Italy. Of the *Codex* the first nine books were known, and then in abridged form, the *Epitome Codicis*. The few remaining copies of the *Digest* and *Novellae* disappeared into libraries, where they were to lie virtually untouched for several centuries. Only a few fragments of these texts remained known. Outside Italy, fragments from the huge mass of Roman jurisprudence were saved thanks to their incorporation in the *leges Romanorum*.

By the sixth century at the latest, legal science as an autonomous discipline as well as legal education had all but disappeared from the West. The Germans did not have any legal science themselves, nor did they develop any after their conquest. They had no distinct class of jurists. With the exception of the clergy, judges and administrators had little if any scholarly education and certainly no legal training. At best, they were practitioners who had built up a knowledge of the law through experience.

153   Natural law and the church

A few traces of Roman jurisprudence survived also in theological works. For example, the *Etymologiae* of the Spanish Bishop Isidore of Seville, a kind of etymological encyclopaedia, contained several references to Roman law and legal sources.

The concept of 'natural law' found its way into early medieval theology. Church Fathers and later theologians were able to indentify with Cicero's ideas on the subject. In *De republica*, Cicero wrote that 'one eternal and unchangeable law will be valid for all nations and all times, and there will be one master and ruler, that is, God, over us all'.[17] The Church Fathers of the second and third centuries had already built on Cicero's definition. God, in creating the world, had created natural law. This was now equated with divine law; it was the reflection of the divine will in nature. According to the Church Father Origen (*c*.181–*c*.254), natural law had been implanted in the human heart and man could recognise it there by virtue of his reason. Origen claimed that all law should be in accordance with natural or divine law to be valid. Augustine and Isidore of Seville shared his opinion. Natural law evolved into a kind of ideal of justice that could act as a touchstone for all law. In doing so, Christian theology

---

[17]   Cicero, *De republica* 3.33.

propped up the Germanic tradition of immutable law. The doctrine also laid the groundwork for a claim by the church to supremacy in law. In the Early Middle Ages, however, these ideas were not further articulated and largely remained dormant.

8   *The emergence of canon law*

154   The organisation of the church under the late Roman Empire

The conversion to Christianity of Constantine the Great and the recognition of Christianity as the empire's official religion by Theodosius the Great triggered a radical transformation of the church. The emperors began to take an active interest in theology, liturgy and church organisation and involved the church in the administration of the empire.

Within a few generations, a church hierarchy and bureaucracy had been established. This required countless regulations and laws. Until the fourth century, the church had produced no more than a handful of laws. Canon law was limited to a few guidelines relating to liturgy, discipline and relations among the faithful. With regard to other matters, such as church property and juridical procedure, Roman law applied.[18] The clergy had not yet set itself apart from the laity, so that their authority and powers did not need to be articulated as yet.

This changed in the fourth and fifth centuries. Imperial constitutions and decisions by universal councils – the assembly of the bishops and other leaders of the whole church – regulated the organisation and operation of the church in great detail. The provincial or local synods of bishops and church leaders worked out separate regulations for the various church dioceses and provinces. The church was given ever greater jurisdiction by the emperors. As the Roman administrative institutions in the West failed or disappeared, the bishops in the various provinces were assigned greater powers as judges and administrators.

155   The growth of canon law

After the collapse of imperial authority and the conquests by the Germans, many bishops tried to cling on to their secular juridical and administrative power. The church claimed jurisdiction over any disputes involving the clergy – *privilegium fori*. It also, with varying success, attempted to obtain or maintain a grip over disputes relating to the

---

[18] 'Ecclesia vivit iure romano: the church lives under the Roman law', from the Frankish *Lex Ribuaria*.

sacraments, such as marriage, and by way of extension over all family law or over the punishments for serious sins. Thus the church was later to claim jurisdiction over any agreements confirmed by oath; for was not perjury a sin?

Following the invasions, the re-Christianisation of Europe in the sixth and seventh centuries and the papal policies to strengthen the unity of the church led to a new wave of lawmaking within the institution. As far as the entire church was concerned, that legislation sprang from the popes – the so-called decretals – or from the universal councils – the so-called decrees or *canones*. It is for this reason that we refer to canon law rather than ecclesiastical or church law. Bishops and provincial synods also promulgated law for their own jurisdictions. Rules of law were taken from the Bible and the writings of the Church Fathers.

The papal decretals underwent an evolution similar to that of the imperial *rescripta* or *decreta*. Initially, these were papal rulings in individual cases. But as they were highly authoritative, they came to be applied *erga omnes*.

156   Early collections of canon law

The earliest collections of canon law go back to the late Roman Empire. Particularly famous were the *Dionysiana*, a collection from the sixth century compiled by a Scythian monk, Dionysius Exiguus. This collection contained both papal decretals and conciliar *canones*. The seventh-century *Hispana* was more extensive and received a wide distribution. During the Carolingian era and even during the crisis of the ninth and tenth centuries, various collections were made. Together with the popes, the Carolingian kings strove for the unification of canon law. Charlemagne asked Pope Hadrian I (772–95) for a compilation of what he regarded to be the prevailing law in the church. In 774, the pope sent the king the so-called *Hadriana*, a revised version of the *Dionysiana*. In 802, the Synod of Aachen decided that all dioceses should apply the *Hadriana* and the *Hispana*. The active ecclesiastical policy of Charlemagne and his son Louis the Pious not only increased the unity of the church but also stimulated the dissemination of the faith and strengthened the implantation of the church and its organisation throughout the Frankish Empire. It was for this reason that all sorts of new laws were promulgated, for example in royal and imperial *capitularia*, in the decades either side of the year 800.

The collapse of royal and papal authority after 850 led in turn to new and radical changes in the life and organisation of the church. The usurpation of the ecclesiastical investiture by secular power brokers stripped large elements of canon law of their relevance. The rapid succession of changes created the need for new collections. During the ninth, tenth and early eleventh century, various collections of canon law were produced at the private initiative of certain clerics. Among other things, these collections were aimed at strengthening the position of the pope and the bishops vis-à-vis the secular rulers. There was no hesitation about including false decretals and *canones* on which the church could base its claims in respect of such rulers. In the ninth century, the so-called *Pseudo-Isidoriana* were compiled in the archbishopric of Reims. Apart from existing legal texts, this book contained false *canones*. Nevertheless, it became one of the most widely distributed works of the period. Another famous and much more reliable compilation was the *Decretum* of Bishop Burchard of Worms (bishop 1000–25). The book also dealt with theological issues.

9   *Correctio*

157   The Dark Middle Ages?

In a survey of the historical development of the Western legal tradition, it is tempting to place the period between 500 and 1000 between brackets and to give it no more than a cursory glance. After the collapse of Roman authority in the West, the law went into decline. Even during the heyday of the Carolingian Empire, it did not prove even remotely possible to approach the level of classical Roman law. The disappearance of Roman law also saw the withering away of legal education and legal scholarship. Until the Renaissance of the Twelfth Century, there was no further question of an autonomous legal science. As such the law of the Early Middle Ages has little significance for the emergence of legal science in the Latin West after the year 1000.

When the revival began, Antiquity became the point of reference for the law, just as in other branches of cultural life. To historians, the Early Middle Ages became an interim period between Antiquity and the new golden age. The period was regarded as no more than a conduit for the writings and knowledge of the Ancients, which had been preserved and copied in the numerous monastic libraries of Europe. As far as the law was concerned, it may be noted that the leading text that was to determine the face of legal science after the year 1000 was Justinian's *Digest*, which was thought to have been lost during the Early Middle Ages. In this regard, the period played a smaller role in the history of the textual tradition in law than it did in other branches of scholarship and science.

This traditional view on the Early Middle Ages is lop-sided and unqualified. Nevertheless, it does have historical merit in itself as it dates back far in time, at least to Renaissance. And as later historians would do, the men of the Renaissance overlooked one thing: the Early Middle Ages may have acted as a conduit, but that did not necessarily make it a passive conduit. The legacy of Antiquity which was taken up during the eleventh and twelfth centuries was the legacy as it had been understood by the scholars and rulers of the Early Middle Ages and adapted to their requirements. The scholars of the Late Middle Ages may have thought that they were entering into a dialogue with Antiquity, but in reality they were turning to an Antiquity as it was perceived and moulded by their medieval forefathers.

158 Augustinian ideology and the Renaissance of the Twelfth Century

The influence of the Early Middle Ages made itself felt in two respects. First, ignoring the Early Middle Ages implies ignoring the Celtic and Germanic contribution to European culture. Elements of Celtic and Germanic culture merged into Roman and Christian culture. The Germanic and Celtic conceptions of government with their focus on the division of power, autonomy and the co-operation between ruled and ruler were to leave deep traces on the political and constitutional evolution after the year 1000. The feudal system, which was to remain of major importance for land ownership and the division of power in the West right up until the French Revolution, was based in part on Germanic tradition and institutions.

Second, the Early Middle Ages produced the Augustinian ideology. That ideology dictated the selection of the textual canon and determined the amendments and falsifications made to the texts and the commentaries to the texts. The *correctio* applied by the scholars of the Early Middle Ages to the ancient texts was in fact a distortion. The Carolingian Renaissance, in particular, was a key factor in this regard. It translated the Augustinian ideology into a political and cultural programme and completed the synthesis of Graeco-Roman, Christian, Celtic and Germanic culture. Although the Carolingian Renaissance had only a limited influence on daily life and this brief flowering of culture was followed by a period of decay, it had an important impact on further developments. When the intellectual elite of the eleventh and twelfth centuries referred back to Antiquity and early Christianity, it did so unconsciously through the lens of the Carolingian Renaissance. Augustinian ideology and the

Carolingian synthesis set the intellectual context in which the revival of culture and science was to start in the eleventh century. The unresolved tension between the ideal of unity at the political, religious and cultural level and the reality of fragmentation and division that formed an inherent part of the Germanic tradition was another part of the inheritance from the Early Middle Ages.

In its first stage, the Renaissance of the Twelfth Century was inevitably a renaissance of Augustinian ideology and of Carolingian views. New ideas only came to the fore as a result of the Renaissance of the Twelfth Century; they were not its cause. That overall intellectual context also had an impact on the new jurisprudence. It influenced the political debates concerning the relation between church and state and between ruler and subjects, for which the 'new law' served as a weapon and instrument. It also provided the theological underpinning and legitimation for the flowering of intellectual life and of science: a flowering in which jurisprudence was to play a leading role.

Further reading

1. On Europe in the Early Middle Ages in general: H. G. Koenigsberger, *Medieval Europe, 400–1500*, London 1987; R. Lopez, *The Tenth Century: How Dark were the Dark Ages?*, New York 1962; R. McKitterick, ed., *The Early Middle Ages: Europe 400–1000*, Oxford 2001; J. M. H. Smith, *Europe after Rome: a New Cultural History, 500–1000*, Oxford 2005; J. M. Wallace-Hadrill, *The Barbarian West, 400–1000*, 2nd edn, Oxford 1985; volumes I–III of the *New Cambridge Medieval History*, Cambridge 1995–2005.

2. On the Franks and the Frankish Empire: J. Dunbabin, *France in the Making, 843–1180*, 2nd edn, Oxford 2000; P. Fouracre, *The Age of Charles Martel*, London 2000; F. L. Ganshof, *The Carolingians and the Frankish Monarchy*, London 1971; R. Gerberding, *The Rise of the Carolingians and the 'Liber Historiae Francorum'*, Oxford 1987; P. Godman and R. Collins, eds., *Charlemagne's Heir: New Perspectives on the Reign of Louis the Pious (814–840)*, Oxford 1990; F. Heer, *Charlemagne and his World*, New York 1975; E. James, *The Origins of France: From Clovis to the Capetians, 500–1000*, London 1982; James, *The Franks*, Oxford 1988; S. MacLean, *Kingship and Politics in the Late Ninth Century: Charles the Fat and the End of the Carolingian Empire*, Cambridge 2003; R. McKitterick, *The Frankish Kingdoms under the Carolingians*, London 1983; J. L. Nelson and M. T. Gibson, eds., *Charles the Bald: Court and Kingdom*, Oxford 1981; J. L. Nelson, *Charles the Bald*, London 1992; P. Riché, *The Carolingians: a Family who Forged Europe*, Philadelphia 1993; J. M. Wallace-Hadrill, *The Long-Haired*

Kings and other Studies in Frankish History, Oxford 1962; I. Wood, *Merovingian Gaul*, London 1993; Wood, *The Merovingian Kingdoms, 450–751*, Harlow 1994.

3. On the church during the Early Middle Ages: R. Fletcher, *The Conversion of Europe: From Paganism to Christianity, 371–1386 AD*, London 1997; Y. Hen, *Culture and Religion in Merovingian Gaul, AD 481–751*, Leyden 1995; R. A. Markus, *Gregory the Great and his World*, Cambridge 1997; K. Morrison, *Tradition and Authority in the Western Church, 300–1140*, Princeton 1969; T. Noble, *The Republic of St Peter: the Birth of the Papal State, 680–825*, Philadelphia 1984; J. Richards, *The Popes and the Papacy in the Early Middle Ages, 476–752*, London 1979; J. M. Wallace-Hadrill, *The Frankish Church*, Oxford 1983.

4. On the intellectual history of the Early Middle Ages: A. H. Armstrong, *St Augustine and Christian Platonism*, Villanova, 1967; Armstrong, ed., *The Cambridge History of Later Greek and Early Medieval Philosophy*, Cambridge 1970; A. K. Bowman and G. Woolf, eds., *Literacy and Power in the Ancient World*, Cambridge 1994; P. Brown, *The World of Late Antiquity*, London 1971; M. L. Colish, *Medieval Foundations of the Western Intellectual Tradition 400–1400*, New Haven and London 1997; M. L. W. Laistner, *Thought and Letters in Western Europe, AD 500–900*, Ithaca 1966; R. McKitterick, ed., *The Uses of Literacy in Early Medieval Europe*, Cambridge 1990; McKitterick, *Books, Scribes and Learning in the Frankish Kingdoms: Sixth to Ninth Centuries*, Aldershot 1994; J. Marenbon, *Early Medieval Philosophy (480–1150): an Introduction*, London 1983; J. Pelikan, *The Christian Tradition: a History of the Development of Doctrine*, 4 vols., Chicago 1971–89; L. D. Reynolds and N. G. Wilson, *Scribes and Scholars: a Guide to the Tradition of Greek and Latin Literature*, 3rd edn, Oxford 1991; P. Riché, *Education and Culture in the Barbarian West, 6th–8th Centuries*, Columbia 1975; Riché, *Ecoles et enseignement dans le haut moyen âge, fin du Ve siècle – milieu du XIe siècle*, 3rd edn, Paris 1999; Riché, *Instruction et vie religieuse dans le haut moyen âge*, London 1981; M. Richter, *The Formation of the Medieval West: Studies in the Oral Culture of the Barbarians*, Dublin 1994; W. H. Stalh, *Martianus Capella and the Seven Liberal Arts*, 2 vols., New York 1971–7; W. Ullmann, *Medieval Foundations of Renaissance Humanism*, London 1977.

5. On Charlemagne, the Carolingian Renaissance and Carolingian church reform: J. Boussard, *The Civilisation of Charlemagne*, London 1968; D. Bullough, *The Age of Charlemagne*, London 1965; Bullough, *Carolingian Renewal: Sources and Heritage*, Manchester 1991; J. Marenbon, *From the Circle of Alcuin to the School of Auxerre: Logic, Theology and Philosophy in the Early Middle Ages*, Cambridge 1981; R. McKitterick, *The Frankish Church and the Carolingian Reforms, 789–895*, London 1977; McKitterick, *The Carolingians and the Written Word*, Cambridge 1989, McKitterick, ed., *Carolingian Culture: Emulation and Innovation*, New York 1994; McKitterick, *Charlemagne: the Formation*

of a European Identity, Cambridge 2008; K. F. Morrison, *The Two Kingdoms: Ecclesiology in Carolingian Political Thought*, Princeton 1964; W. Treadgold, ed., *Renaissances before the Renaissance: Cultural Revivals of Late Antiquity and the Middle Ages*, Stanford 1984.

6. On (early) medieval political thought: J. H. Burns, ed., *The Cambridge History of Medieval Political Thought c.350–c.1450*, Cambridge 1988; J. Canning, *A History of Medieval Political Thought, 300–1450*, London 1996.

7. On Germanic and Frankish kingship: P. S. Barnwell, *Emperors, Prefects and Kings: the Roman West, 395–565*, London 1992; Barnwell, *Kings, Courtiers, and Imperium: the Barbarian West, 565–725*, London 1997; G. Koziol, *Begging Pardon and Favor: Ritual and Political Order in Early Medieval France*, Ithaca 1992; K. Leyser, *Communications and Power in Medieval Europe: the Carolingian and Ottonian Centuries*, London 1994; M. McCormick, *Eternal Victory: Triumphal Rulership in Late Antiquity, Byzantium and the Early Medieval West*, Cambridge 1986; H. Mitteis, *The State in the High Middle Ages*, Amsterdam 1975; J. L. Nelson, *Politics and Ritual in Early Medieval Europe*, London 1986; J. M. Wallace-Hadrill, *Early Germanic Kingship in England and on the Continent*, Oxford 1971; C. Wickham, *Early Medieval Italy: Central Power and Local Society, 400–1000*, London 1981.

8. On the idea of empire and Charlemagne's coronation of 800: G. Barraclough, *The Medieval Empire: Idea and Reality*, London 1950; R. Folz, *The Coronation Of Charlemagne: 25 December 800*, London 1974; J. Muldoon, *Empire and Order: the Concept of Empire, 800–1800*, London 1999; R. E. Sullivan, ed., *The Coronation of Charlemagne: What Did it Signify?*, Boston 1959; W. Ullmann, *The Carolingian Renaissance and the Idea of Kingship*, London 1969.

9. On feudality and the seigniorial system: J. Beeler, *Warfare in Feudal Europe, 730–1200*, Ithaca and London 1973; M. Bloch, *Feudal Society*, 2nd edn, 2 vols., London 1962; Bloch, 'How and Why Ancient Slavery Came to an End', in *Slavery and Serfdom in the Middle Ages: Selected Essays by Marc Bloch*, Berkeley 1975, 1–31; W. Davies, 'On Servile Status in the Early Middle Ages', in M. L. Bush, ed., *Serfdom and Slavery: Studies in Legal Bondage*, London 1996, 225–46; G. Duby, *The Three Orders: Feudal Society Imagined*, Chicago 1980; F. L. Ganshof, *Feudalism*, 3rd edn, London 1964; D. Herlihy, *The History of Feudalism*, New York 1970; S. Reynolds, *Kingdoms and Communities in Western Europe, 900–1300*, Oxford 1984; Reynolds, *Fiefs and Vassals: the Medieval Experience Reinterpreted*, Oxford 1994; W. Rösener, *The Peasantry of Europe*, Oxford 1994; C. Wickham, 'The Other Transition: From the Ancient World to Feudalism', *Past and Present*, 103 (1984) 3–36.

10. On the legal history of the Early Middle Ages: R. Bartlett, *Trial by Fire and Water: the Medieval Judicial Ordeal*, Oxford 1986; P. Classen, ed., *Recht und Schrift im Mittelalter*, Konstanz 1977; W. Davies and P. Fouracre, eds., *The Settlement of Disputes in Early Medieval Europe*, Cambridge 1986; J. Foviaux,

De l'Empire romain à la féodalité, vol. I, Paris 1986; F. L. Ganshof, *Frankish Institutions under Charlemagne*, Providence 1968; S. L. Guterman, *From Personal to Territorial Law: Aspects of the History and Structure of the Western Legal-Constitutional Tradition*, New York 1972; F. Kern, *Kingship and Law*, Oxford 1939; P. D. King, *Law and Society in the Visigothic Kingdom*, Cambridge 1972; E. Levy, *West Roman Vulgar Law: the Law of Property*, Philadelphia 1951; Levy, *Weströmisches Vulgarrecht* II: *Das Obligationenrecht*, Weimar 1956; G. Kobler, *Das Recht im frühen Mittelalter*, Cologne and Vienna 1971; M. Lupoi, *The Origins of the European Legal Order*, Cambridge 2000; R. McKitterick, 'Some Carolingian Law-Books and their Function', in B. Tierney and P. Linehan, eds., *Authority and Power: Studies on Medieval Law and Government presented to Walter Ullmann on his 70th Birthday*, Cambridge 1980, 13–29; P. Wormald, *The Making of English Law: King Alfred to the Twelfth Century* I, Oxford 1999.

11. On (early) medieval canon law: J. A. Brundage, *Medieval Canon Law*, London 1995; P. Fournier and G. Le Bras, *Histoire des collections canoniques en Occident depuis les fausses décrétales jusqu'au Décret de Gratien*, 2 vols., Paris 1931–2; G. Fransen, *Les collections canoniques* (Typologie des sources du moyen âge occidental 10), Turnhout 1973; A. Firey and R. Reynolds, *Early Collections of Canon Law and their Manuscripts: a Vademecum*, Toronto 1993; J. Gaudemet, *Les sources du droit canonique, VIIIe–XXe siècle*, Paris 1985; Gaudemet, *L'église dans l'empire romain (IVe–Ve siècles)*, 2nd edn, Paris 1989; Gaudemet, *Eglise et cité. Histoire du droit canonique*, Paris 1994; G. Le Bras, *Institutions ecclésiastiques de la Chrétiente médievale*, 2 vols., Paris 1959–64.

12. For English translations of the Salic Law: K. Fischer Drew, ed., *The Laws of the Salian Franks*, Philadelphia 1991; T. Rivers, ed., *The Salic and Ripuarian Laws*, New York 1991.

4

Auctoritas
(the Late Middle Ages, c.1000–1453)

A Politics and the state

1 *The revival of Europe around the year 1000*

Très peu d'hommes – des solitudes qui vers l'ouest, ver l'est s'étendent, deviennent immenses et finissent par tout recouvrir – des friches, des marécages, des fleuves vagabonds et les landes, les taillis, les pacages, toutes les formes dégradées de la forêt qui laissent derrière eux les feux des broussailles et les ensemencements furtifs des brûleurs de bois – ici et là des clairières, un sol conquis cette fois, mais qui pourtant n'est qu'à demi dompté; des sillons légers, dérisoires, ceux qui ont tracés sur une terre rétive des outils de bois traînés par des bœufs maigres …[1]

159 Climate change and food production

With these words, the French historian Georges Duby (1919–96) in a few deft strokes conveyed an image of western Europe at its darkest hour; that of an underdeveloped continent, where for most people life was confined to an open place in an immense, dark forest; of small agricultural communities, struggling to survive against the elements and the dangers of war, hunger and disease.

The turning point came during the decades before and after the year 1000. New developments took place in virtually all areas of social and cultural life, at first slow and unnoticed, then faster and clearer. At the end of the eleventh century, this revival culminated in what Haskins called the 'Renaissance of the Twelfth Century'. This late medieval

---

[1] 'A mere handful of men – unending emptiness stretching so far west, north, and east that it covers everything – fallow land, fens and wandering rivers, heaths, woods and pastureland, every conceivable type of erstwhile forest leaving behind it brush fires and the woodburners' furtive sowing – clearings here and there, wrested from the forest but still only half-tamed; shallow pitiful furrows that wooden implements drawn by scrawny oxen have scatched on the unyielding soil …' Georges Duby, *Le temps des cathédrales: L'art et la société 980–1420*, Paris 1976, 11, translation by Eleanor Levieux and Barbara Thompson, *The Age of the Cathedrals: Art and Society, 980–1420*, London 1981, 3.

Renaissance marked the beginnings of the rise of the West. It was also with this Renaissance that the continental legal tradition and legal science took off.

Climate change triggered the revival of Europe. Experts have established that, between the ninth and twelfth centuries, average temperatures rose. This allowed more land to be cultivated, especially in the north-west and on higher ground. At the same time, agricultural innovations led to an increase in productivity. The introduction of the watermill and the windmill made it easier to work iron. Iron ploughs turned the soil better than had the former wooden appliances. The invention of the harness allowed the use of horses as draught animals, instead of only oxen. Three-field crop rotation allowed land to remain fallow only every third year instead of every second year. As a result of all these improvements, the productivity in cereal farming increased by around 50 per cent: where previously two grains were harvested for each grain sown, now three were harvested. Net food production doubled.

160   Industry, trade and the revival of city life

Improved food production led to demographic growth, which was sustained until the fourteenth century. It also allowed for new labour specialisation. Farmers wanted to sell their surplus production for other, particularly manufactured, goods. This led to the revival of craft industry and trade, and of a money economy. Apart from local trade within and between nearby domains, international trade flourished. Commodities and products that were only to be found in certain areas of Europe were traded all throughout the West. During the eleventh century, regular trade routes between the Low Countries and northern Italy were opened up. Every spring, traders from both sides would make their way to the annual fair in the County of Champagne – roughly halfway between the Low Countries and Italy. Later, these fairs lost their position in the north–south trade and were replaced by the annual voyage of Italian cargo ships to Bruges in the County of Flanders, the most important trading port of north-western Europe in the thirteenth and fourteenth centuries. After the year 1000, major Italian trading ports such as Venice, Pisa and Amalfi reconnected Europe to the existing east–west trade in the Mediterranean between the Arab caliphates in Egypt and the Middle East on the one hand and the Arab kingdoms in Spain and the Maghreb on the other. With international trade, international banking developed.

The flowering of trade and industry led to the revival of city life. Professional craftsmen and merchants left the country and established themselves in existing towns – often diocesan seats – or in new population centres. Many towns gained legal autonomy from their local lords. A new class, that of the free citizens or burghers of these towns, arose. This made the third estate even more heterogeneous. Apart from free and bonded country dwellers, the third estate now included all kinds of burghers among its numbers, from mere proletarians, through small business owners to wealthy merchants and bankers.

The country was also subject to social change. From the twelfth century onwards, a process of legal emancipation started in western Europe. Many serfs were granted freedom and became free tenants. For the remaining serfs, bonded labour was often abolished or substituted for new dues. Through these measures, local lords sought to stem the exodus from the country to the towns and to sustain the production levels for their estates. In other areas of Europe, serfdom was tightened in order to achieve the same end. Large rural estates were formed in eastern Germany, Poland, Hungary and the Baltic. Heavy burdens were laid upon serfs, making them little more than slaves.

The economic progress and diversification increased both the possibilities and the need for education and scholarship, in the field of law, among others. Growing prosperity also allowed the arts to flourish. Intellectual and cultural changes closely followed in the footsteps of economic revival.

161   The crisis of the fourteenth century

Economic growth lasted until the early fourteenth century. Thereafter, agricultural production stagnated and demographic growth had reached a critical level. Food production could no longer keep up with the needs of an increased population. After 1300, western Europe once again found itself caught up in the traditional spiral of hunger, war and disease. In many parts of western Europe, the rural economy was dislocated. Desperate to preserve the incomes of their estates, local lords pushed through all sorts of reforms. These were often at the expense of the rural population, causing unrest and uprisings. In the course of the fourteenth century, various parts of western Europe suffered major peasant revolts, such as that in Flanders under the leadership of Zannekin (1323–8), the *Jacquerie* in the environs of Paris (1358) and the Peasants' Revolt led by Wat Tyler in England (1381). Regimes tottered and rulers had more need than ever for foreign and military successes in order to ensure the loyalty of the aristocracy and to prop up their thrones. Weakened by hunger, the population became increasingly susceptible to epidemics. Between

1346 and 1349, the Black Death ravaged Europe. In the space of just a few
years, a third, if not more, of the population of Europe perished. Villages,
towns, even entire regions were depopulated. The crisis marked the end
of a lengthy period of progress. In the short term, the Black Death and
subsequent epidemics of pestilence led to an improvement in the lot of
the survivors. Both in the country and in the towns, manual labour was
in short supply, which led to a rise in wages. But in the somewhat longer
term, the crisis deepened the gap between rich and poor. Laws were introduced to counter the increase in wages and, particularly as far as the crafts
were concerned, to stifle competition. Around 1500, the circumstances of
those at the bottom of society, particularly in the towns, were worse than
two centuries earlier.

2   The expansion of the West

162   The end of the invasions

By the start of the eleventh century, the West had overcome the external
threats to its existence. The invasions by Vikings, Magyars and Saracens
stopped or were beaten off. There are various explanations for this. First,
climate change made life at the northern and eastern fringes of Europe
easier and diminished the need for immigration, conquest and plunder. Second, the military reorganisation that had followed the collapse
of royal authority started to pay off. Throughout Europe, local magnates
filled the power vacuum and organised local defences, especially by
building castles and fortifying population centres. The invaders – who
were more intent on plunder than on conquest – were ill equipped to deal
with this kind of warfare and encountered ever more resistance. Third,
some of the invaders settled in Europe and were assimilated in the Latin
West. These groups of warrior-nomads and traders infused new blood
into the West. After their defeat by Otto the Great at Lechfeld in 955, the
Magyars were no longer a threat. In 1001, the Hungarian King Stephen
(1001–38) was sent a crown by the emperor and pope. This symbolised the
assimilation of the former invaders into the Latin Christian world. In the
centuries thereafter, Hungary evolved into one of the biggest kingdoms
in the Latin world. Until the Turks conquered the country in 1526, it
acted as a military bulwark against Islam. Groups of Vikings established
themselves in England, Normandy and southern Italy. The Danish King
Cnut (Canute) II the Great ruled over Denmark, Norway and England
(1017–35). In 911, the French King Charles the Simple (893–923) granted
the Viking leader Rollo the territory around the Seine estuary, known

since as Normandy. A century and a half later, his descendant William the Conqueror (1066–87) conquered England (Battle of Hastings, 1066). The Norman leader Robert Guiscard (d. 1085) and his successors prised Sicily and southern Italy from the grasp of their Islamic and the Byzantine rulers, founding one of the most modern kingdoms of the age. In 1059, the pope, who claimed suzerainty over the southern part of Italy, recognised their claims.

163   The crusades

After the invasions of Europe had come to an end, the West counter-attacked. Emperor Otto the Great and his immediate successors embarked on an expansion towards the east. During the tenth and eleventh centuries, Hungary, Bohemia and Poland were converted to Christianity and brought within the orbit of the Latin West. In the course of the eleventh century, the Danish, Norwegian and Swedish kings abjured the Germanic gods and converted to the church of Rome. Over the next few centuries, the entire Baltic area, including Finland, was colonised by the Danes, Sweden and the Teutonic Order, a religious-military order of German knights which had grown out of the crusades. Population growth in western Europe led to emigration to the east (*Drang nach Osten*). Thousands of farmers from Germany and the Low Countries moved to Russia, Poland and the Baltic. The West expanded into central and eastern Europe. The Vikings colonised large parts of Scotland and Ireland, pushing on to Iceland, Greenland and even Canada.

Halfway through the eleventh century, the Latin West also began to affirm itself in relation to the two major cultures in the Mediterranean, the Byzantine Empire and the Arab kingdoms. Pope Leo IX (1049–54) demanded the recognition of his supreme authority by the Greek Orthodox patriarch in Constantinople. The consistent refusal by the Orthodox bishops led to the final breakdown of the unity between the Latin church in the West and the Greek church in the East (1054).

From the eleventh century onwards, the Arab kingdoms were regarded as the principal enemy of Latin Christianity. Apart from the recapture of southern Italy and Sicily by the Norseman, there was also the re-conquest or *Reconquista* of the Iberian peninsula. Since the time of Charlemagne, the southern fringe of the Pyrenees in Spain was dotted with a number of small, Christian kingdoms: Aragon, Navarra, Castile and Leon. During the course of the eleventh century, these kingdoms expanded. By the end of the century, the larger part of the Iberian peninsula had been conquered at the expense of the Islamic Caliphate of Cordoba. In

1085, Toledo, in the centre of Spain, was captured; only Andalusia, in the southernmost part of Spain, remained Islamic. In addition to Aragon (with Catalonia), Castile-Leon and Navarre, the kingdom of Portugal was founded. The Catalans – a people of merchants and seafarers – extended their power over the western Mediterranean, capturing the Balearic Islands and Sardinia and driving out the Muslims there. Around 1300, Sicily and, during the fifteenth century, southern Italy were also added to the kingdom of Aragon. At the end of the Middle Ages, the Spanish and Portuguese increasingly mounted raids and expeditions against the Islamic cities in the Maghreb and began exploring the coast of West Africa. In this way, the *Reconquista* gradually evolved into the expansion of Europe through the Atlantic.

The struggle against Islam was not confined to the western part of the Mediterranean. In 1096, the First Crusade departed for the Holy Land. This and later crusades against the Arabs in the Middle East and Egypt were based on a wide range of motives. In the early phases, the crusade to the Holy City of Jerusalem was an important act of faith and redemption, more so than any other pilgrimage. Over time, the crusading in Spain, other parts of the Mediterranean and eastern Europe gained similar religious significance. But the conquest of new lands also promised riches and opportunities for advancement for all who partook. For the pope and the secular rulers of the West, the crusades provided an affirmation of their leadership as defenders of Christianity. The Fourth Crusade of 1204 showed how easily greed and ambition could take the upper hand. In that year, the crusaders allowed themselves to be turned away from their original purpose as they attacked Constantinople, the capital of the Christian Byzantine Empire. After a brief siege, they captured the city, thereby (temporarily) destroying the Eastern Roman Empire. The Latin Empire (1204–61), led by a Flemish emperor, was short lived but did enable the Venetians and Genoese to build up a large trading empire in the Greek world. In 1261, the Byzantines recaptured their capital and the Eastern Roman Empire was restored.

The West's temporary successes in the East were due not just to its own military power. The protracted wars against the Arab kingdoms and the Persians had left the Eastern Roman Empire seriously weakened. The Arab-Islamic world itself was politically divided. In addition, in the thirteenth century, the Islamic world had to deal with the onslaught of the Mongols of Genghis Khan (*c.*1162–1227) and his successors. Also central Europe was threatened. In 1241, the Mongols defeated an army of the Teutonic Order in Silesia.

164   The rise of the Ottoman Empire and the fall of Constantinople

In the fourteenth century, expansion towards the east came to an end. As early as the eleventh century, Turks from central Asia had migrated to the Anatolian peninsula. The Seljuk Turks conquered the larger part of the Byzantine territory in Anatolia after the Battle of Manzikert in 1071. Mongolian invaders in turn destroyed their empire. In the ensuing chaos, a dynasty of warlords, that of Osman (1288–1326), managed to establish its authority over other Turkish warlords. Around 1350, the Ottoman armies penetrated the Balkans. In the space of a few decades, they established their authority over Greek Orthodox kingdoms such as Serbia and Bulgaria, which had previously gained their independence from Constantinople. In 1396, the Ottomans defeated a crusader army from the West near Nicopolis on the Danube. Among the captured crusaders was John the Fearless, later Duke of Burgundy (1404–19). After further wars against the Mongols and campaigns of conquest in the Balkans and Asia Minor, halfway through the fifteenth century the Ottomans turned against the last remnant of the Eastern Roman Empire, its capital Constantinople. In 1453, Sultan Mehmet II (1451–81) captured the city. The 'Second Rome' was renamed Istanbul. The Turkish Sultan adopted the Greek title *basileus* from the Eastern Roman emperors. By doing so, the Ottoman Turks claimed to be the heirs of Rome. With the conquest of Constantinople, the Ottoman Turks at a stroke became the biggest power in the Mediterranean. They not only sealed off the eastern Mediterranean to further Western expansion but were also to turn against the West itself in succeeding centuries. The final remnants of the Venetian and Genoan empires in the East were destroyed by the second half of the seventeenth century. In the meantime, however, Italy and central Europe had already long been in the firing line of Turkish expansion.

3   *The re-emergence of central authority*

165   The rise of new principalities

During the ninth and tenth centuries, local magnates had filled the power vacuum left by the collapse of royal authority. This led to the far-reaching political and legal fragmentation of western Europe. At the same time, this reduction in scale and the multiplication of power centres increased the grip of 'government' on society.

Gradually, some of these local power brokers succeeded in overshadowing their neighbours and extending their power over larger territories. In Flanders, Baldwin Iron Arm (d. 879), Count of the *pagus Flandrensis* in the vicinity of Bruges, and his successors systematically extended their sphere of influence to all the counties between the North Sea and the River Scheldt. The Norsemen in the Seine estuary carved out a large duchy for themselves at the expense of neighbouring lords. In the remainder of France and the Low Countries, large counties, duchies and ecclesiastical principalities were formed. In Germany, the tribal dukes of the Saxons, Bavarians, Franks and Swabians and the bishops filled the vacuum.

In the course of the tenth century, the Carolingians finally left the stage. The various royal thrones fell to new dynasties of former regional lords, who sought to restore royal authority and to recapture the royal powers (*regalia*) from other regional and local rulers. Although a number of great rulers and warlords, such as Otto the Great, managed to do so, their success was generally short lived. The same applied to large regional principalities such as Lorraine and Burgundy. The 'empires' that capable warlords and administrators were able to build in the span of one or two generations often collapsed as quickly as they had emerged.

166   Feudal overlordships

The rapid rise and fall of these great power complexes during the tenth, eleventh and most of the twelfth century can be explained by the weakness of their structural and institutional base. An extensive administrative and legal apparatus was lacking. The Ottonian emperors and the Norman and Plantagenet rulers in western France failed to set up institutions ensuring effective control over their entire empire. It may be for this reason that the most effective and lasting monarchies of the eleventh and early twelfth century were the smaller ones, such as Sicily-Naples, England and the County of Flanders.

In larger power complexes, such as the Ottonian Empire, strong monarchs were able to achieve temporary supremacy. Their success was, however, personal in nature. In fact, they were dependent on the co-operation of the regional secular and ecclesiastical power brokers. It was only through them and their effective control over their smaller territories that the ruler held any real power over most of his empire. The ruler's power was that of an overlord and his rule over most of his territory and people, who were not truly 'his', was indirect. In order to ensure the loyalty of the regional power brokers, the ruler was dependent on his military supremacy or on well-understood self-interest on the part of the regional elites. As of time immemorial, this required the ruler continually to endow them with riches and honours. To this end, new conquests and the spoils of war were necessary.

The personal character of royal power was tied up with the feudal system. The king was the supreme liege; the most important dukes, counts and ecclesiastical princes were his immediate vassals. They obeyed the king according to the terms and constrictions of their feudal contract. Traditional notions of kingship from the Frankish tradition, or of the king as God's deputy on earth, or as the personification of the secular, public authority in the Christian-Roman tradition, had receded into the background. The king ruled not so much over a territory or a people as over his vassals. For this reason, the kingdoms of the tenth to early twelfth century can be characterised as feudal kingdoms. These were loose collections of principalities and seigniories bound together by the personal feudal relationship between the ruler on the one hand and the regional princes and local lords on the other. The rulers made efforts to regain local power from these lords, but these attempts did not rest on a strong institutional base and generally met with little success. The feudal kingdoms overarched the principalities or seigniories but neither controlled nor displaced them. These feudal power complexes did not as yet constitute integrated principalities in their own right. They were feudal overlordships rather than feudal states.

167   *Regnum et patria*

The thirteenth and fourteenth centuries saw the start of a new stage in the centralisation of power. In many parts of western Europe, princes and kings began to strengthen the administrative machinery of state, creating new, central political and juridical institutions. They gradually extended their powers at the expense of the local lords. As they became somewhat less dependent on the intermediation of these lords, the king's rule became more direct – at least for some aspects of government. With time, the ruler's power came to be understood more in territorial and less in personal terms. The feudal 'states' grew into true principalities, often referred to as *regnum* (realm or kingdom) or *patria* (fatherland). These terms applied not just to the actual kingdoms such as France but also to regional principalities such as Flanders or Normandy. The term *patria* indicates that people increasingly identified themselves with a 'country' and less with an ethnic group or a ruler to which they were personally bound. This shift also manifested itself in the titles of kings and princes. From the twelfth and thirteenth centuries onwards, rulers gradually began to style themselves as the ruler of their country (France, England) and no longer as the ruler of their people (the Franks or French, or the English).

In England, France and the Iberian kingdoms, this transformation of the feudal overlordship into the feudal state transpired at the 'national' level. In the Holy Roman Empire, where the power of the emperor was severely weakened during the thirteenth century, it only occurred at the regional level.

4 The struggle between emperor and pope

168 Empire and church before the Gregorian Reform

The death of Emperor Otto III (983–1002) signalled the end of the Ottonian dynasty in the Holy Roman Empire. The Salo-Franconian dynasty, which emerged as the victor from the wars of succession, ruled over the empire until the beginning of the twelfth century. Halfway through that century followed the Hohenstaufen, who with Frederick I Barbarossa (1152–90), Henry VI (1190–97) and especially Frederick II (1212–50), brought three of the most remarkable rulers of the Middle Ages to the throne. Like their Ottonian predecessors, the Salo-Franconian and Hohenstaufen dynasties did not limit their ambitions to Germany. Conrad II (1024–39) was the first Franconian emperor to invade Italy and to be crowned emperor by the pope. The union between the kingdoms of Germany and Italy and the imperial crown remained intact.

The empire had easily been the largest and most powerful monarchy of the tenth and eleventh centuries. Royal authority was vested on two pillars: the approval of the German tribal dukes and the co-operation of the church. Through the Imperial Church, the bishops and abbots were incorporated into the system of secular government. The emperors provided support for the great monastic reform of that period. Emperor and church reformers were allies in the attempt to break the control of local secular lords over church institutions.

The great emperors of the tenth and early eleventh century had also enlisted the papacy in their cause. By the tenth century, papal authority over the Western Church had become no more than an empty slogan, while the pope had lost his secular power over middle Italy as well. The papal throne fell under the domination of the local nobility of Rome itself. The German kings who came to Rome in order to be crowned emperor sought to extract the papacy from local politics. In principle, the pope – the Bishop of Rome – was elected by the people of Rome. As the successors of the Roman emperors, the Ottonian and Hohenstaufen emperors assumed the right to nominate their own candidate for acclamation by the Roman people. In this way, Otto III was able to elevate his preceptor and mentor, the learned Gerbert of Aurillac, to the papacy (Sylvester II, 999–1003). The emperors contributed towards the restoration of the pope's supremacy over the church. In the view of Otto III and his successors, the emperor and the pope were the two leaders of Latin Christianity. Which of them had the ascendancy was not a matter of any doubt to Otto.

169   The Gregorian Reform and the early phases of the Investiture Controversy

By granting support to the monastic reform and to the papacy, the emperors ended up biting their own tail. Halfway through the eleventh century, the papal *Curia* embarked upon its own reform of the church, known as the Gregorian Reform after Pope Gregory VII (1073–84). One of the focal points of the reform was the struggle to wrestle the church from secular, and especially imperial, control. More specifically, the conflict turned on the role played by the emperor in the appointment to higher church offices. In 1059, Pope Nicholas II (1059–61) entrusted the nomination of the pope to the hands of a college of ecclesiastical dignitaries, the cardinals. Gregory VII himself denied the emperor the right to invest bishops and abbots with the symbols of their office (*investire*). The struggle between emperor and pope for control of the church consequently became known as the Investiture Controversy.

The struggle for power over the church escalated. Emperor Henry IV (1056–1106) responded to Gregory's attack by deposing him and appointing a new pope. As supreme secular ruler of the Latin West, he regarded himself as the protector of faith and church. In the spirit of Charlemagne, Henry IV arrogated the right if necessary to correct the ecclesiastical hierarchy. For his part, the pope excommunicated the emperor and exhorted the German nobility no longer to obey him. The objective alliance between the pope and the leading German nobility proved effective. In the winter of 1077, the emperor left for Canossa, imploring the pope's forgiveness. The reconciliation proved to be only temporary.

In 1122, emperor and pope reached a provisional compromise with the Concordat of Worms. Henceforth, the election of its prelates was to be a matter for the church. The ruler could no longer invest the prelates with the symbols of their spiritual power – ring and staff – but only confer on them their secular, feudal office or fief. A distinction was drawn between the spiritual and secular role of the bishops and abbots. This was an important step towards secularisation and the separation of church and state.

With the Concordat of Worms, the pope had realised his predecessors' original ambition: independence of the church from the emperor. This was a heavy blow for the emperor. Not only had his prestige suffered severely from the successive defeats; the Concordat also broke his control over the clerical offices. The system of the Imperial Church, under which important secular offices were entrusted to the clergy, now turned against the emperor. In addition, the successive collisions with the church and the excommunications by the pope had undermined the emperor's legitimacy. For the leading nobles, the ecclesiastical sanctions against the emperor provided grounds for revolt or for exacting major concessions from him. The erosion of imperial power proved irreversible.

170 The Hohenstaufen and the collapse of imperial authority

The Hohenstaufen attempted to restore imperial authority. While his power in Germany was being curbed by the powerful dynasty of the Welfs under Henry the Lion (1129–95), Emperor Frederick I Barbarossa focused on Italy. The Investiture Controversy now entered a second stage, that of the struggle for supremacy in the West. Was secular power supreme, and could the emperor depose the pope, or was it the other way round? The conflict intensified when, at the end of the twelfth century, the Hohenstaufen laid claim to the Norman kingdom of Naples-Sicily by virtue of marriage. The Papal State was now at risk of being encircled by its Hohenstaufen enemies.

The accidental death of Frederick in 1190 during the Third Crusade and the premature death of his son Henry VI in 1197 prevented the Hohenstaufen from attaining victory. Henry's son and successor was the infant Frederick II, who was raised in Palermo. The Hohenstaufen lost control over Germany and the imperial crown and were barely able to hang on to power in their new kingdom of Naples-Sicily. At the same time, a particularly powerful figure ascended the papal throne in Rome: Pope Innocent III (1198–1216).

The pontificate of Innocent III is regarded as the heyday of papal power in western Europe. Innocent III claimed without further ado that the pope, as Christ's vicar on earth, bore supreme authority, spiritual as well as secular. Through his intervention, the emperor and kings were each invested with their share of secular authority. In order to weaken the emperor, Innocent supported various western European kings in their rejection of the emperor's supremacy and succeeded in demanding recognition by various kings as their liege. Even King John of England (1199–1216) had to accept the pope as his suzerain.

One prince who saw himself forced to do the same was the under-age Frederick II for his kingdom of Sicily. But after he had gained power in Germany and become emperor, the conflict between pope and emperor was rekindled. Frederick II managed to establish his authority over Naples and Sicily well enough through his policies of institutional and legal reform. In the remainder of Italy and Germany, however, his power, apart from a few brief episodes, remained largely theoretical. His death in 1250 marked the end of the emperor's bid for supremacy.

The new dynasty of the Austrian Habsburgs that first ascended the throne in 1273 had little real power. Its authority was limited to the territories already governed directly by them as hereditary rulers, its so-called *Hausmacht*. The empire evolved into a loose entity of hundreds of imperial estates, including secular and ecclesiastical principalities and free imperial towns, as well as countless small seigniories. As before, the emperor was elected, now by seven secular or ecclesiastical princes, the Electors. Imperial power was limited. In order to exercise that power, the emperor was dependent on the co-operation of the Electors and the Imperial Diet, that is, the assembly of the estates of the empire. The leading princes within the empire, such as the dukes of Bavaria and Saxony and the king of Bohemia, conducted their own foreign policy, independently of and often against the emperor. As king of Italy, the emperor retained supreme suzerainty over northern Italy until the French Revolution, but in reality that amounted to little. To an even greater extent than their German counterparts, the princes and towns of Italy acted as independent powers. They no longer even had any diet or assembly with the emperor.

171   The crisis of the papacy in the fourteenth century

The papal victory in the Investiture Controversy proved to be pyrrhic. During the Investiture Controversy, the popes found allies with the various kings of Europe who disputed the claims laid by the emperor to supreme sovereignty over the Latin West. On more than one occasion the pope rejected imperial claims for authority over other secular rulers. However, by giving in to the desire for sovereignty of the kings of France, England and Castile against the emperor's superior authority, the pope in the long run undercut his own claims to universal supremacy. Since the days of Charlemagne and Otto the Great, the emperor and pope had jointly been the two heads of the one Latin Christian world. Their claims to universal supremacy were as the flipsides of the same coin. In the struggle between emperor and pope for universal supremacy in the West, the unity of the West itself perished. Once the emperor had been weakened to the point that the Western kings no longer needed the pope's support, they lost any reason for tolerating papal supremacy in secular affairs. Furthermore, the growing separation of the spiritual and the secular set in motion by the popes themselves with the Gregorian Reform increasingly frustrated the papal claims at the secular level. The universal spiritual authority of Rome also came under fire. By continually using and abusing their spiritual role to fight their political battles, the popes had brought themselves into discredit.

When Pope Boniface VIII (1294–1303) staked his claim to papal supremacy in secular as well as in spiritual affairs, he ran into a rejection not by the emperor but by the most powerful ruler in Europe at that time, the French King Philip IV the Fair (1285–14). Philip felt secure enough in his own realm to confront Rome. In 1303, he had the pope taken prisoner. The 'coup of Agnani' marked the end of the pope's secular supremacy in Europe. A few years later the new pope, the French Clemens V (1305–14), left Rome for Avignon, at that time on the border with France. During the Avignon period, the papacy lost much of its political independence to the French monarchy. After the return to Rome in 1377, a schism occurred in the church. In 1378, a conflict arose between the newly elected Pope Urban VI (1378–89) and a large part of the cardinals, who elected a counter-pope. For a period of forty years, during the Great Schism (1378–1417), the West had two popes: one in Rome and a 'French' pope in Avignon. The Council of Constance (1414–18) put an end to the Schism by deposing both popes and designating a new pope, Martin V (1417–31). After 1417, the papacy managed slowly to recover. The pope regained his position as spiritual leader of the Latin West. Martin V and his immediate successors managed to break the power of the universal council (the assembly of all bishops) and to restore papal supremacy over the church, but were no longer able to lay claim to secular leadership. Their political role was reduced to the Papal State and Italy.

172 Guelfs and Ghibellines

By the fourteenth century, the conflict between emperor and pope as a fight for supremacy over the West was over. The conflict, however, lived on in Italy. Many scholars of the fourteenth, fifteenth and sixteenth centuries, including the poet Dante Alighieri (1265–1321) and the civilian Bartolus de Sassoferrato (1314–57), joined in the debate. The continuation of the old debate in Italy may be explained by the political situation in the peninsula. Despite all the efforts to the contrary, the emperors had never succeeded in restoring the political unity of the old *regnum Italiae*. The old kingdom had collapsed into dozens of principalities and city-republics. The struggle between the two universal powers of the West, which had always been focused on Italy, provided an opportunity for these local powers to enhance their autonomy by manoeuvring adeptly between the parties. In addition, all sorts of local disputes between ruling dynasties and especially between factions within the city-republics drew for their inspiration on the struggle between emperor and pope. If, for example, the leading faction or family in a city such as Florence, Milan or Pisa opted in favour of the emperor, the opposition would side with the pope. The parties referred to themselves as Ghibellines – after the Hohenstaufen royal family – or Guelfs – after their important German competitors the Welfs who, with the support of the pope, had on several occasions produced a counter-emperor. Even after the emperor had as good as lost his power and the pope had even been driven out of Italy temporarily, the struggle between emperor and pope and between Guelfs and Ghibellines remained the theoretical and political backdrop to the struggle for power among local dynasties and factions.

5   The Western kingdoms

173   The demise of imperial universal authority

At no point in medieval history were the emperors successful at having their claims to universal authority or universal monarchy widely recognised outside the Holy Roman Empire itself. France, which was one of the successor states of the old Carolingian Empire, and the kingdoms on the periphery of Europe in the west (England and the Iberian kingdoms), the north (Denmark, Sweden and Norway) and the east (Poland and Hungary) retained or won their sovereignty in secular matters. Of the new Christian kingdoms that the Germanic emperors had helped form, only Bohemia remained within the empire. The idea of the emperor as secular head of the West was kept alive in political thought until after the Middle Ages, but it had little real substance to it. A score of large, sovereign power complexes emerged in western Europe.

174   France: the Capetian and Valois kingdom

In 987, the Carolingian dynasty in the western Frankish kingdom fell from power. The new king, Hugo Capet (987–96), came from a dynasty that during the tenth century had won control over Paris and the Île-de-France. Hugo Capet and his descendants held the French throne in the family for generation after generation, but their actual power was confined to their own fiefs in Paris and Île-de-France, the royal domain. During the eleventh century, the Capetian kings even had difficulty in getting their authority recognised by the nobility and clergy within the royal domain. Outside that area, royal authority was largely theoretical. As suzerain, the king could lay claim to the fealty and service of the great dukes and counts of France, but in practice was generally unable to do so.

Aided by their adviser Abbot Suger of Saint-Denis (*c.*1081–1151), the French kings Louis VI (1108–37) and Louis VII (1137–80) were able to strengthen their position within the royal domain and to extend their sphere of influence. Further afield, however, they came up against three powerful vassals, each of whom ruled a territory larger than their own. To the north lay the powerful County of Flanders. In the south, where the authority of the French king was barely acknowledged and where a different language (*langue d'oc*) was spoken, were the lands of the counts of Toulouse, extending to the Mediterranean. The western part of France, from the Somme to the Pyrenees, had ended up in the hands of the Plantagenets by inheritance, conquest or marriage. In 1154, the leader of that house, Henry II (1154–89), Count of Anjou, ascended the throne of England, thereby bringing more than half the kingdom of France under the control of the English king.

The ascendancy of the French kingdom truly began with Philip II August (1180–1223). Through diplomacy, legal manoeuvring and warfare, Philip II was able to enlarge the royal domain several times over. In 1214, he defeated a coalition of English and Flemish forces and the Welf Emperor Otto IV (1198–1218). Philip II was able to lay his hands on Normandy and Poitou. The Duchy of Brittany fell into the hands of another family, while King John of England could only hold on to the Duchy of Guyenne in south-western France. Philip II and his son Louis VIII (1223–6) supported the crusade against the Cathars or Albigensians, a heretical sect with a considerable following in the County of Toulouse. The crusade ended with the massacre of the Cathars and provided an excuse for the annexation of Toulouse and the Languedoc. Of the three powerful principalities, only that of Flanders survived. Philip IV the Fair was able temporarily to conquer the county (1298), but was forced to concede most of it again after being defeated at the Battle of the Golden Spurs (1302). Philip II, Saint Louis IX (1226–70) and Philip IV made a major contribution towards strengthening the administrative and legal apparatus of central government.

The rule of Philip IV was the high watermark for the French monarchy in the Middle Ages. Around 1300, France was the most powerful kingdom in the West, but it quickly fell from that position. Following the death of the last of the sons of Philip IV in 1328, the throne went to a junior branch of the Capetians, the Valois. Seeking to prevent the descendants of Philip's daughter from ascending the throne, the French nobility invoked an allegedly ancient custom that barred women from assuming or passing on the throne. In the fifteenth century, it was claimed that this custom had been part of the Salic Law and that it was part of the immutable, fundamental laws of the realm.

Succession through the female line would have brought Edward III (1327–78), king of England, to the throne of France. Edward did not let matters rest but launched an attack in 1337 with the support of the Flemish towns; this was the start of the Hundred Years War (1337–1453). This protracted conflict was in fact a succession of wars with periods of relative peace in between. At several times, the English succeeded in conquering large parts of France and came close to final victory. A few years after the Battle of Agincourt (1415), they even managed to negotiate a treaty with the aid of the powerful Philip the Good, Duke of Burgundy (1419–67), in consequence of which the throne passed to Henry VI of England (1422–61/ d. 1471). The entire area north of the Loire as well as Guyenne was then in English hands. Only the intervention by Joan of Arc (1412–31), the Maid of Orleans, could turn matters around. She succeeded in lifting the siege of Orleans and having the Valois prince Charles VII (1422–61) crowned in Reims. Once the Duke of Burgundy had left his English ally in the lurch in 1435, the French were able to drive the English back. In 1453, the English possessions were down to Calais alone, thus putting an end to a long period of war, destruction and political crisis in France. During this period, the French kings had lost much of their control over the country. Now a new period of reconstruction got underway.

175   Norman and Plantagenet England

At the death of King Edward the Confessor (1042–65), three pretenders to the English throne came to the fore. Harold Godwinsson, the most powerful earl in England, seized power. His two opponents both had Viking blood in their veins. In the early eleventh century two Norsemen, Swein (1013–14) and Canute the Great (1017–35), had already sat on the English throne. The two pretenders of 1065 called on all sorts of family ties with the former English royal house of Edward the Confessor. The Norwegian King Harold Hardrada invaded northern England in 1066.

Harold Godwinsson managed to defeat his Norse namesake, only to perish a few weeks later in the Battle of Hastings against William the Conqueror, Duke of Normandy.

In the years that followed, the Normans consolidated their grip over England. William and his sons inherited a country that had already enjoyed a certain degree of central administration under its Anglo-Saxon and Scandinavian kings. As conqueror, William was able to bend the institutions and customs even further to his will. William appropriated all land ownership to the crown, introducing feudality at a single stroke. The king became owner of and supreme liege over every scrap of land. The old Anglo-Saxon aristocracy was stripped of numerous of its estates, which were instead given to the Norman and French knights who had crossed the Channel with William. Both the old English aristocracy and the new nobility henceforth held their lands as feudal fiefs from the king. Towards the end of his reign, William had a survey of all existing land titles compiled (the Domesday Book). The introduction of a uniform, countrywide legal system for landholding – the feudal system – provided an important basis for the extension of royal authority. Thanks to the conquest, the English kings were less troubled by the opposition of the landholding aristocracy than were their French counterparts. Against the old Anglo-Saxon landholding aristocracy, the king established a new aristocracy of Norman and French origins that was loyal to the king and dependent on his favour.

Following the death of William's third son, Henry I (1100–35), England found itself caught up in a struggle for succession, from which the French count Henry II Plantagenet (1154–89) emerged victorious in 1154. Through inheritance and marriage, he also became Duke of Normandy and Guyenne and controlled the entire western part of France. The French territories that they held as fiefs from the French king were more important to the Plantagenets than the relatively small and thinly populated England. Although Henry II and his sons spent much of their reign in France, Henry played a major role in the establishment of central government and royal justice in England. Henry II found his efforts opposed by the church. This English Investiture Controversy concerning the independence of the church reached its peak when Henry had the Archbishop of Canterbury, Saint Thomas à Becket, murdered (1170). Ultimately the English king obtained the right to appoint the bishops. To a much greater extent than in the empire, the church remained a source of support for royal power in England.

Opposition to the king by the nobility and senior clergy stiffened in the course of the thirteenth century. The dividing lines between the old Anglo-Saxon and the new Norman elite blurred. In addition, the kingship had been weakened during the reigns of Richard the Lionheart (1189–99) and John Lackland (1199–1216) by the protracted absence of the former during the Third Crusade and the defeats suffered by the latter against France. After his defeat at Bouvines in 1214, John found himself facing a baronial rebellion in England. In 1215, he was forced to accept Magna Carta, setting limits on royal power. A council of twenty-five nobles and clergy was established to supervise the king's compliance with the agreement. During his long reign, Henry III (1216–72) was increasingly required to take account of the involvement by the nobles, clergy and even the third estate. It was out of the meetings of the estates that the English Parliament grew. The English kings of the fourteenth and early fifteenth century devoted the larger part of their energy and resources to their wars against France and Scotland, for which they badly needed the support of the English nobility, clergy and towns. On the other hand, the elite itself had a stake in the wars of conquest in the north and on the continent. At times of war, there was a relatively close co-operation between the king and the estates, while in times of peace, such as under the government of Richard II (1378–99), there could be bloody clashes. However, despite a number of conflicts over the royal succession and attempted coups, the build-up of royal power in England came earlier and was more effective than in France.

176   The Low Countries: from the Duchy of Lorraine to the Burgundian Netherlands

Under the Treaty of Meersen (870), the Low Countries had been assigned to the German kingdom. Only the area west of the River Scheldt – the greater part of the later County of Flanders – came under the French crown. The rest of the Low Countries became part of the Duchy of Lorraine. In the course of the tenth and eleventh centuries, that duchy disintegrated. Power was usurped by counts and local barons, some of whom were able to extend their power over their neighbours. Gradually a score of medium-sized principalities were established in the Low Countries. Apart from the County of Flanders – partly a French and partly a German fiefdom – these were all fiefs of the German king or emperor. In reality, however, these territories located on the edge of the empire enjoyed a large measure of autonomy. In the south, present-day Belgium, the most important principalities were the County of Flanders, the Duchy of Brabant (from the thirteenth century onwards in personal union with the small Duchy of Limburg), the County of Hainault, the prince-bishoprics of Liège and

Cambrai, the Duchy of Luxemburg and the Margraviate of Namur. In the north, the present Netherlands, there were the counties of Holland, Zeeland and Gueldres (later duchy) as well as the large prince-bishopric of Utrecht with the Oversticht. In Frisia, local communities of farmers succeeded in keeping their autonomy.

From the eleventh to the fourteenth century, the various dukes, counts and bishops extended their power within their territories, strengthening their grip over the local nobility and clergy. Particularly in Flanders, Brabant and Liège, however, they found themselves increasingly contending with a new power: the towns. From the twelfth century onwards, the Low Countries, especially the southern Netherlands, developed into one of the most prosperous regions of Europe. First Flanders and later Brabant, Liège and to a lesser extent Holland played a leading role in international trade and industry. The trade between Flanders and Italy was the backbone of international trade in the West. The Flemish towns of Bruges, Ghent and Ypres were among the most prosperous and populated towns in western Europe. During the fourteenth century, Brabant towns such as Antwerp, Brussels and Louvain came to the fore. In Flanders, Brabant and Liège, and also in Holland, the prince was required to take account of the assembly of the estates, which was dominated by the towns. Various monarchs in the Netherlands were obliged to accept limitations on their power in the form of charters along the lines of King John and Magna Carta.

At the end of the fourteenth century, the political landscape of the Low Countries underwent a significant change. As a result of his marriage to the daughter of the Count of Flanders, Philip the Bold, Duke of Burgundy (1364–1404) and son of the French king, obtained a permanent foothold in the Low Countries. Thanks to the marriage policies of his grandfather Philip and his father, John the Fearless (1404–19), Philip the Good (1419–67) gained control over Brabant-Limburg (1430) as well as Hainault, Holland and Zeeland (1433). Later he also acquired Namur and Luxembourg (1451), to which his son Charles the Bold (1467–77) added Gueldres in 1473 through conquest. Philip the Good installed a number of his family members – generally his bastard sons – as bishops of Liège, Utrecht and Cambrai. Thus the larger part of the Low Countries came under a single dynasty, that of the Burgundians, through a personal union. This meant that the various principalities continued to exist as separate legal entities but did have one and the same prince. As lord of the wealthy Burgundian Netherlands, Philip the Good was one of the most powerful princes of western Europe. Charles the Bold attempted to link up his northern and Burgundian lands by annexing the now small Duchy of Lorraine and to have himself crowned king, but his violent death at Nancy in Lorraine (1477) put an end to the dream of a Burgundian kingdom.

6   *The Gregorian Reform and the Investiture Controversy*

177   Cluny

The Gregorian Reform of the late eleventh century was preceded by a movement of monastic reform. During the course of the tenth century, efforts had been made all over western Europe to reform monastic life, with the abbeys of Cluny in France, Gorze in Germany and Glastonbury in England playing a leading role. The reform movement had a dual purpose: the restoration of monastic discipline and the suppression of the influence of the local secular lords. These aspirations fitted in with the former politics of Charlemagne and Louis the Pious. With the support of the emperor, pope and regional princes, many abbeys threw off the yoke of the local secular lords. Cluny, in particular, had a huge influence and became an example for numerous religious foundations. During the course of the eleventh century, hundreds of monasteries were founded that recognised the authority of the abbot of Cluny. Towards the year 1100, the abbot of this French abbey stood at the head of a network of some thousand monasteries and was one of the most powerful men in the West.

178   The Gregorian Reform

With the Gregorian Reform, the papacy assumed the leading role in ecclesiastical reform and extended it to the whole clergy, including bishops and parish priests. The Gregorian Reform had the same two objectives as that of Cluny: the restoration of church discipline and the emancipation of the church from secular control. On top of that there came a third objective: the establishment of papal authority over the entire church.

The restoration of discipline was aimed specifically at the clergy. Attempts were made at eradicating a series of abuses which were widespread among the clergy, such as nicolaism, that is, non-observance of celibacy. Associated with that was nepotism: the passing on of ecclesiastical benefices to the relatives of former prelates. Another problem was the widespread use of buying and selling ecclesiastical benefices, or simony. In suppressing these and other abuses, Rome wished not just to restore the moral prestige of the clergy but more especially to set it apart from the rest of the population. By indulging in simony, nicolaism and nepotism the bishops, abbots, monks and priests were behaving no differently from secular lords. Simony and nepotism were the ecclesiastical variants of what the rules of feudal inheritance were for secular offices and lands. The struggle against these abuses fitted in with the programme of strengthening the transcendent position of the church and fitted seamlessly into the Augustinian tradition.

The reform of ecclesiastical discipline tied in with the second objective of the Gregorian movement: the emancipation of the church from secular control. Whereas in the past the emperor and pope had cooperated in order to curtail the grip of local lords over their 'own' churches, the pope now turned against his former imperial protector, demanding the independence of the church from any form of secular control, especially that of the emperor. With time, as the position of the pope grew stronger and that of the emperor weaker, Rome was to reverse the roles and defend the supremacy of the pope over the emperor.

The Gregorian Reform put an end to the co-operation between the two heads of Christianity – the emperor and pope – that had existed since the days of Charlemagne. Since the Carolingian age, the Latin West had gradually become aware of its own identity. Although the West had been divided since the death of Louis the Pious, the ideal of the unity of the West persisted. Throughout the Middle Ages and well into the Renaissance, the West was to regard itself as a religious, cultural and, to some extent, political and legal entity, Latin Christendom or *christianitas*. From the Renaissance onwards, the term *respublica christiana* or Christian republic was commonly used to indicate this idea.

The idea of unity had two foundations: the renovation of the Western Roman Empire and the unity under the one Roman Catholic Church. Until the Gregorian Reform, the emphasis was on the second. The Latin West was the *populus christianus*, the Christian people belonging to the Roman Church. At the head of this people stood two leaders: the emperor, exercising secular power, and the pope, exercising spiritual power. Pope Gelasius had already expressed this idea of two powers in the fifth century. At no stage, however, had the church and the pope been able to achieve the strict separation of the two powers or attain a position of equality. The kings and emperors of the West accordingly regarded themselves as the guardians of the church for its secular affairs, and ultimately as its correctors, if it failed in its spiritual task. They were the military and political protectors of the church, who ensured its effective organisation and operation. In that sense the Merovingian, Carolingian and Ottonian rulers did not hesitate to issue legislation concerning the organisation of the church or religious education. Many princes insisted on the right to intervene if the faith were placed at risk by the maladministration or abuses of the senior prelates, extending if necessary to the deposition of those clerics. Around the year 1000, many secular rulers had an important say in the selection of the ecclesiastical officeholders in their domains.

The Gregorian Reform called all this into question. As early as 1059, imperial involvement in the election of the pope was rejected: henceforth the pope would be nominated by a group of ecclesiastical prelates, the cardinals. The clergy of the diocese of Rome would then acclaim the candidate, without reference to the nobility or ordinary people. In 1179, the procedure for the election of the pope by a now more extensive college of cardinals was laid down in detail. In his *Dictatus papae* of 1075, Pope Gregory VII placed the entire system of the Imperial Church under review. Any form of secular interference with the church was rejected. The papal supremacy over the church and all the bishops was also confirmed. Gregory VII arrogated the right to depose the emperor. The supremacy of spiritual over secular power was reflected in the rule that princes might kiss the feet only of the pope and not those of the emperor as in the case of the Byzantine court ceremonial. Bishops and abbots were forbidden to accept the insignia of their ecclesiastical office from the hands of secular lords. Secular involvement in the selection of ecclesiastical officeholders was rejected.

179   The two swords

The Investiture Controversy began as an attempt by Rome to counter secular interference with the church but evolved into a debate concerning the question as to who bore supreme power in *christianitas*: the emperor or the pope. The conflict between emperor and pope began around 1070 and lasted until the fourteenth century. In the course of the thirteenth century, the dispute widened into a general debate concerning the relation between church and state, involving other secular rulers apart from the emperor. This debate was to last until the nineteenth century.

The Investiture Controversy is of great significance for the emergence of political thought. The debate was not confined to the world of theology; lawyers – both canon and civilian – joined in from the very start. Thus the Investiture Controversy made a major contribution towards the development of an autonomous legal science.

Many propositions concerning the relation between pope and emperor drew on the old text of Pope Gelasius I, which distinguished two powers within Christianity:

> Two there are, august emperor, by which this world is chiefly ruled, the
> sacred authority [*auctoritas*] of the priesthood and the royal power [*pot-
> estas*]. Of these the responsibility of the priests is more weighty in so far as
> they will answer for the kings of men themselves at the divine judgement.
> You know, most clement son, that, although you take precedence over
> all mankind in dignity, nevertheless you piously bow the neck to those
> who have charge of divine affairs and seek from them the means of your
> salvation, and hence you realize that, in the order of religion, in matters
> concerning the reception and right administration of the heavenly sacra-
> ments, you ought to submit yourself rather than rule ... [2]

Until the Gregorian Reform, the popes had never consummated the
full implications of this distinction between the two powers. Now this
changed. In one of his judgments, Pope Gregory VII referred to Gelasius's
text, but also wrote 'that priests are deemed to be the fathers and masters of kings and princes'.[3] By relating Gelasius's words to relevant biblical
fragments, supporters of the papal position developed the doctrine of the
two swords,[4] whereby the two powers were represented as two swords
transferred by Christ to those in authority on earth. This doctrine became
established in canon law through the *Decretum Gratiani* (*c.*1140), the
most important collection of canon law of the Middle Ages.[5]

From the eleventh to the fourteenth century, the debate on the relation between pope and emperor and between church and state turned
on the correct interpretation of the two swords doctrine. Two traditions
came into being. On the one hand, there was the tradition that defended
the equality and mutual autonomy of those powers. According to the
adherents of this tradition, Christ had bestowed the sword of spiritual
power on the pope and that of secular power on the emperor. According
to an alternative tradition, developed by the civil lawyers, God had
bestowed secular power on the people, who had in turn delegated it
through the *lex regia* on the emperor. The adherents of these dualist

---

[2] Letter from Pope Gelaius I to the Emperor Anastasius (494), translation from Brian
Tierney, ed., *The Crisis of Church and State, 1050–1300*, Toronto 1988, 13–14.

[3] *Decretum Gratiani*, d. 96 c. 9 (my translation).

[4] 'Governments hold no terror for the law-abiding but only for the criminal. You wish to
have no fear of the authorities? Then continue to do right and you will have their approval,
for they are God's agents working for your good. But if you are doing wrong, then you will
have cause to fear them, for they are God's agents of punishment bringing retribution
on the offender.' Romans 13:3–4. 'Lord, they said, we have two swords here. Enough, he
replied.' Luke 22:38.

[5] D. 96 c. 10.

traditions recognised that the spiritual power had a higher standing, but rejected any interference by the spiritual leaders in the secular sphere. The pope did not appoint the emperor and was consequently also unable to depose him.

On the other hand, there was a tradition, particularly among theologians and canonists, that defended the primacy of the pope over the emperor. According to this tradition, which sought and found support in the *Decretum Gratiani*, Peter – the apostle and first pope – had received the swords of both spiritual and secular power from Christ. The pope had then delegated secular power to the emperor and other rulers. The pope stood at the origin of all earthly power, and could thus depose all rulers. Under this doctrine, some of the medieval popes laid claim to suzerainty over the Latin West. The notion that the emperor was the protector of the church was now also used against him. In view of his obligation to defend the church, the emperor was a functionary or *minister* (servant) of church and pope. For this reason, Pope Innocent III claimed in his decretal *Venerabilem* (1202) the right to determine whether or not the German king, who was chosen by the Electors, was suitable for appointment to the office of emperor, since the latter was the military protector or, if one prefers, the general of the pope.[6]

The advocates of the supremacy of the pope in secular matters were also able to draw on another line of argument. This went back to the *Donatio Constantini* (*Donation of Constantine*), according to which the Roman Emperor Constantine the Great was said to have transferred secular power over Rome to the pope. The text, which is now known to have been a forgery from around the year 800 and the authenticity of which was already contested in the Middle Ages, had already been used beforehand to substantiate the papal authority over Rome and middle Italy. Since the ninth century, it had also been used to provide a basis for claims of papal supremacy over the secular rulers. Through its inclusion in the *Decretum Gratiani,* the text became firmly established in canon law and frequently made an appearance in debates concerning papal power. It did, however, suffer from the drawback that it gave the pro-imperialists ammunition to point out the ultimately imperial origins of papal authority. The more the emperor identified himself with his Roman forebears, the more the *Donatio* lost its powers of persuasion for the papal party.

[6] X. 1.6.34.

7 *The rise of the papal monarchy*

180 *Plenitudo potestatis*

The Investiture Controversy not only led to a debate on the relation between church and state but sparked off a more general debate on the relation between ruler and subjects in both the church and the secular world. The Gregorian Reform initiated an attempt by the papacy to vest its authority over the church. Apart from doctrines on the supremacy of the pope over secular authority, theologians and canonists also developed a defence of the supremacy of the pope within the church.

From before the fall of the Western Roman Empire, the Bishop of Rome had already been recognised as the foremost bishop in the West. Since the days of Gregory the Great, many popes had tried to convert the idea of the pope as *princeps inter pares* into a genuine form of supremacy and authority over the other bishops. Gregory VII launched a major offensive to this end.

In his *Dictatus papae* (1075), Gregory VII appropriated the right to depose or transfer bishops. He declared his authority to be universal. New doctrines on the origins of papal authority were articulated. Before, the common view had been that Christ had bestowed spiritual power on the Apostle Peter, the first Bishop of Rome. The pope exercised that power as Peter's successor, as *vicarius Petri*. This did not, however, essentially distinguish him from the other bishops, who were also *vicarii Petri* within their particular dioceses. For this reason, the doctrine was now defended that the pope received his power directly from the hands of Christ. He was not the successor of Peter, the first bishop, but the *vicarius Christi*, Christ's deputy, or even *vicarius Dei*, God's deputy on earth.

The twelfth century saw the emergence of the doctrine of *plenitudo potestatis* (fullness of power). Whereas the bishops enjoyed limited power, the pope had *plenitudo potestatis*. The pope was not the first bishop but the hierarchical superior of all bishops. He could issue them with commands and had the right to intervene in the matters of their bishopric and to act in their stead.[7] According to some canonists, *plenitudo*

---

[7] According to Johannes Teutonicus (*c.*1170–1245/6) 'the authority of the pope is without limits, that of other bishops is limited because they are called to a share of the responsibility not to the fullness of power' ('Papae auctoritas plena est, aliorum episcoporum semiplena est, quia ipsi sunt in partem sollicitudinis vocati non in plenitudinem potestatis'), d. 11 c. 2 v. *plena auctoritate*, translation by Kenneth Pennington, 'Law, Legislative Authority, and Theories of Government', in J.H. Burns, ed., *The Cambridge History of Medieval Political Thought c.350–c.1450*, Cambridge 1988, 434.

potestatis also meant that the pope was above the law: he could change the law and promulgate new law,[8] but also disregard it in specific cases. For the majority of the canonists, this applied only to ordinary human law. The pope remained subject to divine and to natural law. Cardinal Hostiensis (*c.*1200–71) distinguished *potestas absoluta* (absolute power) from *potestas ordinaria* (ordinary, everyday power). Only in the exercise of his absolute power was the pope able to disregard the law. There was no unanimity among canonists concerning the power of the pope within the church. Opposed to the defenders of supreme papal power, there were many scholars who argued for the limitation of that power.

181   Corporatism within the church

The debate on the relation between the pope and the bishops gave rise to the ideas of corporatism within the church. The church was seen as the *corpus Christi*, literally the body of Christ, the continuing presence of Christ on earth. In contrast to secular power, which in the context of feudalism had become the sum total of numerous personal hierarchical relationships, the church formed a body on its own. The church was an abstract, eternal and immutable entity that existed independently of its constituent parts. The death or birth of a single Christian, even the death of the pope, did not in any way change the identity of the church as an institution. In the course of the twelfth and thirteenth centuries, this gave rise to the idea of the church as a *corpus* with its own legal personality, that is, as a *persona ficta*. The term *universitas* was drawn from Roman law. The church was a *universitas fidelium*, a community of believers. The addition or loss of an individual believer did not essentially change the whole.

These concepts in turn sparked off the development of a complex political and legal debate on the balance of power within the church. The church as a fictitious legal entity was not a natural phenomenon but a legal fiction, the limits, organisation and operation of which had to be spelt out. This was done in canon law.

The idea of the church as a body – a corporation – was a powerful metaphor. Like a physical body, the church was an autonomous and at the same time composite entity. Its parts – its several categories of members – all derived their purpose from the part they played within the body. A metaphorical debate arose concerning the relationship between

---

[8] 'He can make something out of nothing' ('de nichilo facit aliquid'). Johannes Teutonicus, *Apparatus ad* 3 Comp. 5.2.3, translation by Pennington.

the head and the rest of the body: a debate concerning the place of the pope within the church. Broadly speaking, two traditions may be distinguished. On the one hand, there was the doctrine of which the great jurist and pope Innocent IV (1243–54) was a propagator, which held that the pope, as head of the body, held absolute power. The head could delegate certain tasks and powers to the members or organs, but all power ultimately originated from the head. On the other hand, there was the tradition that advocated mixed government by the pope and the church, of which Cardinal Hostiensis was one of the best-known representatives. This moderate school of thought distinguished three kinds of matters: those that only concerned the head, those that only concerned the body and those that concerned the whole. Whereas the first two could be primordially handled by the head or the body respectively – with limited consultation of the other party – the third category of affairs required an agreement to be reached between the head and the body, that is, between the pope and the church. This tradition inspired the conciliar movement of the fourteenth and fifteenth centuries.

182 Papal jurisdiction

Between 1050 and 1300, the popes were successful at transforming the church into a centrally governed monarchy. Historians frequently refer to the medieval papal church as the first modern 'state' in Europe.

Between the collapse of the Carolingian Empire and the Gregorian Reform, the pope had effectively been little more than the Bishop of Rome. Just like other bishops, he governed his diocese with the co-operation of its clergy, regularly convening in a synod. New laws and rules were made within this synod. The synod of the diocese of Rome also acted as a court of law, with the bishop-pope acting as judge. He would be advised by the priests in attendance but would decide and deliver the judgment himself.

Halfway through the eleventh century, it had become customary for prelates from other Italian dioceses to attend the Roman synod. With the Gregorian Reform, the synods were systematically expanded into universal councils of the entire Western Church. This culminated in the large universal councils of the Late Middle Ages, such as the First Lateran Council of 1123 or the Fourth Lateran Council of 1215. At this point, the convocation and chairing of universal councils by the pope affirmed his ascendancy over the church.

Gregory VII and his successors strengthened the central government of the church. As Bishop of Rome, the pope traditionally held a *curia* or council consisting of the most important priests in his diocese. This body was now transformed into a consistory of cardinals: an assembly of church dignitaries that was concerned no longer just with Rome but with the entire church. The consistory or college evolved into a group of some thirty cardinals, which obtained a monopoly over the election of the pope. In Rome, the cardinals were charged with specific administrative responsibilities, for which they surrounded themselves with secretaries. Slowly but surely there arose a professional and specialised bureaucracy of cardinals and priests appointed by the pope.

A rigid hierarchical structure was established within the church. Parish priests were subject to the bishops, who in turn were subject to the archbishops. Right at the top was the pope, assisted by his *curia*. The pope was the supreme legislator, the supreme administrator and the supreme judge. Between the eleventh and fourteenth centuries, the popes enacted a continuous stream of legislation, either on their own or through universal councils. The pope claimed supreme jurisdiction over the church. He could arrogate each single case, either as a judge of first instance or on appeal against a lower ecclesiastical court. Anyone could appeal to Rome in order to submit his case to the pope. In order to keep up with the stream of legal cases, from the thirteenth century onwards, popes started to delegate their powers to auditors. During the Avignon papacy, a separate papal court, known as the *Rota*, grew from this practice. The name, meaning wheel, may derive from the shape of the room where the court sat, or from the fact that the various auditors would relieve each other. Gradually, various specialised courts emerged, including one for financial cases. At the request of one of the parties, Rome could also empower a local prelate, bishop or abbot to hear a case on behalf of the pope.

Another important instrument for Rome's control over the church was the dispatch of legates. These were cardinals sent by the pope to an archdiocese. As deputies of the pope, the legates stood apart from and above the local church hierarchy. They could administer justice and promulgate laws in the name of the pope. Through its legates, Rome held the entire church in a strong grip.

183   Conciliarism

The Avignon exile marked the beginning of the decline of the papacy. Within the church, a counter-movement got underway. During the period before and after the Great Schism various universal councils were convened. The councils sought to alleviate the papal crisis but at the same time provided the opportunity to redefine the balance between the pope and the bishops. The conciliar movement defended the participation of the councils in the administration of the church. According to the conciliarists, the pope required the assent of the council for determining dogmas and promulgating laws. Radical thinkers, such as Marsilius of Padua (*c*.1275–1343) and the theologian Jean Gerson (1363–1429), defended the supremacy of the councils over the pope. In the event of dispute, the council had the last word. The Council of Basel (1431), which convened against the pope's will, confirmed its own supremacy. This was, however, to prove the last convulsion of the conciliar movement: by this time, the Schism was as good as over and the pope had retaken his position in Rome. Towards the end of the fifteenth century, Rome had restored its spiritual leadership over the West. The conciliar intellectual heritage continued to exist outside the church and contributed towards parliamentarianism.

8   *The emergence of secular political thought*

184   The concept of empire

The territorial power base of the German emperors was smaller than that of their Carolingian predecessors. Whereas Charlemagne ruled over the larger part of the Latin West, the new emperors' sphere of power was confined to Germany and Italy. The empire was not, however, a territorial concept. As early as his victory at Lechfeld in 955, Otto the Great, in the tradition of the Roman generals, was declared *imperator* by his troops. Until his coronation by the pope in 962, his claim to the title of *imperator* was based on the fact that, like Charlemagne, he ruled over various peoples. Thanks partly to the coronation by the pope, however, new dimensions were added to the concept of empire in the decades either side of the year 1000.

The emperorship came with the crown of the old *regnum Italiae*, to which the German kings had laid claim since the tenth century. Thus, it became the monopoly of the German kings. Under Otto III and Conrad II, the concept of empire had been further articulated. To a greater extent than their Carolingian predecessors, the new emperors placed the emphasis on the Roman, Christian and hence universal nature of the empire. To some extent, the focus on universality served to compensate for reality. During the course of the eleventh century, the emperors started to style themselves as 'Roman' emperors, and even as 'Roman' kings of Germany. In 1254, the name 'Holy Roman Empire' was used for the first time.[9]

---

[9]   The emperors were not, however, dubbed 'Holy Roman Emperor' as they are incorrectly in modern historiography. None of them could, after all, lay claim to holiness.

As 'Roman' emperor the new emperor laid claim to primacy in the West, to 'universal monarchy'. As the heir of the Western Roman emperor, he was the secular head of the Latin West. Otto the Great and his successors expressed this by appointing kings in the new Christian kingdoms in the east such as Poland, Bohemia and Hungary and acting as suzerains. But they were never able to have their claims of suzerainty acknowledged in the territories to the west of Germany and Italy. The Christian nature of the emperorship lay in the claim that the emperor was the secular head of the *populus Christianus*. Otto III and Conrad II regarded themselves as the secular guardians (*defensores*) of the church.

The concept of empire was the politico-juridical dimension to the ideal of the unity of Western Christianity. In itself, it implied not direct authority over the whole Latin West – the emperor only had direct authority as king of Germany and Italy – but a limited and poorly defined secular, 'universal' primacy.

185   Legitimisation of power

For the legitimisation of his power, the emperor drew on a mixture of doctrines and traditions. His authority as German and Italian king came from the concurrence of and acclamation by the leading nobles. The imperial crown may have been placed on his head by the pope, but according to the great emperors of the tenth and eleventh centuries this did not imply that imperial power came from the pope. At most it symbolised, just like the anointing of kings did, that the emperor had received his power directly from God. The pope was only the ceremonial and sacramental instrument of God's will. In the same way that the Frankish kings had used their anointing in order to blur the dividing line between the secular and spiritual spheres, so the emperors used their coronation by the pope. Like his Frankish predecessors, the German king/emperor was not just *rex/Caesar* but also *sacerdos*, invested with sacramental power. This served to justify intervention in ecclesiastical and spiritual matters. The lack of any clear distinction between the two spheres of power gave the emperor the opportunity to strengthen his power over the church.

The Investiture Controversy put an end to this unequal and stormy alliance between emperor and pope. All sorts of scholars – especially jurists – joined in on the emperor's side in the intellectual debate concerning the relations between secular and spiritual power. The propagandists of the emperor kept up their end in the debate about the two swords doctrine. Only a radical minority asserted that the emperor had received both swords from God or Christ, subsequently delegating the sword of spiritual power to the pope. The balance of power in this field forced the defenders of the imperial position on to the defensive. The claim of imperial supremacy was relegated to the background and its proponents had to take satisfaction from defending the independence of secular power from spiritual power. The two swords doctrine was interpreted in the sense that the emperor had received his power directly from Christ or God, without mediation by the pope or church.

While this interpretation of the two swords doctrine might serve to refute papal supremacy, it nevertheless failed to take imperial power out of the religious sphere sufficiently. Now that the centuries-old alliance between emperor and pope had disintegrated, the emperors sought a legitimation of their power that was as far removed from the church as possible. In this way, the Investiture Controversy provided a stimulus for the development of secular political thought. This did not go so far as to call into question the divine origin of political power, but the role of the church was eliminated wherever possible.

186   Appeal to Roman law

The inspiration for a new, secular theory on the origins of secular power was found in Roman law. Frederick Barbarossa is known to have consulted the great Roman lawyers of his time. These reverted to the Roman *lex regia*, whereby the Roman people allegedly had transferred their power to the Roman emperor.[10] As heir of the Roman *Caesares*, Frederick was the holder of that power. The fact that the transfer of power preceded the recognition of the church by Constantine by three centuries made it abundantly clear that the church played no role whatsoever in the origin of imperial power. The people had received their original power from God, but had passed this on to the emperor without mediation by the church. The possible democratic consequences of this ascending theory of power were countered by the proposition that the transfer of power was total and irrevocable. Other jurists, such as Azo (*c.*1150–1220), however, added that the people could revoke their delegation. This tradition would flourish, just like the conciliar movement in the church, during the fourteenth and fifteenth centuries and would provide an impetus for the more democratic streams of thought after the Middle Ages.

---

[10] 'A decision given by the Emperor, has the force of a statute. This is because the populace commits to him and into him its own entire authority and power, doing this by the *lex regia* which is passed anent his authority.' D. 1.4.1.

As late as the fourteenth century, the emperor had his defenders in Italy. In his treatise *De monarchia* (1307/8), the poet Dante Alighieri expressed his desire for the restoration of Italian unity under the emperor. Dante hoped that this would put an end to the unceasing political unrest in and between the Italian cities and principalities. Dante also opposed the secular claims of the pope. According to Dante, only the political unity of the West could ensure peace. Providence had designated the Roman emperor as ruler of the West, to which the birth of Christ under the first Roman emperor bore testimony. The emperor had furthermore received his power directly from God. Secular power was independent from spiritual power. Dante recognised that the pope too had received his spiritual power directly from God. This Marsilius of Padua rejected in his *Defensor pacis* (1324), arguing that the pope owed his authority to the assent of the people.

187   Aristotelian thought

In the same way that the position of the pope was under consideration in the church, so too was the position of the emperor in relation to his subjects actively under discussion on the secular side. Roman law and the Justinian codes were also important sources of inspiration in this regard. The identification with late Roman emperors such as Constantine and Justinian provided the new emperors with ammunition. The constitutional model of the Roman Empire was diametrically opposed to the feudal reality of the German Empire. It was a model in which the emperor towered over everything else as a genuine sovereign and stood at the fount and origin of all political and legal power. The relation between the emperor and his subjects was of a different dimension from that among all other persons. In classical Roman law, the distinction between private and public law had already been touched upon. The advocates of imperial power drew inspiration from the Roman model in order to project the emperor as supreme legislator and judge.

The Roman jurisprudence of the Late Middle Ages produced various approaches to the relation between the emperor, his subjects and the law. The debate widened into a debate on the relation between secular rulers and their subjects in general. The most important maxims taken from the Justinian codes on which the discussion turned were 'what pleases the emperor, has the force of law' ('quod principi placuit, legis habet vigorem') and 'the emperor is not bound by the law' ('princeps legibus solutus est').[11]

---

[11] D. 1.4.1 and D. 1.3.31.

Advocates and opponents of imperial authority used the same textual fragments to defend the most divergent propositions. Only a minority of the medieval jurists used these aforementioned maxims to argue that the emperor was above the law and could disregard it at will. The great gloss-ator of Roman law, Accursius (d. 1263), gave one of the most influential interpretations of these textual fragments and was a foremost representa-tive of mainstream political thought in the thirteenth century. According to Accursius, these and other maxims could be taken to mean that the emperor could change the law by introducing new statute law, but that this did not grant him the right to disregard the law, including his own, at will. Although many jurists accepted that all authority in the empire came from a delegation of part of his *imperium* by the emperor, some disputed that the emperor was at liberty to revoke such delegation as he pleased. As against the maxim of *princeps legibus solutus* there stood a text from the *Codex*, *Digna vox*, stating that it was befitting for the emperor to declare himself bound by the law.[12]

The rediscovery in the course of the twelfth and thirteenth centuries of the most important writings of Aristotle, including his *Politika*, rendered new arguments both for the emancipation of secular power from the spir-itual and for the limitation of imperial power, and by extension that of any secular ruler. Aristotle referred to man as 'a political animal', claiming that it was natural for man to organise himself in political communities.[13] First, this offered another argument for defending the autonomy of polit-ical authority from the church. Whereas under the Augustinian ideology, the state was instrumental to church and faith, the secular sphere became autonomous. Second, the claim that political organisation came from man's social nature provided a strong philosophical basis for an ascend-ing theory of power, while the ultimate divine origin of political power could be preserved through God's creation of man and human nature. Both elements – secularisation and the ascending theory of power – were combined into the articulation of a new, now secular purpose of secular power: serving the *bonum commune* or common good. Both the canon-ist Huguccio (d. 1210) and the great theologian Saint Thomas Aquinas (*c.*1225–74) argued that a law was only valid if it was reasonable and there-fore served the common good.

---

[12] C. 1.14.4 (Codex): 'It befits the majesty of the ruler to profess that he as emperor is bound by the laws' ('Digna vox maiestate regnantis legibus alligatum se principem profiteri') (my translation).

[13] *Politika* 3.4.2–3.

188   Corporatism

The corporatist and conciliar traditions in the church had a bearing on the debate concerning the relation between secular rulers and their subjects. Along the lines of the *universitas fidelium*, other *universitates* or corporations were also recognised, such as the *universitas professorum et studentium* (the universities) and the *universitates civium* (the towns). The identification of these secular communities as *universitates* involved a break with the logic of the feudal system. Whereas under the feudal system, everyone's position was determined by their personal relationship with their liege and vassals and the political community was the sum of all those links, the *universitas* existed in its own right. It was defined not in terms of the legal relations among its members but in terms of the legal relations of the members to itself. In principle, all members were subject to the *universitas* in the same way, according to the rules applying within the corporation. The *universitas* ideal contributed towards the gradual emancipation of public law from private law, or rather, from the law at large that was highly private in nature. The most important example of a political *universitas* was the town. It was a community of free and equal citizens – the burghers – who governed themselves and stood outside the feudal context.

Corporatist thinking with its metaphor of the body was also applied to kingdoms and to the empire. In the context of the debate concerning the limitation of the ruler's power, corporatist thinking, in line with the example of conciliarism in the church, was of major significance. A leading and original thinker in this field was the physician and theologian Marsilius of Padua, who viewed the political community as a *universitas civium*. The political community was autonomous. Public authority had been bestowed upon the ruler by the people.

189   *Superiorem non recognoscens*

Roman law was also harnessed to the defence of the emperor's universal dominion over the Latin West, of universal monarchy. A central passage was 'I am master of the world [*dominus mundi*]',[14] a statement made by the Roman Emperor Antoninus Pius, the precise implications of which were hotly debated among jurists in the Late Middle Ages. But not even the staunchest defence of the emperor's supremacy on the basis of Roman law could prevent the universal power of the emperor from becoming an empty slogan after 1250. Thanks in part to the collision between the two universal powers, the kings outside the Holy Roman Empire had

---

[14] D. 14.2.9.

managed to strengthen their position towards the end of the twelfth century. The popes actively supported them in rejecting imperial supremacy. In 1202, Pope Innocent III declared in his papal bull *Per Venerabilem* that the French king need not recognise any higher authority in secular affairs. The jurists translated this into the maxim *rex imperator in regno suo* (the king is emperor in his own realm). Thus the supremacy of the emperor was rejected, or rather absorbed by various kings.

Aristotelian thought on the natural origin of the 'state' was also to play a role in this debate. The fact that political entities were formed through the spontaneous coming together of individuals implied that different independent political communities could exist. The *communitas* formed in this way was a *communitas perfecta* (perfect community) that derived its legitimation from its natural origin and not from its participation in a greater whole. This too represented a break from Augustinian political thinking, under which all political structures were subordinate to the one, true church and defended the ideal of a single empire. The most important Roman lawyer of the fourteenth century, Bartolus of Sassoferrato, distinguished between imperial supremacy *de iure* and *de facto*. The Italian city-republics were subject to the emperor *de iure*, but were *de facto superiorem non recognoscentes* (recognising no higher authority). For these reasons, they could wage war, a prerogative of the highest authority. The description *superiorem non recognoscens* was later displaced by the concept of *supremitas* (sovereignty), literally meaning the highest position or supreme power and also expressing the absence of any higher authority. It was not until the sixteenth century that a more positive connotation was given to this concept.

The rejection of the universal claims of the emperor and the crisis in papal authority dealt heavy blows to the ideal of the political and legal unity of Europe. Secular authority was dispersed over dozens of 'sovereign' monarchies and republics that would not tolerate any interference whatever in their affairs by the emperor, at most granting him ceremonial primacy. During the fourteenth century and the early decades of the fifteenth century, Rome's universal claims in ecclesiastical affairs once again came under challenge. Nevertheless, the ideal of the *respublica christiana* survived the Middle Ages.

9 The feudal overlordships until 1200

190 The feudal and seigniorial systems

In the centuries after the year 1000, the feudal and seigniorial systems determined the political and legal context of most of the rural population of western Europe. The system expanded throughout the West. From the eleventh century onwards, the feudal and seigniorial systems were formalised in rules and procedures that defined and laid down the rights and obligations of lords, vassals, tenants and serfs. Around 1100, feudal law in Italy was described in a number of books, the *Libri feudorum*, which were to be added later to the texts of the Justinian collection and studied at the faculties. In other countries as well, feudal law, like seigniorial law, found its way into the law books.

From the twelfth century onwards, serfdom was on the decline. Personal serfdom disappeared or was relaxed. Villeins evolved into leaseholders, liable for paying a fixed rent in coin or kind to the lord. Bonded labour was replaced by money payments or simply abolished. With the gradual restoration of central authority, the local lords lost royal powers they had previously usurped, such as high justice, the mint and military command. In terms of the day-to-day administration of their seigniory, however, the local lords and communities retained a large measure of autonomy. Lower justice over civil cases and petty crimes, the promulgation of local laws, the organisation of agriculture, and the levying of local taxes and rents remained matters for the seigniory. The lord continued to exercise his local powers in his own name. Often, his power was not regarded as delegated and could not simply be revoked. Moreover, centralisation was not a linear process: during the Late Middle Ages and even during the Renaissance certain rights, such as that of high justice, would sometimes be resold to local lords.

191   The feudal overlordship

The restoration of centralised authority at the regional or national level took place in two stages. During the first stage, which lasted till around 1200, the defenders of royal power primarily invoked feudalism and the traditional instruments of power attached to kingship. During a second stage, new institutions and instruments of power were developed. For the first stage, we can best speak of the kingdoms and large regional principalities as feudal overlordships; for the second, they can be seen as feudal states.

The feudal overlordship of this first stage was actually a collection of different regional and local seigniories and other politico-juridical entities of all kinds, secular as well as ecclesiastical, the rulers of which recognised the supreme authority of the same prince on a variety of legal bases, feudal and other. The prince's authority was largely indirect as it was dependent on the intermediate authority of his chief vassals. The abstract notion of the state was not far developed yet. 'State authority' was nothing more than the sum of the prince's powers and rights in relation to the different parts of his composite realm, and its subjects. In the first place, as suzerain the king stood at the top of the feudal pyramid within his realm. In the second place, there was the old, Frankish tradition of kingship. During the crisis of the West, royal authority had become largely eroded and the public power of the king and the counts had become feudalised. Even so, the kingship retained a special public and sacral character.

Charlemagne had universalised the feudal system in order to bind the great magnates and warriors more closely to himself. After the division of the Carolingian Empire at Verdun, feudalism became counter-productive. Under the last Carolingians, the focus shifted from the rights of the liege to the rights of the vassal. The great vassals used and abused their position in order to strengthen their autonomy and weaken royal authority. The feudal system gave impetus to the process of decentralisation. Around the year 1000, the tide began to turn. As Charlemagne had done, in order to reassert their authority, various kings, including the Ottonian emperors, used and spread the feudal system in an attempt to enforce their rights of suzerainty. The general introduction of feudal landholding by William the Conqueror in England is just the most notable example of these policies.

Under the feudal system, the prince could appeal to the personal allegiance of his immediate vassals. Feudal law did not, however, give him any authority over his sub-vassals. It was up to the immediate vassals of the sovereign to impose their obligation upon their own vassals. To this extent, the feudal kingdom functioned through a chain of personal and direct relationships of allegiance that came together at the top in the person of the suzerain.

After the year 1000, the obligation of the vassal to assist his lord with 'aid and counsel' was elaborated into a fixed set of particular obligations. Military service, for example, was restricted to a set number of days per year, for example, fifty. Counsel meant that the vassals were obliged to help their lord with the administration of his territory. The prince governed his realm with the aid of his *curia*. On this sat the most important vassals and prelates, as well as a number of court officials. Court offices were often also given to representatives of the feudal nobility. Generally speaking, only the vassals and prelates from the region where the sovereign was residing or passing through at the time would be present for the *curia* session. The *curia* deliberated under the leadership of the prince on all the affairs of state: the administration of the royal domain, taxation, diplomacy and the conduct of war. It also acted as the royal court of law. Its composition meant that it was the place where the prince met with the power elite of the realm.

Princes built up their power by strengthening their position as feudal overlords. They faced the challenge of suppressing the depersonalisation of the feudal system and refocusing on the personal bond between liege lord and vassal. They exploited all the means offered by feudal law to regain control over important fiefdoms. In the event of the death of a vassal without direct heirs, the fiefdom would revert to the liege lord. The latter could then attempt to retain the fief or give it to a relative or friendly magnate. When the Flemish Count Charles the Good (1119–27) was murdered in Bruges in 1127, his liege lord, King Louis VI of France, sought to install his favourite in Flanders. The kings also tightened the personal links with their most important vassals, regularly convening the *curia* and obliging their vassals to take part. The kings selected an elite group from their vassals who were allowed to call themselves *pairs* (*pares*, peers) and who formed a college of companions around the king (such as the *collège des pairs de France*) within or beside the *curia*.

Particularly in the smaller feudal principalities, princes sought to secure a direct grip over the local administration. Within the feudal kingdoms as well as regional principalities, the old Carolingian counties now survived as administrative subdivisions of the principality, later called *bailliages* or *sénéchaussées* in France (shires in England). At the head of these stood a castellan or a viscount (sheriff in England) who commanded the royal castle and garrison if there was one. The castellan represented the prince within the region, exercising control over the aldermen's bench. Since these offices were generally given as feudal fiefs to the local magnates and were also feudalised, this system in the longer run did not prove an effective instrument of strengthening central authority in most countries of the West.

10   *The feudal state after 1200*

192   The reassertion of public authority

Although feudalism remained an important factor, in the feudal state of the second stage the focus shifted to the 'public law' aspect of royal authority. Following in the tradition of the emperors of the Holy Roman Empire, the sovereigns of Europe sought inspiration in Roman law and the Roman emperorship. From the amalgam of Roman law, Germanic, Christian and feudal traditions, the defenders of royal authority distilled a doctrine and a myth of kingship. In addition to being the suzerain, the prince once again became the bearer and embodiment of public authority.

Before 1200, princes had mostly used the instruments feudality offered them to assert central authority. But these proved insufficient. The power of the liege was personal and limited. As feudal lord, the prince could not claim to be of a different order to his vassals themselves. As the holder of a public and sacred office, however, he did.

Even after 1200, the restoration of central authority was a long and difficult process. Gradually, princes began to reclaim traditional royal rights and prerogatives relating to the defence of the realm, taxation, the mint and high justice, and to exercise them again. Over some prerogatives, the princes claimed an exclusive right; over others, they did not. In 1158, at the Imperial Diet in Roncaglia, Emperor Frederick Barbarossa promulgated a list of royal prerogatives and powers that belonged exclusively to the king (*regalia* or *iura regia*). For this, Frederick appealed to the *quattuor doctores*, the four great doctors or scholars of Roman law.

193 Bureaucratisation

Gradually, the central apparatus of government was strengthened and expanded. A new category of councillors claimed its place in the royal *curiae*, that of university-schooled royal officials – mostly jurists and theologians. Many of these did not stem from the leading, landholding noble families. They were appointed and paid by the prince, and lacking a noble background and personal power base, were often completely dependent on him for their political power and social standing. With time, this group formed a new nobility of officeholders (*noblesse de robe* in France), to be distinguished from the old landholding and chivalrous nobility (*noblesse d'épée*).

The emergence of this new class led to professionalisation, bureaucratisation and specialisation. The councillor/jurists acted as secretaries or notaries of the prince and provided the first step towards the creation of a central bureaucracy. The new officials took over the more technical aspects of government, such as the treasury and the administration of justice.

In consequence, the *curia* gradually lost its feudal character. In France, the *collège des pairs de France*, the assembly of the twelve greatest nobles, continued to exist as a separate body. The curia itself now evolved into a genuine council or *conseil*. It was no longer a consultative or participatory body where the monarch met his great vassals but an advisory council and executive body in the service of the prince.

New specialised councils split off from the royal council. Financial councils such as the exchequer in England and the *Chambres des Comptes* in France emerged. At the royal court, a chancellery was established, a kind of secretariat under the direction of the chancellor. The chancellery drew up official documents. It was responsible for all correspondence and played a crucial role in the co-ordination of government activities. Also judicial institutions emerged from the former *curia*.

At the regional and local level, princes often set up a second power circuit next to the old one. Next to the castellans, princes now often appointed other officials to represent them, such as bailiffs, seneschals, provosts (in France and the Low Countries), *podestà* (in Italy) or justiciars (*judiciarii*, in England). They took over the tasks of the castellan in matters of justice and taxation and stood under strict central control. Even so, in various areas, these offices gradually became feudalised as well.

11   The limits of royal power in the Late Middle Ages

194   Lords and towns

During the Late Middle Ages, central authority reasserted itself all over western Europe, if not at the national than at the regional level. But although many kings and princes were successful in expanding their territorial and institutional power, they still had to take account of and compete against local power brokers.

First, the landholding nobility and the church retained a strong position in rural areas. Seigniorial and ecclesiastical lords had to give up some of the royal powers and prerogatives they had previously usurped, but still retained all sorts of other powers and rights under the feudal and seigniorial systems. As seigniorial lords, they in principle exercised those tasks in their own name. Moreover, to a large extent, kings and princes were also dependent on the co-operation of these power magnates to assert royal authority farther down the hierarchy on the latter's own vassals and people.

Second, princes increasingly had to reckon with the towns. Often, an objective alliance was formed between the princes and the emerging towns, in their mutual struggle with local lords. Many towns owed their freedoms and privileges to the prince. These were then laid down in town charters granted by the prince. In certain parts of Europe, however, such as the Low Countries, Germany, northern Italy and northern France, with time the towns evolved into powerful political players and redoubtable competitors to the prince.

195 *Universitas civium*

Towns formed separate jurisdictions of their own, as they gained immunity from the jurisdiction of the ordinary aldermen's benches of the shires, the seigniorial and the feudal courts. The towns were administered by their own aldermen's benches. The town aldermen could be appointed by the prince or be elected by the burghers. The aldermen's bench, together with the mayors and town councils, laid out the mutual rights and obligations of the prince and the town in fiscal, juridical and military affairs. The prince generally retained a measure of control over the town's bench, as he also did over the ordinary aldermen's bench. Thereto, he appointed a representative such as a bailiff or a *podestà*.

The towns broke free from the world of feudalism. They did not fit into the network of personal relations that dominated government authority until the end of the twelfth century. Within the towns, there was a much higher degree of juridical equality than in the countryside. In principle, all burghers fell likewise under the jurisdiction of their own town bench. The towns formed an autonomous, abstract body politic, a *universitas civium*. They were a league of sworn members who had taken an oath to uphold the peace and law of the community. This collective oath symbolised the break from the traditional ties of personal dependency, as the burghers had sworn loyalty to the community and not done homage to a lord. This democratic foundation provided them with an element of legitimacy to distance themselves from the local lords in the surrounding rural areas and even from the prince.

196 Dualism

Princes not only had to deal with the opposition of local lords and towns to inroads against the latter's autonomy. As the central government gained in power, so the local powers had a growing interest in having or obtaining a say in it. The thirteenth and fourteenth centuries were marked by numerous attempts, peaceful and not so peaceful, by the nobility, the clergy and/or the towns to rein in royal power and to ensure themselves of a certain degree of participation in central government. In many cases, royal power was curbed as kings were forced to accept a certain participation by the estates in government. This is referred to as the dualism between the prince and the estates.

Over the thirteenth and fourteenth centuries, many princes found themselves obliged to conclude compacts, known as quasi-constitutional texts, with their subjects, in which they had to accept limitations on their power. The Peace of Konstanz in the year 1183 between the emperor and the Lombard League from northern Italy and Magna Carta of 1215 in England are the most familiar examples, while in the Low Countries there was the *Joyeuse Entrée* ('Joyous Entry') of the Duke of Brabant (1356). In Magna Carta, King John was obliged to promise to respect and honour the personal privileges and property rights of all free persons. The charter also laid down that a free man could be punished only after being tried by his peers and after due process of law. A council of high nobles and prelates would supervise the king's compliance with the charter.

These quasi-constitutional texts were agreements between the prince and the representatives of the estates and laid the foundations for shared government between the prince and the three estates – the nobility, clergy and third estate. The last category particularly included the towns. The vast majority of people, the commoners in the countryside, went unrepresented.

197   Estates and parliaments

Dualism became institutionalised in the Late Middle Ages. From time to time, the prince would convene the representatives of estates, of his own accord or at the urging of the estates themselves, to consult them and to negotiate with them. Often, these 'parliaments' had evolved from the old feudal *curiae*. In the Spanish kingdoms, this evolution was already taking place at the end of the twelfth century. Here, the meeting of the estates was given the name Cortes. In England, Parliament emerged during the reigns of Henry III (1216–72) and Edward I (1272–1307). It was split into two chambers, the House of Lords, the assembly of the great nobles and prelates who had previously formed part of the *curia*, and the House of Commons, with representatives of the gentry and the towns. In France, the first assemblies for the entire kingdom, known as the *Etats Géneraux* or Estates-General, were held in the fourteenth century. Provincial estates were also held in the various parts of the realm. In most other parts of the continent, the estates organised themselves, as in France, into three groups or chambers: the nobility, the clergy and the third estate. In many cases, each estate carried equal weight, irrespective of its numerical strength. In the Low Countries, assemblies of the estates were held in most of the principalities in the course of the fourteenth century. The first Estates-General for the entire Burgundian Netherlands was not held until 1464.

In principle, the estates were convened at the initiative of the prince. They were not in permanent session. The powers of the estates were partly laid down in quasi-constitutional texts but were largely based on custom. The exact rights and obligations of the prince and the estates were subject to an ongoing power struggle. The most important powers of the estates related to legislation and taxation.

The prince often promulgated new laws in consultation with and with the assent of the estates. Although many jurists claimed that the prince could make laws without the consent of the people, in many countries it became customary, if not obligatory, for the king to legislate 'in parliament'. The prince was the legislator, but the people 'accepted' the law. This was consistent with the rule from canon law which stipulated that a statute that had fallen into disuse became void.

The income of the prince, other than the revenues of his own domains, came from a variety of direct and indirect taxes. As suzerain and as king, the prince could tax certain activities and forms of income. Outside these ordinary, traditional rights of taxation (*consuetudines*), however, he was not allowed to levy any new taxes without the consent of the estates. One of the most important reasons for convening the estates was to plead for special taxes to be raised. If the prince, generally in times of war, needed additional resources he was obliged to turn to the estates. In exchange for meeting the request, the estates were often able to exact political or legal concessions from the prince.

The Late Middle Ages were marked by two important constitutional and political developments. On the one hand, most of the kings and princes in Europe were successful at enhancing their authority at the expense of local and regional rulers. On the other hand, they also had to accept a growing participation by the estates at the central level. Both contemporary constitutionalism, in the sense of the limitation of state power by means of a constitution, and parliamentarianism can trace their distant origins to this period.

B   Culture and the law

1   *The awakening of the West and the rebirth of legal science*

Anno a passione Domini millesimo, memorate cladis penurias subsequente, sedatis nimborum imbribus respectu divine bonitatis et misericordie, cepit leta facies celi clarescere … ethereis flare placidaque serenitate magnanimitatem conditoris ostendere; telluris quoque tota superficies amicaliter virens frugum abundantiam funditus inopiam expellendo portendere.[15]

---

[15] 'In the thousandth year after the death of our Lord the rain has stopped falling from the thunder clouds, as desired by God in his goodness and mercy. The heavens began to laugh … showing rest and in peace the magnanimity of the Creator. The entire surface

198   The expansion of the text canon

At the end of the tenth century, fear roamed through the Latin West. It was expected that a thousand years after the birth of Christ – or was it Christ's passion and resurrection? – the world would come to an end. Even after the years 1000 and 1033 had passed, many continued to think that the Final Judgment was upon them. Others, such as the Burgundian monk Rudulfus Glaber, thought they saw a new dawn on the horizon. In the end, the year 1033 did not bring the Apocalypse. It became the year of birth of one of the greatest thinkers ever produced by the West: Saint Anselm of Canterbury (1033–1109).

The Renaissance of the Twelfth Century (1070–1225) marked the intellectual reawakening of the Latin West. The revival of trade and industry as well as the growth of towns and cities created the conditions for the flourishing of education, knowledge and science. By the early thirteenth century, the Latin West had attained a level of intellectual and cultural life that had not been experienced since the fourth century.

The revival started off within the intellectual and institutional framework of the previous age. The ideology of the early Renaissance of the Twelfth Century was the Augustinian ideology. At the inception, the same canon of ancient texts and commentaries thereon formed the basis of its scholarship. The Renaissance of the Twelfth Century was, however, swiftly to transcend these origins. The abbey schools lost their leading position to the cathedral schools, which in turn had to make way for that great creation of the twelfth century, the university. The canon of classical texts was adapted and supplemented. The intellectual lens through which these texts were studied changed. In the thirteenth century, Europe developed a new ideology to replace Augustinianism: Thomism.

Intellectual renewal came from three main sources. Three new textual traditions were to enrich the existing material. First, there was the rediscovery of the Justinian *Digest*. Second, there was the development of canon law with a *corpus* of its own, a consequence of the Gregorian Reform and the Investiture Controversy. These two movements began around 1070 and marked the beginning of the Renaissance of the Twelfth Century. Third, there was the rediscovery – chiefly between 1140 and 1250 – of the leading works of the Greek philosopher Aristotle. While the adoption of the Aristotelian texts and ideas came too late to influence fundamentally the Renaissance of the Twelfth Century itself, it was to

of the Earth was covered with sweet green and an abundance of fruits that drove out hunger.' Rudulfus Glaber, *Historiae* 4.5 (my translation).

give the intellectual resurgence of Europe a second impetus from around 1225/50.

It was within the context of the Renaissance of the Twelfth Century that European jurisprudence and the continental legal tradition emerged. The rediscovery of Roman law and expansion of canon law led to a revival of the systematic study of the law. Legal training was introduced and a new class of professional and educated jurists emerged. The common law tradition, which is less indebted to the medieval study of Roman law, also emerged from the twelfth century onwards. The emergence of legal science was, however, more than a sprig on the lush tree of the Renaissance of the Twelfth Century; it was also one of its roots. It was precisely in the study of an old – the Justinian – and the creation of a new – canonical – textual canon that the medieval Renaissance established one of its initial great achievements. It was also in that context that the crowning glory of the Renaissance, scholasticism, first came to fruition.

2   Early scholasticism (1070–1225): epistemology

199   From early to late scholasticism

Scholasticism was the backbone as well as the pearl in the crown of the Renaissance of the Twelfth Century. The term refers both to the theory of science (that is, the epistemology) and to the scientific methodology which was dominant during the Late Middle Ages. Scholasticism became the chief doctrine and method of the primary intellectual institution of the Late Middle Ages, the university, which it was to remain until the sixteenth and even seventeenth century. We can distinguish early scholasticism (1070–1225) from late scholasticism (after 1225). To a large extent, it was the input from Aristotelian texts that prompted the renewal of late scholasticism.

As a scientific method, scholasticism was first developed and applied in the field of Roman law. In terms of the ideological foundations of its epistemology, however, it drew on the writings of a number of eleventh-century theologians and heavily depended on the Augustinian tradition. The most important of these theologians of early scholasticism was Anselm, the Italian Archbishop of Canterbury from 1093 onwards. Anselm's was a leading voice in two great debates of the twelfth century.

200   Faith and reason

The first debate pertains to the question as to how knowledge and truth are attained: by faith or by reason? Entirely in the Augustinian tradition,

Anselm defends the supremacy of faith. Divine revelation is the ultimate source of all knowledge and of truth. Any form of knowledge is, ultimately, possible only because God has revealed it. In addition, however, Anselm assigns a more active role to reason than the church had done since the time of Gregory the Great. In that sense, Anselm is more faithful to Augustine than the 'Augustinians' of the Early Middle Ages.

For Anselm, reason is a supplementary instrument for attaining knowledge and insight. Reason allows one to understand more effectively the truths that one already 'knows' thanks to faith. Anselm's attitude towards the relationship between faith and reason is summed up in the words 'Credo ut intelligam', 'I believe so that I may understand'. In order to discern the truth, faith is necessary. Those who do not believe are unable to accept the doctrines and dogmas. He who does believe, however, can seek to capture with his reason what his heart already believes and holds dear.

The role of reason remains secondary. It is an instrument for explaining and defending the articles of faith. There are no contradictions between the revealed truth and the conclusions to which reason leads. In practice, the role of reason is confined to countering any objections against faith human reasoning might lead to, so anchoring the doctrines of faith in rational understanding. However, with these and similar propositions, the early theologians of the Renaissance of the Twelfth Century opened the door to the rise of rational thought and science.

201   Realism and nominalism

The second debate concerned *universalia* and *realia*. The debate centred on a textual fragment from the *Isagoge* by the Neoplatonist Porphyry. It concerned the question of whether *universalia* (that is, the general concepts or ideas) had any reality. Two schools of thought arose: the realists, including Anselm, who posited the reality of the *universalia*, and the nominalists, such as Johannes Roscellinus (c.1050–1120), who argued that only the *realia* (earthly phenomena) were real and that *universalia* were just *nomina* (names), creations of the human mind. Anselm's realism became the official ideology of the church. The views of Roscellinus and the Parisian theologian Peter Abelard (1079–1142) were condemned by the church.

Although Anselm was not himself directly influenced by Plato's idealism and subsequent Neoplatonic interpretations, his realism confirmed the Platonic tradition in Western thought. True knowledge comes not from the understanding of the physical world and the phenomena in it, but from insight into the *universalia*, the general concepts roaming beyond its confines. Physical phenomena at the most refer as symbols to the higher, metaphysical reality of the *universalia*,[16] but do not contain reality in themselves.

202   Medieval rationalism

Realism explains the rationalism of scholasticism. True knowledge and understanding come not from the observation of man and nature but through general concepts and ideas. The scientist of the twelfth century does not look for new knowledge and insights in the physical world through observation; instead he seeks knowledge within the confines of his own mind and soul. Anselms's famous proof for God's existence illustrates this well:

> Assuredly, this [being] exists so truly that it cannot even be thought not to exist. For there can be thought to exist something which cannot be thought not to exist; and this thing is greater than that which can be thought not to exist. Therefore, if that than which a greater cannot be thought could be thought not to exist, then that than which a greater cannot be thought would not be that than which a greater cannot be thought – which is contradictory. Hence, something than which a greater cannot be thought exists so truly that it cannot even be thought not to exist. And You are this [being], O Lord, our God. Therefore, O Lord my God, You exist so truly that You cannot even be thought not to exist.[17]

3   Early scholasticism (1070–1225): method

203   The scholastic paradigm: authority

It was against these theological backgrounds that scholasticism developed into a scientific method around 1100, first of all in the study of Roman law (around 1100), then in theology (around 1120) and canon law (around 1140).

The scholastic démarche departed from the notion that God had revealed truth to humankind. That revelation was laid down in the Bible, which had been inspired by God. The quest for truth and knowledge must necessarily be based on the reading, study and interpretation of the Bible.

---

[16] 'Omnis mundi creatura, quasi liber et pictura nobis est in speculum' ('Each creature on earth is to us a mirror like a book or a painting'). Alanus van Rijsel (1125/30–1203), *Parabolae* (my translation).

[17] *Proslogion* 3, translation by Jasper Hopkins, *A New, Interpretative Translation of St Anselm's Monologian and Proslogion*, Minneapolis 1996.

Greek, Roman and early Christian writings shared to some extent the authority of the Bible. Attributing authority to Greek, Roman and early Christian writings was no break with the past. Augustine had already sanctioned their study. He had held the knowledge of the Greeks and the Romans useful to the study of the Bible. Scholasticism adopted the entire classical textual canon of Greek, Roman and early Christian writers as preserved and handed down by the monks in the Early Middle Ages. To these, they also added newly discovered and newly written texts.

The core belief behind scholasticism was that truth as revealed to man by God was to be found in this textual canon. This clearly applied to the Bible and the works of the Church Fathers, but in the wake of Augustine and other Church Fathers, it was accepted that God had also lifted a corner of the veil for other, pagan, authors and revealed some of the truth to them. The writings of philosophers such as Plato and Aristotle, Roman poets such as Virgil, historians such as Livy, orators such as Cicero and Quintilian (c.35–100) and scientists such as Euclid, Pliny (23/4–79) and Galen (129–99), were intensively analysed and commented upon.

For the scholastics, all these texts held *auctoritas*, authority. They had claims on the truth in the sense that the full, irrefutable and perfect truth as revealed by God to man lay hidden in them. This had two implications. On the one hand, apart from faith, only the study of these texts could lead to truth. On the other hand, the correct understanding of the texts could result in true knowledge. Like the Bible, these authoritative texts were considered sacred sources of knowledge and of truth.

204   Dialectics

These idealistic beliefs and expectations about these texts were, of course, naive and unrealistic. No unequivocal, irrefutable and perfect truth could emerge from the huge tradition of thousands and thousands of pages of text written over a period of two millennia. Between the various texts and within major works themselves such as the Bible and the *Digest*, there were countless inconsistencies as well as outright contradictions. Given the many centuries that had elapsed, many of the texts had become superseded by evolution or were simply no longer comprehensible. In addition, most of the texts had become corrupted by translation and copying. A huge gap separated the idealism with which people embarked on the quest for knowledge in the authoritative sources and the state of reality.

The scholastic method bridged this gap. The scholastics developed a logical apparatus for text interpretation. The aim was to analyse and interpret the text in such a way that expectations were met and the one irrefutable Truth had been distilled from it. The difficulties experienced in doing so proved to be incentives to develop new and more sophisticated logical instruments of textual interpretation.

Logic as an instrument for textual exegesis is the core of scholasticism. The medieval scholastics developed a complex logical apparatus that allowed them to eliminate contradictions and systematise the knowledge and truths revealed in the texts or, more accurately, that they saw as being revealed in them. A primary example of these logical instruments was the *distinctio*. By distinguishing situations which appeared at first glance to be identical, contradictions in the texts could be explained away. It will come as no surprise that it was the students of Roman case law who shone in this regard and that they were the first to develop 'scholasticism'. The opposite of the *distinctio* was the *aequiparatio* (literally, equating equal with equal).

The logical démarche of scholasticism was dialectical. Logic, one of the three disciplines of the *trivium*, was known as *dialectica* (dialectics). Teachers and scholars made particular use of *quaestiones* (questions) and *disputationes* (disputes). A question or proposition would be debated. The basic assumption underlying the debate was that the authoritative texts would provide an unambiguous answer to each and every question. The texts' authority required as well as guaranteed this. A number of texts would be quoted in support of the proposition (*sic*, yes) as well as a series of texts refuting the proposition (*non*, no). By the application of *distinctiones* and other logical reasonings, one would arrive at an unambiguous conclusion. Two of the earlier twelfth-century works written in accordance with this dialectic method were *Sic et non* (*Yes and no*) by Peter Abelard (around 1130) and *Concordia discordantium canonum* (*The unity in the disunity of the canons*) by the canonist Gratian (before 1140).

Scholasticism was based on faith in the authority of the text. Through the rational analysis and interpretation of the text, the scholar would arrive at the truth, which he could then profess. In the words of Saint Bonaventura (*c.*1217–74), 'one needed first of all to believe in it, secondly to understand what one believed and thirdly to pronounce what one understood. Faith is based on authority, understanding on reason and pronouncement on the acceptable and comprehensible use of language.'[18]

---

[18] 'Primo contigit ipsam credere, secundo creditam intelligere, tertio intellectam dicere vel enuntiare. Credere autem est per autoritatem, intelligere per rationem, dicere per catholicam et rationabilem locutionem.'

205   Book learning

Scholastic wisdom was book learning. The quest for knowledge took place wholly within the confines of texts and the mind. Experimental research, based on the observation of nature, was not valued. Medieval medicine, as it was studied at the universities from the eleventh century onwards, provides a striking example thereof. At first sight, this was the subject closest to nature, more so than theology or law. But the human body was not studied through its observation. University training largely consisted of the analysis, interpretation and discussion of the traditional views as contained in the ancient sources, especially in the works of the Roman Galen. At the core of Galen's system was the doctrine of the four humours or bodily fluids. Disease meant that there was an imbalance between these fluids. Fever was a sign that there was too much blood in the body. Therefore, bleeding was the common treatment for fever. For centuries to come, even after the discovery of the circulation of blood by William Harvey (1578–1657), university-trained doctors in Europe swore by treating their patients in this way, sometimes bleeding them to death. Experience that this did not work was no match for the authority of Galen and his medieval commentators. Besides the learned *doctores*, there were also surgeon-barbers, who effectively performed surgical interventions such as amputations, the extraction of teeth and the treatment of wounds. These practitioners did live and work in the real world. The division of roles between the learned doctor who made the diagnosis and prescribed the cure and the surgeon-barber who administered the treatment illustrates how scholasticism had breathed new life into the classical distinction between *scientia* or *prudentia* (science, scholarship) and *ars* (skill, expertise and craftsmanship). Scholarship and nature had become distant bedfellows.

206   The autonomy of reasoning and science

The core beliefs underpinning scholasticism were consistent with Augustinian ideology. It helped scholasticism to find speedy acceptance. Scholasticism departed from the same belief in the revelation and authority of Christian and ancient texts as the Augustinians had held. It legitimised the use of reason as a purely instrumental device, in the service of the one, divine truth. In that sense, scholasticism as originally conceived was conservative. It began as an effort to realise the Augustinian ideal of the unity, timelessness, universality and totality of knowledge.

Much more important than this conclusion, however, is that scholasticism granted a space to human reasoning. With time, this space would grow. The use of reason was justified as an effort to bridge the gap between the physical world reality and divine truth, but it was the journey itself, rather than its end, that came to matter most. Dialectics and its products might be regarded only as stepping stones on the road to God, but gradually they became structures in their own right. From generation to generation, scholasticism and its arsenal of knowledge became more extensive and complex and, for the scholar, the means – reason in the service of God – became the end: *l'art pour l'art*, or more strictly *la science pour la science*. In the same way that church building over the course of the twelfth century slipped from the service of God to the 'self-idolisation of human abilities, to which God had just become an alibi', so also did scholarship go down this path.[19] Nothing demonstrates this more effectively than the previously mentioned *Sic et non* by Peter Abelard which, while putting forward arguments for and against each proposition, left the final judgement to the reader. In doing so, he appeared to say that not the one true knowledge but reasoning itself mattered. It is from Abelard that we have the statement 'Intelligo ut credam', 'I understand in order that I might believe'. Faith does not precede understanding; instead, understanding is necessary in order to believe.

The emergence of rational thought as a value in itself detracted from the Augustinian ideal of unipolarity, timelessness, universality and totality. The one and true knowledge was equated to the truth desired by the scholar himself. Once again it should come as no surprise that legal science took the lead. The absolute authority of the claims to truth made on the basis of the authoritative texts was gradually eroded. That was, however, a process that was not to be completed until the twentieth century. Truth became more relative, less timeless and less universal.

The totality of truth and the indivisibility of all truth perished much more quickly. Before the Renaissance of the Twelfth Century there was just one scholarly discipline, theology. The seven *artes liberales* only prepared for the one real discipline, spanning all available knowledge: theology. The twelfth century changed this. The growth of the textual canon and the increase in the mass of available knowledge necessitated specialisation. Even before the year 1100 the first, new disciplines broke free from theology: law and medicine. Gratian's book also conferred autonomy on canon law, independent of theology. The Augustinian model of unity disintegrated.

[19] Raoul Bauer, 'De draagwijdte of the twaalfde eeuw', in Raoul Bauer, J. de Visscher, H. VandeVondele and D. Van Den Anweele, *De twaalfde eeuw. Breuklijn in onze beschaving*, Amsterdam and Antwerp 1984, 116 (my translation).

4   Late scholasticism (1225–1453): synthesis and dissent

207   The rediscovery of Aristotle

From the second half of the twelfth century onwards, new ideas started to take shape. The ideal of unity from Augustinian ideology receded into the background as the focus shifted to nature and its diversity. The rediscovery of the writings of the Greek philosopher Aristotle stimulated this. The thirteenth century witnessed the emergence of a new synthesis that was to replace the Augustinian ideology: Thomism.

During late Antiquity, the writings of Aristotle had, with a few exceptions, been lost. Not Aristotle but Plato dominated late Roman philosophy and early Christian philosophy. Plato's works and ideas were copied, translated into Latin, summarised and commented upon. The majority of the works by his great disciple, however, did not attract any interest. They were not translated, and with the decline of the knowledge of Greek many of his writings were lost to the Latin West.

Aristotle was, however, studied in the Byzantine Empire and the Islamic world. Arab and Jewish scholars translated the majority of his works into Arabic or Hebrew and wrote commentaries on them. Two of the most important of these scholars were Ibn Sina or Avicenna (980–1037) from Persia and Ibn Rushd or Averroes (1126–98) from Cordoba. Through trade as well as through the re-conquest of Sicily and Spain and the crusades, contacts between the Arab world and the West intensified from the late eleventh century onwards. It was through these contacts that Aristotle's writings once again penetrated the West. The Arab and Jewish scholars who stayed on in the now Christian parts of southern Europe translated their Arab and Hebrew texts and commentaries of Aristotle into Latin for their 'new masters'. At the very point at which the Islamic world rejected Averroes's radical ideas and left the path of Aristotelism, the West struck down that same path.

208   Thomism

Aristotle's writings and their radical interpretation by Averroes led to fierce clashes within the theological faculties of Europe. To the Dominican friar and theologian Saint Thomas Aquinas (c.1225–74) falls the merit of articulating a synthesis of the prevailing scholastic views from the Augustinian tradition and a number of elements from the Aristotelian tradition. As David Knowles put it, Aquinas did more than just 'baptise' Aristotle; he built on the latter's work to construct his own synthesis.[20] Aquinas's speedy canonisation in 1323 conferred canonical blessing on the Thomistic synthesis. As in the case of the term 'Augustinianism', the term 'Thomism' ultimately refers to more than the ideas and writings of Aquinas. It is an intellectual tradition that dominated the official ideology of the church from the early fourteenth century onwards and inspired the mainstream in Western thinking.

The most important contribution of Aristotelism was the revaluation of natural philosophy. In contrast to the Platonic–Augustinian tradition, physical nature – including human nature – was not considered a distorted reflection of the higher, metaphysical reality. It was a reflection, but not a distorted one. Earthly phenomena were imperfect but carried the potential of the ideal reality within them. Thomistic ideology tore down the dividing wall between the physical and the metaphysical worlds. The two dimensions grew closer; the divide became permeable.

209 The ideology of the Gothic church

The revaluation of the natural had already started before the influence of Aristotelian philosophy was brought to bear. It was already reflected in the theology of light of Suger, Abbot of Saint-Denis and first patron of Gothic architecture. Suger based his ideas on the writings of Dionysius the Aeropagite (fifth–sixth centuries), the patron saint of Suger's abbey of Saint-Denis. Suger contends that God is light. God's uncreated and creative light permeates all creation and links heaven to earth. Each creature and each human being participates in this divine light. Through the light, man is illuminated by God's mercy and goodness; through the light, he reverts to God.

This theology is at the heart of Gothic architecture. The evolution from Romanesque – or Norman in England – to Gothic art marks the transition from early scholasticism and the Augustinian tradition to the late scholastic revaluation of nature. Romanesque churches are closed, massive constructions. They are veritable fortresses with heavy stone walls and vaults, towers, thick pillars, low ceilings and small windows. Inside darkness reigns. At the altar, at the east end of the church, some concentrated light is let in through small windows in the apse and transept, thereby creating a mystical atmosphere. Decorations, such as frescoes and relief sculpting, are largely confined to the interior. With the exception of the

---

[20] David Knowles, *The Evolution of Medieval Thought*, 2nd edn, London and New York 1988, 233.

entrance porch, the exterior goes largely undecorated. The architecture symbolises the contrast between the physical world outside the church and the house of God. Outside, the world is sinful, repellent and dangerous. Inside, in the house of God, peace and quiet prevail.

The Gothic church is entirely different. It is a structure of light. The vaulting, spires and towers ascend to heaven. The walls have been worked opened: the churches are skeletons of pillars, abutments and flying buttresses. Light streams in from all quarters through the large, high stained-glass windows. Inside and outside, the church is laden with decorations, frescoes, paintings and statues. Gothic architecture symbolises the fusion between the physical world and the divine; the church is the place where they touch.

210   *The revaluation of natural reality*

Thomism fits in with this theology of the light. The divine light is equated with reason. Man, created in God's image, is, like his Creator, a rational being. Creation, stemming from divine reason, is also rational. It is an imperfect, because unperfected, reflection of supreme reason. The natural order is rational, in the sense that it answers to the natural laws laid down by God's creative intellect. Reason allows man to understand nature. Nature is no longer a distorted representation of divine reality; it can help to discern the truth.

Aristotelism and Thomism closed the gap between the physical and the metaphysical from both directions: nature became more divine as the divine became more natural. Thus the political community was once again perceived as a natural autonomous body (*communitas perfecta*). Similarly, the focus on the sacramental in Christian religion lessened somewhat as faith became more a matter of personal belief; the church gave up something of its claims to being outside the physical world. The monopoly of the clergy and the ecclesiastical hierarchy on the mediation between God and man was eroded in favour of each man's personal adherence to Christian dogmas and ethics.

211   Faith and reason, reason and observation

Thomas Aquinas's ideas also had an impact on Christian epistemology. According to Aquinas, there are two ways to understand truth: faith and reason. In the footsteps of his teacher Albert the Great (Albertus Magnus, 1193/1207–1280), Aquinas argues that these are two autonomous paths. Faith and reason lead to the same truths, but do so independently of one another. One does not need to believe in order to reason or reason in order to believe. It is a matter not of 'credo ut intelligam' or 'intelligo ut credam' but of 'credo aut intelligo', 'I believe or I understand'. Even so, the Dominican assigned greater weight to faith. If reason leads to a conclusion different from church dogma, an error of judgement must have been made. In this way, Aquinas averts the tension between new discoveries in scholarship and the old traditions. In addition, there are a few articles of faith or mysteries such as the Holy Trinity that cannot be explained by reason. Within its particular field, reason, like faith, is autonomous, but its domain is smaller than that of faith. With these propositions, Albertus and Aquinas largely sanction the process of emancipation of reason, which started in the late eleventh century.

Aquinas joined forces with the realistic mainstream and confirmed the reality of the *universalia*. His realistic stance does not, however, imply any rejection of the value of the *realia*. Reason does not exclude the observation of the physical world; on the contrary, observation now becomes the precondition to rational thought.[21] Since all nature has been created by divine reason and answers to the laws of the natural reason laid down by God, it is intelligible by human reason and provides accurate information. By studying nature and human behaviour, man is capable of understanding the *quiditas*, or 'whatness' of each phenomenon. *Quiditas* refers to the essential characteristics of each object or living creature. For instance, by studying various trees, man is capable, through induction, of discerning the general, essential characteristics of the category or genus of 'tree', as well as those of the various species of trees. The human mind actively processes the data provided by the senses until it arrives at the *quiditas* or 'whatness'. Such insights then make it possible to define and comprehend the *universalia*. Once these are known, man can reason back deductively to the level of the concrete manifestations, and the general concepts regain their function as explanations of the physical, particular phenomena. In doing so, the deductive pattern of reasoning of scholasticism is supplemented by inductive reasoning. The Aristotelian *topika* returns in full force. The Thomistic synthesis reconciles the revaluation of nature in all its richness and diversity from the Aristotelian tradition with the Augustinian *ordinatio ad unum*. The study of reality is instrumental to understanding God.

---

[21] 'The mind can perceive nothing that has not previously been perceived by the senses' ('nihil est in intellectu, nisi prius fuerit in sensu'). See Knowles, *Medieval Thought*, 236.

212   Late medieval nominalism

These ideas opened the door to the direct observation and study of physical reality. Medieval scholarship was now able to break free from the confines of book learning. Nevertheless, the mainstream of Western scholarship remained faithful to the rationalist approach and those arguing for effective experimental research were no more than a minority. The leading group in the latter category were the nominalists from the Franciscan Order of the late thirteenth and early fourteenth century such as Roger Bacon (1214–92) and William of Ockham (*c.*1290–1349), both of whom were at some time at Oxford.

Bacon and Ockham reject the reality of the *universalia*. Only the physical, particular phenomena are real. 'Ockham's razor' states that it is unhelpful to duplicate reality by creating general concepts. It is not the *realia* – which are natural – that need to be explained but the *universalia*, which are artificial. Ockham argues in favour of observation and experimental research. The human mind is capable of construing general categories and concepts in order to classify and define the observed particular phenomena. Whereas for Aquinas the spirit recognises the *universalia*, for Ockham the spirit creates them. 'Universalia sunt nomina': the general concepts are but names. Bacon and Ockham are at the beginning of a tradition of experimental research that was long to lead a slumbering existence before burgeoning in seventeenth-century England.

The Franciscan theologians took duality between faith and reason further. According to Ockham, these are not two separate paths to one single truth; they lead to a 'different truth'. Faith and reason each has its own field of application in which it has something to teach. Faith brings insight into the divine and the metaphysical, while reason – or strictly speaking observation and thinking – brings understanding of the physical. Faith is unable to teach us anything about nature or reason anything about God. In taking this line, Ockham took a fundamental step towards the definitive emancipation of reason and science from the ambit of church and faith, while at the same time knocking away the foundations beneath theology in the sense of a reasoned approach to God. Secularisation in the sense of the separation of God and nature emerged at its clearest in the nominalism of the medieval Franciscans.

The nominalist theologians assign a key place to the divine will in creation and set limits on the role of divine reason. God has created the world on the basis not of His reason but of His will. As such, we are unable to understand God but can only believe in Him. Furthermore, since God can and does intervene arbitrarily in nature and history, the world does not answer to immutable, rational laws of nature, intelligible for human reason. There are no *universalia* that provide an explanation for everything; and no universal laws by which things and creatures abide, no higher forms to which the world answers. Or as William of Baskerville, Ockham's *alter ego*, says in Umberto Eco's magisterial novel *The Name of the Rose*, 'In order for there to be a mirror of the world, it is necessary that the world has a form.'[22] *Quod non.* For this reason, there is no point in looking for general forms or concepts. The physical world is full of diversity and behaves erratically. It is not for man to seek an overall, all-embracing explanation; instead he must plumb into the depths of creation in all its richness, diversity and individuality. Not reason but will drives creation.

This tension between reason and will goes back to the antitheses that already existed in the early Christian tradition, but which were not articulated in such clear propositions until the fourteenth century. With the canonisation of Thomas in 1323, Thomistic realism gained the upper hand and nominalism was pushed into the background.

5   *The rise of the universities*

213   Cathedral schools

Until the eleventh century, with the exception of a few royal schools, schooling in the *artes liberales* was only to be had in monasteries and abbeys. It was in their schools that the revival of education and intellectual life first took off. The abbey of Bec in Normandy was among the foremost centres of learning in the eleventh century. Both Lanfranc (*c.*1010–89), chancellor of William the Conqueror and later Archbishop of Canterbury, and Anselm of Canterbury were abbots there.

The revival of city life brought a change to the intellectual setting of the West, as first cathedral schools and then universities emerged. To a cathedral, a chapter of canons was attached. Canons were priests who took care of liturgy in the cathedral and helped the bishop with the administration of the diocese. Most cathedrals had a school to educate and train future priests and canons. In the course of the eleventh century, cathedral schools increasingly started to take in students who did not intend to become priests. The revival of industry and trade and the emergence of banking increased the need for schooling. Urban culture proved conducive to the flourishing of arts and learning. Gradually, the

---

[22] Umberto Eco, *Il nome della rosa*, Milan 1980, 127.

cathedral schools diversified their teaching and went beyond the classical curriculum of the *trivium*, theology and liturgy. Famous cathedral schools of the eleventh century included Chartres, Amiens and Reims. At the beginning of the twelfth century, these were displaced by the Parisian schools, at which one of the teachers was the great Abelard. In the late eleventh century, some Italian towns organised their own schools. These schools, such as that of Bologna, specialised in grammar and rhetoric.

214   The emergence of the university

Around the beginning of the twelfth century, another newcomer announced itself: the university as a school for 'higher' education. In order to qualify as a university there had to be at least one 'higher' faculty, that is, higher than the *artes* where the *artes liberales* were taught. During the Middle Ages – and indeed right up to the nineteenth century – there were four faculties: theology, Roman or civil law, canon law and medicine.

The oldest schools to be given the name of faculty or university were Salerno (medicine) and Bologna (civil law). Although Bologna was to remain one of the most important law schools in Europe, Salerno found itself rapidly overtaken, for example by Montpellier. After 1120, the cathedral school of Notre Dame in Paris evolved into a faculty of theology, for a long time one of the leading schools of theology in Europe. In the course of the twelfth and thirteenth centuries, universities were founded all over Europe. Early foundations in Italy included those of Rome, Perugia, Modena, Vicenza, Arezzo, Padua and Naples. In the twelfth century, the first university in England, Oxford, emerged. Cambridge was founded in 1209 when a group of professors and students left Oxford. In Spain, there were Palencia, Lerida, Huesca and Salamanca; in France, Toulouse and Orleans certainly deserve mention apart from Montpellier. In the course of the fourteenth and fifteenth centuries, the network of universities spread eastwards and northwards. In 1348, Emperor Charles IV (1346–78) founded a university in Prague; Cologne followed in 1388. In 1425, the Duke of Brabant founded the first university in the Low Countries: Leuven. As a reward for the courageous resistance it displayed towards the Spanish besiegers, the city of Leyden was awarded its university in 1575.

The term university – *universitas* – referred to the community of professors and students who gave and received instruction at the *studium generale*, the term by which the actual 'university' was designated in the Middle Ages. Right from the beginning, the European universities were international schools. More prestigious faculties such as those of law in

Bologna or theology in Paris attracted faculty and students from all over Europe, who would form nations (*nationes*). In Bologna, the *nationes* were in turn grouped into two large *universitates*, the *ultramontani* or non-Italians and the *citramontani* or Italians. Teaching activities took place at a *schola*. In the early days, this was simply the house of the tutor. Wealthy benefactors had *collegiae* (colleges) built to house students from a particular country. The college system applied particularly outside Italy; it was certainly not restricted to only Cambridge and Oxford where it still exists.

The universities became the backbone of Western intellectual life. Many students and professors would move from one city to another in the course of their career. Everywhere in Europe, the same language was used at the universities: Latin. The curriculum was everywhere based on the same canon of authoritative texts. Students would often choose or switch to a particular university in order to attend lectures by a renowned professor.

The oldest universities may be divided into two categories, reflecting their origins. On the one hand, there is the model of Bologna and on the other, that of Paris. The Bologna Law School was founded by its own prospective students or their sponsors. The city magistrates wished for Roman law to be taught at Bologna. They themselves engaged a learned doctor and set up the school. The universities of the Bologna type – which were in the minority – were 'students' universities', managed and governed by the students. They imposed an exacting regime on the professors, with a rigorous curriculum and strict regulations. The second type, that of Paris, was easily the more common. These universities had evolved out of existing cathedral schools, as the Paris faculty of theology had grown from the Paris cathedral school. This type may also be regarded as including the universities founded by the prince or the church. These institutions fell under the authority of their founder, often the bishop or archdeacon, the most important priest in the cathedral after the bishop. The distinction between the two forms of administration lost its significance when the pope decreed in 1219 that doctorates could be awarded only by an archdeacon. This provided the church with a formal grip over university education.

215 Scholasticism and university education

This decree was just one step in the gradual formalisation and standardisation of university education. The university curriculum consisted of two stages. Before being able to enrol at one of the four higher faculties, a student had to go through the *artes* faculty, where instruction was provided in the *artes liberales*. Just as before, this primarily concerned the *trivium*, whereas the *quadrivium* was reduced to a minimum. Within the *trivium*, a shift took place, with grammar losing pride of place in favour of logic or dialectics, the leading subject of scholasticism.

After passing the final examination at the *artes* faculty (generally after five or so years) a student could opt for one or more of the higher faculties with a view to graduating as bachelor (*baccalaureus*) or licentiate. At the Law School in Bologna, it took five years to become a bachelor in law and a further eight years before one could take the licentiate examination. Theological training in Paris took eight years.

The core of the instruction consisted of the daily *lectura*. At the Bologna Law School, the *professor ordinarius* gave daily lectures from 7 a.m. to 9 a.m. from the first twenty-four books of the *Digest* or the first nine books of the *Codex*. From 2 p.m. to 4 p.m. and from 4 p.m. until 5.30 p.m. there followed the *lecturae extraordinariae* from other texts. The professor would read out the actual texts as well as the standard commentaries on them. In doing so, he would quote a number of texts that would appear to be in contradiction and provide the solution. Gradually, at the urging of the students, a strict programme was set out stipulating what texts were to be covered when. A professor who failed to do so would be fined. For this reason, professors banned their students from intervening during classes. In order to overcome this restriction two new types of teaching were introduced, the *repetitio* and the *quaestio disputata*. During the *repetitio*, a textual fragment would be analysed in depth by the professor or another lecturer. During a *quaestio disputata*, a question would be examined on the basis of the *sic et non* method, under which students would generally take part in the discussion. The various methods of teaching corresponded closely to the scholastic method. Scholasticism came into full flowering in the context of university education. Right from the earliest days of the universities, teaching and academic research were bound up together. This has remained the unique characteristic of the university to the present day.

6   *The rediscovery of Roman law*

216   The school of Pavia

The rediscovery of the *Digest* provided an important impetus for scholasticism and was one of the great intellectual root causes of the Renaissance of the Twelfth Century. The growing complexity of society consequent upon the rise of the city, the revival of international trade and the strengthening of central authority was also reflected in matters of law. In the course of the eleventh century, the need arose for a sophisticated legal system. Roman law provided the answer.

Roman law had never completely disappeared from Italy. Until the eleventh century, the Byzantine Empire had retained some enclaves in southern Italy where Roman law was applied. The customary law of most of the towns and principalities of the peninsula had grown on Roman foundations. It was a form of vulgar Roman law. The *Institutes* of Justinian were known. Of the first nine books of the *Code*, a summary had been made but this was extremely rare. The *Digest* and *Novellae* were all but lost, except for a few fragments of the latter. There had long ceased to be any higher education or systematic study of the complex Roman law.

In the eleventh century, the first law school emerged in Pavia, the capital of the *regnum Italiae*. The curriculum did not include so much Roman law as a collection of Lombard customary and statute law. This compilation followed the system of the *Institutiones* and the *Code* and was accompanied by commentaries. The quality was not comparable with that of ancient Roman law. The later scholars of Roman law referred to it as the *ius asinium*, the law of asses.

217   The rediscovery of the *Digest* and the School of Bologna

The major breakthrough came at the end of the eleventh century when a copy of the Justinian *Digest* was discovered. Justinian had introduced his compilation of laws in Italy in 554, upon his re-conquest of the peninsula. In the course of the seventh century, the text of the *Digest* had largely been lost. During the eleventh century, the interest in reverting to Roman law, and particularly to the *Digest*, grew. Somewhere during that century, a copy of the *Digest* was found and copied into the *Codex Secundus*. This copy held many interpolations as well as errors. It probably derived from the so-called *Littera Pisana*, a complete copy of the *Digest* from the sixth century which was held at Pisa, until the Florentines took it to their city after their capture of Pisa in 1406. This copy was brought to light again only in the fifteenth century and was thus unknown to the late medieval civil lawyers or 'civilians'.

It is known that Irnerius (*c*.1055–1130) lectured on the *Digest* and other parts of the Justinian collection at Bologna from around 1100. Before Irnerius, a certain Pepo is said to have given instruction on the *Digest* in that town. It was also in Bologna that Irnerius and others drew up the standard edition of the *Digest* on the basis of the *Codex Secundus* and a number of other fragments, which was to be used in all European law schools in the Middle Ages. Together with the *Code*, an entire copy of which was also discovered, the *Institutions*, which had never been lost, and the *Authenticum*, a medieval compilation from the *Novellae*, this formed the *Littera Vulgata* or *Littera Boloniensis*, the medieval version of the Justinian collection. The humanists were later to give the Justinian textual canon the name *Corpus iuris civilis*.

The medieval *corpus* of Roman texts was divided into five parts. The *Digestum vetus* covered books 1 to 24.2 of the *Digest*, the *Infortiatum* books 24.3 to 35.2.82, and the *Digestum novum* the remainder up to the end of the *Digest*. The *Code* comprised all the first nine books of the Justinian *Codex*. Together with the *Institutiones* and the *Authenticum*, the latter three formed the *volumen parvum*. The *Authenticum* contained not just Justinian texts but also a number of later texts. Over the course of time, even a few texts from the time of Frederick Barbarossa were added. The *Libri feudorum*, a Lombard compilation of feudal law from the tenth and eleventh centuries, was included in the medieval *corpus*.

It was the textual canon of the Justinian texts that was studied and taught throughout the Latin West at the faculties of the *ius civile*. During the *lectura*, the texts would be read out and furnished with commentaries, while during the *quaestiones*, legal questions were answered on the basis of textual fragments from the Justinian compilation.

The study of Roman law took off in Bologna. After the modest beginning with Pepo and Irnerius, the School of Law grew rapidly. The generation after Irnerius was dominated by the *quattuor doctores* (the four doctors): Bulgarus, Hugo, Jacobus and Martinus Gosia. Among other things, they were consulted by Emperor Frederick Barbarossa in his struggle with the pope and the Lombard towns. After them, the number of scholars and students grew by leaps and bounds. Even before 1200, the Bologna Law School boasted hundreds, if not a thousand students. Legal faculties in which Roman law was taught sprang up all over Europe. Once again an autonomous class of jurists arose: the civilians.

7 The glossators

218 Glosses

The earlier generations of civilians (until 1263) are known as the glossators. After them (from 1263) came the commentators. The glossators originated in Bologna with Irnerius, but within the course of a few generations, they spread over Europe. The early glossators greatly contributed to the development of the scholastic method.

The glossators' primary aim was to disclose the Justinian texts. Their intellectual endeavours in disclosing and understanding these texts were part and parcel of their lecturing on Roman law. The literary output of the glossators consisted primarily of *glossae* (glosses), annotations written in the margin around the original text. Sometimes brief comments were also inserted between the lines. Some glosses offered only a basic, literary clarification on points of vocabulary or syntax. Others went deeper into the material content of the law. The glossators aimed not just at explaining the text but also at discovering the ideal law hidden within the authoritative fount of legal wisdom that was the Justinian collection. Thus parallel places were cited – that is, references to fragments on the same subject – and contradictions reasoned away. The glossing of the Justinian canon contributed significantly to the development of the scholastic arsenal of logic text interpretation.

The challenge faced by the glossators was enormous. The *Corpus iuris civilis*, and the most prestigious element of the *Corpus*, the *Digest*, did not form a systematic, internally consistent, let alone comprehensive textbook of Roman law. It was basically an anthology of Roman jurisprudence, produced over a period of several centuries. The subjects covered in the *Digest* were, more or less, logically ordered over fifty books and hundreds of subtitles. Within the subtitles, the logical ordering of subjects had not been taken far. A great many subjects were covered in various places. Above all, however, it was the casuistic nature of ancient Roman law that presented a gigantic challenge to the scholastic glossators. The *responsa* from classical Roman jurisprudence that made up the *Digest* had not been drawn up with a view to turning Roman law into a consistent, complete, universal and timeless, perfected legal system, as medieval jurists professed. They were designed only to resolve specific cases. The compilers of the Justinian collection had attempted to eliminate any contradictions. They had, however, been far from successful in doing so for the whole *Digest*, let alone the entire *Corpus*. The deeper the glossators dug and the more they analysed the *ius civile*, the more frequently they were confronted by the enormity of their ambition to provide a consistent interpretation of Roman law.

The glossators strove to mould the material into a coherent system. While glossing the textual canon was a necessary first step towards this end, the gloss itself provided anything but an ideal framework for systematisation. The glossators were bound to the sequence of the text, so that the treatment could hardly be any more logical or systematic than the Justinian collections themselves. By indicating parallel places and providing a detailed explanation of certain fragments, some of the glossators tried to overcome this problem. However, the sophistication of Roman casuistry and the complexity of the material were formidable obstacles on the way to systematisation.

From the start, the glossators were no mere scholars. Pepo and his immediate successors often provided a learned opinion on a case pending in court based on Roman law. Although the bond between jurisprudence and legal practice at the time of the glossators was certainly not as strong as it was in Roman times, it nevertheless existed.

219   Azo and Accursius

Glosses were written down by the professor himself (*glossa redacta*) or by the students during his *lecturae* (*glossa reportata*). The glossing of the *Corpus iuris civilis* was a cumulative undertaking, with the glosses being added to from generation to generation. Thus it could happen that a new professor inherited the copy of the Justinian collection from his predecessor and simply continued adding glosses in the margin. In this way *strata*, or layers of glosses, accompanied certain passages. Later these would be summarised by a new glossator and reworked into a more logically ordered *apparatus*. Subsequently, these might be further added to or revised by the glossators. In this way, a number of important apparatuses were produced around 1200 by leading jurists, such as the Bolognese professor Azo (*c*.1150–*c*.1220/30).

The endpoint of the glossing activities of this first school of medieval Roman law was the *Glossa Ordinaria* of Accursius (*c*.1185–1263). Based partly on the work of Azo and his contemporary Hugolinus de Presbiteris, this Bolognese professor drew up a gloss apparatus that rapidly became the reference point for future jurists. The *Glossa Ordinaria* is not the original work of one man – even though it is difficult to overestimate his intellectual achievement – but the culmination of one and a half centuries of text interpretation. Accursius selected material from the available glosses, which he then rewrote and supplemented until it was regarded by his contemporaries as sufficiently comprehensive and exhaustive to claim that the glossing work had now been completed. The death of Accursius in 1263 brings the age of the glossators to an end.

Apart from the actual glosses, the Bolognese and other glossators also produced other genres of legal literature. Particular reference deserves to be made to the *summae* or summaries of one or more titles or books from the *Corpus*. In the *summa*, the author approached the text more freely. Where the gloss explained the text line by line, sometimes even word for word, the *summa* was a summary – with interpretations – of a larger part of it. The author had greater freedom to order the material. The summary was also an invitation to abstraction, the formulation of general rules and the definition of general concepts, thereby transcending the level of case law. The most famous *summa* was the *Summa codicis* of Azo, a synthesis of the entire Roman law, written down in the order of the *Code*. Finally, there were also *brocardica*, brief catchphrases summarising a particular legal rule. Many of the Latin quotes often found in textbooks to this day date from this time and not from the Roman period. These *brocardica* were memory aids for the student. They helped develop the abstraction and formulation of general rules and principles. A similar effect may be attributed to the *paratitla*, the titles that the glossators placed above the various parts of the *Corpus*.

8   The commentators

220   Bartolus and Baldus

The civilians who came after Accursius are known in historiography as the post-glossators or the commentators. The differences between the glossators and commentators did not emerge all of a sudden. They were the result of a slow and gradual shift in the approach to Roman law that had already started with the later glossators. It would be well into the fourteenth century before the commentators came into their own. The changes between the two schools were at least in part a consequence of the shift from early to late scholasticism.

The first law school to introduce a new style and method was that of Orleans in France. The pioneers thereof were Jacques de Révigny (d. 1296) and Pierre de Belleperche (d. 1308). The representatives of this school are not generally included among the commentators but they are regarded as their trail-blazers. The first commentator is Cinus de Pistoia (1270–1336), who introduced the ideas from Orleans in Bologna. Apart from the proto-humanist Petrarch, his pupils included the greatest of all medieval jurists: Bartolus of Sassoferrato (1314–57), professor in Perugia from 1342 to his death. After his death, the legal scholars we now designate as commentators were referred to as Bartolists.[23] The second most important commentator is undoubtedly Bartolus's student Baldus de Ubaldis

---

[23] *Nemo iurista nisi Bartolista*, 'no one is a lawyer without being a Bartolist'.

(1327–1400). Their commentaries on the *Corpus iuris civilis* enjoyed huge authority among the commentators of the fourteenth to sixteenth centuries. In many cases, they were found to have laid down the *communis opinio*, or generally accepted opinion, from which it was, according to Baldus, foolhardy to depart. In Castile, it was even laid down by law in 1449 that if the law had nothing to say on a particular topic, one should consult Bartolus and Baldus. In the course of the sixteenth century, scholasticism, and hence also Bartolist jurisprudence, was exposed to competition from humanism, the intellectual driving force of the Early Modern Age (1453–1648).

221   Commentaries

The single most important difference between the glossators and the commentators concerns their autonomy from their source, the Justinian collection. Whereas the glossators stuck closely to the actual text, its order and system – or lack of it – the commentators took more distance from it. The shift is best illustrated by the respective literary output of the two schools. What the gloss apparatus was for the glossators, the commentary was for the commentators. The gloss provides an explanation of a given word or phrase in the *Corpus iuris civilis* it annotates. The commentary provides a substantive analysis of a particular passage or part of it. The difference lies not just in the length of the fragment under consideration, but also and more especially in the degree of interpretive freedom exercised by the author. The glossator is bound to the order of the glossed text and limits his 'comments' to the issue at hand. The commentator is at liberty to arrange his comments as he sees fit and will have less hesitation about drawing on other legal rules and concepts, including those from other sources, than those touched on in the text being commented upon. The canonist Huguccio (d. 1210) stated:

> There is a distinction between the commentary, the gloss and the text ... the commentary is a discussion based not just on the coherence of the words but of the contents ... A gloss is an interpretation of the meaning of the letter of the text itself, looking not just at the content but also at the words of the text itself.

It should be noted once again that the difference between glossators and commentators evolved gradually. The *Glossa Ordinaria* contains all sorts of glosses that are barely to be distinguished from later commentaries. Furthermore, the commentary arose in the same context as the gloss, namely that of the *lectura*, except that the professor no longer gave his commentary word by word or sentence by sentence following the text under examination, but set out his observations on the text in its entirety.

This more autonomous approach towards the textual tradition and the focus on its substance stimulated a more systematic and logical treatment of the material. It invited the commentators to discuss questions and cases that did not come up in Roman law but were of relevance to contemporary practice. For example, a response to a commentary on the *Corpus* raised all sorts of issues concerning maritime law, commercial law and feudal law, which were totally unknown to the Romans. Such a treatment was, however, conditional upon the existence of a *sedes materiae* or point of reference in the *Corpus*, since instruction was confined to the *Corpus* and this was all that was written about.

The distinction between glossators and commentators may be understood in terms of a shift from text to content. Both approaches are scholastic in the sense that they strive to find the ideal law in their authoritative source. Where the glossator, however, is concerned with the question: 'What does the *Corpus iuris civilis* say?', the commentator concentrates on the question: 'What is the ideal law?'

222   From text to content

This shift from text to content helps explain why the commentators expanded their textual canon. The concern was not just with interpreting the *Corpus* but with understanding the 'law'. It was, consequently, logical to draw on other, authoritative legal sources to address a point of law. In the first place, that was the *Glossa Ordinaria*. Accursius's gloss itself became the object of study and was regarded as authoritative. This constituted a kind of meta-interpretation of the text. Later, the commentators often referred to the work of older commentators, especially Bartolus and Baldus, as sources of authority. In addition, however, a link was established between Roman law and other legal systems. Above all there was canon law, which, with the *Corpus iuris canonici*, was given a fixed textual tradition and which, from the second half of the twelfth century onwards, had also been taught at university. Many medieval jurists studied both laws.[24] Gradually, sources from contemporary customary and statute law were subject to scholarly study.

The growing concern about the material content of the 'law' was tied up with the commentators' growing involvement with contemporary legal

---

[24] They might then be awarded a *utriusque iuris* degree, in both laws.

practice. In contrast to the other form of university law – canon law – Roman law was not applied in the courts, at least not in most parts of Europe. It was a learned, professorial law. Nevertheless, many civilians were frequently asked for advice on contemporary problems. On the basis of Roman law, combined in some cases with other textual sources, they would issue a learned opinion concerning a pending case.

The double démarche of the commentators, the focus on content and the application of Roman law in contemporary legal practice, drove them away from their original source, Justinian's *Corpus*. Although they continued to refer for all their opinions to the authority of this text, they would deal with it in a remarkably free way. Paradoxically enough, it was the sacrosanct nature of the text that led scholars to interpret it ever more freely and indeed to take liberties with it and even distort it until one attained the desired outcome for a certain problem. The preconception that the text contained for each problem an unequivocal solution and that it carried in it the absolute truth degenerated into the reality that each jurist strove to find 'his truth' in the text. Making this possible and preserving the link to the source of authority required a good deal of mental gymnastics. Fragments were torn out of context and given a new meaning. Texts that were in no way related to each other – dealing, for example, with public law and private law respectively – were combined in order to form a new rule. With the aid of scholastic logic, it became possible to draw almost anything from the texts of Roman law. The great commentators of the fourteenth and fifteenth centuries built up a new system of learned law out of Roman law far beyond what the ancient Romans would have recognised as theirs.

223   Commentaries, treatises, *consilia*

The most important literary production of the commentators consisted of extensive commentaries on the *Corpus*, or parts of it. We may regard the commentaries of Bartolus and Baldus on the *Digest* as the high point of medieval legal scholarship. In the form of commentaries on the various parts of the *Digest* they set out their views on all sorts of legal subjects, both within and without Roman law.

Whereas the commentaries ultimately followed the sequence of the *Corpus*, this no longer applied to treatises. These were monographs dealing exhaustively with a well-defined subject in a systematic order selected by the author. The treatises were studded with references to the *Corpus* and other texts, but the author fitted these in where it seemed logical. In the course of the fourteenth and fifteenth centuries, treatises were written on the most wide-ranging of topics. To Bartolus, an impressive number of treatises, long as well as short, have been attributed.

The third major genre of the commentators was the *consilia* or advices. In these, the commentators answered a legal question that had arisen in a particular case or political dispute. The *consilia* were for the commentators what the *responsa* had been for the ancient legal scholars. They differed radically from them in that the *consilia* comprised detailed analyses of the legal issue in question. In this field too, Bartolus and Baldus were prolific and put their contemporaries and successors in the shadow.

9   Classical canon law (1140–1378)

224   The growth of canon law and the Gregorian Reform

Together with the development of Roman jurisprudence, the development of canon law was one of the great accomplishments of the Renaissance of the Twelfth Century. During the two centuries after the Gregorian Reform, the popes transformed the church into a papal monarchy with an effective central administration. In this process, canon law played an essential role. In order to put into effect its claim to autonomy from secular power, the church needed not just its own ecclesiology but also its own body of law regulating the internal working of the church. Setting the clergy apart from the rest of society implied that its statute had been defined in fine detail. The growth of canon law was further boosted by the individualisation of religious faith. Before the Renaissance of the Twelfth Century, faith was primarily ritualistic and collective. The Church played a mediating role between God and the faithful. That role was externalised by the continued repetition of the sacraments in liturgy. In this way, one sought to obtain God's grace for Christianity as a whole. With the Gregorian Reform, the emphasis shifted from collective salvation to the salvation of each individual soul, from the Last Judgment as a judgment on mankind as a whole at the end of times to an individual judging upon each person's death. The individual's faith, morals and behaviour throughout his or her life span, the number and nature of their sins or good deeds determined the outcome of this judging. Did the soul ultimately go to heaven or to hell? How long did someone need to spend in Purgatory until his or her soul was sufficiently purified to ascend to heaven? This new theology placed sin and its expiation and punishment at the heart. Canon law – criminal law as well as the law concerning the sacraments such as marriage – translated this new concern into a system of sanctions and punishments.[25] The church claimed jurisdiction for the ecclesiastical courts over all infringements that could be classed as sins.

After the Gregorian Reform, canon law swelled in size and gained rapidly in terms of quality. The period between the Gregorian Reform and the Great Schism marked the high point of canon law. This is referred to as the period of classical canon law. Canon law detached itself from theology, evolving into an autonomous system of law distinct but not totally detached from Roman law. An autonomous, authoritative textual canon arose, and canon law became the subject of independent scholarship at separate university faculties. In this way, just like Roman law, it became a learned law.

225   Applicable law

The quantitative growth of canon law went along with the increase in the jurisdiction of the ecclesiastical courts. In contrast to the other form of learned law – Roman law – canon law was applied in court, in the ecclesiastical courts. In the context of medieval Europe, this meant that its application was very wide indeed. The church had jurisdiction in respect of certain categories of litigants (*ratione personae*). It claimed the exclusive right to judge the clergy. The clergy enjoyed immunity from the secular courts, the *privilegium fori*. They included not just the monks, nuns and priests but also all those who had received more minor orders and were only part of the church on a temporary basis, like students. The claim did not go uncontested and many members of the clergy did in fact end up before secular courts. The laity, however, could also appeal to the ecclesiastical courts in all sorts of cases. The claims of the church *ratione materiae* were extensive, allowing it to claim jurisdiction over any unlawful deeds or offences that could be described as sins. Here again, the church's claims were not uncontested and often its jurisdiction was not exclusive. Apart from violations of the faith and offences against the church such as heresy, also included were all sorts of cases that at one and the same time came under secular law. Since breaking a promise was a sin – and if a promise had been made under oath, it was also the sin of perjury – breach of contract came within the sphere of the church. Similarly, the church guaranteed compliance with treaties between princes, which were generally confirmed under oath. In this indirect way, the pope, the

---

[25] See on this subject Harold Berman, *Law and Revolution: the Formation of the Western Legal Tradition*, Cambridge, Mass. and London 1983, 165–98.

church and canon law played a predominant role in the law of nations. Everything to do with the sacraments, such as marriage law, also came under canon law.

226   Gratian

The growth of canon law was in the first place the work of the popes. Whereas not a single papal statute law (decretal) appeared between the end of the ninth century and the Gregorian Reform, some 2,000 were promulgated between 1159 and 1241. Through their *canones*, the universal councils also added numerous new laws.

In contrast to Roman law, canon law had no autonomous textual tradition on which to fall back. That textual tradition was now created in the form of authoritative compilations of canonical texts. These compilations still contained all sorts of theological or Roman law texts, but gradually the canon law became dominant. At the end of the eleventh century, Burchard, Bishop of Worms, put together an important compilation, known as the *Decretum*. A century later, Ivo, Bishop of Chartres (c.1040–1115), made various compilations: the *Decretum*, the *Panormia* and the *Tripartita*. In his *Panormia*, Ivo contributed to the early development of the scholastic method in the field of canon law.

The oldest part of what was ultimately to become the authoritative text of canon law, however, was the work of Gratian (Gratianus). It is traditionally assumed that Gratian was a monk who taught law in Bologna, but even that little piece of information is contested. By 1140, Gratian had compiled a canonical collection known as the *Concordia discordantium canonum* or the *Decretum Gratiani*. This *Decretum* was more than just a simple collection of texts relevant to canon law; the author also immediately applied the scholastic method to his textual material. First, the material was ordered by subject, as Gratian's immediate predecessors had also done. Second, and more importantly, the scholastic method was applied to the compilation. The numerous sources and texts cited on each topic often contradicted one another, in part or in whole. By introducing a hierarchy for the sources and by the use of scholastic dialectics – especially the *distinctio* – Gratian sought to arrive at unequivocal answers to the issues raised. The first part of his book consists of 101 distinctions addressed by use of the *sic et non* method. In the second part, 36 *causae* (cases) are considered in detail. The latter part, in particular, betrays the fact that the *Decretum Gratiani* was written for teaching purposes.

Gratian laid the foundations for a jurisprudence of canon law. Among other things, he introduced elements from Roman jurisprudence into such law. His book acquired great authority throughout Europe and became the basic text for the academic study of canon law, driving out all other compilations. The book was the subject of study at the schools of canon law established in Bologna and elsewhere in Italy and Europe. In the same way that the *Corpus iuris civilis* was disclosed by the glossators, Gratian's own work was glossed. The first person to add glosses to the work was Paucapalea, as early as 1148. Other noteworthy glossators of canon law include Rufinus (d. *c.*1192) and Huguccio (d. 1210), both attached to the school of Bologna. The standard gloss, the *Glossa Ordinaria* of the *Decretum Gratiani*, was that of Johannes Teutonicus (d. *c.*1245). Since the ecclesiastical glossators studied the *Decretum Gratiani*, they were also known as decretists. Their line of approach and literary output was *mutatis mutandis* the same as that of the glossators of Roman law.

227   *Corpus iuris canonici*

The *Decretum Gratiani* was not the endpoint in the development of classical canon law. The great period of papal legislation had had not yet commenced in 1140. In the two centuries after Gratian, popes and councils produced a mass of new laws. Selective collections of the new rules were put together in various phases, this time on the instruction of the pope. In contrast to the work of Gratian, which was a private initiative and as such lacked official legal authority, these were official collections that were published as codes of law. The first of these collections of decretals was the *Liber decretalium Extra decretum vagantium* (Book of the decretals outside the *Decretum*), or for short the *Liber Extra*.[26] This collection, made by the Catalan monk Ramon de Peñaforte (*c.*1180–1275), was published in 1234 by Pope Gregory IX (1227–41). Gregory IX ordered the universities of Bologna and Paris to teach his *Liber Extra* as the official law of the church. All canonical texts that had come into being after the *Decretum Gratiani* and had not been included in the Gregorian collection lost their force. This provision indirectly gave the work of Gratian papal endorsement as the main source of canon law for the pre-1140 period. The *Liber Extra* consisted of five volumes. The next supplement was consequently given the name *Liber Sextus* (1298, under the pontificate of Boniface VIII). In 1314, under Clemens V, there followed the *Constitutiones Clementinae* and in 1325, the *Extravagantes* of John XXII. All these texts, from the *Decretum Gratiani* to the *Extravagantes* plus a number of minor

---

[26] This is generally referred to as X. Fragments from the *Decretum* are referred to by d. (*distinctio*) or c. (*causa*).

supplements and corrections, were amassed in 1582 into the *Corpus iuris canonici*, the code of canon law. This continued to apply until it was succeeded in 1917 by the first *Codex iuris canonici*, which in turn had to give way to the new *Codex* of 1982.

Like the *Decretum Gratiani*, the decretal collections, as authoritative texts, became the object of academic study at university. And in the same way that the glossators of Roman law were succeeded by the commentators, a comparable evolution happened among the scholars of canon law. The canonical 'commentators' who studied the new collections were given the name decretalists. One of the most influential of these was no less than Baldus of Ubaldis. Other important names were Pope Innocent IV (Sinobaldo de' Fieschi, 1243–54), Cardinal Hostiensis (Henricus de Segusio, *c*.1200–71) and Johannes Andreae (*c*.1270–1348). Apart from Innocent IV, a number of the other great popes of the twelfth and thirteenth centuries were also important canonists. The crisis of the papacy in the fourteenth century brought an end to the golden age of canon law.

10   *The* ius commune

228   Interaction between Roman and canon law

Legal historians refer to the learned law of the Late Middle Ages as the *ius commune*. *Commune* (common) indicates that this law was common to the whole of the Latin West. It was taught and studied at all law faculties throughout Europe. The jurists formed an international elite in the same way as the representatives of other academic disciplines.

This *ius commune* had two pillars: Roman law and canon law.[27] Roman law was in essence only a professorial, learned law. Canon law was learned law, as well as applicable law. The *ius commune* was more than the sum of two separate parts. Before the Gregorian Reform, the church applied Roman law in all sorts of areas. After 1070, a considerable number of concepts and rules of Roman law continued to find their way into canon law. Through the ecclesiastical judiciary, concepts and rules of Roman law were spread to all corners of the Latin West. Moreover, the commentators and the decretalists used each other's sources and writings in their study of Roman and canon law. Since many had studied both Roman and canon law, this was self-evident. As scholastics, the commentators and decretalists strove to find an unambiguous, authoritative answer

---

[27] The learned Roman law also included some feudal law. The *Libri feudorum* were added to the medieval version of the Justinian collection.

to each and every legal problem. In their endeavours, they articulated a mass of legal rules, concepts and institutions which had their roots in the Roman and canonical textual traditions but at the same time transcended them. It was the interaction between the two branches of the *ius commune* that was most responsible for the originality and creativity of medieval jurisprudence. The outcome of that interaction is in fact the *ius commune*. Baldus, who wrote an important commentary on both the *Digest* and the decretals, made a major contribution to bringing the two legal systems together.

Allowing for a broad generalisation, it may be argued that to this amalgam of the *ius commune*, Roman law contributed legal technique and sophistication and canon law the general principles. From the rich casuistry of the Justinian collection, the medieval jurists distilled thousands of concepts, institutions, rules and procedures. The moral/theological foundations and origins of canon law rendered it a less formalistic or technical kind of law and placed the requirements of justice more in the forefront. The great principles of private law that to this day form the common foundation of the great continental law systems were in most cases first formulated in canon law. By confronting Roman law with canon law, the medieval scholars recognised the limitations of the formalistic and often overly technical Roman law. Canon law inspired solutions for dealing with this. In this way, the path was prepared for the ultimate absorption of general principles of canon law into Roman law and the sacrifice of some of the technicality of Roman law. Matters had not, however, yet reached this stage in the fourteenth and fifteenth centuries; it would fall to the natural lawyers of the seventeenth and eighteenth centuries to take the process to its completion.

229   Principles of tort and contract law

Two examples may clarify the respective functions of canon and Roman law within the *ius commune*, one from tort law and one from contract law. As noted earlier, Roman law did not contain any general principle on tort. It did, however, specify a number of provisions for well-defined particular injuries. A number of theological texts indicated that property which one has taken unjustly had to be restored before the sin could be forgiven. Through the *Decretum Gratiani*, these found their way into canon law.[28]

---

[28] 'If another person's property, which has been the object of sin, could be returned and is not returned, there is no true but a simulated penance. Where a person acts with truth, the sin will not be forgiven unless that which was taken away is returned'; c. 14, q. 6, c. 1

In the thirteenth century, Thomas Aquinas argued that the restoration needed to consist of an equivalent compensation.[29] In the seventeenth century, Hugo Grotius formulated the modern principle of liability.[30]

The second example concerns the origins of consensualism in contract law. Consensualism means that any agreement, whatever its substance – in so far as it is not inherently unlawful – and whatever the way it came about, is binding and enforceable. Roman law never accepted this as a principle. Roman contract law distinguished various forms of contracts defined either in terms of their content (purchase, hire, partnership and mandate) or their form of origin. Outside this extensive but ultimately limitative list of contracts there were also the formless contracts (*pacta nuda*). These were not enforceable but only constituted natural obligations. The legal concept of the *bona fides* (good faith) brought Roman law close to consensualism but the procedural foundations of *bona fides* and the weakness of the moral argument for it prevented that step from being taken. It was once again thanks to Gratian that a number of relevant biblical and theological texts found their way into classical canon law.[31] The relevant text held that people had to abide by their word. Breaking one's word was a sin. In this way, breach of contract became a punishable offence under canon law. *Pacta sunt servanda*, 'agreements are binding', was a principle of ecclesiastical law well before it penetrated into secular law.[32] Baldus, among others, brought ecclesiastical and Roman law together in this respect. He confronted the freedom of contract in canon law with the limitations of the more technical Roman law and extended solutions for softening the latter. According to Baldus, it was enough for a contract to have a *causa* (cause) for it to be not a *pactum nudum* but a *pactum vestitum* and hence to be enforceable. In doing so, Baldus closed the gap between the two legal systems, thereby smoothing the path for the inclusion of the principle of freedom of contract in Roman law. The natural lawyers of the seventeenth century, including Grotius, were to clear this last hurdle. From there, the principle found its way to the great codifications of civil law.[33]

(from a letter of Saint Augustine). Included in *Liber Sextus* as 'the sin is not forgiven if that which was taken away is not given back'. See also c. 12, q. 2, c. 11.1 (letter from Pope Gregory I) (my translations). Also see X.5.36.9 on the restoration of damage.

[29] *Summa theologiae* SS q. 62, art. 2 re 2.

[30] Hugo Grotius, *Inleidinge tot de Hollandsche Rechtsgeleerdheid*, The Hague 1631, 3.32.7.

[31] 'Plain Yes or No is all you need to say,' Matthew 5:37.

[32] '*Universi dixerunt, pax servetur pacta custodiantur*', X. 1.35.1.

[33] Art. 1134 *Code civil*.

11   *The medieval doctrine of natural law*

230   Divine, natural and human law

The notion of natural law had already been incorporated in Christian doctrine in the late Roman Age by the Church Fathers. Irenaeus (*c*.130–200) and Origin (*c*.185–254) equated natural law with the will of God. God had created nature, laying down certain rules and laws: natural law. No distinction was made between divine law and natural law. Origin and later Church Fathers such as Augustine and Isidore held that in order to be valid, human, positive law had to be in accord with divine law or natural law. Gratian adopted the equivalence between divine law and natural law and the supremacy of natural law over human law:

> The human race is ruled by two things, namely, natural law and usages. Natural law is contained in the Law [of Moses] and the Gospel …[34]
>
> … Everything that has become accepted in usages or in writings is invalid if it is in contravention of natural law.[35]

The revaluation of nature in late scholasticism prompted the theologians of the thirteenth century to assign more autonomy to natural law from divine law. This made the relation between divine law and natural law into a point of scholarly contention. Broadly speaking there were two opposing opinions.

The majority opinion was articulated by Thomas Aquinas. In the wake of other theologians of the thirteenth century, Aquinas emphasised the rationality of creation. Nature is an external reflection of the creative, rational intellect of God. Nature, and consequently natural law, is comprehensible to human reason. God, who is Reason, respects the laws of nature and does not intervene in them of his own free will. Natural law may be discerned in two ways: thanks to revelation – in the Bible and the Law of Moses – and thanks to reason. As seen by Aquinas, the eternal, immutable law manifests itself in two separate ways in the world: in the *lex divina* (divine law) through revelation and in the *lex naturalis* (natural law), which is inherently present in the human mind. The two are separate bodies of law that can be discovered via various paths but can never be in contradiction to one another. Aquinas's doctrine of natural law is a faithful application of his general epistemology. Human reason is furthermore equipped to deduce more specific rules from the general rules of natural law. As opposed to the primary natural law, this secondary natural law is

---

[34] D. 1 a. c. 1.   [35] D. 8 p. c. 1.

not immutable but can adapt to the changing circumstances of time and place. The rules of the secondary law of nature which apply universally to all people form the *ius gentium* (the law of nations). In addition, rules may be deduced that apply only to certain peoples. This is human law (*ius humanum*). This can never be in contradiction to divine or natural law. As seen by Aquinas, natural law is therefore the reflection of the scholastic ideal law.

The second view is that of the great nominalists of the thirteenth and fourteenth centuries, especially Ockham. The English Franciscan emphasises the role of God's free will. Not reason but the will of God lies at the basis of creation. Since God is also able to intervene in nature at any point and to set aside the laws of nature through his divine will, natural law provides a poor frame of reference for understanding, let alone controlling, the world. This school of thought laid the intellectual basis for the notion that human beings, following the example of God, are able to create law on the basis of their free will and that they are therefore not subject to universal, immutable laws.

12 Ius commune *and* ius proprium: *reception and acculturation*

231 The plurality of legal systems

The unity which marked legal scholarship was in no way reflected in legal practice. Throughout the Latin West, there were thousands of politico-legal entities, ranging from empire and sovereign kingdoms, over principalities, bishoprics and abbeys to the towns and rural seigniories. All these entities formed separate jurisdictions with their own courts and own legal system: the *ius proprium*. The legal discrimation between the different classes combined with the principle of *iudicium parium* further multiplied the number of jurisdictions and law systems. Distinct courts were set up for the clergy, nobles, burghers, free men and serfs, and for particular groups such as the urban trades and guilds or the professors and students at the *studia generalia*. The rise of central authority from the eleventh century onwards did not bring a dramatic change in this respect. The autonomy of the lower courts was cut back and their powers limited, but they retained a large measure of autonomy under or, more generally, beside the central courts.

In terms of content and form these numerous *iura propria* stood a world apart from the learned law. At the outset of the Late Middle Ages, in most parts of the Latin West, the law consisted largely of unwritten, local customs. Statute law was often scarce. Particularly in the larger jurisdictions such as important towns, the customary law (*droit coutumier*) was gradually developed through the interpretations by the courts into a more sophisticated system of case law.

All this leads us to pose the question as to why thousands upon thousands of young men throughout Europe took the trouble of studying Roman law, which was not the applicable law in the vast majority of the courts in Europe? Why should they spend years far from home in order to study a foreign legal system at huge personal and financial cost? The fact that they did so indicates the enormous prestige enjoyed by Roman law. Roman law was indeed not applicable in most courts of the Latin West. Together with its counterpart, canon law, however, it embodied the ideal of what law could and should be. The learned law was taught and studied in order to enhance and disseminate understanding of that ideal. In the early days of scholasticism, this was reason enough. However, the more the walls between the worlds of jurisprudence and practice crumbled, the more the ambition grew to translate learning into practice. The learned law became a source of inspiration for legal practitioners in their efforts to improve their own particular law systems and the administration of justice. The learned law overarched the huge diversity of law within Europe. As well as being an ideal, it now also became an objective: the ultimate idea of law in Platonic terms, or supreme potentiality in Aristotelian terms. The *ius commune* was the lighthouse by which the numerous vessels of law in Europe were all required to set their course. In order to be an improvement any change in the law needed to bring that law closer to the *ius commune*. The numerous university-trained jurists who gradually filled the benches of central and other important courts were instrumental in steering that course.

232   Reception and acculturation

The improvement of the *ius proprium* through the influence of the *ius commune* proved more than just an ideal, gradually also becoming reality. From the twelfth century onwards, the learned law started to have an impact on the *ius proprium*. This happened in two different ways: through reception and acculturation. Reception of learned law refers to the adoption of particular concepts and rules of material law into the *ius proprium*. Acculturation of the *ius proprium* refers to the formal adaptation of it to the 'culture' and forms of the learned law.[36]

---

[36] This distinction and the terminology are of Dirk van den Auweele, although the two concepts have been defined somewhat differently here; see Dirk van den Auweele and

Two phases may be distinguished in the dual process of reception and acculturation during the Late Middle Ages. The first of these began as early as the twelfth century and involved the gradual intake of elements of Roman law via canon law. Canon law had traditionally been under the influence of Roman law and had incorporated a good many elements from it. Through the application of canon law in the ecclesiastical courts, certain elements of Roman law consequently penetrated into ecclesiastical legal practice and were thus spread all over Europe. This then provided the basis for these elements to make their way, in a second phase, into secular courts. One example of the reception of Roman law in canon law is the adoption of Roman law concepts such as *contractus* and *pactus* from contract law. An example of acculturation is the development, in the twelfth and thirteenth centuries, by the ecclesiastical courts of new procedures that were clearly inspired by Roman law. These procedures are commonly referred to under the collective name of Romano-canonical procedure. They differed from the traditional customary procedures in that writing played a far greater role in the former than in the latter. Much greater use was made of written documents, such as notarial deeds, for evidentiary purposes. Witness statements were written down. The judgment was still rendered orally but was also written down.

Another important innovation was the shift from an accusatory to an inquisitional procedure in canon penal law. The *per inquisitionem* procedure was first allowed by Innocent III in 1199 in order to prosecute certain abuses among the clergy. In the course of the thirteenth century, this was taken further by the Inquisition for the prosecution of heresy. Under an accusatory procedure the perpetrator is prosecuted by the victim, the latter's next of kin or a third party, but in all cases by a private individual acting in his own name. The litigants are on an equal footing. In an accusatory process, the judge generally plays a fairly passive role. It is the parties who introduce arguments and evidence; the judge or jury listens, but provides little direction. Under the inquisitorial procedure, the perpetrator is prosecuted by an official. In the ecclesiastical *per inquisitionem* procedure that was done by the court itself. The judge could even instigate prosecution in the absence of any complaint, *ex officio*. Whereas the purpose of a criminal trial under the old procedure was to render justice to the victim, it now was to punish the offender – so that he would expiate

Michel Oosterbosch, 'Consilia juridica Lovaniensia. A propos de trois recueils d'avis juridiques du XVe siècle', in Fred Stevens and Dirk van den Auweele, eds., *Houd voet bij stuk. Xenia iuris historiae G. van Dievoet oblata*, Leuven 1990, 105–48.

his sin and save his soul. The court itself also played an active role in tabling evidence. Thus the Inquisition itself ordered investigative measures and oversaw their implementation. Higher appeal also developed within the ecclesiastical court system. Popes and bishops often delegated their legal authority to local representatives. In this case, litigants could appeal to the higher authority against the judgment of the lower court, in the same way that appeal could be made to the Roman emperor in the context of the *cognitio extraordinaria*.

During the second phase, secular law too fell under the influence of Roman and canon law. The speed and degree of reception and acculturation differed greatly. Broadly speaking, the process of 'Romanisation' may be said to have been quicker and more far-reaching in the south than in the north of Europe. France was divided from east to west into two legal cultures, *les pays du droit coutumier* (the lands of customary law) in the north, and *les pays du droit écrit* (the lands of written law) in the south. In Italy, southern France and Spain the reception and acculturation was already under way in the thirteenth century. To the north, this did not take place until the fourteenth, fifteenth or even sixteenth century. In England, which had already started to develop its own 'national' law by the late twelfth century, the Romanisation was much more limited. The faster and greater acceptance of Roman law in the south may be explained by the fact that the *iura propria* had retained much more of the old Roman law than the systems in the north, which had been particularly subject to Germanic and Celtic influence. In these parts of Europe, customary law was for a large part based on vulgar Roman law. Consequently, the learned law was regarded in these regions as the overarching system, of which the local customary law was a divergent, vulgarised variant.

The difference between south and north was translated into two different kinds of reception of Roman law. In the south, Roman law was regarded as *lex scripta* (written law). The *Corpus iuris civilis* was accepted as binding law or legislation. On the basis of the doctrine endorsed by most of the glossators that a local custom was allowed to depart from the law, it was regarded as supplementary law. If local law had nothing to say about the problem in question or failed to provide a suitable solution, the *Corpus* and hence the learned Roman law would be applied. Upon the promulgation of the *Liber Augustalis*, a compilation of legislation for the kingdom of Sicily in 1231, Emperor Frederick II laid down that the *ius commune*, of which Frederick considered Lombard law also to be part, would be considered supplementary statute law. Other emperors had taken the same line for the *regnum Italiae* on the grounds that the *Corpus* of Emperor

Justinian was also the law of the current emperor. In the north, Roman law was considered to be the *ratio scripta* (reason put into writing). If local law failed to provide an adequate answer, one should turn to the *ius commune* for intellectual inspiration but not apply it as binding law.

233 Aspects of acculturation

For the acculturation of the *ius proprium* during the Late Middle Ages, three major examples may be quoted. First, the written word came to play a much bigger role in judicial procedure – as well as in government administration. The Romano-canonical procedures were adopted first and foremost in the central, royal courts which emerged in various countries during or after the thirteenth century. At the same time, there was a shift from the accusatory to the inquisitorial procedure in criminal cases. Prosecution was initiated not by the judge but by a distinct court official, such as the bailiff. Criminal justice gradually moved out of the sphere of private law into that of public law. The growing significance of the written word resulted in the recording of customary and case law. This at one and the same time constituted a first step towards the academic study of the *ius proprium*.

At the start, the recording of customary law or a court's judgment was often a private, individual undertaking. An alderman, registrar or bailiff would decide to write up the customary and case law of his jurisdiction or various jurisdictions for his own use. A simple law recording does not go beyond the reporting of separate legal rules or cases and judgments in which the rules appeared, without any logical order. A law book presupposes a certain degree of systematisation. The rules are classified by subject and selected, while more general and clear rules will often be formulated from various cases. Sometimes the cases and rulings will not be directly quoted. Treatises are systematic and comprehensive treatments of one or more subjects, an entire part of the law or even a whole law system. This genre did not emerge until the fifteenth and sixteenth centuries. Important examples of medieval recordings are the *Coutumes de Beauvaisis* by Philippe de Beaumanoir (around 1280) of northern France, the *Somme rural* by Jehan Boutillier of Tournai (1393–6) and the *Rechtsboek van Den Briel* by Jan Matthijssen (d. 1423). For maritime law, there were two important collections of customary law, the *Consolato del Mar* (Barcelona, thirteenth/fourteenth century) and the *Rôles d'Oléron* (French and Dutch, thirteenth/fourteenth century).

The recording of customary law could also be undertaken by order of the authorities. The systematic recording and keeping of legal rulings by the court itself provides an initial example. In the Parliament of Paris, set up after 1250 by Louis IX as a royal court, the rulings were first recorded in 1263 (*Olim*, 'there was once …'). The recording and confirmation of customs in royal, local or municipal statute law is a second form of official recording.

The recording of the *ius proprium* was a precondition to its academic study, although no genuine jurisprudence along the lines and methods of the learned law can be said to emerge until the sixteenth century in most of Europe – with England constituting the most significant exception. The fact that the recordings were made in the vernacular and not in the language of learning alone prevented them from being regarded as truly scholarly. Moves towards the learned study of the *ius proprium* are, however, to be found in late medieval law texts. The logical ordering of the material is in itself an act inspired by the learned law. Classifications and concepts drawn from Roman law were also used. Some texts included learned law. The *Somme rural* dealt not only with local customary law but also with Roman and canon law. In this way, the learned law affirmed its role as *ratio scripta*. It provided the intellectual context within which the *ius proprium* operated and helped overcome the latter's shortcomings.

Finally the rationalisation of the evidentiary law may be cited as an example of legal acculturation. Until the twelfth century, the use of ordeals was widespread. The best-known form was the legal duel. In addition, there were all kinds of ordeals such as ordeal by fire and ordeal by hot and cold water. From the end of the twelfth century onwards, resistence against their use grew. The Fourth Council of Laterans (1215) banned the duel. Although remnants of trial by ordeal persisted until well into the modern age, they were sharply on the decline by the thirteenth century. In their place, a new law of evidence, that of the *preuves savantes* or *preuves légales* from Romano-canonical procedure, took over. This was a system whereby a certain value was assigned to each form of evidence – a written document or a witness statement. By adding up all these one arrived at *plena probatio* (full evidence). Only once this had been achieved could the judge hand down a ruling. A plea of guilty was regarded as full evidence. The latter explains the emergence of legal torture at the end of the Middle Ages. This rigorous system bears witness to a lack of confidence in the powers of judgment of the judges. The step from a blind faith in divine judgment to faith in human judgment proved too great. Only in England, where trial by ordeal increasingly fell into disfavour even before the learned law had come into its own, did this system fail to strike a popular chord. Instead, the judgment was left to a jury, in whose power of judgment there was confidence.

234   Unification

Most kings promoted the study and reception of Roman law. The German emperors, who regarded themselves as the successors of Justinian, mobilised Roman law in their struggle against the pope. Justinian law offered a sound base for a doctrine legitimating and strengthening the power of the sovereign. Finally, as a law common to all, Roman law was a useful instrument to enhance the political and legal unity of the realm. The unification of the law is of major importance for political unity and administrative efficiency (*unum sit ius ut unum est imperium*, 'may the law be one even as the kingdom is one').

The French kings had initially resisted Roman law. Thus the study of Roman law was forbidden in Paris in 1219 by Pope Honorius III (1216–27) at the request of Philip II Augustus. The French kings regarded the Roman law as the law of the emperor and feared that acceptance of the supremacy of Roman law would strengthen the emperor's claims to supremacy. The Papal Bull *Per Venerabilem* and the idea that the king was emperor in his own realm removed those objections. The theoretical division of the emperorship meant that Roman law could now be regarded as the inheritance of each small emperor and each king in the West.[37] From the thirteenth century onwards more and more rulers, including the French kings, began to invoke Roman law.

13   *Legislation in the Late Middle Ages*

235   Royal charters

In most legal systems, customary law as interpreted and developed by the courts was the main source of law. Statute law played only a marginal role in the creation of new law. The prince's role was to guarantee, enforce and correct the law, not to change it. Traditionally, royal statutes were used to confirm or clarify the law rather than to modify, let alone to replace it. During the crisis of royal authority between the end of the ninth and the eleventh century, kings only rarely acted as legislators.

Royal legislation returned on the tail of the restoration of central authority. From the twelfth century onwards, national and regional

---

[37] Thus the principle of 'rex imperator in regno suo' is also to be found in the *Siete Partidas*, a legal compilation from Castile of the thirteenth century: 2.1.5.

princes became more active legislators. In the earlier stages, legislation amounted to little more than the recording and confirming of existing laws and privileges. Generally speaking these statutes, or 'charters', were aimed at a particular jurisdiction, a certain territory or class within it. Princes would grant privileges and immunities to towns while at the same time laying down the conditions and limits of their immunity and autonomy. In the second half of the twelfth century, the Count of Flanders, Philip of Alsace (1168–91), promulgated a series of charters for the various towns in his county. In the thirteenth century, other regional princes would follow his example. The charters confirmed or described in detail the rights and obligations of the ruler and his subjects in respect of administration, justice, property and taxation. These charters could be real statute law in the sense of unilateral decisions by the legislator or, more commonly, compacts between the legislator and his subjects. In the context of dualism, which presupposes the participation of the representatives of the estates in legislation, the difference is rather formal. These charters were often used to make adjustments or additions to the existing customary law. Thus certain customs that were regarded as unjust (*mala consuetudo*) were abolished.

236   Peace of the land

A common form of legislation in the Late Middle Ages was the peace of the realm or the land, or public peaces (*Landsfriede*). These were royal statutes confirming the rights and immunities of the entire realm or of a particular territory or class. The prince stated he would uphold these by using his *bannum*. With these peaces, the rulers wished to put an end to the endemic violence in society. In feudal society, the nobility held certain rights to self-help, that is, to use force in order to enforce their rights. The royal peace placed limits on such powers, substituting royal jurisdiction for it. Only under the authority of the prince could force be used to enforce a right. The royal peaces stood in the tradition of the church's initiative to promote and impose peace. From the tenth century onwards, bishops as well as the pope had promulgated Truces or Peaces of God. These forbade the use of force against certain categories of people such as children, women, the elderly and clerics, or during certain times of the year. Like the Truces and Peaces of God, royal peaces generally stipulated the taking of an oath on the peace. With that oath, people subjected themselves to the royal peace and hence to the prince's jurisdiction. *Pax et iustitia*, peace and justice, were bound together. The royal peaces extended in the first place to the weak and to groups in need of special protection. Often,

comprehensive royal peaces were promulgated on the occasion of the
departure of the prince abroad, for example at the start of a major war or
a crusade. One of the common purposes of the royal peaces was to bring
high justice, particularly in the field of criminal law, under the control of
the prince and wrest it from local control, at the same time withdrawing
it from the sphere of private law. All sorts of offences came under the prohibitions spelled out in the royal peaces. An offence against the peace not
only wronged its victim, but also constituted a violation of the peace of
the land. For this reason, the prince had it prosecuted through his bailiffs
and other judicial officials. A similar evolution occurred in the towns:
these were confederacies of which the members swore to abide by the laws
and maintain the peace of the town. Certain offences were regarded as
infringements against the peace and prosecuted as such.

Over time, legislation was increasingly used to change the law and
introduce new law. The examples of the Roman emperors – particularly
Constantine and Justinian – and the pope were invoked in support of
the right of the king to legislate. Various emperors and kings followed
the example of Justinian by attempting to make a more comprehensive
'code' of law. The two most important examples in the Late Middle Ages
were the previously mentioned *Liber Augustalis* (1231) promulgated by
Frederick II for Sicily and Naples and the *Siete Partidas* of Alfonso X the
Wise (1252–84) for Castile.

14   *The administration of justice during the Late Middle Ages*

237   Plurality of jurisdictions

The fragmentation of political authority at the end of the Early Middle
Ages also led to the fragmentation of the administration of justice. Each
territorial entity and each class constituted a separate jurisdiction with
its own administrative and judicial body and own law. Since there was
no separation of powers, this body held administrative, judicial and, at
times, legislative authority. With the collapse of royal authority, the role
of the royal court – the *curia* – was reduced. In addition, the princes, and
in many cases even the counts, had lost control over the county courts.
In most of the counties, the office of count had become hereditary under
the feudal system and the count had usurped the royal rights, which he
now exercised in his own name. When the old counties were subsequently
amalgamated into larger regional fiefdoms, such as Flanders, Brabant or
Holland in the Low Countries or Normandy in France, the old county
courts of aldermen continued to exist as the court of the bailliage under

the control of a local lord. Apart from these courts of aldermen there arose numerous other courts, such as the feudal and seigniorial courts, town benches, the ecclesiastical courts and the courts of trades, guilds or universities.

As in the field of legislation, the kings and princes resumed a greater role in the administration of justice during the Late Middle Ages. This did not mean that all these other courts lost all significance or disappeared altogether. The king's jurisdiction increased in competition with that of these local and regional courts. In certain areas, the rulers were able to acquire exclusive legal powers for certain matters, but often litigants had a choice of various courts.

238   Royal jurisdiction

In the first place, the rulers sought to restore their supervision over the courts throughout the land. To this end, first castellans and then bailiffs were appointed to the courts in the bailliages. These acted as the prince's deputies. They commanded the court of aldermen to pronounce a judgment and were responsible for its enforcement. They also exercised control over the court and were able to act in the event of denial of justice or false judgment. This they would report to the prince, who could then impose sanctions on the court in question. In many cases, the royal representatives lost the right to preside over court hearings, thereby ceasing to act as judges in the old style. This traditional power of supervision on the part of the prince was not confined to the courts of aldermen of the bailliages, which had replaced the former county courts; the rulers also had their representatives in most of the towns. The town benches had after all won their immunity from the courts of the bailliages, often through a charter granted by the prince.

In the second place, in the same way as their great example, Charlemagne, the princes of the Late Middle Ages sought to extend their own jurisdiction. There were various ways in which this could be done. One was to make use of their supervisory powers over the local and regional courts. If a court was guilty of denial of justice or false judgment, proceedings could be instituted with the royal *curia* by the injured party or sometimes by the royal deputy. Where previously the ruler would refer the matter back to a different court, it now became customary for the ruler to take on the case. He would hand down judgment himself and act as judge in the modern style. The members of his *curia* would still advise him but the ruler himself now decided upon the judgment. Another form of control was a procedure whereby the court of a minor legal jurisdiction would seek advice on the law from a higher court. This could also be the ruler. These two procedures, together with the Roman and ecclesiastical models, lay at the basis of the system of higher appeal. As appeal judge, the prince also acted as a judge in the modern style. Through these and other procedural detours, rulers were able to extend their judicial powers, positioning themselves at the head of a truly hierarchical judiciary.

Finally, the princes also extended their jurisdiction in first instance. To this, the royal peaces contributed significantly. In these laws, the princes specified a number of individuals and rights that they were taking under their protection. In many cases, disputes in these areas could be submitted directly to the prince. Most princes claimed jurisdiction in all disputes involving their personal domains and also reserved jurisdiction over certain offences.

239   Royal courts

At the outset, the prince exercised his jurisdiction, as he did all his powers, with the aid of his *curia*. The expansion of royal jurisdiction and the increasing complexity of cases brought before the *curia* necessitated a certain specialisation. Following the example of the popes and bishops, secular princes delegated their judicial powers to specific members of the *curia*. From the thirteenth century onwards, these were mainly civilians or canonists. These royal councillors met in session at regular times and dispensed justice in the name of the ruler. Later these 'courts' split off altogether from the royal *curia*, and became autonomous and permanent institutions in their own right. In France, the Parliament of Paris, first established by Louis IX in the second half of the thirteenth century, grew into a true royal and supreme court during the next century. The Count of Flanders followed this example in 1386 with the Council of Flanders. The other principalities in the Low Countries did not obtain sovereign courts until the fifteenth century (Holland and Zeeland 1428, Brabant 1430) or even, for the northern provinces, the sixteenth century.

15   *The birth of the common law in England*

240   Common law and the learned law

Although the learned law made its way across the Channel to the ecclesiastical courts and universities of England, it had a far smaller influence on the development of English law than it had on the continental legal systems, or even that of Scotland. The most important explanation stems from the fact that by the time the reception of the *ius commune* into secular law had properly started – the fourteenth century – England already had its national law. England consequently did not require the *ius commune* to unify its law. Furthermore, that common law was already too far developed to admit external influence to the same extent as on the continent. This does not, however, mean that the learned law exerted no influence whatsoever: all kinds of legal concepts, institutions and rules from the learned law found their way into the common law, often through the mediation of canon law.

241   Writs

Even before the Norman conquest of 1066, Anglo-Saxon England already had a tradition of centralised, royal government, but the conquest certainly strengthened the conditions for an early unification of English law. It gave the central government more leeway with regard to local power elites than most kings enjoyed on the continent.

In Anglo-Saxon England, the ordinary administration of justice was dispensed by gatherings of free men at the level of the shires and the hundreds. These were administered by the earl, assisted by the shireman or hundredman. From the tenth century onwards, royal officials – the reeves (and hence shire-reeve, or sheriff) – were appointed to exercise control over the shires and hundreds. In addition, there were seigniorial courts, in which the local lords exercised their personal jurisdiction over their dependants. At the national level, there was the royal Witan, which travelled around the country with the king. The king and his Witan supervised the administration of justice but also handed down justice in matters directly affecting the king.

The Normans did not make *tabula rasa*; the king did, however, consolidate his grip. The Witan was replaced by the *curia regis*. When land ownership was feudalised by William the Conqueror, the *curia* instantly became the highest feudal court. William allowed the shires, now called counties, and hundreds to remain in existence. The county court obtained jurisdiction over civil and criminal cases, at the expense of the hundred courts. The seigniorial courts, often in the hands of Norman nobles, became more important, fitting in well with the new feudal structure. From time to time, the king would send members of the *curia regis* to the counties in order to check on the sheriffs and courts.

The foundations of the later common law were laid during the reign of King Henry II Plantagenet (1154–89). In the Assizes of Clarendon (1166), Henry decided to send out 'justices on eyre' to hear a large number of cases throughout the kingdom. The fact that members of the *curia regis* could also be commissioned to hear legal cases was not new, but from the time of Henry II onwards it became a fixed system and their powers were greatly expanded into a General Eyre in the *commission ad omnia placita*. Apart from trying offences that were regarded as violations of the royal peace (known as pleas of the crown), disputes concerning royal properties (royal pleas) and complaints against royal officials, the justices on eyre could also hear ordinary, civil cases (common pleas). In the thirteenth century, the king had to accept that the General Eyre, which assigned general powers to the itinerant royal judges, would be called only every seven years. In its place, the judges were sent out with more specific commissions in order to hear certain types of cases. This did, however, allow the king to respond more effectively to existing needs or opportunities. The measure certainly did not hold back the advance of royal justice. Whatever the case, it was possible from the thirteenth century onwards for cases to be submitted to the itinerant royal judges anywhere in England. They allowed the king to exert his jurisdiction throughout the land.

Royal administration of justice had two typical features. First, the assizes were a jury-based system. This had its roots in Anglo-Saxon practice. The lawsuit was presided over by the justices of assize, but the verdict was given by jurors (that is, persons who had been sworn in), twelve in number. In England the system of grand juries was retained until 1933; in the USA, it remains in place. Second, there was the system of writs – written documents promulgated by the royal chancellor under the Great Seal of the king. These were royal commands directed to the king's officials, such as the justice on eyre. Their aim was to protect a right or to put an end to a wrong. The king instructed the official to ensure that a particular dispute was handled by the court and would if necessary lay down certain measures to be taken. The writs were therefore legal actions on the basis of which the justices on eyre could handle a particular case on behalf of the king. The party wishing to institute proceedings would apply for a writ from the chancellery in Westminster in order to gain access to the courts throughout the realm or at Westminster. Writs became standardised as early as the thirteenth century. The common law was a body of writs, royal commands or prohibitions imposed by the courts in certain cases in order to enforce a right. The writs may be compared with the *legis actiones* or the *formulae* in Roman law. Like Roman law, common law is consequently primarily a set of actions applied to a growing number of cases. An example of a writ is that for entry (*ad terminum qui praeteriit*):

> The king to the sheriff of N., greeting. If A. shall give you security for pursuing his claim, then put by gage and safe pledges B. that he be before

our justices at Westminster [on such a day] to show why, with force and arms, he entered into the manor of I., which T. demised to the said A. for a term which has not yet expired, and took and carried away the goods and chattels of the said A. to the value [etc.] found in the same manor, and ejected him the said A. from his farm aforesaid, and offered other outrages against him, to the grave damage of the selfsame A. and against our peace. And have there the names of the pledges and this writ. Witness etc.[38]

242   Royal courts

During the course of the thirteenth century, various royal courts split off from the *curia regis*. On the one hand there was the King's Bench, which travelled around the country with the king. Apart from that, there was the Common Bench or the Court of Common Pleas, which became permanently based in Westminster in the early thirteenth century. These two central courts held jurisdiction for different sorts of cases. The King's Bench had jurisdiction over wrongs, where the king might be thought to have an interest, while the Common Pleas dealt with claims between individuals. During the course of the thirteenth century, the King's Bench was also permanently established at the palace of Westminster. In addition, there was the Court of Exchequer, which particularly dealt with cases touching the royal revenue.

Although the royal courts found a permanent home in Westminster, the system of itinerant judges remained in force. The courts were in session in Westminster for only a limited period of time. Proceedings would be instituted by means of a writ. The proceedings into the facts, however, would still generally be held in the local court, where the case would be submitted to a local jury. One or two royal judges would be delegated to preside over the proceedings (*nisi prius*). This could be done during the period in which the court was not in session. The judgment would in turn be rendered in Westminster itself. In this way, an early centralisation of royal justice was combined with a presence throughout the realm. The royal courts steadily arrogated to themselves more and more cases, at the expense of the older county courts and the seigniorial courts – although these remained formally in existence, some until well into the twentieth century.

It was the three royal courts with their seat in Westminster which, through the interpretation of the law and the precedents they set, were responsible for the development of the common law. The common law

---

[38] John Baker, *An Introduction to English Legal History*, 4th edn, London 2002, 545.

was made the object of learned commentaries as early as the thirteenth century. *De legibus et consuetudine Angliae*, associated with Henry de Bracton (d. 1268) and generally referred to simply as Bracton, rapidly became an authoritative source of common law and would remain so for centuries. In fact, until William Blackstone (1723–80) wrote his commentaries, no other similar treatise covering the whole law would appear.

With the common law, England had its own, national law by the end of the fourteenth century. In contrast to the continent, the royal courts were not required to turn to the learned law in order to attain legal unification. The second stage in the reception of the learned law – that of Roman law in the secular courts – made little impact in England.

16 Auctoritas

243 *Auctoritas*

The rediscovery of Roman law at the end of the eleventh century marks the beginnings of the continental legal tradition. The flowering of Roman and canon jurisprudence took place within the broader context of the Renaissance of the Twelfth Century. The budding European jurisprudence was closely bound up with scholasticism.

Medieval jurisprudence differed fundamentally from classical Roman law. Classical jurisprudence was *ars*; it was pragmatic and concerned with practice. Legal study meant in the first place technical mastery of the law. The aim of the classical jurist was to apply the existing law as effectively as possible. Medieval, scholastic jurisprudence, by contrast, was *scientia*: it was idealistic and not predominantly directed at legal practice. Its object was to discover and understand 'the law' in its most perfected manifestation. That ideal law was sought not in legal practice but in authoritative sources, that is, the surviving texts of Justinian and the authoritative sources of canon law. Their *auctoritas* guaranteed that the perusal and scholastic interpretation of these texts would ultimately bring to light the immutable and universal 'truth of the law'. Like their counterparts in theology and medicine, the early scholastic jurists did not consider that the study of reality – in their case the practice of law – could add anything. This purely scholastic approach did not mean that the medieval legal scholar could already be regarded as a genuine systematist; for that they were still too dependent on their textual sources. Particularly in the case of Roman law, the case law-based and unsystematic nature of the source material prevented scholars from articulating a logical and comprehensive system based on clearly defined general principles. In that regard,

e more successful. It was not until the Late Middle Ages
..tual preconditions were in place for turning law into a
..d of scholarship as envisaged by Cicero. The systematisa-
..rocess that was not to be completed until the eighteenth and
..i centuries.

.. the scholastic ideology determined the approach to Roman law
a.. .e selection of sources and texts used, it did not result in slavish
adherence to the texts. On the contrary, it stimulated thought and even
creativity. The faith in the authority, immutability and universality of
texts that were hundreds of years old and stemmed from a different civilisation forced the scholastic jurists into all sorts of mental gymnastics
and interpretive wizardry in order to validate the claims to truth of these
texts. Scholastic superstition was unable to prevent each legal scholar
from seeking and finding arguments in the text in favour of 'his' ideal
truth and 'his' interpretation.

In accordance with the revaluation of natural reality in later scholasticism, the interaction between jurisprudence and legal practice, although
never absent, gradually increased. The rapprochement between the study
of law and practice occurred first of all in canon law and subsequently
through the direct reception of Roman law into the secular *ius proprium*.
By giving legal advice in pending cases, university professors became
directly involved with the application of the learned law in practice. As
members of royal courts and councils, university-trained jurists played
an important mediating role in the reception of and acculturation to
Roman law by municipal law.

The ultimate purpose behind the reception and acculturation was
to improve the existing municipal law. Little of this, however, came as
yet from the scholarly study of municipal law; if anything the converse
applied, of adapting municipal law to the learned law. The higher level of
sophistication and its written and learned nature were important elements
behind the learned law's appeal. For the time being, however, the gap
between the ideal of the *ius commune* and the *ius proprium* remained too
wide. The convergence began during the Late Middle Ages but, depend-
ing on the region and the branch of law in question, was ultimately not
completed until the seventeenth, eighteenth and nineteenth centuries.

Further Reading

1. On Europe in the Late Middle Ages: M. Barber, *The Two Cities: Medieval
Europe, 1050–1320*, London and New York 1992; C. Brooke, *Europe in the*

Central Middle Ages, 962–1154, 3rd edn, London and New York 2000; D. Hay, *Europe in the Fourteenth and Fifteenth Centuries*, 2nd edn, London and New York 1990; G. H. Holmes, *Europe: Hierarchy and Revolt, 1320–1450*, 2nd edn, Oxford 2000; W. C. Jordan, *Europe in the High Middle Ages*, London and New York 2001; J. H. Mundy, *Europe in the High Middle Ages, 1150–1300*, 3rd edn, London and New York 2000; volumes IV–VII of the *New Cambridge Medieval History*, 1998–2004.

2. On the expansion of Europe and the crusades: J. A. Brundage, *Medieval Canon Law and the Crusader*, Madison 1969; D. Lomax, *The Reconquest of Spain*, London and New York 1978; F. McLynn, *1066: the Year of Three Battles*, London 1999; J. J. Norwich, *The Normans in Sicily*, London 1970; J. R. S. Philips, *The Medieval Expansion of Europe*, Oxford 1998; S. Runciman, *A History of the Crusades*, 3 vols., Cambridge 1951–4; C. Tyerman, *God's War: a New History of the Crusades*, London and New York 2006.

3. On the church, the Investiture Controversy and the papacy: A. Black, *Monarchy and Community: Political Ideas in the Later Conciliar Controversy, 1430–1450*, Cambridge 1970; U.-R. Blumenthal, *The Investiture Controversy: Church and Monarchy from the Ninth to the Twelfth Century*, Philadelphia 1988; H. E. J. Cowdrey, *Pope Gregory VII, 1073–1085*, Oxford 1998; C. Morris, *The Papal Monarchy: the Western Church from 1050–1250*, Oxford 1989; F. Oakley, *The Conciliarist Tradition: Constitutionalism in the Catholic Church, 1300–1870*, Oxford 2003; K. Pennington, *Popes and Bishops: the Papal Monarchy in the Twelfth and Thirteenth Centuries*, Philadelphia 1984; I. S. Robinson, *The Papacy, 1073–1198: Continuity and Innovation*, Cambridge 1990; R. W. Southern, *Western Society and Church in the Middle Ages*, London 1970; B. Tierney, *Foundations of the Conciliar Theory: the Contribution of the Medieval Canonists from Gratian to the Great Schism*, Cambridge 1955; Tierney, *The Crisis of Church and State, 1050–1300*, Prentice-Hall 1964; H. Tillman, *Pope Innocent III*, London 1980; W. Ullmann, *The Growth of Papal Government in the Middle Ages: a Study in the Ideological Relation of Clerical to Lay Power*, 3rd edn, London 1970.

4. On feudal power complexes and the feudal state: D. Abulafia, *Frederick II: a Medieval Emperor*, London 1988; C. T. Allmand, *The Hundred Years War*, Cambridge 1988; J. W. Baldwin, *The Government of Philip Augustus: Foundations of French Royal Power in the Middle Ages*, Berkeley 1986; F. Barlow, *The Feudal Kingdom of England, 1042–1216*, 4th edn, London 1988; H. Fuhrmann, *Germany in the High Middle Ages, c.1050–1200*, Cambridge 1986; J. Gillingham, *The Angevin Empire*, London 1984; E. M. Hallam, *Capetian France, 987–1328*, London 1980; B. Hill, *Medieval Monarchy in Action: the German Empire from Henry I to Henry IV*, London 1972; E. Kantorowicz, *The Emperor Frederick the Second, 1194–1250*, London 1957; B. Lyon, *A Constitutional and Legal History of Medieval England*, 2nd edn, New York 1980; A. Marongiu, *Medieval Parliaments: a Comparative Study*, London 1968; A. P. Monahan, *Consent,*

Coercion and Limit: the Medieval Origins of Parliamentary Democracy, Leyden
1987; H. Mitteis, *The State in the Middle Ages: a Comparative Constitutional
History of Feudal Europe*, Amsterdam 1975; P. Munz, *Frederick Barbarossa:
a Study in Medieval Politics*, London 1969; E. S. Procter, *Curia and Cortes in
Leon and Castile, 1072–1295*, Cambridge 1980; E. Searle, *Predatory Kinship and
the Creation of Norman Power*, Berkeley 1988; J. R. Strayer, *On the Medieval
Origins of the Modern State*, Princeton 1970; Strayer, *The Reign of Philip the
Fair*, Princeton 1980; D. Willoweit, *Deutsche Verfassungsgeschichte. Vom
Frankenreich bis zur Teilung Deutschlands*, 2nd edn, Munich 1992.

5. On political and constitutional thought: A. Black, *Political Thought in
   Europe 1250–1450*, Cambridge 1992; J. M. Blythe, *Ideal Government and the
   Mixed Constitution in the Middle Ages*, Princeton 1992; J. H. Burns, ed., *The
   Cambridge History of Medieval Political Thought c.350–c.1450*, Cambridge
   1988; J. Canning, *The Political Thought of Baldus de Ubaldis*, Cambridge 1987;
   M. P. Gilmore, *Argument from Roman Law in Political Thought, 1200–1600*,
   Cambridge, Mass. 1941; J. C. Holt, *Magna Carta*, 2nd edn, Cambridge 1992;
   R. W. Kaeuper, *War, Justice and Public Order: England and France in the Later
   Middle Ages*, Oxford 1988; E. Kantorowicz, *The King's Two Bodies: a Study in
   Medieval Political Theology*, Princeton 1957; Kantorowicz, *Mourir pour la patrie
   et autres textes*, Paris 1984; A. McGrade, *The Political Thought of William of
   Ockham*, Cambridge 1974; K. Pennington, *The Prince and the Law, 1200–1600:
   Sovereignty and Rights in the Western Legal Tradition*, Berkeley 1993; G. Post,
   Studies in Medieval Political Thought: Public Law and the State, 1100–1322,
   Princeton 1964; B. Tierney, 'The Prince is not Bound by the Laws: Accursius and
   the Origins of the Modern State', *Comparative Studies in Society and History*,
   5 (1962) 378–400; Tiernty, *Religion, Law and the Growth of Constitutional
   Thought, 1150–1650*, Cambridge 1982; W. Ullmann, *Medieval Political Thought*,
   London 1965; Ullmann, *Principles of Government and Politics in the Middle
   Ages*, London 1966; Ullmann, *Law and Politics in the Middle Ages*, Cambridge
   1975; C. N. Woolf, *Bartolus of Sassoferrato: His Position in the History of
   Medieval Political Thought*, Cambridge 1913.

6. On the Renaissance of the Twelfth Century: R. L. Benson and G. Constable, eds.,
   Renaissance and Renewal in the Twelfth Century, Oxford 1982; G. Duby, *The
   Age of the Cathedrals: Art and Society, 980–1420*, London 1981; C. H. Haskins,
   The Renaissance of the Twelfth Century, Cambridge, Mass. and London 1927;
   R. N. Swanson, *The Twelfth-Century Renaissance*, Manchester and New York 1999.

7. On the significance of the Renaissance of the Twelfth Century for the law:
   H. J. Berman, *Law and Revolution: the Formation of the Western Legal Tradition*,
   Cambridge, Mass. and London 1983; J. A. Brundage, *The Medieval Origins of
   the Legal Profession: Canonists, Civilians, and Courts*, Chicago 2008.

8. On intellectual life in the Late Middle Ages: F. B. Artz, *The Mind of the
   Middle Ages, AD 200–1500: an Historical Survey*, Chicago and London 1980;

A. B. Cobban, *The Medieval Universities: Their Development and Organization*, London 1975; M. Colish, *Medieval Foundations of the Western Intellectual Tradition, 400–1400*, New Haven and London 1997; H. De Ridder-Symoens, *A History of the University in Europe*, vol. I, Cambridge 1992; G. R. Evans, *Old Arts and New Theology: the Beginnings of Theology as an Academic Discipline*, Oxford 1980; S. Ferruolo, *The Origins of the University: the Schools and their Critics, 1100–1215*, Stanford 1985; E. Grant, *The Foundations of Modern Science in the Middle Ages: Their Religious, Institutional, and Intellectual Contexts*, Cambridge 1996; D. Knowles, *The Evolution of Medieval Thought*, 2nd edn, London and New York 1988; N. Kretzmann, A. Kenny and J. Pinburg; eds., *The Cambridge History of Later Medieval Philosophy*, Cambridge 1982; J. Marenbon, *Later Medieval Thought (1050–1350): an Introduction*, London 1991; R. W. Southern, *Scholastic Humanism and the Unification of Europe*, 2 vols., Oxford 1995–2001; W. Ullmann, *Medieval Foundations of Renaissance Humanism*, London 1977.

9. On Roman law during the Middle Ages: J.-M. Aubert, *Le droit romain dans l'oeuvre de Saint Thomas*, Paris 1955; K. Bezemer, *What Jacques Saw: Thirteenth Century France through the Eyes of Jacques de Revigny, Professor of Law at Orleans*, Frankfurt 1997; F. Calasso, *Medio Evo del Diritto*, vol. I, Milan 1954; E. Cortese, *Il rinascimento giuridico medievale*, Rome 1992; Cortese, *Il diritto nella storia medievale*, 2 vols., Rome 1995; R. Feenstra, *Fata Iuris Romani. Etudes d'histoire du droit*, Leyden 1974; Feenstra, *Le droit savant au moyen âge et sa vulgarisation*, Aldershot 1986; A. Gouron, *La science du droit dans le midi de la France au Moyen Age*, Aldershot 1984; E. Kantorowicz and W.W. Buckland, *Studies in the Glossators of the Roman Law*, Cambridge 1938; P. Koschaker, *Europa und das Römische Recht*, Munich 1947; H. Lange, *Römisches Recht im Mittelalter*, 2 vols., Munich 1997–2007; A. Padoa-Schioppa, *Il diritto nella storia d'Europa. Il medioevo*, vol. I, Padua 1995; C. Radding, *The Origins of Medieval Jurisprudence: Pavia and Bologna 850–1150*, New Haven 1988; E. Schrage, *Das Römisches Recht im Mittelalter*, Darmstadt 1987; E. Schrage and J. Dondorp, *Utrumque Ius. Eine Einführung in das Studium der Quellen der mittelalterlichen gelehrten Rechts*, Berlin 1992; J. A. C. Smith, *Medieval Law: Teachers and Writers, Civilian and Canonist*, Ottawa 1975; W. Ullmann, *Jurisprudence in the Middle Ages*, London 1980; P. Vinogradoff, *Roman Law in Medieval Europe*, 3rd edn, Oxford 1961; F.C. von Savigny, *Geschichte des römischen Rechts im Mittelalter*, 7 vols., 2nd edn, Heidelberg 1834–51.

10. On medieval canon law: J. A. Brundage, *Medieval Canon Law*, London and New York 1995; Brundage, *The Profession and Practice of Medieval Canon Law*, Aldershot 2004; G. Fransen, *Décrétales et les collections décrétales*, Turnhout 1972; J. Gaudemet, *La formation du droit canonique mediéval*, Aldershot 1980; R. Helmholz, *The Spirit of Classical Canon Law*, Athens, Ga. 1996; S. Kuttner, *Harmony from Dissonance: an Interpretation of Medieval Canon Law*, Latrobe, Calif. 1960; Kuttner, *Gratian and the Schools of Law, 1140–1234*, London

1983; Kuttner, *Studies in the History of Medieval Canon Law*, Aldershot 1990; Kuttner, *Medieval Councils, Decretals and Collections of Canon Law: Collected Essays*, 2nd edn, Aldershot 1992; Kuttner, *History of Ideas and Doctrines of Canon Law in the Middle Ages*, 2nd edn, Aldershot 1992; P. Landau, *Kanones und Dekretalen: Beiträge zur Geschichte der Quellen des kanonischen Rechts*, Goldbach 1997; G. Le Bras, C. Léfebvre and J. Rambaud, *L'âge classique, 1140–1378: Sources et théorie du droit*, Histoire du droit et des institutions de l'église en occident 7, Paris 1965; W. P. Müller, *Huguccio: the Life, Works and Thought of a Twelfth-Century Jurist*, Washington 1994; J. R. Sweeney and S. Chodorow, eds., *Popes, Teachers and Canon Law in the Middle Ages*, Cornell 1989; W. Ullmann, *The Church and the Law*, London 1975; A. Winroth, *The Making of Gratian's Decretum*, Cambridge 2000.

11. On natural law: J. Finnis, *Aquinas: Moral, Political, and Legal Theory*, Oxford 1998; A. J. Lisska, *Aquinas's Theory of Natural Law: an Analytical Reconstruction*, Oxford 1996; B. Tierney, *The Idea of Natural Rights: Studies on Natural Rights, Natural Law and Church Law, 1150–1625*, Atlanta 1997.

12. On customary law, legislation and the judiciary in the Late Middle Ages: R. Bartlett, *Trial by Fire and Water: the Medieval Judicial Ordeal*, Oxford 1986; A. Harding, *Medieval Law and the Foundations of the State*, Oxford 2002; F. Kern, *Kingship and Law in the Middle Ages*, Oxford 1939; J. M. Powell, *The Liber Augustalis or Constitutions of Melfi*, Syracuse, N.Y. 1971; J. H. Shennan, *The Parlement of Paris*, London 1968; E. N. van Kleffens, *Hispanic Law until the End of the Middle Ages*, Edinburgh 1968.

13. On the historical development of the common law: J. H. Baker, *An Introduction to English Legal History*, 4th edn, London 2002; P. Brand, *The Origins of the English Legal Profession*, Oxford 2002; A. Harding, *The Law Courts in Medieval England*, London 1973; J. Hudson, *The Formation of the English Common Law: Law and Society in England from the Norman Conquest to Magna Carta*, London 1996; S. Milsom, *Historical Foundations of the Common Law*, 2nd edn, London 1981; R. C. van Caenegem, *The Birth of the English Common Law*, 2nd edn, Cambridge 1988; as well as the volumes from the *Oxford History of the Laws of England* already published.

14. On the learned law in England: J. Barton, *Roman Law in England*, Milan 1971.

5

Emulatio
(the Early Modern Age, 1453–1648)

A   Politics and the state

1   A new dawn?

Hamlet: What news?
Rosencrantz: None, my Lord, but that the world's grown honest.
Hamlet: Then is doomsday near.[1]

244   The Italian Renaissance

More than a century before the Italian Renaissance, Petrarch (1304–74) had already announced the dawn of an age, an age of revival. The epoch between the fall of the Roman Empire and his own time – the Middle Ages – he described as an age of decay and barbarism. This chronology of decay and revival was to grow into one of the most enduring myths in European historiography. Most eighteenth- and nineteenth-century historians held to the view that the advent of modern, Western civilisation began with the Italian Renaissance and with humanism in the fifteenth and sixteenth centuries.

Since the publication of Haskins's *The Renaissance of the Twelfth Century* (1927), these views have been revised. The foundations of Western civilisation were laid not by the Renaissance of Leonardo da Vinci (1452–1519), Michelangelo Buonarotti (1475–1564), Raffaello Sanzio (1483–1520) and Desiderius Erasmus (*c.*1466–1536), but by the older Renaissance of Anselm, Abelard and Gratian. The rediscovery of Antiquity began not in the fifteenth century but in the late eleventh century. But what then, in the light of all this, was the significance of the Italian Renaissance within the evolution of Western civilisation? Is it still correct to speak of a caesura between the Middle Ages and the Modern Age?

The response to the latter question is undeniably yes. The fifteenth century brought a number of important changes that ushered in a new

---

[1] William Shakespeare, *Hamlet* 2.2.

era in the political and cultural history of the West. The changes may be seen as part and parcel of a general revival of western Europe following the stagnation and decline that marked the fourteenth century. Many intellectuals of the Renaissance thought about their own times, as Petrarch already had, in terms of revival and renewal. Although the term 'Renaissance' did not obtain general currency until the nineteenth century, the great artists, thinkers and politicians of that period often considered themselves the trail-blazers of a new age.

245   The Ottoman Empire

Western historians have proposed various dates to demarcate the Middle Ages from the Modern Age. Each of these symbolises one of the major changes that announce the beginning of a new era. The oldest date, which is the one preferred here, is 1453. In that year, the Ottoman Turks conquered the city of Constantinople, the last but one remnant of the Eastern Roman Empire. Five years later, the last Byzantine bulwark, Trabzon on the Black Sea, fell into their hands. Between 1453 and 1526, the Turks overran the larger part of the eastern Mediterranean and the Balkans. The Battle of Mohacs (1526) brought Hungary under their domination. In 1529, their failure to take Vienna put a stop to their westward expansion. The Ottoman Empire became the leading power in the Mediterranean and was to remain so well into the seventeenth century. The larger part of southern Europe lived under the threat of Turkish power. This had major consequences for Europe. First, Italian trading republics such as Venice and Genoa saw their empires in the East crumble in the course of the fifteenth, sixteenth and seventeenth centuries. Second, the Ottoman ascendancy also severely jeopardised any realistic hope for expansion to the Levant for the greater, dynastic powers of the West. Third, in the somewhat longer run, this stimulated the shift of the centre of gravity of culture, politics and economics from the Mediterranean to the North Sea. The year 1453 was also the year in which the Hundred Years War between France and England came to an end. For the French monarchy, the victory over the English marked the start of the restoration of its domestic authority and the re-emergence of France as one of the leading powers in the West. In England, the defeat in France led to a major dynastic conflict over the succession, the Wars of the Roses (1455–85), which was ultimately to bring a new dynasty to the throne, the Tudors. The great Tudor monarchs, Henry VII (1485–1509), Henry VIII (1509–47) and Elizabeth I (1558–1603), turned their country into a medium-sized power that was to play a significant role in the balance of power between the two major European powers of the sixteenth century, France and the Habsburg Empire based around Spain.

246   The Age of Discovery and the rise of Spain

The second date is 1492, the year in which Christopher Columbus (1451–1506) reached America. The discoveries in the Atlantic Ocean had already started at an earlier point: around 1400, Portuguese ships were already sailing down the coast of western Africa. Columbus's journey was sponsored by the most important competitors of the Portuguese, Isabella the Catholic (1474–1504) of Castile and Ferdinand the Catholic of Aragon (1479–1516). Whereas the Portuguese sought to find a route to India around Africa, Columbus set out to reach the Indies by travelling around the world in a westerly direction. Columbus's plan failed, but his discovery of the New World led to the formation of the Spanish world empire. Around 1520, Hernán Cortés (1485–1547) and Francisco Pizarro (c.1471–1541) overran the indigenous empires in Mexico and Peru. In the meantime, in 1495, the Portuguese Vasco da Gama (c.1469–1524) became the first European to reach India via the Cape of Good Hope. In the early decades of the sixteenth century, the Portuguese established a commercial empire in the Indian Ocean, from which they brought spices and other luxury products to Europe. With the concurrence of the pope, the Spanish and Portuguese kings claimed the monopoly over navigation and commerce outside Europe. In 1493, Pope Alexander VI (1492–1503) promulgated the Bull *Inter Caetera* in which he divided the non-European world between the Spanish and Portuguese crowns. One year later, the Iberian kings confirmed the principle of the division under the Treaty of Tordesillas, although they drew different dividing lines in the Atlantic. After the fleet of the Portuguese navigator Fernando Magellan (1480–1521) had demonstrated by the circumnavigation of the globe (1519–1522) that the world was indeed round, a second dividing line had to be drawn through the Pacific Ocean. The other countries of the West did not accept the Iberian monopoly. During the second half of the sixteenth century, French, English and Dutch seafarers broke the Iberian monopoly over the Indies, in their own turn founding commercial empires and colonies. The year 1492 was also the year in which the *Reconquista* or re-conquest of Spain by the Christians from Islam was completed. In that year, Ferdinand and Isabella captured the Moorish kingdom of Granada in the southern part of the Iberian peninsula. This success heralded the rapid emergence of

Spain as the leading power in Europe and the greatest challenger to the Ottoman Turks in the Mediterranean.

247   Protestantism

Finally, there is the year 1517. In that year, the German Augustinian monk Martin Luther (1483–1546) nailed his ninety-five theological theses to the door of the All Saints Castle Church in Wittenberg. This marked the beginning of the Reformation and the end of the unity of church and faith in the Latin West. By 1648, Europe was, roughly speaking, divided into a Catholic south and a Protestant north. Italy, Spain, Portugal, France, the Southern Netherlands, southern Germany, Bohemia and Poland remained Catholic, while Scandinavia, northern Germany, the Northern Netherlands, England and Scotland went over to one of the Protestant churches. Before this point had been reached, a number of bloody wars of religion were waged. Although Europe continued to label itself as the *respublica christiana* for more than a century, the last remnants of the universal authority of the pope over the West had disappeared by 1550. The rejection of papal authority and canon law knocked away the political and legal pillars on which the *respublica christiana* stood, plunging it into a protracted crisis. No higher power stood in the way of the absolute sovereignty of the great princes and republics any longer. The sovereign state established itself on the ruins of the unity of the Latin West.

2   *Recovery, crisis and the formation of aristocratic society*

248   Economic revival and stagnation

Following upon the crisis of the fourteenth century came a new period of economic and demographic growth, which lasted to around 1600. As in the eleventh century, climate change led to fewer harvest failures and allowed more land to be taken into cultivation. There were not, however, any fundamental improvements in agricultural techniques. The production coefficient rose only slowly to no more than five. In the long run, food production was unable to keep pace with the demographic evolution. Towards the year 1600, Europe, with 75–80 million people, had a greater population than around 1300. The critical point in the ratio between population and food production was once again exceeded and a new period of scarcity set in. The warmer period came to an end around 1540. From that time onwards, Europe was in the grip of a minor ice age. The perpetual circle of famine, disease and war returned with a vengeance.

249 Trade and industry

The demographic expansion led to a new upsurge in trade and industry. The traditional trade flows in Europe and the Mediterranean were restored, with northern and eastern Europe more heavily involved in this traffic than before. Poland and the Baltic regions became important exporters of cereals and shipbuilding materials to the West. During the Middle Ages, Italy acted as the hub for the importation of luxury products from the East and the Indies. The fall of Constantinople did not put an abrupt end to the Levantine trade. It does not suffice to explain why Portugal and Spain opened an alternative route to the Indies. First, the Portuguese discoveries pre-dated 1453. Second, the Turkish sultans did not conquer the major trading routes via Syria and Egypt until 1516–17, after the voyages by Columbus and Vasco da Gama. Third, Venice and Genoa managed to remain important players in East–West trade for a considerable time to come.

The fall of Constantinople in 1453 may not immediately have destroyed the strong position of the Italian city-republics in international commerce, but it was nevertheless one certain factor in the long-term, gradual shift of the centre of gravity from Italy to the North Sea. Over the course of the sixteenth century, Italy lost its dominance in international trade. The Portuguese and Spanish explorers opened up new routes to the Indies, thereby bringing to an end the Italian monopoly over the importation into Europe of silk and spices. Seamen from the western countries, such as the Netherlands and England, penetrated the Mediterranean. Halfway through the seventeenth century, the bulk of the carrier trade on the seas around Europe was in Dutch hands.

The sixteenth century also saw changes in industrial production. During the Late Middle Ages, traditional craft industry, such as textiles, was concentrated in the towns. Northern Italy and the Netherlands were the most important centres of urban craftsmanship. Now town craftsmen increasingly had to reckon with competition from the country. The large merchant houses encouraged cottage industry among farming households as this was cheaper. Urban industry increasingly focused on luxury products such as fine clothing, weapons, jewels and art, thereby responding to the increased demand for luxury and display among the aristocracy and the urban elite. These developments were also to the disadvantage of the Italian towns, although a number of large cities such as Venice, Milan and Florence were themselves centres of luxury industry. With the emergence of the new industries, imports of such products from the eastern part of the Mediterranean lost some of their importance.

250   Money economy

During the Late Middle Ages, the great city-republics of northern Italy controlled a large part of international banking activities. Florence, Venice and Genoa managed to remain important banking centres throughout the fifteenth and sixteenth centuries, but in this area too they were exposed to increasing competition. Thanks to the discovery and exploitation of silver mines in central Europe, a number of German families built up an international financial network. They owed their success to co-operation with leading royal houses. In this way, the Fuggers of Augsburg obtained a monopoly over a significant proportion of the silver mining in southern Germany in exchange for loans to the Habsburgs. This German ascendancy proved, however, to be short lived. With the opening up of silver mines in Potosi in Bolivia from 1545 onwards and Zacatecas in Mexico several years later, the money market became swamped by cheap silver and money, the latter reaching the European economy through Seville. Since the Spanish rulers and elites used this money to pay for imported products and Spain neglected to build up its own industry, the silver coinage was distributed throughout Europe, and Spain ceased to be a competitor for Italy and the Netherlands in the field of industry. The influx of silver from the New World radically changed the balance of power in international banking. With the slump in silver mining in central Europe, the large German banking dynasties such as the Fuggers no longer occupied centre-stage; the ascendancy switched to the Iberian peninsula with Seville and to the Netherlands with Antwerp and, after 1585, Amsterdam. The Genoese, who took over from the Fuggers the role of bankers for the Habsburgs from 1530 onwards, were able to play a leading role in the European monetary economy for another century.

From the sixteenth century onwards, central governments began to assume a more active role in the economy. In order to pay for their large courts and governmental apparatus and to fund their continuous wars, the leading princes of the West needed vast amounts of money. For this purpose, they relied on loans from the great banking houses of Europe such as the Fuggers in Augsburg or the Doria in Genoa who in return received all kinds of economic privileges – often in the form of monopolies of exploitation or trade. The entrepreneurs and rulers of Europe became mutually dependent. Their co-operation laid the foundation for a capitalist monetary economy with a European dimension. Networks of large family businesses and alliances in which trade, industry and the monetary system were interlinked spread all over Europe. In order to increase their earnings, the rulers encouraged the luxury industry and sought to limit exports of precious metals and imports of luxury products. This was later to give rise to mercantilism.

The rapid increase in population, the rise of the luxury industries and imports of cheap money led in the course of the sixteenth century to a constant rate of inflation of between 2 and 3 per cent. In today's terms, that may not appear much, but for people in the sixteenth century the steady devaluation of the money came as a shock. It meant a break from the medieval economy where the fixed value of land had formed the basis for all wealth. Inflation caused serious problems for both rich and poor. The fact that agricultural production was unable to keep pace with demographic growth led to a rise in food prices, while wages remained stable. Between 1500 and 1600, day labourers, both those in the countryside and those in the towns, became impoverished. On the other hand, the fact that copy-hold rents also remained fixed for long periods of time meant that many farmers were temporarily better off, while some of the landed gentry grew poorer.

251   Social relations

Demographic growth led to a trek from the country to the towns. The population of old existing towns multiplied. Towards 1600, Paris and Naples had 200,000 inhabitants; in addition there were a further ten cities with 100,000 inhabitants within or around their walls. The abrupt economic changes led to an increase in social inequality between 1450 and 1600. In order to defend themselves against inflation or new competitors, the elites in the towns and the country took all sorts of measures that undercut chances for social mobility and further weakened the economic position of the poor. In the towns, the gap between the established, independent master craftsmen and the day labourers widened. The guilds and trades tightened up their regulations in order to preserve the interests of their constituencies. The expanding numbers of destitute day labourers and proletarians threatened social and political stability. In rural areas, the landed gentry dealt with inflation by increasing rents, imposing new charges or evicting farmers from their lands and replacing them by day labourers. In many cases, this led to peasants' revolts, such as the Peasants' War in southern Germany of 1524–5. In different parts of eastern Europe, such as Poland, Ukraine and Russia, farmers enjoyed even less legal protection. There, systematic exploitation by the gentry reduced thousands of farmers and their families to effective slavery. In sum, all over Europe, the economic developments of the sixteenth century condemned millions of people – especially those who had to live on the fruits of day labour – to poverty, while the rich steadily improved their position.

252   Aristocratic culture

Not only relations between rich and poor were put under strain. Among the wealthy classes of the population, the balance of power also shifted. During the Late Middle Ages, a new, economic elite had emerged in the towns: the wealthy merchants, bankers and craftsmen. This new, urban elite had largely contributed to the cultural and economic innovations of the twelfth, thirteenth and fourteenth centuries. At the head of large, wealthy and powerful towns, the urban elites formed a power that princes and the traditional, noble aristocracies had to reckon with.

The sixteenth century redrew the balance to the advantage of the nobility. The succession of major wars, the ongoing centralisation of power by the princes, the alliances between the greatest banking and merchant houses and the royal dynasties, and the successive financial crises brought about by inflation and warfare resulted in a relative weakening of the political and economic position of the urban elites. Although most towns saw their population rise and many became more wealthy as new markets were opened up, they lost much of their political autonomy and their grip over the rural economy. Old medieval centres such as Florence, Pisa, Siena, Bruges, Ghent, Augsburg or the Hanseatic towns on the coasts of the Baltic Sea went into decline. Those towns that had not switched to the new luxury industries found themselves facing major competition from the emerging cottage industry. The increase in food prices further undercut the ascendancy of the towns over the countryside.

The turnaround had not just an economic but also a social and cultural dimension. The ascendancy of royal power in most of Europe stimulated aristocratic culture. Although the nobility, like the urban elites, often opposed the policies of centralisation by the monarchy, the leading nobility was gradually absorbed into the royal apparatus of government. The kings and princes gathered the leading members of the nobility and the clergy around them in their royal households. The royal court provided a model for the landed nobility and the higher clergy to copy in their country palaces and manors. After the fifteenth century, the royal dynasties and noble aristocracies retook the lead from the urban elites in the field of artistic patronage.

The social and cultural aspirations of the urban elite themselves worked to the advantage of the aristocracy. The highest aim of the rich urban patricians was not to gain recognition as a separate class but to become nobles themselves. Most patrician families tended to invest their fortunes in rural estates and manors after one or two generations in the hope of acceding to the ranks of the aristocracy. The triumph of the nobility over the urban elite in the sixteenth century did not prevent social mobility. The 'nobility' included not just the traditional landed and military nobility; jurists, civil servants and wealthy traders and bankers could also ascend to the ranks of the noble aristocracy through their wealth, marriage or royal favour.

The weakening of the urban elites in favour of the nobility needs to be measured primarily in relative terms. In absolute numbers, the towns generally progressed in terms of population and wealth in the Early Modern Age. The crisis of the period between 1350 and 1450 was not as radical as that of the ninth and tenth centuries. The economic level from which people departed in 1450 was several times higher than that on which the revival of the eleventh century had been built. The volume of trade and industry was greater in the sixteenth century than it had been in the early fourteenth century, as was the number of well-to-do nobles, merchants and master craftsmen. There were also more jurists, physicians, theologians and artists than in the Late Middle Ages. The elite culture had a broader base than before. This put the international character of the elite under pressure. The numerous merchants, intellectuals and artists had less opportunity than hitherto of finding work in foreign countries. Each country and each large region had its own supply. The Renaissance remained an international movement but nevertheless saw the beginning of the formation of separate, national cultures, of which the use of the vernacular as the language of culture was just one expression.

3   The end of religious unity

253   The papacy during the Renaissance

During the Avignon Exile (1307–77) and the Great Schism (1378–1417), the papacy found itself in a state of crisis. The Avignon Exile brought the pope under the domination of the French king and damaged his authority. During the Schism, the balance of power between the pope and the great princes of the West tilted further in favour of the latter. Competing popes constantly had to beg the favour and support of the secular rulers. In addition, during his stay outside Italy, the pope had lost his grip on the city of Rome and the Papal State.

It was not just in the political field that the pope's power had shrunk; the papacy had also lost much of its religious and moral authority. The palace and court in Avignon soaked up money, accounting for a large part of the church's income and taxes. The ecclesiastical machinery of government and canon law was increasingly used as an instrument to garner money, while the pastoral function of the first bishop of the West receded into the background. Criticism of the riches of the church and the opulent lifestyle of the higher clergy spiralled.

After the restoration of unity in the church at the Council of Constance, Pope Martinus V (1417–31) re-established the papacy in Rome. During the fifteenth and early sixteenth century, Martinus's successors gradually managed to regain control over Rome and the Papal State, and the pope once again became a political force in Italy. The popes also increasingly acted as secular princes. The great Renaissance popes Alexander VI, Julius II (1503–13), Leo X (1513–21) and Clemens VII (1523–34) have gone down in history more as princes and conquerors than as church leaders. None of the popes of that era, however, was able to match the power and authority over the Latin West of their predecessors in the thirteenth century. Never again would a pope be able to claim the secular leadership of the Western world.

The restoration of unity and the return to Rome enabled the *Curia* to re-establish a firm grip over the administrative machinery of the church. There was, however, no moral reversal. When the popes returned to Rome in the early fifteenth century, they found the city reduced to rubble. During the next century, aided by many rich cardinals and prelates, they embarked on a huge building programme, of which the new Saint Peter's Basilica and the Vatican Palace were the crowning glories. The huge expense of this process seduced the popes into using the church once more as a money-making machine.

254   Lutheranism

The moral decay of the papacy sparked off a response within the church. The German monk and theologian Martin Luther began his protests in 1517 in response to the sale of indulgences by Rome: a practice whereby those with money were able to assure themselves of a speedier acceptance into heaven. Initially, it was not Luther's intention to break with Rome. He demanded a series of reforms to restore morality and piety among the clergy, for which reason his action and the later Protestant movements in the sixteenth century became known under the collective denominator of the Reformation. He found himself driven ever further by the unbending attitude taken by Rome and Emperor Charles V (1519–58). In 1521, his movement broke away from the church, rejecting the authority of the entire ecclesiastical hierarchy, including the pope. Luther rapidly obtained the support of a number of German princes, who saw Lutheranism as a means of reducing the grip of the church over their territories and of seizing the lands and wealth of the church. The support for Lutheranism also fitted into their struggle against the efforts by Charles V, the defender of the church, to increase his power in the Holy Roman Empire. The two great Scandinavian kingdoms, Sweden (1527) and Denmark (1536), as well as the German Order (1525), converted to Lutheranism.

Lutheran theology may be summarised in two brief catchphrases. *Sola scriptura* (only through Scripture) means that the Bible alone provides the basis for Christian dogma and doctrine. Luther calls for a return to the original church, the church of Christ and the first Apostles, as portrayed in the New Testament. All later dogmas, liturgy and institutes must be rejected. The existence of a separate clergy, the sacrament of confession, the dogma of transubstantiation and canonisation of saints are refuted. The monastic system had to go as well. *Sola fide* (only through faith) means that one can achieve salvation of one's soul only through personal faith and piety. Here Luther links up with an evolution that dated back to the Late Middle Ages. Since the twelfth century, the emphasis within the church had shifted from sacramental ritual as an instrument of salvation to the personal faith and piety of each individual Christian. With Luther, the break from the liturgical significance of the sacraments was complete. The clergy and the ecclesiastical hierarchy lost their most essential function, the administration of the sacraments. Thereby the theological foundations for setting the clergy apart from the laity and from the lay world collapsed. In the Lutheran churches, the community of the faithful retook control over the ecclesiastical structure.

Luther rejected the independence of the church and of the ecclesiastical hierarchy from secular authority. For its secular interests, the church came under the tutelage of secular rulers. This made Lutheranism particularly attractive to many such rulers. At a stroke, they were able to liberate themselves from the interference of the Roman *Curia* while at the same time eliminating a competing source of power in their territories: the local high clergy. In that sense Lutheranism brought about a twofold nationalisation of the church: it came under the control of the ruler and became a 'national' rather than a universal church.

255 The Peace of Augsburg

The schism within the church led to political tensions within the German Empire between the emperor and the Catholic and Lutheran

Reichsstände. In 1530, during the Diet of Augsburg, the attempt at reconciliation between Charles V and the Lutheran princes failed. The latter then forged an alliance known as the Schmalkaldic League. On account of foreign wars, Charles V refrained for a long time from armed intervention. Moreover, he still held hopes that the unity of the church could be peacefully restored by means of a general council. In 1546, one year after the beginning of the Council of Trent, which was attended only by the Catholic clergy, Charles V commenced hostilities against the Protestants. The Schmalkaldic War was the first of a long list of religious wars in the empire and in Europe, of which the Thirty Years War (1618–48) was to be the last. In 1555, peace was concluded in Augsburg between Charles V and the forces of the Schmalkaldic League. Each prince was allowed to determine the religion – Catholic or Lutheran – of his subjects. With this principle, encapsulated in the words *cujus regio, ejus religio* (whose the region, his the religion), the Diet gave up the hope of restoring the religious unity of the empire, while at the same time guaranteeing religious unity within each of its principalities.

256   Calvinism and Anglicanism

Apart from the Lutherans, several other Protestant movements broke away from the Roman church. The most important of these was Calvinism, which was more radical than Lutheranism. The founder of this reform movement was the Frenchman John Calvin (1509–64), who emphasised austerity and the purity of faith. If Luther had only rejected the autonomy of an ecclesiastical hierarchy, Calvin collapsed the distinction between secular and spiritual authority altogether. The political community could not be viewed in isolation from the community of the faithful. In Geneva, Calvin experimented with a theocracy, under which the leaders of the faithful also undertook the administration of secular affairs. The Calvinist movement was militant and rapidly spread all over Europe. In the second half of the sixteenth century, Calvinism took root not just in Switzerland and a number of principalities of the empire, but also in France, the Netherlands, Bohemia, Hungary, Poland and Scotland. In all these countries, there arose sharp religious and political conflicts between the Protestants and the Catholic rulers and church. Only in the Northern Netherlands, some parts of the empire and Scotland were these resolved in favour of the Protestants.

The Anglican Church was the third of the three great Protestant churches. The breakaway of the Anglican Church was primarily political in motivation, the immediate cause being the desire on the part of Henry

VIII to repudiate his wife, Catherine of Aragon (1485–1536), the aunt of Charles V. Catherine was beyond child-bearing age and had borne only one surviving daughter. Henry feared that if he died without male issue, this would give rise to a new civil war. When the pope refused to annul his marriage, Henry resorted to more radical methods. In 1534, Parliament in London passed the Act of Supremacy declaring the king rather than the pope to be the sovereign head of the Church of England. Shortly afterwards, Henry had the monasteries dissolved and appropriated their lands and properties. Over the next few decades, the Church of England evolved somewhat in the direction of Protestantism, but many aspects of Catholic theology and organisation were kept. The ecclesiastical hierarchy of priests, bishops and archbishops remained intact.

257   Counter-Reformation

The Lutheran Reformation was not the first protest movement within the church and also not the last, but it was the first to result in a permanent schism within it. For this, Rome to a considerable extent had itself to blame. Despite the urging of Charles V and other Catholic rulers, Rome long refused to enter into the debate on church reform and to take Luther's criticisms seriously. From the 1520s onwards, Charles V called for a universal council to address reform. This was not held until 1545, in Trent. The Tridentine Council (1545–63) came too late for any reconciliation between the various Christian groups. Instead of promoting reconciliation, the Council became the launch-pad for a counterattack against the Reformation: the Counter-Reformation.

The Council of Trent approved a series of measures that left the Catholic Church better prepared for its struggle against the Reformation. Some of these were aimed at the worst abuses among the clergy, while others sought to sharpen Catholic doctrine and to strengthen Rome's grip over the church in matters of theology and liturgy. The Council confirmed and strengthened the mediating, sacramental role of the clergy. Liturgy was further refined. As against the austerity and strictness of Protestantism, the church offered a new liturgy and new artistic language, that of the baroque. Baroque art evoked the faith in a dramatic, often theatrical way, inspiring awe and emotion. The vivid depiction of God, Christ, the saints, as well as the dogmas and mysteries, appealed directly to the imagination and inner feelings of devotion, and were meant to dissipate all doubt about the truth of the Catholic doctrines, many of which the Protestants contested. The training of the clergy was another focal point of the Counter-Reformation. A network of seminaries in all the dioceses would provide the church with a huge army of well-trained priests. This met one of the most important criticisms of the Protestants: the low intellectual and moral standards of the parish priests.

The Council of Trent was a turning point in the struggle for the soul of the Latin West. During the century after Trent, Rome managed to stem the rise of Protestantism and regain some of the lost ground. The Reformation was pushed back and defeated in France, Poland, Bohemia, Hungary and the Southern Netherlands. Towards 1648, the borders of the Catholic and the Protestant worlds were all but settled. The south remained loyal to Rome, while the north went its own way. The dividing line went straight through the Netherlands and the Holy Roman Empire.

258   Church and state

The partial success of the Counter-Reformation was largely due to the support of several secular princes. The Habsburg kings of Spain, Philip II (1558–98), Philip III (1598–1621) and Philip IV (1621–65), as well as their cousins, the Habsburg emperors Ferdinand II (1619–37) and Ferdinand III (1637–57), projected themselves as the defenders of the Roman Church. In France too, the monarchy engaged in the struggle against the Calvinist minority, the Huguenots. The pope was, however, to pay for this support. The great Catholic monarchs supported the Counter-Reformation in an effort to restore or safeguard religious unity among their subjects. They helped the pope in his fight against Protestantism and, as such, shored up his spiritual leadership over the church, but rejected any interference in secular affairs. The political supremacy of the pope was history. The balance between church and state tilted in favour of the latter. The princes wanted to re-establish the church as an instrument of power in state affairs and as a means of unification of their territories. Modelling themselves on their Protestant counterparts, Catholic princes demanded a say in the administrative affairs of the church as well. In most countries, the kings strengthened their grip over the appointment of the higher clergy. In France, the influence of the king over the appointment of bishops had already been strengthened thanks to the Concordat of Bologna (1516), an agreement between the French King Francis I (1515–47) and Pope Leo X. The church saw itself forced to allow the diversion of some of its income to the royal treasury. The right of *placet*, under which papal decisions could obtain legal force in the realm only after the prince had signified his approval, was gradually extended. In consequence, canon law lost much of its universal validity. The 'nationalisation' of the churches was not confined to the Protestant countries.

4   The collapse of the respublica christiana and the struggle for hegemony in Europe

259   Crusading ideal

The fall of Constantinople and the rapid expansion of the Ottoman Empire caused panic in the Latin West. With the fall of the Eastern Roman Empire, Italy and Germany came into the frontline of the struggle between Christianity and Islam. For the first time since the tenth century, the survival of the Latin West seemed in jeopardy. In 1480, the Turks occupied Otranto in southern Italy. In 1499, they conducted a predatory raid in the vicinity of Vicenza. With Hungary (1526) the last buffer between the Turkish Empire and the Holy Roman Empire disappeared. In 1529, Suleiman the Magnificent (1520–66) laid siege to Vienna.

Fear of the Ottomans sparked off a revival of the crusading ideal in Italy and the West. In order to mount a joint counteroffensive against the Ottomans, peace among the Christian princes of Europe needed to be established first. Peace within Christianity and the plans to conduct a crusade resounded loudly within diplomatic discourse from 1453 onwards. Various popes attempted to put both ideas into practice. In 1517, Pope Leo X even announced a five-year truce for the entire West. The attempt failed, like all the others.

260   The collapse of the respublica christiana

The revival of the crusading zeal and the ideal of unity within Christianity proved to be the death throes of the medieval respublica christiana. Towards 1530, the ideal lay in ruins. Instead of uniting them, the crusading ideal divided the great princes of the West. Plans to mount an offensive against the Turks foundered on the ambitions of the most powerful rulers of Europe to lead the crusade and so be recognised as secular leader of the West, as its monarcha universalis. The key to leadership over the respublica christiana was hegemony over Italy. The peninsula not only was the cradle of Latin Christianity but also formed the seat of the old empire. Furthermore, an offensive against the Turks could best be launched from Italy. From 1494 to 1530, an almost uninterrupted series of wars raged between the emperor, Spain and France, with Italy as the prize. In the course of the struggle, the pope, as head of the Papal State, lost much of his prestige and independence. The Sack of Rome by the soldiers of Emperor Charles V in 1527 (sacco di Roma) illustrates the fiasco of the respublica christiana: the troops of the secular leader of the West and the protector of the church had laid waste to the seat of the spiritual leader of the church.

The schism in the church and the wars of religion were the *coup de grâce* for the medieval ideal of unity. The Reformation destroyed the foundations on which the traditional universal claims of the pope and emperor were based. Even Charles V who, as king of Castile and Aragon, Archduke of Austria and Lord of the Netherlands, possessed an enormous power base, could not seriously aspire to vest his overlordship, in whatever form, over the Latin West. Any ambitions he might have had in that direction foundered on the alliance between the French king and the Protestant princes. The co-operation (from 1536 onwards) between Francis I of France and Sultan Suleiman in their struggle against Charles and the Habsburgs dealt another death-blow to the medieval ideal of Christian unity.

261   Endemic warfare

Together with the wars of religion the protracted struggle between the Habsburg kings of Spain and the Valois kings of France plunged Europe into a political and institutional crisis. The religious divisions dislocated the West. Where faith had once been the foundation of unity, now it was the cause of dissent. Virtually constant warfare marked the period between 1494 and 1648.

First, there were the numerous wars against the Turks. The crusading ideal notwithstanding, the burdens of these wars were borne by the countries in the frontline: the hereditary lands of the Habsburgs in Austria, the larger Italian states such as Venice, Spain – which, through its control over Naples, Sicily and Sardinia dominated the western Mediterranean – and the pope.

Second, there was the constant rivalry between the two leading dynasties of the West, the Habsburgs and the Valois, for hegemony over Europe. The Valois had emerged victorious from the Hundred Years War against the English (1453). Charles VII (1422–61) and Louis XI (1461–83) had succeeded in consolidating their power and expanding it at the expense of the great aristocratic families. Charles VIII (1483–98), Louis XII (1498–1515) and Francis I turned their sights on Italy. With the invasion of the Italian peninsula in 1494, Charles VIII launched a lengthy conflict with Spain for hegemony over Italy and ultimately the entire West. For a period of thirty years, the two great powers of the day were locked in combat in and around the peninsula. This changed when the Habsburg Charles V, who was already lord of the Burgundian Netherlands since 1506, inherited Castile, Aragon, Sardinia and Sicily in 1516 from his maternal grandparents, Ferdinand of Aragon and Isabella of Castile. From Ferdinand,

Charles also inherited claims to the kingdom of Naples. In 1519, he inherited the Austrian hereditary lands from his paternal grandfather, Emperor Maximilian (1493–1519) and was elected emperor. Towards 1530, Charles had all but driven the French out of Italy and had established Spanish hegemony there.

The victory of the Habsburgs in Italy did not lead to recognition of their hegemony over Europe. Francis I and his successors found new allies in the Protestant princes of the empire and continued to fight the Habsburgs. Upon his abdication in 1555/6, Charles V carved up his empire. His son Philip II (1555–98) was given Spain and the Habsburg possessions in Italy (Naples, Milan and the islands), the Netherlands and the Spanish colonies in America. Charles's brother Ferdinand I retained Austria, Bohemia and what remained of Hungary, and succeeded Charles as emperor. Until 1648, Spain remained the strongest power in Europe, but it could not hope – as it did not – to attain universal leadership over the West. Philip II and his successors did, however, like to portray themselves as the protectors of the Catholic Church and as effective leaders of the Catholic world. This too was resolutely contested by the Catholic kings of France.

Third, the struggle between the Habsburgs and the Valois for hegemony over Europe was nothing other than an extreme manifestation of the sort of war inherent in the dominant political structure of the Early Modern Age: the dynastic state. The great countries of the West, such as France, Spain, England, Sweden and the Habsburg lands in Austria and the Netherlands, were no contiguous, unified states. They consisted of various medieval realms and principalities kept together in personal union under one and the same ruler. They were power complexes within which the ruling dynasty was the main binding element. The dynasties often held the different parts of their possessions under various titles: enfeoffment, inheritance, purchase, conquest, cession under a peace treaty, marriage. The fact that the members of the great dynasties were continually intermarrying, together with the plurality and complexity of the laws and the fact that claims often went back centuries, left few areas in Europe that were not contested by various families. If only for this reason there were numerous dynastic wars. Furthermore, many of the dynasties, such as the Habsburgs in Spain, the Tudors in England and the Orleans (a branch of the Valois) in France, had come to power only recently. In many cases, they had no more than a precarious grip on the throne. The stability of the regime was dependent on the success and reputation of the prince. Traditionally, military victories remained an important means for a ruler to secure the allegiance of the great nobility.

dynastic state [margin annotation]

lands contested [margin annotation]

Innovations in warfare were also one of the reasons why war became endemic in the European system from the sixteenth century onwards. The advent of artillery and handguns resulted in far-reaching changes in the way in which war was waged. These changes are known in historiography under the name of the Military Revolution (sixteenth and seventeenth centuries). Armies became many times bigger. The armies of Charles V and Francis I – the most powerful monarchs of the early sixteenth century – numbered around 50,000. During the Thirty Years War, the greatest monarchs had around 150,000 men under arms. Around 1700, the army of Louis XIV (1643–1715) of France numbered in the order of 400,000. The monopoly of chivalry over professional warfare had been broken. This was the period of large mercenary armies. The introduction of artillery, the increase in the size of armies and the construction of large fortresses made warfare far more expensive. This had two major consequences. On the one hand, only the greater powers, such as the sovereigns of the larger countries, could field an efficient army. The feudal lords and smaller rulers were obliged to drop out or ally themselves to a greater power. On the other hand, the great princes found themselves in a vicious circle of internal centralisation and foreign conflicts. The high cost of war forced them to develop instruments efficiently to mobilise the human and material resources within their territories. To this end, a central bureaucracy and efficient taxation were crucial. This in turn resulted in revolts by the elite and the people, which the rulers were only able to suppress thanks to their large and expensive armies. Precisely this domestic necessity of a strong army made foreign wars more likely.

Fourth, there were the religious wars. The first great religious wars were also civil wars within certain countries. Apart from the wars in the empire during the reign of Charles V, there were the protracted conflicts in France (1562–98 and 1624–9) and the Eighty Years War in the Netherlands (1568–1648).

Fifth, during the sixteenth and early seventeenth century, various countries regularly fell victim to internal political conflicts. In many cases, this concerned revolts by the aristocracy, sometimes in alliance with the clergy or urban elites, against the attempts at centralisation by the rulers. On more than one occasion, political conflicts and religious wars were intertwined. Thus the wars between the German Protestants and the emperor or the Eighty Years War (1568–1648) between the Northern Netherlands and Spain were as much political as religious in nature.

262　The Thirty Years War and the Peace of Westphalia

All these wars and conflicts culminated after 1618 in a great, brutal and bloody war that was to hold central Europe in its grip for three decades: the Thirty Years War (1618–48). The war began as a political and religious conflict between, on the one hand, the Catholic emperor and a number of German Catholic princes and, on the other, various German Protestant princes. It coincided with the final stage of the struggle between the Protestant Northern Netherlands and the Spaniards (1621–48). Denmark (1625–1629), Sweden (1630–48) and finally France (1635–48) were drawn into the war. In its final stage, it evolved into a clash between the two leading great powers, France and Spain (1635–59). As had previously been the case with regard to Italy, control over Germany now became the object of the struggle for hegemony in Europe. Since the time of Charles V, France had been encircled on three sides by Habsburg dominions. Cost what it might, France wanted to prevent the emperors from gaining control over Germany and so tightening the Habsburg stranglehold.

The Peace Treaties of Westphalia of 1648 brought an end to the Thirty Years War in the empire and the Eighty Years War in the Netherlands. Under the Treaty of Munster of 30 January 1648, Philip IV of Spain renounced his claims to the eight rebel provinces in the Netherlands. In doing so, he recognised the political independence of the Republic of the United Provinces of the Northern Netherlands. The two peace treaties of 24 October 1648, signed in Munster and Osnabruck, put an end to the struggle between the various princes and cities within the Holy Roman Empire and sealed the peace between the Habsburg emperor and his allies, and France and Sweden. The war between France and Spain did not come to an end until the Treaty of the Pyrenees in 1659.

The peace treaties of 24 October 1648 ended the last great religious war in the Holy Roman Empire and western Europe. They involved a religious compromise under which the equality of the three great Christian religions – Catholicism, Lutheranism and Calvinism – and the principle of *cujus regio, ejus religio* were endorsed.[2] Differences in religion should no longer prevent princes from maintaining peaceful relations and provided no justification for war. The treaties contained some important constitutional arrangements and regulated the mutual rights

---

[2] Now, however, subject to the provision that a prince could no longer change the religion of his province, thus freezing the situation of 1624.

and obligations of the emperor, the 300-plus Estates (*Reichsstände*) represented in the Imperial Diet and the 1,500-plus members of the College of Imperial Knights. The estates preserved their right to establish military alliances with one another and with foreign powers, as long as these were not aimed at the empire and the emperor. The Thirty Years War and the Peace of Westphalia destroyed the chances of the Habsburg emperors to convert the empire into a centrally administered monarchy. The treaties, which became part of the constitution of the empire, confirmed the division of power. The Habsburg encirclement of France was punctured and, divided as it was, Germany was unable to constitute any threat to France or the other European powers. With the Treaty of the Pyrenees (1659), Spain acknowledged the superiority of France, which now became the leading power in Europe.

263   The significance of Westphalia

During the 1640s and 1650s, civil wars afflicted many of the major countries of Europe. Spain had to deal with revolts in Naples (1647), Catalonia (1640–53) and Portugal (1640–68), the last managing to gain independence. In France, there was the great Fronde (1649–53); in England there was the civil war that ended with the beheading of Charles I (1625–49) and the subsequent republic under Oliver Cromwell (1599–1658) from 1649. By around the year 1660, the great civil wars had come to an end. In most cases, they ended with the central government victorious. In England, the monarchy was restored in 1660 with Charles II (1660–85).

The years between 1640 and 1660 mark the end of a protracted period of international political crisis in western Europe, a transition that is best symbolised by the Peace of Westphalia. Contrary to what has been and is still held by many scholars, Westphalia did not lay the foundation for the modern law of nations.[3] It did, however, put an end to the long religious and political crisis within and among the great powers. For a full century, that crisis had prevented the emergence of a new legal order to replace the defunct *respublica christiana*. With the pacification of the empire at the political and religious levels, Westphalia helped create the relative stability that was required in order to develop a new, stable political system and a new legal order, that of the modern law of nations. The so-called 'Westphalian' order of the European system of sovereign states was laid out not at, but after Westphalia.

---

[3] Which in modern scholarship is, paradoxically, often also referred to as the classical law of nations.

5 Sovereignty in political thought

264 External and internal sovereignty

The political crisis into which the West was plunged around 1530 was structural. The entire legal edifice of the medieval order was torn down. In the absence of a new order, Europe found itself in a structural vacuum. It was not until after 1648 that the sovereign state became sufficiently formed to shore up a new, stable political and diplomatic order.

Sovereignty has two dimensions. First, there is external sovereignty, that is, the absence of any higher authority. The collapse of the *respublica christiana* around 1530 achieved this for most of the great monarchies and republics of Europe. Internal sovereignty presupposes that the sovereign ruler or sovereign body is the sole original source of law and public power. All other public institutions derive their authority from sovereign delegation. Both external and internal sovereignty may be seen in absolute or relative terms. Relative sovereignty applies only to certain powers and rights, absolute sovereignty to all powers and rights. Most European countries truly became internally sovereign only after the French Revolution. In many cases, however, a considerable level of internal sovereignty was attained after the great revolts of the mid-seventeenth century.

The rise of the modern sovereign state was a lengthy process which began during the Renaissance of the Twelfth Century and was only completed during the nineteenth century. It left the state an abstract, political entity that was both externally and internally sovereign. At its inception stood the medieval order of the *respublica christiana*: an amalgam of various political entities, ranging from the emperor and the pope with their claims to universal authority to the smallest rural fiefdoms. These all stood in a hierarchical relationship with one another. In that sense, the concept of external sovereignty employed by the medieval legal scholars was no more than relative. *Superiorem non recognoscens* was the ruler who, de facto if not de iure, acknowledged no higher authority. Every kingdom, dominion, bishopric, abbey, city or rural legal circle was by tradition subject to the two universal powers. Since imperial power had been conceived of as divided among the great kings of the West since the thirteenth century and the emperor's authority was no longer recognised outside the Holy Roman Empire, this left just the pope and the church as the overarching powers. Ranged above all the various legal systems was the one *ius commune*, of which only canon law could base its claims to universality on reality. The sixteenth century saw the collapse of the medieval system of *respublica christiana* and the start of a new age. First, the loss of religious unity around 1530 achieved absolute external sovereignty for the great princes and republics of Europe. Second, the schism in the church and the collapse of religious unity fostered the process of secularisation. Third, the 'state' broke free from the hierarchical continuum of political entities that had been the medieval order. The 'state' began to monopolise the most important elements of public power, being conceived as a unique and exceptional *corpus* or body politic, fundamentally different from all others. The emancipation of public law from ordinary law, which had already begun in medieval jurisprudence, now picked up speed. The state transcended the personal relations of allegiance that had dominated political reality in the Middle Ages. It established its exceptional character in a new doctrine, that of external and internal sovereignty.

265   The discourse of political thought

The crisis of the European political order in the early sixteenth century stimulated the intellectual debate on government and the relations between the sovereigns and rulers of Europe. Whereas before these themes had been covered in theological and juridical literature, political thought now began to grow into a discourse of its own, with its own literature. From 1600 onwards, public law broke free from the *ius commune*. Self-standing treatises on matters of internal public law or on the law of nations appeared. These developments did not mean that the entire legacy of theology and scholarly law was thrown overboard. The humanist authors of the Early Modern Age who wrote about politics and public law continued to refer to medieval literature. This did not, however, prevent them from elaborating their own discourse.

266   The Machiavellian provocation

The emancipation of political thought had various dimensions. One of these was secularisation. The Florentine diplomat and historian Niccolò Machiavelli (1469–1527) is one of the most controversial but also most frequently cited political thinkers in history. In his two most famous works, *Il principe* (*The Prince*) and the *Discorsi*,[4] Machiavelli analysed statecraft on the basis of Roman and recent history. In contrast to the writers of the medieval 'mirrors for princes', he did not present an ideal image of the virtuous ruler but outlined reality in all its rawness. The sharp, cynical portrayal elicited a considerable response. In the century and a half after the publication of his works, a mass of anti-Machiavellian writings

---

[4] A commentary on the first ten books of the work of Titus Livius.

appeared in Europe. The counter-reaction was unable to disguise the fact that with his work, Machiavelli had helped set the agenda for the early modern debate on politics and political morality. The anti-Machiavellian literature was in fact an ongoing, gradual retreat by generations of authors who wanted to salvage what they still could from the old medieval world, the foundations of which Machiavelli had shaken so fundamentally. In order to reconcile their 'morality' with the reality that Machiavelli had portrayed, they were, however, obliged to move ever closer to his way of thinking. However extreme Machiavelli's views may have appeared, they were little other than an unadorned and honest articulation of political reality setting out the extreme consequences of the new ideas concerning politics, law and society that were typical of the Renaissance and humanism. In that sense, Machiavelli was an extreme but also representative exponent of his age.

Like the humanists, Machiavelli breaks with the medieval approach to history. He regards history not as the fulfilment of the divine plan for mankind but as the sum total of human decisions and actions and the blows of fortune. Machiavelli distinguishes three forces that determine history. First of all, there is *necessità* (necessity). These are the given facts of the natural world and the world to which human beings are subject, but which are also known in advance. Second, there is *fortuna* and third, *virtù*. Traditionally, *virtù* meant moral virtue, but under Machiavelli's pen it comes to imply a resolute sense of purpose or effectiveness – referring to its etymological basis, manliness – in maintaining the state and remaining in power. *Virtù* presupposes that one takes account of necessity and enters it within one's calculations and decisions. Someone with a large amount of *virtù*, who makes proper preparations, is less susceptible to the vagaries of fortune than one who does not.[5] Machiavelli discerns a number

[5] 'I am not unaware that many have thought, and many still think, that the affairs of the world are so ruled by fortune and by God that the ability of men cannot control them. Rather, they think that we have no remedy at all; and therefore it could be concluded that it is useless to sweat much over things, but let them be governed by fate … Nevertheless, so as not to eliminate human freedom, I am disposed to hold that fortune is the arbiter of half our actions, but that it lets us control roughly the other half. I compare fortune to one of those dangerous rivers that, when they become enraged, flood the plains, destroy trees and buildings, move earth from one place and deposit it in another. Everyone flees before it, everyone gives way to its thrust, without being able to halt it in any way. But this does not mean that, when the river is not in flood, men are unable to take precautions, by means of dykes and dams, so that when it rises next time, it will either not overflow its banks, or, if it does, its force will not be so uncontrolled and damaging … I conclude then, that since circumstances vary and men when acting lack flexibility, they are successful if their methods match the circumstances and unsuccessful if they do not.' Niccolò Machiavelli,

of historical laws of human behaviour. It is useful to study the past, as it teaches us how people will behave in a certain situation.

For Machiavelli, a competent ruler is resolute, effective and morally flexible. Whereas the medieval authors in their mirrors for princes held up the image of a virtuous prince, Machiavelli in his *Il principe* holds up the image of a successful prince – a deliberate send-up of the genre. Not magnanimity, compassion or loyalty but decisiveness, resolution, flexibility and perspicacity are the qualities of the good prince. Genuine greatness does not lie in the observance of Christian morality but in spectacular deeds and, in particular, success.[6] Not morality but success itself is the criterion used by Machiavelli to distinguish good from bad policies. Power thus becomes its own purpose. The right of self-preservation is at the same time the highest right and highest duty of the prince, as it is for each individual. Politics no longer finds its legitimation in morality or in faith but in itself. It is the declaration of independence of politics.

In various places in his work, Machiavelli questions whether a ruler should observe morality (*bontà*, goodness) and uphold religion. The answer is that it is desirable for a ruler to respect the prevailing morality, and certainly to appear to do so. In this way, the ruler can avoid becoming hated. But where necessary to achieve his goals, morality may be brushed to one side. A ruler may, for example, break his word if that works out to his advantage. Agreements with rulers and treaties have relative value only.[7] Morality is instrumental, being at the service of politics and not vice versa. In the words of Machiavelli: 'a bad deed is excused by its result'.[8] Machiavelli also regards religion as an instrument of power. It is a means of keeping the populace calm and making them obey the laws and the rulers.

These attitudes towards history and politics were in direct opposition to the prevailing views in the Late Middle Ages. Machiavelli wrenched politics out of the grasp of the church and Christian morality, giving it its

Il principe 25, translation by Quentin Skinner and Russell Price, *Machiavelli: The Prince*, Cambridge 1988.

[6] 'I certainly think that it is better to be impetuous than cautious, because fortune is a woman, and if you want to control her, it is necessary to treat her roughly [literally, to beat and abuse her].' Machiavelli, *Il principe* 25.

[7] 'Everyone knows how praiseworthy it is for a ruler to keep his promises, and live uprightly and not by trickery. Nevertheless, experience shows that in our times the rulers who have done great things are those who have set little store by keeping their word, being skilful rather in cunningly confusing men; they have got the better of those who have relied on being trustworthy.' Machiavelli, *Il principe* 18.

[8] 'Conviene bene, che, accusandolo il fatto, lo effetto lo scusi': Machiavelli, *Discorsi* 1.9.

own finality and logic. In doing so, he took a step towards the total secu-larisation of politics. On his deathbed, Machiavelli related that he had had a dream, in which he had seen a procession of holy people on their way to heaven. In a second procession, on the way to hell, he saw the great political thinkers of Antiquity. Machiavelli said that he hoped he might be allowed to spend eternity with the second group – meaning that the aim of the politician was not heaven but earthly success.

Machiavelli did not so much develop his own political theory as describe the practices of the Romans and the rulers in the Italy of his own day whom he had observed as a historian and as a politician. He uncom-promisingly described the extreme consequences of a process of secular-isation that had got under way in the Late Middle Ages and reached full maturity in the Italian city-states of the fifteenth century. Machiavelli demonstrated to his contemporaries and succeeding generations the extreme implications that the collapse of the *respublica christiana* – then still in the future – and the crisis of the medieval legal and political system would have. However much he was opposed, his work marked an irre-versible step towards an autonomous, secular political discourse.

267   Jean Bodin

The French jurist Jean Bodin (1530–96) has been acclaimed the father of the modern concept of sovereignty. His most famous work, *Les six livres de la République* (1576), was published in the midst of the French Wars of Religion. Like Machiavelli, Bodin takes the view that only a strong ruler can bring peace and tranquillity; otherwise chaos and civil war loom. In his works, Machiavelli had a number of pointed things to say about the egotism, unreliability and violent tendencies of man. Bodin took a similarly negative view of human nature. His political doctrine too was designed to strengthen central power and to liberate it from all competi-tion. In contrast to Machiavelli, however, he did not seek a solution in the lifting of all moral or legal restrictions on the exercise of political power. His political doctrine legitimated the independence or sovereignty of the supreme state authority vis-à-vis foreign and domestic powers, without, however, eliminating all moral and legal barriers.

Bodin defines the concept of *souveraineté* as 'that absolute and per-petual power vested in a commonwealth'.[9] To some extent, he copies the

---

[9] 'La souveraineté est la puissance absoluë et perpétuelle d'une Republique.' Jean Bodin, *Les six livres de la République*, Paris 1576, 1.8, translation by M. J. Tooley, *Jean Bodin: Six Books of the Commonwealth*, Oxford 1967.

papal *plenitudo potestatis.* By 'absolute' he indicates that sovereign state power is bound neither internally nor externally to a higher or different authority. Bodin fleshes out the concept of internal sovereignty, distinguishing a number of powers or competencies of the state that form part of the *merum imperium* of the sovereign. The concept of *merum imperium* stems from medieval jurisprudence. It means original, undelegated power. That power is consequently inalienable. According to Bodin, the *merum imperium* of the sovereign includes the appointment of ministers, legislation, the declaration and termination of war, supreme jurisdiction and the power to grant pardon for capital crimes.[10] The sovereign may delegate the exercise of those specific powers to other officials, but they can never have it on their own account. Other powers may belong originally to subordinate magistrates. With this, Bodin does not go as far as the humanist jurist Andreas Alciatus (1492–1550), who considers that all public power stems originally from the sovereign. In a material sense, internal sovereignty for Bodin is not absolute but relative: it should apply only to the essential state powers indicated.

Bodin associates the terms 'republic' – to be understood as commonwealth – and 'sovereignty' with one another. Only the republic is sovereign and only a sovereign entity is a republic. Furthermore, like sovereignty, the republic is everlasting. The 'sovereign state' consequently breaks loose from the amalgam of political entities, ranging from the *respublica christiana* through kingdoms, principalities, city-republics, ecclesiastical territories, seigniories to the smallest villages and hamlets, thereby obtaining its own, unique character. The 'state' no longer occupies a place within the hierarchical continuum of entities all of which hold and exercise an element of the *imperium* or public power, but sets itself up independently as the sole source of true 'sovereign' power. The other entities must disappear as bearers of sovereign power and be subjected to the 'state'. The state is conceived of as perpetual and transcends the person of the ruler himself. It is not the sum total of all legal relations between the rulers and his subjects, but is a transcendent and autonomous body politic. Bodin is often cited in historiography as one of the forefathers of royal absolutism on the basis of his doctrine of the indivisibility of sovereign state power. In fact, Bodin did not consider sovereign power to be indivisible; this is largely a reinterpretation. Bodin does not defend the proposition that all

---

[10] Jean Bodin, *Methodus at facilem historiarum cognitionem* (1566), ed. Pierre Mesnard, *Oeuvres philosophiques de Jean Bodin*, Paris 1951, 174–5; see also *Les six livres de la République* 1.10.

state power springs from a single source or that the sovereign powers are at all times exercised by a single sovereign body. He does not in any way rule out the ability of the sovereign to delegate part of his power. His doctrine fits in perfectly with the efforts by the great princes of his age to monopolise the most important powers of state and to eliminate the independent power of the church, the great vassals and the cities in key areas of foreign policy and domestic administration. Bodin supports them in this aim because he thinks that the division of sovereign power leads to civil war and internal unrest.

Bodin also takes up the debate initiated by the medieval jurists on the subjection of the prince to the law. Here too, he refrains from taking an extreme, absolutist stance. According to Bodin, the sovereign is *legibus (ab)solutus* in the sense that he may amend the laws and is not personally bound by them – a position that was already held by certain medieval jurists. The prince is, however, bound by a number of fundamental laws. He is subject to the rules of divine and natural law – such as the inviolability of private property – to the law of nations and to *les lois impériales*, the fundamental constitutional rules of the realm. The prince must honour his agreements, including those with his subjects. Many medieval ideas on the limitation of sovereign power are preserved in Bodin.

Bodin links up with the tradition of contractual power going back to medieval canon law and the practice of the quasi-constitutional texts. This tradition obtained a new currency in the course of the sixteenth century in the theories on the right to resistance – the resistance of the people against the unlawful or unjust actions of the prince. This was a right that Calvinism, in particular, defended. The contractual basis for government authority and the duty on the part of the sovereign to abide by his agreements with his subjects was one of the angles from which the right to resistance was defended.

268   Suarez

Bodin and the great Protestant political thinkers of the sixteenth and seventeenth centuries such as the French scholar François Hotman (1524–90) were greatly influenced by humanism. On the Catholic side, the scholastic tradition remained well represented. During the course of the sixteenth century, scholasticism went through a renewal thanks to the endeavours of some Spanish theologians, civilians and canonists: the so-called second scholastic or neo-scholasticism. The Jesuit Francisco Suarez (1548–1617) was among the most influential political thinkers of this movement. His writings influenced Hugo Grotius (1583–1645).

In the wake of Aristotle and Thomas Aquinas, Suarez recognises that people have a natural inclination to organise themselves into political communities subject to a political power. The existence of the *polis* (meaning here the political community) and the exercise of power by the ruler find their legitimisation in nature itself. The ruler receives his power through a delegation from the people. According to Suarez, this delegation is necessitated by nature. According to other neo-scholastics such as Juan de Mariana (1536–1624), it is the outcome of a choice freely made by the people. Delegation in that case marks the transition from the natural state to the political state. The rule of natural law is replaced by that of positive (that is, man-made) law. For Suarez, the natural and political states coexist. However, under both variants of contract theory – that of natural law and that of positive law – the origin of state power lies with the people and each individual citizen. As the creator of nature, God is the ultimate source of state power, but the ruler has not received his power directly from God. Suarez nevertheless regards the transfer of power from the people to the ruler as irrevocable, although that does not eliminate the ability of the people to rebel if the ruler's deeds threaten the existence of the people and the state. Other forms of bad government the people have to put up with. Sovereign power is not absolute, but at the same time the people do not have the right continually to judge the sovereign. Only in extreme circumstances can the sovereign be called to a halt. The positive law variant of contract theory leaves greater freedom in determining the details of the contract, including the right of resistance.

As Bodin, Suarez presented a doctrine that strengthened the position of the sovereign rulers but nevertheless imposed limitations on the unbridled exercise of royal authority. The vast majority of political thinkers in the sixteenth and seventeenth centuries recognised the sovereign to be bound to higher norms and laws, such as divine or natural law, or the fundamental laws of the realm. But there was far less consensus when it came to the question of how this subordination had to be imposed. In fact, most writers did not acknowledge the existence of any external enforcement mechanisms to induce the prince to abide by the higher laws, putting all trust in the prince's conscience. In this respect, it may be said that in various countries the control by the estates over the sovereign was weakened and that doctrine followed suit. Nevertheless, there is no question of absolutism in the strict sense of the word within the main currents of political thought in the sixteenth and early seventeenth century.

6 The emergence of the law of nations

269 Medieval *ius gentium*

During the Middle Ages, the law of nations did not exist as an autonomous body of law. The rules which regulated the mutual relations of princes and republics were part of the law at large. The medieval law of nations (*ius gentium*) drew on a plurality of sources, including custom, feudal law and the learned *ius commune*.[11]

As there was as yet no sovereign state, which monopolised its external relations, set apart from other categories of bodies politic, there was no need for an autonomous law of nations that applied exclusively to this one category. The personal dimension in public authority made it natural to apply rules of private law to the relations between rulers. Thus treaty law was to a large extent a particular form of contract law.

The *ius commune* in general and canon law in particular were not only sources of inspiration for the *ius gentium*; they also gave it legitimacy. Both had 'universal' authority in theory; canon law also held it in reality. The universal jurisdiction of the ecclesiastical and above all the papal courts provided the *ius gentium* with an enforcement mechanism.

270 The crisis of the international legal order

The second quarter of the sixteenth century saw the collapse of the old political and legal order of the Latin West. The Reformation caused around half of Europe to reject the authority of the pope, the ecclesiastical courts and canon law, knocking away the common foundations on which the authority of the *ius gentium* rested. The gradual 'nationalisation' of civil jurisprudence eroded its relevance as a common source of authority as well. The discoveries and colonisation outside Europe set another challenge to the existing legal order. The old *ius gentium*, the authority of which was derived from Roman and canon law, was impractical for relations with indigenous peoples who were neither Christian nor Roman. The emergence of externally sovereign powers put yet another strain on the old *ius gentium* that partook in the *ius commune* and was based on a conception of order as a hierarchical continuum of bodies politic.

Halfway through the sixteenth century, it became clear Europe needed a new law which would embrace relations with the non-European world and regulate relations between fully fledged sovereigns of different

---

[11] As of the Middle Ages, the term *ius gentium* came to be used to refer to the law regulating the relations between independent powers.

religions. The political and religious divisions in Europe delayed the articulation of that new law for a century. Not until the Peace of Westphalia was there sufficient stability to provide the basis for a new law of nations. This then became the modern law of nations. It was premised on the principle of state sovereignty and was designed to regulate the relations between externally and internally sovereign states. The modern law of nations could only be articulated once the internally sovereign state was sufficiently in place. In most parts of Europe, this was only after the age of great rebellions had ended, around 1660. Between the collapse of the *respublica christiana* with the achievement of external sovereignty (1530) and the emergence of the internally sovereign state (1660) lay a period of great turmoil. During this time, the West lacked a common and stable legal order.

271   Francisco de Vitoria

The crisis stimulated intellectual debate on international relations and the *ius gentium* in the course of the sixteenth and seventeenth centuries. The Spanish neo-scholastics made a significant contribution. Foremost among them were Francisco Suarez and the Dominican theologian Francisco de Vitoria (c.1480–1546) of the University of Salamanca.

Vitoria and the other neo-scholastics assign a central place to natural law. As human nature is universal – now to be understood in the true sense of the word – so is natural law. It provides a basis for regulating the relations between peoples from different religions, ethnic origins and legal systems. To Vitoria, natural law applies universally but still, it is not completely secular. Medieval theologians commonly held to the view that, as God had created human nature, only true Christians could correctly understand it. Vitoria still attributes a special role to the church in declaring what the precepts of natural law are.

Vitoria distinguishes *ius gentium* from natural law. According to Vitoria, there are two kinds of law of nations, one natural and one human. The natural law of nations is derived from the rules of natural law. The source of the human law of nations is the *consensus maioris partis totius orbis* (the consent among the greater part of the world).[12] It finds its basis in the consent among the peoples but must nevertheless always be in accordance with natural law.

Vitoria rejects the universal authority of the pope and the emperor. Outside Christianity or the empire, they do not have any positive legal

---

[12] Francisco de Vitoria, *Relectio de Indis* 3.1.8, ed. and translation in Anthony Pagden and Jeremy Lawrance, *Vitoria: Political Writings*, Cambridge 1991.

authority, especially in relation to unbelievers. Vitoria recognises the political communities of the indigenous peoples in America as *communitates perfectae* in the sense of autonomous bodies politic. Like the Christian communities, these communities have their origin in human nature and natural law. Their political institutions hold public authority and can, therefore, not be pushed aside by the Europeans. As such, the Christian explorers cannot simply lay claim to their territories. Natural law guarantees the same natural rights to the pagans as to the Christians. This did not, however, prevent Vitoria and the other neo-scholastic thinkers ultimately justifying the Spanish and Portuguese conquests in the New World.

272   Hugo Grotius

Apart from the neo-scholastics, several civilians made their contribution to the articulation of the modern law of nations. The Italian jurist Albericus Gentilis (1552–1608), who became Regius professor of civil law at Oxford, deserves to be mentioned here. Like other civilians writing on the subject, he was heavily influenced by humanist political thought and jurisprudence.

The same went for the Dutch humanist Hugo Grotius (1583–1645), who also drew on the works of the neo-scholastics. His *De Iure Belli ac Pacis libri tres (Three Books on the Law of War and Peace)* (1625) is traditionally regarded as the first autonomous and comprehensive treatise on the laws of nations. It conferred on Grotius the title of 'father of modern international law' – a paternity that is increasingly contested. At any event Grotius's book was the standard work in the field for more than a century, relegating its predecessors to the shadows.

Grotius too distinguishes the law of nations from natural law. Natural law is universal and immutable. In the celebrated passage 'Etiamsi daremus non esse Deum' from the *Prolegomena* to his *De Iure Belli ac Pacis*, the Dutch humanist indicates that natural law applies and is intelligible to all peoples, irrespective of their faith. In doing so, he breaks away, more explicitly than Vitoria, from medieval natural law, which was primarily Christian.[13] Grotius also draws a distinction between a natural (*ius gentium primarium*) and a human or positive law of nations (*ius gentium secundarium*). The latter consists of customs and treaties. Both are

---

[13] 'What we have been saying would have a degree of validity even if we should concede that which cannot be conceded without the utmost wickedness, that there is no God ...' *Prolegomena* 11, translation by Francis W. Kelsey, *Hugo Grotius: On the Law of War and Peace*, Classics of International Law, Oxford and London 1925.

founded on consent – expressly in treaties or tacitly in custom – among sovereigns. Despite the fact that they recognise no higher authority, sovereigns are bound by their agreements. *Pacta sunt servanda*, the duty to stand by your agreements, is a precept of natural law to which everyone is subject. With this, Grotius provides a basis for a binding legal system governing the relations between sovereigns. With this, he answers the Machiavellian provocation.

7   The rise of the dynastic state

273   The dynastic state

In the transformation of the medieval order to that of the modern, sovereign state, the sixteenth and early seventeenth century form an era of transition. The Reformation brought an end to the universal authority of the pope and of canon law in temporal matters. By the 1530s, the great princes and republics of Europe, first the Protestant and somewhat later the Catholic, shed the last vestiges of the papal authority in temporal matters and thus achieved absolute, external sovereignty. Thereby, they broke free from the hierarchical continuum that had been the *respublica christiana* and transformed themselves into a unique sort of body politic, essentially different from all others. In many cases the process of state formation went hand in hand with territorial expansion. With few exceptions, the successful states were dynastic power complexes.

274   Exclusion and inclusion of the aristocracy

The true realisation of the modern dynastic state presupposes the achievement of, if not absolute, then at least far-reaching relative internal sovereignty through a process of centralisation and monopolisation of power. Jean Bodin's doctrine effectively catches the historical evolution in this respect. In most dynastic states, the process of centralisation took place at two levels – national and local – and at two speeds. At the national level, the sovereigns sought to monopolise the most important powers of state. As Bodin had indicated, this concerned the conduct of war, foreign relations, legislation and supreme jurisdiction. The autonomy of the nobility, the church and the towns was broken in these areas. The great vassals and prelates were no longer permitted to conduct an independent foreign policy or to wage war against one another. The sovereign attempted to minimise the input of the estates in legislation. The role of the royal courts as appellate or supreme courts was expanded, although it should be noted that in many countries the royal courts themselves became centres of opposition towards the king.

The monopolisation of sovereign state power by the ruler at the national level did not mean that the nobility, clergy and top layer of the third estate could be totally banned from national governance. The rulers sought as far as possible to secure the loyalty of their most powerful and most notable subjects. Their elimination as independent, competing sources of power was made possible only by their inclusion in government. The feudal nobles lost their military autonomy but returned as officers in the royal army. Senior offices in government and, even more so, at the royal courts were assigned to the leading members of the three estates.

275   Royal power

As in the Middle Ages, the prince was the heart of the whole governmental apparatus. Royal authority rested on various traditions. Sovereign power was in the first place based on the acceptance by and consent of the leading classes, that is, the three estates. The prince was the supreme knight and the military leader of the country, for which reason the personal reputation of the sovereign as commander of the army and defender of his realm remained highly important. He was the feudal suzerain. He was the secular protector of the church. Outside the Holy Roman Empire, most of the princes in Europe – who had less to fear from papal claims to supremacy – had not renounced the divine legitimisation of their power. The king was the Lord's anointed. In various countries, such as France, the prince was also believed to have sacred or miraculous powers. Above all, however, princes increasingly identified with the realm. The sovereign prince was no ordinary liege or bearer of political rights and obligations like so many others. He was the embodiment of public authority and accordingly escaped the normal networks of allegiance characteristic of the old political order. The Roman law tradition of imperial power remained of significance for the formation of this modern conception of state, public law and kingship. As *rex imperator in regno suo* the king was the successor of the Roman emperors in his realm. The Roman emperorship provided a model for strong kingship. The notions of emperor and empire obtained different connotations from those under the great German emperors of the Middle Ages. The concept of 'empire' lost its dimension of universality. The 'empire' no longer encompassed the entire Latin West but only the sphere of influence of a particular ruler. The terms 'empire' and 'emperor' did, however, retain the meaning of dominion over various peoples or countries at once. The notions of empire and emperor were used in order to legitimate the power of a single ruler over various peoples and to consolidate the unity of that 'empire'. Spain, France and England all referred to themselves as 'empires'. The terms were also used for the establishment of the colonial empires outside Europe. Modern imperialism was at hand.

276   Court and government

Royal courts played an instrumental role in the centralisation of power within the dynastic state. Kings no longer constantly travelled about but established themselves in or in the vicinity of the capital. Philip II built a new capital in Madrid, setting up his court in the nearby Escorial. The French kings too gave up their itinerant existence in the course of the sixteenth century and provided the government with a permanent seat in or near Paris. The royal courts were not just the seat of government but also the place where the king gathered his most important subjects around him. The ruler would secure the loyalty of the leading notables through patronage. Court culture became the model for a new type of relationship between the ruler and his subjects. The relationship was no longer that of feudalism, whereby liege and vassal entered into reciprocal legal obligations with one another; instead it was an informal *patronus–cliens* relationship. The king was the patron, showering his nobles with honours and gifts as and when he saw fit. The highest honour for a peer was to be appointed as chamberlain in the king's household. Court offices provided access to the ruler and to more favours, for both the noble himself and for his clients. Direct or indirect access to the king became the stepping stone to wealth and power. Whoever controlled the channels to the king governed the land. But that was a prize which was made hard to attain. A complicated and strict court ceremonial elevated the ruler far above his subjects and widened the gap between him and the leading nobility. In this way, the royal court was turned into an arena where the greatest nobles vied with one another for royal favour, thus serving the king's ultimate purpose of keeping them in check.

The gathering of his most important subjects at court was coupled with a movement to separate the real work of government from the court and to keep the courtiers away from real power. On the fringes of or outside the court, there arose a network of government councils and secretariats where policy was made. The only individuals who could move freely from the court to the government and back again were the prince and his most important confidants or ministers. Some kings, such as Philip II in Spain and Elizabeth I in England, maintained personal control over the process of government. Others, such as Philip III and Philip IV in Spain or Louis XIII (1610–43) in France, confined themselves to their role at the court and left the process of government to a kind of prime minister, such as the Duke of Lerma (1553–1625) and the Count-Duke of Olivares (1587–1645) in Spain or Cardinal Richelieu (1585–1642) and Cardinal Mazarin (1602–61) in France. Apart from a general council, various other councils were set up. These eroded the power of the former central council in which the leading nobility and clergy were generally strongly represented. Often a small, limited council with direct access to the ruler was established that concerned itself primarily with foreign policy. In England that was the Privy Council, and in France the Conseil des Affaires. Separate, specialist councils were set up for the governance of certain parts of the kingdom or for certain subjects. These bodies advised the monarch or his main minister and proposed decisions. The monarch or his main minister would then approve or reject them. Apart from the councils, there were secretaries of state and ministers who presided over the royal bureaucracy, controlled the agenda for the king and the councils, and prepared the documents. The king increasingly selected his top councillors and ministers himself, from the aristocracy, the church or the upper middle classes as he saw fit. The term minister was well chosen: they were servants of the prince, who were made, elevated and if necessary brought low again by the prince.

277   The decline of dualism

In the course of the sixteenth and especially the seventeenth century, the role of the estates at the national level was curtailed. In the great monarchies of Europe, the rulers sought to govern without the estates or the parliament. This meant that financially they had to get by on their ordinary incomes. In some countries, such as France, the general assembly of the estates was not convened for a long time (between 1614 and 1789), although a smaller assembly of the highest notables (Assemblée des Notables) was sometimes called. In several countries, princes also managed to legislate without real consultation of the estates.

278   Local administration

At the local level there was far less, if any, question of monopolisation of public authority by the prince and central government. Local and provincial public authority did not derive exclusively from the sovereign: feudal lords, ecclesiastical princes and even towns and corporations had their own jurisdiction and authority, which stemmed only in part if at all from sovereign delegation. The process of centralisation at these levels was gradual and took the form of co-operation between the prince and the local notables. The sovereigns were unable to eliminate or break local administrations and could only infiltrate them or secure their loyalty through patronage. From a pragmatic viewpoint, that was indeed the most sensible option. In the light of the limited possibilities for transport and communication, the fragmentation of local authority over all sorts of differing structures made it possible for the elite and the government to exercise a much tighter grip over the country than would have been possible for a single centralised government. It was preferable to infiltrate this network and try to take it over than to make efforts to destroy it and replace it. Where this did not achieve sufficient results, the central government sought to engage with the competition by sending its own, centrally appointed officials to the provinces and towns. The *intendants* appointed by Louis XIV (1643–1715) in the provinces, in addition to the existing governors, form an example thereof. They too, however, were obliged to co-operate with the existing administrations. Lower and ordinary jurisdiction often remained with the nobility, the clergy and the local institutions such as town councils and aldermen's benches. In most countries, such as France and Spain, taxation was not centrally administered and different rules applied in different parts of the kingdom. Tax farming applied virtually everywhere, with the exception of England. Under this system, private financiers would advance the taxes for a certain area to the ruler, then collect the revenues themselves from the taxpayers. This led to abuse and reduced governmental control. More generally, the rulers had no success, not even in Spain or France, in harmonising regional and local structures. Spain remained a personal union of various kingdoms, while France remained an amalgam of various categories of provinces and legal jurisdictions each subject to its own rules and subject to the crown in various ways.

279   The myth of absolutism

The dynastic state is sometimes described as absolutist. The term absolutism suggests that the sovereign power was unlimited, but in reality this was not the case. First, the prince was required to heed the local elites. The plurality of the law and the diversity of political organisation throughout the realm set limits to the efficiency of central government. Second, while it was possible to clip the wings of the nobility and higher clergy as national power brokers, they were not entirely subjugated. Their inclusion and the conflict and political compromise that went along with it was the price for their allegiance to the crown. Reference has already been made to the great rebellions of the mid seventeenth century. These were often prompted by resistance on the part of the elite to royal centralising policies. The system did, however, also provide for legitimate brakes on sovereign power. In France, there was the rule that the monarch should abide by the fundamental laws of the kingdom, as expressly recognised by Louis XV (1715–74). The highest courts, the Parlements, arrogated the role of custodians of the law and customs of France, by reserving the right to refuse registration of the king's legislation, thereby preventing it from coming into force.

In this regard, it should be noted that the person and personality of the prince – or of his prime minister – were of the utmost importance for the success of government. The entire apparatus was built around the prince and owed its legitimisation to him. A strong government and strong state needed a strong monarch. The great princes of the sixteenth and seventeenth centuries were forceful personalities and hard workers. Charles V, Francis I, Philip II and later Louis XIV are the most notable examples. A weak or under-age ruler who, furthermore, was unable to rely on a strong prime minister, was apt to lead to political instability and the weakening of central government. Examples include the rule of the lazy Philip III of Spain or the under-age Louis XIII, who came to the throne at the age of nine.

280   Religious unity

Unity of faith was instrumental to the success of the dynastic state: the Reformation led not just to religious division but also to political tensions. The rulers sought to use faith as an element of national unity, particularly since there was little if any cultural or linguistic homogeneity in most of the great monarchies. People identified with their village, town, city or at most region in which they lived. For many centuries, religion had been virtually the sole reality of daily life which bound people together over the borders of their local village or town. The idea that there could be various religions and churches was unwelcome and cut across the desire for unity and centralisation. Now that the independent political power of the church had declined, it could once again be used by the rulers as an instrument of power.

281   The dynamics of state formation

The process of centralisation fed on itself. Centralisation increased the ability of the ruler to mobilise the human and material resources of his realm. This made the sovereign ever more powerful and increasingly elevated him above his domestic competitors. This in turn led to greater centralisation. The result of the process was that a large part of the resources came to be controlled by a single bureaucracy. It is precisely this that explains the huge dynamic exerted in the Modern Age by the states in Europe at the domestic, diplomatic, military, economic and colonial level. In most of the great countries of Europe, centralisation had, after the period of the great revolts in the mid-seventeenth century, reached the point where we may refer to internal sovereignty. The central – generally monarchical – government had acquired a quasi-monopoly over the waging of war, foreign policy and national legislation. The aristocracy, the church and the cities remained a factor within the central government but, at least at national level, were no longer able to make a stand against it.

282   Italy

Until the French Revolution, as king of the *regnum Italiae*, the emperor of the Holy Roman Empire was the suzerain of the northern Italian princes and city-republics. However, his effective power south of the Alps was very limited. The *regnum* had no central government and the emperor was not involved in the day-to-day administration of its various parts. His suzerainty served mainly to legitimate Habsburg military expeditions and political interventions in the peninsula. Thus Charles V used his position as emperor in order to bestow the Duchy of Milan, to which both his family and that of the French king laid claim, on his son Philip II (1540).

Italy consisted of a patchwork of several dozen principalities and city-republics. Five of these powers dominated the peninsula: the Papal State, the kingdom of Naples, the Duchy of Milan and the republics of Venice and Florence. After a protracted series of wars, and particularly in response to the Turkish threat, these five concluded the Treaty of Lodi in 1454. With a number of minor interruptions, the peace held for forty years. During this time, the balance of power between the big five was preserved at the initiative of Lorenzo il Magnifico dei Medici, the strong man of Florence (1469–92). This process, which was to inspire later thinkers to formulate the doctrine of the balance of power, implied that continually changing coalitions were needed to prevent one or more players from gaining hegemony. Hegemony is achieved if one power within a certain system – like the Italian states system – becomes stronger than any likely coalition of opponents put together. In the background the fear lurked that one of the Italian states, if it felt threatened, might seek foreign intervention, for example by France, Spain or the emperor, and that Italy would be trampled underfoot.

Two years after the death of Lorenzo this fear was realised. At the invitation of the Duke of Milan, Ludovico il Moro Sforza (1452–1508), Charles VIII of France invaded Italy (1494). His objective was to conquer the kingdom of Naples to which the French royal dynasty laid claim. Through the maternal line of the house of Orleans-Valois to which they belonged, Charles's successors Louis XII and Francis I had also had a claim on Milan. The French invasion induced Ferdinand of Aragon, who was also a pretender to the throne of Naples, to react. In the protracted conflict between France and Aragon/Spain, ruled since 1516 by Charles V, the latter emerged as victor in 1530. Naples fell into the hands of Charles V and his Spanish successors; in 1540 Milan also became a Habsburg possession. From 1530 to 1713 Spain held hegemony over Italy. The other principalities retained their internal autonomy but were incapable of conducting an independent foreign policy, with the exception of the Papal State, Venice and, to a lesser extent, Savoy.

The revival of interest in Antiquity that occurred with the Italian Renaissance and humanism had a strong political dimension to it. In the Florentine Republic and elsewhere, humanist scholars referred to the Roman Republic as a model for their own republican ideals. Republican humanism, known as civic humanism, had its peak during the early fifteenth century, but its roots stretched back in time as far as the late thirteenth century. As the Medici, a powerful banking family, strengthened their grip over the Florentine Republic and became, as from 1434 with Cosimo the Elder (1434–64), its effective rulers, the republican dimension of humanism was scaled down. In 1494, in the wake of the French invasion, the Medici fell from power and were expelled from Florence. The republic was restored (1494–1512). It was in this republican government that Machiavelli played an important political role. But thanks to the election of two Medici cardinals as pope – Leo X and Clemens VII – the Medici were able to restore their control over the city. With the consent of Charles V, the Medici transformed the Republic of Florence in 1532 into the Duchy and later Grand Duchy of Tuscany. Another large republic, Siena, was incorporated in 1559. The republican ideal of early humanism gave way to the sovereign model. Venice and the Swiss Confederation did survive as republics.

283   France: from Valois to Bourbon

After its victory in the Hundred Years War, the Valois dynasty restored its grip on France. Louis XI (1461–83) systematically expanded the royal domain. Anjou, Provence, Picardy and even the Duchy of Burgundy (1477) were united with the crown. The coming to power of the house of Orleans with Louis XII and Francis I brought their lands also under the king. Brittany fell to the crown through marriage. The revolt by the Duke of Bourbon (1525) provided Francis I with the excuse to confiscate the huge territorial complex of the house of Bourbon in central France.

The central governmental apparatus was expanded. The Grand Conseil – the successor of the *curia regis* – lost its political functions and continued as a court of law. Apart from a number of cases in first instance, the council handled appeals against the parliaments. The number of its members was fixed and a permanent residence built. As early as 1484, the Conseil Etroit was split off from the Grand Conseil, becoming the true royal council. Established in order to assist the underage Charles VIII, the Conseil Etroit included the princes of the blood and a number of high-ranking members of the nobility and the clergy. In the 1520s, Francis I set up a Conseil Privé for administrative affairs and taxation. After 1550, the Conseil Etroit evolved into a council fashioned by the king in order to provide him with personal advice on foreign policy and the great political issues of the day. At that time, it became known as the Conseil des Affaires.

Religious wars and dynastic crises held back the further extension of royal power in the second half of the sixteenth century. After the death of Henry II (1547–59), three of his sons succeeded one another in quick succession: Francis II (1559–61), Charles IX (1561–74) and Henry III (1574–89). They were all weak figures who were dominated by their mother, Catherine de Medici (1519–89), and became the playthings of the warring factions among the leading nobility and religious denominations. Between 1563 and 1598, the country was plagued by a series of bloody wars of religion that deprived France of its ability to act as one of the great powers of Europe.

The death of the childless Henry III brought his distant cousin, Henry of Bourbon-Navarre, leader of the Huguenots, to the throne. Henry IV (1589–1610) was required to fight a protracted civil war and furthermore had to contend with an intervention by Spain, which aimed at preventing a Protestant from ascending the throne in France. Henry IV converted to Catholicism – giving expression to his pragmatic motives with the words 'Paris vaut bien une messe' – and secured internal peace. The war with Spain came to an end in 1598 with the Peace of Vervins. The same year, Henry IV promulgated the Edict of Nantes granting religious freedom to the Huguenots. As a guarantee against fresh persecution, the

Huguenots were given a number of fortified towns, such as La Rochelle. In 1629, Cardinal Richelieu broke the independent political power of the Huguenots by seizing that town. In 1685, Louis XIV revoked the Edict of Nantes, bringing to an end the tolerance displayed towards the Protestants. This was the latest triumph of the ideology of unity of faith: 'un roi, une loi, une foi'.

With the accession of Henry IV, the process of centralisation was resumed. Under Cardinal Richelieu and Cardinal Mazarin, the independent military power of the nobility, the clergy and the Protestants was broken for good. Royal hold over the local and provincial administrations was gradually strengthened and taxes increased. The Fronde (1649–53) was the last great attempt by the nobility, church and upper classes to turn the tide through the use of force. Upon the death of Mazarin and the assumption of power by the now of-age Louis XIV (1661), the monarchy in France was genuinely sovereign, in the sense that Bodin would have understood the term. Under Cardinal Richelieu's ministry (1624–1642), France assumed its role in Europe as a counterweight to Spain.

284 France: *parlements*

The establishment of sovereign monarchy severely undercut dualism in France, at least at the national level. At the provincial level, the estates (*les États*) continued to play a role, but at the national level, they disappeared. The first Estates-General (*les États-Généraux*) were convened as early as the fourteenth century. The fact that they had, in co-operation with the provincial states, transferred much of their fiscal power to the sovereign meant that they were convened less frequently after 1450 and never achieved the significance Parliament had in England. During the religious wars, the Estates-General met more frequently, but even so were unable to take advantage of the weakness of the monarchy. The last Estates-General before the French Revolution met in 1614, during the minority of Louis XIII. The monarchy then managed to govern for 175 years without calling a meeting of the estates at national level. In their stead, an Assemblée des Notables was convened from time to time. This was dominated by the nobility.

The strongest institutional opponents of the king were no longer the estates but the highest courts, the various *parlements* such as those of Paris, Rouen, Bordeaux, Dijon or Toulouse. The members of the *parlements* formed virtually the top layer of the *noblesse de robe*, that is, the most senior members of the legal profession who had penetrated the ranks of the aristocracy and whose magistracies often passed from father to son.

The *parlements* acted as courts of appeal and had a strong grip over the lower courts, regarding themselves as the custodians of the laws and customs. They supervised compliance by all – including the sovereign – with the fundamental laws of the kingdom, such as the rules of succession, the inviolability of the royal domain and respect for private property. The *parlements* had the right of remonstration. The king was the legislator, but before his statutes could enter into force they had to be registered by the *parlements*. The councillors could refuse to do so if the statute contravened fundamental law and could propose amendments. The king could respond to the amendments or could come to the *parlement* himself, take up his place on the *lit de justice*, and order that registration proceed. The *parlement* was, after all, his court, having been split off from the royal council under Louis IX. The evolution of the *parlements* is just one example of how royal institutions went their own way and how they could evolve from instruments of sovereign power into brakes on that power.

285   Spain: the Catholic Kings to the Habsburgs

At the end of the Middle Ages, the Iberian peninsula consisted of five kingdoms: Castile, Aragon, Navarre, Portugal and Islamic Granada (*al-Andalus*). Through the marriage of Ferdinand of Aragon and Isabella of Castile, the Catholic Kings, the two most important kingdoms formed a union (1474). Although from the sixteenth century onwards, the name 'Spain' was often used, it remained in essence a personal union between Castile and the various regions of which Aragon consisted (Aragon, Catalonia, Valencia, Sardinia, Sicily and later Naples). In 1492, Granada was conquered, and in 1512, Navarre south of the Pyrenees. Between 1580 and 1640, Portugal was united to the Spanish crowns through a personal union.

Through the marriage of the heir to Ferdinand and Isabella, Joanna the Mad (1479–1555), with Philip the Fair (1478–1506), son of the Emperor Maximilian of Habsburg (1477–1482) and Mary of Burgundy and himself lord of the Burgundian Netherlands (1482–1506), the Spanish territories ended up in Habsburg hands in 1516 upon the death of Ferdinand. By 1519, Charles V, son of Philip and Joanna, was King of Castile, Aragon, Sardinia and Sicily, Archduke of Austria and ruler of the Burgundian Netherlands. To these, his brother Ferdinand I (1530–64) added Bohemia and the crown of Hungary. In Italy, Naples and Milan were subjugated, while in America, Mexico and Peru were conquered. After the abdication by Charles V, under which he left the dominions around Austria and the imperial throne to his brother, Spain and King Philip II remained the true centre of Habsburg power.

286 Habsburg Spain and its empire

The Catholic Kings Ferdinand and Isabella and their Habsburg successors conducted a policy of centralisation. The Habsburgs did not succeed in forging their various possessions into a single state. In strict legal terms, the Habsburg complex remained a personal union in which the sole factor of unity was the monarch. It was, however, perceived as something more than that: the Spanish–Habsburg complex became an *imperium* or empire. The new concept of empire rejected the ideal of universality of the Middle Ages: the empire brought together various kingdoms under one prince. From the beginning, the Spanish–Habsburg sovereigns were advised by one royal council and by the same ministers for the administration of all their territories. This *curia regis* evolved into a 'central government' for the entire empire. Under Philip II and his successors, the Consejo de Estado, the Council of state of Castile, became the main advisory body for the great political affairs of the Spanish–Habsburg Empire. Supporting this central council was a network of further councils with responsibility for the various territories (Aragon, Italy, the Netherlands, Portugal and the Indies) or for certain subjects, such as the waging of war, the Inquisition and public finances. In addition to the councils, there were *juntas* in which some important councillors and ministers debated on a particular issue. The councils and *juntas* produced a stream of *consultas* (recommendations) that were submitted to the king or his *valido* (favourite and prime minister). All this did not, however, lead to the transformation of Spain, let alone the entire Habsburg Empire, into a single state. Centralisation went little beyond the concentration of the work of the king, as ruler of all these territories, in a single location, namely Madrid. There was no question of any standardisation of legislation, of the administration of justice or taxation, or even of defence. When Olivares attempted to introduce a more centralised system of military mobilisation and finance in the 1620s and 1630s with the Union of Arms, this provoked unrest and revolt.

The process of centralisation progressed further within some of the various constitutive parts of the Spanish–Habsburg Empire than they did on the level of the whole empire. That applied in the first place to the core realm of the empire, Castile, where Ferdinand and Isabella and also Charles V were able to secure the loyalty of the nobility and clergy by granting them important privileges, including tax immunities. The nobility was drawn into the administration of the empire through the great orders of chivalry, the central administrative councils, the royal court, the army and the diplomatic service. Since the relations between the nobility, clergy and sovereign, including those at the fiscal level, were clearly laid down, the king no longer invited the nobility and clergy to participate in the assembly of the estates of Castile, the Cortes. Only the towns were still represented in the Cortes, and that representation was curtailed. From the rule of Charles V onwards, the Cortes were unable to take an effective stand against the king in matters concerning the kingdom. At the local level, the king left the urban elites alone. Like the nobility, the great merchants took advantage of the opportunities that the Habsburg Empire afforded them. In the other parts of Spain – the kingdoms of the Aragonese crown – the Cortes retained more of their power and dualism remained intact. The efforts by Philip IV and Olivares to put an end to that power resulted in the major revolt of 1640, as a result of which Olivares was brought down (1642).

287   England: from Tudors to Restoration

Two years after the defeat of England in the Hundred Years War, a war of succession broke out in 1455 between the two branches of the royal house, the Yorks and the Lancasters. In 1485, the Wars of the Roses were resolved in favour of a branch of the house of Lancaster, the Tudors. Henry VII (1485–1509) and his Tudor successors Henry VIII (1509–47), Edward VI (1547–53), Mary I (1553–8) and Elizabeth I (1558–1603) restored peace and expanded the central government. Henry VIII separated the court and the organs of government from one another. Parliament and the secretariats remained in Westminster, while the king, court and his personal councillors, united in the Privy Council, moved to Whitehall. Presiding over the royal machinery of government was the chancellor. In the course of the sixteenth century, various state secretaries were added. These were appointed and dismissed by the king and generally did not belong to the high nobility. Apart from the common law courts, which became ever more independent, justice, known as 'equity', was also dispensed by the chancellor. Special courts were established, particularly in criminal matters. The Star Chamber was a dreaded instrument by which the king imposed his authority. Here not just common offenders but also political opponents were subjected to torture and summary justice. Under the Tudors, Parliament lost much of its power and prestige. Statute law continued to be passed by the 'King in Parliament', but in reality Parliament often behaved as an obedient voting machine. When Parliament was not in session, the king governed by means of royal proclamations, although it was possible for these to be revoked later by Parliament. During the course of the sixteenth century, Parliament was convened less and less frequently.

After the death of Elizabeth, the Stuart King James VI of Scotland ascended the thrones of England and Ireland as James I (1603–25). James's attitudes towards kingship were radical and absolutist. He sought to govern without Parliament. Similarly, his son Charles I (1625–49) was able to rule from 1629 to 1640 without convening Parliament. By means of the Star Chamber and arbitrary arrests, Charles I suppressed the growing opposition. His attempts to impose the Anglican Book of Common Prayer on the Presbyterian Church in Scotland led to an armed revolt there and war against England. Out of financial necessity, Charles convened Parliament in Westminster in 1640. The ensuing political conflict developed into a civil war between king and Parliament, which was ultimately to cost Charles his crown and his head. The republic or Commonwealth that was established in consequence proved to be of short duration; in 1660, Charles's son Charles II ascended the thrones of England, Scotland and Ireland.

288   The Holy Roman Empire: the failure of centralisation

The Holy Roman Empire forms the great exception to the move towards centralisation in western Europe in the Early Modern Age. As a result of the emperor's defeat during the Investiture Controversy, his authority in the empire crumbled. The Romano-German kingship, to which the title of emperor was linked, remained subject to election. From the fourteenth century onwards, the emperor was chosen by seven imperial Electors.[14] The emperor governed the empire in co-operation with the estates, united in the Imperial Diet. The latter consisted of the Electors, the other secular and ecclesiastical princes, and the representatives of the imperial towns. In contrast to most of the other great princes of the West, the emperor was unable to expand his power during the fifteenth and sixteenth centuries. Even the monopolisation of warfare and foreign policy proved beyond his grasp. The religious divisions and wars of religion were an important cause of the inability of the Habsburgs – who had occupied the imperial throne without interruption since 1440 – to build up a central monarchy. The Peace of Westphalia (1648) sealed this failure.

In 1648, the Holy Roman Empire consisted of 314 estates (*Reichsstände*) represented in the Diet, and some 1,500 imperial knights. The Imperial Constitution, of which the Peace of Westphalia formed part, laid down

---

[14] The king of Bohemia, the Electors of Saxony, Brandenburg and the Palatinate, the archbishops of Mainz, Cologne and Trier. During the Thirty Years War the Elector of Bavaria was added.

that in the event of internal dispute there should be a waiting period of three years before one should resort to arms. The estates could not use force against the empire or the emperor. In fact, the three-year rule was a step backwards from the medieval imperial public peaces. Apart from the Diet, the most important effective central institution was the Imperial Chamber of Justice or *Reichskammergericht*. This supreme court was established by Maximilian upon the promulgation of the Public Peace of 1495. Among other things, its task was the peaceful resolution of disputes among the estates. It stood entirely in the tradition of the medieval royal adjudication and arbitration. The Peace of Westphalia confirmed its role, but limited it by setting the period of truce at three years. As long as they did not turn against the empire and the emperor, the estates were permitted to conduct their own foreign policy, to conclude alliances and to put troops into the field. During the early sixteenth century, an imperial council, the *Hofrat*, emerged, but to a large extent its activities concerned the Habsburg dominions in Austria and Bohemia. This clearly illustrates that already at that stage, the establishment of a monarchy throughout the empire was beyond reach. This failure of centralisation at the imperial level did not, however, prevent a certain degree of centralisation from being introduced within the great principalities such as Austria, Bavaria and Saxony.

289   The Netherlands: from Burgundians to Habsburgs

After the violent death of Charles the Bold at Nancy in 1477, his twenty-year-old daughter Mary of Burgundy came to power in the Burgundian Netherlands. The French king Louis XI made use of the instability in the Netherlands to annex the Duchy of Burgundy. With the support of her spouse, Archduke Maximilian of Habsburg, the later emperor (1493–1519), Mary was able to ward off further French expansion. After Mary's death the Netherlands devolved upon her son Philip the Fair (1482), and after his untimely death, upon her grandson, the future Charles V (1506).

Charles V united virtually all the provinces of the Netherlands. His territories in the Netherlands were referred to as the Seventeen Provinces. The Prince-Bishopric of Utrecht became a secular dominion. Gueldres and Frisia also came under Charles's control. Only the Prince-Bishopric of Liège remained independent. Upon the Peace of Madrid (1526), the feudal ties of Flanders and Artois to France were broken. Appeal to the Parliament of Paris against the judgments of the Council of Flanders was no longer possible. As emperor, Charles V managed to weaken the bonds between his territories in the Low Countries and the Holy Roman Empire. The Pragmatic Sanction (1546) laid down that the same rules of succession would apply in the Seventeen Provinces, so that the personal union was guaranteed. Under the Transaction of Augsburg (1548), the Dutch provinces within the empire were united into a single legal circle, the Burgundian Circle (*Kreits*), and were absolved from the jurisdiction of the Imperial Chamber of Justice.

The Habsburg rulers of the Netherlands continued the centralising policies of their Burgundian predecessors. Under Philip the Good, a council had been set up to help the ruler with the administration of his various provinces. There was also a chancellor, who presided over the royal civil service. Charles V extended the central government by the establishment of the Collateral Councils (1531): the Council of State, concerned with general and foreign policy, the Privy Council, advising on domestic and legal affairs, and the Council of Finance. Each of the provinces had a governor or stadholder who replaced the sovereign in the latter's absence. For the Netherlands as a whole, a viceroy or governor-general was appointed when the sovereign was abroad. From the time of Charles V this was nearly permanent, while from Philip II onwards it was permanent. In most cases, the governors-general were members of the Habsburg dynasty. In the course of the sixteenth century, virtually every province hitherto lacking one was given a central court, known as the provincial Council of Justice (Frisia 1499, Utrecht 1530, Gueldres 1547, Overijssel 1553). For the Netherlands as a whole, a central court was established, the Great Council of Mechelen (1504). Previously, Charles the Bold had already tried to establish a central court, the Parliament of Mechelen (1474–7), but this had disappeared upon his death. The new body had final jurisdiction over all disputes, but this was not recognised by certain provincial councils. Apart from provincial estates, there were also the Estates-General for the Netherlands as a whole. This body, which first met in 1464, was an assembly of the representatives of all Burgundian and later Habsburg provinces in the Low Countries. It met more frequently in the course of the sixteenth century.

290   The Netherlands: the Dutch revolt

The centralisation policy of Charles V led to dissatisfaction and outright rebellion, although under his regime the opposition remained within bounds. Charles V was born in Ghent, spoke the language of the local elite (French) and had considerable affinity with the leading classes. Matters differed when it came to his son Philip II, who was born and raised in

Spain. From his base in Madrid, Philip II resolutely continued his father's policy of centralisation. He gave the governor-general, his half-sister, and her government on the ground little leeway and paid little heed to the growing opposition among the nobility and the wealthy towns in the Low Countries. As a strict Catholic he also came down heavily on the growth of Calvinism in his northern dominions.

The deeper causes of the rebellion against Philip II must be sought in the opposition on the part of the elite towards the policy of centralisation conducted by Madrid. The dissatisfaction with that policy battened on to the growing religious disunity and ensuing unrest. The dispute escalated when Philip II sent an army to the Netherlands in 1566 in order to restore his authority. William of Orange (1531–84), the richest noble in the Low Countries and confidant of Charles V, fled to Germany in order to return in 1568 with an army of mercenaries. After initial defeats, the tide started to turn in 1572. By 1576, Spanish power in the Netherlands had been all but expunged. The Estates-General were unable to restore the peace or to reach a compromise with Philip. The radicalisation of the Calvinist minority drove the Catholics back into Spain's arms. In the years after 1579, Alexander Farnese (1520–89), Duke of Parma, the new Spanish governor-general, managed to re-conquer the Southern Netherlands, leading to a split between the rebellious north and the submissive south. The unity of the Netherlands was a thing of the past. The Spanish king was not to recognise the division of the Netherlands until 1648, after eighty years of war.

291   The Republic of the United Provinces: the monarchical republic

After the attempt at pacification by the Estates-General in 1576 had failed, seven northern provinces joined forces in 1579 in the Union of Utrecht. The alliance of Holland, Zeeland, Utrecht, Gueldres, Overijssel, Groningen and Frisia proved a permanent one. The seven provinces agreed to wage the struggle against Spain collectively. They would conduct a joint foreign policy and field a single army. This naturally required a basic administrative and financial machinery. In 1581, the northern provinces promulgated the Act of Abjuration deposing Philip II as their sovereign.

These two documents constituted the birth certificates of the Republic of the United Provinces. This was not a unitary state but a loose alliance of seven – and after the accession of Drenthe, eight – 'sovereign' mini-states. In fact they continued to form part of the empire until after the Peace of Westphalia, but since the Transaction of Augsburg that had entailed the bare minimum. Following the deposition of their prince, the 'sovereignty' resided with the estates of each of the provinces. The intention was not, to begin with, to remain without a sovereign. Efforts were made on several occasions to appoint a new prince, but without lasting success. At the same time, the dethronement of the sovereign did not bring dualism to a complete end. Even after Philip II had been deposed, the office of stadholder – that is, the sovereign's deputy – curiously enough continued to exist. That office became all but permanent from the 1570s onwards and was filled in all the provinces by members of the house of Orange-Nassau. The descendants of William the Silent and later of his brother monopolised the stadholdership. The stadholders were provincial officials who were temporarily deputising for a number of limited sovereign powers. By holding the office in several of the most powerful provinces, however, the stadholders from the house of Orange evolved into key figures in the Republic. They also acted as captains- and admirals-general of the Union, were in charge of the war effort and played a major role in foreign policy. With the stadholders, the Republic retained a monarchical element. In the seventeenth and eighteenth centuries there were, however, various periods in which there were no stadholders. After the restoration of the house of Orange following the last of these episodes, the joint stadholdership of all the provinces became hereditary (1748). In the Europe of sovereigns, the Republic was not, after all, so exceptional.

The most important organ at the confederal level was the Estates-General. This was a permanent assembly of representatives from the seven original members of the Union (Drenthe was not represented). Although the Estates-General were entitled 'sovereign powers' that was not in fact so, except as representatives of the genuine sovereigns, the provincial estates. The Estates-General discussed all the affairs of the Union, such as foreign policy, warfare and the administration of the territories that had since been captured from the Spaniards, such as Northern Brabant (Den Bosch 1629, Breda 1637) and Maastricht (1632), the so-called Generality Lands (*Generaliteitslanden*). In addition, there was a Council of State, the task of which was primarily executive. After the secession from the south, the jurisdiction of the Great Council of Mechelen was no longer recognised. No new central court superior to the provincial legal councils for the eight provinces was appointed. Holland and Zeeland did, however, set up a common High Council where appeals could be lodged against the judgments of the courts of Holland and of Zeeland (1581). In general, it may be said that the Northern Netherlands, like the rest of the

German Empire, remained an exception in the field of centralisation, which did not go beyond the provincial level.

292   The Southern Netherlands: the Spanish restoration

With the Union of Utrecht in January 1579, the seven northern provinces responded to the Union of Arras that had been forged two weeks earlier between a number of southern provinces and Alexander Farnese. In the subsequent years, Farnese and his successors managed to re-conquer the southern provinces, including the larger parts of Flanders and Brabant. Following the fall of Breda in 1637, the border was largely established where the border between the Netherlands and Belgium remains to this day. The Habsburg regime in the Southern Netherlands was restored. The old institutions, such as the Collateral Councils, the governorship-general and the Great Council of Mechelen, continued as before. In addition, the number of permanent secretariats was extended and the governor-general was assisted by *juntas*. In 1598, Philip II transferred the Netherlands to his daughter Isabella (1598–1633). Isabella and her husband, Archduke Albrecht of Austria (1598–1621), governed as sovereign princes. After the death of Albrecht, the Southern Netherlands reverted to Spain. Isabella continued to rule as governor-general until her death. Albrecht and Isabella and their successors managed to restore sovereign authority and political unity in the Southern Netherlands, but did not succeed in putting an end to local and provincial autonomy.

B   Culture and the law

1   Renaissance and humanism

> Verum enimvero quo magis superiora tempora infelicia fuere, quibus homo nemo inventus est eruditus, eo plus his notiris gratulandum est, in quibus (si paulo amplius adnitamur) confido propediem linguam Romanam vivere plus, quam urbem, & cum ea disciplinas omneis iri restitutum.[15]

293   The Italian Renaissance: a European movement?

The view that the Italian Renaissance marked the revival of the Latin West after a millennium of darkness is as old as the Italian Renaissance

---

[15] 'The more inauspicious the bygone times were due to the absence of genuine scholars, the more we should be gratified by this age, during which, if we continue to do our best, there is in my view no doubt whatever that the language of Rome and hence all the arts and sciences will speedily be restored to a fuller glory than in Rome itself.' Lorenzo Valla, *Elegantiae Linguae Latinae* 1 (1449) (my translation).

itself, in fact older, as it goes back to the works of the fourteenth-century Italian scholar Petrarch. Although the negative portrayal of the Middle Ages by the standard-bearers of the Renaissance and later historians has proved untenable, the self-appraisal of the Renaissance as a transfer from darkness to light is a historical fact in itself. In its rediscovery of Antiquity, the Italian Renaissance was not unique: all the great cultural movements of the Middle Ages referred in one way or another to the Romans. If Antiquity had already been rediscovered, what then was the significance of the Italian Renaissance? The answer is that the new Renaissance dealt with Antiquity in a different way. Antiquity was re-rediscovered.

Humanism is to the Italian Renaissance what scholasticism is to the Renaissance of the Twelfth Century. It is its intellectual backbone. Humanism dates from around 1400, the Renaissance from the second quarter of the fifteenth century. The humanists had their forerunners, the so-called proto-humanists like Petrarch and others, reaching back to the early fourteenth or even late thirteenth century. In their initial stage, Renaissance and humanism centred around the city-republics of northern Italy, especially Florence. During the course of the fifteenth century, both movements spread to the other states of the peninsula. Around 1450, they penetrated the papal court. Around 1500, Rome superseded Florence as the centre of Renaissance artistic production. Princes and popes hired artists and scholars in order to turn their courts and capitals into centres of art and learning, seeking thereby to show their riches, power and refinement to the outside world and thus to enhance their reputation. The wars in Italy after 1494 accelerated the export of the Renaissance and humanism throughout Europe. The *sacco di Roma* in 1527 brought to an end the high point of the Renaissance and humanism in Italy. During the sixteenth and early seventeenth century, the two movements took root in almost all the countries of Europe, including central Europe and even Russia. Renaissance and humanism coincided with the rise of the sovereign state and the collapse of the politico-legal unity of the West. Throughout Europe, Renaissance and humanism adapted to local circumstances. Around 1600, it was no longer possible to speak of a single European Renaissance or a single European humanism, but only of many 'national' variants.

The fact that the Renaissance and humanism began in northern Italy is readily explained. The political and legal order of northern Italy greatly differed from that of the rest of Europe. Feudalism had not had the same impact as it had elsewhere; the elites in the great towns and city-republics had been more successful at wresting power from the hands of the landed aristocracy than they had been elsewhere in Europe. There were also cultural differences. As in other parts of Europe, scholasticism dominated the study of law, medicine and theology, but in the arts, it had somewhat less of a role inside than outside Italy. In the arts schools of northern Italy, which in many cases were run by the towns, the *ars dictaminis* – rhetoric – held place of pride. These arts schools would prove an important breeding ground for humanism. In addition, factors such as the ideal of poverty in the popular Franciscan Order and Byzantine influence meant that Gothic architecture – the art of scholasticism – had not become so lavish, or flamboyant, in Italy and that Romanist influences had remained stronger.

294   The humanist paradigm: relative authority

The term humanism to indicate the fifteenth-century cultural movement was first used in 1808. It derives from an expression the 'humanists' had already used in the fifteenth century in order to refer to their activities: *studia humanitatis*. That was in turn taken from Cicero. It referred to the teaching and study of various disciplines central to the humanist démarche: grammar, literature, rhetoric, (political) history and ethics.

Like scholasticism, humanism was a method of analysing and interpreting classical and early Christian texts. It did so, however, from a totally different angle. The humanists rejected the absolute authority – the *auctoritas* – of the text canon. For the humanists, these texts had only relative authority. The humanists acknowledged that the classical texts were creations of the human mind, products of a bygone age, drawn from a historical civilisation. They did not contain within themselves the complete, perfect and timeless truth. To understand them properly, one had to relate them to the context of time and place from which they originated.

That approach sprang from a new understanding of history, which had already been articulated by Petrarch. The medieval scholastics did not regard Antiquity as a bygone, historical age. Medieval historiography was based on the assumption that human history was the preordained fulfilment of God's plan. The fall of the Western Roman Empire was not viewed as a fundamental caesura. The centuries before and after the fall of the Western Empire all belonged to the sixth and final historical era, that of Christianity. Antiquity was not thought of as a past age; medieval man felt that he belonged to the same civilisation as the Romans, certainly the Christian Romans. This helps explain why the text canon from Antiquity was thought of not as a historical legacy of a lost civilisation but as the source of a timeless and hence current truth. The *auctoritates* were studied not in order to discover Antiquity but in order to apply them to the contemporary age itself. Scholasticism aimed at extracting the timeless and hence current truth from the texts.

This interpretation of history was rejected by Petrarch, the other proto-humanists and their later successors. They regarded Antiquity as a historical period that had come to an end with the fall of the Western Roman Empire. Antiquity had given way to a long period of decline, the Middle Ages; its text canon was an heirloom of the past. The more the proto- and early humanists learned about ancient history, the more they saw how the recent past and their own times differed from Antiquity, and how bleak they seemed in comparison.

The classical text canon was now ascribed the authority of historical sources bearing witness to the lost civilisation and past history of the Greeks, Romans and early church. It merited study not because it contained the absolute truth but because it provided a glimpse of the most developed and revered civilisations ever. These texts were not of divine but of human origin. However, the classical and early Christian authors were far superior to those of the Middle Ages and even of their own times. Only by studying and imitating Antiquity could one hope to achieve the same level. Antiquity became the example to follow, the civilisational role model. Instead of *auctoritas*, the key concept in studying the ancient texts became *emulatio*: the emulation or imitation of classical and early Christian civilisation. In the twelfth century, John of Salisbury (c.1115–76) had written of the medieval thinkers that they were like dwarves sitting on the shoulders of giants and therefore could see further. The humanist 'dwarf' now wished to become a 'giant' himself.

Despite the sacred respect for the ancient sources, scholasticism had, paradoxically enough, led to a notably lapsed treatment of the classical sources. In order to make good upon their expectations regarding the authority of the texts, the scholastics often indulged in very extensive interpretations of the texts; they were concerned, after all, not with their authenticity or with the historical accuracy of the significance which they attached to them, but with teasing out what could be represented as absolute truth. That approach now came in for severe criticism. The humanists accused their scholastic predecessors and contemporaries of having traduced, corrupted and misused the legacy of Antiquity. The humanist method was aimed at understanding the ancient sources in a historically correct manner. The relativisation of the authoritativeness of the classical textual canon led to a more respectful treatment of the texts. Whereas the scholastic applied and if necessary adapted Antiquity to his own age, the humanist dreamt of adapting his own age to the example of Antiquity.

295   A historical method

Whereas scholasticism was primarily concerned with a logical interpretation, the humanist method of interpretation was historical and philological. In the first place, the historical approach meant that, in order to understand a Greek, Roman or early Christian text correctly, it had to be read against the background of the historical context in which it had been written. The humanists laid the foundations of the historical method. The study of a text assumed familiarity with the background and motives of the author and an understanding of the political, cultural, socio-economic and institutional context. Humanism entailed first and foremost the historical study of Graeco-Roman Antiquity and the early church, for which reason the historiography and relevant literature of Antiquity gained greatly in importance for the light they threw on the period itself. The works of authors such as Herodotos, Thucydides, Cicero, Livy and Tacitus were tracked down and, as soon as they had been discovered, closely analysed. The focus on philosophy, theology, medicine and law somewhat diminished. This shift in and broadening of the perspective also involved a switch in historical focus. Medieval scholasticism was primarily concerned with imperial Rome and the early Christian sources. The texts of Plato, Aristotle and several others were used in order to study Greek philosophy. These texts were, however, read only in Latin translation and knowledge of them was to a significant extent determined and formed by late Roman, Arabic and Jewish interpretations. The humanists broadened the spectrum. Ancient Greece was rediscovered on its own terms. More Greek authors and texts were discovered, analysed and (re-)translated. This is one of the most important substantive differences between the medieval renaissances and the new Renaissance. In addition to Latin and Roman Antiquity, Greek civilisation became the object of study. There was also a shift of emphasis with regard to the Romans: in addition to the imperial age, the spotlight was now also trained on the late republican era – the age of Cicero. The motives for doing so were primarily political.

296   A philological method

In the second place, humanism was philological and concerned with text criticism. The humanists realised that the manuscripts of ancient texts they used were not original but highly corrupt medieval copies. The frequency with which the manuscripts had been copied and the analysis to which they had been subjected had distorted the texts. Apart from slips of the pen, the copying had given rise to grammatical errors, the wrong explanation of abbreviations and incorrect splitting of words. Apart from formal or lexical errors, substantive mistakes had also crept in. Unfamiliar words were left out or replaced. Passages that were not understood were deleted; other fragments that contradicted a favoured proposition or were considered not to be of interest were left out, abridged or summarised. On top of that, accidentally or otherwise, medieval text fragments such as glosses and commentaries had ended up in the texts themselves as though they were part of the original, the so-called interpolations. Finally, passages were added to certain texts, or certain 'ancient' texts were in fact entire falsifications. According to the humanists, in order to arrive at a correct historical interpretation of the classical texts, it was necessary to return to the authentic source. The medieval corruptions were tracked down and corrected; the medieval glosses and commentaries were the object of little interest. In some respect Martin Luther's *sola fide, sola scriptura* was a religious translation of humanism.

The humanists accused the scholastics of having corrupted the Latin language. The Latin which they wrote, or in which they copied and quoted the ancient texts, was a miserable variant of classical Latin. Classical Latin became identified with the age of Cicero, Virgil and Livy. The language of these authors – especially of Cicero – was held up as a model and minutely analysed. The orations, letters and treatises of the great Roman orator were one of the most important focuses of humanism. By studying his work and that of other classical authors, the humanists aimed to restore Latin to its former glory. In their own writings, they sought to compete with the ancients. Petrarch, for example, did so by writing letters to some of the ancients, such as Cicero.

Linguistics was also important for the correct interpretation of the classical texts. In order to understand the text properly, it was necessary to know the language as it stood at the time of writing. The Latin of Cicero was different from that of Ulpian or Augustine. Linguistic analysis implied the study of the historical evolution of language. This was, and is, a precondition for historical text interpretation. Words and sayings change their meaning over time. One of the most important of the early humanists, the Roman scholar Lorenzo Valla (1407–57), defended these propositions in his *Elegantiae Linguae Latinae* (*The Beauty of the Latin Language*), a kind of linguistic guide to Latin. His work was taken further in the *Adagia* by the great Dutch humanist Erasmus.

It is in this context that we need to consider the revival of the study of Greek and the biblical languages of Hebrew and Aramaic. The Latin translations of numerous ancient texts in Greek, Hebrew or Aramaic were corrupted. The increasing relations between the Catholic and the Greek Orthodox churches in the fourteenth and fifteenth centuries brought Italy into direct contact with the Greek world. Before the collapse of the Byzantine Empire, many Greek scholars fled to the West. With their aid, a number of humanists learned Greek. New and better translations into Latin were made of the works of Plato, Aristotle and other great classical authors, as well as of the Greek patristics. A growing number of humanists learned Greek. Erasmus, who devoted a large proportion of his energy to the philological study of the Bible, also wanted to restore Hebrew to its rightful place. In Louvain, he founded the Collegium trilinguae, the trilingual college for the study of Latin, Greek and Hebrew. Erasmus himself had little if any knowledge of Hebrew. Even among humanists, knowledge of Hebrew remained rare.

297   Critical text edition

The philological dimension of humanism also included text criticism. Text criticism was a method which, with the aid of linguistic, contextual and technical arguments, sought to reconstruct an original classical text by the study and comparison of the various (corrupt) versions of that text. A critical edition of the text would then be issued, accompanied by notes. The humanist text editions differed markedly from their medieval predecessors. For many centuries, the humanist editions served in education and scholarship as the classical, authentic texts. Many editions survived with little if any emendation and remain in use to this day.

One of the most familiar examples of the application of the humanist method is the *De donatione Constantini* by Lorenzo Valla. The *Donatio Constantini* (*The Donation of Constantine*) was the deed whereby Emperor Constantine the Great was said to have transferred authority over the city of Rome and the West to Pope Sylvester I (314–35). The deed, which had found its way into the *Decretum Gratiani*, was an authoritative text on which the popes based their claims to supremacy over secular rulers before, during and after the Investiture Controversy. Lorenzo Valla wrote his work on this so-called imperial constitution on behalf of the king of Naples, whose kingdom the pope laid claim to. In his treatise (1440), the humanist scholar demonstrated on the basis of historical and philological arguments that the text was a fake dating from the ninth century. Modern historians have established that the text did indeed date from around 800 and that it had been produced in the context of the struggle between the pope and the Byzantine emperor. Valla's treatise is an example of how the humanist method could undermine the authority of ancient sources, even those of ecclesiastical origin.

Humanism received a great boost from the invention of the printing press in the second half of the fifteenth century. This new technology made it possible for text editions to be printed in unlimited numbers without any new errors creeping in. Furthermore, printing enabled the distribution of books on a much greater scale. This contributed towards the distribution of knowledge and scholarship outside the great intellectual centres – the universities – and increased the pace and geographical range of communication among scholars throughout Europe.

298   Civic humanism

Scholasticism was aimed at the speculative interpretation of the classical *auctoritates*. The basic discipline was logic; theology, law and medicine were the main areas of application. Humanism shifted the emphasis to the *artes*, especially the two other subjects constituting the *trivium*: grammar and rhetoric. Apart from linguistics, grammar covered the study of classical literature, history and ethics. These were literary disciplines, but the interest in them was largely prompted by practical motives. The study of classical grammar and rhetoric made it possible to express oneself elegantly as well as accurately in speech and writing. Humanism first obtained a foothold in northern Italy, especially the city-republics of Tuscany, of which Florence was the most important. As in the case of the Athens of Pericles (495–429 BC) and the Rome of Cicero, these were aristocratic republics in which the members of a governing elite of a few hundreds or thousands competed with one another for power and popular favour. In the scene of city politics, eloquence was an instrument of power. In the same way that education in rhetoric, language, literature, political history and public morality had become established in Athens and Rome because of its political uses, so also its revival in Italy is to be explained. The Florentine humanists of the early fifteenth century translated their republican ideals into a literary, historical and ethical educational programme. For the Florentine official and historian Leonardo Bruni (1370–1444), the Roman Republic was the model.[16] As

---

[16] Bruni's history of Florence is now available in English translation: *History of the Florentine People*, ed. and translated by James Hankins, Cambridge, Mass. and London, 3 vols., 2001–7.

he saw it, Caesar and Augustus – the founders of the empire, and held up as heroes in the Middle Ages – sounded the death-knell of liberty. In terms of moral philosophy, the Graeco-Roman republican tradition also served as a source of inspiration. *Virtus* (virtue) was understood as the involvement of the citizen in the administration and interests of the *polis* (the city-republic): civic virtue.

When humanism made its way into the courts of the princes of Italy and Europe in the course of the fifteenth and sixteenth centuries, the republican, political programme receded into the background. Interest in imperial Rome revived. In the field of ethics, the focus shifted from the pleas of the early Roman Stoics such as Cicero in favour of political involvement to those of the later Stoics such as Seneca (4 BC–AD 65) in favour of keeping a distance from political events. The literary-historical programme was substantively revised but remained intact methodologically.

299   The impact of humanism on Western culture

The rise of humanism did not put an end to scholasticism. For a long period of time, both movements existed side by side and competed with one another. Humanism did not take the academic scientific establishment, the universities and the church, by storm. Instead, it remained a fairly marginal movement that developed primarily outside the traditional institutions of scholarship and learning. To a large extent, humanism flourished outside the universities. The humanists established their own schools, such as those at the courts of the dukes of Ferrara and Mantua in the fifteenth century, and devoted their energy to the establishment and reform of the secondary schools based around the *studia humanitatis*. At the universities, they obtained their strongest foothold in the faculties of the *artes*, first and foremost in Italy. Only in the sixteenth century did humanist influence tell in the civil law schools, first in France and later in the Protestant countries. Even then and there, however, scholasticism still had an impact. This later phase of humanism was marked far more by a blending of the scholastic and humanist approaches, or by the gradual transformation of the basic scholastic assumptions under the influence of humanism. Humanism was first and foremost a historical and philological movement. It did not propose its own comprehensive worldview, although through the study of classical philosophical texts it brought new fundamental insights into the intellectual discourse. As such, it did not replace the scholastic worldview all by itself, but only prepared the way for the articulation of a new ideology. In that sense, humanism is a transitional movement in between scholasticism and the modern rationalism of the post-1648 period.

The most important consequences of humanism for the development of Western culture may be summarised as follows. First, humanism stimulated the intellectual emancipation of the West. It diminished the authority of the text canon from absolute to relative. The classical sources offered testimony of the highest human achievements, which were to be emulated as a 'role model', but their authority was neither absolute nor sacred. Although the humanists deeply revered the classics, they placed Antiquity in perspective and reduced it to what it truly was: a historical epoch. Intellectually speaking, the step from absolute authority to the best model to be emulated was a big one. Thereafter, the further relativisation of the claims to authority of Antiquity, from the example always to be followed to the one to be followed generally or sometimes, was a gradual one. Room was made for independent reflection and evaluation of the instances and circumstances in which Antiquity deserved imitation or not. Halfway through the seventeenth century, the ancient text was no longer sufficient in itself as an argument to substantiate a particular proposition.

Second, the historical approach to Antiquity stimulated interest in and appreciation for other cultures and epochs, and particularly for the contemporary age. Apart from Graeco-Roman Antiquity, the great historians of humanism such as Bruni, Machiavelli and Francesco Guicciardini (1483–1540) also studied recent Italian history. They found numerous stories and examples in Antiquity that deserved imitation but which also served as an explanatory model for human behaviour. Parallels with contemporary events or the recent past were eagerly drawn. Interest in the vernacular was also on the rise. In the wake of the great Florentine poet Dante, humanists increasingly wrote not just in Latin but also in the vernacular such as Italian, French, Spanish or English. This was consequential to the recognition that language too was a human creation, and hence context-bound and time-bound.

Third, humanism speeded up the process of secularisation. Humanism was not in itself a secular movement. The textual canon of the humanists extended equally to the biblical and patristic tradition as it did to the classical, pre-Christian texts. While the humanist method could be applied to both, pre-Christian Antiquity provided the humanists with the model for a more secular civilisation. The Graeco-Roman civilisation had been a deeply religious one, but in a different way from medieval Christianity. Classical religion was pantheistic, the divine being immanently present in nature. In contrast to medieval Christianity, it was not oriented towards the metaphysical or the afterlife. The Greek and Roman Hades did not provide an attractive prospect of eternity; the ancients directed their energy and ambitions to their earthly lives. The heroes of classical civilisation were the great conquerors and political leaders who, driven by personal ambition, had imprinted their mark on their own age. It was these examples that inspired the writers and leaders of the Renaissance. Machiavelli's work abounds with reverence for the great Roman heroes. In choosing their papal names, Alexander VI and Julius II sought to associate themselves with the two greatest generals of Greek and Roman history. Humanism marked the beginning of a gradual process of sacralisation of man and nature, that was to reach its high point in the twentieth century. Secularisation had major consequences for scholarship. The study of God and the metaphysical was confined to theology; disciplines which had man and nature as their object gained an ever greater independence from theology and came to flourish. In that sense, humanism did no more than provide a fresh boost and an additional dimension to the process of intellectual secularisation that had begun as early as the eleventh century. The Renaissance of the Twelfth Century had justified the study of the physical world in terms of its instrumentality for understanding the divine. Humanism prepared the next step: the study of man and nature on their own terms. In this respect, humanism certainly had much in common with fourteenth-century Franciscan nominalism.[17]

Fourth, humanism shifted the focus from the static and the collective to the dynamic and the individual. The study of Antiquity inspired the notion that man was perfectible. As opposed to what was the case in medieval Christianity, the ancients did not perceive of their earthly life as a preparation for the afterlife. Their bleak view of the afterlife caused them to confine their energies and ambitions for happiness and self-realisation to the temporal world. Rather than metaphysical, much of ancient philosophy was ethical. Humanism propagated the individual moral and intellectual development of man. For this, it took inspiration from currents of classical philosophy such as Platonism, Stoicism and scepticism. In doing so, humanism opened the door to the individualisation and mutability of

---

[17] In general, it may be said that humanism displayed considerable affinity with the nominalist movements of, among others, the Franciscans, with their emphasis on free will and the individual, as compared with the rational and universal in the Thomist tradition of natural law.

society. The former in turn tied in with the move towards a more personal profession of faith as had already commenced in the Late Middle Ages and which offered an important springboard for Protestantism.

300   The art of the natural

Renaissance art reflected the shift from the metaphysical to the natural. The differences between medieval and Renaissance sculpture illustrate this well. When medieval artists sculpted the human body to depict Christ or biblical figures, they did not faithfully represent it. Heads, hands and bodies were often out of proportion and human figures were highly static and stylised. This sprang not (just) from a lack of technical skill but was also prompted by theological motives: the figures were instrumental and symbolic. Sculptures were not freestanding statues but were incorporated in the church walls. They represented a higher, supernatural order. Christ above the tympan of a church extending an excessively large hand symbolised the way in which He was welcoming the faithful to Him.

The difference with Renaissance art becomes clear if one takes a look at the most famous example of Renaissance sculpture, the *David* by Michelangelo (1504). Relief sculpture is replaced by a freestanding statue, the aim of which is primarily aesthetic. *David* is a biblical subject, but it is hardly the biblical story that informs the sculpture. Along the lines of the great sculptors of classical Antiquity, Michelangelo wanted to create as realistic a representation as possible of his ideal of the human body. From the Renaissance onwards the objective of plastic art became the faithful representation of nature and man. Art no longer referred to the metaphysical but portrayed physical reality.

301   Humanism and the seventeenth century

It is difficult to pinpoint precisely when humanism came to an end. Humanism was not an all-embracing philosophy and did not propagate an all-embracing worldview. It was a scholarly and educational programme that grafted itself on to the dominant worldview and gradually transformed it. Only with the rationalism and scientific revolution of the seventeenth century was a new worldview articulated. The time it took for that transition to happen differed from country to country. In general terms, it may be said that in most countries the synthesis between humanism and the old, prevailing scholastic models took place somewhere between 1550 and 1650. In the meantime, great scholars such as Cartesius (René Descartes, 1596–1650) and Grotius (Hugo de Groot,

1583–1645) – themselves children of humanism – laid the foundations for a new conception of God, man and world.

2   Humanist jurisprudence

302   Littera Pisana

In his *Elegantiae Linguae Latinae,* Lorenzo Valla severely criticised the glossators and commentators of Roman law, accusing them of a lamentable mastery of the Latin language and a total lack of style. This made it impossible for them to understand Justinian law, since legal scholarship turned on the interpretation of words and texts. The first precondition to that end was mastering the classical language and written style, on which point the medieval and contemporary jurists failed dismally in comparison with their classical predecessors.

Valla's attack on the late medieval and contemporary civilians was taken further by other humanists. The Italian Politianus (Angelo Poliziano, 1454–94), a friend and protégé of Lorenzo de Medici, claimed that the Justinian texts used by the commentators differed greatly from the original. Politianus suggested that there was a better text than the *Littera Bononiensis*, namely the manuscript F, held in Florence. This was in fact the *Littera Pisana*, which was transferred to the Medici library in Florence after the conquest of Pisa in 1406. According to Politianus, this was the original copy of the *Digest* that was sent to the pope by Justinian around the year 550 and on which later manuscripts, such as the *Littera Bononiensis,* were ultimately based. Politianus wanted manuscript F itself to be used for the reconstruction of the Justinian texts. After Lorenzo de Medici had allowed him to consult the manuscript, he embarked on his critical edition of the *Digest*. In 1553, a full and critical printed edition of the *Digest* was published by Lelio Torelli and Antonio Agustin.

303   Bourges and the *mos gallicus*

Valla and Politianus outlined the contours for a programme of humanist jurisprudence. During the first half of the fifteenth century, humanism penetrated the world of legal scholarship. The humanist school did not displace the commentators. On the contrary, the commentators continued to control most law schools throughout Europe. The humanist jurists did, however, succeed in establishing themselves in some French law schools. The University of Bourges, established in 1464, became the centre of humanist jurisprudence in the sixteenth century. The Italian Alciatus (Andrea Alciato, 1492–1550) introduced humanism there (1529). Great humanist jurists such as Cuiacius (Jacques Cujas, 1522–90), Donellus (Hughues Doneau, 1527 91) and François Hotman (1524–90) worked there. Humanist legal scholarship is often referred to as *mos gallicus* (the French style), in contrast to *mos italicus* (the Italian style) of the commentators. Many of the great humanist jurists, in France and elsewhere, were Protestants. *close textual approach*

In canon law, the scholastic tradition remained stronger and the influence of humanism was smaller. The high point of canon jurisprudence was, however, over. The most important innovations in the Catholic world during the seventeenth and eighteenth centuries were consequential to the endeavours of princes to strengthen their grip over church and faith. National variants of canonical jurisprudence arose. Canon law is not discussed in further detail below.

304 *Corpus Iuris Civilis*

The early humanist jurists focused on restoring the authentic Justinian text canon and the correct historical interpretation of Roman law. These scholars applied the historico-philological programme of the *studia humanitatis* to the field of law. In the wake of Politianus, the first humanist jurists embarked on reconstructing the authentic Justinian texts. This concerned the *Digest* as well as the other parts of the Justinian collection. They certainly did not all follow the proposition that manuscript F was the original text. Cuiacius, the most important humanist jurist in the field of text criticism, argued that in order to determine what was the original text it was also necessary to look at the actual meaning of the laws contained therein. Did the proposed interpretation of the passage in fact generate a relevant result? Was the legal rule meaningful? Was it consistent with the overall body of Roman law?

A large part of the humanists' endeavours consisted of stripping the sources of their medieval glosses and commentaries. This proved a major challenge as not all glosses could be readily identified as such. Many had found their way into the text itself. The medieval jurists had also consciously incorporated new words and lines in order to give credence to a particular legal or political proposition. Medieval laws and treaties, such as the *Libri feodorum* and the *Pax Constantiae*, which were added to the *Authenticum*, were omitted from the new editions. On the other hand, the humanists added a number of Greek texts to the *Novellae*, the collection of the statutes of Emperor Justinian himself. These additions were to do with another important point of criticism expressed by the humanists with regard to the Bartolists: *Graeca non leguntur* (Greek texts are not read). In contrast to their medieval predecessors, many humanists were proficient in Greek and tried to restore the Greek texts to their original form. Thus the Frisian jurist Viglius of Aytta (1507–77) published the *Paraphrases of Theophilus*, a Greek version of Justinian's *Institutes*.

Among the great humanist jurists of the first generation, the French Budaeus (Guillaume Budé, 1467–1540), the German Zasius (Ulrich Zäsi, 1461–1536) and, of course, the Italian Alciatus must be mentioned. They dedicated themselves to eliminating the glosses and commentaries from the texts, and to the philological and historical interpretation of the Justinian collection. Cuiacius built on the work of the first generation. With him, the hunt for interpolations really took off. In 1583, Denis Godefroi (1549–1622) published the entire Justinian codification in a humanist edition. His publication, which was given the title *Corpus Iuris Civilis*, remained the classical edition for education and scholarship until the modern edition by Theodor Mommsen replaced it in the late nineteenth century.

305   A legal history of the Romans

Philological analysis and text criticism were instrumental to the most important aim of the humanists: the correct, historical interpretation of Justinian law. The humanists accused the Bartolists of taking liberties with Roman law. The Bartolists aspired to understand Roman law not as the Romans had intended it but in a way that served their own needs. The more the Bartolists concentrated on the current application of Justinian law, the more they departed from historical reality. The humanists, to the contrary, aimed for a correct historical interpretation of Roman law and this at each of the phases of its evolution. They realised that in order to understand Roman law properly they needed to know more about the social context in which it had emerged. In his *Annotationes*, Budaeus provided a catalogue of substantively incorrect interpretations made by the Bartolists. The humanists also acknowledged that the Roman legal texts were informative on Roman society. They were aware that the Justinian codification, especially the *Digest*, was a collection of texts drawn from different epochs of Roman history. A number of humanists sought to reconstruct the original texts collected in the *Digest*, such as the Law of the Twelve Tables. The reconstruction of the original sources on which the compilers of the *Digest* had drawn is referred to as palingenesis. Studies on the law and institutions in various periods in Roman history appeared. As early as 1515, the French scholar Aymar du Rivail published a work on archaic Roman law and the Law of the Twelve Tables.

3   The influence of humanism on the further development of jurisprudence

306   Humanism and Bartolism

Some legal historians have accused the humanists of detracting from the relevance of Roman law for legal practice. The humanists certainly included scholars whose interest in Roman law was purely antiquarian and who turned the study of Roman law into an erudite, specialist undertaking. Even so, the accusation is incorrect. Pure humanist jurisprudence, in the sense of a historical-philological study of Roman law, was too limited in nature to encompass the entire field of legal scholarship and bend it to its will. With a few exceptions, Bartolism remained dominant in most law schools throughout the greater part of the sixteenth century. Humanism could influence general jurisprudence to any meaningful extent only by shedding its purely historical-philological character and going down a road where it could be reconciled with the needs of legal practice.

Although it may at first sight appear surprising, this was possible without the humanists needing to deny their basic principles. The humanists accused the Bartolists of applying Roman law to practice to the extent that they took liberties with the correct historical interpretation of Roman law. The humanists placed the emphasis on the correct historical understanding of Roman law. This did not, however, necessarily prevent them from continuing to use this most sophisticated of all legal systems as a source of inspiration for their own time and to address current legal problems.

The combination of a humanist approach to Roman law with Bartolist pragmatism is often explained as though the two activities existed side by side. The humanistic legal scholar was obliged to bow to the needs of education and practice. As a humanistic dilettante he was able to engage in the historical and philological study of Roman law, but as a professional jurist at the university, in legal practice or in government he did not hesitate to apply Roman law to contemporary questions. The interaction between humanism and Bartolism reaches, however, much deeper. Gradually, the two methods evolved towards one another and became closely intertwined. Bartolism, which continued to dominate most of the European law schools, fell under the influence of humanism. The result was a new type of legal scholarship. In reality, there were numerous variants and gradations, whereby the humanist dimension could be greater or smaller. In many cases, we may justifiably refer to a moderate humanist jurisprudence; in other cases it would be better to refer to Bartolism with a smaller humanistic influence: the *usus modernus pandectarum*.

307   Moderate humanism

A good example of moderate humanist jurisprudence may be found in the Leuven Law School during the first half of the seventeenth century. At that time, humanism blossomed both in the arts and in the law faculties. Professors of Roman law, such as Petrus Gudelinus (1550–1620) and Diodorus Tuldenus (d. 1645), were clearly influenced by the great humanists from the arts such as Eyricius Puteanus (1574–1646) and Nicolaus Vernulaeus (1583–1649). They used the achievements of humanist text criticism and historical interpretation for their commentaries on the *Corpus Iuris Civilis*. But neither did they shy away from using Roman law to address current legal problems. Furthermore, they often drew from the works of medieval glossators and commentators. However, contrary to what the scholastic civilians did, they did not attribute absolute authority to the *Glossa Ordinaria* or the *opinio communis* of the great commentators. They treated the writings of Accursius, Bartolus and Baldus as just another historical interpretation of Roman law and freely debated them. In modern historiography, this moderate humanism is sometimes referred to as the *via media* (the middle way).

308   Humanist jurisprudence and legal practice

What now were the characteristics of this moderate humanist jurisprudence? What was the impact of humanism on the development of jurisprudence in general? First, humanism led to the relativisation of the authority of Roman law. The medieval jurists ascribed absolute authority to the Justinian texts, as they did to the canonical sources. Some of the medieval writings, in particular the *Glossa Ordinaria* and the writings of the greatest commentators and decretalists had gained similar authority. The Roman and canon law sources bear witness to a perfect, timeless and universal law. It was consequently sufficient to study these texts in order to find the ideal legal solution for each contemporary problem. In their quest for the ideal law, the scholastic jurists could confine themselves to the study of the *auctoritates* of the law. The humanists regarded the ancient Roman law sources not as authorities but as evidence of the best legal system man had ever devised. Roman law merited study as a model, an example. It was the most developed and sophisticated legal system ever and consequently deserved imitation. But it was also bound to the circumstances of time and place and could not therefore simply be applied to current questions as it stood. The study of Roman legal history brought the insight that there had not been a single system of Roman law but that it had evolved over time. This led to a further relativisation of its authority.

These new insights resulted in a reversal of the relations between Roman jurisprudence and legal practice. Because Roman law was perfect and timeless, the commentators considered that it should provide an appropriate solution to any current legal issue. The result was that the commentators interpreted and reinterpreted Roman law fairly freely until it provided a solution to the issue in question. In fact, they subjected Roman law to the needs of practice. The humanists regarded Roman law as a model, an *exemplum*. Rather than adapting Roman law to the needs of practice, they tried to bring current law more closely into line with Roman law by adapting it, as far as this was relevant and useful, to Roman law.

In order to achieve this, the humanist jurist had to go beyond the study of Roman law. He himself had to discover and articulate the best legal system for his own age. Roman law formed the most important source of information to that end but could not be adopted literally as it stood. For some current questions, Roman law did provide a suitable answer. That would then be adopted in the sense that the law would be brought into line with the Roman model. If Roman law did not provide an answer, another solution would be sought. Sometimes Roman law provided only a partial solution. Then it would be built on to devise a new, more suitable answer. If this was done, and Roman law was adapted and transformed in the process, that would be done consciously. The result was no longer presented as a literal transplant from Roman law but as a deliberate adaptation. In this way, historical reality no longer had to be distorted. The critical reflection on the correct, historical interpretation was followed by a critical reflection on the use of a historical law for contemporary purposes. The key question was no longer, 'What does Roman law say?' or 'What is the ideal law?' but 'What would be the best possible law in these circumstances?'

309   Expansion of the text canon

Second, the relativisation of Roman law enhanced scholarly interest in other legal systems. If Roman law was no more than an example, there could be other examples. The question of 'What would be the best possible law?' did not have to be resolved on the basis of Roman law alone. This approach provided the humanists with the opportunity to extend their field to the medieval scholarship of Roman and canon law, which may also be regarded as historical. Despite all their critique of Bartolism, the humanists continued to draw on the works of Accursius, Bartolus, Baldus and other medieval jurists. The accomplishments of these writers and other jurists were not rejected. If anything, the humanists sought to improve upon their works by making use of them. Their historical and philological errors were criticised and corrected, but the often sophisticated legal discourses were used to argue certain points. Apart from the texts of the medieval jurists, historical examples from practice – relating to the Jews, Greeks, Romans or later periods – as well as customs, legislation or treaties could serve as sources of inspiration. Under the influence of humanism, legal scholarship became eclectic. Roman law and canon law remained dominant but lost their monopoly over truth.

310   Ius proprium — local laws

Third, humanism provided a stimulus for the academic study of the *ius proprium*, in most cases customary law. Until the sixteenth century, with few exceptions, secular jurisprudence was tantamount to the study of Roman law. Now, customary law started to be studied in the sense that it was ordered, analysed and commented upon according to the methods, terminology and system of Roman jurisprudence.

311   The 'nationalisation' of law

Fourth, the academic study of current law went along with the gradual 'nationalisation' of law. The unification or harmonisation of the law was part and parcel of the centralising policies of the emerging sovereign state. Humanist jurisprudence contributed towards this. On the one hand, Roman law came to be studied and interpreted in various ways in different countries of Europe. On the other hand, in several countries steps were made or attempted towards forging a single system of national law out of the many legal systems within the country. In practice, this proved to be overambitious, but some jurists began construing a system of national law in their writings. They generally did so by systematically describing the customary laws as applied in the most important court or courts of law in the country, using the methodology of the learned, Roman law. Where this was necessary or desirable, they would amend, supplement or correct these laws with the aid of concepts, precepts and institutions taken from or inspired by Roman law. Certain humanists – particularly from Protestant quarters – went a step further and wanted to limit the use of Roman law as far as possible. The French jurists François Hotman and Molinaeus (Charles Dumoulin, 1500–66) are good examples thereof. The latter is known for his commentaries on the customary law of Paris (1538), in which he cast doubt on the authority of the medieval jurists. In his *Oratio de concordia et unione consuetudinum Francorum* he made the case for a unified French customary law. The gaps in the law needed to be filled not by resort to Roman law but by seeking inspiration in the various systems of customary law in the country. Two generations later, Antoine Loysel (1536–1617) was to distil a kind of highest common denominator from the leading systems of customary law in France in his *Institutes Coutumières* (1607).

312   The system of the *Institutes*

Fifth, the humanist jurists provided the impetus for a more systematic study of Roman law. The relativisation of Roman law meant that the humanist jurists were able to dispense with the classification of the law that had traditionally been used by the commentators. As long as the literary production consisted of glosses, commentaries and summaries of the *Digest* and *Codex*, the jurists were bound to the system of the *Digest* or the *Codex*. The humanists departed from this. Their literary production consisted mainly of treatises. In this way, a subject – extending even to the entire body of law – could be handled according to the logical needs of the subject in question, with its own ordering and framework. Even when presenting their works as commentaries on parts of the *Corpus Iuris Civilis* – which they did for the purposes of university education – the humanist jurists would adopt the same practice and divide up their 'commentary' as they saw fit. For the study of private law, the system of the *Institutes* was adopted. The threefold division into persons, property and actions laid the basis for the later classical threefold division of the civil law (persons, property and obligations). Duarenus (François Douaren, 1509–59) had already argued in favour of adopting the system of the *Institutes*. Following in the footsteps of Cicero, he held that in order to be a genuine science, the law needed to be handled in accordance with a system that began with the general and worked towards more concrete rules. The *Institutes* provided a good start in that direction. His contemporary Connanus (François Connan, 1508–51) and Donellus were the first to follow that advice and to base their work on the system adopted by the *Institutes*. Donellus drew the distinction between substantive subjective rights and procedural rights. This led him to classify obligations, which were covered under actions in the *Institutes*, as a third part of the material civil law. The first sixteen of the twenty-eight books of his *Commentaria iuris civilis*, Donellus devoted to substantive law; the last twelve to procedural law. In respect of substantive law, he drew a distinction between the rights that were truly ours (the law of persons and the law of property) and the rights that we enforce upon others (the law of obligations).

313   History as an instrument of intellectual emancipation

Humanism, both in law and elsewhere, resulted in an increase of intellectual freedom. The ancient sources had lost their claims to absolute authority and validity. Roman law continued to enjoy widespread respect. However, the aim of studying it was no longer its application but its *emulatio*. The example of the Romans was no longer to be imitated in all cases, but became a source of inspiration from which one might or might not draw in order to improve on the existing law. That created the need for a criterion to determine when Roman law should be adopted and when it should not. That criterion was to be designated in the seventeenth century: reason. Humanistic legal scholarship took an essential step in the transition from *auctoritas* to *ratio*.[18] The historical interest in a legal system going back a thousand years turned out to be an intellectual *reculer pour mieux sauter*.

314   *Usus modernus pandectarum*

In the modern literature on legal history, another school of thought is often distinguished from the humanist: the *usus modernus pandectarum*.[19] That movement arose in the late sixteenth century and centred on Germany. In a certain sense, it concerned a continuation of Bartolism. From the fifteenth century onwards, the reception of the learned law had come up to speed in the empire. Law courts increasingly adopted the Romano-canonical procedure. In 1495, the Imperial Diet decided that the Imperial Chamber of Justice should apply Roman law as supplementary law. If customary law did not offer a definitive answer, the judges would have to turn to Roman law. Since it was often difficult to demonstrate the existence of a customary legal rule, Roman law was regularly applied. The scholarly opinions by civil law professors on current cases were greatly valued in Germany. In 1532, Charles V had ordered that judges who had no university training themselves must seek counsel at the nearest law school on matters of Roman law.[20] The idea that the Holy Roman Empire was the perpetuation of the Roman Empire set the reception of Roman law on a solid basis.

The *usus modernus pandectarum* was a form of neo-Bartolism in the sense that Roman law was studied with a view to its application to current

---

[18] The humanists referred to a transition from the validity of Roman law *ratione imperii* (because of the empire) to *imperio rationis* (on the authority of reason).

[19] Named after the book by Samuel Stryk (1640–1710).

[20] Art. 219 of his great ordinance on criminal law, the *Carolina*.

issues. The proponents of the movement did not hesitate to adjust and distort the rules and concepts of Roman law in accordance with the needs of practice. The movement did not, however, entirely escape the influence of humanism. Some representatives of the *usus modernus* made use of the improved understanding of Roman law to which humanist scholarship had led.[21] This did not prevent them from also applying it to current situations, for which purpose they also had to interpret it ahistorically. Like the Bartolists before them, the adherents of the *usus modernus* selected fragments and rules from the Justinian texts which they tore out of context and interpreted freely. They no longer did so, however, on the basis of the timeless, universal *auctoritas* of these texts; the absolute claims to truth of Roman law were surrendered. The advocates of the *usus modernus* felt obliged to advance arguments other than the timeless *auctoritas* of Roman law in order to legitimate their actions. Like the more humanistic legal scholars, they found these in the intrinsic quality of the law. It provided a model, not authority. Reference was also made to recent or contemporary laws based on Roman law. Within the Holy Roman Empire, there remained the argument that Roman law was the positive law of the empire and the emperor. The advocates of the *usus modernus* realised that, in contrast to the Bartolist approach, theirs was ahistorical and defended it on the basis, among others, of the relative authority – the best model – and not on timeless claims to truth. But whatever the basis of support, the representatives of the *usus modernus* did not invariably decide in favour of the reception or adoption of the Roman model. The latter demonstrates that the *usus modernus pandectarum*, which may be regarded as the most faithful perpetuation of Bartolism, also illustrates the gradual rapprochement between *mos gallicus* and *mos italicus*. It stands at one of the two extremes of the variants in the synthesis between the two approaches, the one in which the emphasis continued to be placed on Bartolism and humanist influence remained smaller. The essential feature of humanism, however, was adopted: the relativisation of *auctoritas*. The distinction between humanist jurisprudence and the *usus modernus pandectarum* has merit, but the differences deserve to be qualified.

---

[21] The Friesian scholar Ulrik Huber (1636–94) chose to disregard this. He argued that all the legal rules in the Justinian codes should be regarded as contemporaneous. That this was not in accord with the true situation was something of which he was aware, and he accordingly considered it necessary to legitimate his viewpoint. Huber resorted to the argument that they had all been promulgated at the same time by Justinian. In his view, the Roman legal rules therefore qualified as positive law on the basis of their inclusion in the imperial law collection.

4   Grotius and Roman-Dutch law

315   The Dutch Elegant School

The evolution of jurisprudence in the Republic of the United Provinces in the seventeenth century offers a good illustration of the impact of humanism on the further development of the law. The great humanist Grotius played a crucial role in this process.

Humanist jurisprudence established itself quite early in the Low Countries, especially at Leuven, the sole law school there until Leyden was founded in 1575. Mudaeus (Gabriel van der Muyden, 1500–60) and Raevardus (Jacob Reyvaert, 1535–68) were the forerunners of legal humanism in Leuven. Scholars in the north included the previously mentioned Viglius of Aytta. From its foundation in 1575, the Leyden Law School came under the influence of humanism. The great French humanist Donellus taught there from 1579 to 1587, having fled from France for religious reasons. He and his successors were behind the flourishing seventeenth-century school of humanist jurisprudence: the Dutch Elegant School. It was not confined to Leyden and had supporters at other universities such as those of Franeker (1585) and Utrecht (1636). The Dutch Elegant School was another example of moderate legal humanism.

316   Grotius and Roman-Dutch law

Hugo Grotius (1583–1645) studied at the Leyden arts faculty at a very young age, from 1595 onwards. There he came in contact with literary humanism. Without having studied much at any law school, he was awarded the title of *doctor utriusque iuris* by the prestigious Law School at Orleans (1598). Over the next few decades, Grotius won international renown as a humanist writer. His works include historical, literary, theological and legal writings. During the 1610s, he became involved in the politico-religious conflict between Stadholder Maurice of Nassau (1584–1625) and the Dutch town regents. After the beheading of the leader of the regent faction, Johan of Oldenbarneveldt (1547–1619), Grotius, who was Pensionary of the city of Dordrecht and an important supporter of Oldenbarneveldt, was condemned to lifelong imprisonment in Loevenstein castle. Just over a year later, he managed to escape in a bookcase and fled to Paris, where in 1634 he became ambassador of the Swedish Queen Christina (1632–54). Grotius was to spend most of the rest of his life in Paris. In 1645, he died in Rostock, after the ship on which he was returning from Stockholm had foundered.

During his imprisonment in Loevenstein, Grotius wrote an important treatise on the law of Holland, entitled *Inleidinge tot the Hollandsche Rechtsgeleerdheit*. In the book, first published in 1631, Grotius described the law of the province of Holland in a systematic way. Grotius limited himself to discussing substantive law and used Donellus's threefold classification into persons, property and obligations. In general, his methodology was closely based on that of Roman jurisprudence but he applied it to the *ius proprium* of Holland, its customary law as applied by the highest courts and its statute law. Where necessary, he supplemented these laws with rules and concepts from Roman law and with precepts from natural law.

Similarly, Arnold Vinnius (1588–1657), professor at Leyden, mixed local customs, Roman law and natural law in his work *In quattuor libros Institutionum imperialium commentarius*. The work of Grotius and Vinnius and various followers gave rise to a new form of learned law, which also found application in the practice of the courts. Simon van Leeuwen (1626–52) named this Roman-Dutch law (1652). This consisted of Dutch customary law supplemented by and systematised along the lines of Roman law. In the course of the seventeenth and eighteenth centuries, this Roman-Dutch law became the model for the other provinces. In Holland and elsewhere this learned mixture was applied in practice and contributed towards the unification of law at the provincial level and, given the dominance of the Holland model, to a certain harmonisation at the national level.[22]

5 Legislation and the judiciary

317 The slow process of harmonisation and unification

In their attempts to centralise government, rulers strove at the harmonisation or unification of the law within their territories. The plurality of jurisdictions arising from the class system and from territorial fragmentation was a major obstacle to efficient central government. The process of unification was an exceptionally long and laborious one that, in most countries of Europe, was not complete until the French Revolution. In the meantime, in the majority of countries, numerous jurisdictions, each with its own court and legal system, continued to exist.

---

[22] To this day Roman-Dutch law remains an important source for private law in South Africa.

362   EMULATIO (THE EARLY MODERN AGE, 1453–1648)

Steps towards the harmonisation of legal systems had already been underway during the Late Middle Ages. Thanks to appellate jurisdiction or the procedure whereby a lower court had to seek counsel from a higher court, more important courts could exert their influence over the development of the law in smaller jurisdictions. This process continued unabated in the Early Modern Age. The academic study of *ius proprium* was largely restricted to the laws of the more important courts and jurisdictions. This allowed them to become more sophisticated and strengthened their chances of influencing or displacing smaller legal systems.

318   Royal legislation

The rulers and governments of the Early Modern Age encouraged this process of harmonisation. In various countries, rulers ordered that the various courts should record their customary law and submit it to the central government for approval and confirmation, a process known as the codification and homologation of customary law. In this way, the ruler sought to strengthen his grip over local and regional law and to inject greater unity. Before the recorded systems of customary law were homologised and confirmed by royal statute, the royal councillors could make changes and improvements, thereby also bringing more unity among different legal systems. Certain customs were simply abolished. The codification and homologation also put a brake on the further evolution of customary law.

France and the Netherlands provide good examples of this movement. In 1454, Charles VII promulgated the Edict of Montil-lez-Tours requiring the recording of customary law. In 1531, Charles V issued a similar instruction for the Netherlands. In the course of the sixteenth century, this instruction had to be repeated several times. This demonstrates the difficulty of putting royal commands into effect. Ultimately 700 systems of customary law were recorded in the Netherlands; 600 of these were abolished. Most of these records were drawn up in the south; the Northern Netherlands largely escaped the process.

The rulers also increased their control over canon law. During the fifteenth century, princes all over Europe started to claim the right of *placet*. This entailed that a canon rule would only come into force in the prince's territories after he had approved (*placet*) it.

The sovereigns used their legislative powers not only to bring more unity to the existing legal systems but also to construct an embryonic form of national law over and above local and provincial law. Most of the royal ordinances to do so concerned procedural law and criminal law, extending the sovereign's powers at the expense of ecclesiastical and local courts. In many cases, the Romano canonical procedure was introduced or elements of it were adopted. Some royal ordinances also laid down the application of Roman law as supplementary law for certain jurisdictions, of which the decision by the German Diet of Worms of 1495 concerning the Imperial Chamber of Justice is an important example. In France, sovereign jurisdiction over matrimonial affairs was extended at the expense of the church under the Edict of Villers-Cotterêts (1539). The great ordinances of Moulins (1566) and Blois (1579), promulgated during the wars of religion, strengthened the control of the king over the judiciary, as well as over the nobility, the army and the universities. In the Low Countries, Charles V and Philip II promulgated sizable ordinances on procedural and criminal law, such as the *Constitutio Criminalis Carolina* of Charles V of 1532 and the two criminal Ordinances of Philip II of 1570.

319   The central courts

Many royal ordinances of the fifteenth and sixteenth centuries aimed at the increase of royal jurisdiction and a more efficient organisation of the central courts. Reception of Roman law, which transcended the local and regional laws, remained an important element in the process of unification and centralisation. The central courts increased their influence and control over the other courts, particularly through the universal extension of the system of higher appeal. In most countries, the central, royal courts obtained supreme, appellate jurisdiction. In France, these were the parliaments and in certain cases the Grand Conseil. In the empire, it was the Imperial Chamber of Justice. In the Netherlands – and after the revolt, just in the Southern Netherlands – the body in question was the Great Council of Mechelen, although its supreme jurisdiction was not recognised by all the provinces. These or other central institutions tightened their grip over the operation and organisation of the local and provincial courts. In the (Southern) Netherlands, this was done by the Privy Council; in other countries too the supervision was exercised by an administrative body. Nevertheless, the many lower courts and legal systems largely retained their original jurisdiction in first instance and generally continued to dispense justice in their own name. This often led to conflicts of jurisdiction between local and other courts. Similarly, the Catholic ecclesiastical courts jealously guarded their jurisdiction, although they found themselves gradually forced to make concessions to the monarchs.

The central as well as the large provincial and local courts continued the reception of Roman law in the Early Modern Age. Many courts adopted the Romano-canonical procedures (on royal command or otherwise) or were inspired by them. Apart from the Imperial Chamber of Justice in Germany, the Scottish Court of Session (1532) also provides a good illustration of the role of the large courts in the reception of Roman law. Here too, the adoption of the Romano-canonical procedure marked the beginning of a more general process of reception. The academic study of customary law accelerated the amalgamation of that law with techniques, concepts and precepts derived from Roman law and jurisprudence. Together with the great collections of case law that were published everywhere in the Early Modern Age, the great legal treatises on customary law were gratefully used and quoted in legal practice. The academic study of the *ius proprium* provided the reception of Roman law with fresh stimulus.

The enhanced jurisdiction and power of the central courts did not necessarily translate into an increase in the prince's power. The great central courts were staffed by a caste of professional jurists, who had often found their way into the ranks of the nobility. Over the course of time, the central courts had obtained greater independence from the prince. In France and elsewhere, the central legal institutions liked to project themselves as guardians of the legal order. They were at the service of the sovereign and the central government, but also acted as the defenders of the rights and liberties of the estates, including their power and autonomy at the provincial and local level. Both the French parliaments and the provincial councils of justice in the Netherlands placed an effective brake on sovereign power.

6   Common law and equity

320   Common law and equity

The same holds true for the common law courts in England. Already in the twelfth century, a system of royal courts with jurisdiction all over the realm had been established in England. Through them, a national system of law, known as the common law, had emerged. The Tudor and Stuart dynasties sought gradually to extend and strengthen royal power at the expense of the estates and Parliament. In doing so they ran into considerable opposition from the old royal courts, which set themselves up as defenders of the law of the land – the common law – regulating the relations between the sovereign and his subjects.

The rulers of the late fourteenth to seventeenth centuries responded to this challenge by establishing new, central law courts. The most important of these was the Court of Chancery. The rigidity and highly technical nature of the common law offered opportunities for the new royal judicial system. With its rigid and limited system of writs, the common law was in many cases unable to offer a just solution. A person seeking justice who felt aggrieved would appeal directly to the king, the highest judge in the land. In the Early Modern Age, these appeals were referred to the chancellor, the king's most important minister, who would issue a ruling outside common law. This was done on the basis of his conscience and sense of justice or fairness, or what was known as equity. Needless to say this led to accusations of caprice and unequal treatment; the dispensation of justice was said to alter 'according to the length of the chancellor's foot'. In the course of the sixteenth and seventeenth centuries, equity in turn evolved into a fixed system of legal rules existing side by side with and outside the common law. Equity rapidly assumed a rigidity equal to that of the common law. English law became a dual law system, under which the shortcomings of the one system were put right by the other system. In 1615, it was laid down that in the event of a conflict between the two systems, equity would prevail. Until 1875, both systems were applied by separate courts. From that point onwards, common law and equity have been applied jointly throughout the judicial system.

321   The role of Roman law

As a result of the rapid unification of customary law into common law in England, the learned law made little headway in the common law courts. With the Reformation, the significance of the ecclesiastical judicial system also declined, and with it the application of the learned canon law. Henry VIII banned the universities from teaching canon law. On the other hand, the Tudor kings promoted the study and reception of Roman law. Henry VIII established chairs in Oxford and Cambridge for the study of the *ius civile*.[23] Roman law influenced equity. The impact of Roman law on the Star Chamber and the Court of Admiralty was even greater. In general, however, the reception of Roman law in England tended to lag behind that on the continent.

---

[23] To this day the Regius professor of civil law continues to teach Roman law (civil law) in Cambridge and Oxford.

7 Emulatio

322 *Emulatio*

In contrast to what had been the case in the late eleventh century, legal scholarship did not lead the way in the articulation of a new scientific model during the Renaissance. Humanism did not penetrate into legal scholarship until late in the day. The history of the relationship between humanism and law may be divided into two phases, overlapping one another partly in time.

The first phase was that of pure humanist jurisprudence. This involved the faithful application of the principles of the *studia humanitatis* to the text canon of Roman law. Encouraged by the leading representatives of Italian humanism, including Lorenzo Valla, the first humanist jurists sought to reconstruct the authentic Roman legal texts as faithfully as possible and embarked on the historical study of Roman law. This new approach to Roman law was underpinned by a fundamentally different attitude towards Roman law and the Justinian collection from that held by the scholastic jurists. The absolute claims to authority of the Justinian texts were abandoned. Roman law deserved to be studied because it was the most developed legal system ever.

In a second phase, that of moderate humanist jurisprudence, humanism became more relevant to jurisprudence at large. In order to achieve this, humanism was required to go beyond the historical-philological discourse. Gradually, there arose a new system of legal scholarship that retained the pragmatism of the Bartolists while at the same time drawing consequences from the basic principles of humanism. If Justinian law had lost its absolute *auctoritas*, it nevertheless deserved to be studied with a view to modelling the doctrine and practice of contemporary law on it. Legal scholars influenced by humanism no longer went in search of the ideal law in the books of Justinian but sought inspiration in them in order to articulate the best possible law. In many cases that could be done by adopting Roman law, while in some cases it had to be adapted and in others simply dropped. The efforts towards the imitation and emulation of Roman law allowed intellectual freedom and creativity to creep into legal thinking. This intellectual emancipation enabled civil jurisprudence to escape from the limitations of the case-law-based tradition in Roman law and to strike down the path of systematisation. Ironically enough, the humanist movement meant that legal scholars continued to regard Roman law as a treasure trove of concepts, precepts and arguments that could be used as one saw fit: precisely the charge that the humanists had levelled against the Bartolists. In contrast to the Bartolists, however, the modern jurists recognised that their treatment of Roman law was a free ranging one, and they no longer sought to take exclusive refuge behind its authority.

Further reading

1. On the Early Modern Age: J. H. Elliott, *Europe Divided, 1559–1598*, London 1968; G. R. Elton, *Reformation Europe, 1517–1559*, London 1963; J. R. Hale, *Renaissance Europe, 1480–1520*, London 1971; H. G. Koenigsberger, *Early Modern Europe, 1500–1789*, London and New York 1987; H. G. Koenigsberger, G. L. Mosse and G. W. Bowler, *Europe in the Sixteenth Century*, 2nd edn, London 1989; D. Maland, *Europe in the Sixteenth Century*, 2nd edn, Basingstoke 1993; Maland, *Europe in the Seventeenth Century*, 2nd edn, Basingstoke 1983; D. Nicholas, *The Transformation of Europe, 1300–1600*, London 1999; G. Parker, *Europe in Crisis, 1598–1648*, London 1979; M. E. Wiesner-Hanks, *Early Modern Europe, 1450–1789*, Cambridge 2006.

2. On international relations and Europe's confrontation with the Ottoman Empire: M. S. Anderson, *The Rise of Modern Diplomacy, 1450–1919*, London 1993; Anderson, *The Origins of the Modern European States System, 1494–1648*, London and New York 1998; A. Ayton and J. L. Price, eds., *The Medieval Military Revolution: State, Society, and Military Change in Medieval and Early Modern Europe*, London 1995; W. Blockmans, *Emperor Charles V, 1500–1558*, Oxford 2002; F. Braudel, *The Mediterranean and the Mediterranean World in the Age of Philip II*, 2 vols., Berkeley 1996; B. Downing, *The Military Revolution and Political Change: Origins of Democracy and Autocracy in Early Modern Europe*, Princeton 1992; D. Eltis, *The Military Revolution in Sixteenth-Century Europe*, London 1995; D. Goffman, *The Ottoman Empire and Early Modern Europe*, Cambridge 2002; J. R. Hale, *War and Society in Renaissance Europe, 1450–1620*, London 1985; R. Lockyer, *Habsburg and Bourbon Europe, 1470–1720*, London 1974; G. Mattingly, *Renaissance Diplomacy*, Boston 1955; G. Parker, *The Military Revolution: Military Innovation and the Rise of the West, 1500–1800*, Cambridge 1988; Parker, *The Grand Strategy of Philip II*, New Haven and London 1998; M. Roberts, *The Military Revolution, 1560–1660*, Belfast 1956.

3. On the discoveries and colonisation: J. H. Elliott, *The Old World and The New, 1492–1650*, Cambridge 1967; Elliott, *Empires of the Atlantic World: Britain and Spain in America, 1492–1830*, New Haven and London 2006; Felipe Fernandez-Armesto, *Columbus*, Oxford 1991; H. Kamen, *Spain's Road to Empire: the Making of a World Power, 1492–1763*, London 2002; L. McAlister, *Spain and Portugal in the New World, 1492–1700*, Minneapolis 1984; A. Pagden, *European Encounters with the New World*, New Haven 1992; Pagden, *Lords of All the World: Ideologies of Empire in Spain, Britain and France, c.1500–c.1800*,

New Haven and London 1995, J. H. Parry, *The Age of Reconnaissance*, London 1963; Parry, *The Spanish Seaborne Empire*, London 1966.

4. On Reformation and Counter-Reformation: R. P. Becker, ed., *German Humanism and Reformation*, New York 1982; E. Cameron, *The European Reformation*, Oxford 1991; C. S. Dixon, *The Reformation in Germany*, Oxford 2002; M. Greengrass, *The French Reformation*, Oxford 1987; A. Levi, *Renaissance and Reformation: the Intellectuel Genesis*, New Haven and London 2002; D. MacCulloch, *Reformation: Europe's House Divided, 1490-1700*, London 2003; A. McGrath, *The Intellectual Origins of the European Reformation*, London 2003; B. Thompson, *Humanists and Reformers: a History of the Renaissance and the Reformation*, Cambridge 1996.

5. On the emergence of the sovereign state in Europe: R. Bonney, *The European Dynastic States, 1494-1660*, Oxford 1991; T. Ertman, *Birth of the Leviathan: Building States and Regimes in Medieval and Early Modern Europe*, Cambridge 1997; S. E. Finer, *The History of Government*, vol. III, Oxford 1999; N. Henshall, *The Myth of Absolutism: Change and Continuity in the Early Modern European Monarchy*, London and New York 1992; P. K. Monod, *The Power of Kings: Monarchy and Religion in Europe, 1589-1715*, New Haven 1999; A. R. Myers, *Parliaments and Estates in Europe to 1789*, London 1975; A. Osiander, *Before the State: Systemic Political Change in the West from the Greeks to the French Revolution*, Oxford 2007; H. Spruyt, *The Sovereign State and its Competitors: an Analysis of Systems Change*, Princeton 1994; P. Zagorin, *Rebels and Rulers, 1500-1660*, 2 vols., Cambridge 1982.

6. On the political and constitutional history of some important countries: F. J. Baumgartner, *France in the Sixteenth Century*, New York 1995; R. Bonney, *Political Change in France under Richelieu and Mazarin, 1624-1661*, Oxford 1978; J. H. Elliott, *Imperial Spain, 1469-1716*, London, 1963; Elliott, *The Count-Duke of Olivares: the Statesman in an Age of Decline*, New Haven and London 1986; G. R. Elton, *The Tudor Revolution in Government*, Cambridge 1953; R. Evans, *The Making of the Habsburg Monarchy, 1550-1700: an Interpretation*, Oxford 1979; M. P. Holt, *The French Wars of Religion, 1562-1629*, 2nd edn, Cambridge 2005; M. Hughes, *Early Modern Germany 1477-1806*, London 1992; J. Israel, *The Dutch Republic: its Rise, Greatness and Fall, 1477-1806*, Oxford 1995; H. Kamen, *Philip of Spain*, New Haven 1997; J. P. Kenyon, ed., *The Stuart Constitution, 1603-1688*, Cambridge 1966; R. J. Knecht, *The Rise and Fall of Renaissance France, 1483-1610*, London 1996; A. W. Lovett, *Early Habsburg Spain, 1517-1598*, Oxford 1986; J. A. Lynch, *Spain, 1516-1598: From Nation State to World Empire*, Oxford 1991; L. Martines, *Power and Imagination: City-States in Renaissance Italy*, New York 1979; R. J. Major, *From Renaissance Monarchy to Absolute Monarchy: French Kings, Nobles and Estates*, Baltimore 1997; D. Parker, *The Making of French Absolutism*, London 1983; G. Parker, *The Dutch Revolt*, London 1977; Parker, *Spain and the Netherlands, 1559-1659*, London

1979; D. Potter, *A History of France, 1460–1560: the Emergence of a Nation State*, London 1995; T. K. Rabb, *The Struggle for Stability in Early Modern Europe*, Oxford 1975; J. H. Shennan, *The Origins of the Modern European State, 1450–1725*, London 1974; J. D. Tracy, *Holland under Habsburg Rule, 1506–1566: the Formation of a Body Politic*, Berkeley 1990.

7. On the Thirty Years War and the Peace of Westphalia: R. G. Asch, *The Thirty Years War: the Holy Roman Empire and Europe, 1618–1648*, London 1997; F. Dickmann, *Der Westfälische Frieden*, 6th edn, Munster 1972; H. Duchhardt, ed., *Der Westfälische Friede*, Munich 1998; G. Parker, *The Thirty Years' War*, London 1984; J. J. Poelhekke, *De vrede van Munster*, The Hague 1948; G. V. Polisensky, *The Thirty Years' War*, London 1971.

8. On political and constitutional thought: H. Baron, *The Crisis of the Early Italian Renaissance: Civic Humanism and Republican Liberty in the Age of Classicism and Tyranny*, Princeton 1966; J. H. Burns, ed., *The Cambridge History of Political Thought, 1450–1700*, Cambridge 1991; F. Chabod, *Machiavelli and the Renaissance*, Cambridge 1958; J. A. Fernandez-Santamaria, *The State, War and Peace: Spanish Political Thought in the Renaissance, 1516–1559*, Cambridge 1977; J. Franklin, *Jean Bodin and the Rise of Absolutist Theory*, Cambridge 1973; S. Gordon, *Controlling the State: Constitutionalism from Ancient Athens to Today*, Harvard 1999; H. Höpfl, *Jesuit Political Thought: the Society of Jesus and the State, c. 1540–1630*, Cambridge 2004; F. Meinecke, *Die Idee der Staatsräson*, Munich 1924; J. G. A. Pocock, *The Machiavellian Moment: Florentine Political Thought and the Atlantic Republican Tradition*, Princeton 1975; Quentin Skinner, *The Foundations of Modern Political Thought*, 2 vols., Cambridge 1978; M. Stolleis, *Geschichte des öffentlichen Rechts in Deutschland*, vol I Munich 1988; D. Wyduckel, *Princeps legibus solutus. Eine Untersuchung zur frühmodernen Rechts-und Staatslehre*, Berlin 1979.

9. On the early modern law of nations: A. Eyffinger, ed., *Compendium volkenrechtsgeschiedenis*, 2nd edn, Deventer 1991; D. Gaurier, *Histoire du droit international; Auteurs, doctrines et développement de l'Antiquité à l'aube de la période contemporaine*, Rennes 2005; W. G. Grewe, *The Epochs of International Law*, Berlin 2000; R. Lesaffer, 'The Grotian Tradition Revisited: Change and Continuity in the History of International Law', *British Yearbook of International Law*, 73 (2002) 103–39; Lesaffer, ed., *Peace Treaties and International Law in European History: From the End of the Middle Ages to World War One*, Cambridge 2004; K.-H. Ziegler, *Völkerrechtsgeschichte*, 2nd edn, Munich 2007.

10. On the Renaissance and humanism: J. Burckhardt, *The Civilization of the Renaissance in Italy*, London 1958; P. Burke, *The Italian Renaissance: Culture and Society in Italy*, 2nd edn, Cambridge 1987; R. Fubini, *Humanism and Secularization: From Petrarch to Valla*, Durham, N. C. 2003; E. Garin, *Italian*

Humanism: Philosophy and Civic Life in the Renaissance, New York 1965;
M. P. Gilmore, *The World of Humanism, 1453–1517*, New York 1952; P. Godman,
From Poliziano to Machiavelli: Florentine Humanism in the High Renaissance,
Princeton 1998; A. Grafton, *From Humanism to the Humanities: Education
and the Liberal Arts in Fifteenth- and Sixteenth-Century Europe*, Cambridge,
Mass. 1986; J. R. Hale, *The Civilization of Europe in the Renaissance*, London
1993; D. Hay, *The Italian Renaissance in its Historical Background*, 2nd edn,
Cambridge 1977; J. Kraye, ed., *The Cambridge Companion to Renaissance
Humanism*, Cambridge 1996; J. Kraye and Martin Stone, eds., *Humanism and
Early Modern Philosophy*, London 2000; P. O. Kristeller, *Renaissance Thought*,
2 vols., New York 1961–5; A. MacKay and A. Goodman, eds., *The Impact of
Humanism on Western Europe*, London 1990; C. G. Nauert, *Humanism and
the Culture of Renaissance Europe*, 2nd edn, Cambridge 2006; R. Porter
and M. Teich, eds., *The Renaissance in National Context*, Cambridge 1992;
A. Rabil, ed., *Renaissance Humanism: Foundations, Norms and Legacy*,
3 vols., Philadelphia 1988; J. Seigel, *Rhetoric and Philosophy in Renaissance
Humanism: the Union of Eloquence and Wisdom, Petrarch to Valla*, Princeton
1968; C. Trinkaus, *The Scope of Renaissance Humanism*, Ann Arbor 1983.

11. On early modern law: H. Coing, *Europäisches Privatrecht, 1500–1800*, 2 vols.,
Munich 1985; H. J. Berman, *Law and Revolution II: the Impact of the Protestant
Reformations on the Western Legal Tradition*, New York 2004; F. Wieacker,
A History of Private Law in Europe with Particular Reference to Germany,
Oxford 1995.

12. On humanist jurisprudence: K. H. Burmeister, *Das Studium der Rechte im
Zeitalter des Humanismus im deutschen Rechtsbereich*, Wiesbaden 1974;
R. Dekkers, *Het humanisme en de rechtswetenschap in de Nederlanden*,
Antwerp 1938; A. P. Th. Eyssell, *Doneau, sa vie et ses ouvrages; l'école de
Bourges; synthèse du droit romain au XVIe siècle; son influence jusqu'à nos
jours*, Geneva 1970; M. P. Gilmore, *Humanists and Jurists: Six Studies in the
Renaissance*, Cambridge 1963; D. R. Kelley, *Foundations of Modern Historical
Scholarship: Language, Law and History in the French Renaissance*, New York
1970; Kelley, *François Hotman: a Revolutionary's Ordeal*, Princeton 1972;
Kelley, 'Civil Science in the Renaissance: Jurisprudence in the French Manner',
Journal of the History of Ideas, 3 (1981) 261–76; G. Kisch, *Erasmus und die
Jurisprudenz seiner Zeit: Studien zum humanistischen Rechtsdenken*, Basel
1960; Kisch, *Gestalten und Probleme aus Humanismus und Jurisprudenz*,
Berlin 1969; Kisch, *Studien zur humanistischen Jurisprudenz*, Berlin and New
York 1972; I. Maclean, *Interpretation and the Meaning in the Renaissance: the
Case of Law*, Cambridge 1992; D. O. McNeil, *Guillaume Budé and Humanism
in the Reign of Francis I*, Geneva 1975; S. Rowan, *Ulrich Zasius: a Jurist in the
German Renaissance*, Frankfurt 1987; E. P. J. Spangenberg, *Jacob Cujas und
seine Zeitgenossen*, Frankfurt 1967; P. Stein, 'Legal Humanism and Legal

Science', *Legal History Review*, 54 (1986) 297–306; H. E. Troje, *Graeca leguntur: Die Aneignung des byzantinischen Rechts und die Entstehung eines humanistischen Corpus Juris Civilis in die Jurisprudenz des 16. Jahrhunderts*, Cologne and Vienna 1971; Troje, *Humanistische Jurisprudenz*, Goldbach 1993; J. Witte, *Law and Protestantism: the Legal Teachings of the Lutheran Reformation*, Cambridge 2002.

13. On the Dutch Elegant School and Roman-Dutch law: M. Ahsmann, *Collegia en colleges: juridisch onderwijs aan de Leidse universiteit, 1575–1630, in het bijzonder het disputeren*, Groningen 1990; A. Cannoy-Olthoff and P. L. Nève, *Holländische Eleganz gegenüber deutschem usus modernus pandectarum?* Nijmegen 1990; R. Feenstra and C. De Waal, *Seventeenth-Century Leiden Law Professors*, Amsterdam 1975; R. Feenstra and R. Zimmermann, eds., *Das römisch-hollandische Recht: Fortschritte des Civilsrechts im 17. und 18. Jahrhundert*, Berlin 1992; G. van den Bergh, *Die holländische elegante Schule. Ein Beitrag zur Geschichte von Humanismus und Rechtswissenschaft in den Niederlanden 1500–1800*, Frankfurt 2002.

14. On the life and works of Hugo Grotius: C. Edwards, *Hugo Grotius, the Miracle of Holland: a Study in Political and Legal Thought*, Chicago 1981; H. J. M. Nellen, *Hugo de Groot: Een leven in strijd om de vrede, 1583–1645*, Amsterdam 2007; C. G. Roelofsen, 'Grotius and the International Politics of the Seventeenth Century', in H. Bull, B. Kingsbury and A. Roberts, eds., *Hugo Grotius and International Relations*, Oxford 1990, 95–131.

15. On the evolution of law and the reception of Roman law in various countries: D. L. Carey Millar and R. Zimmerman, eds., *The Civilian Tradition and Scots Law*, Berlin 1997; H. Conrad, *Deutsche Rechtsgeschichte*, Vol. II, Karlsruhe 1966; J. P. Dawson, *The Oracles of the Law*, Ann Arbor 1968; B. Diestelkamp, *Recht und Gericht im Heiligen Römischen Reich*, Frankfurt 1999; R. H. Helmholz, *Roman Canon Law in Reformation England*, Cambridge 1990; B. Hermesdorf, *Römisches Recht in den Niederlanden*, Milan 1968; G. Strauss, *Law, Resistance and the State: the Opposition to Roman Law in Reformation Germany*, Princeton 1986; R. C. van Caenegem, *Le droit romain en Belgique*, Milan 1966.

6

Ratio
(the Modern Age, 1648–1914)

A Politics and the state

1 The Modern Age

This is the generation of that great Leviathan, or rather (to speake more reverently) of that mortall God to which wee owe under the immortal God, our peace and defence.[1]

323 The French Revolution and the Modern Age

In the spring of 1789, the French Revolution broke out. In the years that followed, the revolutionaries spread their radical ideas at the points of their bayonets throughout Europe. Even the final defeat of Napoleon and the restoration of the monarchy in France in 1815 could not erase the Revolution. A return to the pre-1789 political regime – the *Ancien Régime* – proved impossible. In all parts of Europe the sovereigns and the old privileged aristocracy henceforth had to share power with the upper middle class, the bourgeoisie. The class system, feudality and royal 'absolutism' were now things of the past.

In the field of law as in others, the Revolution caused a watershed. Legal reform stood high on the revolutionary agenda. Napoleon Bonaparte (1799/1804–15) pushed through the codification in France. The French conquest of a large part of Europe ensured that the Napoleonic codes were introduced outside France. In many countries, the end of the *Ancien Régime* spelled the end of the *ancien droit*.

It may come as a surprise that the French Revolution is not treated here as a break between two epochs but falls in the middle of the Modern Age (1648–1914). The French Revolution went a long way towards realising the political and legal programme of modernity, which was largely laid out in the late seventeenth and the eighteenth century. However radically and suddenly the Revolution may have struck Europe, the resultant

---

[1] Thomas Hobbes, *Leviathan* 17, ed. Richard Tuck, *Hobbes: Leviathan*, Cambridge 1996.

social, political and legal model was no *creatio ex nihilo*. The impact of
the Revolution should not blind us to the continuity between the decades before and after 1789. The fundamental worldview of the late *Ancien
Régime* does not differ in essence from that of the early nineteenth century. Before 1789, modernity was still in the making, while after 1815 it
was more in place; but in both cases faith and confidence in the unbridled
possibilities of human reason were central. In addition, this periodisation does greater justice to the country that largely escaped the French
Revolution, partly because it had already realised some of the most
important achievements of that Revolution by its own revolution a century before: Great Britain.

324   The highpoint of modernity

The nineteenth century marks the high point of the modern, western
European civilisation. Modernity with its emphasis on the human capacity for reason provided the framework for unparalleled progress in the
fields of science, technology and economics. With the constitutional and
parliamentary monarchy and the protection of individual rights under
the rule of law, a politico-legal model arose in western Europe that provides a model for the rest of the world to the present day. Within Europe,
the lower classes called ever louder for a share in the increased prosperity
and opportunities modern civilisation had brought. That aim was to be
achieved in the twentieth century. A large part of Europe's success during the nineteenth century was made possible by its domination over
other continents and peoples. The nineteenth century marked the aegis
of Europe's global dominance through its large colonial empires. The colonies footed a good part of the bill for Europe's economic success.

2   The Industrial Revolution

325   Agrarian Revolution

Since pre-classical Antiquity, agriculture had always formed the backbone of the world's economy. The Industrial Revolution of the late eighteenth and nineteenth century would change that. It caused a spectacular
growth in the industrial output of Europe and North America and led to
an enormous increase in trade within and outside Europe. By the early
twentieth century, for the first time in history, more people would work in
industry and commerce than would farm the lands.

   The Industrial Revolution was preceded by an Agrarian Revolution.
From the second half of the seventeenth century onwards, agricultural

production was on the rise in western Europe. The Agrarian Revolution started off in England, the Southern Netherlands and Catalonia. During the early eighteenth century, it spread to the rest of western and central Europe. Eastern Europe, where the landed gentry continued to exploit the rural population and invested little in innovation, lagged behind.

From the mid-seventeenth to the late nineteenth century, the amount of farmed land in and outside Europe increased dramatically. The Habsburg re-conquest of Hungary from the Ottoman Turks (1699) and the Russian expansion towards the Black Sea opened up new lands to feed the European population. By the late eighteenth century, North America was an important exporter of agricultural produce to Europe. Further colonisation of lands in North America, Argentina and Australia during the nineteenth century would make Europe even less dependent upon itself to feed its population.

During the seventeenth and eighteenth centuries, several new crops such as potatoes and maize were imported from the New World into Europe. The potato not only led to a more varied diet for the European population, but also provided an alternative in case the grain harvest failed. Different technical and scientific innovations, such as more sophisticated methods of crop rotation and fertilisation, as well as increasing specialisation, enhanced productivity.

For the first time in centuries, the cycle of hunger and disease was broken. Although there would be more periods of famine in the nineteenth century – as after the failure of the potato harvest in 1845–8 – these were now fewer and further apart. The time of the great epidemics was also over. The last epidemic of pestilence in Scotland dates from 1649, in England from 1665, in Spain from 1685, in France from 1720 and in Italy from 1743.[2] In eastern Europe and the Ottoman Empire, pestilence recurred until the late eighteenth century. Improved health care and hygiene reduced the impact of other epidemic diseases on demographic evolution. Between 1700 and 1800, Europe's population grew from 118 million to 187 million.[3] A century later, the old continent accommodated 400 million people.[4]

326   Mercantilism

The European states started to intervene more actively in the economy of their countries in order to increase the tax basis for their ever-growing

---

[2] From Jeremy Black, *Eighteenth-Century Europe*, 2nd edn, London 1999, 5.
[3] Black, *Eighteenth-Century Europe*, 1.
[4] J. M. Roberts, *Europe, 1880–1945*, 3rd edn, London 2001, 12.

armies and navies. During the seventeenth and much of the eighteenth century, in several of the leading countries of Europe, mercantilism set the agenda of economic policy. In the mercantilist credo, economic competition between the European states was a zero-sum game. The total volume of commerce and wealth was believed to be constant so that economic growth by one state would always be at the expense of the others. In consequence, economic competition was seen as an inherent part of the political rivalry between states.

The economic policy of Louis XIV's minister Jean-Baptiste Colbert (1619–83) is often quoted as the textbook example of mercantilism. The backbone of Colbert's policies was the creation of a positive trade balance by stimulating the production and export of manufactures and the import of raw materials and by restricting the export of raw materials and the import of manufactures. He invested in some segments of craft industry such as silk and metal production. Also, he tried to enhance France's share of the cargo trade in and outside Europe. For this, he invested in maritime infrastructure and the shipbuilding industry. Within France, tolls and customs were abolished or at least harmonised as much as possible. In relations with other countries, they served as instruments to strengthen the domestic economy and damage that of the other countries.

327   Workshops

Overall, during the second half of the seventeenth and the eighteenth century, commerce and industry continued to expand in western and central Europe. The two fastest growing sectors were colonial trade and rural cottage industry. Both sectors were or became capital intensive. Whereas urban craft industry was run by small family businesses, cottage industry increasingly fell under the control of rich investors – from the aristocracy as well as the urban elites – who supplied the raw materials and bought the manufactures from the cottage labourers. During the eighteenth century, increasing numbers of investors took to setting up large workshops in which they employed scores of day labourers. This allowed them to gain a tighter grip on the production process and enhance productivity. Technical innovations and changes, such as the general use of wind- and watermills in textile and metal production, also made the concentration of labour in larger workshops necessary.

These evolutions stimulated international banking and money lending. The centre of the international money economy now shifted definitively from Italy and Spain to north-western Europe. During the sixteenth century, Antwerp still had to compete with Genoa, Venice and Seville as major centres of international banking. By the early seventeenth century, Amsterdam had become the financial centre of Europe. A century later, London had displaced Amsterdam as the leading financial hub of the expanding Western economy. After 1900, London had to cede the place of honour to New York.

328   The Industrial Revolution

The first industrial use of the steam engine by James Watt (1736–1818) in the English textile industry in the 1780s is often quoted as the event which started off the Industrial Revolution. Although the Industrial Revolution built on processes that had already been underway for much of the eighteenth century – such as the emergence of large manufactories – it really was a 'revolution'. The introduction of the steam engine allowed human beings to break through the natural limitations human labour has set on economic growth. In the course of a few generations, the basic tenets of traditional economic thought, like mercantilism, were displaced by a new theory of unlimited economic growth.

Industrialisation first took off in Britain. The fact that the industrial steam engine was a British invention does not provide sufficient explanation for this. The expansion of commerce, the building of a colonial empire and the development of agriculture and cottage industry had provided Britain with a large domestic and colonial consumer market and with enough capital to invest. The isolation of the British economy from continental Europe during the Napoleonic Wars further stimulated British industry.

The First Industrial Revolution lasted from the 1780s until halfway through the nineteenth century and had two major phases. Britain took the lead in both. From Britain, industrialisation spread to the continent, first to Belgium, and then to the other countries of western and central Europe. For industrialisation to reach Russia and Turkey, one had to wait until the early twentieth century, or even until after the First World War.

The first phase was that of the industrialisation of the textile industry. Over time, the introduction of the steam engine led to mass production of cheaper textiles, with which the traditional urban and cottage craft industry could not compete. Cotton came to replace wool as the most important commodity. The cotton industry was inextricably bound to the colonial economy. The Northern American and Asian colonies constituted primary consumer markets for European industrial products. In Asia, local manufacturing was destroyed in the process. The profits were used to purchase more raw materials and to finance the slave trade. The industrial use of steam engines as well as its use in households multiplied the demand for coal. Steam engines were also used for coal mining – in fact, their first use dates back to the late seventeenth century. Even more so than the industrialisation of textile production, coal mining led to the concentration of labour and the emergence of important industrial cities.

The second phase was that of the steel industry. This demanded far greater investments than the industrialisation of textile production. The construction of railways provided both the demand and the capital to make the industrialisation of steel production viable. The first railway in Britain dates from 1825. The USA (1827), France (1828), Belgium (1835), Germany (1835) and Russia (1837) followed quickly.

329 Industrial society

Industrialisation had multiple consequences. First, there was the introduction of mass production and its standardisation. Large plants with hundreds and sometimes thousands of workers displaced the old traditional craft workshops and cottage manufacturing. To reduce the costs, production had to be standardised as much as possible. Mass production, mass communication, the tailoring of consumer demand to a regularly updated common denominator of taste called fashion, bureaucratic government with its armies of civil servants who with their standard forms and procedures processed myriad petitions and decisions ... these were all characteristic of the industrial society that came out of the Industrial Revolution.

Second, the Industrial Revolution stimulated urbanisation. Already during the seventeenth and eighteenth centuries, the level of urbanisation had greatly increased. But this was dwarfed by the growth of urban population centres in the nineteenth and twentieth centuries. Old towns expanded; new cities emerged close to coal mines and harbours.

Third, the Industrial Revolution marked the triumph of the bourgeois elite over the old landed aristocracy. To a large extent, this was as much a process of amalgamation as one of displacement. Because of industrialisation, industrial production and trade for the first time became economically more significant than agricultural production. Mass production and the explosion of trade allowed the bourgeoisie to amass fortunes in the space of a few decades that outdid those of the traditional landed aristocracy many times over. Increasingly, the demands of industrial and commercial investors came to dictate the economic policies of the state, often to the detriment of the landowners. The victory of the proponents of free trade during the second half of the nineteenth century clearly illustrates this. In most countries of Europe, landowners tried to protect domestic agricultural production against cheap imports from the colonies by advocating trade restrictions on food import. The industrialists for their part favoured free trade because this would lower food prices and thus allow them to pay lower wages to their labourers.

Fourth, there was the emergence of a new social class, that of the industrial labourers. Demographic growth and the increase in agricultural productivity provided an ever larger supply of cheap labour for the emerging industries. The collapse of traditional manufacturing further swelled the ranks of the unpropertied labourers. After the first phases of industrialisation, sharp competition within and between the industrialised countries of Europe and North America took off. To sustain the competition, industrialists resorted to two measures: trade restrictions to stem the import of foreign industrial products and the reduction of production costs. The latter meant that the wages of industrial labourers were under constant pressure. Labourers were forced to work long hours; women and even children had to work for minimal wages in the factories in order to provide the family with enough income to survive. Working and living conditions were appalling. From the 1830s onwards, the outcry for change grew louder. The first advocates for social justice came from the ranks of the liberal bourgeoisie. During the second half of the nineteenth century, labourers started to organise themselves in trade unions and co-operative societies. Many adopted the ideology of the great socialist thinkers such as Karl Marx (1818–83).

3   Europe conquers the world

330   Commercial empires and early colonisation

The Industrial Revolution rode on the back of the working class and the world beyond Europe. The rapid industrialisation of Europe would not have been possible without the colonial empires in America, Africa, Asia and Oceania.

The colonisation of the world by Europe had begun as early as 1500 with the great discoveries by the Spaniards and the Portuguese, who were the first to establish a global empire. The Portuguese colonies in Brazil, along the African coast and in the Indies were primarily trade settlements. The Spaniards in Latin America penetrated more deeply inland, destroying the great indigenous empires of the Aztecs in Mexico and the Incas in

Peru and colonising their lands. In the interior, they discovered important silver mines that were to provide wealth and power for the Spanish monarchy for centuries. Large groups of Europeans settled in Mexico and Peru, as well as in the Caribbean.

From the end of the sixteenth century onwards, the Spaniards and Portuguese ran into competition from other Europeans, especially the English, French and Dutch. They too acquired trade settlements in the Caribbean, Africa, America and the Indies. During the seventeenth century, the Republic of the United Provinces evolved into the strongest maritime power in the world, conquering a large commercial empire in the East Indies. Apart from acquiring trade bases along the routes to the Indies, the three new colonial powers set about conquering the interior of North America. In the Caribbean, Canada and on the east and south coasts of what is now the United States, colonies were established to exploit the natural resources and farming possibilities of the land. Plantations were laid out for the cultivation of products for the European market, such as sugar and cotton. A triangular trade arose between Africa, America and Europe. Ships sailed from Europe to Africa, loaded with European products in order to buy black slaves; from there they sailed to America, where the slaves were required to work the plantations; and the crops grown in America were in turn brought to Europe. The growing demographic pressures in Europe led to an increase in immigration to the western continent and from 1788 to Australia as well. The colonists seized more and more land and increasingly engaged in traditional farming. In the course of the nineteenth century, North America was to become an important supplier of cereals for Europe.

331 European imperialism in the nineteenth century

The Industrial Revolution increased the economic importance of the colonial empires. Industry needed raw materials from the various continents and the colonies provided important and secure markets for industrial products. Whereas the relations with Asia and, to a lesser extent, Africa had in the past been primarily commercial in nature and the European presence was confined to some coastal bases, it now became clear that the colonisation of the interior could yield greater economic benefits. Ruling the interiors in the Indies and Africa made it possible for the colonising powers to exploit the raw materials themselves instead of buying them. Furthermore, indigenous industries such as the cotton industry could be brought to a standstill, making the native population dependent on European products.

[handwritten margin note: 7 Years War]

The late eighteenth and the nineteenth century saw a race between the European powers – led by Great Britain and France – for dominion over the interiors of Asia, Africa and North America. The Seven Years War (1756–63) between Britain and France was not just a European war but also a colonial one that sealed the expulsion of the French from Canada and India. With the colonisation of Australia in 1788 and New Zealand in 1841, London also assured itself of dominance in that part of the world. The takeover of the Cape Colony from the Dutch during the Napoleonic Wars in 1806 had also given the British a firm foothold in southern Africa. From there, British colonists were to vest their power over almost all of East Africa in the course of the nineteenth century, from the Cape to the Nile delta. During the same century, the French built up a great colonial empire in western Africa, the Maghreb and Indochina. The Netherlands extended its power in the East Indies over the entire archipelago known as the Netherlands Indies. At the end of the nineteenth century, King Leopold II of Belgium (1865–1909) obtained an immense empire in central Africa, Congo, which he left to the Belgian state upon his death. The Russian tsars extended their European empire across Siberia to the Bering Strait and the Pacific. The European colonists on the north-east coast of America, who had declared independence from London in 1776 and proclaimed the United States of America, began the great trek westwards in the nineteenth century, seizing the entire area from the Atlantic to the Pacific. Towards the beginning of the First World War, virtually the entire world, with the exception of Japan, China, Siam, Liberia and Ethiopia, was in European hands.

Even so, the first cracks in European dominance were evident from the end of the eighteenth century onwards. In 1776, thirteen British colonies on the east coast of North America declared independence. After seven years of fighting, this fact was recognised by the British crown in 1783 (Treaty of Paris). During the first few decades of the nineteenth century, the Spanish and Portuguese colonies in Latin America cut their ties with the motherland. The new states on the western continent were, however, all European creations that applied the European model of civilisation.

4   The Ancien Régime

332   The rise of bureaucratic government

With the exception of England, the monarchy managed to strengthen its position in virtually all the great countries of western Europe in the late seventeenth and early eighteenth century. The 'absolute' monarchy reached its high point in what is referred to as the *Ancien Régime*. The France of Louis XIV (1643–1715) and Louis XV (1715–74) provides the historical model for the 'absolute' monarchy of that period.

The century after Westphalia saw the steady rise and expansion of centralised, monarchical government. Bureaucracies expanded. Within the royal councils an increasing number of specialised secretariats were set up, with growing numbers of civil servants and councillors. As ministers, the royal councillors bore responsibility for a particular aspect of government. The diplomatic service was somewhat professionalised.

As before, warfare remained the engine of state formation. Between 1648 and 1815, numerous wars were fought between the great powers of Europe. These were hugely expensive. From the second half of the seventeenth century, most princes had a standing army in peacetime. Previously most monarchs – with the exception of the Spanish king – had no more than a small army in peacetime, consisting of an extensive royal guard, garrisons in strategically located forts and cities, a small fleet and the artillery. In the event of war, mercenaries – generally foreign – would be drawn upon. Louis XIV and Frederick William, the Great Elector of Brandenburg and Duke of Prussia (1640–88), broke with tradition, maintaining a large standing army in peacetime. This ensured that the system of mercenaries gradually fell into desuetude. Officers and soldiers gained permanent employment in the king's service. Fewer foreigners were recruited; the nationalisation of warfare had begun. Most of the other countries of Europe gradually followed the French example. In the early eighteenth century, Prussia introduced a limited form of conscription.

Almost constant warfare and the introduction of a standing army pushed government spending to ever higher levels. In order to generate greater income for the government, the civil service had to be strengthened. This not only meant a larger and better equipped central administration but also necessitated tighter control by the central government over the provincial and local authorities. Louis XIV, for example, appointed *intendants* to exercise control over the provincial and local administrations. These were civil servants appointed at his discretion, with powers equal or superior to those of the traditional governors, who normally belonged to the high nobility. In 1683, Louis issued a decree bringing the municipal finances under the authority of the central government and its *intendants*.

Nor did the church escape the tentacles of the sovereign state. In France, the Southern Netherlands and Spain the sovereigns encouraged

placet

greater autonomy on the part of the church vis-à-vis the pope and Rome. The *placet* was generalised. Ecclesiastical judges and jurists often favoured the nationalisation of canon law. The great sovereigns promoted the unity of faith among the population. Louis XIV even went so far as to revoke in 1685 the 1598 Edict of Nantes, which had provided for religious toleration. Thousands of Huguenots who refused to convert were forced to leave France. Many fled to the Republic of the United Provinces, Britain or North America.

333   The territorial state

Following on from the feudal state (thirteenth–fifteenth centuries) and the dynastic state (sixteenth–seventeenth centuries) came the territorial state of the eighteenth century – although the term dynastical-territorial state would be even better. The expansion of central government was accompanied by a process of de-personification of the regime. In the sixteenth- and seventeenth-century dynastic state, the prince was very much the heart and soul of the state. The success of the central government stood or fell by the personality of the prince. The great princes of the sixteenth and seventeenth centuries were shrewd if not intelligent, as well as hardworking. The drawback was that they organised their administration in such a way that less gifted or conscientious successors were bound to get into difficulties. However, the larger, more specialised and professional the machinery of government became, the more the role of the prince shrank. During the course of the eighteenth century, the 'monarchy' was institutionalised and evolved into a collective government. Whereas in 1500, there was no such thing as the 'state' independent of the person of the sovereign, the latter now gradually became a symbol for a larger, collective and abstract identity consisting of a multiplicity of institutions and organs.

The great monarchies of western Europe had emerged from the often accidental grouping of various kingdoms and dominions in the hands of a single dynasty. The monarchy or kingdom was often a personal union between the different possessions of the dynasty. Now the state obtained an autonomy of its own. From having been the possessor of the state, the monarch now became the supreme state official and representative. '*L'état, c'est moi*,' words which Louis XIV allegedly uttered in 1654, worked in both directions.

This emergence of the sovereign state as an abstract body politic had started in the Late Middle Ages with the efforts by the great dynasties to obtain more direct control over their territories by the extension of the central machinery of government and the suppression of the nobility and the clergy. The Military Revolution of the sixteenth and seventeenth centuries had assured victory on the part of the sovereigns. The latter expanded their governments into genuinely modern, bureaucratic systems. Now this state machinery developed a dynamic of its own and, as it were, absorbed the sovereign himself. The territorial state had become an autonomous unit. The territory of the state was the historical outcome of the dynastic rights of the sovereign, but now obtained a value in its own right. The state was identified with its territory. That territory was jealously guarded. The borders were for the first time clearly demarcated and systematically strengthened; foreign interference was an attack on sovereignty and was to be opposed at all costs. The notion that sovereigns could cede territories by marriage, inheritance or sale was increasingly resisted, as evidenced by the numerous episodes during the eighteenth century in which the normal rules of the dynastic and feudal succession were set aside in order to safeguard the higher interests of state. The state not only transcended the sovereign who brought and kept the territory together and who defended and governed it with the aid of the army and the bureaucracy; the state was now also the army and the bureaucracy.

334   Aristocratic government

All this did not mean that political and legal unification had been achieved. While external sovereignty might be absolute, internally it remained relative in the face of legal plurality and class discriminations. The sovereigns managed to increase their grip over local and regional government only gradually and laboriously. In most countries of western Europe, the regime rested on a precarious balance of power between the sovereign and the nobility and the higher clergy. Princes tried as much as possible to remain free in the choice of their leading ministers, civil servants and military commanders. Great princes such as Louis XIV in France, Maria Theresa (1740–80) in Austria and Frederick II (1740–86) in Prussia were able to do so for the most important positions. Nevertheless, princes were limited in their choices as they needed to secure the loyalty of the aristocracy to their regime by allowing them to participate in it. The senior positions in the towns, provinces, courts, central government, army and diplomacy constituted the reward for loyalty to the monarchy on the part of the scions of noble families. The monarchs were in many cases obliged to appoint sons to succeed their fathers as ministers or councillors. In France, the sale of offices by the sovereign to the heirs of previous office-holders became general practice.

This illustrates the built-in tension within the monarchical regimes. On the one hand, after the 1660s, in most countries of Europe, the monarchy had established its supremacy over the aristocracy. In the struggle between the prince and the aristocracy, the third estate – especially the urban elites – had often of old chosen the side of the prince against the nobility and clergy. On the other hand, the monarchy had assured itself of the co-operation of the same nobility and clergy by compensating them for their loss of autonomy and political freedom with active participation in the regime. Inevitably, this new alliance between king and aristocracy weakened the position of the third estate. In the course of the sixteenth and seventeenth centuries, princes had often used members of the urban, professional elites to staff their bureaucracy. In this way, leading families from the third estate had managed to penetrate the higher offices of state and, with time, join the ranks of the nobility. As the nobility witnessed a decline in its actual power from the second half of the seventeenth century onwards, it closed ranks. The sale of offices ensured that new men would have greater difficulty in attaining the top tiers of central government and entering the ranks of the nobility. In this way, the political amalgamation of the two great secular elites, the noble aristocracy and the urban, professional elite, was slowed down if not frustrated in most countries of continental Europe. That was also the case in France. Halfway through the eighteenth century, the chances for members of the urban elites to penetrate the highest levels of central government were smaller than before.

At the same time, however, in some countries, the social, cultural and economic differences between the urban elite and a large part of the nobility – with the exception of the top tiers of the landed nobility such as princes, dukes and marquesses – shrank and both secular elites increasingly merged into one. This was particularly true in Great Britain where the gentry and the top of the third estate practically merged into one class. To some extent, it was also the case in France. But in the latter country, the members of the new secular elite which resulted from this process felt blocked in their political and administrative aspirations by the central government and those members of the traditional aristocracy who did not care for sharing power. This led to ever-growing tensions within the *Ancien Régime*.

5   The *Ancien Régime* contested

335   Ideologies of absolutism

These tensions were reflected in political thought. Whereas many writers of the seventeenth century took up the defence of royal absolutism, others built on the old constitutional tradition which had its roots in medieval jurisprudence and conciliar thought and gave it a new direction, that of political liberalism.

In France, Jacques-Bénigne Bossuet (1627–1704), preceptor to Louis XIV's son and later Bishop of Meaux, counts among the staunchest defenders of royal authority. In his *Politique tirée des propres paroles de l'Ecriture sainte*, which he wrote largely to instruct the Dauphin, Bossuet defended the divine origins of royal powers. The king had received his authority directly from God and his authority resembled that of God. The king's power, like God's, was that of a father over his people.

> We have seen that kings hold the place of God, who is the true Father of the human race. We have also seen that the first idea of power that there was among men, is that of paternal power; and that kings were fashioned on the model of fathers. Moreover, all the world agrees that the obedience, which is due to public power, is only found (in the Decalogue) in the precept which obliges one to honour his parents.[5]

Like a father, the king had to take care of his people and work for their wellbeing. He was bound to divine law and justice, but no earthly power could take him to account or had a right to disobey him because of the injustice of his actions or commands. The absoluteness of royal authority was seen as necessary to avoid civil unrest and to safeguard the security of all.

> The kings are subjects, like the others, to the equity of the laws; both because they must be just, and because they owe to the people the example of justice-keeping; but they are not subject to the penalties of the laws …
>
> If there is in the state an authority capable of stopping the course of public power, or of hampering its exercise, no one is safe.[6]

In Britain, the cause of absolutism was taken up by King James I (1603–25) and Robert Filmer (1588–1653), author of *Patriarcha*. Filmer too likened the power of the king to that of a father over his family. It found its origins in nature and divine creation.

336 Hobbes

A third advocate of royal absolutism in Britain was Thomas Hobbes (1588–1679). Hobbes wrote his main political treatise, *Leviathan* (1651),

---

[5] Jacques-Bénigne Bossuet, *Politique tirée des propres paroles de l'Ecriture sainte* 3.3, translation by Patrick Riley, *Bossuet: Politics Drawn from the Holy Scripture*, Cambridge 1999.
[6] Bossuet, *Politique tirée* 4.1.4 and 6.

against the background of the English Civil War. As Bodin and Bossuet had done, Hobbes put his trust in a strong, central government to safe-guard peace and security within the realm.

Hobbes takes the state of nature as the point of departure of his polit-ical philosophy. In the state of nature, before there is an organised civil society, all men are equal. They are all subject to the same natural obliga-tions and enjoy the same natural rights or liberties. Man's first obligation is that of self-preservation, for the pursuit of which he holds the right to do everything necessary, including the use of force. 'The Right of Nature, which Writers commonly call *Jus Naturale,* is the Liberty each man hath, to use his own power, as he will himselfe, for the preservation of his own Nature.'[7] Hobbes rejects the existence of an objective morality in nature. Each man's interest determines what is good or not. In Hobbes's system, this moral individualism did not have as yet far-reaching consequences because in civil society man loses his natural freedom. But it would have in nineteenth- and twentieth-century liberal political thought.

Because of their equality and their natural dispositions, men will come to desire the same, scarce goods. Thus, each man becomes another's enemy (*homo homini lupus*). Therefore, the desire for self-preservation leads to a permanent state of 'warre of every one against every one', which ends by putting everybody's life in jeopardy: 'And the life of man [is] soli-tary, poore, brutish, and short.'[8]

> And because the condition of Man ... is a condition of Warre of every one against every one; in which case every one is governed by his own Reason; and there is nothing he can make use of, that may not be a help unto him, in preserving his life against his enemyes; It followeth, that in such a condition, every man has a Right to every thing; even to one anothers body. And therefore, as long as this naturall Right of every man to every thing endureth, there can be not security to any man, (how strong or wise he ever be), of living out the time, which Nature ordinarily, alloweth men to live. And consequently it is a precept, or generall rule of Reason, That every man ought to endeavour Peace, as farre as he has hope of obtaining it; and when he cannot obtain it, that he may seek, and use, all helps, and advantages of Warre.[9]

To escape from this anarchy, man decides to leave the state of nature and institutes a 'commonwealth', a civil society or state. This is done by enter-ing a social contract. In this contract, all men surrender their natural

---

[7] Hobbes, *Leviathan* 14.64.   [8] Hobbes, *Leviathan* 13.62–3.
[9] Hobbes, *Leviathan* 14.64.

liberties, including the right to use force, to the commonwealth. To enforce
the contract, a sovereign authority is established to which the members of
the commonwealth subject themselves and upon which all natural liberties and powers are bestowed. The sovereign himself, the *Leviathan*, alone
retains his natural liberties; by consequence, his rights and liberties are
unlimited, as is his authority.

The humanist thinkers of the fifteenth and sixteenth centuries had
already placed self-preservation at the heart of their political system.
In the writings of Hobbes, this humanist tradition, to which Grotius
adheres, is further developed. Hobbes, as Machiavelli and many other
humanist thinkers before him, holds a negative view of human nature.
Man is naturally inclined to discord and violence. Only by suppressing
human nature can peace and security be achieved. Therefore, man must
leave the state of nature behind and institute a commonwealth. Therefore,
all public power must be concentrated in one single sovereign power.

Because sovereign power is the first and last safeguard of public peace
and security, each action that disturbs the internal order is an attack on
sovereign state power. Only the sovereign has the right to use force. The
state's subjects do not have a right of resistance. However, if the state
proves incapable of safeguarding peace and security, it loses its reason for
existence and its subjects are no longer held to obedience. But as long as it
has the power to uphold public power, it can do so and quell any attempt
at subverting it. In a system wherein might is the legitimisation of the
state and its law, might is right.

337 Locke

The Englishman John Locke (1632–1704) may be considered the foremost
representative of the constitutional tradition in the seventeenth century.
He is one of the founding fathers of modern political liberalism. His *Two
Treatises of Government* (1679–81, published 1690) provide an answer
to the absolutist doctrines of Filmer and Hobbes. As Hobbes had done,
Locke uses the concepts of the state of nature and the social contract to
explain the origins of public authority.

However, Locke has a far less negative view of human nature and
on the state of nature than Hobbes. In Locke's view, nature not only
bestows liberties or rights upon man, but also duties. To each man's
right answers another man's obligations. The right to life, liberty and
property is limited by the duty to respect another man's life, liberty and
property. Self-preservation may be man's first duty to himself, but his
right to pursue it is restricted by the obligation to respect another's right

to self-preservation. With Locke, the state of nature is more organised than with Hobbes. Rights and obligations are equally balanced and morality is not determined solely by man's proper interests. Men also have a right to enforce their claims upon other men and to hold them to their duties under natural law. This Locke refers to as 'executive power'. As this power can also be executed collectively, it forms the foundation of governing power. In Locke's system, political power is natural and precedes the state.

Men did not leave the state of nature solely because of the need to suppress human nature and man's natural inclination for violence. According to Locke, the origin of the social contract must be sought in property. At the beginning of times, all goods were common property. But by adding their labour to certain goods, men attained ownership over them. The state was then instituted to protect and enforce the rights of men with regard to their life, liberty and property.

In Locke's vision, man did not subject himself totally to the state through the social contract. He envisages the social contract as a kind of trust, in which the state receives certain well-defined powers over its citizens to attain certain well-defined ends. Public authority is instrumental as well as restricted; it is subject to its purpose, the common good. Contrary to what Hobbes held, in Locke's view, the ruler too is party to the social contract. Similar to his subjects, he has also ceded his natural liberties to the community.

With his theory of social contract and entrusted power, Locke lays the foundations for one of the basic tenets of modern political liberalism: the limitation of state power. In Locke's view, the state does not hold absolute power over its citizens, but has only limited authority. As the liberty and power of the individual were limited in the state of nature by man's natural duties, and as state power is derived from these, state power itself is restricted. In Britain after the Glorious Revolution (1688) and on the continent after the French Revolution, this idea would be translated into practice through the constitutional protection of certain fundamental rights and liberties which were declared to be beyond the reach of normal state power, such as the freedom of conscience and religion, free speech and the right to property.

Because state power is instrumental and limited, the people also retain the right to resistance, according to John Locke. The citizens have not ceded their natural rights and liberties completely, but only to the extent that it is necessary to preserve their life, liberty and property. A residue of natural rights stays with the people. As public authority has been bestowed upon the state government in trust, the people retain the right to change the government, even to revolt, in case the trust is broken.

§338   Separation of power

The notion that public power is contractual, instrumental and restricted by its end, the common good, has its roots in the medieval constitutional tradition. But, in contrast to most other early modern constitutionalist thinkers, Locke also proposes a mechanism to make the limits on governmental power effective: the doctrine of the separation of powers. In the state of nature, man had two different kinds of power: the power to do everything necessary for his preservation and the power to enforce his rights upon others. Within the state, the former evolved into the legislative power, the latter into the executive power. Under the social contract, the people cede their natural rights and liberties and delegate these to the state. The majority forms a legislative authority which lays down the fundamental rules concerning life, liberty and property. The executive power receives the right to enforce these rules upon the people:

> The first Power, *viz. of doing whatsoever he thought fit for the Preservation of himself*, and the rest of Mankind, he gives up to be regulated by Laws made by the Society, so far forth as the preservation of himself, and the rest of that Society shall require; which Laws of the Society in many things confine the Liberty he had by the Law of Nature.
>
>   *Secondly*, the *Power of punishing* he wholly *gives up*, and engages his natural force ... to assist the Executive Power of the Society, as the Law thereof shall require.[10]

Locke does not distinguish judicial power from the executive power. The legislative power belongs to parliament, the executive power to the king and his ministers. The executive power is accountable and subject to the legislature. The people retain the power to dissolve the legislature. This is manifested through regular elections. Apart from the legislative and the executive power, there is a third power: the federative power, which is the external function of the state.

339   Montesquieu

The political thought of John Locke and other British philosophers of the seventeenth and eighteenth centuries exerted great influence on the French *philosophes* of the Enlightenment. In his *De l'esprit des lois* (1748),

---

[10] John Locke, *The Second Treatise on Government*, 129–30, ed. Peter Laslett, *Locke: Two Treatises on Government*, 2nd edn, Cambridge 1967.

the French jurist Charles de Secondat, Baron de Montesquieu (1689–1755), takes up Locke's idea of the separation of power and transforms it into the classical doctrine of the *trias politica*. From the legislative and executive branch of government, he separates the judiciary as a third power. The legislative branch is supreme. It promulgates the laws which the executive has to apply and the judiciary has to enforce. The executive is accountable to the legislative power. The division of powers and the mutual checks and balances within the system guarantee the limitation of state power and the freedom of the citizens: 'Le pouvoir arrête le pouvoir' ('power must check power').[11]

Montesquieu is a representative of the political thought of the Enlightenment, the dominant cultural and intellectual movement of the eighteenth century. The Enlightenment built on the scientific revolution and the rise of rationalism of the seventeenth century. Based on an almost unlimited faith in the possibilities of human reason, it was reflected into a social and political programme of personal liberty and equality. In nature, men, as rational beings, are born free. Even after the state of nature has been left behind and states have been instituted, man still needs to be perceived of and treated as a rational being. By consequence, the state has to respect and safeguard some natural rights and liberties which are inherently bound up with the human condition. The Enlightenment thinkers desired the realisation of these ideas and the theory of social contract through the introduction of written constitutions and declarations of fundamental rights and liberties. In these texts, the limits of state power and the sphere of individual liberty would be mutually defined.

In addition to being free, men are also equal by nature. The Enlightenment, however, did not propose a radical programme of social equality. The Enlightenment was an elitist movement, the constituents of which were to be found among the nobility, the clergy and the higher tiers of the third estate. Its political programme is one of resistance against the legal discriminations between the three parts of the elite, which were increasingly lagging behind the amalgamation of these elites at the social and economic level and helped, in several countries, the governing elite of the prince and his closest aristocratic allies to monopolise governmental power. The Enlightenment proposed the abolition of feudalism and the legal discrimination between the three estates with its many immunities

---

[11] Charles de Secondat de Montesquieu, *De l'esprit des lois* 11.4, translation by Anne M. Cohler, Basia C. Miller and Harold S. Stone, eds., *Montesquieu: the Spirit of the Laws*, Cambridge 1989.

and privileges. In more general terms, Enlightenment thinkers aspired to a more rational organisation of the state. They aimed at the territorial and legal unification of the state through a unification of the law and a drastic reform of the judiciary and administrative institutions.

340   Rousseau

Among the political philosophers of the Enlightenment, Jean-Jacques Rousseau (1712–78) stands out as one of the most original and radical. Rousseau does not share in the optimism about human progress most *philosophes* propagated. According to Rousseau, in the state of nature, man is morally superior, freer and happier than in civil society. Civilisation has corrupted natural man and has led to inequality between men.

Although Rousseau believes that civilisation has corrupted man, he also believes that it can perfect him. Man can learn and improve himself. However, for this to happen, it is necessary to make a break with the past and the civil society as it exists, and to start all over. This *tabula rasa* does not imply that man has to return to the state of nature to stay there, but that he has to make a new social contract in which the mistakes of the old are corrected and which achieves liberty and equality.

All this leads to a fundamental dilemma. Whereas the purpose of the state is human liberty, its institution supposes the subjection of the individual to the state.

> To find a form of association that will defend and protect the person and goods of each associate with the full common force, and by means of which each, uniting with all, nevertheless obey only himself and remain as free as before. This is the fundamental problem to which the social contract provides the solution.[12]

Rousseau's social contract is more encompassing than Locke's. Through it, man surrenders all his natural rights and liberties to the community. Nevertheless, man's subjection differs from that in the Hobbesian state. Man subjects himself not to a separate state power, external to the contract, but to the community itself, of which he is a member. In this sense, his subjection is to himself.

Central to Rousseau's conception of the state is the *volonté générale*. This does not equate to the will of the majority, or the broad consent among the people; rather, it expresses the general interest. True liberty comes from the voluntary subjection to and identification with the general will. As

[12] Jean-Jacques Rousseau, *Du contrat social* 1.6.4 (1762), translation by Victor Gourevitch, *Rousseau: the Social Contract and Other Later Political Writings*, Cambridge 1997.

the achievement of individual liberty comes from the individual's subjection to the general will and the general interest, the individual is to
be absorbed completely into the commonwealth. Individual liberty and
public morality coincide. The community can force the individual to be
subject to the common will: 'On les forcera d'être libre.'[13]

Rousseau clearly parts company with Locke's liberalism. According to
Locke, man was naturally free and retained at least part of this freedom
through his accession to the social contract and the state. With Rousseau,
the social contract and the subjection to the state constitute a step towards
man's realisation of his freedom. Man is not free yet, but he should become
so through his subjection to the general interest and the general will. The
state's power, therefore, is not limited but total.

In Rousseau's ideal state, the people themselves are sovereign. The
people embody the general will and express it. The state coincides not
with its government, but with the people. It is not the prince, but the
nation. Rousseau's doctrine sounds the death-knell for the dynastic state
and ushers in the nation-state.

The general will is laid out in the laws. Legislative power belongs to the
nation. But because direct democracy is not feasible in large countries, it
is transferred to popular assemblies. These do not represent the people,
in the sense that they freely make decisions in the name of the people.
They are mandated by the people to enact the general will into laws. The
practical implications thereof are hard to surmise, but it could mean that
the members of the legislature can act only within the confines of a strict
programme on the basis of which they were elected. Rousseau does not
provide a clear and practical answer to the question of how the general
will manifests itself. In fact, he does not come much further than a reference to the broad consent among the people.

Rousseau's political thought had a great impact on some of the more
radical political currents of the French Revolution. His doctrine provided
intellectual ammunition to the Jacobins and the *Terreur*. His extreme
democratic views and his doctrine of popular sovereignty inspired the
radical Revolution as well as later totalitarian ideologies, such as communism and fascism. In the claim of representing and knowing the general will lurks a justification for suppressing individual liberty: 'on les
forcera d'être libre'. To the absolutist royal state of Hobbes, Rousseau
added the totalitarian nation-state.

---

[13] Rousseau, *Du contrat social* 1.7.

≫341 Smith

The Scottish philosopher Adam Smith (1723–90) can be considered the intellectual father of modern, economic liberalism. In his *An Inquiry into the Nature and Causes of the Wealth of Nations* of 1776, Smith claims that all economic and social organisation flows from man's propensity to barter and trade. A nation's wealth stems from three sources: land, labour and capital; this threefold division is reflected in the class divisions within society in landowners, labourers and capitalists. All other groups, such as the clergy and government officials, are not productive as they do not contribute to the nation's wealth.

A nation's wealth is determined by the outcome of its trade relations with others. The trade balance in turn results from a myriad individual decisions. The determinant factor in human decision-making is self-interest. Smith, however, believes that the pursuit of self-interest in the end also serves the common interest, as people will understand it to be in their own interest to take into account the interest and rights of others. Smith thus does not share the negative perception of human nature that Hobbes had. As with Locke, for Smith, the state of nature is not completely chaotic. The 'invisible hand' of the market provides a certain order. Therefore, it is unnecessary and even detrimental for the state to completely supersede the natural order and restrict the natural liberty of men.

Nevertheless, the market needs a certain political organisation and regulation, which the state has to provide. The state should confine itself to guaranteeing a proper functioning of the market, as it is the market, and not the state, that creates prosperity. The state should only take care of external and internal security, infrastructure, education and cultural policy. Also, it should protect people from illicit exploitation by others.

Smith acknowledges man to be selfish and driven by his proper interest. But he perceives this self-interest as a force to the good, the common good. It is the motor of economic growth and progress. Smith added an economic theory to political liberalism. In the past, the economy had primarily been thought of in terms of the enhancement of a state's power through the growth of its demographic and tax basis. In Smith's mind, the interests of the state and the citizen coincide; it is the economic interest of the individual which drives the market and determines a nation's wealth. Together, political and economic liberalism sanction the notion that the state's ultimate purpose lies in the enhancement of its citizens' welfare and happiness and that the common good is best served by the pursuit of individual happiness.

394   RATIO (THE MODERN AGE, 1648–1914)

342 Bentham

Individual happiness was central to yet another ideology of the late eighteenth century: utilitarianism. The jurist Jeremy Bentham (1748–1832) is the foremost representative of this current. With utilitarianism, the rupture with the old doctrines which subjected all human endeavours to the eternal afterlife, the common good or an objective morality, is completed. The utilitarians promote man's individual happiness to the highest purpose of man and society on earth. Although the utilitarian is not necessarily an atheist, he holds that God does not intervene directly in human life and that the afterlife should not determine man's life on earth. The common interest is nothing but the total sum of all men's personal happiness. The purpose of society should therefore be 'the greatest happiness for the greatest number'.[14] The pursuit of one's own interest is perfectly moral. Society should make those choices and pursue those policies which promote the greatest total amount of happiness. Political choices must be made on the basis of a 'happiness' cost/benefit analysis.

343 Liberalism

The great political and economic theories of the eighteenth century laid the basis for the ideology of the liberal bourgeoisie which took power in western Europe and North America during the nineteenth century. This liberal ideology adopted elements from the political thought of Hobbes, Locke, Montesquieu, Smith and Bentham, combined them and vulgarised them.

Man is viewed in atomistic terms. Like atoms, man is a self-standing actor whose behaviour is determined by the workings of some general and universal natural laws upon him. The striving for self-preservation and personal happiness is man's first and foremost natural instinct. As with atoms, the natural laws, however, guarantee that the pursuit of individual happiness of all people also serves the common interest. In the case of human behaviour, these laws are the laws of the market, the laws of supply and demand. Human nature does not prevent a rational ordering of society. By consequence, it should not be suppressed. To the contrary, man's natural egoism forms the basis of the wealth of the nation.

The state should not suppress man's natural liberty or the proper workings of the market. It should guarantee them. In the first place, the state should guarantee personal security, property and contractual freedom.

---

[14] Jeremy Bentham, *Introduction to the Principles of Morals and Legislation*, 1, 1781, addition from 1822 at note 5, ed. New York 1988.

Furthermore, through the organisation of ideologically neutral education and its cultural policies, the state can help people to develop themselves so that they can participate in the market. But this was not the main concern of the liberal bourgeoisie. The bourgeoisie wanted to control the state in order to break down the legal discriminations of the *Ancien Régime*; to harness state power to its economic interest and to suppress the lower, unpropertied classes. The more radical ideas of Rousseau and his followers found a hearing among those whose interests and ambitions were frustrated by the liberal state.

6 The English Revolution

344   The Stuarts and the Protestant succession

In contrast to the case in most countries of continental Europe, the British monarchy did not manage to strengthen its position during the course of the seventeenth century. In the struggle between the crown and the elite, the latter emerged victorious.

The accession to the throne of the Stuart dynasty in 1603 marked the beginning of a new and lengthy period of conflict between crown and Parliament. James I and his son Charles I tried to rule without Parliament. Since new taxes could be levied only with the consent of Parliament, however, they were obliged to convene that representative body on several occasions. After acceding to the throne in 1625, Charles tried to persuade both Houses to assign taxes to him for the duration of his rule. Parliament refused. The Third Parliament under Charles, that of 1628, submitted the Petition of Rights to the king in exchange for a new tax. The Petition stands in the old tradition of quasi-constitutional texts, beginning with Magna Carta. Although drawn up in the form of a petition submitted by the subjects that was graciously accepted by the king, it was in fact an Act passed 'by the King in Parliament'. The Petition of Rights confirmed that no taxes could be raised without parliamentary consent. A free man could be punished only after due process of law and in accordance with the law of the land. The king was unable to deprive anyone of their liberty without trial.

> I. Humbly show unto our Sovereign Lord the King, the Lords Spiritual and Temporal, and Commons in Parliament assembled, that whereas it is declared and enacted by a statute made in the time of the reign of King Edward I, commonly called *Statutum de Tellagio non Concedendo*, that no tallage or aid shall be laid or levied by the king or his heirs in this realm, without the good will and assent of the archbishops, bishops, earls,

barons, knights, burgesses, and others the freemen of the commonalty of this realm …

III. And whereas also by the statute called *The Great Charter of the Liberties of England*, it is declared and enacted, that no freeman may be taken or imprisoned or be disseized of his freehold or liberties, or his free custom, or be outlawed or exiled, or in any manners destroyed, but by the lawful judgments of his peers, or by the law of the land.

IV. And in the eight-and-twentieth year of the reign of King Edward III, it was declared and enacted by authority of Parliament, that no man, of what estate or condition that he be, should be put off his land or his tenements, nor imprisoned, nor disinherited nor put to death without being brought to answer by due process of law.

Following the Restoration of the monarchy in 1660, Charles II, the son of Charles I, initially pursued a cautious policy. With French support he did, however, seek to reduce his financial dependence on Parliament and granted the Catholics greater rights. Parliament feared the succession by Charles's brother, James II, who was Catholic. In 1679, the Commons sought to exclude James from the succession, but the Lords refused to co-operate. In the same year, Charles II was obliged to accept the Habeas Corpus Act. This laid down that nobody was to be arrested arbitrarily and guaranteed that anyone who was arrested would rapidly appear before a judge. The name comes from an old writ whereby the king ordered that the prisoner be brought before a court for his case to be heard.

The accession of James II (1685–8) saw a new escalation in the conflict between crown and Parliament. The foreign and religious sympathies of the new sovereign were even more at variance with those of Parliament than had been those of his brother. In 1688, a number of political leaders in Parliament moved to give the crown to James's Protestant daughter Mary and her spouse, Stadholder William III of Orange (1672–1702). William landed in England with an army in that same year; James II fled to France. During the next few decades, his descendants in the house of Stuart were to make a number of efforts to regain the throne with the support of the English Catholics and the Scottish clans. The final attempt by James's grandson, Bonnie Prince Charles (1720–88), ended dramatically at the Battle of Culloden (1746). This was to be the last land battle ever fought on British soil.

345 The Bill of Rights

The Glorious Revolution of 1688 not only guaranteed the succession to the throne by a Protestant but also meant the start of parliamentary monarchy in Britain. William III was not satisfied to rule as prince-consort by the side of his spouse, Mary II (1688–94), demanding recognition from Parliament as king in his own right. In exchange, the new rulers were required to accept the Bill of Rights (1689). The Bill states that through numerous violations of the rights and freedoms of his subjects, James II had abdicated the throne. The succeeding articles set limitations on royal power and organise the relations between king and Parliament. The Bill states that the king must abide by the laws and is unable to amend or suspend them without the consent of Parliament. Only Parliament has the power of taxation and only Parliament may permit the king to maintain a standing army in peacetime. The control of government finances and the army by Parliament were also later to become the two main instruments in other countries whereby the people's assembly maintained control over the executive power. The text provides for the free election of Members of Parliament, in a manner determined by Parliament. This accordingly undermines the right of the king to convene or dissolve the two Houses at will.

> I. That the pretended power of suspending the laws or the execution of laws by regal authority without consent of Parliament is illegal; …
>
> II. That the pretending power of dispensing with laws or the execution of laws by regal authority, as it hath been assumed and exercised of late, is illegal; …
>
> IV. That levying money for or to the use of the Crown by the pretence of prerogative, without grant of Parliament, for longer time, or in other manner than the same is or shall be granted, is illegal; …
>
> VI. That the raising or keeping of a standing army within the kingdom in time of peace, unless it be with consent of Parliament, is against law; …
>
> VIII. That election of members of Parliament ought to be free;
>
> IX. That the freedom of speech and debates or proceedings in Parliament ought not to be impeached or questioned in any court or place out of Parliament …

The Act of Settlement (1701) excluded the male Stuarts, that is, the descendants of James II, from acceding to the throne. It provided for the Protestant house of Hanover to come to power after Mary's sister Anne (1702–14) died. In 1714, George I (1714–37) of Hanover assumed the throne. In the meantime, the personal union between England and Scotland was transformed in 1707 into a constitutional union, Great Britain. The Scottish parliament was dissolved and Scotland obtained direct representation in

Westminster. Since the Devolution of 1998, Scotland has once again its own parliament at Holyrood on the outskirts of Edinburgh.

346   A parliamentary monarchy

During the early eighteenth century, Parliament managed to strengthen its position. Britain became the first parliamentary and constitutional monarchy in Europe. Parliament continued to consist of two Houses. The House of Lords contained both the aristocracy and the clergy. The members of the House of Commons were elected on the basis of a limited system of suffrage. Only those with property were able either to vote and to stand for election. Under the Hanovers, the role of the king within the executive branch of government rapidly declined. George I and George II (1737–60) ceased presiding over Cabinet meetings. That role was henceforth fulfilled by one of the king's ministers. Although ministers were formally appointed by the king, the composition of the government more or less reflected the majority in Parliament. The latter annually voted on the budgets to be allocated to the government, thereby making it difficult for any party to govern against the will of Parliament. From the early seventeenth century onwards, the House of Lords ceased vetoing budgetary legislation. This became a constitutional custom establishing the supremacy of the Commons.

7   *Enlightened absolutism*

347   Enlightened princes

The British model acted as a source of inspiration for continental political thinkers, such as Montesquieu, but it was nowhere copied. Throughout Europe, princes and their closest aristocratic allies anxiously defended and, in many countries, even consolidated their hold on power. Even in the most important republic of Europe – the United Provinces – the monarchical element became stronger. In 1748, the princes of Orange were able to convert the stadholdership into a hereditary position.

Even so, the monarchies of Europe did not escape the influence of the Enlightenment and its political programme. In central and eastern Europe, various rulers adopted elements of the Enlightenment programme in order to conduct an active policy of reform. The alliance between the absolute monarchy and the Enlightenment is not as surprising as it might seem at first sight. The rulers and the philosophers shared a number of concerns. The rational organisation of government and law called for by the Enlightenment could only enhance the administrative efficiency of the central government. The ideal of equality advocated by the Enlightenment ran counter to the privileges of the two highest estates. Although these provided the main sources of support for the monarchical regime in most countries, the nobility and the clergy also acted as the biggest check on royal power. The erosion of the traditional privileges of the estates would subject every citizen equally to the prince's authority. The desire for equality translated itself into a policy of national unification of government and law. The Enlightenment offered the sovereigns a progressive programme for realising an old dream, that of putting an end to the traditional, historical rights and privileges of their most powerful subjects.

The most important enlightened rulers of the eighteenth century were Frederick II of Prussia (1740–86), Maria Theresa of Austria (1740–80), her son Joseph II (1765–90) and Catherine II the Great of Russia (1762–96). Enlightened absolutism remained absolutist in the sense that the ruler did not give up any of his or her power. But it was enlightened because the sovereign's policy was placed at the service of his or her subjects' well-being, and was no longer directed one-sidedly towards the interests and reputation of the sovereign and the dynasty. The enlightened sovereigns of the eighteenth century promoted agriculture, trade and industry, for example by means of large-scale public works to improve transportation. In fact, this was a continuation of the mercantilist policies of the seventeenth century. The policy benefited not just the treasury but also the population. The government also interfered in the schooling system. After the expulsion of the Jesuits from Austria, secondary schools were administered by the state. Universities also came under state control. Frederick II welcomed the same Jesuits with open arms to his Protestant Prussia. In the Austrian dominions, compulsory education for children aged between six and twelve was introduced in 1774. At the religious level, there was greater tolerance for adherents of other Christian denominations and for Jews. The training of the clergy was brought under state control. Similarly, the enlightened rulers introduced major changes in the field of law and justice. They made attempts at codifying the law and sought to replace the many existing law courts by a rationally structured pyramid of courts. In the wake of what was advocated by enlightened philosophers such as Cesare Beccaria (1738–94), the rulers devoted themselves to the humanisation of criminal law by the limitation of corporal punishment and the abolition of torture.

The active reform policies of the enlightened absolutists in Germany and Russia were only partially successful. On the one hand, the enlightened rulers ran into considerable resistance among the elites, whose political power and freedoms were threatened by the policy of centralisation. On the other hand, the reforms did not go far enough for the progressive, enlightened members of these same elites. In very few instances was the alliance between the ruler and the aristocracy dismantled to such an extent as to put an end to the privileges of the nobility, the class system or feudalism. Central Europe was not to prove immune to the Revolution.

8   The American Revolution

348   The War of American Independence

The first great revolution that shook the *Ancien Régime* to its foundations did not, however, take place in Europe – and was also directed against one of the most liberal of all monarchical regimes, Britain. In 1776, thirteen British colonies on the north-east coast of America declared independence from the British crown. The underlying cause of the rupture was disagreement on foreign policy. The American colonists felt frustrated in their desire to expand westwards against the French colonists and their native American allies by the British policies of appeasement. In the years before 1776, tensions had also arisen over British taxation and the refusal by the London government to have the colonies directly represented in the Westminster Parliament ('no taxation without representation'). These last two grievances served to justify the revolution, but did not cause it.

On 4 July 1776, representatives from the different colonies adopted the Declaration of Independence. The Declaration has its intellectual roots in the liberal tradition of John Locke. The power of the government is conditional. The administrators must ensure the inviolable rights of the people. If the government fails to fulfil its tasks, the people can dismiss and replace it.

> We hold these truths to be self-evident, that all men are created equal, that they are endowed by their Creator with certain unalienable Rights, that among these are Life, Liberty and the pursuit of Happiness. That to secure these Rights, Governments are instituted among Men, deriving their just powers from the consent of the governed. That whenever any Form of Government becomes destructive of these ends, it is the Right of the People to alter or to abolish it, and to institute a new Government ...

For the purpose of setting up their new government, the Founding Fathers sought inspiration in the ideals of political liberalism and the

Enlightenment. The different states united in a loose federation through the Act of Confederation (1776). In 1781, the confederation was renamed the United States of America. Two years later, the British government under George III (1760–1820) recognised the independence of the USA under the Treaty of Paris. With the support of the French, the Americans had won their war of liberation.

349   The Constitution of the United States

In 1787, the Federal Constitution of the USA was completed. It stands in the liberal tradition. The constitution is a kind of social contract through which the people establish and organise the state. It establishes the institutions of state and determines their composition, jurisdiction and workings.

> We, the people of the United States, in order to form a more perfect Union, establish justice, insure domestic tranquility, provide for the common defense, promote the general welfare, and secure the blessings of liberty to ourselves and our posterity, do ordain and establish this Constitution for the United States of America.[15]

The constitution transforms the USA from a loose federation into a federal state. The federation is given a limited number of powers summed up in the constitution such as foreign policy, common defence, the currency, international trade, general welfare and the observance of the rights and freedoms. Although the residual powers reside with the individual states, the federal government has steadily but radically extended its sphere of influence over the past two centuries.

The separation of powers is strictly implemented. Legislative power is assigned to Congress, consisting of the House of Representatives, in which each state is represented in proportion to its population, and the Senate, to which each state may send two delegates. The head of the executive branch is the president, who is elected. This democratic legitimisation withdraws the president from the political control of Congress. Only through impeachment may the president be removed from office, for example, for committing a criminal offence. The other members of the executive branch, the members of the cabinet, are appointed by the president. The president can veto an act of Congress. Congress can set the presidential veto aside with a two-thirds majority in both houses. The independence of the judiciary is guaranteed.

---

[15] *Constitution of the United States*, Preamble.

350   Constitutional review

The highest federal court is the Supreme Court. In *Marbury* v. *Madison* (1803), the Court ruled that it can review whether federal legislation is in accordance with the constitution and refuse to apply it if it is not, thus effectively voiding it. This is consistent with the doctrine of the social contract by Locke. Through the constitution, the people entrust part of their liberties and rights to the state. The constitution not only determines the way in which that power must be exercised, it also lays down its limits. Even the legislative branch is subject to it: it is not the legislator but the people who are ultimately sovereign. Constitutional review guarantees that the highest federal institutions respect the will of the people. The words of Chief Justice John Marshall (1755–1835) in *Marbury* v. *Madison* are a tribute to liberal political doctrine:

> That the people have an original right to establish, for their future government, such principles, as in their opinion, shall most conduce to their own happiness, is the basis on which the whole American fabric has been erected. The exercise of this original right is a very great exertion; nor can it, nor ought it, to be frequently repeated. The principles, therefore, so established are deemed fundamental. And as the authority from which they proceed is supreme, and can seldom act, they are designed to be permanent.
>
> This original and supreme will organizes the government, and assigns to different departments their respective powers. It may either stop there, or establish certain limits not to be transcended by those departments.
>
> The government of the United States is of the latter description. The powers of the legislature are defined and limited; and that those limits may not be mistaken, or forgotten, the constitution is written. To what purpose are powers limited, and to what purpose is a limitation committed to writing, if these limits may, at any time, be passed by those intended to be restrained? The distinction between a government with limited and unlimited powers is abolished, if those limits do not confine the persons on whom they are imposed, and if acts prohibited and acts allowed, are of equal obligation. It is a proposition too plain to be contested, that the constitution controls any legislative act repugnant to it; or that the legislature may alter the constitution by an ordinary act.
>
> Between these alternatives there is no middle ground. The constitution is either a superior, paramount law, unchangeable by ordinary means, or it is on a level with ordinary legislative acts, and, like other acts, is alterable when the legislature shall please to alter it.
>
> If the former part of the alternative be true, then a legislative act contrary to the constitution is not law; if the latter part be true, then written constitutions are absurd attempts, on the part of the people, to limit a power in its nature illimitable.

> Certainly all those who have framed written constitutions contemplate them as forming the fundamental and paramount law of the nation, and consequently, the theory of every government must be, that the act of the legislature, repugnant to the constitution, is void …
>
> If an act of the legislature, repugnant to the constitution, is void, does it, notwithstanding its invalidity bind the courts, and oblige them to give effect? Or, in other words, though it be not law, does it constitute a rule operative as if it was law? This would be to overthrow in fact that which was established in theory; and would seem, at first view, an absurdity too gross to be insisted on.

In 1789, a Bill of Rights, which stated the fundamental rights and freedoms, was added to the constitution. The most important of these were freedom of religion, freedom of speech and freedom of the press (First Amendment), the right to bear arms (Second Amendment) and due process of law (Fifth Amendment). In the course of the nineteenth and twentieth centuries, further amendments were added.

9   The French Revolution

351   The causes and nature of the French Revolution

The deeper, underlying cause of the French Revolution of 1789 was the growing rupture between the royal government of Louis XV (1715–74) and his grandson and successor Louis XVI (1774–92), and an increasing part of the French elite. During the second half of the eighteenth century, France's economy went through a process of modernisation. A growing number of the elite, coming from all three estates, involved themselves with commercial, industrial, maritime and colonial activities and investments. Many fell under the spell of the Enlightenment and proposed a reform and rationalisation of government, the tax system and the law which would bring more unity, transparency and efficiency.

In the three decades before the Revolution, the royal regime became increasingly alienated from France's elite. Apart from a few scandals which weakened the authority of the monarchy, there were two main reasons for this. First, the royal government failed to bring sufficient reform. Halfway through the eighteenth century, a reform movement led by the Parliament of Paris pitted the government against part of its traditional power base, the top of the *noblesse de robe*. The government was successful in quelling the rebellion and reasserting its authority, but achieved this at the price of weakening its power base and destroying the credit of the parliament and the leading jurists as the standard-bearers of reform.

It pushed the opposition further away from the circles of government. Apart from some half-hearted attempts at reform under Louis XVI, the royal regime progressively entrenched itself among the more conservative members of the aristocracy and clergy. The court of Versailles, a few dozen miles from the capital, increasingly came to symbolise the king's isolation from his people. Second, there was the defeat against France's traditional enemy, Britain, in the Seven Years War. Not only had this defeat destroyed France's colonial empire and damaged the interests of those who had invested in it, it also weighed heavily on the nation's pride and self-esteem. The victory in the War of American Independence, which was largely won by the French for the Americans, did not bring solace as it had crippled the state's treasury and only fuelled the elite's main criticism of the royal government: that its failure to reform the tax system, the royal administration and the law crippled the economy and weakened France as a great continental and colonial power. When in 1788, state bankruptcy forced the king to convoke, for the first time since 1614, a meeting of the Estates-General to discuss tax reform and, above all, new taxes, the volcano erupted.

The French Revolution has often been described as the *coup d'état* of the liberal bourgeoisie against the alliance of the king, the nobility and the higher clergy. This is an oversimplification. In its initial phase, the Revolution was an elitist bid to reform royal government and its main support came from the top ranks of the urban elite, the third estate. But it had wide support from among the ranks of the nobility and the clergy as well. In a sense, the bourgeois elite was rather a product than a cause of the Revolution. The abolition of feudality and the system of the three estates with its legal discriminations with time led to the formation of a new, broad, social, economic and political elite. Although the period of the Restoration would be marked by further tensions between town and country elites, between a bourgeois elite and the aristocracy over issues like the role of the church in education, the balance of power between the king and the legislature and free trade, the Revolution was successful at tearing down the juridical barriers between the three elites and preparing the way for domination by a more unified propertied elite.

352   National Assembly

After a failed attempt to raise new taxes through the co-operation of the Assemblée des Notables in 1787 and in the face of the state's bankruptcy, in 1788 Louis XVI took the fateful decision to convene the Estates-General in Versailles in order to push through a tax reform. Apart from the representatives of the nobility and clergy, all through France 610 men were elected to speak for the third estate. Many of these hailed from the middle classes of professionals and shopowners; a significant number held university degrees, in particular in law. Supported by the more enlightened members from the first two estates, these men came to Versailles to make their demands for a radical reform of the state.

During the meeting of the Estates-General in May 1789, some members demanded that the estates should be reformed into a general assembly that would represent the whole nation as one single body so that each member would have an equal vote. After the king had repeatedly rejected this demand, a large group of members of the Estates-General proclaimed itself the National Assembly (*Assemblée Nationale*) on 17 June. When, in reaction, it was rumoured that the king threatened to dissolve the assembly, they left the royal palace and retreated to the tennis court at Versailles. The members of the National Assembly did not consider themselves any longer the representatives of their estates and their local communities, but representatives of the one and indivisible French nation. On 9 July, the National Assembly arrogated to itself the power to make a constitution.

353   The Revolution of 1789

The Revolution of June 1789 erupted because the desire for reform of a great part of France's elite was frustrated by the royal government's intransigence. In its initial phase, it was a *coup d'état* by one part of the elite to wrest control over the royal government from the power brokers that held it in their grasp. But the Revolution soon started to radicalise. The bad harvest of 1788 and harsh winter of 1788/9 had brought many of the urban and rural poor to the verge of starvation. The civil unrest this caused both in the countryside and in the cities, especially in Paris, combined with the political stand-off at Versailles; the situation spiralled out of control. In the short run, the popular revolts served the political agenda of the revolutionaries at Versailles. On 14 July 1789, at the instigation of the revolutionaries, a crowd stormed the Bastille. The capture and destruction of the royal prison in Paris held high symbolic value. In the month to follow, throughout France, the people rose and took up arms, often targeting as much the properties of the local rich as the symbols of governmental authority. After the failure of the discredited government to protect their properties, the higher and middle classes started to organise their own protection by taking control over local government and forming civil militias, the National Guard. These were staffed with members of the middle and lower propertied classes, often small land and property owners who stood themselves on the verge of poverty but were the easiest targets for the rioting populace. The militias, the *Sansculottes*, would become the storm troopers of the Revolution while at the same time protecting the property of the higher and middle classes.

The events of July finally forced Louis XVI to cave in and recognise the National Assembly. On 4 August, the Assembly abolished all legal discrimination between the estates as well as their privileges and immunities. Not only the nobility and the clergy, but also the merchants and craft guilds lost their privileges and economic monopolies. A few years later, in 1793, the feudal system of land ownership was terminated. On 26 July 1789, the *Déclaration des droits de l'homme et du citoyen (Declaration of the Rights of Man and Citizen)* was issued. Later that year, the taxes for the church were abolished and all ecclesiastical properties confiscated and put up for sale. The *Constitution civile du clergé* of 12 July 1790 forced the clergy to subject itself to state control. In September 1791, the first constitution of France was approved, turning France into a parliamentary and constitutional monarchy. The *Déclaration* was absorbed into the constitution.

354   The *Déclaration* of 1789 and the constitution of 1791

In its first Article, the *Déclaration* guarantees all citizens equality before the law, thus realising one of the main points from the political programme of the Enlightenment. The Article does not guarantee economic equality, but it abolishes all legal distinctions and discriminations between the estates. It also does away with all forms of bondage and servitude. It opens the door to a societal organisation based on merit, and not on class distinction.

The *Déclaration* serves the interest and concerns of the higher and middle classes. It guarantees the traditional civil liberties such as freedom of opinion and the press. It does not stipulate the freedom of association. One of the main points of the revolutionary platform of 1789 was the abolition of the economic privileges of the trade and craft guilds: the Act of Le Chapelier abolished and forbade all professional corporations and associations. Freedom of education was not provided for in the *Déclaration*. The revolutionaries wanted, after all, to wrest the schools from the control of the church.

The drafters of the *Déclaration* mixed elements of Rousseau's political thought with that of the more traditionally liberal political philosophers. Article 6 held that the legislation reflected the general will. In Article 3, it is stated that sovereignty belongs to the people. But the *Déclaration* also set great store by the natural liberties of all people. The state can limit these liberties only to safeguard and protect other people's rights (Article 4). This can be done only by the legislature (Article 5). With this, and contrary to what Article 3 held, sovereignty was effectively transferred from the nation to the Assembly.

1. Men are born and remain free and equal in rights. Social distinctions may be founded only upon the general good.

2. The aim of all political association is the preservation of the natural and imprescriptible rights of man. These rights are liberty, property, security and resistance to oppression.

3. The principle of all sovereignty resides essentially in the nation. No body nor individual may exercise any authority which does not proceed directly from the nation.

4. Liberty consists in the freedom to do everything which injures no one else; hence the exercise of the natural rights of each man has no limits except those which assure to the other members of the society the enjoyment of the same rights. These limits can only be determined by law.

5. Law can only prohibit such actions as are hurtful to society. Nothing may be prevented which is not forbidden by law, and no one may be forced to do anything not provided for by law.

6. Law is the expression of the general will. Every citizen has a right to participate personally, or through his representative, in its foundation. It must be the same for all, whether it protects or punishes. All citizens, being equal in the eyes of the law, are equally eligible to all dignities and to all public positions and occupations, according to their abilities, and without distinction except that of their virtues and talents.

7. No person shall be accused, arrested, or imprisoned except in the cases and according to the forms prescribed by law. Any one soliciting, transmitting, executing, or causing to be executed, any arbitrary order, shall be punished. But any citizen summoned or arrested in virtue of the law shall submit without delay, as resistance constitutes an offence.

The constitution of 1791 introduces the separation of powers in France. The legislative power is exercised by an Assembly, which is directly elected by the people. Franchise is restricted to all men over the age of twenty-five who pay a minimal amount of taxes. The king and his ministers hold the executive power. The king appoints his ministers; they are accountable only to him. Before a parliamentary act enters into force, the king needs to ratify it. In other words, the king can veto an act of parliament. The independence of the judiciary is guaranteed through the direct election of its members by the people. The judges do not hold the right of constitutional review but have to apply the legislation at all times. In other words, the independence of the judicial power guarantees not so much the 'rule of law' as the 'rule of the legislation'. It does not protect the citizens against all unlawful actions by the state, including the legislature, but only against actions by the executive that contravene existing legislation.

The constitution does away with all old territorial divisions and jurisdictions. In their stead comes a nationwide, uniform division of the territory in *départements* and *communes* which were all strongly controlled by the central government in Paris. All old courts are disbanded and replaced by a uniform hierarchy of courts. At one stroke, the administrative and legal unification of the country is achieved. With it, internal sovereignty is accomplished.

355   The end of the monarchy

Started as a coup of the elite and the intellectuals, the political Revolution quickly spread to the lower middle classes of small land and property owners, such as craftsmen and shopkeepers. During the first two years, a programme was pursued that served the purposes and interests of these groups. The parliamentary monarchy with its limited suffrage guaranteed ambitious and intelligent men a chance to rise to the highest offices of state, while the ambitions of the largest part of the population, the lower classes, were kept in check. The abolition of legal class discrimination, the feudal system, the economic privileges and monopolies took away the brakes on the free accumulation of wealth and property and enhanced the freedom of trade and industry. The abolition of feudal landholding and the sale of church property allowed the emergence of a new class of property owners. Many leaseholders thus became owners of their own lands and farms. In this way, a large middle class of small proprietors – farmers, shopkeepers, craftsmen – emerged. Ever since, these groups have had a leading voice in French politics.

King Louis XVI's flight from Paris to Germany and his arrest at Varennes in 1791, together with the outbreak of the war against Austria and Prussia, led to a further radicalisation of the Revolution. The Assembly was dominated by two great factions. On the right side sat the Girondins who were supported by the higher classes and who defended the new status quo. On the left sat the more radical Jacobins. These represented the more radical of the middle classes of small owners and intellectuals and were supported by the *Sansculottes*.

In August 1792, Louis XVI was deposed by the Assembly. This constituted a great victory for the Jacobins. In September 1792, a new parliament, the National Convention, was elected. Through manipulation of the election – there was only a 10 per cent turnout – the radicals obtained a large majority in the new parliament. The Republic was promulgated and the former king, now known as Louis Capet, was condemned to death. On 21 January 1793, he was guillotined on the Place de la Concorde. In June 1793, the Jacobins, led by the jurist Maximilien Robespierre (1758–94), staged a coup.

356   Robespierre and the Jacobin *Terreur*

The Jacobin coup signalled a new phase of radicalisation of the Revolution. Robespierre and his adherents were deeply influenced by Rousseau. They proposed a radical reform of society. At the political level, the Jacobins proposed to achieve true popular sovereignty through the extension of the right to vote and by strengthening the supremacy of the legislative over the executive power. The Jacobins perceived themselves as the revolutionary, enlightened vanguard that would liberate the French nation from the chains of oppression, if necessary by force. The Jacobin regime was marked by the *Terreur*. In slightly over a year, Robespierre and his cronies sent thousands of their ideological opponents and political competitors, including many Jacobins, to the guillotine. The introduction of a new calendar symbolised the radical break with the *Ancien Régime*.

The radicalisation had been fuelled by the war. By 1792, revolutionary France was confronted by a broad coalition of European dynasts who wanted to contain the Revolution, if not turn it back. The radicalisation of the Revolution allowed the French state to mobilise more people and more means for its war effort. The old royal, professional army was transformed into a popular army of conscripts (*levée en masse*). In the new army, not birth, family or money, but talent and merit were the criteria for promotion. This allowed a new generation of young, dynamic and enterprising generals to come to the fore. Of these, Napoleon Bonaparte (1769–1821) was the most spectacularly successful. After some initial defeats, the new army could turn the tide and would assure France of two decades of military supremacy on the European continent. The mobilisation of the nation for the war put an end to the era of internationally composed, professional mercenary armies. War was nationalised.

357   The constitution of 1793

In September 1793, the Convention accepted a new constitution. This time, the list of fundamental rights and liberties preceding the actual constitution did stipulate the freedom of association and of education. For the first time, it also included some economic rights, such as the right to labour (Article 21). Article 1 of the actual constitution affirms the unity of the French state: 'The French Republic is one and indivisible.' The legislative power is exercised by the Legislative Body (*Corps législatif*), which is elected by all male citizens. The Legislative Body proposes laws to the nation, which then has to ratify them through a referendum. Apart from this, the Legislative Body can also promulgate decrees. The Legislative Body selects the members of the government, the executive council (*conseil exécutive*), from a list made up by the voters. The government has little autonomy and is subject to the legislature. The constitution of 1793 translated Rousseau's popular sovereignty into constitutional reality.

But this constitution never entered into force. Its application was suspended because of the war. This illustrates the dilemma the Jacobins found themselves in from the moment they took power. On the one hand, they were the proponents of a far-reaching democratisation. But on the other hand, this would have led to their downfall. The Jacobins were not a popular movement, but a radical vanguard of intellectuals, often lawyers and journalists. Their only constituency was the more radical members of the middle classes. Their economic policies served the purposes of these groups, to the detriment of the old aristocracy and urban elites, and of the lower classes. As long as the constitution was suspended, the Jacobins ruled France by means of small executive committees, such as the Comité du salut public and the Comité de Sureté générale, and with the aid of a professional bureaucracy and a large police force. It was the rule of the revolutionary vanguard.

358   Directoire

Robespierre and the Jacobins fell from power on 9 Thermidor of the revolutionary year II (27 July 1794). Now that France was winning the war, support for the regime with its excesses of violence evaporated. Robespierre and his main allies were sent to the guillotine in their turn. The Convention, the same one which had been elected in September 1793, now issued a new constitution (that of the year III), which installed the regime of the Directoire, dominated by the Girondins.

To prevent new excesses, the new constitutional settlement provides for a far-reaching division of state power. The legislative power is divided between two chambers: the Conseil des 500 and the Conseil des anciens. The first chamber initiates new legislation, which the members of the second chamber – all married or widowed men – can only approve or reject. The executive power is in the hands of a five-man Directoire, who are elected by the Conseil des anciens on the recommendation of the 500. The constitution of the Year III also contains a declaration of fundamental rights. The new regime proved highly unstable. It enjoyed little support throughout the country and was constantly attacked both from the radical left and the counter-revolutionary right.

359   Napoleonic France

The military successes of the revolutionary armies led to the emergence of a new power within the French state: that of the generals and the armed forces. On 18 Brumaire of the year VIII (9 November 1799), the most successful of these generals, Napoleon Bonaparte, staged a coup and assumed power. He installed a new executive of three consuls, with himself as the first consul. In 1804, he had himself voted and crowned Emperor of the French. The Revolution was at an end.

The constitution of the Year VIII restored the supremacy of the executive power within the state. This would be further strengthened under the empire. The legislative power is now divided among three bodies. The members of the Senate are co-opted and appointed for life. It appoints in its turn the 150 members of the Tribunat and the 300 members of the Corps législatif. Only the first consul can table new legislation. The proposals are prepared by the Council of State (*Conseil d'État*), which consists of bureaucrats rather than politicians. The Tribunat debates the proposal, the Corps législatif puts it to the vote and the Senate submits it to a constitutional review. Judges are appointed by the first consul, rather than elected by the people as before.

Napoleon's regime brought political stability and economic progress. It enjoyed the support not only of the armed forces, but also of the bourgeoisie and the propertied middle classes, the economic interests of which he safeguarded. His well-deserved reputation as a great general, which he carefully cultivated, sustained his popularity among the masses. Napoleon also put an end to the conflict with the Catholic Church by making the Concordat of 1801 with the pope. The church accepted the loss of its property but the state would henceforth pay salaries to church officials within the country. A new alliance between church and state was brokered. This time, the state was clearly in the driving seat.

Under the regime of Napoleon, many of the more radical achievements of the French Revolution were turned back. His rule constituted a return to the constitutional monarchy of 1791, or even before. The liberal bourgeoisie, however, held on to most of the gains it made in the early phases of the Revolution. Its economic position and its juridical equality with the former aristocracy were guaranteed.

10   Europe and the French Revolution

360   Napoleon's empire

The radicalisation of the French Revolution triggered a series of wars, which would last for almost a quarter-century (1792–1815). On several occasions, revolutionary France practically stood alone against a broad coalition of European powers. The royal houses of Europe saw the Revolution – particularly after the deposition and beheading of Louis XVI – as a threat to the stability of their own thrones. In addition, however, classical great power politics played a role. London had traditionally sought to prevent continental Europe from being dominated by a single power, which would then have the resources to threaten Britain and its colonial empire. The successes of the French revolutionary armies from 1794 onwards turned London into the irreconcilable foe of the Revolution and Napoleon. Even when Napoleon had overrun virtually all of Europe, Britain continued the war effort by itself.

In 1792, war broke out between France on the one side and the Emperor Francis I, the brother-in-law of Louis XVI, and Prussia on the other side. For the more radical revolutionaries who took power in its wake, the war evolved into a crusade to spread the Revolution and liberate the other peoples of Europe from oppression by their princes. France became the revolutionary model, and the French people the enlightened vanguard of Europe. Initially, the French revolutionaries could count on a good deal of sympathy in other countries. But shortly, many groups felt deterred by the radicalisation of the Jacobin regime and instability of the Directoire regime. After a few years, in most countries, French support wavered.

In the end, it was the French popular army that conquered Europe and spread the Revolution. The *levée en masse* gave rise to a revolution in the conduct of war. A new and sudden increase in the scale of the armies, daring and unorthodox tactics, rapid movements, and above all the idealism and enthusiasm of the French soldiers broke the backbone of the old, professional armies of the *Ancien Régime*. After initial defeats, the tide turned. By 1795, the Austrians had been driven out of the Southern Netherlands, which remained part of France until the fall of Napoleon. Under the Treaty of Campo Formio (1797), the Austrians had to concede defeat. The war in Italy was won by the young Bonaparte. Under Napoleon's rule, France brought the larger part of Europe under its control. After Napoleon had defeated Austria, Russia and Prussia (1807), his hegemony was as good as total. The French Empire stretched from the Southern Netherlands, the Rhineland and northern Italy to the Dalmatian coast. The German Empire was abolished (1806) and replaced by a loose confederation of French satellite states, the Confederation of the Rhine (*Rheinbund*). One of the largest of these satellites, the kingdom of Westphalia, was given to Napoleon's brother Jérôme (1784–1860) to rule. Francis I could still call himself emperor, but now of Austria, as Francis II. He lost all his Italian possessions; his daughter Marie-Louise (1791–1847) was married off to Napoleon (1810). Naples fell into the hands of Napoleon's elder brother, Joseph (1768–1844). When some time later he became king of Spain (1808), Napoleon's loyal general and brother-in-law Joachim Murat (1767–1815) was made king of Naples.

361 The Batavian Republic and the Kingdom of Holland

The Republic of the United Provinces did not escape the Revolution and French domination. As early as the 1780s, a group of enlightened revolutionaries, the Patriots, had made their presence felt in the Republic. In late 1794, the French general Charles Pichegru (1761–1804) invaded the Northern Netherlands. In his wake followed the Patriots who had previously fled to France. Stadholder William V of Orange fled on 18 January 1795 to England. The Batavian Republic was born.

The new leaders modelled their revolution on the French Revolution. The Estates-General were dissolved and replaced by the National Assembly. This had a double meaning. As in France it was a break with the estates system. In addition, the Netherlands was transformed from a confederation of states into a unitary state. The Estates-General had been a congress of representatives from the seven provincial estates. Sovereignty resided with each of the latter. The National Assembly was the emanation of the one, sovereign Dutch people. The Netherlands was to remain a unitary state after the fall of Napoleon and was in fact to become one of the most centralised countries in Europe – a choice supported in particular by the Province of Holland, as the unitary state enabled it to make full use of its demographic and economic weight. Previously, the confederal model had always acted as a brake on the domination of the Netherlands by Holland (and Zeeland).

Along French lines, the National Assembly aspired to promulgate a constitution. Political divisions slowed the process. It took until 1798 for the first Dutch constitution, the *Staatsregeling voor het Bataafse volk*, to be adopted. Ultimately, there was a fresh coup with the object of sidelining the conservative proponents of the former confederal model. This illustrates that in the Netherlands too the radical concepts of the Revolution were shared by no more than a small minority.

The *Staatsregeling* of 1798 implemented the separation of powers to a certain extent. The legislative branch was placed in the hands of the Representative Body (*Vertegenwoordigend Lichaam*), the members of which represented the entire people and not their province. The executive was in the hands of the five-member Executive Directory (*Uitvoerend Bewind*). Class distinction, seigniorial rights and the feudal system were abolished. The constitution laid down the fundamental rights and freedoms.

The Batavian Revolution turned the Netherlands into a French satellite state. The Hague was, however, an unreliable partner for Paris. The alliance with France in the war against Britain – the traditional ally of the Netherlands – was unnatural and damaged the economic interests of the Dutch regents in Holland and Zeeland. Dutch support for the continental blockade – Napoleon's economic boycott of Britain – was lukewarm. Paris was moreover irritated by the lack of enthusiasm in The Hague for a range of revolutionary policies and by the slow pace of reform.

In 1805, Napoleon intervened, arranging for power to be placed in the hands of Rutger Jan Schimmelpenninck (1761–1825), the former Batavian ambassador in Paris. Schimmelpenninck established an autocratic regime modelled on that of Napoleon's own. That too, however, failed. One year later, Napoleon had the Batavian Republic transformed into the Kingdom of Holland, installing his brother Louis (1778–1846) on the throne. When he too failed to obtain a sufficient grip he was recalled to Paris. In 1810, the French emperor simply incorporated the Netherlands into the French Empire. The ten departments of which the Kingdom of Holland had consisted became ten French departments. This situation lasted until the liberation in 1813.

362   The fall of Napoleon

Dutch history illustrates how the external policies of the French Revolution evolved from liberation to oppression. The radicalisation of the Revolution from 1792 onwards and Napoleon's autocratic regime alienated first the more moderate advocates of the Revolution, and subsequently virtually all revolutionaries in Europe. Except in the earliest days of the war, the French troops were rarely welcomed as liberators. Nor did they behave as such. The idea of the French nation as the vanguard of the Revolution made it possible to bridge the gap between the revolutionary ideal of liberation and the reality of oppression. When that ideal was buried by Napoleon, this left nothing but occupation and oppression. Resistance, no longer confined to the conservative groups calling for a return to the *Ancien Régime*, broke out in many countries of Europe. Napoleon's domination acted as a spur for nationalism, uniting people across political dividing lines and rousing revolutionary forces against the French emperor.

It was not, however, these nationalists who brought about Napoleon's fall but a coalition of Spanish conservative forces, the Russian tsar and the British. Although Napoleon had subjugated the entire continent, he had never managed to subdue Britain. After the defeat at the Battle of Trafalgar (1805), Napoleon could not hope any longer to overcome British naval power. Meanwhile, London could use French dominion over Europe to expand its colonial empire at the expense of other powers, such as Spain and the Netherlands. The most successful revolt against Napoleonic rule was in Spain. From 1808 onwards, the French troops were involved in a *guerrilla* (small war) against Spanish aristocrats and farmers, supported by a British expeditionary force led by Arthur Wellesley, the later Duke of Wellington (1769–1852). In 1812, Napoleon invaded Russia. His army reached and sacked Moscow, but was unable to force the tsar to sue for peace. During the retreat, Napoleon lost virtually his entire army. The result was the formation of a new anti-Napoleon coalition. At the Battle of the Nations near Leipzig in 1813, Napoleon suffered a major defeat. In 1814, he was forced to abdicate and was exiled to Elba. A few months later he managed to escape and recaptured the French throne. On 18 June 1815, the French army was defeated by an Anglo-Prussian army commanded by Wellington at Waterloo, just south of Brussels. This time, Napoleon was imprisoned on the island of Saint Helena in the southern Atlantic. The Napoleonic Age was over; the Restoration could begin.

11   *The Restoration and the bourgeois age (1815–1914)*

363   Vienna and the Bourbon Restoration

Napoleon's downfall left the four victors – Britain, Russia, Austria and Prussia – with the opportunity to redraw the map of Europe and to turn back some of the achievements of the Revolution. This was done at the Congress of Vienna (1814–15).

One of the great architects of the Europe of Vienna was the Austrian chancellor, Prince Klemens von Metternich (1773–1859). Metternich wanted to return as far as possible to the *Ancien Régime*, but realised that after two decades it was no longer possible totally to obliterate the Revolution; that would only lead to further revolutions. What the monarchies of central Europe needed was peace and stability. This was certainly true for the Austrian Empire; it had more to fear than just political revolution. Nationalism, which was on the rise, constituted a mortal threat to a composite empire such as Austria–Hungary with so many different ethnic groups within its borders.

In France, Louis XVIII (1814–30), the brother of the beheaded Louis XVI, was placed on the throne. The restoration of the Bourbons was a fact. A constitution was introduced, albeit in the form of a charter voluntarily granted by the new king to his subjects (*Chartre octroyée*). This reflected the fact that sovereignty lay not with the people but with the king. The king voluntarily accepted a number of curbs on his power. The separation of powers was retained, but parliament had no political control over the government. It could only impeach the king's ministers for criminal activities (from 1816 onwards). The king, the Chambre des Pairs and the Chambres des Députés formed the legislature. The king appointed the members of the First Chamber, who were drawn from the aristocracy of the *Ancien Régime* or the nobility created under Napoleon. The members of the Second Chamber were elected on the basis of a restrictive tax-based voting system created in the time of Napoleon. Only the king had the right to initiate legislation. He was the head of the executive branch of government. The independence of the judiciary, the new judicial system and the new codes of the Napoleonic age were left unimpaired.

The Bourbons were also restored in Spain. Northern Italy largely came under Austria; in other parts of the peninsula the former dynasties were reinstated. The Netherlands was transformed into a kingdom. William I (1813–40), the son of Stadholder William V, ascended the throne in 1813 as Sovereign Ruler. A year later, he became the first king of the Kingdom of the Netherlands. The Congress of Vienna added the larger part of the Southern Netherlands (Belgium) to this territory. In addition William I, as Grand Duke of Luxemburg (consisting of both the present Grand Duchy and the Belgian province), also became a member of the German Confederation. The Holy Roman Empire was not restored. In its place came the German Confederation (*Deutsche Bund*), a loose confederation of forty-one states, thirty-seven principalities and four free cities, of which the Austrian Empire and the greatly enlarged Kingdom of Prussia were the most important. The many ecclesiastical principalities and imperial cities that had been swallowed up by several German princes during the Napoleonic era were not restored.

364 The Kingdom of the Netherlands

William I had a new constitution promulgated for the United Kingdom of the Netherlands. This he introduced against the will of the majority of those eligible to vote in Belgium. The new constitutional model retained the principal achievements of the Revolution, at least at formal level. In fact, it was largely based on the Napoleonic model of strong government. The rights and freedoms survived in the constitution and the separation of powers was retained. The parliament – the Estates-General – consisted of two chambers. The First Chamber was appointed by the king, while the members of the Second Chamber were elected by the provincial estates. Those estates were elected by the three estates: the knights, the towns and the landowners. The right to vote was limited to the propertied classes. While this represented a return to the old class divisions, it did not detract from the dominance of the bourgeoisie in a country in which the nobility had in fact not been a major factor for a considerable time. Belgium and the Netherlands each obtained fifty-five representatives in the Second Chamber, even though the population of Belgium was nearly twice that of the Netherlands. The king did not have the exclusive right to initiate legislation but the chambers could not initiate legislation without the king's consent. In certain areas, the king could rule by decree. In 1822, William I revoked the jurisdiction of the courts in administrative matters. Despite the reintroduction of the name Estates-General for the parliament and of the name provinces for the departments, the unitary state remained intact. The new legal structure was barely touched. Instead of the Cour de Cassation in Paris, the High Council (*Hoge Raad*) now became the highest court in the land. And although efforts were made to replace the existing French legal codes, the ideal of codification itself survived.

365 The compromise of 1815

The Restoration of 1815 was a compromise. Whereas the monarchy was everywhere restored and the old dynasties of the *Ancien Régime* regained their lost thrones, some of the most important achievements of the French Revolution could not be reversed.

With few exceptions, the principle of equality before the law survived. Although most countries continued to have aristocratic titles – many of these handed out under Napoleon – membership of the nobility no longer carried with it any legal discrimination. It had political implications, though. In many countries, like Britain, France and the Netherlands, the noble aristocracy – old or new – controlled the higher chamber of parliament and felt closely allied to the king.

The churches too were unable to restore the position they held before the French Revolution. The Revolution had brought about the separation between church and state. The state no longer projected itself as the defender of a single religion; freedom of religion was included as a fundamental right in most constitutions. The unity of religion was no longer a precondition for the unity of the state. Even so, the heirs of the French Revolution held an ambiguous attitude towards church and faith. On the one hand, they wanted a secular, civil society. They professed belief in utilitarianism: the pursuit of happiness on earth. The liberals wanted to keep education out of the hands of the church and called for the organisation of state education or even for the monopolisation of education by the state. On the other hand, they were aware that faith offered a moral framework to justify their lifestyle and economic interests and to control the people. In many countries, close relations between the state, the elite and the higher clergy remained. The churches were consequently unable to detach themselves entirely from political tutelage, while they also retained a major influence in political circles. The clergy continued to be drawn from the upper strata and the middle class of the population. The payment of salaries by the state guaranteed direct control over the clergy by the political system. To a large extent, the churches remained national churches, as also in Catholic countries. In the latter case, opposition came from the Ultramontanes, who sought the restoration of absolute authority by the pope over the church, at the expense of state interference. There were also sharp clashes between conservatives and liberals concerning education. Was the church still permitted to organise education, or should this be fully taken over by the state? In most countries, such as France, Belgium and the Netherlands, a compromise was arrived at under which both forms coexisted.

These and other contentious issues resulted in the formation of political parties within the bourgeois and noble elites, with a split into liberal and Christian-conservative parties.

366   The call for liberal reform

Nevertheless, the liberal bourgeoisie did not meekly accept the status quo of 1815. Given its numerical strength and economic position, its members could hope to occupy the political field sufficiently in due course to turn the state to their hand. The liberal forces in France and other countries of western Europe sought amendments to the constitution serving to reduce the control of the king over the executive and legislative branches. The introduction of political accountability of ministers to parliament was designed to turn them into 'servants' of the people's assembly, rather than of the king. The appointment of the members of the first, aristocratic chamber was forced to give way to more democratic methods. Thanks to the tax-based or competence-based suffrage, the bourgeoisie could be certain of obtaining an electoral majority. The control of the judiciary over the government had to be strengthened, thereby providing a bulwark against government interference. At the economic and social level, the liberals dreamt of a minimal state. This would create the climate in which merchants, industrialists and landowners could pursue their financial interests. The safeguarding of public order and the protection of property and freedom of contract were the primary tasks of the state. This meant that the state needed to deploy its monopoly of violence to keep the masses in check. There was little consensus among liberals on free trade. While the merchants advocated free trade, industrialists – particularly in the early stages of industrialisation – generally pressed for trade restrictions in order to cope with foreign competition. It was not until the late nineteenth century that this issue receded into the background and free trade became the rule, and then only temporarily. Most industrialised countries, however, continued jealously to protect their colonial markets.

367 Nationalism

The liberal opposition was not the only challenge faced by the princes of the Restoration. Nationalism was another. Nationalism was a foster child of the Enlightenment. Universalism comes naturally to the rationalist credo of the Enlightenment: since all men are by nature rational beings, they are fundamentally equal. There was, however, no political basis on which to build a programme of universal equality among the peoples. Moreover, the 'universalism' of the Enlightenment was translated into an ideal of civilisation: the European, enlightened civilisation was the most advanced, for it was the most rational. To it fell the burden – the 'White man's burden', in the words of Rudyard Kipling (1865–1936) – of enlightening the rest of the world. Therefore, it had first to rule it. European imperialism was justified in terms of a humanitarian ideal. At the same time, the civilisational argument turned the Enlightenment into a seedbed for the later doctrines concerning white supremacy. The Enlightenment could only obtain a foothold in the leading political circles of a country by supporting the government's policies of national centralisation and unification. Even the internationalism of the Revolution proved unable to overcome this.

Nationalism had even more intellectual roots in the Enlightenment. In his *De l'esprit des lois*, Montesquieu argued that differences between the laws of various countries in Europe are natural, even if all the laws are based on the one human reason. These differences are due to all sorts of factors such as geography, climate, religion, the political system, the economic situation and the national mentality. All this means that each country has its own laws and that those laws exude their own spirit: *l'esprit des lois*.

> Law in general is human reason in so far as it governs all the peoples of the earth; and the political and civil laws of each nation should be only the particular cases to which human reason is applied. Laws should be so appropriate to the people for whom they are made that it is very unlikely that the laws of one nation can suit another.
>
> Laws must relate to the nature and the principle of the government that is established or that one wants to establish, whether those laws form it as do political laws, or maintain it, as do civil laws.
>
> They should be related to the physical aspect of the country; to the climate, be it freezing, torrid, or temperate; to the properties of the terrain, its location and extent; to the way of life of the peoples, be they plowmen, hunters, or herdsmen; they should relate to the degree of liberty that the constitution can sustain, to the religion of the inhabitants, their inclinations, their wealth, their numbers, their commerce, their mores and their manners.[16]

The German philosopher Friedrich Wilhelm Hegel (1770–1831) argued that history was the learning process of the collective memory of the people, the *Volksgeist*. The history of a nation was both cause and outcome of its own 'spirit' or nature. From acknowledging the particularity of each nation to claiming its superiority proved to be a small step in the context of early nineteenth-century Europe.

French domination gave wings to nationalism in many countries of Europe. The opposition against French oppression transcended ideological and class divisions. The ideal of the nation-state offered an intellectual substructure: now that the state no longer belonged to the sovereign but to the people, it had to belong to the people in question and not to an alien people. Separatist movements reared their heads in multi-ethnic

---

[16] Montesquieu, *De l'esprit des lois* 1.1.3, translation by Anne M. Cohler, Basia C. Miller and Harold S. Stone, eds., *Montesquieu: the Spirit of the Laws*, Cambridge 1989.

states, such as Austria-Hungary or the Ottoman Empire. In Germany and Italy, the nationalists dreamed of a unified German or Italian state. Congress Europe came under pressure.

368 The revolution of 1830

In many cases, the liberal and nationalist oppositions found one another and joined forces. In general, these more radical opposition movements could not draw on massive support among the population but were often small factions, seeking legitimisation in the theory of the revolutionary advance guard.

In the early 1820s, Europe was hit by a first wave of revolutions. Of these the Greek rebellion (1821–9) against Ottoman rule was the most successful. With, in particular, British support, Greece managed to gain its independence. A second, larger revolutionary wave hit Europe in 1830. This revolution sealed the victory of the liberal bourgeoisie over the restoration.

In July 1830, the liberal opposition in France forced the Bourbon King Charles X (1824–30) to abdicate. The more liberal prince Louis-Philippe d'Orléans (1830–48), from a junior branch of the house of Bourbon, assumed the throne. The constitution of 1814 was transformed into a genuine constitution (*charte constitutionelle*), to which the king pledged allegiance. Parliament would oversee compliance with the constitution and hence control the king. The idea of popular sovereignty was partly restored by designating the king no longer as king of France but as king of the French. The king lost the right to promulgate general decrees or to veto legislation.

The revolution of 1830 assured the liberal bourgeoisie of political power in France. The movement spilled over into other countries. In August 1830, a riot broke out in Brussels. On 4 October, the provisional government formed by the rebels declared the independence of Belgium. The uprising was by the Francophone bourgeoisie and aristocracy of Belgium. After a brief diplomatic tussle, the European powers recognised Belgian independence and Britain forced The Hague to accept it under the Treaty of London. William I was permitted to retain the eastern half of his Grand Duchy of Luxembourg, and a part of Limburg, the present Dutch province of that name, was allocated to the Netherlands. William I refused to ratify the treaty until 1839.

The Belgian constitution of 1831 was the most liberal in Europe at the time. Belgium became a constitutional and parliamentary monarchy. The executive power was vested in the king and the ministers appointed by him. The king was not accountable to parliament; every one of his actions had to be co-signed by a minister who assumed political responsibility for it. The legislative power was shared by the king, the Chamber of Representatives and the Senate. The king as well as all the members of parliament had the right to propose legislation. The king, as the third branch of the legislature, still had to confirm legislation passed in parliament but it rapidly became a constitutional custom that the king could not withhold his assent. The Chamber and Senate were elected directly on the basis of a system of tax-based suffrage. The conditions for election to the Senate were such that the aristocracy and landowners were in the majority. The judiciary had the right to review all government actions and decisions in terms of their legality and refuse to apply them if they failed the test. The Belgian constitution did not, however, provide for constitutional review of legislation. The legislative power was sovereign. This is consequential to applying Rousseau's theory of people's sovereignty to a system of representative democracy, which renders superfluous the limitation of state power as discussed by Locke. In this regard, sovereignty is vested both de facto and de iure not in the people but in parliament. The people's sovereignty slips over into the sovereignty of the legislature; as in the French constitution of 1791, the rule of law becomes the rule of the legislature. Without checks on the constitutionality of the law, the state is subject not to the law as intended by the constitution but to the law as understood by parliament.

369   The revolution of 1848 and its consequences

The revolutionary wave of 1830 and a new wave of revolutions in 1848 brought further liberalisation to most countries of western Europe. Even Britain, which had largely remained aloof from the revolutionary waves on the continent, did not escape entirely on this occasion. The Reform Act of 1832 implemented a reform of the electoral system whereby the preponderance of the rural gentry was reduced and the power of the urban bourgeoisie increased. In central, southern and eastern Europe, the autocratic monarchs survived, but ultimately there too the liberal bourgeoisie was able to push through some of its programme. Before 1830, many of the southern German states had a constitutional charter; after 1830, a number of states obtained a genuine constitution. Austria and Prussia obtained a constitution in 1848, but in the case of Austria this was withdrawn just a year later and replaced by a chartered constitution, which was then rescinded in 1851. In 1861, Austria ultimately became a constitutional monarchy. In 1867, the country was converted into the dual monarchy of

Austria-Hungary, a personal union with two governments and parliaments. Prussia developed its own constitutional model after 1848. Various aspects of the programme introduced by the bourgeoisie upon the revolution of 1848 were reversed. Prussia was a constitutional monarchy, but the monarch retained his ascendancy over parliament. There was no question of popular sovereignty. Parliament consisted of two chambers. Suffrage was confined to the wealthier class, while the members of the Herrenhaus were drawn from the nobility or were appointed by the king. The system reflected the actual balance of power. In Prussia, the regime continued to rely heavily on the old landed gentry. The bourgeoisie had managed to guarantee fundamental rights and freedoms but politically played second fiddle. The most important power of the Haus der Abgeordneten was that of setting the annual budget. When the chamber refused to do so, however, the king and his chancellor often took no notice and continued to govern without such consent. The supremacy of the monarchy was also retained in the German Empire after the unification of 1871. The unification was a success for the Prussian monarchy and the army, the leaders of which were drawn from the Prussian aristocracy. The German parliament had two chambers, the Bundesrat with representatives appointed by the constituent states, and the Reichstag, whose members were directly elected. Under the constitution of 1871, the chancellor and the government were accountable to the emperor alone and not to parliament. Since the government needed parliament in order to approve its finances and its legislative proposals, there was in fact a certain sharing of power. In practice, it was a constant tug-of-war between the government and parliament, with both sides exacting concessions. The conservative aristocracy governed through the emperor and the chancellor, while the bourgeoisie expressed its views through parliament.

Halfway through the nineteenth century, there were two different kinds of regimes in Europe. In the west and the north there were the most liberal regimes, as in Britain, Belgium and, from 1848 onwards, the Netherlands. Here the liberal middle classes were in the ascendancy and the power of the king had been greatly curtailed. In the centre, east and south, as in Austria and Prussia, the monarch and the traditional aristocracy consisting of the nobility and landowners continued to retain greater power. At the same time, however, this predominance was able to survive only while the precarious alliance between the nobility and the higher bourgeoisie remained in place. The regimes in these countries generally had to contend with nationalist movements. Europe split into a liberal north and west and a conservative central, southern and eastern part.

370   Radical opposition

As the nineteenth century progressed and industrialisation spread, the power elite found itself increasingly challenged by the working class. By the second half of the nineteenth century, the latter developed a class consciousness which the proletariat had previously never had. The struggle between rich and poor became a struggle between two classes, each with its own ideology.

During the French Revolution there were already movements in support of the political and social rights of the poor, especially the urban proletariat. These movements were harnessed to the Revolution by the bourgeoisie or were suppressed. During the first half of the nineteenth century, the working class had not yet succeeded in organising itself as a political movement or in developing real political clout. Its interests were defended on the political forum by progressive, radical liberals and by small, revolutionary splinter groups. The biggest mass movement of that period, the Chartist Movement in Britain in the 1830s and 1840s, was a spectacular failure.

The radical liberals who were engaged in legal opposition and their more revolutionary counterparts who did so through illegal, often violent means were in fact the heirs of the Jacobins. They sought the extension of suffrage and the improvement of the lot of the working class. Suffrage was indeed extended throughout Europe with the relaxation of the financial and other requirements, but it was not made universal yet and did not extend to the poorer strata of society.

371   The triumph of the liberals

The first revolutionary wave to be regarded as a people's revolution dates from 1848. Even then, however, the fruits of the unrest sown by the lower classes were plucked by the liberal bourgeoisie and middle classes in most countries. A republic was declared in France. The victory by the more radical liberal forces was largely overturned upon the election as president of Louis Napoleon, the son of Napoleon's brother Louis, who became emperor under the name Napoleon III (1852–70). Even though there was general suffrage for the Chamber, the predominance of the emperor and an elitist Senate meant that this far-reaching democratic measure had little effect. Not until the defeat in the Franco-Prussian War of 1870 did France become a republic again, this time with a highly liberal constitution. In the Netherlands, King William II (1840–8) had the constitution amended at the behest of the liberal politician and law professor Johan Rudolf Thorbecke (1798–1872). Political ministerial responsibility was introduced. The Second Chamber of the Estates-General was henceforth to be directly elected while the First Chamber was to be composed of representatives appointed by the members of the provincial estates. The Meerenberg decision by the High Council in 1889 was to impose further limits on the power of the king and to establish the authority of the Estates-General even more firmly. According to the court, the king had only those powers which the constitution expressly assigned to him.

372   Marxism and reformist socialism

During the second half of the nineteenth century, the working class managed to extend its political power. Socialist and communist thinkers gave the working class a political ideology of its own. The German intellectual Karl Marx places the class struggle in a historical context. Marx has a dialectical view of history. In the Hegelian tradition, Marx presents history as a natural process of thesis and antithesis resulting each time in a new synthesis. This does not lead to stability but provides the grounds for a new antithesis. For Marx, the modern, liberal state is not the final point in its historical evolution but a transitional phase. The state is the instrument of the capitalist elite to defend its economic power and dominate the working class. Since economic relations determine society as a whole and labour is the most important production factor, this situation cannot last. Marx not only calls for a class struggle, in the sense of the revolt of workers against capitalists, but also predicts it. In doing so, he is in fact taking the economic reasoning of Adam Smith a step further. Labour, and not capital, brings about productivity and welfare. The workers and not the capitalists must dominate. The victory of the proletariat in the class struggle will put an end to the existing political and legal order. The final result is a classless society in which everyone contributes and participates equally through his labour. The state – the machinery of oppression by the capitalist owners – then loses *raison d'être*. In order to achieve all this, the workers must obtain control over the means of production such as the factories, machinery and land. Individual property – on which the capitalists base their economic and political power – must be abolished.

Marxism became one of the many strands of thought of the labour movement. Together with other socialist and communist schools of thought, it marked the break with the radical liberals. The workers' movement would improve its lot not through co-operation with the wealthier classes but by struggling against them. This newly won autonomy became the lever for the success of the labour movement. The formation of separate organisations such as trade unions and co-operatives, each with its own newspapers, shops and social facilities, gave the left the necessary pull and political autonomy. For the time being, however, this did not lead to the overthrow of the bourgeois state in any part of Europe. By means of the systematic extension of the right to vote and by making a start on the social policy to improve the lot of the working class, the bourgeois state was able to absorb the labour movement sufficiently. In Germany, the first steps were taken towards social legislation and the social protection of workers as early as the 1880s. Other countries followed from the 1890s or 1900s onwards. On the left, there was growing dissent between the diehard communists, who favoured the class struggle, and reformist socialists, who sought gradual reform and participation in the political life of the state. The churches also became increasingly engaged with the lot of the poor. The Papal Encyclical *Rerum Novarum* (1891) of Pope Leo XIII (1878–1903) offered Catholics the necessary opening to establish Christian workers' movements and Christian-democratic parties allowing co-operation among the classes.

12   The European states system: diplomatic history

373   Louis XIV and William III

The Treaties of Westphalia symbolised the end of the crisis into which Europe had been plunged by the Reformation and the collapse of the *respublica christiana*. The religious and constitutional settlements that the 1648 treaties established for the Holy Roman Empire created a level of stability such as Germany had not known in more than a century. The attempt by the Habsburg emperors to extend their power over the entire empire had failed. The empire remained a loose federation of more than three hundred imperial estates of which just a few – such as Austria, Brandenburg-Prussia, Bavaria and Saxony – were genuine players at the European level. The great empire was unable to constitute a threat to its neighbours. After 1648, religious divisions ceased to play a dominant part in European diplomacy. Alliances were no longer formed along the dividing lines between the great Christian denominations, and religion was no longer considered a cause for war.

The defeat of Spain in the war against France (1635–59) marked a shift in the balance of power in Europe. With the annexation of Alsace and Franche-Comté, France had not just broken the Habsburg encirclement but also assumed the leading role in Europe. In the second half of the seventeenth century, European politics was dominated by the expansion of France and the efforts on the part of a growing coalition of states to keep it at bay. Under the government of Louis XIV, France conducted a number of wars of aggression against its neighbours, especially the Spanish possessions in the Southern Netherlands (1665–8, 1672–9, 1689–97). The French border gradually moved northwards, resulting in a breach between Paris and its traditional ally, The Hague. The Republic saw itself forced to defend its traditional enemy Spain against France. The French annexation of the Spanish Netherlands had to be averted at all cost: *Gallicus amicus, sed non vicinus.*[17] The accession to the British throne of the Dutch Stadholder William III (1689) led to a close alliance between London and The Hague. Britain gradually took over the role of leading maritime power from the Republic and embarked on its colonial expansion. On the European continent, it had no territorial ambitions, but that did not make Britain stand aloof from the great power politics of Europe. British domination of the North Sea and the English Channel was vital in order to assure its domestic security. To make all this possible, it was essential to prevent any continental power from securing dominance over Europe. In particular, it was necessary for the estuaries of the great rivers in the Netherlands as well as the Flemish ports, offering as they did good operating bases for an invasion of England, to remain out of the hands of any great power. London aimed at a divided continent, in which the great powers were too busy keeping each other at arm's length to turn to the sea and attack Britain. William III may be regarded as the architect of the British policy towards Europe that London conducted without interruption from the end of the seventeenth century to the Cold War (1947–90).

374 The balance of power and the War of Spanish Succession

The doctrine of the balance of power formed the backbone of Britain's grand strategy. According to the doctrine, the key to security was to safeguard a balance of power between the great powers of Europe, so that no power could achieve hegemony and thereby threaten the sovereignty of other states. The doctrine both safeguarded and limited sovereignty. If a power became too great, other powers would join forces to clip its wings. The balance did not prevent war. On the contrary, it was often used to justify war. But it limited the effects of war. Because the balance had to be maintained at all times, no power would be allowed to make too substantial gains out of a war. In seventeenth- and eighteenth-century Europe, there were few wars that resulted in total victory or the dismemberment or destruction of a major power.

---

[17] 'France as friend, but not as neighbour.'

The Spanish War of Succession (1700–13) illustrated all this. In 1700, Charles II (1665–1700), the last Habsburg king of Spain, died without issue. In his will, he left his entire empire to a grandson of Louis XIV, Philip V of Anjou (1700–46). The two other pretenders, the Austrian Habsburgs and the Elector of Bavaria, did not accept this outcome. But neither did William III. The dynastic union between France and the Spanish Empire with its possessions in Italy, the Netherlands and Latin America radically disturbed the balance of power both inside and outside Europe. Great Britain, Austria and the Republic declared war on France. This was to be the last great war for the Sun King and the first he lost. When, however, in 1711 the Austrian pretender to the Spanish throne, Archduke Charles, inherited the Austrian dominions upon the death of his brother and, as Charles VI, became emperor (1711–40), this created a situation that was unacceptable to London, namely the restoration of the empire of Charles V. At the peace negotiations in Utrecht, London steered a course whereby France was spared as much as possible. Under the Peace of Utrecht (1713), the Spanish Empire was carved up. Charles VI was given the Southern Netherlands and a number of Spain's Italian possessions. Philip V retained Spain and the overseas possessions, but was required to renounce his rights to the French throne. The dynastic rules of succession and the sovereignty of both countries were set aside in order to guarantee the balance of power in Europe. France retained all its possessions. London grabbed Gibraltar and Minorca, thereby providing itself with bases for its fleet in the western Mediterranean.

375 Limited wars, limited changes

Despite many wars, the European states system of the eighteenth century was fairly stable. Constantly changing alliances and coalitions ensured that the effects of wars on the positions of states remained relatively limited. Often, peace negotiations would start while the fighting still went on. Victories in battle degraded into arguments at the negotiating table and were rarely decisive.

The balance of power put the great powers centre-stage. The great powers (France, Austria, Great Britain and, as the century went on, also Russia and Prussia) assumed responsibility for the stability of Europe. At conferences and in treaties, they would agree on a settlement which they would then impose on the smaller powers, if necessary by force. The small powers generally paid the bill for the safeguarding or restoration of the balance of power between the great powers. The partition of Poland between Russia, Austria and Prussia (1772, 1793, 1795) offers the most cynical cxample thereof.

The diplomacy of the late *Ancien Régime* was a matter not for the countries or peoples but for the royal dynasties and their governments. Foreign policy and warfare were the preserve of the prince. In their mutual relations, states remained dynastical to a greater extent than on the domestic front. War too was the affair of the dynasts and of their professional armies and extensive bureaucracies. The people were surely expected to foot the costs of war, but ideally they were not supposed to die in it.

376   Total war and the nation-state

The French Revolution overturned all this. The French revolutionaries turned warfare into a struggle of the nation. Wars no longer concerned a scrap of land here or there but were ideological confrontations for which the entire nation was mobilised. A new increase in the scale of war took place. Where the biggest armies under the *Ancien Régime* had numbered around 400,000, Napoleon had more than twice that number under arms. In the dynastic and territorial state, warfare was a matter for the prince; in the nation-state it was a matter for the entire nation. In the course of the nineteenth and twentieth centuries, the nationalisation and massive increase in scale of war was taken further. Towards the beginning of the twentieth century, the object of war was the destruction not of the enemy army but of the enemy nation. The First World War was fought with national armies numbering millions.

377   The Concert of Europe

The European leaders who met at the Congress of Vienna sought a diplomatic restoration. The balance of power had to be restored. Under pressure from London, France was saved from dismemberment. It retained its borders of 1792 and was rapidly readmitted to the club of the five great powers. In this way, the pre-1789 balance of power was restored, at least on the surface. Austria and Prussia made territorial gains, but in fact only the latter country was left more powerful. Ethnic divisions and the threat of national uprisings crippled the Austrian colossus.

The Congress of Vienna sought to counter fresh French expansion. A cordon of strong buffer states was created to hem France in. Prussia acquired the Rhineland – and hence the basis for its industrial expansion and emergence as a leading continental power – while Austria obtained a large slice of Italy. Through the expansion of both Austria and Prussia a second balance within the balance was created in Germany. In this way, Germany was kept divided so that it could not threaten the rest of Europe, but its main powers were strong enough to contain France. The lands of the house of Savoy were greatly expanded to become the kingdom of Piedmont-Sardinia. Belgium and Luxembourg were given to the Dutch King William I.

London retained a few of the colonies it had occupied during the war such as the Cape in South Africa and the island of Ceylon, which it had seized from the Netherlands, as well as Malta. Under pressure from the Russian Tsar Alexander I (1777–1825), who had projected himself as the custodian of the conservative order, a Holy Alliance was formed between Russia, Austria and Prussia. This alliance of conservative princes appropriated to itself the task of suppressing each uprising, revolution or challenge to the existing order. As time went by, the alliance was unable to prevent the liberal bourgeoisie from overturning the restoration again, nor could it stop a number of changes to the international architecture of Europe, such as the independence of Greece and Belgium.

Nevertheless, the Congress of Vienna was a success. The restored balance of power ushered in a period of peace of unparalleled length. The great powers were all apprehensive of war, fearing that a new general mobilisation of the population would lead to revolutions. The post-1815 balance of power differed fundamentally from that before 1789. Under the *Ancien Régime*, the great powers found themselves continually at war or on a war footing with one another. With the exception of Britain, they sought almost constantly to extend their territories in Europe. The balance of power did not exclude warfare; it only guaranteed that gains and losses would remain limited. After 1815, the European great powers sought to preserve the peace and the status quo through constant consultation. Wars were avoided at all cost. Until the Crimean War in 1854, there was not a single major war in Europe. Leaving aside the conflict in the Balkans, the Franco-Prussian War of 1870 was also followed by a lengthy period of peace. Even the collapse of the Ottoman Empire and the Balkan War of the 1870s did not trigger great power wars. Under the system of the Concert of Europe, all major matters of concern were sorted out by the five great powers at multilateral conferences. The architect of this new balance of power policy was, besides Metternich, the British statesman Lord Castlereagh (1769–1822).

378   German unification and the disruption of the balance of power

Stability on the continent was radically disturbed by the process of Italian and German unification. In 1866, war broke out between Austria and

Prussia. Prussia, governed by its brilliant Chancellor Otto von Bismarck (1815–98), won a rapid and convincing victory, thereby taking over the leadership of the German Confederation from Vienna. During the years that followed, Bismarck conducted a resolute policy aimed at the unification of Germany under Prussian leadership and without Austria. In 1870, Bismarck provoked a war with Napoleon III. In a lightning campaign, the German armies defeated France and Napoleon III was overthrown. The German Empire was proclaimed in the Hall of Mirrors at Versailles. The Prussian King William became Emperor William I (1870–88) and Bismarck became German chancellor. In the meantime, Italy had achieved unification at the initiative of King Vittorio Emanuele II of Piedmont-Sardinia (1848–78) and his prime minister, Camillo Benso di Cavour (1810–61). The Austrians were driven out of Italy and the pope lost his state, locking himself up in his palace in the Vatican. In 1929, the fascist prime minister Benito Mussolini (1883–1945) was to conclude a concordat with the pope under which the Vatican was recognised as a sovereign state. The German and Italian processes of unification were coupled with what might be termed the nationalisation of nationalism. Spurred on by Bismarck, the conservative Prussians took over the nationalist movement in Germany from the revolutionary groups. Bismarck mobilised the energy emanating from the nationalist ideology for the dream of a German Empire. In Italy, the government of Piedmont-Sardinia, in a precarious alliance with revolutionary patriots such as the legendary Giuseppe Garibaldi (1807–82), followed a similar course. In the coming years, in many parts of Europe, the feelings of nationalism were also to be mobilised on behalf of the state; something for which Europe was to pay a heavy price after 1914.

The unification of Germany and defeat of France disrupted the balance in Europe. The rapid emergence of Germany as an industrial power and the economic and demographic stagnation of France during the last decades of the nineteenth century widened the gap. In Germany, Europe had a new potential hegemonic power. By means of a sensible and cautious policy, Bismarck managed to ward off the disquiet that this had aroused, for example, in London. He refrained from building a large fleet and set limits on his country's colonial aspirations. By means of a network of alliances, Bismarck ensured that no great power would have reason to wage war against Germany or could be certain of Germany's support in the event of war.

In 1888, William II (1888–1918), a youthful and ambitious emperor, came to power in Germany, Bismarck was sidelined and Berlin plunged

itself into colonial adventures. Under William II, Berlin began building up its military power on land and at sea. Before the turn of the century, the European great powers had become involved in an arms race.
Conscription was introduced in many countries; Prussia already had conscription before unification. The German threat and the alliance between
Berlin and Vienna drove Paris and Moscow into each other's arms. The
colonial and maritime aspirations of William II even induced London to
give up its traditional policy of remaining outside alliances ('England has
no permanent friends; it only has permanent interests'). Britain teamed
up with France and Russia to form the Triple Entente (1907). The cards
had been shuffled; the First World War was at hand.

13   *The European states system: the modern law of nations*

379   Natural and positive law of nations

The collapse of the *respublica christiana* and the crisis of the international
legal order greatly stimulated the scholarly debate on international
relations from the second quarter of the sixteenth century onwards.
Gradually, the law of nations emerged as an autonomous discipline, independent of theology and the *ius commune* and with its own discourse and
literature. Until the second half of the eighteenth century, Grotius's *De
iure belli ac pacis libri tres* (1625) was the most authoritative work on the
law of nations.

Most writers on the law of nations of the seventeenth and eighteenth
centuries stood in the tradition of natural law. To them, natural law constitutes the basis for the law regulating the relations between sovereign
states. Under the pen of the natural lawyers, the law of nations becomes a
highly prescriptive set of rules, embodying the ideal of natural justice and
rationality as applied to international relations.

One of the most radical spokesmen of the School of Natural Law was
Samuel Pufendorf (1632–94). Pufendorf held the first chair in natural
law and the law of nations to be established at a university (at Heidelberg,
1661). In his view, the law of nations is natural law applied to sovereign
states. It is logically derived from natural law and has no other foundations than natural justice and rationality. Pufendorf rejects the existence
of an autonomous positive law of nations based on human consent. As
natural law, the law of nations is enforceable only *in foro interno*, in conscience. Its laws constitute natural obligations. It is not enforceable *in
foro externo*, that is, by an external power. Pufendorf draws the logical

consequences from Hobbes's political doctrine. The sovereign monarchs may be compared with Leviathans in the state of nature. They are the only ones in their states not to have given up their natural rights and freedoms. Within the states, positive law prevails; among the states, the natural state and natural law prevail. No external, higher power can impose the application of natural law on the sovereign. Hobbes and Pufendorf are heirs of Machiavelli and in turn stand at the beginning of the tradition of 'deniers of international law', who reject the binding force of such law. This was – ironically enough – to reach a pinnacle among the positivists of the nineteenth century.

Christian Wolff (1679–1754), his follower Emer de Vattel (1714–57) and other natural lawyers do not go so far. Vattel's *Le droit des gens ou principes de la loi naturelle* (1758) was largely based on Wolff's *Jus gentium methodo scientifica pertractatum* (1749), translated into French, made more readable and accessible and amended on some points. Vattel's work became highly influential, particularly among diplomats and practitioners, and displaced Grotius's treatise as the standard textbook on the law of nations for more than half a century. Following Wolff, Vattel distinguishes between a natural or necessary and positive or voluntary law of nations. The necessary and voluntary laws of nations are both general in application. Whereas the voluntary law of nations cannot contravene natural justice, it can adapt it and lower its standard to the needs of the society of sovereign states. It is based on common consent among the nations and is expressed in their pacts and practices. As general consent can almost never be established, it has to be presumed. Here Vattel ties the voluntary law back in with the necessary. If a rule contravenes natural justice, common consent cannot be presumed. Apart from the two categories of general law of nations, there are two categories of particular law of nations, applicable only to those states whose consent to the rules can be established: the conventional and customary law of nations.

With other writers, natural law receded more into the background as they focused on describing contemporary state practice, sometimes making suggestions for improvement. They concentrated on the study of the positive sources of the law of nations: treaties, customs and diplomatic practice. The most important representatives of this so-called positivist current were the Dutch-Roman lawyer and judge Cornelius van Bynkershoek (1673–1743), Johann Jakob Moser (1701–85), professor at the Tubingen Law School, and Georg-Friedrich von Martens (1756–1821), diplomat and professor at the Göttingen Law School.

380 ¶ The law of nations in traditional historiography

The Treaties of Westphalia had created the conditions of stability in which a new European legal order could emerge. From Westphalia to the end of the *Ancien Régime* runs a string of important peace treaties that came to form the core of the political and legal order of Europe. These treaties were generally the outcome of multilateral peace conferences at which virtually all the great powers were represented, such as those of Nijmegen (1678–9), Ryswick (1697), Utrecht/Rastadt (1713–14), Aachen (1748) and Paris/Hubertusburg (1763).

The emergence of the internally sovereign state led to the gradual monopolisation of its external relations by its central government. By the second half of the seventeenth century, this process was largely complete in most European countries. The waging of war, the conclusion of treaties, and the posting and accreditation of diplomats were henceforth the exclusive preserve of the sovereign. Great vassals, towns and ecclesiastical princes lost their autonomy on the international plain. The great exception was formed by the more than three hundred German estates, which under the Treaty of Westphalia retained their right to conclude alliances with foreign powers.

State sovereignty forms the foundational principle of the European states system and its modern law of nations, which emerged in the century *after* Westphalia. Traditional historiography has often ascribed three essential characteristics to the modern law of nations. First, the sovereign states are the sole subjects of the law of nations. Only they are the bearers of rights and obligations under it. This is reflected in the doctrine of dualism, under which two spheres of law are separated from one another: the inter-state and intra-state sphere. Within the state, municipal law applies to the exclusion of the law of nations. Among the states, the law of nations applies to the exclusion of municipal law. Individuals are not subject to the law of nations and cannot invoke it in municipal courts. Sovereigns cannot be subject to the law of another land. For this reason the immunity of diplomats as representatives of their sovereign under the modern law of nations is quasi-absolute.

Second, the sovereign states are also the sole authors of the law of nations. This opens the way to voluntarism, meaning that sovereign powers are bound only by rules that they have voluntarily consented to. This consent can be given either expressly, in treaties, or tacitly, through state practice constituting customary law.

Third, the sovereign states are also the sole enforcers of the law of nations. The law of nations is externally enforceable, but in the end, the sanction will often come down to self-help, potentially forcible self-help. This is expressed in the doctrine of legal war, which came to supplement, albeit not displace, the doctrine of just war. The just war doctrine was a product of late medieval theology and jurisprudence. Thomas Aquinas had moulded it into its classical form. For a war to be just, it had to fulfil three conditions. *Primo*, it had to be waged by a sovereign (*auctoritas principis*). *Secundo*, the belligerent needed to have just cause (*causa iusta*). This meant that the war constituted a kind of self-help to defend, enforce or restore a right that had been wrongfully injured by the enemy and for which he refused compensation. In this sense, war was a form of unilateral enforcement of law and justice. *Tertio*, the war had to be waged under a righteous intention (*recta intentio*), for a just purpose, such as just and stable peace. In principle, a just war was discriminatory. Only one side could have justice on his side, making the other belligerent unjust. In consequence, only the just side had a right to wage the war and could thus benefit from the laws of war, such as the right to ransom, loot or conquer. In a context of sovereign states, where there was no higher, external authority – that is, other than God – to judge on the justice of each belligerent's claim, this discriminatory concept of war became highly impractical. Therefore, authors such as Gentili and Grotius had constructed a second conception of war: that of legal war. Under a legal war, both sides were granted the right to wage the war and the laws of war benefited them equally. For a war to be legal, it sufficed that it was waged by a sovereign and that it was formally declared. In fact, this meant that sovereigns could freely decide when to resort to war.

381 Sovereignty and European order

This traditional, extremely 'Hobbesian' characterisation of the modern law of nations is in dire need of far-reaching qualification. Sovereignty was unquestionably the leading principle in the modern law of nations but, at the same time, that law also constituted an attempt to regulate sovereignty and hence overcome the chaos into which Europe had been plunged since the Reformation. It was an effort to bring order to a world of sovereign states. Its point of departure may have been the Hobbesian natural condition of war by all against all, but it purported to create a more stable legal order. In this sense, the modern law of nations was not unequivocally Hobbesian, or 'Westphalian',[18] but was a fundamentally dualistic system.

---

[18] In modern scholarship, the term 'Westphalian' is widely used to indicate the European states system and its law premised on the principle of state sovereignty, although it has

None of the three characteristics noted above was ever realised in full. Dualism was never absolute. At all times the law of nations contained rules which were directly applicable to private persons. Peace treaties granted rights to state subjects, for example, with regard to restitution of property seized during war, which they could then have enforced by the municipal courts. There was also a whole body of customary law on navigation, maritime warfare and reprisal, applied by the municipal Admiralty Courts, which were directly applied to private persons. Nor was voluntarism carried to its ultimate consequences: in reality numerous rules were adopted from the ancient Roman and canonical traditions and from natural law. The proposition that this was done with the tacit consent of the states does not entirely stand up to scrutiny. Some rules, such as self-defence and the binding force of treaties, were so fundamental that they were not liable for discussion. The fairly general acceptance of the *clausula rebus sic stantibus* actually sustains this. According to that doctrine, sovereigns are not bound by treaties if the circumstances under which the treaty was concluded have radically altered. While this doctrine weakens the binding force of treaties, it also confirms the principle. The *clausula* forms the exception to the rule. Moreover, whereas they applied the conception of legal war to the practices of war (the laws of war or *ius in bello*) and peacemaking (*ius post bellum*), states still took trouble elaborately to justify their resort to force (*ius ad bellum*). For this, until well into the eighteenth century, they operated a language that was still very much reminiscent of the just war tradition, although increasingly the discourse of political interest slipped in. Nevertheless, the freedom of states to wage war and conclude and break alliances with one another was at once enhanced and curtailed by the balance of power and the great powers principle. Those principles were aimed at defending state sovereignty, but also at reconciling it with the common interests of Europe.

382 ☩ The French Revolution and the nation-state

The most important legacy of the French Revolution to the international order of Europe was the nation-state. In the nation-state, the people – all if not represented by its elected officers – and not the prince were sovereign and embodied the state. In the nation-state, diplomacy and warfare too were the concerns of the nation and not the preserve of the prince. Even if the sovereigns in 1815 formally reassumed their prerogative over

---

been established now that Westphalia itself contributed but little to the formation of the modern law of nations.

foreign policy, diplomacy was in most countries no longer separable from the economic interests of the elite. Similarly, the nationalisation of war by the *levée en masse* was no longer reversible. The ideology of the nation-state gave the state much greater leverage to mobilise the population for a struggle against its enemies than was open to the dynastical and territorial state. The consequences of this were to turn the twentieth century into the bloodiest in history.

383   Modern international law

In the course of the nineteenth century, modern international law – as it was now called[19]– reached full maturity. Popular sovereignty and the concept of the nation-state strengthened the claims to sovereignty for the state in a way dynastical sovereignty never could. The language of the state's political interest, which was now the interest of the people itself, further displaced the language of justice and the common good. The justifications for war became less elaborate and used the language of justice less often, although the fact that there were remarkably few inter-European wars after 1815 may also be part of the explanation for that.

The nineteenth century also marked the heyday of legal positivism in international law. The positivist *credo* is twofold. Only rules that have been accepted by the states are valid in international law (voluntarism) and all rules to which a state has consented are binding upon it, regardless of the question of whether they are in accordance with natural law or any other transcendent standard of justice or not (consensualism). The vast majority of nineteenth-century international lawyers rejected natural law as the source of international law and found themselves therefore confronted with the difficult riddle of what constituted the basis for the binding character of international law. Those who did not, such as John Austin (1790–1859), denied any external authority to international law.

Although by the mid-seventeenth century the law of nations had largely completed its formal emancipation from the *ius commune*, the impact of general principles and of institutions, conceptions and rules of, in particular, private law had remained substantial all through the seventeenth and eighteenth centuries. Natural law acted as a conduit between the law at large and the law of nations. In the nineteenth century, international law strengthened its autonomy. Particularly among continental lawyers, international law was claimed to be of a whole different order to any other

---

[19] In the English language, the term 'international law' was introduced by Jeremy Bentham (1748–1832).

ıt applied to states and not to persons. The former answered to
rules of morality and necessity than the ordinary citizenry, namely
of the reason of state (*raison d'état*). By consequence, rules of private
should not – directly or by analogy – be applied to states.

Once again, the picture in practice was not as one-sided as the writings
of the great nineteenth-century authors might lead one to believe. The
Concert of Europe brought order and limited the free arbiter of states.
Under pressure from the ever-increasing importance of public opinion, the first initiatives were taken to place limits on the conduct of war.
Particularly during the second half of the nineteenth century and in the
early days of the twentieth century, the sheer body of international law
greatly expanded. Attempts at codifying important parts of international
customary law through multilateral conventions were made, with some
success. The Peace Conferences at The Hague in 1899 and 1907 codified
a large part of the laws of war and led to the foundation of the Permanent
Court of Arbitration in the same city. On a more technical level, concepts
and rules that had their roots in private law – often in Roman or canon
law – and had already made their way into the law of nations were still
applied and even new analogies and transplants were made.

B   Culture and the law

1   The scientific revolution and the emergence of rationalism

They therefore to right belonged, so were created, nor can justly accuse
their maker, or their making, or their fate, as if predestination overruled
their will, disposed by absolute decree or high knowledge: they themselves
decreed their own revolt, not I: if I foreknew, foreknowledge had no influence on their fault, which had no less proved certain unforeknown. So
without least impulse or shadow of fate, or aught by me immutably foreseen, they trespass, authors to themselves in all both what they judge and
what they choose; for so I formed them free, and free they must remain,
till they enthrall themselves ...[20]

384   The scientific revolution of the seventeenth century

The ideologies of the liberal bourgeoisie and of the nation-state of the
nineteenth century were indebted to the modernism of the Enlightenment
of the eighteenth century, which in turn had its roots in the scientific
revolution and rationalism of the seventeenth century. Spectacular new

---

[20] John Milton, *Paradise Lost* 3, 111–25, London 1667; John Milton, *The Complete English Poems*, London 1909, 204–5.

insights and discoveries in science and hitherto unknown technological progress marked the scientific revolution. The innovations widened the gap between science and revelation. Scholastic epistemology, which still set the tone in many universities and ecclesiastical circles, became untenable. Humanism had already greatly increased the intellectual freedom of the elite. With the scientific revolution of the seventeenth century, a huge step was taken towards further intellectual emancipation.

385 Galileo

As early as the sixteenth century, the Polish astronomer Nikolas Copernicus (1472–1543) had demonstrated that the sun did not revolve around the earth but that the earth, like all the other planets, revolved around the sun. In the early seventeenth century, the Italian mathematician and astronomer Galileo Galilei (1564–1642) substantiated heliocentrism with the aid of a powerful telescope and detailed mathematical computation. Thanks to Galileo, the theory of heliocentrism became widely disseminated. Heliocentrism was totally at variance with the cosmology of the church. The idea that man was God's highest creation and was made in God's image and likeness was challenged. Galileo was condemned by the church in 1633.

Galileo also held radical convictions regarding epistemology. He did not totally reject revelation. According to him, God had given mankind two books from which it could draw the truth: the Bible and nature. Each dealt with a different aspect of reality. Nature taught about the physical world, while the Bible dealt with the metaphysical dimension. The Bible did not teach anything about nature. It just spoke about natural phenomena by way of allegory in order to impart something about God and divine reality. Galileo had much in common with the Franciscan nominalists of the fourteenth century.

It was not just in the area of astronomy that the seventeenth century saw remarkable progress. Important discoveries were made in the fields of physics, chemistry, botany, biology and medicine, setting modern man on a collision course with the old authorities. So the discovery of the blood circulation by William Harvey (1578–1657) tore down the entire received wisdom on medicine based on Hippocrates, Galen and Avicenna, as taught at the universities.

386 British experimentalism

During the seventeenth century, two great epistemological traditions emerged: 'British' experimentalism and 'continental' rationalism. The

British tradition had its roots in the fourteenth-century nominalism of Roger Bacon and William of Ockham. The philosopher, scientist, lawyer and statesman Francis Bacon (1561–1626) recycled some of the basic tenets of nominalism. The British empiricists hold, just like Galileo, that direct observation of natural phenomena is the only source of true information about the physical world. Through experiment, the scientist can observe nature. If repeated experiments consistently produce the same results or, alternatively, explicable differences, it becomes possible to formulate general scientific laws on the basis of inductive reasoning. Thomas Hobbes applies the empirical method to philosophy, treating reality as a chain of cause and effect. Man is capable of discovering the causes by observing the consequences. Hobbes also takes the view that only the external observation of the natural world can disclose the laws governing those causal relations. In his *Essay Concerning Human Understanding* (1690), John Locke rejects the existence of innate ideas. All human knowledge is ultimately based on external or internal observation or experience. This generates an arsenal of factual knowledge. By means of induction, man is then able to build up more complex ideas and insights. Knowledge is the outcome of observation, followed by inductive reasoning within the human mind. The Scottish philosopher David Hume (1711–76) argues that the veracity of causal relations determined by the human mind can never be definitely established. Hume is the founding father of modern scepticism.

In contrast to the radical nominalists of the fourteenth century, the mainstream of British experimental thinkers of the eighteenth century did not reject the existence of general concepts, ideas and laws. In line with the medieval nominalists, they acknowledged the role of the divine will in creation. The will, not reason, is the determining factor. God's will is free and not subject to reason. Consequently, it is not subject to the laws of reason and nature, which He himself had created. Nevertheless, these laws operate and are worth discovering. God may not be subject to the laws of reason but in His goodness He does not generally overrule them and leaves nature untouched. This attitude prevents the modern experimentalists from falling into the trap that had ensnared many of their Christian and Islamic predecessors and counterparts. The rejection of the existence of general concepts and laws had meant in the past that the study of nature had been considered irrelevant; God could at any point suspend the workings of the natural world. As such, true knowledge lay in the discovery of God's will and hence in the authority of faith.

387 Cartesian rationalism

The father of the 'continental' rationalist tradition is the French philosopher René Descartes (Cartesius, 1596–1650). The point of departure for Descartes is methodical or systematic doubt. Man can only attain certain and true knowledge by first casting doubt on everything and challenging all assumptions.

> The first was never to accept anything as true that I did not know evidently to be such; that is to say, carefully to avoid haste and bias, and to include nothing more in my judgments than that which presented itself to my mind so clearly and so distinctly that I had no occasion to place it in doubt.[21]

For this process to lead to certain knowledge, however, one should arrive at a first indubitable, axiomatic truth to serve as the foundation for all other knowledge. Descartes found this in human thought itself, which produces the evidence for one's own existence ('cogito ergo sum').

> But, soon afterwards, I noticed that although I wanted thus to think that everything was false, it was necessary that I, who was thinking this, be something. And noting that this truth: *I think, therefore I am*, was so firm and well assured that all the most extravagant suppositions of the sceptics were incapable of shaking it, I judged that I could accept it without scruple as the first principle of the philosophy for which I was searching.[22]

This first axiomatic truth which he finds in his own rationality leads Descartes to conclude that all proposals that the mind is capable of producing through rational deduction from this first truth and that are of the same clarity and precision must also be true. In this way, he achieves certainty about God's existence. The mind is capable of imagining a perfect, infinite, omniscient and omnipotent being. Since the mind is not itself perfect and infinite, that being cannot have arisen from the mind itself but must have been put in it. On the basis of these first certainties about the existence of God, the mind and its cognitive power, Descartes develops his rationalist epistemology. By means of deductive reasoning the human mind is able to deduce new laws from the first certainties. These truths in turn form the basis for more concrete laws that one can derive from them, and so on. Ultimately, reason is capable of pervading the whole natural world.

[21] René Descartes, *Discours de la méthode* 2.141, 1637, translation by Paul J. Olscamp, *Descartes: Discourse on Method, Optics, Geometry, and Meteorology*, Indianapolis and Cambridge 2001.
[22] Descartes, *Discours* 4.158.

According to Descartes, nature is intelligible. God, through His divine reason, has created nature so that it is ruled by immutable and universal laws. These govern the chains of causes and effects, of which the world and history consist. Because these laws are rational, human reason can comprehend nature. Those who understand the laws of nature are capable of explaining and predicting natural events. Descartes understands the natural world in terms of movement and extension. In the same way as a machine, nature obeys a number of mechanical principles or laws. These may be expressed in terms of mathematical laws and formulae. For Descartes, mathematics is the language that human reason has developed and with which it is able to comprehend and demonstrate the laws of nature. Descartes believes that the most complex phenomena can be understood by approaching them through the methods of geometry (*more geometrico*), as a combination of numerous simple and comprehensible elements.

> The long chains of reasoning, so simple and easy, which the geometers customarily used in order to arrive at their most difficult demonstrations, had given me occasion to imagine that all things that can be understood by men follow from one another in the same way, and that, provided only that we abstain from accepting as true anything which is not, and always follow the order that is necessary to deduce each from the other, there can be none so remote that we cannot eventually come upon it, or so hidden that we cannot discover it.[23]

The Cartesian epistemology as developed by Descartes and his followers, among whom Gottfried Wilhelm Leibniz (1646–1716) should be mentioned, is rationalist. It presupposes the congruence between nature and the human mind. According to the Cartesians, man is rational, as is nature. The laws of nature are innate to the human soul and spirit, which is immortal, although man has forgotten them at birth. Systematic observation of nature by means of experimental research is superfluous. Only by means of pure deductive reasoning based on the first axioms stored in the mind can man hope to rediscover the laws of nature. True knowledge can only be rediscovered by the mind in itself.

The Cartesian epistemology is hugely optimistic about the possibilities of the human mind. The latter is not just capable of explaining reality as a whole; departing from a single axiom, the mind can also capture all of reality in a single ideal construction, such as mathematics, devised by the mind itself without need for direct observation of nature. The compact of

---

[23] Descartes, *Discours* 2.142.

this rationalist constructivism was felt in the sciences, and not just those concerned with physical reality. It argues in favour of science as systematisation. Science is the creation of an ideal construct embracing all individual phenomena by placing them into larger categories and bringing them under more general laws.

⚘ 388 Newton

Modern science combines elements from both traditions. Experimental research is carried out in order to test hypotheses first developed through rational thought and through prior experience. The results of these experiments are used in order to support, reject or modify the hypothesis. Abstract deduction and inductive generalisation constantly interact. This was also the method used by the most important and successful representative of the scientific revolution, Isaac Newton (1642–1727). Newton articulated and substantiated some of the most fundamental laws of physics. His laws of motion and gravitation were believed to explain the behaviour all natural bodies, from the biggest, such as heavenly bodies, to the smallest here on Earth. To many of his contemporaries, Newtonian physics appeared to confirm the proposition that the world is one great machine, governed by a number of timeless and universal laws. However, Newton himself also held that not all in nature, and in particular in nature's evolution through time, could be explained by these natural laws and that some things would remain mysterious and could only be known through divine revelation.

2 Modernism and the Enlightenment

389 Modernism

At the end of the seventeenth century, the French author Charles Perrault (1628–1703) published an essay entitled *Parallèle des anciens et des modernes*. In it, Perrault engaged in the debate over whether the ancient Greeks and Romans were superior to the moderns or not. He concluded that the moderns had indeed surpassed most of the Greek and Roman achievements. In consequence, there was no reason to turn to Antiquity any longer.

Perrault's view was certainly not uncontested, but it does reflect some of the basic assumptions of the mainstream in intellectual life in the eighteenth century. *Emulatio* had been successful; modernism was born. This sounded the death knell for Latin as the common language of diplomacy and learning. French, the language of the leading political and cultural power, took over the role of Latin.

Modernism rejected both the scholastic *auctoritates* and the example of Antiquity as a source of knowledge and truth. The criterion for true knowledge became the test of reason. What human reason recognised as truth, was true; what it rejected as false, was false. For the time being, this did not necessarily imply the rejection of the possibility of objective and universal truth, as the sceptics would have it. On the contrary, most thinkers held to the firm belief that there was a single Reason operating in nature and in each human being and that correct application of rational thought led to a single, unambiguous truth. The international community of scientists and scholars, particularly those engaged in the study of physical reality, managed to achieve consensus on many issues. Newtonian physics laid the foundations for modern science and remained dominant throughout the eighteenth and the larger part of the nineteenth century.

390   The Enlightenment credo

Modernism led to the articulation of a new worldview, that of the Enlightenment. 'Enlightenment' is the name for a broad cultural movement that spread all over Europe, reaching its high point halfway through the eighteenth century (1720–80). Although it became contested from the second half of the century onwards, the basic assumptions of the Enlightenment remained fundamental throughout the nineteenth and even twentieth centuries. The Enlightenment embodies the basic ideology of modern, Western civilisation. The postmodern counter-currents of the twentieth and twenty-first centuries exist only through a dialectical relation with the modernist ideology. The great debates from the recent past and of our own time predominantly turn around the Enlightenment credo.

The Enlightenment's roots stretched back to seventeenth-century Britain but the movement reached its pinnacle in France and Germany in the eighteenth century. It was an elitist movement which spread all over the continent. It influenced the French Revolution and the bourgeois regimes of the nineteenth century.

The enlightened 'philosophers' – from the contemporaneous French term *philosophes*, actually meaning all kinds of Enlightenment intellectuals or thinkers – had an unbounded faith in the possibilities of human reason. All through the seventeenth and eighteenth centuries there raged a debate as to whether the world was completely intelligible (Leibniz) or not (Newton, Voltaire). In the following paragraphs, this debate will be ignored and the Enlightened credo as it stood in its purest and most radical form will be explained. Whether or not one adhered to this to the full, it was after all these radical ideas that underpinned the whole Enlightened discourse, to whatever degree.

391 Positivism

One of the basic assumptions underlying the Enlightenment discourse is mechanism. The world is a machine and nature an endless chain of cause and effect. These causal relationships are governed by a number of immutable and universal natural laws. This makes nature and the world – totally or largely – intelligible: human reason is capable of comprehending, controlling and improving the world.

That intelligibility is not confined to the world of physical phenomena. The triumph of reason is the triumph of mankind. Man and his behaviour are studied more than ever before – even more than under humanism. Theology – the great science of the Middle Ages – recedes into the background. Human behaviour is subject to the laws of nature as is physical reality. Human history too is a chain of causes and effects ruled by natural laws and can therefore be rationally explained. The scientific revolution and the Enlightenment extend to law, politics and the economy. During the nineteenth century, a number of other aspects of human behaviour become the object of scientific study along the lines of the exact sciences. Sociology and psychology offer two important examples thereof.

The scientific positivism of the nineteenth century is a sprig on the tree of the Enlightenment. Positivism holds that, as nature and man are governed by general, universal and immutable laws, it is possible to attain exact knowledge in all areas of natural and human reality. As these laws are reflected in natural and human reality, so their effects can be observed. Positivism rests on a double assumption about the relation between true knowledge and its source (observable fact) which is formally similar to the scholastic epistemological credo on its source (the authoritative texts): observation of fact leads to exact and true knowledge and exact and true knowledge can only arise from the observation of fact.

From the second half of the nineteenth century onwards, the theory of evolution of Charles Darwin (1802–89) gave a new impetus to the belief in the intelligibility of human behaviour and history. All live species are determined by the natural laws of evolution, of the survival of the fittest. They continually adapt to their environment; those who do so best survive. This theory indicates that man like other animals is a natural being. His behaviour is consequentially scientifically explicable. Furthermore, the constant perfection of man also appears to be a natural law. For the proponents of positivism, Darwin's theory of evolution was a huge triumph.

The claim that even man could be understood by means of empirical/rational research seemed vindicated.[24]

✗392   Enlightenment optimism

The Enlightenment, which brought about the liberation and triumph of reason, constitutes a fundamental caesura in human history according to the Enlightenment philosophers. The Enlightenment is considered as the point in history at which mankind liberates itself from any form of suppression of free, rational thought. The times of darkness are over. In the words of the German philosopher Immanuel Kant (1724–1804):

> Enlightenment is man's release from his self-incurred tutelage. Tutelage is man's inability to make use of his understanding without direction from another. Self-incurred is this tutelage when its cause lies not in lack of reason but in lack of resolution and courage to use it without direction from another. *Sapere aude.* Have courage to use your own reason – that is the motto of enlightenment.[25]

The Enlightenment's advocates are modernists. As Voltaire (François-Marie Arouet, 1694–1778) writes in his *Siècle de Louis XIV*, his age is one of the best in history. The Enlightenment frees mankind from the chains of suppression. It is the beginning of an age of unparalleled and continuing progress. Where previously history was an ongoing sequence of progress and decay, the future brings only growing prosperity and welfare. The emancipation of reason will enable man to take his fate into his own hands and continually improve it. This makes the Enlightenment fundamentally ahistorical. The study of the past is only useful in as far as it allows one to discern, through the recurrent patterns of human behaviour, the immutable and universal laws of nature that determine human behaviour. The past thus should be studied not because it determines man, but because it offers observable information about what determines man. This view was to contribute during the nineteenth century to the development of historiography into a genuine scientific discipline. For the Enlightenment thinkers themselves, however, historiography remains primarily a literary and philosophical activity.

The Enlightenment consummates the process of emancipation from Antiquity that, paradoxically, humanism and the Renaissance started. It

---

[24] Matthew Kneale has written a splendid, satirical novel, *English Passengers* (London 2000), on the theory of evolution.

[25] Immanuel Kant, *Was ist Aufklärung*, 1783, translation by Lewis W. Beck, *Immanuel Kant: Foundations of the Metaphysics of Morals and What is Enlightenment*, Indianapolis 1959.

stands at the juncture at which man places reason at the forefront and consequently breaks with the past. Mankind liberates itself from oppression and irrationality. Western man, who for centuries has been looking backwards, now turns around and starts to look forwards. The giants of the past now seem like dwarfs. Only a few periods in history, such as the century of Socrates, the century of Cicero or the Renaissance, find merit in the eyes of the Enlightenment thinkers: these are oases of reason in the desert of history. But, under the modernist credo, their achievements too have already been surpassed.

393   Deism

Nor does religion escape the assault of the Enlightenment. Many *philosophes* are advocates of deism. Deism is consequential to mechanism. The deists believe in God and divine creation. They believe that God has created nature and man with His reason and subjected them to the operation of rational laws. Here the metaphor of the *dieu horlogier* or divine watchmaker comes to the fore. The world is like a watch: it is a mechanism of cogs and springs, the movements of which are governed by the laws of gravity. Like a watchmaker, God has created the mechanism of the world but, since then, had ceased to interfere in the world. He does not intervene and leaves nature untouched. Any further interpretation of faith and religion is not the work or will of God but that of man and nature. Specific forms of religions and religious institutions are human creations. The Enlightenment thinkers consequently call for religious tolerance, particularly for the various Christian denominations and the Jews. During the second stage of the French Revolution, the Jacobins sought to introduce a kind of secular, national religion based on deism.

394   Liberty and equality

The Enlightenment was also translated into a programme of social and political emancipation. All suppression or censure of free thought is condemned. Many of the *philosophes* clashed with both secular and spiritual authorities. Some were forced to flee abroad. At some point in their lives, both Voltaire and Rousseau had to leave France to avoid a worse fate.

The Enlightenment stands not just for freedom but also for equality. Each man is endowed with reason and has been given certain inalienable rights and freedoms by nature. Therefore, men are fundamentally equal. The Enlightenment strives for the abolition of the legal discrimination between the estates, although in real terms, most of the elitist *philosophes* are primarily concerned with improving the position of the top layers of the third estate and much less with the rest of it. The national unification of the law fits into this programme.

395   Legal reform

The Enlightenment thinkers also push for legal reforms. They denounce the existing situation. The plurality of legal systems, sources and institutions, and the complexity of many legal rules, which are often organically grown and not rationally planned, have made the law inaccessible and incomprehensible to most people. It has turned the law into the instrument of the governmental and juridical elites to conserve and strengthen their position. A radical simplification and rationalisation of the legal system will lead to greater legal certainty and equality. The Enlightenment thinkers believe in the possibilities of intellectually construing a rational legal system which, since it is reasonable, would be timeless, universal and comprehensible to all. Similarly, the judiciary needs to be radically reformed.

3   *The modern School of Natural Law*

396   Grotius

The modern doctrine of natural law was the reflection of rationalism in legal scholarship. The School of Natural Law had a particular following in Germany, but also had an impact in other countries such as the Dutch Republic, Sweden and France. It reached its high point in the second half of the seventeenth century and first half of the eighteenth century.

The Dutch humanist Hugo Grotius may be considered the founder of the modern School of Natural Law. We may regard him as the counterpart in the humanities to what Descartes was for the sciences. One of his achievements was to secularise natural law by detaching it from Christianity.[26] According to Grotius, natural law is innate to each human being. Both man and nature are rational. And although man has been created by God, even non-believers are capable, as rational beings, of discovering natural law and comprehending it. Until the seventeenth century, natural law was primarily the domain of theologians and canon lawyers, such as the Spanish neo-scholastics. Now it had also evolved into an important branch of secular jurisprudence.

According to Grotius, man differs from all other living beings by virtue of his reason. This provides him with the capacity to distinguish good

---

[26] Suarez had also already taken that step.

from evil. Furthermore, man is a social animal. Man has a natural inclination to live together with his fellow men, Grotius calls this man's *appe-
titus socialis* (social inclination). Natural law, which derives from man's
rationality and social nature, is reasonable and expresses natural justice.

> Man is, to be sure, an animal, but an animal of a superior kind, much far-
> ther removed from all other animals than the different kinds of animals
> are from one another; evidence on this point may be found in the many
> traits peculiar to the human species. But among the traits characteristic
> of man is an impelling desire for society, that is, for the social life – not of
> any and every sort, but peaceful, and organized according to the measure
> of his intelligence.[27]

Natural law consists of a number of moral-legal principles that each reasonable person will consider natural and spontaneously recognise as
reasonable. Like nature itself, they are timeless and universal. Grotius
indicates what he considers to be the basic principles of natural law:

> This maintenance of the social order, which we have roughly sketched,
> and which is consonant with human intelligence, is the source of law
> properly so called. To this sphere of law belong the abstaining from that
> which is another's, the restoration to another of anything of his which
> we may have, together with any gain which we may have received from
> it; the obligation to fulfil promises, the making good of loss incurred
> through our fault, and the inflicting of penalty upon men according to
> their deserts.[28]

Positive law, covering both the law of nations and the civil law of any
country, is based on agreements among people. The natural law rule *pacta
sunt servanda* renders them binding.

Grotius cherishes the ambition to turn law into a systematic science –
something which, according to him, no one has been able to do before.
Natural law provides an outcome. Because it consists of general and
unchangeable principles, it may readily be systematised. Legal science
should take natural law as its starting point and, at least initially, must
relegate positive law to the sidelines. The great, unchangeable principles of
law may be found in natural law, on the basis of which the great classifications can be made.

> Many heretofore have purposed to give to this subject a well-ordered
> presentation; no one has succeeded.
> And in fact such a result cannot be accomplished unless – a point which
> until now has not been sufficiently kept in view – those elements which

---

[27] Grotius, *De Iure Belli ac Pacis*, Prol. 6.   [28] Grotius, *De Iure Belli ac Pacis*, Prol. 8.

come from positive law are properly separated from those which arise from nature. For the principles of the law of nature, since they are always the same, can easily be thought into a systematic form; but the elements of positive law, since they often undergo change and are different in different places, are outside the domain of systematic treatment, just as other notions of particular things are.

If now those who have consecrated themselves to true justice should undertake to treat the parts of the natural and unchangeable philosophy of law, after having removed all that has its origin in the free will of man; if one, for example, should treat legislation, another taxation, another the administration of justice, another the determination of motives, another the proving of facts, then by assembling all these parts a body of jurisprudence could be made up.[29]

Grotius himself does not go so far as to base the entire law on natural law and to disregard the positive law or the old scholarship of the *ius commune*. In his great work on the laws of war and peace of 1625, he discusses not just the general principles of natural law and the natural law of nations he deduces from this, but also the legal rules of positive law arising from treaties or state practice.

397 Law of reason

The natural lawyers of the late seventeenth and eighteenth centuries took up the challenge as laid out by Grotius and indeed tried to 'discover' and intellectually reconstruct a whole and complete system of natural law that would provide a just solution to each and every human problem on the basis of a few axiomatic precepts of natural justice. Because it is rational, as is the whole creation, it should be possible for the human mind to discover and reconstruct such a law wholly within itself, through abstract deductive reasoning. No reference needs to be made to positive law such as legislation, treaties, custom, case law and even ancient jurisprudence. These are all mutable laws and impede systematisation. This natural law is also referred to as *Vernunftrecht* (law of reason).

The result of this thought process should be a genuinely scientific legal system. It should be complete in the sense that it provides a solution for any potential dispute. It should be internally consistent and intelligible to all. Furthermore, it would ideally also be universal and if not immutable, then adaptable to shifting circumstances without changing its basic precepts.

---

[29] Grotius, *De Iure Belli ac Pacis*, Prol. 30–31.

398 German and French natural lawyers

Many natural lawyers still drew on Roman law for their expositions of natural law. According to them, natural justice had found no better expression in human law than in Roman law. Many principles, concepts and rules of Roman law and civilian jurisprudence were considered to be reasonable and just and were therefore adopted into the natural law. The criterion is not the authority of Roman law or its exemplary function but simply its conformity with reasonableness. In his *Nova methodus discendae docendaeque jurisprudentiae* (1667), the philosopher, mathematician and jurist Gottfried Wilhelm Leibniz recognises that Roman law remains the foremost source for law and justice. However, Roman law needs to be divested of its structure and system, which have grown not rationally but historically. The law needs to be systematised *more geometrico*, that is, along the lines of geometry.

Some of the German natural lawyers did seek to describe an entire legal system along purely idealistic lines. One of these was Samuel Pufendorf. His natural law is embedded in a Christian context and is heavily imbued with moral philosophy. In *De iure naturae et gentium* (1672) and *De officio hominis et civis iuxta legem naturalem* (1673), Pufendorf works out an ideal law of nature and of nations in detail. God has bestowed upon man the natural inclination to love God and his fellow men. The sense of duty towards God, his fellow men and himself that is innate to each man forms the basis of natural law. From this, Pufendorf derives the binding force of the given word and hence of promises and agreements. People must also respect each other's property. Each person is held to loyalty to the community of which he forms part, such as the family or the state. The law of obligations, the law of property, family law and public law spring from this.

Two other leading representatives of the German *Vernunftrecht* are Christian Thomasius (1655–1728) and Christian Wolff. Wolff's main work, *Ius naturae methodo scientifica pertractatum* (1740–8), marks the intellectual high point of modern natural law. Wolff creates an intellectual system of natural law that realises many of the claims of the underlying rationalist and constructivist ideal. His deductive arguments do indeed approximate the methods used by the exact sciences. Wolff inspires the idea that jurisprudence should confine itself to basing its judgments as closely as possible on general legal principles, without any external input.

For France, reference must be made to Jean Domat (1625–96). He too works on the basis of a number of Christian, moral premises from which he derives more concrete rules *more geometrico* in his *Les lois civiles dans leur ordre naturel* (1689–94). Domat arrives at a new classification of civil law that was later to be adopted by the German legal scholars of the nineteenth century and which from there found its way to the *Bürgerliches Gesetzbuch*.

399   Natural law and the universities

The modern School of Natural Law was primarily a German affair, but even there it did not conquer the academic establishment totally. The natural lawyers gained the ascendancy in certain new and progressive universities such as Halle and Göttingen, but in most universities the *usus modernus pandectarum* remained dominant. This did not mean that the natural law tradition failed to exert any influence on these faculties of law, but most university professors left matters at a compromise between natural law and Roman law, the latter being said to contain natural reason. In addition, Roman law remained an instrument for change. In the divided empire, it was as before an instrument of choice for those who dreamt of national unification. In addition, in the eighteenth century, in many European countries, universities did not stand at the head of scientific and intellectual progress. They were conservative institutes in which there was little innovation, and where one's origins were more important than talent and industry. This intellectual fall-back assumed particularly dramatic proportions in England, where education and science had become all but marginalised in the elitist subculture of Oxbridge. The universities were displaced as the leading centres of intellectual progress by new institutions such as the Royal Society (1660) in England or the Académie des Sciences (1666) in France and by the informal circles of *philosophes* who met in the salons of Paris and other cultural centres.

4   The codification movement in Germany

400   The inspiration for the codification movement

During the eighteenth century, inside and outside the circles of Enlightenment thinkers, the ambition grew to replace existing law by a system of codes. The modern codification movement differed substantially from the Justinian codification. The latter was a compilation of existing law. It was exclusive in the sense that everything not contained in it was abolished, but it did not lead to the creation of new law. The ambitions of the advocates of the new codification went further. They wished to abolish the entire mass of existing law and replace it. This time the replacement would be not just formal but also substantive; the codes would introduce new law. That ideal of new law was inspired by the Enlightenment and by the School of Natural Law.

The modern codification movement was in many respects the translation into practice of the ideals of modern natural law. The codes would establish a new and much improved legal system. The advocates of codification shared the conviction of the natural law lawyers – as they themselves also often were – that man was capable of formulating a legal system that was complete, consistent, clear and comprehensible to all. Ideally, this new system of law would also be universal and immutable, at least on the level of its general principles if not in their particular application in detailed regulations.

The codification movement also tied in with the political programme of the Enlightenment. Under the separation of powers, the introduction of new law belonged to the province of the legislature. Existing law with its multiplicity of legal sources and mutually contradictory rules had to be replaced by a clear-cut system of legal rules that were all drawn from a single source. This would make the law more certain and comprehensible. The power of the aristocratic judiciary would be broken. In a system of codified law, the judge would only have to apply the law as it stood on the books. Since the law was clear, certain and internally consistent there was no longer any place for interpretation. In the words of Montesquieu, the judge would simply be 'la bouche de la loi'.

In the context of the European states system, codification would have to be attempted at the level of the states, not at any 'universal' level. Whereas this implied surrendering the universalist aspirations of natural jurisprudence and the Enlightenment, this was not a major point of contention among natural lawyers and Enlightenment thinkers. Whereas most consistently claimed the universality of human nature and of the general precepts of natural law, most also acknowledged that in their particular applications these precepts had to be adapted to particular circumstances. Montesquieu's argument along these lines was perhaps one of the best known and best elaborated, but the idea preceded him and was widespread. Thus the potential gap between universalist idealism and political pragmatism was bridged.

The codification movement grafted itself on to the emergent sovereign state, in which it found a natural ally. The replacement of all existing law by a single national code would at a stroke accomplish the national unification of law. As statute law, all law would also spring from the legislator, the sovereign in most countries.

401   The Prussian codification

The first princes to embark upon a general codification of the law were some of the enlightened absolutists from Germany. The first example comes from Bavaria, where the *Codex Maximilianeus Bavaricus civilis* was issued in 1756 on the instructions of Elector Max Joseph III (1745–77). The text was the work of Wiguläus von Kreittmayr (1705–90). The code made no claims to exclusivity. In the event that the code proved incomplete, the learned Roman law would be invoked. There was little influence from natural law on the code.

Matters were different in Prussia and Austria. In 1714, King Frederick William I (1713–40) of Prussia instructed the faculty of law in Halle, where Christian Thomasius was professor, to codify private law. In the spirit of natural law, the code would be concise and clear. The project came to nothing. A quarter of a century later, in 1738, the king reissued the order for codification. This time, he stipulated that the code should be based on Roman law. Frederick William's successor, Frederick II, withdrew the instruction and now commanded a general codification of the law on the basis of the law of reason. The particular nature and circumstances of the realm had to be taken into account. Rules of Roman law could be adopted only if they were in accordance with natural law and did not detract from the code's systematic consistency. As Justinian had done, Frederick II issued a ban on scholarly interpretation. Samuel van Cocceji (1679–1755), who was assigned to lead the codification project, was unable to complete it. His work was taken over by Johann Heinrich Casimir von Carmer (1720–1801) and especially by Carl Gottlieb Suarez (1746–98). Both were heavily influenced by natural law.

The *Allgemeines Landrecht für die Preussischen Staaten* was introduced in 1794. It comprised no fewer than 19,000 articles. Apart from private law, it also covered public law, criminal law, commercial law, ecclesiastical law and even feudal law. The system of the code stemmed from the works of Pufendorf and Wolff. It departed from general principles which were then applied in myriad detailed rules and regulations. In the tradition of natural jurisprudence, the code starts by laying out the foundational principles of the organisation of state, society and law:

> Par. 82. Men's rights are determined by their birth, class, actions and events to which the legislation has attached certain effects.
>
> Par. 83. The general rights of men are founded in their natural liberty to pursue their own interest without, however, any encroachment upon the rights of other men.[30]

---

[30] My translation.

In their desire to make a comprehensive and complete code of law, the authors of the *Allgemeines Landrecht* created a code that was too elaborate and detailed to be easily manageable and comprehensible. A special *Gesetzkommission* held the authority to give out authentic interpretations of the code. The code breathes the conservative spirit of the Prussian state, preserving feudal law and class discrimination. But all the king's subjects were equally subject to the king's legislation.[31]

402   The Austrian codification

In Austria, Maria Theresa commissioned work on codification as early as 1753. The committee that was established was instructed to base the code on the *ius commune*. Natural law would be applied to improve and supplement the learned law where necessary. The first draft was completed in 1766. This *Codex Theresianus* met with opposition from both conservative and progressive forces. The former contested the code since it would end the autonomy of the different composite parts of the monarchy. The latter group found too much of the old learned law and too little of the natural law. The great defender of this latter school of thought was Karl Anton von Martini (1726–1800). Partly in response to his arguments, further work was carried out on a code that was simpler and clearer. In 1786, Joseph II ultimately introduced a first part of the code as the *Josephinische Gesetzbuch*. The civil code as a whole was not completed until 1811. It is the work of Franz von Zeiller (1751–1828). With 1,502 articles, the *Allgemeines Bürgerliches Gesetzbuch* introduced in 1811 is remarkably concise. It has remained the Austrian civil code to this day. It uses both natural law and Roman law. It is a modern code which, among other things, abolishes the legal discrimination between the estates.

5   The French Revolution and codification

403   Codification in the *Ancien Régime*

From the outset, one of the programmatic points of the French revolutionaries of 1789 was the codification of the law. The codification would put an end to the numerous different jurisdictions and legal systems throughout France and would subject all citizens to the same rules, irrespective of class or place of residence. The codification would achieve equality before the law. In the *Déclaration des droits de l'homme et du citoyen*, the supremacy of the legislature was indicated in various places. Article 4 laid down that only through legislation could the natural rights of the citizens

---

[31] 'The laws of the state apply to all citizens, without any distinction of class, rank or sex': Par. 22.

be limited, while Article 8 laid down the principle of legality in criminal law. On 5 July 1790, the Constituent Assembly ordered the codification of the law: 'the civil laws will be reviewed and reformed by the legislators, and a general code with simple and clear laws which are in accordance with the constitution will be made'.[32]

For all their revolutionary fervour, the ambition for codification placed the revolutionaries in a long tradition. Since the end of the Middle Ages, the French kings had always tried to enhance the role of royal legislation. Legislation was the instrument par excellence for the central ruler to bring innovation and unity to the law. During the fifteenth and sixteenth centuries, there had been the codification and homologation of customary law. Under Louis XIV and Louis XV, some major royal ordinances codifying entire branches of law had been issued. These statutes applied to the whole realm and thus led to a partial unification of the law. The *Ordonnance civile pour la réformation de la justice* (1667) had reformed civil procedure. Commercial law was the subject of the *Code sur le commerce* (1673), which fitted in with the mercantilist policy of Colbert. The same applied to the *Ordonnance sur le commerce des mers* and the *Ordonnance de la Marine*, both of 1681. Under Louis XV, three parts of private law were revised: donations, testaments and fidei-commissa in the *Ordonnance sur les donations* (1731), *Ordonnance sur les testaments* (1735) and the *Ordonnance sur les substitutions fidéicommissaires* (1747). The chancellor Henri-François Daguesseau (1668–1751) was the great promoter of these.

The French revolutionaries decided to embark on the complete codification of the law. For the civil code, they could draw on the work of Robert Joseph Pothier (1699–1772). A magistrate from Orleans, Pothier had in his numerous treatises provided a survey of private law, starting from Roman law and the customary law of Orleans, which he compared with other systems of customary law in France. In this way, he arrived at a systematic account of what could be regarded as a 'French' system of civil law. His best-known work concerns the law of obligations, *Traité des obligations* (1761). The compilers of the French codes made grateful use of Pothier's treatises. In itself, that was contrary to the ambition of breaking totally with the law of the *Ancien Régime* and replacing it by new law. In practice, things did not go so far: *l'esprit des lois* was too strong.

404   Napoleon and the codification

During the first turbulent decade of the Revolution, the codification did not progress very well. Two drafts of a civil code were submitted to

---

[32] My translation.

parliament but rejected. The drafts were the work of a committee headed by Jean-Jacques de Cambacèrcs (1753–1824). A number of statute laws were adopted in specific areas of civil law, such as marriage and divorce (1792), civil status (1792), illegitimate children (1793), hereditary succession (1794), and mortgages and transfer of title for realty (1798). In the field of criminal law, there were the *Code pénal* (1791) and the *Code des délits et des peines* (1795).

The codification was pushed through by Napoleon Bonaparte. In 1800, he appointed a limited commission of four members to compile a civil code. The four members were François Tronchet (1726–1806), Jean Portalis (1746–1807), Félix Bigot de Préameneu (1747–1825) and Jacques de Maleville (1741–1824). They hailed from various parts of the country and from different legal backgrounds in Roman law and customary law. The draft was submitted to the Court of Cassation and discussed at length in the Council of State, where Napoleon himself took part in various deliberations and pushed through his views in various areas. The *Code civil*, also known as the *Code Napoléon*, was introduced in 1804. The Civil Code came into force not just in what is now France but also in territories annexed to France, such as Belgium and northern Italy. With many amendments, it continues to apply to this day in France, Belgium and Luxembourg. In Switzerland it applied until 1912, and in Poland until 1946. The code was also introduced in the French and Belgian colonies. It has had a major impact on civil law in many countries inside and outside Europe, especially in the Latin world. The Italian code of 1865 was inspired by the French Civil Code. The same may be said of the Spanish *Codigo civil* of 1867, which in turn had its impact on Latin America.

405 ⭐ The *Code Napoléon*

In many respects, the *Code Napoléon* of 1804 is a compromise between the ideals of the Enlightenment thinkers and pragmatic realism. It answers to the conservative policies of partial restoration of the Napoleonic regime. It is innovative but nevertheless largely draws on existing law. As Portalis says in his *Discours préliminaire* to the *Code*, not everything that is ancient needs to be rejected: 'All that is old has been new. It is most essential to imprint upon the new institutions a certain character of permanence and stability that will allow them to become old'.[33] Portalis acknowledges that law results from historical evolution. In doing so, he rejects the intellectual claims of rationalist constructivism and questions the revolutionary approach to law by the Enlightenment and the revolutionaries. The

---

[33] My translation.

compilers of the *Code Napoléon* aimed at clarity, completeness and stability, but realised that these goals would remain unattainable:

> At the beginning of our deliberations, we have been stricken by the opinion, so widely held, that for the making of a code, a few precise texts on each subject will suffice and that it is all a matter of simplification by foreseeing everything.
>
> *To simplify all* is a matter on which we have to elaborate. *To be able to do all* is a goal which it is impossible to attain.

Since it is impossible to foresee everything and to guarantee the total completeness of the law, Portalis opens the door to judicial interpretation. He also rejects a ban on scholarly interpretation.

> If the law is clear, one has to apply it; if it is obscure, one has to work its dispositions out in more detail. If there is no rule, then one has to turn to custom or equity. Equity is an appeal to natural law in case positive law is silent, contradictory or obscure.

The outcome of all these and other considerations is a fairly concise and practical code. A theoretical introduction concerning the general principles of natural law is lacking.

406   The *Code civil* and the bourgeois state

The *Code civil* of 1804 is a mixture of old law and a number of new ideas stemming from the French Revolution. Its 2,281 articles have their roots in customary law, Roman law, canon law, the ordinances of Chancellor Daguesseau and the works of jurists such as Domat and Pothier. Of the three great principles on which the edifice of the *Code* was erected, two clearly convey the atmosphere of the Enlightenment. They are at the same time pillars of the bourgeois state. These are the virtually unlimited right of property and contractual freedom. The third principle is marital power. The latter was primarily a concern on the part of Napoleon.

> Art. 544. Property is the right to use and control things in the most absolute manner provided this use and control are not prohibited by the law.[34]
>
> Art. 1134. Agreements legally formed are like a statute for those who have made them …[35]

---

[34] Translation by Catherine Deplanque, 'Origins and Impact of the French Civil Code', *Association française pour l'histoire de la justice* (2007) 1–5.

[35] Translation by Hugh Beale, Arthur Hartkamp, Hein Kötz and Denis Tallon, eds., *Cases, Materials and Text on Contract Law*, Ius Commune Casebooks on the Common Law of Europe, Oxford and Portland, Oreg. 2002, 118.

Pothier advocated a three-way division of private law into persons, property and actions. This arrangement had its roots in the *Institutes* and had been further refined by Donellus. This was now more or less taken over by the *Code civil*. Under 'actions' (that is, the way in which property was acquired) came the law of obligations, marital property law and the law of succession.

Under Napoleon's rule, the *Code de procédure civile* (1806) and the *Code de commerce* (1807) also came into force. These rested on the great ordinances of Louis XIV. Criminal law and the law of criminal procedure were laid down in the *Code pénal* (1810) and the *Code d'instruction criminelle* (1810).

6   Codification in the Netherlands

407   Codification under French domination

Like France, Belgium and the Netherlands offer a good illustration of the impact of politics upon the codification process. After Belgium had been overrun and annexed by France, French law came into force (1797). When the French codes were introduced in France, they also came to apply in Belgium. In the Netherlands, the codification was part and parcel of the reform programme of the revolutionaries of 1795. The First Constitution of 1798 contained a codification article laying down that the entire body of law would be codified within two years.

Shortly after the constitution came into force, a twelve-member committee went to work. The Amsterdam jurist Hendrik Constantijn Cras (1739–1820) was the dominant figure in the subcommittee responsible for the civil code. Cras called for a code that was as complete as possible and left as little room as possible for interpretation by the courts. The civil code could not, however, bypass the existing law in the Republic. Grotius's *Inleidinge tot de Hollandsche Rechtsgeleerdheit* was taken as the starting point. This immediately created the risk that the codification would turn into a kind of legal colonisation by Holland. The codification project fell victim to serious political contention.

These and other points of discussion led to bitter disputes within and around the committee, thereby greatly slowing down its work. The fact that a rapid codification came to nothing was, however, also partly due to the lack of support for the Revolution in The Hague. After the assumption of power by Schimmelpenninck and later King Louis, Napoleon took the view that the Netherlands should simply adopt his codes, as had happened in some French satellite states in Germany. Louis, however, was not prepared to entertain this idea; there were too many differences between the French legal tradition and that of Roman-Dutch law. Louis found a compromise in a revision of the *Code Napoléon*. The *Wetboek Napoleon ingerigt voor het Koningrijk Holland* was introduced in 1809. More than just a translation, this was a revised version of the French emperor's legal code. A number of typical Dutch elements were included in it, but the structure of the code and the majority of the articles were taken from the *Code Napoléon*. After the annexation by France of the Kingdom of Holland, the code was withdrawn. On 1 March 1811, the French codes came into force in the former Dutch kingdom. In the meantime, a criminal code had also come into force, the *Crimineel Wetboek voor het Koningrijk Holland*. That too now had to make way for its French counterpart.

408   The Dutch Civil Code of 1838

Upon his installation as king of the Netherlands, William I indicated that he favoured a national codification of the law, especially of civil law. The codification was an achievement by the Revolution that it was no longer possible or desirable to reverse, as it assured the unity of the law and the dominance of the central government and was a symbol of equality among the population. The existing French codes needed, however, to be replaced by Dutch codes. In 1814, a committee embarked on its task. It was dominated by the Leyden professor Johan Melchior Kemper (1776–1824). Following the addition of Belgium to the Kingdom of the Netherlands, the draft of the Dutch committee – the 1816 Draft – was submitted to a committee of three Belgian jurists. The chairman of this group was the Liège magistrate Pierre Thomas Nicolaï (1763–1836), who came from a very different legal tradition from Kemper. The clashes between Kemper and Nicolaï would become the stuff of legend and greatly frustrated the work on the civil code in the following years.

The 1816 Draft was unacceptable to the Belgian delegation. Nicolaï and the Belgian jurists failed to see the need for a distinct Dutch codification. They felt comfortable with the existing Napoleonic texts. If there had to be a national code, it was not clear what that 'national' should consist of. The Dutch and Belgian legal traditions differed widely. In Belgium customary law was dominant, while in the Netherlands, thanks to Roman-Dutch law, Roman jurisprudence was more important.

After a further draft, that of 1820, had been rejected by the Estates-General, a third text was completed in 1829. After Kemper's death the struggle between north and south over the code had petered out. With his opponent no longer on the scene, Nicolaï was able to turn the work on the code – now in the Second Chamber of the Estates-General – to his hand. The draft of 1829 was highly Belgian in nature; in other words it resembled the *Code Napoléon*. That code was accepted and was to be introduced on 1 February 1831. Matters took a different turn, however, with the secession by the southern part of the country. Whereas the now independent Belgium kept the Napoleonic code, the Netherlands decided to go through with making a civil code of its own. This was finally introduced in 1838. Ironically enough, this code too was largely a carbon copy of the Napoleonic code. The new criminal code was completed in 1886. The new code of criminal procedure was not introduced until the *Wetboek van Strafvordering* of 1921.

7 *The Exegetic School and legal positivism*

409 The revolution in jurisprudence and the Exegetic School

The codification triggered a revolution in jurisprudence. Since its emergence in the eleventh century, Western jurisprudence had been idealistic in the sense that its main aspiration was to articulate an ideal law and to perfect the law, or at the very least to improve it as much as possible. According to many, that ideal had now been achieved through the codification of the law, and legal scholarship should now restrict itself to understanding and teaching the codes. Although the French legislator did not go as far as the Prussian king in banning scholarly interpretation of the codes, the sheer existence of the codes inevitably limited the room for manoeuvre for legal scholars.

The Exegetic School consummated the codification in jurisprudence. It was primarily a Franco-Belgian school, but it also had its impact on other countries, including the Netherlands. The school only emerged a generation after the introduction of the French codes. The leading jurists of the first few decades of the nineteenth century had their juridical formation under the law of the *Ancien Régime*. Their commentaries on the codes included a good deal of traditional law. Philippe Antoine Merlin de Douai (1754–1838) commented on the new civil code on the basis of the ancient legal sources. Jacques de Maleville (1741–1824) interpreted the *Code civil* primarily in the light of the preparatory works and of traditional jurisprudence. The German scholar Karl Salomo Zachariae (1769–1842) reverted to the old system of Roman law to explain the *Code civil* to his German readership.

It took a new generation for a truly new jurisprudence to arrive. This new post-revolutionary generation had been educated at the new imperial faculties of law that were established in 1808. Their legal training consisted of little more than the exposition or exegesis of the codes. During classes, the codes were interpreted and commented upon article by article. Particularly in the early period, references to case law or legal theory were rare: both stemmed from the *Ancien Régime* and were regarded as superseded and, above all, reactionary.

From the teaching at university, the exegetic approach spread to the legal literature. The work of the great French and Belgian exegetes consisted of detailed commentaries on the *Code civil* and the other codes. The French exegetes include Alexandre Duranton (1783–1866), Raymond Théodore Troplong (1795–1869) and the duo of Charles Aubry (1803–83) and Frédéric-Charles Rau (1803–77). The last worked on the commentaries of Zachariae and continued to adhere to the system that was customary in traditional German jurisprudence. In Belgium, the Ghent professor François Laurent (1810–87) was the leading representative of the Exegetic School.

410   Legal and legislative positivism

The Exegetic School reduced the study of the law to the study of the codes. Its proponents are legal, or even better, legislative positivists: only the legislator determines what the law is, and what the legislator determines is law. Their commentaries on the codes correspond as closely as possible with the text. The exegetes advocate as literal an interpretation of the codes as possible; it is not the spirit of the law but the letter of the law that counts. In doing so, they minimise the role of jurisprudence and the judiciary in the formation and interpretation of the law. As time went by, that position became less and less tenable. In reality the law courts – especially the highest courts such as the French and Belgian Court of Cassation – played a growing role in the interpretation of the law and increasingly had to find creative ways of filling the gaps in the codes.

The exegetes opposed any direct appeal to natural law, even if some accepted its existence. The exegetes are consistent representatives of the positivism that dominated legal scholarship in many countries of Europe throughout much of the nineteenth century and continues to set the tone for many jurists to the present day. Legal positivism in law is the carbon copy of positivism in the sciences. It seeks to turn the law into an empirical science along the lines of physics or biology. The subject matter of that science must confine itself to positive, observable law. This comprises the legal rules which have been introduced according to the formal procedures provided therefore in the legal system. In those countries where the law has been codified, these are the codes and any other later statutes. In these countries, legal positivism is the same as legislative positivism. Positivism leads to a formal approach to the law. It rejects the proposition that for a law to be valid it must be in accordance with the precepts of a transcendent normative system, such as natural law. For a law to be valid, it suffices that it is in accordance with the procedural rules for creating law. All hierarchy of norms is internal to the positive law itself. The law exists in and of itself and answers to its own, formal logic. Law is law if the law says so. In doing so positivism threatens to sever the link with social reality. Law need not be tested for its justness or social utility. Such testing is superfluous since the formal laws of a parliamentary democracy ensure that the law is automatically in accordance with justice and general welfare. In that sense, legislative positivism is the translation into legal theory of the system of representative democracy combined with popular sovereignty.

8 Romanticism

411   The Enlightenment and Romanticism

At the end of the eighteenth century, a new cultural movement emerged: Romanticism. Of all great historical cultural movements Romanticism is the hardest to grasp in rational terms. It was in fact barely a movement at all. By definition, it rejected any form of institutionalisation or even a consistent social, political or cultural programme. Romanticism is a collective name for a complex of attitudes, ideas and artistic expressions. It had many subcultures and has exerted its influence on many aspects of social life.

Romanticism is often portrayed as a reaction against the Enlightenment's one-sided focus on reason. While that is correct, the relationship between the Enlightenment and Romanticism is a complex one. The two movements stand in a dialectical opposition. Romanticism reacted against the Enlightenment but also came out of it. In fact, the current within Enlightenment thinking, represented by Newton, Voltaire and most clearly by Rousseau, which challenged the view that all nature was rational and intelligible is sometimes referred to as pre-Romanticism. After all, the intellectual fathers of Romanticism were some of the greatest Enlightenment thinkers, not only Rousseau but also Hegel.

The Romantics rejected the belief in the complete intelligibility of man and nature of the radical Enlightenment. They took the pre-Romantic argument further by focusing on emotion and sensitivity for man's engagement with himself, his fellow men and the world. But as in the Enlightenment, the personal development of the individual was central to Romanticism.

Romanticism had its adherents among the old and new elites, the aristocracy, the bourgeoisie and the middle class. It found acceptance in different intellectual and artistic circles. The movement reached its high point somewhere between 1780 and 1820, but its impact on Western culture continues to be felt until this day. Successive generations of artists and thinkers have been influenced by it. The modern novel, Hollywood and the music industry are all indebted to Romanticism. Although it is certainly possible to cite many examples of purely Romantic artists and intellectuals, the main significance of Romanticism is not that of an autonomous movement. Its greatest impact and significance was and remains that of bringing greater balance into a society in which rational thought and economic progress were and are dominant. Liberal society emerged from the Enlightenment, but received a good dose of feeling from Romanticism as a counterweight.

412   Sense and sensitivity

The Romantic obsession with emotion has manifested itself in many different forms and given rise to the most divergent attitudes and forms of behaviour. In the arts, Romanticism has been particularly influential in music and literature. In the world of learning, it has exerted a strong influence on historiography but also on jurisprudence. Through its glorification of valour, the drive for action and passion, it also inspired the numerous revolutionary and nationalist splinter groups of the early nineteenth century.

Whereas the pre-Romantics cast doubt on the total intelligibility of man and nature, the Romantics reject it outright and place that rejection at the heart of their worldview. Mankind and nature are not governed by eternal and universal laws; they are unpredictable and not totally intelligible. Romanticism opposes the reduction of man and nature to intelligible objects of rational analysis. Man is by nature sensitive and emotional. Rational thought has corrupted him. Rousseau's *retour à la nature* is one of the catchphrases of the Romantics. The Romantics do not study nature, they admire it and are inspired by it. Nature becomes an allegory for their feelings and an inexhaustible source of inspiration for the artist.

413   The return of history

Romanticism breaks with the ahistorical approach to the past of the Enlightenment. The world is not the result of a pre-ordained order; history is no more determined by natural laws than man and nature are. The present results from a historical process of evolution, in which individual decisions, feelings and chance all play a role. History is not wholly intelligible and must not be approached rationally, but must be reconstructed as an evocative narrative story. But even if history itself is not explicable, it does explain where the present comes from.

During the nineteenth century, a Romantic form of historiography emerged. Its qualities are literary rather than scientific and often constituted a form of escapism from present reality. Romanticism did, however, also exert a more general influence on historiography in that it led to a revival of interest in the past. The emphasis is not so much on seeking to explain history but on nostalgia for other and better times: times before reason turned everything to its hand. Romanticism focuses on totally different eras compared with the Enlightenment: the Middle Ages – especially the Dark Middle Ages – are intensively covered. This fits in with the preference of the Romantics for anything that is not intelligible and therefore irrational, occult and magical. Hence comes the fascination with the Dark Ages, the *Völkerwanderung* and the Germanic conquerors of the Roman Empire, of which little is known. The Germans are depicted as fierce warriors, whose wild nature was still uncorrupted by civilisation or Christianity and who brought down the weakened and effeminate civilisation of the Romans; their ancient customs and religion are eagerly studied and at the same time mystified. The *Nibelungenring* by the German composer Richard Wagner (1813–83) or the collections of German sagas and legends in the fairy tales by Hans Christian Andersen (1805–75) or the Grimm brothers Jakob (1785–1863) and Wilhelm (1786–1859) bear witness to this.

414   Nationalism and the creation of the past

Romanticism triggered a religious revival in western Europe. Religion becomes a refuge for human emotions and the glorification of the inexplicable. Romanticism also grafts itself on to nationalism. The notion that the special nature of each people is determined by its past and the identification of that past with Hegel's *Volksgeist* or national spirit provide powerful encouragement for nationalism. A nation is no more dominated by timeless and universal rules than an individual. Both can determine their own lot through their deeds, their feelings and the choices that they

make on the basis of their free will. Romanticism and nationalism tie up
in most countries of Europe in the creation of the narrative of a heroic
and/or dramatic national past. In Germany that goes back to the time of
the great migrations and the heyday of the Holy Roman Empire, in France
to the time of Clovis and Charlemagne, in Spain to the *Reconquista* and
the heroic days of El Cid. The Netherlands has its glory days in the Dutch
Revolt and the seventeenth century, the Golden Age. In Scotland and
Belgium, novelists dip into Antiquity and the Middle Ages in search of
great heroes. Ambiorix, the leader of the Eburones, a Belgian tribe, who
led a rebellion against Caesar, assumes mythical proportions. With his
historical novel *The Lion of Flanders* on the Battle of the Golden Spurs
of 1302, Hendrik Conscience (1812–83) – unintentionally – gave the
Flemish people its past and identity. 'He taught his people to read' may be
correct; 'he turned his people into a people' equally so. The novels by Sir
Walter Scott (1771–1832) and the poems by Robert Burns (1759–96) about
William Wallace, alias Braveheart, created an upsurge in nationalist feeling in Scotland.

9.   *The Historical School, Pandect Science and codification in Germany*

415   Savigny

The Congress of Vienna put an end to the dream of a unified Germany
held by the liberal nationalists. As the country remained divided, so did
the law. To remedy this, some nationalist jurists and politicians sought to
introduce the French legal codes throughout Germany; others wanted a
German codification. Both projects were politically unfeasible.

But there were also opponents of codification among the German
jurists. The most vocal of these was Friedrich Carl von Savigny (1779–
1861), professor in Berlin. In 1814, he published a pamphlet entitled *Vom
Beruf unserer Zeit für Gesetzgebung und Rechtswissenschaft*, in which he
protested against the demands for the rapid codification of German law.
His resistance is based on a wholly different vision of the development of
the law from that of most defenders of codification. As the father of the
Historical School, Savigny had a profound impact on nineteenth-century
German legal scholarship.

In his pamphlet of 1814 and in other writings, Savigny takes issue with
the basic assumptions of the School of Natural Law. The law does not
derive rationally from a number of universal and immutable precepts and
cannot therefore be discovered *more geometrico* through mere rational

reasoning. The law is a product of historical evolution. Just like a living organism, it grows and changes over time, in the same way that 'the tree grows from its roots'. In this regard, Savigny connects with the historical vision of Romanticism. The law is the outcome of a centuries-long evolutionary process and of the traditions and customs of the people, but also of the more technical accomplishments of professional jurists, such as the German civilians.

> When a scientific province, such as ours, has been cultivated by the unbroken exertion of many centuries, a rich inheritance is offered to us who belong to the present. It is not merely the mass of truth won which falls to our share; every direction essayed by the intellectual powers, all efforts of past time, be they fruitful or abortive, are also good for us as pattern or warning and thus we are in some sense in the position of working with the united powers of centuries passed away. If now we would, through indolence or conceit, neglect this natural advantage of our position and in a superficial treatment leave to chance how much of that rich inheritance is to influence our culture, we should then be dispensing with the priceless benefits inseparable from the nature of real science – the communion of scientific convictions and at the same time with the constant, living, progress without which that communion might pass over into a dead letter.[36]

416   Roman law and German jurisprudence

Savigny's main objection against a speedy codification is that it would freeze the spontaneous, historical evolution of the law. Hegel believed that history evolved towards a final purpose and end. Through its history, a nation's spirit is formed. Once that formation is complete, history has run its course. For Savigny, the same goes for the nation's 'legal spirit'. According to him, the endpoint of the legal formation of the German nation has not been reached yet.

In order to unify German law, the historical development of German law must be allowed to continue. For Savigny, not the code of his own Prussia nor the ancient Germanic customary law constitutes the 'German' law, but the learned Roman law. At first glance, it may appear surprising that Savigny advances Roman law as the law of a people that most decidedly did not form part of the Roman Empire. His vision is, nevertheless, defensible. The academic study of Roman law took off in Germany in the Late Middle Ages. It was applied for many centuries in the Imperial Chamber

---

[36] Friedrich Carl von Savigny, *System des heutigen Römischen Rechts*, vol. I, Berlin 1840, ix–x, translation by William Holloway, *System of the Modern Roman Law*, vol. I, Westport 1867.

of Justice and was the overarching law of the Holy Roman Empire. The learned civilians – the university professors – enjoyed huge prestige and for a long time had steered the development of the law in Germany.

Savigny induces the German jurists to go a step further than their predecessors. The study of Roman law has to be continued but its primary object should be the construction of a consistent and complete legal system. Once jurisprudence has completed that construction, legal evolution would be at an end. Then, and only then, the law could be codified. Justinian law would provide the building blocks, and the centuries-old tradition of civilian jurisprudence the system and the dogmas. Roman law should be stripped of all the non-Roman elements that had been added to it down the centuries. Savigny does not argue for a return to a pure historical humanism. He is clearly a product of moderate humanism and *usus modernus pandectacum* and their dynamic tensions that had dominated German civilian jurisprudence for two centuries. According to Savigny, the object of sifting out the later additions to Roman law is not a correct, historical insight but the reconstruction of pure and clear-cut concepts and precepts. If the reconstruction of the original Roman law serves that purpose, this should be done. If not, Savigny does not hesitate to sacrifice the historical reality to the higher purpose of German civilian jurisprudence. On that point, Savigny partakes in the tradition of the many legal scholars who, under the influence of humanism and the ideal of systematisation propagated by Aristotle and Cicero, work towards a more rational systematisation of the law. Among those, Donellus is particularly admired by Savigny.

417   Savigny and the School of Natural Law

The drive for systematisation also betrays that Savigny does not completely escape the influence of the School of Natural Law and of the codification he opposes. He concedes that he has the same objectives as the advocates of codification, but his method is different.

> We are agreed as to the end in view: we desire a sound system of law, secure against the encroachments of caprice and dishonesty; as also, the unity of the nation, and the concentration of its scientific efforts upon the same object. For this end, *they* are anxious for a code, which, however, would only produce the desired unity for one half of Germany, and separate the rest by a line of demarcation, more strongly marked than before – I see the proper means in an organically progressive jurisprudence, which may be common to the whole nation.[37]

---

[37] Friedrich Carl von Savigny, *Vom Beruf unsrer Zeit für Gesetzgebung und Rechtswissenschaft*, Heidelberg 1814, 161, translation by Abraham Hayward, *Of the Vocation of Our Age for Legislation and Jurisprudence*, London 1831.

The endpoint of the law pursued by Savigny is a genuine scientific legal system, a pyramid of general principles and particular, clearly defined rules.

> As regards the substance, the most important and difficult part is the completeness of the code, and upon this point we have only fully to comprehend the following proposition, in which all agree.
>
> The code, then, as it is intended to be the only law-authority, is actually to contain, by anticipation, a decision for every case that may arise. This has been often conceived, as if it were possible and advantageous to obtain, by experience, a perfect knowledge of the particular cases, and then to decide each by a corresponding provision of the code. But whoever has considered law-cases attentively, will see at a glance that this undertaking must fail, because there are positively no limits to the actual varieties of actual combinations of circumstances ...
>
> But there is certainly a perfection of a different kind, which may be illustrated by a technical expression of geometry. In every triangle, namely, there are certain data, from the relations of which all the rest are necessarily deducible: thus, given two sides and the included angle, the whole triangle is given. In like manner, every part of our law has points by which the rest may be given: these may be termed the leading axioms. To distinguish these, and deduce from them the internal connection, and the precise degree of affinity which subsists between all juridical notions and rules, is amongst the most difficult of the problems of jurisprudence. Indeed, it is peculiarly this which gives our labours the scientific character.[38]

But those rules and principles must be German and can only grow from the German legal experience and past.

Savigny's relation to the German tradition of natural law is equivocal. He rejects the ahistorical claims of the natural lawyers, but believes in the possibility and necessity of constructing a complete and consistent legal system. As said above, the process of rational deduction plays a great part therein. Savigny is also a modern positivist, in the sense that he believes this construction can only be achieved on the basis of observable and thus historical law. For him, this should be Roman law.

Savigny takes issue with the support of the cause of codification by the School of Natural Law. He reacts against the two legal strongholds of the Enlightenment – the School of Natural Law and the codification movement – but even so is unable to escape their influence. The Hegelian and historical inspiration provides a counterweight to the rationalism of the Enlightenment, but does not entirely dispose of it.

---

[38] Savigny, *Vom Beruf*, 21–3.

418   Germanic law

Even before the death of its founder, the Historical School split into two groups: the Romanists, following most closely in the footsteps of Savigny, and the Germanists.[39] The Germanists start from the same basic assumption of the historical evolution of the law as Savigny, but do not agree with him that the learned Roman law constitutes the core of the German legal experience. In their view, the essence of German law needs to be discovered in Germanic law. Civilian jurisprudence, they argue, has actually held back the development of German law. According to the Germanists, Germany has consequently missed the opportunity to develop its own national law based on German traditions and customs, along the lines of the common law in England. The Germanists are even more than the Romanists influenced by Romanticism and nationalism. Their vision grows out of the marked interest among artists and historians in the old Germanic nations and the time of the *Völkerwanderung*. The Germanists immerse themselves enthusiastically in the history of Germanic law and medieval customary law. Important Germanists include Karl Friedrich Eichhorn (1768–1854) and Jakob Grimm.

419   Pandect Science

Savigny immersed himself in Roman law, writing a monumental treatise on the historical development of Roman law since the time of Justinian, outlining its evolution through the Middle Ages. In his eight-volume *System des heutigen Römischen Rechts* (1840–9), he sets the stage for the completion of his programme: the intellectual creation of a dogmatic system based on Roman law.

Savigny was unable to complete his work. The representatives of the *Pandektenwissenschaft* would do so. They are the true heirs of Savigny. The Pandectists set themselves the task of building up a complete and internally consistent legal system. The concrete legal precepts and concepts they use are taken from Roman law. In their eagerness to construct a system that would answer all current legal questions, they do not hesitate to interpret Roman law idiosyncratically. The most important representative of Pandect Science is Bernard Windscheid (1817–92), the author of *Pandektenrecht* (1862–70).

---

[39] To this day there is a *Romanistische* and a *Germanistische Abteilung* – in addition to a *Kanonistische* section – of the authoritative *Zeitschrift der Savigny-Stiftung für europäische Rechtsgeschichte*.

Like Savigny's system, Pandect Science is a highly eclectic school of thought taking inspiration from many currents in historical jurisprudence. It has its roots in the philosophy of Hegel, natural law, the *usus modernus pandectarum* and humanism. All this comes together in its initial purpose: the opposition to a speedy codification that would terminate the historical evolution of German civilian jurisprudence and end the ascendancy of the German juridical establishment. Pandect Science does not escape the influence of legal positivism. Its representatives are primarily concerned with constructing an internally logical, autonomous scientific system the rules of which are derived from their logical consistency with the system and not from their social effects. Like the Exegetic School, it rejects any testing against higher normative standards outside the law or against reality.

420   *Bürgerliches Gesetzbuch*

Ultimately, Pandect Science was unable to prevent codification. The unification of Germany in 1870 created the political base for the unification of the law. The Pandectists, who dominated the German faculties of law, had the choice of staying on the sidelines or of co-operating. On the grounds that the development of German law was now sufficiently advanced and had achieved completion, many opted in favour of the latter. The *Bürgerliches Gesetzbuch*, introduced in 1900, was accordingly also primarily the work of the Pandectists, Windscheid's masterwork being its most important source.

421   *Interessenjurisprudenz*

Both within and outside Germany, towards the end of the nineteenth century, opposition against legal positivism grew. Influenced in some cases by the works of Karl Marx, a new generation of jurists argued that the conception of the law as an independent and self-contained logical system served only the political, economic and social agenda of the propertied bourgeoisie and aristocracy. The reaction against Pandect Science went hand in hand with the political emancipation of the working class.

The new schools of thought perceived law as an instrument of social and economic policy. The jurist must take into account the effects the law had on society. In Germany, Rudolf von Jhering (1818–92) – himself a leading Pandectist – accused his colleagues of other-worldliness. The adherents of the new movement argued that the Pandectists were guilty of *Begriffenjurisprudenz*. The correct definition of a concept and its place within the complex of their cherished legal system were more important than the impact of the concept or rule on society. The new school of thought favoured *Interessenjurisprudenz*. A legal rule had to be selected with a view to the social interest that it did or did not defend. Comparable movements, such as legal realism in the Anglo-American world, emerged in other countries as well. The sociology of law came into being in the wake of this movement.

10   Judicial reform

422   Judicial reform and revolt

The programme of the Enlightenment and the French Revolution also included a programme for judicial reform. There was to come an end to the plurality and diversity of legal systems and the associated proliferation of jurisdictions and courts.

In Austria, Emperor Joseph II implemented a far-reaching reform as early as the 1780s. In 1786, he reformed the judiciary in the Southern Netherlands. The thousands of law courts in the various provinces of the Austrian Netherlands were abolished in 1787 at a single stroke of the pen. This amounted to the seizure of power by the central government in Vienna and Brussels. Most of these judicial institutions, such as the provincial councils of justice, were more than just law courts: generally speaking, they also had administrative powers. Like the parliaments in France before the Revolution, they were also the bulwarks of provincial autonomy and the custodians of the privileges and freedoms of the estates. The old institutions were replaced by a rational and hierarchical system of courts. The Southern Netherlands were subdivided into nine *Kreitsen*. A threefold hierarchy of law courts was introduced: a single Sovereign Council of Justice, two courts of appeal and sixty-three courts of first instance. The reform sparked off a revolution in the Southern Netherlands headed by the estates of Brabant: the Brabant Revolution of 1789. This was a conservative revolution by the privileged classes who sought to defend their rights and uphold local and provincial autonomy. The Austrians were temporarily driven out and the United States of Belgium declared independence. In 1790, Leopold II (1790–2), Joseph's successor, managed to re-conquer the Southern Netherlands. A few years later, the Austrians were finally driven out of the country by the French revolutionaries.

423   The French Revolution and judicial reform

The rationalisation of the judicial institutions was also rapidly undertaken in France after 1789. The reform was already in place in 1791, but was amended several times. As a result of the French expansion, the French judicial structure was also introduced in other countries, such as present-day Belgium and Netherlands and different parts of the former empire. Separate law courts were established for civil, commercial and criminal affairs. A hierarchical structure was set up for each branch of the law. In the case of civil law, there was a four-tier structure with cantons, districts (*arrondissements*), resorts for the courts of appeal and a single national jurisdiction. At cantonal level there was the judge of the peace and at district level a court of first instance. Each resort had a single court of appeal (competent to hear civil, commercial and criminal cases), while for the country as a whole there was a single court of cassation. After the Restoration, the latter became known in the Netherlands as the High Council. There were three types of criminal courts of first instance: the police court for misdemeanours, the correctional chambers at the court of first instance for most felonies and the court of assizes for the most serious crimes. Appeal against judgments in the former two courts could be lodged with the court of appeal. There was no possibility of appeal – only cassation – against judgments reached in jury trials at the court of assizes.

11   *The relative resistance of the common law*

424   Blackstone and the consolidation of the common law

In the course of the eighteenth and nineteenth centuries, England was largely spared the wave of renewal and revolution that flooded the continent. The country had already had its political revolution in the seventeenth century and had had a national legal system for centuries. The evolution of the law in England was more gradual.

The common law remained dominant in England. By consistently adding new interpretations to the law of the land, English judges were able to renew the law from within. The competition from equity became less intense. Equity was transformed into a body of positive law as well, from which sprang no more renewal than from the common law. As of 1875, the distinction between common law and equity courts was abolished and the courts could apply both systems side by side. In comparison with the continent, legislation continued to play a minor, supplementary role in the formation of the law. Jurisprudence never held the central place in legal practice it had on the continent. Lawyers were educated not at the universities but at the Inns of Court, where they were trained in the practices of the courts. At the end of the eighteenth century, William Blackstone

(1723–80) wrote a summary of the common law, *Commentaries on the Laws of England* (1765–8), which continues to enjoy great authority in England to this day. Traces of the Enlightenment may be discerned in his work. Blackstone attempted to portray the common law in a clear and comprehensible manner and to demonstrate its reasonableness. It was in fact a response to the Enlightenment: England already had its enlightened legal system.

425   Bentham and reform

Jeremy Bentham (1748–1832), the father of modern utilitarianism and a leading jurist, did not share this view. Bentham pushed for a revolution in English law in the form of a general codification. He did not, however, present himself as a follower of continental rationalism; not the rational coherence of the system but the social utility of each legal rule should provide the criterion for the compilation of the codes. Bentham, who was held in great respect and also had a high reputation outside England, was unable to realise his dream in his own country.

Nevertheless Bentham's ideas had an impact. They did not lead to a departure from the common law, but encouraged simplification on utilitarian grounds. During the 1830s, a good many old laws and customs that had fallen into disuse were abolished. The statutes that were retained were compiled, to the benefit of legal certainty. The most important reform concerned the system of writs. Instead of a limited number of legal remedies for well-defined issues, a single general writ was introduced with which a case could be brought before the court (1832–3). The formalism of common law was consequently reduced and legal renewal – especially by the judges – was facilitated.[40] The different courts now applied both common law and equity. The legal structure was simplified (1873–5). The old common law courts and the Court of Chancery were absorbed into a new, central court: the High Court of Justice. This also involved the abolition of the distinction between common law and equity, so that the courts could now select and apply rules from both systems. A system of appeal was introduced along continental lines. A Court of Appeal for all England was established in London with, above it, the Law Lords in the House of Lords. Eventually in 1971, the assize courts were abolished and the Crown Court, with particular jurisdiction for some criminal offences, was instituted. The High Court, Crown Court and Court of Appeal together form the Supreme Court of Judicature. Outside London, there are now county

---

[40] In 1980, the writ disappeared entirely.

courts (1846) and magistrates' courts. The county courts bear no resemblance to their medieval namesakes. The county courts have particular jurisdiction for minor civil cases, and the magistrates' courts for the majority of criminal offences. In the course of the nineteenth century, the legislature began to play a more active role in the creation of new law, especially outside the sphere of private law.

12   Ratio

426   The triumph of the legislature

The modern doctrine of natural law completed a gradual process of intellectual emancipation that had already begun with the rediscovery of Roman law in the eleventh century. The Renaissance of the Twelfth Century marked the origins of an autonomous jurisprudence in Europe. The law became the object of systematic and rational study by a caste of professional jurists trained for that purpose. Their thought was, however, dominated by and embedded in the claims to authority of the ancient text canon. Humanism resulted in a relativisation of that authority and opened the door to a more independent assessment of the value of these sources. Modernism constituted the declaration of independence from that past. Human *ratio* or reason was, as a mirror of rational nature, sufficient in itself to understand nature, man and society.

The triumph of reason liberated jurisprudence from the confines in which it had been kept by the wholly distinct character and structure of Roman law. For the first time, it became possible to cut through the ties of existing traditions, classifications and methods of argumentation. That was the work of the modern natural lawyers.

The French Revolution made possible the realisation of part of the modernist credo. The French codification was a compromise between the ideals of the Enlightenment and reality as it gave the old traditions a place. At the same time, however, it ushered in a new era in the law. At a stroke, the national unification of the law was achieved. What the French kings had been unable to do, the revolutionaries achieved. Legal discrimination and diversity made way for a single, relatively consistent and complete legal system. The political revolution with its separation of powers and the assumption of legislative power by the people gave the legislature the authority to exact a monopoly over the formation of the law. Jurisprudence and custom – the traditional bulwarks of the privileged classes against the claims of the sovereign ruler – were swept away by the new sovereign: the nation. During the course of the nineteenth and twentieth centuries, the legislature would have increasing difficulty in making good its claims to exclusivity, but right up to the present day, legislation remains the most important source of law in virtually all countries of the civil law tradition. Jurisprudence – the engine of renewal since the Late Middle Ages – has given up its place of honour. *Ratio* had led to the triumph of the *natio*.

Further reading

1. On the general history of the Modern Age: M. S. Anderson, *Europe in the Eighteenth Century, 1713–1789*, 4th edn, London 2000; J. Black, *Eighteenth-Century Europe*, 2nd edn, London 1999; T. Blanning, *The Pursuit of Glory: Europe, 1648–1815*, London 2007; F. L. Ford, *Europe, 1780–1830*, 2nd edn, London 1989; H. Hearder, *Europe in the Nineteenth Century, 1830–1880*, 2nd edn, London 1988; E. Hobsbawm, *The Age of Revolution, 1789–1848*, London 1962; Hobsbawm, *The Age of Capital, 1848–1875*, London 1975; Hobsbawm, *The Age of Empire, 1875–1914*, London 1987; O. Hufton, *Europe: Privilege and Protest, 1730–1789*, London 1980; J. M. Roberts, *Europe, 1880–1945*, 3rd edn, London 2001; J. Sperber, *Revolutionary Europe, 1780–1850*, London 2000; J. Stoye, *Europe Unfolding, 1648–1688*, London 1969; G. Treasure, *The Making of Modern Europe, 1648–1780*, London 1985.

2. On modern political thought: P. Anderson, *Lineages of the Absolutist State*, London 1974; R. Antonio, *Marx and Modernity: Key Readings and Commentary*, Malden, Mass. 2003; S. Avineri, *The Social and Political Thought of Karl Marx*, Cambridge 1968; Avineri, *Hegel's Theory of the Modern State*, Cambridge 1972; R. Barny, *Le triomphe du droit naturel: la constitution de la doctrine révolutionnaire des droits de l'homme (1787–1789): des théories parlementaire ou rousseauisme*, Paris 1997; J. Brückner, *Staatswissenschaften, Kameralismus, und Naturrecht*, Munich 1977; A. Cobban, *Rousseau and the Modern State*, London 1964; J. Daly, *Sir Robert Filmer and English Political Thought*, Toronto 1979; J. Dunn, *The Political Thought of John Locke*, Cambridge 1982; E. Eisenach, *Narrative Power and Liberal Truth: Hobbes, Locke, Bentham and Mill*, Lanham 2002; J. Franklin, *John Locke and the Theory of Sovereignty*, Cambridge 1978; J. Heideking, *Republicanism and Liberalism in America and the German States, 1750–1850*, Cambridge 2002; M. Hulliung, *Citizens and Citoyens: Republicans and Liberals in America and France*, Cambridge, Mass. 2002; T. Jessop, *Hobbes*, London 1964; A. Kahan, *Liberalism in Nineteenth-Century Europe: the Political Culture of Limited Suffrage*, London 2003; H. J. Laski, *The Rise of European Liberalism*, London 1936; C. MacPherson, *The Political Theory of Possessive Individualism: Hobbes to Locke*, Oxford 1962; C. McKinnon, *Liberalism and the Defence of Political Constructivism*, London 2002; K. Martin, *French Liberal Thought in the Eighteenth Century: a Study of Political Ideas from Bayle to*

Condorcet, New York 1963; R.S. Masters, *The Political Philosophy of Rousseau*, Princeton 1976; J Miller, *Rousseau: Dreamer of Democracy*, New Haven 1984; J. Muravchik, *Heaven on Earth: the Rise and Fall of Socialism*, San Francisco 2002; A. Patterson, *Early Modern Liberalism*, Cambridge 1997; G. Parry, *John Locke*, London 1978; J.G.A. Pocock and R. Ashcraft, *John Locke*, Los Angeles 1980; Q. Skinner, *Visions of Politics: Hobbes and Civil Science*, Cambridge 2002; J.L. Talmon, *The Origins of Totalitarian Democracy*, New York 1960; J. Tully, *A Discourse on Property: John Locke and his Adversaries*, Cambridge 1980; L. Whaley, *Radicals: Politics and Republicanism in the French Revolution*, Stroud 2000; P. Zagorin, *A History of Political Thought in the English Revolution*, New York 1966.

3. On the Glorious Revolution and the English constitutional system: G. Burgess, *Absolute Monarchy and the Stuart Constitution*, New Haven 1996; J. Clark, *Revolution and Rebellion: State and Society in England in the Seventeenth and Eighteenth Centuries*, Cambridge 1986; E. Cruickshanks, *The Glorious Revolution*, London 2000; C. Hibbert, *The Intellectual Origins of the English Revolution Revisited*, Oxford 2001; J. Miller, *The Glorious Revolution*, 2nd edn, London 1997, J.R. Jones, *Liberty Secured? Britain before and after 1688*, Stanford 1992.

4. On the revolutionary period, its constitutional consequences and the nation-state: R. Asprey, *The Rise and Fall of Napoleon Bonaparte*, 2 vols., New York 2001; N. Aston, *Religion and Revolution in France, 1780–1804*, London 2000; K.M. Baker, *The French Revolution and the Creation of Modern Political Culture*, Oxford 1987; T. Blanning, *The French Revolution: Class War or Culture Clash?*, London 1998; M. Bouloiseau, *The Jacobin Republic, 1792–1794*, Cambridge 1984; W. Doyle, *The Origins of the French Revolution*, Oxford 1988; Doyle, *The Oxford History of the French Revolution*, 2nd edn, Oxford 2002; D. Dowe, *Europe in 1848: Revolution and Reform*, New York 2001; J.S. Fishman, *Diplomacy and Revolution: the London Conference of 1830 and the Belgian Revolt*, Amsterdam 1988; F. Furet, *Penser la Révolution française*, Paris 1978; G. Lefebvre, *La Révolution française*, Paris 1962; Lefebvre, *Napoléon*, Paris 1953; P. McPhee, *The French Revolution, 1789–1799*, Oxford 2002; J.M. Roberts, *The French Revolution*, Oxford 1978; S. Schama, *Patriots and Liberators: Revolution in the Netherlands, 1780–1813*, New York 1977; Schama, *Citizens: a Chronicle of the French Revolution*, New York 1989; A. Soboul, *Précis d'histoire de la Révolution Française*, Paris 1962; A. Sorel, *Europe and the French Revolution*, London 1969; D. Sutherland, *The French Revolution and Empire: the Quest for a Civic Order*, Malden, Mass. 2003; J. Swann, *Politics and the Parlement of Paris under Louis XV, 1754–1774*, Cambridge 1995; C. Tilly, *European Revolutions, 1492–1992*, Oxford 1993.

5. On nationalism and the nation-state: P. Browning, *Revolutions and Nationalities: Europe, 1825–1890*, Cambridge 2000; O. Dann, *Nationalism*

in the Age of the French Revolution, London 1987; R. Gildea, *Barricades and Borders: Europe, 1800–1914*, 3rd edn, Oxford 2003; E. Hobsbawm, *Nations and Nationalism since 1780: Programme, Myth, Reality*, Cambridge 1990; H. Schulze, *State, Nation and Nationalism: From the Middle Ages to the Present*, London 1996.

6. On diplomatic history and the law of nations: M. S. Anderson, *The Ascendency of Europe, 1815–1914*, 2nd edn, London 1985; M. Belissa, *Fraternité universelle et intérêt national (1713–1795). Les cosmopolitiques du droit des gens*, Paris 1998; Belissa, *Repenser l'ordre européen (1795–1802): de la société des rois aux droits des nations*, Paris 2006; L. Bély, *L'art de la paix en Europe. Naissance de la diplomatie moderne XVI–XVIIe siècle*, Paris 2007; J. Black, *European International Relations, 1648–1815*, New York 2002; P. Bobbit, *The Shield of Achilles: War, Peace and the Course of History*, London 2002; P. Kennedy, *The Rise and Fall of the Great Powers*, New York 1987; H. Kissinger, *Diplomacy*, New York 1994; M. Koskenniemi, *The Gentle Civilizer of Nations: the Rise and Fall of International Law, 1870–1960*, Cambridge 2001; E. Luard, *The Balance of Power: the System of International Relations, 1648–1815*, London 1992; D. McKay and H. M. Scott, *The Rise of the Great Powers, 1648–1815*, London 1983; P. W. Schroeder, *The Transformation of European Politics, 1763–1848*, Oxford 1994; A. J. P. Taylor, *The Struggle for Mastery in Europe, 1848–1918*, Oxford 1954.

7. On rationalism, Enlightenment and postivism: T. C. W. Blanning, *The Culture of Power and the Power of Culture: Old Regime Europe, 1660–1789*, Oxford 2002; J. Bury, *The Idea of Progress: an Inquiry into its Origin and Growth*, New York 1987; P. Gay, *The Enlightenment: an Interpretation*, 2 vols., London and New York 1966–9; N. Geras, *The Enlightenment and Modernity*, London 2000; D. Goodman, *The Republic of Letters: a Cultural History of the French Enlightenment*, Ithaca and London 1996; P. Hazard, *The European Mind: the Critical Years, 1680–1715*, New Haven and London 1953; Hazard, *European Thought in the Eighteenth Century: From Montesquieu to Lessing*, Ann Arbor 1963; N. Hampson, *The Enlightenment: an Evaluation of its Assumptions, Attitudes and Values*, London 1968; U. Im Hof, *The Enlightenment: an Historical Introduction*, London 1997; J. Israel, *Radical Enlightenment: Philosophy and the Making of Modernity, 1650–1750*, Oxford 2001; Israel, *Enlightenment Contested: Philosophy, Modernity, and the Emancipation of Man, 1670–1752*, Oxford 2006; D. Outram, *The Enlightenment*, 2nd edn, Cambridge 2005; J. G. A. Pocock, *Barbarism and Religion*, 4 vols., Cambridge 1999–2008; P. Schouls, *Descartes and the Enlightenment*, Edinburgh 1989; A. Soboul, *Le siècle des lumières*, Paris 1977.

8. On the School of Natural Law and legal science under the *Ancien Régime*: E. Barker, *Natural Law and the Theory of Society, 1500–1800*, Cambridge 1934; K. Haakonssen, *Natural Law and Moral Philosophy: From Grotius to the Scottish Enlightenment*, Cambridge 1996; K. Haakonssen, ed., *Grotius, Pufendorf and*

Modern Natural Law, Aldershot 1999; T. Hochstrasser, *Natural Law Theories in the Early Enlightenment*, Cambridge 2000; Hochstrasser, *Early Modern Natural Law Theories: Contexts and Strategies in the Early Enlightenment*, The Hague 2003; R. Tuck, *Natural Rights Theories: Their Origin and Development*, Cambridge 1979; G. van den Bergh, *The Life and Work of Gerard Noodt (1647–1725): Dutch Legal Scholarship between Humanism and Enlightenment*, Oxford 1988.

9. On the codification: A.-J. Arnaud, *Les origines doctrinales du Code civil français*, Paris 1969; P. P. Bernard, *The Limits of Enlightenment: Joseph II and the Law*, Urbana, Chicago and London 1979; M. John, *Politics and the Law in Late-Nineteenth-Century Germany: the Origins of the Civil Code*, Oxford 1990; J. Musset, *Naissance du Code civil an VII–an XII, 1800–1804*, Paris 1989; H. E. Strakosch, *State Absolutism and the Rule of Law: the Struggle for the Codification of the Civil Law in Austria, 1753–1811*, Sydney 1967; P. van den Berg, *The Politics of European Codification: a History of the Unification of Law in France, Prussia, the Austrian Monarchy and the Netherlands*, Groningen 2007; A. Watson, *The Making of the Civil Law*, Cambridge, Mass. 1981.

10. On legal science during the nineteenth century: B. Bouckaert, *De exegetische school. Een kritische studie van de rechtsbronnen en interpretatieleer van de 19de eeuwse commentatoren van de Code Civil*, Antwerp 1981; A. Bürge, *Das französische Privatrecht im 19. Jahrhundert: zwischen Tradition und Pandektenwissenschaft, Liberalismus und Etatismus*, 2nd edn, Frankfurt 1995; D. R. Kelley, *Historians and the Law in Post-Revolutionary France*, Princeton 1984; E. Polay, *Ursprung, Entwicklung und Untergang der Pandektistik*, Szeged 1981; M. Reiman, *Historische Schule und Common Law: die deutsche Rechtswissenschaft des 19. Jahrhunderts im amerikanischer Rechtsdenken*, Berlin 1993; J. Whitman, *The Legacy of Roman Law in the German Romantic Era: Historical Vision and Legal Chance*, Princeton 1990; D. Wisner, *The Cult of the Legislator in France, 1750–1830: a Study in the Political Theology of the French Enlightenment*, Oxford 1997.

Epilogue

7

Voluntas
(the Post-Modern Age, 1914–2004)

1 The end of modernity

Now that we are almost settled in our house
I'll name the friends that cannot sup with us
Beside a fire of turf in th'ancient tower
And having talked to some late hour
Climb up the narrow winding stair to bed.
Discoverers of forgotten truth
Our near companions of my youth
All, all are in my thoughts tonight being dead.[1]

427   The First World War and the challenge to modernism

When the war broke out in August 1914, the Anglo-Irish romantic poet
William Butler Yeats (1865–1939) was too old to sign up. While Yeats himself escaped the horrors of the western front, he saw how a generation of
young men was decimated on the battlefields of the Great War. When the
armistice was declared on 11 November 1918, the war had claimed more
than ten million lives. In the next few years, millions of people were to
perish from hunger, disease, enfeeblement, civil war and outright genocide, particularly on Europe's eastern fringes.

The First World War sent a psychological shockwave through Europe,
overturning the certainties of the intellectual, economic and political
elites. The war affected Europe to its core. The decades either side of the
turn of the century marked the high point of modern, European civilisation. Since human reason had liberated itself from all kinds of oppression, science and technology had taken off. The natural world appeared
to have few if any secrets left to reveal. The invention of the telephone,
radio and aeroplane vindicated man's claims to be master of creation.
Industrialisation brought unparalleled wealth and enabled Europe to

---

[1]   William Butler Yeats, *In memory of Major Robert Gregory,* from *The Wild Swans at Coole,*
New York 1919.

conquer the world. Europe itself experienced a lengthy period of relative peace. In due course, science would fully reveal the workings of the
human mind and would render human behaviour predictable and con-
trollable. In the meantime, new horrors, such as that of the Terror and the
Napoleonic Wars, were totally ruled out in the age of reason.

The First World War (1914–18) brutally and unexpectedly put an end
to this dream. To the informed observer, the outbreak of war in the summer of 1914 will not have come as a total surprise, but no one could have
foreseen that the war would prove to be so protracted and bloody. The
soldiers departed for the front in the summer of 1914 with a song on their
lips, convinced that they would be home by Christmas. Modern weaponry, rational statesmen and the balance of power would ensure that
the war was short and limited and that a new and stable balance would
quickly be found. Modern technology and new weaponry led, however,
to huge casualties and the stalemate of trench warfare that was to last for
years. The logic of the balance of power and coalition politics failed. It had
not only been unable to prevent the war but had caused it and rendered a
rapid compromise impossible. The nation-state showed its true face in the
total mobilisation of the population and the economy in what became a
new kind of war: a war for total victory and the total annihilation of the
enemy. Modernity did not prevent the First World War; it caused it. The
optimism of the Enlightenment and the faith in the rationality of humankind were buried in Flanders Fields.

428   Age of extremes

The historian Eric Hobsbawm dubbed the twentieth century the age of
extremes.[2] The epigram is well-chosen. On the one hand, the twentieth
century was that of the crisis of modern European civilisation, the low
points being the two world wars, the Holocaust and the murderous dictatorships of Adolf Hitler (1889–1945), Joseph Stalin (1879–1953) and Mao
Tse-Tung (1893–1976). It was the century in which optimism and faith
in the rationality of humankind crumbled away. It was also the century
in which the European powers lost their empires and the old continent
was forced to acknowledge the supremacy of Russia and the United States.
On the other hand, the post-1945 period was for most people in western
Europe unquestionably the best period in history in which to have lived.
Economic prosperity reached unparalleled levels and for the first time
in history virtually all classes of society benefited from this. Thanks to

[2] Eric Hobsbawm, *Age of Extremes: the Short Twentieth Century, 1914–1991*, London 1994.

democracy, the rule of law, the protection of human rights and European integration, a level of safety and freedom was guaranteed throughout much of the continent for which there was no parallel in history. The 'age of extremes' may therefore be regarded as a tale of highs and lows and of huge clashes between conflicting ideologies and forces, but with a largely happy ending.

The generations that escaped the Second World War and the Soviet regime may certainly regard things in this light. All this does not, however, eliminate the fact that the twentieth century ushered in the end of modern European civilisation. Modernity did not disappear with the First World War but was increasingly subject to debate in the course of the twentieth century, first of all by the intellectual and artistic elites and later by the public in general.

It will be up to the historians of future centuries to interpret the true significance of the twentieth century in the *longue durée* of history. It may be that it will later be seen as a transitional period between the period of modern European civilisation and a new civilisation. What name that civilisation will bear cannot be predicted, but at any event it is probable that this civilisation will be not a European but perhaps an Atlantic or even a global one. It is also too early for a definitive name for the era that began with the First World War. For the present we refer to this period as 'post-modern', that is, the age after modernity.

2   Voluntas

429   Utilitarianism and materialism

The twentieth century did not break entirely with the modern worldview of the Enlightenment. The unbridled faith in human reason was called into question, nuanced and challenged in certain respects but continued to provide the foundation for the European civilisational model. Even the two most extreme political ideologies that contested the modern, liberal states – communism and fascism – were indebted to the Enlightenment. Communism shared with liberalism the faith in rational thought, while fascism found its *raison d'être* in contesting it.

Ratio remained the foundation beneath the European civilisation but was increasingly coloured by four other factors: utilitarianism, materialism, individualism and voluntarism. Utilitarianism elevated the maximisation of the happiness of the greatest number of people into the purpose of the state; the state at the service of the people (that is, the nation-state). Utilitarianism is a sprig on the tree of the Enlightenment.

It turns reason as it were into the instrument of 'social utility', namely the greatest happiness of the greatest number. It departs from the belief that human reason is capable of comprehending mankind and society and predicting and controlling human behaviour.

Utilitarianism ties in with two other important trends of the twentieth century, materialism and individualism. 'Happiness' is understood one-sidedly in terms of material welfare. Part of the explanation for this is provided by the dominance of the positive sciences in the ideological discourse of the West. In contrast to emotional and spiritual welfare, material prosperity is quantifiable. Needless to say, various counter-movements to that one-sided materialism arose during the course of the century. Still today, however, it remains dominant – all counter-currents from punk through ecologism and new age to anti-globalism notwithstanding.

During the twentieth century, individualism tied in with this utilitarianism. The nineteenth and twentieth centuries turned the political and economic liberal doctrine into a caricature of itself. The liberal bourgeoisie reduced liberalism to the reign of individual freedom. The idea that the individual also bore responsibility for the functioning of society faded into the background. Individualism consequently received a huge boost. The main thing that was to survive in the collective memory from Adam Smith's subtle and complex thinking was the idea of the 'invisible hand'. If everyone is given the freedom to pursue his own interests, this will lead to the maximum welfare. The effect of individualism on materialistic utilitarianism was that society had to be organised in such a way as to give everyone the maximum opportunities for self-development and to achieve what they considered their greatest, personal happiness.

430   Reason and will

All these trends were consummated in the ideology of voluntarism. The relation between rationalism and voluntarism is a complex one. On the one hand, voluntarism assigns primacy to people's freedom of choice. On the other hand, mainstream voluntarism departs from the assumption that rational thought is the best instrument for maximising human happiness, but subjects it to the individual choices and desires of human beings.

First, voluntarism claims for each individual the freedom to determine and pursue his or her own ends within certain limits. In itself, this is a consistent application of the liberal ideology, but in practice, it came unstuck. Individualism with its focus on the material dimension went much further than the great liberal thinkers of the eighteenth century had in mind. The balance between self-interest and the common interest and between freedom and social responsibility inherent in the thinking of Locke and Smith fell by the wayside.

Second, there is an inherent tension between voluntarism and rationalism. That tension forms part of the European intellectual tradition and goes back to the debate between realists and nominalists in the Late Middle Ages and to the discussion as to whether creation was a rational deed or an act of will on the part of God. Voluntarism mobilises rational thinking for the realisation of its goals, but also inevitably clashes with it. Reason does not always produce the result people want. The voluntarist responds by bending reality to his will. In its most extreme form, voluntarism leads to the rejection of reason. This attitude stems back to nineteenth-century Romanticism and nationalism. During the twentieth century, these tendencies found radical expression in fascism and religious fundamentalism. Even apart from these extreme manifestations, however, it cannot be denied that the prevailing ideology of western Europe during the twentieth century contained a marked voluntarist dimension. The ambition to achieve one's own objectives, even at the expense of the truth, had become a widely propagated way of life by the turn of the twentieth century. However, as against this – particularly during the last four decades – an awareness evolved that physical and human reality imposes limits on progress and self-development. It may be that this is a precursor for a new, more balanced interpretation of the Western, liberal model of civilisation.

3   The excesses of Enlightenment and revolution: communism

431   The Russian Revolution

The architects of the Vienna peace settlement wanted at all costs to prevent new wars from breaking out for fear of new revolutions. The First World War demonstrated that their fears were not unfounded. The human and economic toll of the war led to serious civil and social unrest in several European countries. The working and agrarian classes, which supplied a large element of the cannon fodder for the war, stirred. The most radical and successful revolution, however, took place not in the Western, industrialised part of Europe, but in Russia.

The revolution broke out in Petrograd in March 1917. The war had severely dislocated the Russian economy. Transport had collapsed, so that large parts of the huge empire – especially the cities – were condemned to starvation. On 15 March, Tsar Nicholas II (1894–1917) was forced to abdicate. Power was assumed by a coalition government of Western-oriented liberals and the leftist Social Revolutionaries led by Alexander Kerensky (1881–1970), who was appointed prime minister. As defenders of the peasantry, the Social Revolutionaries called for the legal emancipation of the peasants and for land reform, under which those working on farms would themselves become landowners. The republic was declared in September 1917.

The moderate regime of liberals and Social Revolutionaries decided to continue the war against Germany and its allies. The government did not wish to leave the Western allies in the lurch and wanted to observe their treaty obligations with London and Paris. The consequence was that the new administration instantly lost support among a large element of the peasantry. The Bolsheviks, the radical leftist movement of Vladimir Lenin (1870–1924), took advantage of this. A group of radicals within the Communist Party, the Bolsheviks enjoyed the support of part of the working class. Lenin realised that in barely industrialised Russia the working class was too small to bring him to power. Now that the Social Revolutionaries had compromised themselves with the peasants, he saw his chance. Lenin promised that if he came to power he would immediately make peace with Germany.

On 6 November 1917, the Petrograd garrison, which had also taken up arms in March, rebelled. The Winter Palace was stormed and seized (the so-called 'October Revolution'). The Bolsheviks assumed power and, together with the Social Revolutionaries, formed a new government, the Council of the People's Commissars. Lenin and his associates immediately pushed through a number of radical reforms. All land was expropriated and transferred to the peasants' soviets, that is, the people's councils in rural areas. As promised, peace negotiations were immediately conducted with Germany, resulting in the Treaty of Brest-Litovsk in March 1918, under which Russia was obliged to cede a great deal of territory. In the months after the October Revolution that brought the Bolsheviks to power, Poland, Finland, Estonia, Latvia and Lithuania gained their independence. Ukraine and the Caucasus also temporarily evaded the grip of the Bolshevik government.

In the elections in late 1917 for a constituent assembly, the Bolsheviks were defeated by the Social Revolutionaries. After parliament had rejected the Bolsheviks' proposal to transfer all its power to the popular councils (the soviets), Lenin had it dispersed by the army. In July 1918, the first communist constitution was adopted. Until 1921, a bloody civil war was waged against the supporters of the tsar, who was murdered together with his family in 1918.

432   Marxism and Leninism

The constitution of July 1918 turned Russia into the first communist state. The ideology of Lenin's Communist Party was based on the economic and historical analysis of Karl Marx. History was marked by class struggle, which would culminate in the final victory by the working class. After that victory was achieved, class distinctions would disappear and everyone would share the same interests. The state, which in the Marxist view was an instrument of oppression, would no longer be needed. But before this 'end of history' could be reached, first the proletariat had to seize power and control the state. Here the Jacobin idea of the revolutionary vanguard came into play, with the leadership of the Communist Party in the predominant role. They would lead the working class in the revolution and help them conquer the state. After that, a dictatorship by the proletariat had to be established. The capitalists and other unwilling parties would be forced by the now communist state to accept the ideal of a society without classes and without property. Once this was done, the state's role would be fulfilled.

The means of production, including capital, had to be made collective; private property was to be abolished. Everyone contributed to society through their labour. As 'workers' all people were considered equal. The individual was subject to the interests of the revolution and, after the takeover of power, the state. The state intervened in every aspect of life. Man had to identify himself with the interests of the revolution and the Soviet state. Communism dictated a totalitarian state.

433   Stalin

In reality, the combination of the radical-leftist ideology with the idea of the revolutionary vanguard produced one of the most brutal and totalitarian dictatorships in world history. After a brief struggle for power following Lenin's death in 1924, the Georgian apparatchik Joseph Stalin came to power.

On paper, the successive Soviet constitutions adopted between 1918 and 1977 appear highly democratic. The Soviet Union and its later communist satellite states called themselves people's democracies. In the Soviet Union and its fifteen constituent republics, legislative power was in the hands of the soviets, which were directly elected by universal suffrage. The ideology of the revolutionary vanguard, however, provided legitimation for the fact that these elections were not free. In practice, only candidates of the Communist Party were allowed to stand for election; sometimes, a kind of official opposition was tolerated. In theory, the government and the soviets were the official organs of state, but in reality the Communist Party controlled the state. The latter created a parallel structure to the organs of state at all levels. The party leaders appointed the government and the members of the soviets, or occupied the most important posts themselves. The communist apparatchiks also took over the army, the secret police and the bureaucracy, and placed the country under tight control.

434   The law in the Soviet Union

Initially the communists were highly suspicious of law and the state, which they saw as the instruments of power and oppression of the bourgeoisie. Now that they themselves held power, however, this changed radically. Public authority and the law were turned into the instruments of power and oppression of the 'proletarian' revolution. The communist rulers designed their own legal system. The independence of the judiciary was enshrined in the constitution. In the face of the ideology of the totalitarian state, the rule of law was, however, powerless, certainly under Stalin's regime. The political discourse prevailed in the law courts. Political trials and outright show-trials were the order of the day. Under the dictatorship of the proletariat, the rule of law, as protector of individual rights, led an uneasy existence.

435   Soviet imperialism

Under the Stalin regime, the Soviet state became almost sacred. The Soviet Union was the bulwark of communism, both for the country's own population and for the rest of the world. A huge apparatus of governments, soviets and civil servants and an extensive system of police and security services was built up. To the external world the Soviet Union was presented as the shining example for millions of workers and peasants oppressed all over the world by capitalism. In reality, the Soviet mission degenerated into brutal imperialism. Even before the Second World War, communist parties all over the world were subject to Moscow's authority. Since the success of the Russian Revolution was considered the paramount concern for all communists, the communist parties in Europe were required to sacrifice their own interests to those of Moscow. After the Second World War and during the Cold War, the communist ideology served as justification for the establishment of a Soviet empire in central and eastern Europe.

During the civil war, Lenin was obliged to permit a certain liberalisation of the economy (the New Economic Policy, 1921). This came to an end after Stalin assumed power. Private land ownership was once again suppressed. By the mid 1930s, nearly all farms had been incorporated into large collective agricultural enterprises. For the ideological glorification of the working class, however, industry became the main focus of the Soviet government. The state took over industry and the distribution sector. By means of five-year plans, Stalin succeeded in a short space of time in turning Russia into an industrialised country. After the victory in the Second World War, the country was ready to dominate the world together with the United States. The price for this success was huge. Any form of opposition was suppressed in the most brutal fashion. The totalitarian ideology of the general interest legitimated the sacrifice of literally millions of individuals on the altar of the revolution. The death toll of the Stalinist regime was therefore vast; according to even the most conservative estimates, tens of millions lost their lives. Stalin once said, 'A single death is a tragedy, a million deaths a statistic.' Under the Soviet dictatorship, the idealism of the Enlightenment and the Revolution suffered its greatest betrayal.

4   The rejection of Enlightenment and revolution: fascism

436   Germany and Versailles

The end of the First World War did not put an end to the turmoil in Europe. The Russian Revolution sent a shockwave through the continent. The lower classes began to stir. In Western democracies such as Britain, France, Belgium and the Netherlands, the ruling classes responded quickly and sensibly to obviate and channel the unrest. In countries such as Germany, Italy and Spain, however, matters took a different course.

Germany emerged from the war as the loser. The Peace of Versailles (1919) bore heavily on the country; the *Diktat* of Versailles was accepted by neither the elite, the general populace nor the army. Until shortly before the armistice of 11 November 1918, the German people had lived under the illusion that Germany was on the brink of victory. Furthermore, the country was unoccupied on 11 November, while the war in the east had been won. From this, there emerged the myth of the stab in the back: the story of how the left had betrayed the army and caused Germany to lose the peace negotiations. A seedbed was created for a programme of national resurgence and revision of the Treaty of Versailles.

By 1930, one party, Adolf Hitler's National Socialist German Workers Party (NSDAP), succeeded in channelling a large part of this dissatisfaction and taking over the leadership of the extreme right in the political spectrum. The extreme right was and is a collective name for all sorts of currents and movements that can differ markedly from one another but nevertheless have certain features in common. The main characteristic of the extreme right – designated below as fascism – is the total rejection of the ideology of the Enlightenment and the liberal state.

437   Fascism

In the first place, fascism represents an extreme form of voluntarism and anti-rationalism, although inevitably it draws on the Enlightenment and the modern concept of the nation-state for many of its arguments and instruments of power. Fascism is an outgrowth from the darker recesses of Romanticism. It is based on the glorification of the irrationality of the human will and springs from the more morbid and self-destructive undercurrents of the Romantic movement. It taps the darkest and most primitive feelings arising from the human subconscious and brings these to the surface. In that sense, fascism is a denial of civilisation itself.

In the second place, fascism is nationalistic. It places the interests of the people above all else. The approach to the people and nationalism is romantic and irrational. The country's own people are regarded as superior: a proposition for which fascists do not refrain from mobilising pseudo-scientific, rational arguments. The greatest threats to one's own nation are internal divisions and the turmoil and anarchy these create. Fascism advocates a strong state in which everyone works towards the same goal.

It is in this idealisation of unity that nationalism and voluntarism abut one another. The fascist ideology does not leave any room for the divisions and individual freedom that are inherent to a liberal democracy under the rule of law. Modern political thinking with its emphasis on the individual rights and obligations of rational and free human beings is rejected. The fascist state is totalitarian. Ideally, the people would consist of a classless mass; also, there is no room for religious diversity. In practice, the most extreme right-wing regimes were obliged to compromise with the economic elites and sometimes with the churches. But there was no place for marginal groups and strongly divergent opinions. In Germany, the struggle for the unity of the nation became channelled not just into a half-hearted battle against the churches, but more particularly into discrimination and even the extermination of various minorities. The Holocaust, which claimed the lives of six million Jews, remains the greatest indictment against fascism.

The governmental model of fascist ideology is based on the glorification of the leader. The leader holds the nation together and leads it to victory. The model of the fascist state is a one-man dictatorship, supported by a tightly led professional bureaucracy. The leader is the incarnation of the determined individual who, by virtue of his will-power and dynamism, makes the impossible come true. It ties in with the romanticism of the tragic hero, who is overcome by death but never gives up. The unity of the nation is strengthened by mobilising it in the struggle against its enemies. It is for this reason that fascism thinks in black and white terms and seeks enemies, conspiracies and plots everywhere. Here again the idea of the revolutionary vanguard, which convinces the people of its true interests and leads it to its true purposes at the expense of all else, comes into play.

438   Mussolini

Fascism scored its first major success in Europe with the assumption of power by Mussolini in Italy in 1922. Italy was a member of the club of victors in the Versailles peace negotiations and had paid a relatively high price for its participation in the war. It was, however, unable to realise its megalomaniacal ambitions in the peace negotiations. Italy too had fallen victim to recession and social unrest in the post-1918 period. Although his party had only a limited number of seats in the Italian parliament, Mussolini managed to become prime minister in 1922. In the space of a few years, he turned the Italian parliamentary democracy into a fascist one-party state. Mussolini remained in power until the Allied invasion of Italy in 1943.

439   Hitler

In Germany, Hitler's NSDAP came to power on the coat-tails of the depression, which hit the country hard after the Wall Street crash in 1929. The party evolved into the largest political party in the country, obtaining some 40 per cent of the votes. After managing to keep Hitler from power for four years, the president, Paul von Hindenburg (1847–1934, president 1925–34), was obliged to appoint Hitler as chancellor in January 1933. Over the next three years, Hitler turned the country into a dictatorship. The power of the *Länder* was broken, other parties were forbidden and, after Hindenburg's death, Hitler had himself elected president by popular acclaim. Along the lines of Stalin's Communist Party, the NSDAP duplicated the state structure within its own organisational structure and systematically took over the powers of the state. At the start of the

Second World War, the control exercised by the NSDAP over Germany was absolute.

440   Autocracies

During the interwar period authoritarian regimes came to power throughout central and southern Europe, with the exception of Czechoslovakia. These regimes, such as that of General Francisco Franco (1892–1975) in Spain and Joseph Pilsudski (1869–1935) in Poland, are often associated with fascism, but that goes too far. These were conservative and autocratic regimes having a much greater affinity with the pre-First World War German conservative tradition. At the same time, most of these regimes unquestionably also had fascistic tendencies, such as the glorification of the strong leader. An autocratic, extreme nationalistic regime also came to power in Japan during the same period.

5   The victory of the liberal state

441   The Long War and the triumph of the liberal state

The American constitutionalist Philip Bobbitt has described the history of the twentieth century in terms of a long war between three different ideologies of the nation-state: liberal, communist and fascist.[3] The Second World War (1939–45) brought victory over fascism, and the Cold War (1947–90) brought victory over communism. The fall of the Berlin Wall sealed the end of a lengthy, ideological and political struggle and marked the triumph of the Western, liberal state.

Seen in terms of the *longue durée*, this analysis is undoubtedly correct, although it does not say anything about the future. The victory of the liberal state was indeed fought out in two wars, one an open war and the other a largely 'cold' one. The success of the liberal model was not, however, attributable solely to the outcome of these international conflicts but rested primarily on the fact that this model provided the most realistic interpretation of the ideal of the greatest happiness of the greatest number and was best placed to bring this about.

442   The liberal welfare state

The First World War put the liberal state under pressure. The lower classes, who had paid the heaviest price for the war, demanded their share

---

[3] Philip Bobbitt, *The Shield of Achilles: War, Peace and the Course of History*, London and New York 2002.

of the spoils of victory. Revolution was in the air throughout Europe. In western and northern Europe as well as in North America, liberal democracies managed to stay in place, but this required far-reaching concessions to be made to the working classes.

The most important of these concessions was the introduction of universal suffrage. During the course of the nineteenth century, the right to vote and to stand for election was systematically extended. Now, it was suddenly opened to all men, and shortly afterwards to all women. The Netherlands introduced universal suffrage for men as early as 1917. In Belgium universal multiple suffrage was rapidly replaced by universal single suffrage in 1919. The constitution was not amended accordingly until a year later. In the Netherlands, women were allowed to vote for the first time in 1922; in the case of Belgium, they had to wait until after the Second World War to vote in general elections.

Thanks to the introduction of universal suffrage, leftist parties won a great deal of ground throughout Europe. In many countries, the left wing had some time before it split into radical communists and moderate socialists or social-democrats. Whereas the former wished ultimately to replace parliamentary democracy and the free market economy by a dictatorship of the proletariat, the socialists had reconciled themselves to the liberal state. They were reformists in the sense that they accepted the model with a view to managing and reforming it from within. The subjection of the communist parties in Europe to Moscow widened the gap between the two left-wing factions and facilitated the recovery of socialism for liberal democracy.

From the 1920s onwards, social-democrats came to power almost everywhere in Europe, generally in coalitions with either Christian-democrats or liberals. The centre-left reconciled itself to the system, becoming a pillar rather than opponent of liberal democracy. Inevitably this, together with a number of other factors, led to a gradual transformation of the liberal state. The most important evolution was undoubtedly the growth of state intervention. This began as early as the First World War and, for all the neo-liberal rhetoric of the past thirty years, continues to hold sway, at least in continental Europe.

The ideal of the limited state and the free market economy became diluted. Not long after the First World War, most countries embarked on an encompassing programme of social reform. The system of social security was built up in order to provide the lower classes with protection against all sorts of risks and to allow them to share in the prosperity. The rights of the working class were extended and laid down in the law. The

two world wars and the 1929 depression forced active government intervention in the economy in the form of an activist monetary policy and
direct investment in the economy in the form of large-scale public works
and the establishment and operation of public utilities, such as airlines,
insurance companies and telephone companies. In the years after the
Second World War, in many countries, the size of the public sector grew
as a result of direct government participation and taxation to more than
50 per cent. The limited state became an active, interventionist state concerned with an ever-growing range of aspects of communal and even private life. Even so, it did not become a totalitarian state: the protection of
the fundamental rights, the principle of the rule of law and the regular
changes in power inherent to democracy proved strong enough to keep
this danger at bay. The free market economy evolved in the direction of
the socially adjusted free market.

443   Liberal democracy

As a result of these changes, the advantages of the liberal political and
economic model now at last were shared by the vast majority of the population. In that sense, the twentieth century saw the realisation of the ideals
of the liberal thinkers of the eighteenth century, despite the opposition and
the egotistical interpretations of this ideology by the bourgeoisie. Bobbitt
distinguishes the twentieth-century state from the nineteenth-century
state. In his view, the latter was a state-nation, while the nation-state
did not arise until the end of the nineteenth century. In the nineteenth
century, the state was – as Marx himself said – the elite's instrument for
mobilising the nation and people for its own purposes. In the twentieth
century, it became the nation's instrument for creating the greatest possible prosperity.

Since the 1920s, politics in most Western democracies has been dominated by three or four large political families that have battled it out for
power, but which have not challenged the system of liberal democracy
itself: social-democrats, liberal-democrats, Christian-democrats and
conservatives. With varying degrees of enthusiasm, these parties all
accepted parliamentary and constitutional monarchy, the separation of
powers, equality of all citizens, the separation of church and state, the
rule of law, human rights and the free market economy based on private
property and contractual freedom, but with social adjustments. In that
sense, they are all liberals, in the broad and historical meaning of the
word. The differences between the movements are generally gradual ones
concerning the extent to which they identify themselves with the overall

programme of liberalism – such as the genuine liberals in the strict sense of the word and some Christian-democratic parties do – or alternatively place certain particular emphases, in the way that the conservatives and other Christian-democrats emphasise the classic, Christian values and the social-democrats the social adjustments to the free market model. Within these main movements, there are, needless to say, a great many more radical elements that only appear to accept the system but want to transform it as they see fit from within. Similarly, there were throughout the entire twentieth century fringe political parties on the extreme left or extreme right that rejected the system. With few exceptions, these have not been successful since the Second World War.

444   The bureaucratic state

In most countries of western Europe, the broad contours of the constitution of the liberal state as laid down in the nineteenth century remained formally in place. The separation of powers, the supremacy of the legislature, the representative democracy, the independence of the judiciary and the protection of fundamental rights remained the basic principles of a liberal state. In reality, however, the system was reformed from within. The executive, the government and the central bureaucracy obtained a clear ascendancy over the legislature throughout Europe. Various reasons may be advanced for this. The most important has undoubtedly been the growing share of the public sector, which resulted in a huge expansion of the bureaucracy in the form of ministerial departments, government enterprises and all kinds of government bodies and agencies. The scale of government administration has consequently grown many times over and the complexity and technicality of politics have risen exponentially. Politics and administration have consequently become less a matter of broad ideological choices that are then converted by parliament into laws. They are rather a matter of hundreds of thousands of small decisions that are the particular preserve of a highly sophisticated bureaucracy. The executive has grown too big, too complex and its workings too sophisticated for the legislative control to be effective.

In many countries, the freedom of action of the legislature has been limited by the need to govern with multi-party coalitions or broad majority parties that in fact cover a variety of persuasions, such as Labour and the Conservatives in Britain and the Union pour un Mouvement Populaire (UMP) in France. The fear of a breakdown of the coalition and a government crisis makes it particularly difficult for the parliamentarians of the majority to criticize the government and vote independently.

This results in rigid discipline among the majority parties in parliament, which is fatal for parliamentary debate. Government proposals are bound to be adopted. The legislative initiative is de facto monopolised by the executive.

The curtailment of government power is guaranteed by judicial protection against specific violations of the law by the government or by parliament. In most European countries, the judiciary has been given greater powers to that end. Almost everywhere there is now an extensive system of administrative jurisdiction, under which the government can be held accountable for its actions vis-à-vis citizens. As a result of a process of liberalisation or decentralisation, a constitutional court has been set up in various countries including Germany and Belgium. The process of European integration and the growth of international law since the Second World War have done away with the dualism between international and national systems of law. Most countries nowadays accept that national rules, including laws, must be in accord with international and European law – in so far as such law has direct application – and have assigned the judiciary powers of review to that end.

6   *The era of the three world wars*

445   The victors of the First World War

The peace agreements concluded in and around Paris in 1919/20 failed to bring political stability to Europe, largely because the three main victorious powers – the United States, Britain and France – did not form a united front. France wanted guarantees for its security, seeking an alliance with London and Washington and the maximum possible weakening of Germany. Germany was required to give up a substantial part of its territory, to pay massive reparations and was suffered to retain only a small army (100,000 soldiers). Britain was not prepared to go along fully with the French demands. London wanted the balance of power in Europe to be restored, so that it could withdraw from the continent as quickly as possible and concentrate on its colonial empire. For this reason, it did not wish to go as far as its French ally in punishing Germany and was wary of entering into a permanent alliance with France.

The United States had entered the war in 1917 at the behest of President Woodrow Wilson (1856–1924, president 1913–21). The underlying explanation for US intervention was the fear that Germany would win the war and hence dominate the continent. This the USA wished to avoid, in the

British tradition of the balance of power. For nearly a century the USA had been the leading power on its continent. That was and remained a comfortable position, which not only guaranteed the United States a large measure of security but also permitted far more room for manoeuvre in the world. The USA was not prepared to grant that position to any other power.[4]

Although the fundamental reason for US intervention had its roots in the traditional doctrine of the balance of power, Wilson was a genuine opponent of this doctrine and the entire diplomatic system of the European Concert. He was, not unjustifiably, convinced that the politics of the balance of power with its coalitions had unleashed the disaster of the First World War. Wilson sought a new world order based not on the balance of power but on international law. The guideline for the peace settlement should be not the interests of the state but the self-determination of the peoples. The security of the states and peoples would be guaranteed by a system of collective security. The League of Nations would put in place an international organisation that would safeguard compliance with the international legal order and maintain peace. Alliances between states would consequently become superfluous.

446   The failure of Versailles

The peace arrangements of 1919/20 were the outcome of protracted negotiations in and around Paris. The bulk of the time was taken up by talks among the leaders of the three main victorious states, which the Italian and later the Japanese leader were allowed to attend. The three leaders were Woodrow Wilson, the British prime minister, David Lloyd George (1863–1945), and his French counterpart Georges Clémenceau (1841–1929). After months of meetings, they reached a laborious compromise which they then imposed unilaterally on the other allies and the defeated countries; the German delegation at Versailles was simply handed the text of the treaty. There was no room for negotiation. That, straightaway, was the second reason for the failure of Versailles. While Germany signed the peace, it in fact never accepted the *Diktat* of Versailles.[5]

The Treaty of Versailles was an impossible compromise. Germany was severely punished, felt itself cheated and was unwilling to accept the new status quo. This created the seedbed for a new war. While France

---

[4] This is the interpretation that the proponents of offensive realism gave to US policy: John Mearsheimer, *The Tragedy of Great Power Politics*, New York and London 2001.

[5] On the peace negotiations: Margaret Macmillan, *Peacemakers: Six Months that Changed the World*, London 2001.

had realised part of its programme with the punishment of Germany, the necessary security guarantee on the part of the USA was not forthcoming. This created a situation in which a peace was imposed on Germany that the country was not to observe wholeheartedly, while on the other hand, France failed to obtain the necessary means to enforce the peace. At Versailles, the allies opted in favour of a punitive peace. Almost straightaway, however, they conveyed the message that they were unprepared or unable to enforce that peace.

This was because Wilson was counting for the enforcement of the peace on the League of Nations, which was founded as a result of the Treaty of Versailles. The League soon turned out to be powerless. Both the losers and the Soviet Union were temporarily excluded. Because the USA Senate refused to ratify the Treaty of Versailles, the USA was unable to accede. The League became a club of the European victors – who did not in fact believe in the instrument.

447   The end of Versailles and the rise of Hitler

The peace settlement of 1919 lasted less than five years. In 1923, Germany refused to pay further reparations. France called on London and Washington to intervene, but they refused. Supported by Belgian troops, the French army occupied the Ruhr. German workers went on strike, so that this action produced nothing. The withdrawal of the French and Belgian troops was disguised in the form of an agreement with Berlin, but in fact it meant the end of Versailles. Paris understandably felt left in the lurch by its main allies and would henceforth not make any further serious effort to enforce the peace conditions or hold in check the German revival.

The passivity of the allies offered Hitler's Germany the room it needed for rearmament and gradual expansion. In 1936, Hitler violated the provision prohibiting the presence of German troops on the left bank of the Rhine. In 1938, there followed the *Anschluss* of Austria and the occupation of the Sudetenland in Czechoslovakia, followed by the full-scale dismantling of the country the next year. Each time the French and British governments had been given the opportunity to turn the tide by acting resolutely; on each occasion they had allowed the opportunity to slip.

448   The Second World War

Hitler was accordingly taken by surprise when Britain and France did suddenly take a firm stand in September 1939. The fall of Czechoslovakia had made it clear to the French and British governments that Hitler had to be stopped, and that this could only be done by force. Shortly after the invasion of Poland by the German army on 1 September 1939, London and Paris declared war on Hitler. In the *Blitzkrieg* of May 1940 the German army overran France, the Netherlands, Belgium and Luxembourg. The British Expeditionary Force was barely able to escape from Dunkirk to England. In the summer of 1940, only Britain, now under the leadership of Winston Churchill (1874–1965), stood between Hitler and total dominion in Europe. In the meantime, Stalin had annexed the three Baltic states and a part of Poland with Hitler's concurrence.

In June 1941, Hitler made the capital error of invading Russia. The initially successful offensive ground to a halt towards winter. At the end of the year, Hitler made his second major error, declaring war on the USA in the wake of the Japanese attack on Pearl Harbor. This gave the US president, Franklin D. Roosevelt (1882–1945, president 1933–45), the excuse he needed for intervention alongside Britain in the war in Europe.

The Second World War was even more destructive than the First. It was a genuine world war waged not just in and around Europe but also in the Far East. The death toll exceeded fifty million. The war was also fought with hitherto unknown brutality, dragging the civilian population into the violence on a far greater scale than before. The Second World War was an ideological and also total war. The First World War had also gradually obtained an ideological dimension, as a struggle between the Western democracies and the more conservative monarchies of central Europe. The Second World War became the struggle between three totally different world orders, of which two had temporarily formed an uneasy alliance. The destruction of the opponent, of its identity and worldview, became the objective. The enemy population was not spared, even by the Western allies. In the communist and, somewhat less, in the fascist states, the domestic population was exploited to the full.

Even with the US intervention, the war in Europe and the Pacific was to last a further three years. In May 1945, Germany capitulated, followed three months later by Japan. The peace settlement of 1945 had already been prepared during the war by the big three: Roosevelt, Stalin and Churchill. This time, the victory over Germany and Japan was total. Both countries abjured their regimes and recent past, and accepted the peace arrangements that had been imposed. Under pressure from the USA, both countries and their allies were rehabilitated and included in the coalition of Western democracies. Thanks in part to US magnanimity, they rapidly put the war behind them. To this day, both countries remain powerful allies of Washington.

449   The Cold War

The Second World War ended Europe's leading position in the world. Towards the early 1960s, the European powers lost the bulk of their overseas colonies. In the space of two decades, Britain and France lost their empires and were relegated to the group of medium-sized powers. By 1960, there were just two great powers left in the world: the USA and the Soviet Union. Europe came under the hegemony of both.

The League of Nations had already been replaced in June 1945 by a new worldwide organisation, the United Nations Organisation. This was given a stronger structure than the League and almost all the countries of the world acceded. Even so, the organisation was able to play no more than a minor role in world politics, for most of the time being crippled by a new conflict that began in the late 1940s: the Cold War.

The Cold War had begun as early as 1947 when it became clear to the USA and its allies that Stalin sought hegemony over as much of Europe as possible. In 1948, President Harry Truman (1884–1972, president 1945–53) decided to call a halt to the Soviet expansion inside and outside Europe. The Americans intervened in the civil war in Greece, helping to defeat the communists in that country. Eastern and central Europe including East Germany were left to Stalin. The rest of Europe teamed up with Canada and the USA in a military alliance, the North Atlantic Treaty Organisation (NATO, 1949), thereby coming under the protection of the US armed forces and the US nuclear umbrella. In that part of Europe, liberal democracy and the socially adjusted free market economy were able to flourish. The period from 1960 in western Europe will undoubtedly go down in the history books as a golden age; the countries of eastern and central Europe largely came under the Soviet yoke, forming the Eastern bloc together with the Soviet Union.

During the Cold War, matters never reached the point of a direct, military confrontation between the superpowers. Open war was held at bay by the threat of a nuclear holocaust. Following the Cuban Missile Crisis (1961), Washington and Moscow managed to achieve a subtle compromise. The two powers continued to confront one another, but spared each other's most direct interests. The Cold War was a clash between two ideologies. It was fought out in a great propaganda battle, by infiltration and destabilisation of the opponent, in an enormous arms race and in small wars on the periphery of the spheres of influence of the two superpowers.

450   Post-Cold War Europe

In 1989/90, after four decades, the West resolved the Cold War in its favour. The Western victory was not the outcome of military victories in the many smaller wars. The two most important regional conflicts, Korea and Vietnam, had in fact resulted in a stalemate and defeat respectively for the United States. The outcome of the Cold War reflected the intrinsic strength of the Western, liberal model and the intrinsic weakness of the communist model. Whereas in the West the vast majority of the population enjoyed an ever rising standard of living and exceptional freedom, the economy in the Eastern bloc failed and the dictatorship weighed ever more heavily. The unstoppable advance of communication made it increasingly difficult for the Soviet dictatorship to seal its own population off from the West, with a consequent loss in credibility of its propaganda. Moscow and the governments of its satellite states in Europe experienced increasing difficulties in keeping their populations in line. In Poland, during the early 1980s, the communist government found itself confronted by the opposition of the Solidarity trade union led by Lech Walesa (b. 1943), who received backing from Pope John Paul II (1920–2005, Pope 1978–2005), the Pole Karol Wojtyla. The last Soviet leader, Mikhail Gorbachev (b. 1931), who came to power in 1985, realised that the situation was no longer tenable and sought change. Gorbachev hoped that the Soviet regime could save itself by adopting various elements of the successful formula of the West. His cautious reforms came, however, too late. Under pressure from the assertive Cold War policy of US President Ronald Reagan (1911–2004, president 1981–9), the Soviet regime imploded. In 1989, the central and eastern European countries freed themselves from the Soviet yoke. The wall that divided Berlin was demolished. A year later, Moscow resigned itself to the reunification of Germany. In 1991, the regime of the Communist Party was overthrown in the Soviet Union. The Union was dissolved and the fifteen republics obtained independence. By means of the Commonwealth of Independent States (CIS) and all sorts of treaty arrangements, the Russian Republic is once again trying to exert some control over the other republics, with varying success. Their inclusion in NATO and the European Union in 2004 has more or less guaranteed the three Baltic countries their independence from Russia.

7   European integration

451   The European Community

After the Second World War, a process of economic, social and political integration got underway in western Europe. The first moves were made as early as the late 1940s. The policy of integration was motivated by the will to avoid further warfare between the western European countries and to form a bloc against the Soviet threat. The USA fully supported the integration, making it a precondition for its economic aid towards the reconstruction of Europe.

European integration was and remains essentially an institutional process, propelled by the political class. Although the integration is predominantly economic, it is prompted by geopolitical objectives. The initial step consisted of the formation of the European Coal and Steel Community (ECSC) in 1950. France, the Federal Republic of Germany, the Netherlands, Belgium, Luxembourg and Italy founded an international organisation with supranational powers over the coal and steel industry. The integration of heavy industry was designed to prevent the Federal Republic of Germany, established in 1949, from steering an independent course.

In 1957, there followed the founding of the European Economic Community with the Treaty of Rome. Together with the ECSC and Euratom (the European Atomic Agency), this formed the European Community (EC). The EC was a free-trade zone with far-reaching integration of economic and monetary policy, the supranational character of which set it apart from most other regional organisations. The institutions of the EC were able to create legal norms with direct application within the legal systems of the member states. This marked a genuine limitation on the sovereignty of those states. During the course of the 1970s and up to 1990, the Community was systematically enlarged. The United Kingdom, Denmark and Ireland acceded in 1973, Greece in 1981, Spain and Portugal in 1986, and Sweden, Finland and Austria in 1992.

452   Extension to the east

After the end of the Cold War, European integration went into higher gear. The reunification of Germany awakened the traditional spectre of German dominance of Europe. In exchange for German unification, the president of France, François Mitterrand (1916–96, president 1981–95) and the British prime minister, Margaret Thatcher (b. 1925), demanded guarantees that the new Germany be firmly anchored in Europe. The threat of German dominance needed to be obviated by means of institutionalised Franco-German co-operation. The German chancellor, Helmut Kohl (b. 1930), recognised the wisdom of this. In autumn 1990, the European countries, the Soviet Union and the USA agreed on the shape of the new European order. Germany was reunited and regained full sovereignty over its territory. It would remain part of NATO. Peace and security in Europe would be guaranteed by chaining down the German eagle in a unified Europe, in which it would then automatically play a leading role together with France.

The treaties of Maastricht (1992) and Amsterdam (1997) were the result of this compromise. The European Community was transformed into the European Union, which obtained powers in the field of internal and external security. The process of integration therefore obtained an increasingly political dimension. In 2002, the single currency became a fact with the introduction of the euro.

The fall of communism opened the door to the inclusion of the countries of the former Eastern bloc in the western European order. The countries of central and eastern Europe adopted the system of liberal democracy under the rule of law and the free market economy. At no point in history have East and West enjoyed such unity as today. The institutional inclusion of the former Eastern bloc countries in the European structure was already set in motion shortly after the fall of the Berlin Wall. These countries rapidly acceded to the Council of Europe which, by means of the European Convention on Human Rights (1950) and the European Court of Human Rights in Strasbourg, guarantees the observance of human rights. In 1999, Poland, the Czech Republic and Hungary were admitted to NATO. In 2004, Estonia, Latvia, Lithuania, Slovakia, Slovenia, Romania and Bulgaria followed. Albania and Croatia were due to join in April 2009. On 1 May 2004, the three Baltic states, Poland, the Czech Republic, Slovakia, Hungary, Slovenia, Malta and Cyprus became members of the European Union. In 2007, Bulgaria and Romania were allowed in.

453   Decentralisation

In parallel with the process of European integration, there has also been a trend towards decentralisation in many west European countries. In 1949, at the foundation of the Federal Republic of Germany, the country reverted to its historical tradition, becoming a federation. As a result of the communal tensions between the Flemish and the Francophones in Belgium, that country was transformed between 1960 and 1993 from a unitary state into a federal state. Most countries in Europe have not gone so far. In France and Italy, regions were established with autonomy in certain areas. Spain was required to grant the Basque country, Catalonia and the Canary Islands a far-reaching form of self-government. In Denmark, a large measure of the powers were transferred to the municipalities. In Britain, Scotland obtained its own parliament and government for the first time since 1707; Wales was also given its own administrative and parliamentary institutions. In this way, the state sovereignty that had been so significantly eroded by European integration came under pressure from below as well. The era of the sovereign state appears to be nearing its end; sovereignty has once again become a highly relative concept.

8   International law

454   Sovereignty and the international community

Although the Treaty of Versailles and the League of Nations were political failures, they remain milestones in the development of international law. They provided the impulse for innovations that were to come to maturity at a later point. The basis of international law remained state sovereignty, as expressly recognised in the 1945 Charter of the United Nations. That sovereignty did, however, become an increasingly relative concept. Modern international law had in any case always been dual in nature: it was based on state sovereignty but was at the same time an effort to control if not limit it. During the second half of the twentieth century, efforts to curb sovereignty and strengthen the international community were stepped up but, to this day, remain only partially successful.

455   International organisations

First, with the League of Nations, the era of international organisations began. Since 1920, hundreds of international organisations have been set up all over the world, both global and regional. Some have general powers; most are specialised. These organisations have become important players in the field of international law and have partly overcome the monopoly of the states as subjects, authors and enforcers of international law.

456   The end of voluntarism in international law

Second, the monopoly of the state over the creation of international law has been diluted. Among the international organisations there are a number, such as the UN and the European Union, that are supranational in nature. Among other things, that means that their institutions, such as the UN Security Council or the Council of Ministers of the European Union, have authority to create binding legal rules through a majority decision. The states that did not vote for these rules are nevertheless bound by them. These majority decisions detract from voluntarism. The same goes for the *ius cogens*. Since the 1960s, the view has gained ground that the rules of international law accepted by the majority of states may even be regarded as coercive law that also applies to states that did not consent to them, the so-called *ius cogens*. This is reminiscent of the proposition by Francisco de Vitoria that the *consensus maioris partis totius orbis* provides a sufficient basis for the rules of general positive 'international law'. The *ius cogens* is highly controversial and is rejected by many – especially powerful – countries.

457   Legalised hegemony

Third, the great powers principle – or legalised hegemony in the wording of Gerry Simpson[6] – became a fundamental principle of the international legal order. That was already reflected in the composition of the organs of the League of Nations, but even more so in the UN Security Council, on which the five great powers – which were also the first five nuclear powers – obtained a permanent seat and the right of veto.[7] The Security Council is responsible for the maintenance of peace and security in the world. It can adopt binding resolutions and has supranational authority. It may also authorise the use of armed force. In that sense, the permanent representation of the five powers on the Council is a recognition that these countries bear special responsibility for the enforcement of the international legal order. The right of veto implies de facto that they cannot themselves be subjected to such enforcement.

458   International adjudication and arbitration

Fourth, there was the establishment of the Permanent Court of International Justice at The Hague after the First World War, called since 1945 the International Court of Justice. Although the jurisdiction of the court is limited to disputes between states that have specifically recognised its jurisdiction and the number of cases to date has remained fairly limited, the court played a major role in the formation of international law in the twentieth century. Its existence provides a symbol for the growing recognition that the international community, like any other community, is, or at least should be, a legal community. Reference must also be made to the growing role of international arbitration. Since the First Hague Peace Conference of 1899 there has been the Permanent Court of Arbitration in The Hague, while permanent law courts or arbitration chambers have evolved out of the various international organisations.

---

[6] Gerry Simpson, *Great Powers and Outlaw States: Unequal Sovereigns in the International Legal Order*, Cambridge 2004.
[7] Apart from the USA and Russia, also China, Britain and France.

459   *Ius contra bellum*

Fifth, the right of states to wage war was radically curbed in the course of the twentieth century, at least on paper. The Peace of Versailles stated that the German aggression was a violation of international law and declared the country to have been unilaterally responsible for the war and all ensuing damage. Upon the formation of the League of Nations, it was laid down that states should in future first seek to resolve their disputes peacefully by means of arbitration or appeal to the Council of the League of Nations. The League had the right to use force against countries that did not abide by these rules or the recommendations of the Council. The Charter of the United Nations in 1945 imposed further restrictions on the *ius ad bellum* (right to war), turning it into a *ius contra bellum* (law against war). The use or threat of armed force between states was expressly prohibited; only individual or collective self-defence against armed attack remained permissible. In addition, the UN Security Council was given the right to use or permit armed force in order to maintain or restore peace and security in the world. In practice, the prohibition of the use of armed force has proved anything but effective. The Security Council and the states of the world have largely accommodated this failure by giving an ever more extensive interpretation to the concept of self-defence, which now encompasses pretty much all forms of use of force by states except blatant aggression.[8]

460   The end of dualism

Sixth, dualism found itself under challenge. The Treaty of Versailles had already begun to break down the dividing wall between the national and international legal orders. The treaty laid down that the German emperor and a number of military leaders would be subject to criminal prosecution for their part in the outbreak of the war and its conduct. The argument that they had acted as organs of a sovereign Germany no longer provided them with immunity. As individuals they were held directly liable under international law. After the Second World War, several dozens of German and Japanese military and political leaders were prosecuted and sentenced by the tribunals of the allied powers in Nuremberg and Tokyo. International criminal courts were set up under the auspices of the UN in Arusha after the genocide in Rwanda and in The Hague

---

[8] See on this, Stephen C. Neff, *War and the Law of Nations: a Historical Survey*, Cambridge 2005.

after the war in the former Yugoslavia. The Treaty of Rome of 1996 provided for the establishment of a permanent International Criminal Court, where people are to be tried for serious violations of the laws of war and crimes against humanity.

The loss of dualism is also reflected in the international protection of human rights. In the wake of the Second World War, the Universal Declaration of Human Rights was adopted in 1948. The declaration summarises the most important fundamental rights, but is not binding law. Later conventions such as the International Covenant on Civil and Political Rights (1966) are, however, binding. In various parts of the world, regional covenants such as the European Convention on Human Rights and Fundamental Freedoms (1950) were adopted. Also, regional international courts ensuring compliance with those treaties, such as the European Court of Human Rights, were established. In Europe, individual citizens can take their case to this court. Conversely, the convention also directly applies in most countries, so that citizens can invoke the convention before municipal courts. There are also regional conventions and courts for the protection of human rights in other parts of the globe. More generally, it may be said that ever more countries have accepted that international law forms part of the national legal order and is therefore applicable in national courts. Monism is on the march.

461 Transnational law

Seventh, international law has ceased to be solely confined to public law – if it ever was. Apart from states and international organisations, other players have also gained a seat on the forum of international law, such as non-governmental organisations (NGOs) and multinational companies. These often powerful and influential organisations have more of an impact on the development and application of international law than many states are able to. The growth in the international traffic of persons, goods and services has been accompanied by an increase in the body of international legal rules regulating these matters. During the course of the twentieth century, thousands of treaties and conventions dealing with matters of private law, such as the contract of sale or trade, came into being. In many cases these treaties are applied directly by national courts or in international arbitration between private individuals or companies. In this way, there gradually arose a mass of worldwide private law within international law, which is often referred to as transnational law.

9   *The relative failure of codification*

462   The evolution of society and the codes

The eighteenth- and nineteenth-century codifications established the supremacy of legislation at a stroke. The ideal of codification consisted of capturing the entire body of law in a number of codes. The codes would be the sole sources of the law. In line with the doctrine of natural law, the codes therefore should be complete, internally consistent and timeless. Most lawyers involved in the making of the major codes were not so naive and understood that their codes would in fact be subject to change. Most did, however, aim at completeness and consistency.

As early as the nineteenth century, it became evident that both completeness and timelessness were no more than pious ideals. The rapid changes in society, economy and politics in the nineteenth century called for all sorts of adjustments and additions, in the form of amendments, new statute law and interpretations by the judiciary and scholars. In the twentieth century, the social, economic and political changes were even more radical, so that the codes became increasingly outdated. Although in most countries the constitution and the codes continue to form the core of the classic branches of the law – constitutional law, civil law, commercial law, criminal law and procedural law – they nowadays form just one source of law beside many others. A panoply of other sources has evolved around the codified texts. Legislation, complemented by all kinds of executive regulations, remains, however, the main source of most national law systems on the continent.

463   Legislative frenzy

The principles underpinning the municipal law systems in continental Europe did not change greatly during the course of the twentieth century, but the nature of the legal system as a whole nevertheless changed. The following general trends may be discerned.

The increasing role of the government and the public sector in society and the economy has been reflected in the growth of a huge bureaucratic machinery penetrating the smallest and farthest reaches of public and private life. In a democracy under the rule of law, that bureaucracy can function only through the means of a complex system of detailed and technical legal rules. In addition, the complexity and technicality of the bureaucracy and the law provide no more than a mirror of what is taking place in society itself. Particularly in recent decades, the body of legislation and governmental regulations has increased hugely. The ever more rapid developments in society and ever growing complexity and technicality of the problems leave government with the constant feeling that it is not managing to respond to the problems and challenges with which society confronts it. But instead of evaluating the entire legal system and challenging the underlying principles of the system, governments react by introducing ever more laws and regulations. Not only is this doomed to failure, but the 'solution' has become part of the problem. Contemporary statute law has in the meantime become a travesty of the ideals of the Enlightenment. Clarity and comprehensibility have been sacrificed to the unattainable ideal of completeness. In that sense, the drama of the law during the twentieth century is that of the entire century: it is the failure of a rationalist ideal that has become self-destructive but has not yet been replaced by a new ideal.

The failure of codification to comply with the ideal of completeness has not led to the abandonment of the ideal of codification. To this day codification continues to be regarded as the means of radically reforming and simplifying the law and making it as complete as possible. In most countries there are (admittedly modest) efforts to codify the new branches of law in general laws. Other countries that had not as yet achieved their own codification of the law did so in the twentieth century. In the Netherlands, a new civil code was made after the Second World War (1947–92). Upon decolonisation, many of the former colonies retained the Western codes, gradually amending or replacing them later with new but often highly similar codes. Various Eastern bloc countries are today working on new codes along Western lines. Some jurists dream of a European codification.

The growth in the number of rules is in the first place evident from the huge number of laws introduced each year in all European countries. Apart from laws amending the codes, there are also numerous particular laws, outside the codes. Moreover, important parts of the law – especially with regard to public law and the public economy – became the object of government regulation.

464   Case law and legal scholarship

The failures of the legislator created room for judicial and scholarly interpretation. Legislation remains the dominant source of law only with the aid of the courts and legal scholars. These find themselves confronted by tangled, often unco-ordinated skeins of statutory rules that frequently contradict one another or are unclear or incomplete. Judges are no longer the *bouche de la loi* who literally apply the law; instead, the judge has become like a workman who takes the most usable tools out of the tool box of statute law, adjusts them to his requirements and then proceeds to work with them. Jurisprudence often plays a mediating role between legislator and the courts, suggesting possible interpretations of the law which are then used by the courts.

465   New branches of the law

The welfare state and the technological society impose new demands on the law. New disciplines such as labour law, social security law, financial law, environmental law, urban planning law, public procedure and medical law saw the light of day during the past century. These grew into independent branches of the law, with their own sources and often with their own logic and specific principles.

466   The rise of the public sector

All this had the effect of blurring the boundaries between public and private law. Governments increasingly concerned themselves with matters traditionally pertaining to private law. The inviolability of property and the freedom of contract were curtailed in order to safeguard social and ecological interests which were considered public. Branches of the law inherently forming part of private law, such as labour law, social security law or business law, obtained a public law look. Public law is expanding rapidly. On the other hand, governments increasingly behave like private institutions and are for their part closing the gap between private and public law. The direct participation by governments in private economic activities has taught them that the organisation and culture of private companies are often more efficient than their own and, under pressure from the revival of liberal economic thinking in the 1980s, this has led them to adopt the uses and practices of private businesses. The private and public sectors are today separated by a grey area of institutions and public enterprises that cannot be said with any certainty to belong to any one particular sphere, such as companies in the utilities sector and the non-profit sector. In some countries, this has even led to uncertainty as to the applicable law (private or administrative) and competent courts for such enterprises. This last fact illustrates that our legal system is collapsing under the weight of its own success.

10   *The partial capitulation of legal science*

467   Codification and legal scholarship

The codification put an end to the leading position that legal scholarship had held in the development of the law in continental Europe since the Late Middle Ages. Legal scholars had always involved themselves to a lesser or greater extent with legal practice, but legal science was also ideological: its main démarche was prescriptive. Moreover, legal scholars held an essentially superior and autonomous position with regard to legal practice. That position the legal scholars derived from the higher ideal aspired to by the science of law, namely the discovery or development of a perfected, complete and consistent legal *system*.

At least in the eyes of the jurists of that time, the French codification went a very long way towards achieving that ideal and deprived legal scholarship of one of its traditional roles and its autonomy. The Exegetic School was the capitulation of jurisprudence to the new reality of the codes. In the future, the role of legal scholarship would be confined to the explanation and instruction of the law. After the codification of civil law in Germany, a similar process took place there albeit to a lesser extent.

468   The quantitative expansion of legal scholarship

Despite this loss of part of its function and its intellectual autonomy, legal science expanded enormously, at least in terms of quantity, in the twentieth and twenty-first centuries, more particularly from the 1970s onwards. At no stage in history have there been so many university-trained lawyers as today; never has Europe had so many legal scholars or were there more scholarly legal publications. The explosion in legal scholarship may to some extent be explained by the democratisation of university education since the 1960s. The past five decades have seen an exponential increase in the number of students, including law students. The numbers of faculty at the law schools consequently swelled into impressive legions of professors, lecturers and other teaching staff. These are all expected to make a contribution to legal scholarship (at least quantitatively) in the form of a continuous stream of publications. The fact that quantity rather than quality has tended to be the norm is another outgrowth of the ongoing dominance of positivism in the discourse of twentieth-century science. Given the huge number of researchers, it is inescapable that the number of publications rather than the number of readers counts towards academic success. The Czech author Milan Kundera hit the mark when he wrote of student dissertations:

> When a society is rich, its people don't need to work with their hands; they can devote themselves to activities of the spirit. We have more and more universities and more and more students. If students are going to earn degrees, they've got to come up with dissertation topics. And since

dissertations can be written about everything under the sun, the number of topics is infinite. Sheets of paper covered with words pile up in archives sadder than cemeteries, because no one ever visits them, not even on All Souls' Day. Culture is perishing in overproduction, in an avalanche of words, in the madness of quantity.[9]

469   Overspecialisation

The legal scholarship of the twentieth century is based on the same foundation as that of French nineteenth-century legal scholarship: the supremacy of legislation. From this, there have arisen two trends, each with its roots in the two hallmarks of nineteenth-century legal scholarship: legal positivism and the instrumental approach towards the law. In the course of the twentieth century, these two essentially conflicting trends became bound up with one another. Even though a more positivistic stance may be discernible in the work of one legal scholar and a more instrumental approach in that of another, it remains fair to say that it is precisely from this conjunction of the two movements that twentieth-century legal scholarship sprang.

The legal positivists of the twentieth century were the heirs of the exegetes of the nineteenth century. They saw the role of legal scholarship as the interpretation of positive law as laid down by the political authorities. As the law became more complex and opaque, the creative input of legal scholarship went through a revival. The role of legal scholarship changed from one of explanation to one of interpretation, supplementation and repair. The inability of the codes to make good on their claims gave rise to the need for systematisation by legal scholarship. By placing the various sources of law side by side, legal science sought to provide the systematic consistency and overview no longer afforded by legislation. Here too, however, the complexity of the law turned out to be an insuperable problem. Since the law had become so complex and huge, the vast majority of legal scholars were forced into far-reaching specialisation. Even in a new field of law such as urban planning law it is extremely difficult to find a specialist who retains the broad view. Systematic surveys by a single author are becoming ever rarer and are being displaced by compilations in which each sub-area of the law is dealt with by a separate specialist.

---

[9] Milan Kundera, *The Unbearable Lightness of Being*, London 1984, translation by Michael Henry Heim.

470   Social engineering

The proponents of an instrumental approach to the law regard the law as a social instrument or means of social engineering. This trend is related to the German *Interessenjurisprudenz* of the late nineteenth century. The rise of this approach to the law in the twentieth century reflects the advent of government intervention and the welfare state. The law not only serves to uphold the existing order but is a political instrument for intervening in and changing society. In the process, the methodology and internal logic of the law are inevitably sacrificed.

471   Positivism and beyond

The teaming up of positivism and the instrumental approach to the law has become externalised in the revival of a limited ambition among legal scholars to improve upon the law. Nowadays, even the most rabid exegetes accept that legal scholarship must not just explain the law but must also make suggestions for improvement. Even so, it is not possible to claim that in doing so legal science has regained its historical autonomy. The legal science of the glossators up to and including the School of Natural Law was based on a more comprehensive ideal than the improvement of existing law. Their goal and *raison d'être* was the autonomous articulation of an ideal law and the *total replacement* of existing law by it. In comparison with these idealists, present-day legal scholars may be regarded as reformists. They are aiming not at a new edifice but at repairs and partial rebuilding. In that sense, present-day legal science has also become a good deal more realistic.

In addition, the partial capitulation of legal science with respect to legal practice has led to another division within legal science, namely that between the specialists of current, positive law and the practitioners of the so-called meta-juridical disciplines such as legal history, legal philosophy, legal theory and sociology of law. All these disciplines are useful instruments at the service of those wanting to articulate an ideal law – even if often their proponents strongly object to that. The irony is that these disciplines have obtained their autonomy and reached a high state of development at the very point at which the 'other' legal scholars had the least interest in these aims. This is at its clearest in the case of legal history. Prior to codification there was no room for an independent study of legal history – particularly in the sense of the history of ancient Roman private law – because Roman law was the subject of most legal scholarship.

As a result of codification, first in France and later in Germany, Roman law lost its role as a source of inspiration for an ideal law. This in turn created room for a purely historical study of the law of the Romans. In the wake of this, and on the model of the Germanists of the Historical School, there was a growth in interest in the legal development of other historical systems and eras. It was therefore the loss of significance of Roman law for current law that made possible the resurgence of interest in the historiography of Roman law. At the same time, all this has not prevented the subject of Roman law from fulfilling a different, more traditional function than that of a subject of legal history at many European law schools to this day. Particularly in southern Europe but also (for example) in some western European and British law schools, Roman law continues to serve as an introduction to private law in general as it provides a large part of the historical basis for the continental systems of private law.

11   1 May 2004 and beyond…

472   The return of history

To some, the accession of ten new member states, including eight former Eastern bloc countries, to the European Union on 1 May 2004 may seem to have consecrated the victory of liberal democracy in Europe. At the same time that the last remnants of the last great totalitarian ideology of the twentieth century are being cleared away in the former Eastern bloc, Europe has achieved the greatest measure of unity in its history.

The optimism of the American liberal philosopher Francis Fukuyama, who claimed that the victory of the liberal West over communism ushered in 'the end of history', was widely shared during the 1990s. Fukuyama considered that the end of the great ideological struggle of the twentieth century also meant the end of the great conflicts.[10] In doing so, he drew on the ideas of Hegel, according to whom history was an ongoing struggle between theses and antitheses, ultimately resulting in the victory of one great synthesis. According to Hegel that was the nation-state; for Fukuyama it was the liberal state.

Some years into the twenty-first century, this optimism is fast fading away. It has become clear that Fukuyama's analysis is valuable as a historical or philosophical thesis but does not have anything to say about the future. The liberal state of today, which is being increasingly reformed and contested, will certainly not be Hegel's definitive synthesis.

[10] Francis Fukuyama, *The End of History and the Last Man*, London 1992.

Just a few years after the end of the Cold War, Samuel Huntington launched an attack on Fukuyama's optimistic view.[11] The struggle between ideologies might be over, he argued, but the clash of civilisations was just beginning. Huntington predicted new conflicts and wars. For the coming decades he predicted a fierce struggle between the West, based as it is on the Latin-Christian tradition, and Islam. For their part, Henry Kissinger (b. 1923) and, more recently, Robert Kagan among many others insisted on the significance and dangers of traditional great power competition.[12]

Huntington, Kissinger and Kagan are right in so far as, with the resolution of the struggle among the three great ideologies of the twentieth century, history has not come to an end. New conflicts are at hand; new threats are disrupting the feast of liberal democracy. But in contrast to what Huntington asserts, it is not a matter of the clash between civilisations or religions. As before, the greatest challenges with which the liberal model is confronted today, both internally and externally, are ideological in nature. Moreover, ideological conflicts are most dangerous when their fault-lines merge with those of opposing great powers.

More extreme parties, challenging liberal democracy, are coming to the fore within Europe. Since the end of the Cold War some of these parties have achieved significant growth in various countries. More worrisome might be that in some countries even some democratic parties move towards more populist and autocratic approaches to politics and that the participation of the social and economic elites and middle classes in the democratic process diminishes. In a televised democracy, where the spotlights are constantly trained upon a very few political leaders, the checks and balances of parliamentary and judiciary control on the popularly elected leaders lose their strength.

Outside Europe, the threats come from religious fundamentalism as well as the revival of autocracy. Religious fundamentalism is not an Islamic monopoly but is to be found in other religions as well. There is no inevitable conflict between the Christian and Islamic worlds as Huntington asserts. The Islamic world is no more of a monolithic block than the secular or 'Latin-Christian' West. Within the Islamic world, an internal struggle is raging, over such issues as the separation between religion and

---

[11] Samuel Huntington, *The Clash of Civilizations and the Remaking of World Order*, London 1997.

[12] Henry Kissinger, *Does America Need a Foreign Policy? Towards a Diplomacy for the Twenty-First Century*, London 2001; Robert Kagan, *The Return of History and the End of Dreams*, London 2008.

state. Fundamentalist movements reject secularisation and contest the basic tenets of the Enlightenment and liberal ideology. Radical fundamentalism is aimed in the first place at the Muslims advocating a more liberal interpretation of Islam, and secondarily at the influence exerted by the secular West on the Islamic world. There is, however, no struggle between the Islamic world and the West; it is a struggle between various approaches towards religion and society in politics, in which the dividing lines run not between but across the civilisations and religions.[13]

During the last decade of the twentieth century, a wave of democratisation hit many parts of the world outside Europe. In the former Soviet republics, in central and eastern Europe, in Latin America and in several Asian and African countries – including South Africa – democratic regimes were established. Even Communist China seemed to be able to escape the wave of democratisation only through the resort to force by the regime at Tiananmen Square in 1989. Over recent years, however, in many of these countries, it seems that democracy has taken only shallow roots, although its forms are often respected. In Russia and other former Soviet republics, as well as in different Latin American countries such as Venezuela, autocracy and populism are reasserting themselves. Most Western countries are more willing to accommodate the Chinese regime today than they were during the 1990s.

473   Fortress Europe?

But the biggest threat to Europe comes not from the outside but from within. European unification is an impressive success story, but it also embraces a fundamental danger: Fortress Europe. Since Europe has relinquished its leading role in the world and achieved unification, the continent has become inward-looking. In the eyes of the rest of the world – not just the Third World but also other industrial countries – there is something of Thomas More's *Utopia* about Europe: an island paradise outside the real world. As a result of the success of its integration, its prosperity, half a century of peace and the rapid integration of the former Eastern bloc, Europe is at risk of becoming further embroiled in a culture of self-satisfaction and a discourse of moral supremacy. Europe has reason to be proud of its achievements in the fields of the economy, the welfare state, democracy, the rule of law and human rights. And it has reasons for disseminating those achievements and trying to persuade the world of the

---

[13] For a forthright and radical interpretation of the ideological dimension in the debate, see Paul Berman, *Terror and Liberalism*, New York and London 2003.

merits of its own ideology. In order to do so, however, it must – together with the other half of the West   be prepared to lead, to assume responsibility and to share. That assumes a totally different set of attitudes on the part of European leaders and the European population of today. In the globalised society, it will be not Europe but the world that provides the perspective from which history will judge our success or failure.[14]

[14] Concerning the differences between Europe and the USA in this field, see Robert Kagan, *Paradise and Power: America and Europe in the New World Order*, London 2003.

INDEX

William II, Emperor of Germany
431–2
William II, King of the Netherlands
424
William III, King of England 396, 427,
428
William V of Orange 413
Wilson, Woodrow 498–9, 500
Windscheid, Bernard 470, 471
Witan 280
Wolff, Christian 433, 451, 454
workshops 375–6
World War I 11, 483–4, 487
World War II 500

Worms, Concordat of (1122)
202–3
writs 280–2

Yeats, William Butler 483
Yourcenar, Marguerite 1, 43
Yugoslavia 509

Zachariae, Karl Salomo 461, 462
Zacharias, Pope 130
Zannekin, Nicholas 194
Zäsi, Ulrich 352
Zeiller, Franz von 455
Zeitgeist 7